THE BOOK OF
MILITARY STRATEGY

ENGAGE BOOKS

The Book of Military Strategy
Sun Tzu, Machiavelli, & Clausewitz

The Art of War
Tzu, Sun 544 BC – 496 BC
Translated by Lionel Giles
First published by Luzak & Co. in 1910
The Prince
Machiavelli, Niccolò, 1469 – 1527
First Published by Antonio Blado
d'Asola in 1532
On War
von Clausewitz, Carl 1780 – 1831
First Published in German by
Dümmlers Verlag in 1832
First Published in English by
N. Trübner in 1873
Text © 2015 Engage Books
Design © 2015 Engage Books

Mailing address:
Engage Books
PO BOX 4608
Main Station Terminal
349 West Georgia Street
Vancouver, BC
Canada, V6B 4A1

www.engagebooks.ca

Cover design by: A.R. Roumanis

Text set in Minion Pro. Chapter headings
set in News Gothic Standard.

ISBN: 978-1-77226-215-5

FIRST EDITION / FIRST PRINTING

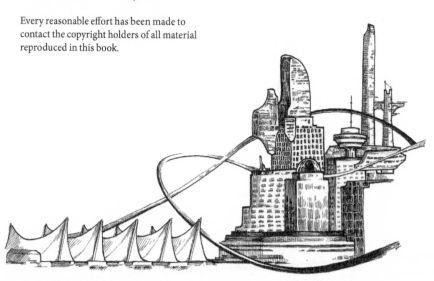

THE BOOK OF
MILITARY STRATEGY

SUN TZU'S
THE ART OF WAR

Translated by
LIONEL GILES

MACHIAVELLI'S
THE PRINCE

Translated by
W.K. MARRIOTT

CLAUSEWITZ'S
ON WAR

Translated by
COLONEL J.J. GRAHAM

1000 COPY LIMITED EDITION

VANCOUVER:
ENGAGE BOOKS
2015

CONTENTS

THE
ART
OF WAR

CONTENTS

INTRODUCTION

Sᴜɴ Tᴢᴜ Wᴜ was a native of the Ch`i State. His *Art of War* brought him to the notice of Ho Lu,[1] King of Wu. Ho Lu said to him: "I have carefully perused your 13 chapters. May I submit your theory of managing soldiers to a slight test?"

Sun Tzu replied: "You may."

Ho Lu asked: "May the test be applied to women?"

The answer was again in the affirmative, so arrangements were made to bring 180 ladies out of the Palace. Sun Tzu divided them into two companies, and placed one of the King's favorite concubines at the head of each. He then bade them all take spears in their hands, and addressed them thus: "I presume you know the difference between front and back, right hand and left hand?"

The girls replied: Yes.

Sun Tzu went on: "When I say "Eyes front," you must look straight ahead. When I say "Left turn," you must face towards your left hand. When I say "Right turn," you must face towards your right hand. When I say "About turn," you must face right round towards your back."

Again the girls assented. The words of command having been thus explained, he set up the halberds and battle-axes in order to begin the drill. Then, to the sound of drums, he gave the order "Right turn." But the girls only burst out laughing. Sun Tzu said: "If words of command are not clear and distinct, if orders are not thoroughly understood, then the general is to blame."

So he started drilling them again, and this time gave the order "Left turn," whereupon the girls once more burst into fits of laughter. Sun Tzu: "If words of command are not clear and distinct, if orders are not thoroughly understood, the general is to blame. But if his orders *are* clear, and the soldiers nevertheless disobey, then it is the fault of their officers."

---

1   He reigned from 514 to 496 B.C.

So saying, he ordered the leaders of the two companies to be beheaded. Now the king of Wu was watching the scene from the top of a raised pavilion; and when he saw that his favorite concubines were about to be executed, he was greatly alarmed and hurriedly sent down the following message: "We are now quite satisfied as to our general's ability to handle troops. If We are bereft of these two concubines, our meat and drink will lose their savor. It is our wish that they shall not be beheaded."

Sun Tzu replied: "Having once received His Majesty's commission to be the general of his forces, there are certain commands of His Majesty which, acting in that capacity, I am unable to accept."

Accordingly, he had the two leaders beheaded, and straightway installed the pair next in order as leaders in their place. When this had been done, the drum was sounded for the drill once more; and the girls went through all the evolutions, turning to the right or to the left, marching ahead or wheeling back, kneeling or standing, with perfect accuracy and precision, not venturing to utter a sound. Then Sun Tzu sent a messenger to the King saying: "Your soldiers, Sire, are now properly drilled and disciplined, and ready for your majesty's inspection. They can be put to any use that their sovereign may desire; bid them go through fire and water, and they will not disobey."

But the King replied: "Let our general cease drilling and return to camp. As for us, We have no wish to come down and inspect the troops."

Thereupon Sun Tzu said: "The King is only fond of words, and cannot translate them into deeds."

After that, Ho Lu saw that Sun Tzu was one who knew how to handle an army, and finally appointed him general. In the west, he defeated the Ch'u State and forced his way into Ying, the capital; to the north he put fear into the States of Ch'i and Chin, and spread his fame abroad amongst the feudal princes. And Sun Tzu shared in the might of the King.

– Ssu-ma Ch'ien (c. 145 B.C. – 86 B.C.)

CHAPTER ONE

Laying Plans[2]

1. Sun Tzu said: The art of war is of vital importance to the State.

2. It is a matter of life and death, a road either to safety or to ruin. Hence it is a subject of inquiry which can on no account be neglected.

3. The art of war, then, is governed by five constant factors, to be taken into account in one's deliberations, when seeking to determine the conditions obtaining in the field.

4. These are:
   (1) The Moral Law;[3]
   (2) Heaven;
   (3) Earth;
   (4) The Commander;
   (5) Method and discipline.

5,6. The *Moral Law* causes the people to be in complete accord with their ruler, so that they will follow him regardless of their lives, undismayed by any danger.[4]

---

2 Ts'ao Kung, in defining the meaning of the Chinese for the title of this chapter, says it refers to the deliberations in the temple selected by the general for his temporary use, or as we should say, in his tent.

3 It appears from what follows that Sun Tzu means by "Moral Law" a principle of harmony, not unlike the Tao of Lao Tzu in its moral aspect. One might be tempted to render it by "morale," were it not considered as an attribute of the ruler.

4 Tu Yu quotes Wang Tzu as saying: "Without constant practice, the officers will be nervous and undecided when mustering for battle; without constant practice, the general will be wavering and irresolute when the crisis is at hand."

7. *Heaven* signifies night and day, cold and heat, times and seasons.[5]

8. *Earth* comprises distances, great and small; danger and security; open ground and narrow passes; the chances of life and death.[6]

9. The *Commander* stands for the virtues of wisdom, sincerity, benevolence, courage and strictness.

10. By *method and discipline* are to be understood the marshaling of the army in its proper subdivisions, the graduations of rank among the officers, the maintenance of roads by which supplies may reach the army, and the control of military expenditure.

11. These five heads should be familiar to every general: he who knows them will be victorious; he who knows them not will fail.

12. Therefore, in your deliberations, when seeking to determine the military conditions, let them be made the basis of a comparison, in this wise: –

13. (1) Which of the two sovereigns is imbued with the Moral law?
    (2) Which of the two generals has most ability?
    (3) With whom lie the advantages derived from Heaven and Earth?
    (4) On which side is discipline most rigorously enforced?[7]
    (5) Which army is stronger?[8]

---

5 The commentators, I think, make an unnecessary mystery of two words here. Meng Shih refers to "the hard and the soft, waxing and waning" of Heaven. Wang Hsi, however, may be right in saying that what is meant is "the general economy of Heaven," including the five elements, the four seasons, wind and clouds, and other phenomena.
6 The five cardinal virtues of the Chinese are (1) humanity or benevolence; (2) uprightness of mind; (3) self-respect, self- control, or "proper feeling;" (4) wisdom; (5) sincerity or good faith. Here "wisdom" and "sincerity" are put before "humanity or benevolence," and the two military virtues of "courage" and "strictness" substituted for "uprightness of mind" and "self-respect, self-control, or 'proper feeling."
7 Tu Mu alludes to the remarkable story of Ts`ao Ts`ao (A.D. 155-220), who was such a strict disciplinarian that once, in accordance with his own severe regulations against injury to standing crops, he condemned himself to death for having allowed his horse to shy into a field of corn! However, in lieu of losing his head, he was persuaded to satisfy his sense of justice by cutting off his hair. Ts`ao Ts`ao's own comment on the present passage is characteristically curt: "when you lay down a law, see that it is not disobeyed; if it is disobeyed the offender must be put to death."
8 Morally as well as physically. As Mei Yao-ch`en puts it, freely rendered, *"espirit de corps* and 'big battalions."

(6) On which side are officers and men more highly trained?[9]

(7) In which army is there the greater constancy both in reward and punishment?[10]

14. By means of these seven considerations I can forecast victory or defeat.

15. The general that hearkens to my counsel and acts upon it, will conquer: let such a one be retained in command! The general that hearkens not to my counsel nor acts upon it, will suffer defeat: – let such a one be dismissed![11]

16. While heading the profit of my counsel, avail yourself also of any helpful circumstances over and beyond the ordinary rules.

17. According as circumstances are favorable, one should modify one's plans.[12]

18. All warfare is based on deception.[13]

19. Hence, when able to attack, we must seem unable; when using our forces, we must seem inactive; when we are near, we must make the

9 Tu Yu quotes Wang Tzu as saying: "Without constant practice, the officers will be nervous and undecided when mustering for battle; without constant practice, the general will be wavering and irresolute when the crisis is at hand."

10 On which side is there the most absolute certainty that merit will be properly rewarded and misdeeds summarily punished?

11 The form of this paragraph reminds us that Sun Tzu's treatise was composed expressly for the benefit of his patron Ho Lu, king of the Wu State.

12 Sun Tzu, as a practical soldier, will have none of the "bookish theoric." He cautions us here not to pin our faith to abstract principles; "for," as Chang Yu puts it, "while the main laws of strategy can be stated clearly enough for the benefit of all and sundry, you must be guided by the actions of the enemy in attempting to secure a favorable position in actual warfare." On the eve of the battle of Waterloo, Lord Uxbridge, commanding the cavalry, went to the Duke of Wellington in order to learn what his plans and calculations were for the morrow, because, as he explained, he might suddenly find himself Commander-in-chief and would be unable to frame new plans in a critical moment. The Duke listened quietly and then said: "Who will attack the first tomorrow – I or Bonaparte?" "Bonaparte," replied Lord Uxbridge. "Well," continued the Duke, "Bonaparte has not given me any idea of his projects; and as my plans will depend upon his, how can you expect me to tell you what mine are?"

13 The truth of this pithy and profound saying will be admitted by every soldier. Col. Henderson tells us that Wellington, great in so many military qualities, was especially distinguished by "the extraordinary skill with which he concealed his movements and deceived both friend and foe."

enemy believe we are far away; when far away, we must make him believe we are near.

20. Hold out baits to entice the enemy. Feign disorder, and crush him.[14]

21. If he is secure at all points, be prepared for him. If he is in superior strength, evade him.

22. If your opponent is of choleric temper, seek to irritate him. Pretend to be weak, that he may grow arrogant.[15]

23. If he is taking his ease, give him no rest. If his forces are united, separate them.[16]

24. Attack him where he is unprepared, appear where you are not expected.

25. These military devices, leading to victory, must not be divulged beforehand.

26. Now the general who wins a battle makes many calculations in his temple ere the battle is fought. The general who loses a battle makes but few calculations beforehand. Thus do many calculations lead to victory, and few calculations to defeat: how much more no calculation at all! It is by attention to this point that I can foresee who is likely to win or lose.[17]

---

14   All commentators, except Chang Yu, say, "When he is in disorder, crush him." It is more natural to suppose that Sun Tzu is still illustrating the uses of deception in war.
15   Wang Tzu, quoted by Tu Yu, says that the good tactician plays with his adversary as a cat plays with a mouse, first feigning weakness and immobility, and then suddenly pouncing upon him.
16   This is probably the meaning though Mei Yao-ch`en has the note: "while we are taking our ease, wait for the enemy to tire himself out." The *yu lan* has "Lure him on and tire him out."
17   Chang Yu tells us that in ancient times it was customary for a temple to be set apart for the use of a general who was about to take the field, in order that he might there elaborate his plan of campaign.

CHAPTER TWO

Waging War[18]

1. Sun Tzu said: In the operations of war, where there are in the field a thousand swift chariots, as many heavy chariots, and a hundred thousand mail-clad soldiers,[19] with provisions enough to carry them a thousand *li*,[20] the expenditure at home and at the front, including entertainment of guests, small items such as glue and paint, and sums spent on chariots and armor, will reach the total of a thousand ounces of silver per day. Such is the cost of raising an army of 100,000 men.

2. When you engage in actual fighting, if victory is long in coming, then men's weapons will grow dull and their ardor will be damped. If you lay siege to a town, you will exhaust your strength.

3. Again, if the campaign is protracted, the resources of the State will not be equal to the strain.

18   Ts`ao Kung has the note: "He who wishes to fight must first count the cost," which prepares us for the discovery that the subject of the chapter is not what we might expect from the title, but is primarily a consideration of ways and means.
19   The "swift chariots" were lightly built and, according to Chang Yu, used for the attack; the "heavy chariots" were heavier, and designed for purposes of defense. Li Ch`uan, it is true, says that the latter were light, but this seems hardly probable. It is interesting to note the analogies between early Chinese warfare and that of the Homeric Greeks. In each case, the war- chariot was the important factor, forming as it did the nucleus round which was grouped a certain number of foot-soldiers. With regard to the numbers given here, we are informed that each swift chariot was accompanied by 75 footmen, and each heavy chariot by 25 footmen, so that the whole army would be divided up into a thousand battalions, each consisting of two chariots and a hundred men.
20   2.78 modern *li* go to a mile. The length may have varied slightly since Sun Tzu's time.

4. Now, when your weapons are dulled, your ardor damped, your strength exhausted and your treasure spent, other chieftains will spring up to take advantage of your extremity. Then no man, however wise, will be able to avert the consequences that must ensue.

5. Thus, though we have heard of stupid haste in war, cleverness has never been seen associated with long delays.[21]

6. There is no instance of a country having benefited from prolonged warfare.[22]

7. It is only one who is thoroughly acquainted with the evils of war that can thoroughly understand the profitable way of carrying it on.

8. The skillful soldier does not raise a second levy, neither are his supply-wagons loaded more than twice.[23]

21   This concise and difficult sentence is not well explained by any of the commentators. Ts`ao Kung, Li Ch`uan, Meng Shih, Tu Yu, Tu Mu and Mei Yao-ch`en have notes to the effect that a general, though naturally stupid, may nevertheless conquer through sheer force of rapidity. Ho Shih says: "Haste may be stupid, but at any rate it saves expenditure of energy and treasure; protracted operations may be very clever, but they bring calamity in their train." Wang Hsi evades the difficulty by remarking: "Lengthy operations mean an army growing old, wealth being expended, an empty exchequer and distress among the people; true cleverness insures against the occurrence of such calamities." Chang Yu says: "So long as victory can be attained, stupid haste is preferable to clever dilatoriness." Now Sun Tzu says nothing whatever, except possibly by implication, about ill-considered haste being better than ingenious but lengthy operations. What he does say is something much more guarded, namely that, while speed may sometimes be injudicious, tardiness can never be anything but foolish – if only because it means impoverishment to the nation. In considering the point raised here by Sun Tzu, the classic example of Fabius Cunctator will inevitably occur to the mind. That general deliberately measured the endurance of Rome against that of Hannibals's isolated army, because it seemed to him that the latter was more likely to suffer from a long campaign in a strange country. But it is quite a moot question whether his tactics would have proved successful in the long run. Their reversal it is true, led to Cannae; but this only establishes a negative presumption in their favor.
22   That is, with rapidity. Only one who knows the disastrous effects of a long war can realize the supreme importance of rapidity in bringing it to a close. Only two commentators seem to favor this interpretation, but it fits well into the logic of the context, whereas the rendering, "He who does not know the evils of war cannot appreciate its benefits," is distinctly pointless.
23   Once war is declared, he will not waste precious time in waiting for reinforcements, nor will he return his army back for fresh supplies, but crosses the enemy's frontier without delay. This may seem an audacious policy to recommend, but with all great strategists, from Julius Caesar to Napoleon Bonaparte, the value of time – that is, being a little ahead of your opponent – has counted for more than either numerical superiority or the nicest calculations with regard to commissariat.

9. Bring war material[24] with you from home, but forage on the enemy. Thus the army will have food enough for its needs.

10. Poverty of the State exchequer causes an army to be maintained by contributions from a distance. Contributing to maintain an army at a distance causes the people to be impoverished.[25]

11. On the other hand, the proximity of an army causes prices to go up; and high prices cause the people's substance to be drained away.[26]

12. When their substance is drained away, the peasantry will be afflicted by heavy exactions.

13,14. With this loss of substance and exhaustion of strength, the homes of the people will be stripped bare, and three-tenths of their income will be dissipated;[27] while government expenses for broken chariots, worn-out horses, breast-plates and helmets, bows and arrows, spears and shields, protective mantles, draught-oxen and heavy wagons, will amount to four-tenths of its total revenue.

15. Hence a wise general makes a point of foraging on the enemy. One cartload of the enemy's provisions is equivalent to twenty of one's own, and likewise a single *picul*[28] of his provender is equivalent to twenty from one's own store.

24   The Chinese word translated here as "war material" literally means "things to be used", and is meant in the widest sense. It includes all the impedimenta of an army, apart from provisions.

25   The beginning of this sentence does not balance properly with the next, though obviously intended to do so. The arrangement, moreover, is so awkward that I cannot help suspecting some corruption in the text. It never seems to occur to Chinese commentators that an emendation may be necessary for the sense, and we get no help from them there. The Chinese words Sun Tzu used to indicate the cause of the people's impoverishment clearly have reference to some system by which the husbandmen sent their contributions of corn to the army direct. But why should it fall on them to maintain an army in this way, except because the State or Government is too poor to do so?

26   Wang Hsi says high prices occur before the army has left its own territory. Ts'ao Kung understands it of an army that has already crossed the frontier.

27   Tu Mu and Wang Hsi agree that the people are not mulcted not of 3/10, but of 7/10, of their income. But this is hardly to be extracted from our text. Ho Shih has a characteristic tag: "The *people* being regarded as the essential part of the State, and *food* as the people's heaven, is it not right that those in authority should value and be careful of both?"

28   Because twenty cartloads will be consumed in the process of transporting one cartload to the front. A *picul* is a unit of measure equal to 133.3 pounds (65.5 kilograms).

16. Now in order to kill the enemy, our men must be roused to anger; that there may be advantage from defeating the enemy, they must have their rewards.[29]

17. Therefore in chariot fighting, when ten or more chariots have been taken, those should be rewarded who took the first. Our own flags should be substituted for those of the enemy, and the chariots mingled and used in conjunction with ours. The captured soldiers should be kindly treated and kept.[30]

18. This is called, using the conquered foe to augment one's own strength.

19. In war, then, let your great object be victory, not lengthy campaigns.

20. Thus it may be known that the leader of armies is the arbiter of the people's fate, the man on whom it depends whether the nation shall be in peace or in peril.

29 Tu Mu says: "Rewards are necessary in order to make the soldiers see the advantage of beating the enemy; thus, when you capture spoils from the enemy, they must be used as rewards, so that all your men may have a keen desire to fight, each on his own account."
30 As Ho Shih remarks: "War is not a thing to be trifled with." Sun Tzu here reiterates the main lesson which this chapter is intended to enforce."

CHAPTER THREE

Attack by Stratagem

1. Sun Tzu said: In the practical art of war, the best thing of all is to take the enemy's country whole and intact; to shatter and destroy it is not so good. So, too, it is better to recapture an army entire than to destroy it, to capture a regiment, a detachment or a company entire than to destroy them.[31]

2. Hence to fight and conquer in all your battles is not supreme excellence; supreme excellence consists in breaking the enemy's resistance without fighting.[32]

3. Thus the highest form of generalship is to balk[33] the enemy's plans; the next best is to prevent the junction of the enemy's forces;[34] the

31 The equivalent to an army corps, according to Ssu-ma Fa, consisted nominally of 12500 men; according to Ts`ao Kung, the equivalent of a regiment contained 500 men, the equivalent to a detachment consists from any number between 100 and 500, and the equivalent of a company contains from 5 to 100 men. For the last two, however, Chang Yu gives the exact figures of 100 and 5 respectively.
32 Here again, no modern strategist but will approve the words of the old Chinese general. Moltke's greatest triumph, the capitulation of the huge French army at Sedan, was won practically without bloodshed.
33 Perhaps the word "balk" falls short of expressing the full force of the Chinese word, which implies not an attitude of defense, whereby one might be content to foil the enemy's stratagems one after another, but an active policy of counter-attack. Ho Shih puts this very clearly in his note: "When the enemy has made a plan of attack against us, we must anticipate him by delivering our own attack first."
34 Isolating him from his allies. We must not forget that Sun Tzu, in speaking of hostilities, always has in mind the numerous states or principalities into which the China of his day was split up.

next in order is to attack the enemy's army in the field;[35] and the worst policy of all is to besiege walled cities.

4. The rule is, not to besiege walled cities if it can possibly be avoided.[36] The preparation of mantlets, movable shelters, and various implements of war, will take up three whole months;[37] and the piling up of mounds over against the walls will take three months more.[38]

5. The general, unable to control his irritation, will launch his men to the assault like swarming ants,[39] with the result that one-third of his men are slain, while the town still remains untaken. Such are the disastrous effects of a siege.[40]

6. Therefore the skillful leader subdues the enemy's troops without any fighting; he captures their cities without laying siege to them; he overthrows their kingdom without lengthy operations in the field.[41]

35 When he is already at full strength.

36 Another sound piece of military theory. Had the Boers acted upon it in 1899, and refrained from dissipating their strength before Kimberley, Mafeking, or even Ladysmith, it is more than probable that they would have been masters of the situation before the British were ready seriously to oppose them.

37 It is not quite clear what the Chinese word, here translated as "mantlets", described. Ts'ao Kung simply defines them as "large shields," but we get a better idea of them from Li Ch'uan, who says they were to protect the heads of those who were assaulting the city walls at close quarters. This seems to suggest a sort of Roman *Testudo*, ready made. Tu Mu says they were wheeled vehicles used in repelling attacks, but this is denied by Ch'en Hao. See supra II. 14. The name is also applied to turrets on city walls. Of the "movable shelters" we get a fairly clear description from several commentators. They were wooden missile-proof structures on four wheels, propelled from within, covered over with raw hides, and used in sieges to convey parties of men to and from the walls, for the purpose of filling up the encircling moat with earth. Tu Mu adds that they are now called "wooden donkeys."

38 These were great mounds or ramparts of earth heaped up to the level of the enemy's walls in order to discover the weak points in the defense, and also to destroy the fortified turrets mentioned in the preceding note.

39 This vivid simile of Ts'ao Kung is taken from the spectacle of an army of ants climbing a wall. The meaning is that the general, losing patience at the long delay, may make a premature attempt to storm the place before his engines of war are ready.

40 We are reminded of the terrible losses of the Japanese before Port Arthur, in the most recent siege which history has to record.

41 Chia Lin notes that he only overthrows the Government, but does no harm to individuals. The classical instance is Wu Wang, who after having put an end to the Yin dynasty was acclaimed "Father and mother of the people."

7. With his forces intact he will dispute the mastery of the Empire, and thus, without losing a man, his triumph will be complete.[42] This is the method of attacking by stratagem.

8. It is the rule in war, if our forces are ten to the enemy's one, to surround him; if five to one, to attack him;[43] if twice as numerous, to divide our army into two.[44]

9. If equally matched, we can offer battle;[45] if slightly inferior in numbers, we can avoid the enemy;[46] if quite unequal in every way, we can flee from him.

10. Hence, though an obstinate fight may be made by a small force, in the end it must be captured by the larger force.

11. Now the general is the bulwark of the State; if the bulwark is complete at all points; the State will be strong; if the bulwark is defective, the State will be weak.[47]

12. There are three ways in which a ruler can bring misfortune upon his army: –

42 Owing to the double meanings in the Chinese text, the latter part of the sentence is susceptible of quite a different meaning: "And thus, the weapon not being blunted by use, its keenness remains perfect."
43 Straightway, without waiting for any further advantage.
44 Tu Mu takes exception to the saying; and at first sight, indeed, it appears to violate a fundamental principle of war. Ts'ao Kung, however, gives a clue to Sun Tzu's meaning: "Being two to the enemy's one, we may use one part of our army in the regular way, and the other for some special diversion." Chang Yu thus further elucidates the point: "If our force is twice as numerous as that of the enemy, it should be split up into two divisions, one to meet the enemy in front, and one to fall upon his rear; if he replies to the frontal attack, he may be crushed from behind; if to the rearward attack, he may be crushed in front." This is what is meant by saying that 'one part may be used in the regular way, and the other for some special diversion.' Tu Mu does not understand that dividing one's army is simply an irregular, just as concentrating it is the regular, strategical method, and he is too hasty in calling this a mistake."
45 Li Ch'uan, followed by Ho Shih, gives the following paraphrase: "If attackers and attacked are equally matched in strength, only the able general will fight."
46 The meaning, "we can *watch* the enemy," is certainly a great improvement on the above; but unfortunately there appears to be no very good authority for the variant. Chang Yu reminds us that the saying only applies if the other factors are equal; a small difference in numbers is often more than counterbalanced by superior energy and discipline.
47 As Li Ch'uan tersely puts it: "Gap indicates deficiency; if the general's ability is not perfect (i.e. if he is not thoroughly versed in his profession), his army will lack strength."

13. (1) By commanding the army to advance or to retreat, being ignorant of the fact that it cannot obey. This is called hobbling the army.[48]

14. (2) By attempting to govern an army in the same way as he administers a kingdom, being ignorant of the conditions which obtain in an army. This causes restlessness in the soldier's minds.[49]

15. (3) By employing the officers of his army without discrimination,[50] through ignorance of the military principle of adaptation to circumstances. This shakes the confidence of the soldiers.[51]

16. But when the army is restless and distrustful, trouble is sure to come from the other feudal princes. This is simply bringing anarchy into the army, and flinging victory away.

17. Thus we may know that there are five essentials for victory:
(1) He will win who knows when to fight and when not to fight.[52]
(2) He will win who knows how to handle both superior and inferior forces.[53]

48 Li Ch'uan adds the comment: "It is like tying together the legs of a thoroughbred, so that it is unable to gallop." One would naturally think of "the ruler" in this passage as being at home, and trying to direct the movements of his army from a distance. But the commentators understand just the reverse, and quote the saying of T'ai Kung: "A kingdom should not be governed from without, and army should not be directed from within." Of course it is true that, during an engagement, or when in close touch with the enemy, the general should not be in the thick of his own troops, but a little distance apart. Otherwise, he will be liable to misjudge the position as a whole, and give wrong orders.
49 Ts'ao Kung's note is, freely translated: "The military sphere and the civil sphere are wholly distinct; you can't handle an army in kid gloves." And Chang Yu says: "Humanity and justice are the principles on which to govern a state, but not an army; opportunism and flexibility, on the other hand, are military rather than civil virtues to assimilate the governing of an army" – to that of a State, understood.
50 That is, he is not careful to use the right man in the right place.
51 I follow Mei Yao-ch'en here. The other commentators refer not to the ruler, as in SS. 13, 14, but to the officers he employs. Thus Tu Yu says: "If a general is ignorant of the principle of adaptability, he must not be entrusted with a position of authority." Tu Mu quotes: "The skilful employer of men will employ the wise man, the brave man, the covetous man, and the stupid man. For the wise man delights in establishing his merit, the brave man likes to show his courage in action, the covetous man is quick at seizing advantages, and the stupid man has no fear of death."
52 Chang Yu says: If he can fight, he advances and takes the offensive; if he cannot fight, he retreats and remains on the defensive. He will invariably conquer who knows whether it is right to take the offensive or the defensive.
53 This is not merely the general's ability to estimate numbers correctly, as Li Ch'uan and others make out. Chang Yu expounds the saying more satisfactorily: "By applying

(3) He will win whose army is animated by the same spirit throughout all its ranks.

(4) He will win who, prepared himself, waits to take the enemy unprepared.

(5) He will win who has military capacity and is not interfered with by the sovereign.[54]

18. Hence the saying: If you know the enemy and know yourself, you need not fear the result of a hundred battles. If you know yourself but not the enemy, for every victory gained you will also suffer a defeat.[55] If you know neither the enemy nor yourself, you will succumb in every battle.[56]

---

the art of war, it is possible with a lesser force to defeat a greater, and vice versa. The secret lies in an eye for locality, and in not letting the right moment slip. Thus Wu Tzu says: 'With a superior force, make for easy ground; with an inferior one, make for difficult ground.'"

54 Tu Yu quotes Wang Tzu as saying: "It is the sovereign's function to give broad instructions, but to decide on battle it is the function of the general." It is needless to dilate on the military disasters which have been caused by undue interference with operations in the field on the part of the home government. Napoleon undoubtedly owed much of his extraordinary success to the fact that he was not hampered by central authority.

55 Li Ch'uan cites the case of Fu Chien, prince of Ch'in, who in 383 A.D. marched with a vast army against the Chin Emperor. When warned not to despise an enemy who could command the services of such men as Hsieh An and Huan Ch'ung, he boastfully replied: "I have the population of eight provinces at my back, infantry and horsemen to the number of one million; why, they could dam up the Yangtsze River itself by merely throwing their whips into the stream. What danger have I to fear?" Nevertheless, his forces were soon after disastrously routed at the Fei River, and he was obliged to beat a hasty retreat.

56 Chang Yu said: "Knowing the enemy enables you to take the offensive, knowing yourself enables you to stand on the defensive." He adds: "Attack is the secret of defense; defense is the planning of an attack." It would be hard to find a better epitome of the root-principle of war.

CHAPTER FOUR

Tactical Dispositions[57]

1. Sun Tzu said: The good fighters of old first put themselves beyond the possibility of defeat, and then waited for an opportunity of defeating the enemy.

2. To secure ourselves against defeat lies in our own hands, but the opportunity of defeating the enemy is provided by the enemy himself.[58]

3. Thus the good fighter is able to secure himself against defeat,[59] but cannot make certain of defeating the enemy.

4. Hence the saying: One may *know* how to conquer without being able to *do* it.

5. Security against defeat implies defensive tactics; ability to defeat the enemy means taking the offensive.[60]

---

57   Ts'ao Kung explains the Chinese meaning of the words for the title of this chapter: "marching and countermarching on the part of the two armies with a view to discovering each other's condition." Tu Mu says: "It is through the dispositions of an army that its condition may be discovered. Conceal your dispositions, and your condition will remain secret, which leads to victory,; show your dispositions, and your condition will become patent, which leads to defeat." Wang Hsi remarks that the good general can "secure success by modifying his tactics to meet those of the enemy."
58   That is, of course, by a mistake on the enemy's part.
59   Chang Yu says this is done, "By concealing the disposition of his troops, covering up his tracks, and taking unremitting precautions."
60   I retain the sense found in a similar passage in ss. 1-3, in spite of the fact that the commentators are all against me. The meaning they give, "He who cannot conquer takes the defensive," is plausible enough.

6. Standing on the defensive indicates insufficient strength; attacking, a superabundance of strength.

7. The general who is skilled in defense hides in the most secret recesses of the earth;[61] he who is skilled in attack flashes forth from the topmost heights of heaven.[62] Thus on the one hand we have ability to protect ourselves; on the other, a victory that is complete.

8. To see victory only when it is within the ken of the common herd is not the acme of excellence.[63]

9. Neither is it the acme of excellence if you fight and conquer and the whole Empire says, "Well done!"[64]

10. To lift an autumn hair is no sign of great strength;[65] to see the sun and moon is no sign of sharp sight; to hear the noise of thunder is no sign of a quick ear.[66]

11. What the ancients called a clever fighter is one who not only wins, but excels in winning with ease.[67]

61 Literally, "hides under the ninth earth," which is a metaphor indicating the utmost secrecy and concealment, so that the enemy may not know his whereabouts."
62 Another metaphor, implying that he falls on his adversary like a thunderbolt, against which there is no time to prepare. This is the opinion of most of the commentators.
63 As Ts'ao Kung remarks, "the thing is to see the plant before it has germinated," to foresee the event before the action has begun. Li Ch'uan alludes to the story of Han Hsin who, when about to attack the vastly superior army of Chao, which was strongly entrenched in the city of Ch'eng-an, said to his officers: "Gentlemen, we are going to annihilate the enemy, and shall meet again at dinner." The officers hardly took his words seriously, and gave a very dubious assent. But Han Hsin had already worked out in his mind the details of a clever stratagem, whereby, as he foresaw, he was able to capture the city and inflict a crushing defeat on his adversary."
64 True excellence being, as Tu Mu says: "To plan secretly, to move surreptitiously, to foil the enemy's intentions and balk his schemes, so that at last the day may be won without shedding a drop of blood." Sun Tzu reserves his approbation for things that "the world's coarse thumb And finger fail to plumb."
65 "Autumn" hair" is explained as the fur of a hare, which is finest in autumn, when it begins to grow afresh. The phrase is a very common one in Chinese writers.
66 Ho Shih gives as real instances of strength, sharp sight and quick hearing: Wu Huo, who could lift a tripod weighing 250 stone; Li Chu, who at a distance of a hundred paces could see objects no bigger than a mustard seed; and Shih K'uang, a blind musician who could hear the footsteps of a mosquito.
67 The last half is literally "one who, conquering, excels in easy conquering." Mei Yao-ch'en says: "He who only sees the obvious, wins his battles with difficulty; he who looks below the surface of things, wins with ease."

12. Hence his victories bring him neither reputation for wisdom nor credit for courage.[68]

13. He wins his battles by making no mistakes.[69] Making no mistakes is what establishes the certainty of victory, for it means conquering an enemy that is already defeated.

14. Hence the skillful fighter puts himself into a position which makes defeat impossible, and does not miss the moment for defeating the enemy.[70]

15. Thus it is that in war the victorious strategist only seeks battle after the victory has been won, whereas he who is destined to defeat first fights and afterwards looks for victory.[71]

16. The consummate leader cultivates the moral law, and strictly adheres to method and discipline; thus it is in his power to control success.

17. In respect of military method, we have, firstly, Measurement; secondly, Estimation of quantity; thirdly, Calculation; fourthly, Balancing of chances; fifthly, Victory.

18. Measurement owes its existence to Earth; Estimation of quantity to Measurement; Calculation to Estimation of quantity; Balancing of chances to Calculation; and Victory to Balancing of chances.[72]

---

68 Tu Mu explains this very well: "Inasmuch as his victories are gained over circumstances that have not come to light, the world as large knows nothing of them, and he wins no reputation for wisdom; inasmuch as the hostile state submits before there has been any bloodshed, he receives no credit for courage."

69 Ch'en Hao says: "He plans no superfluous marches, he devises no futile attacks." The connection of ideas is thus explained by Chang Yu: "One who seeks to conquer by sheer strength, clever though he may be at winning pitched battles, is also liable on occasion to be vanquished; whereas he who can look into the future and discern conditions that are not yet manifest, will never make a blunder and therefore invariably win."

70 A "counsel of perfection" as Tu Mu truly observes. "Position" need not be confined to the actual ground occupied by the troops. It includes all the arrangements and preparations which a wise general will make to increase the safety of his army.

71 Ho Shih thus expounds the paradox: "In warfare, first lay plans which will ensure victory, and then lead your army to battle; if you will not begin with stratagem but rely on brute strength alone, victory will no longer be assured."

72 It is not easy to distinguish the four terms very clearly in the Chinese. The first seems to be surveying and measurement of the ground, which enable us to form an estimate of the enemy's strength, and to make calculations based on the data thus obtained; we are

19. A victorious army opposed to a routed one, is as a pound's weight placed in the scale against a single grain.[73]

20. The onrush of a conquering force is like the bursting of pent-up waters into a chasm a thousand fathoms deep.

---

thus led to a general weighing-up, or comparison of the enemy's chances with our own; if the latter turn the scale, then victory ensues. The chief difficulty lies in third term, which in the Chinese some commentators take as a calculation of NUMBERS, thereby making it nearly synonymous with the second term. Perhaps the second term should be thought of as a consideration of the enemy's general position or condition, while the third term is the estimate of his numerical strength. On the other hand, Tu Mu says: "The question of relative strength having been settled, we can bring the varied resources of cunning into play." Ho Shih seconds this interpretation, but weakens it. However, it points to the third term as being a calculation of numbers.

73   Literally, "a victorious army is like an I (20 oz.) weighed against a *shu* (1/24 oz.); a routed army is a *shu* weighed against an I." The point is simply the enormous advantage which a disciplined force, flushed with victory, has over one demoralized by defeat." Legge, in his note on Mencius, I. 2. ix. 2, makes the I to be 24 Chinese ounces, and corrects Chu Hsi's statement that it equaled 20 oz. only. But Li Ch`uan of the T`ang dynasty here gives the same figure as Chu Hsi.

CHAPTER FIVE

Energy

1. Sun Tzu said: The control of a large force is the same principle as the control of a few men: it is merely a question of dividing up their numbers.[74]

2. Fighting with a large army under your command is nowise different from fighting with a small one: it is merely a question of instituting signs and signals.

3. To ensure that your whole host may withstand the brunt of the enemy's attack and remain unshaken – this is effected by maneuvers direct and indirect.[75]

---

74   That is, cutting up the army into regiments, companies, etc., with subordinate officers in command of each. Tu Mu reminds us of Han Hsin's famous reply to the first Han Emperor, who once said to him: "How large an army do you think I could lead?" "Not more than 100,000 men, your Majesty." "And you?" asked the Emperor. "Oh!" he answered, "the more the better."

75   We now come to one of the most interesting parts of Sun Tzu's treatise, the discussion of the *cheng* and the *ch`i.* As it is by no means easy to grasp the full significance of these two terms, or to render them consistently by good English equivalents; it may be as well to tabulate some of the commentators' remarks on the subject before proceeding further. Li Ch`uan: "Facing the enemy is *cheng*, making lateral diversion is *ch`i.* Chia Lin: "In presence of the enemy, your troops should be arrayed in normal fashion, but in order to secure victory abnormal maneuvers must be employed." Mei Yao-ch`en: "*ch`i.* is active, *cheng* is passive; passivity means waiting for an opportunity, activity beings the victory itself." Ho Shih: "We must cause the enemy to regard our straightforward attack as one that is secretly designed, and vice versa; thus *cheng* may also be *ch`i.*, and *ch`i.* may also be *cheng.*" He instances the famous exploit of Han Hsin, who when marching ostensibly against Lin- chin (now Chao-i in Shensi), suddenly threw a large force across the Yellow River in wooden tubs, utterly

4. That the impact of your army may be like a grindstone dashed against an egg – this is effected by the science of weak points and strong.

5. In all fighting, the direct method may be used for joining battle, but indirect methods will be needed in order to secure victory.[76]

6. Indirect tactics, efficiently applied, are inexhaustible as Heaven and Earth, unending as the flow of rivers and streams; like the sun and moon, they end but to begin anew; like the four seasons, they pass away to return once more.[77]

7. There are not more than five musical notes, yet the combinations of these five give rise to more melodies than can ever be heard.

8. There are not more than five primary colors (blue, yellow, red, white, and black), yet in combination they produce more hues than can ever been seen.

---

disconcerting his opponent. [Ch'ien Han Shu, ch. 3.] Here, we are told, the march on Lin-chin was *cheng*, and the surprise maneuver was *ch'i*." Chang Yu gives the following summary of opinions on the words: "Military writers do not agree with regard to the meaning of *ch'i* and *cheng*. Wei Liao Tzu [4th cent. B.C.] says: 'Direct warfare favors frontal attacks, indirect warfare attacks from the rear.' Ts'ao Kung says: 'Going straight out to join battle is a direct operation; appearing on the enemy's rear is an indirect maneuver.' Li Wei-kung [6th and 7th cent. A.D.] says: 'In war, to march straight ahead is *cheng*; turning movements, on the other hand, are *ch'i*.' These writers simply regard *cheng* as *cheng*, and *ch'i* as *ch'i*.; they do not note that the two are mutually interchangeable and run into each other like the two sides of a circle [see infra, ss. 11]. A comment on the T'ang Emperor T'ai Tsung goes to the root of the matter: 'A *ch'i* maneuver may be *cheng*, if we make the enemy look upon it as *cheng*; then our real attack will be *ch'i*., and vice versa. The whole secret lies in confusing the enemy, so that he cannot fathom our real intent.'" To put it perhaps a little more clearly: any attack or other operation is *cheng*, on which the enemy has had his attention fixed; whereas that is *ch'i*., which takes him by surprise or comes from an unexpected quarter. If the enemy perceives a movement which is meant to be *ch'i*., it immediately becomes *cheng*."

76 Chang Yu says: "Steadily develop indirect tactics, either by pounding the enemy's flanks or falling on his rear." A brilliant example of "indirect tactics" which decided the fortunes of a campaign was Lord Roberts' night march round the Peiwar Kotal in the second Afghan war.

77 Tu Yu and Chang Yu understand this of the permutations of *ch'i* and *cheng*." But at present Sun Tzu is not speaking of *cheng* at all, unless, indeed, we suppose with Cheng Yu-hsien that a clause relating to it has fallen out of the text. Of course, as has already been pointed out, the two are so inextricably interwoven in all military operations, that they cannot really be considered apart. Here we simply have an expression, in figurative language, of the almost infinite resource of a great leader.

9. There are not more than five cardinal tastes (sour, acrid, salt, sweet, bitter), yet combinations of them yield more flavors than can ever be tasted.

10. In battle, there are not more than two methods of attack – the direct and the indirect; yet these two in combination give rise to an endless series of maneuvers.

11. The direct and the indirect lead on to each other in turn. It is like moving in a circle – you never come to an end. Who can exhaust the possibilities of their combination?

12. The onset of troops is like the rush of a torrent which will even roll stones along in its course.

13. The quality of decision is like the well-timed swoop of a falcon which enables it to strike and destroy its victim.[78]

14. Therefore the good fighter will be terrible in his onset, and prompt in his decision.[79]

15. Energy may be likened to the bending of a crossbow; decision, to the releasing of a trigger.[80]

16. Amid the turmoil and tumult of battle, there may be seeming disorder and yet no real disorder at all; amid confusion and cha-

78 The Chinese here is tricky and a certain key word in the context it is used defies the best efforts of the translator. Tu Mu defines this word as "the measurement or estimation of distance." But this meaning does not quite fit the illustrative simile in ss. 15. Applying this definition to the falcon, it seems to me to denote that instinct of *self restraint* which keeps the bird from swooping on its quarry until the right moment, together with the power of judging when the right moment has arrived. The analogous quality in soldiers is the highly important one of being able to reserve their fire until the very instant at which it will be most effective. When the "Victory" went into action at Trafalgar at hardly more than drifting pace, she was for several minutes exposed to a storm of shot and shell before replying with a single gun. Nelson coolly waited until he was within close range, when the broadside he brought to bear worked fearful havoc on the enemy's nearest ships.
79 The word "decision" would have reference to the measurement of distance mentioned above, letting the enemy get near before striking. But I cannot help thinking that Sun Tzu meant to use the word in a figurative sense comparable to our own idiom "short and sharp." Cf. Wang Hsi's note, which after describing the falcon's mode of attack, proceeds: "This is just how the 'psychological moment' should be seized in war."
80 None of the commentators seem to grasp the real point of the simile of energy and the force stored up in the bent cross- bow until released by the finger on the trigger.

os, your array may be without head or tail, yet it will be proof against defeat.[81]

17. Simulated disorder postulates perfect discipline, simulated fear postulates courage; simulated weakness postulates strength.[82]

18. Hiding order beneath the cloak of disorder is simply a question of subdivision; concealing courage under a show of timidity presupposes a fund of latent energy;[83] masking strength with weakness is to be effected by tactical dispositions.[84]

19. Thus one who is skillful at keeping the enemy on the move maintains deceitful appearances, according to which the enemy will act.[85] He sacrifices something, that the enemy may snatch at it.

81 Mei Yao-ch`en says: "The subdivisions of the army having been previously fixed, and the various signals agreed upon, the separating and joining, the dispersing and collecting which will take place in the course of a battle, may give the appearance of disorder when no real disorder is possible. Your formation may be without head or tail, your dispositions all topsy-turvy, and yet a rout of your forces quite out of the question.
82 In order to make the translation intelligible, it is necessary to tone down the sharply paradoxical form of the original. Ts`ao Kung throws out a hint of the meaning in his brief note: "These things all serve to destroy formation and conceal one's condition." But Tu Mu is the first to put it quite plainly: "If you wish to feign confusion in order to lure the enemy on, you must first have perfect discipline; if you wish to display timidity in order to entrap the enemy, you must have extreme courage; if you wish to parade your weakness in order to make the enemy over-confident, you must have exceeding strength."
83 The commentators strongly understand a certain Chinese word here differently than anywhere else in this chapter. Thus Tu Mu says: "seeing that we are favorably circumstanced and yet make no move, the enemy will believe that we are really afraid."
84 Chang Yu relates the following anecdote of Kao Tsu, the first Han Emperor: "Wishing to crush the Hsiung-nu, he sent out spies to report on their condition. But the Hsiung-nu, forewarned, carefully concealed all their able-bodied men and well-fed horses, and only allowed infirm soldiers and emaciated cattle to be seen. The result was that spies one and all recommended the Emperor to deliver his attack. Lou Ching alone opposed them, saying: "When two countries go to war, they are naturally inclined to make an ostentatious display of their strength. Yet our spies have seen nothing but old age and infirmity. This is surely some ruse on the part of the enemy, and it would be unwise for us to attack." The Emperor, however, disregarding this advice, fell into the trap and found himself surrounded at Po-teng."
85 Ts`ao Kung's note is "Make a display of weakness and want." Tu Mu says: "If our force happens to be superior to the enemy's, weakness may be simulated in order to lure him on; but if inferior, he must be led to believe that we are strong, in order that he may keep off. In fact, all the enemy's movements should be determined by the signs that we choose to give him." Note the following anecdote of Sun Pin, a descendent of Sun Wu: In 341 B.C., the Ch`i State being at war with Wei, sent T`ien Chi and Sun Pin against the general P`ang Chuan, who happened to be a deadly personal enemy of the later. Sun Pin said: "The Ch`i State has a reputation for cowardice, and therefore our adversary despises us. Let us turn this circumstance to account." Accordingly, when the army had crossed

20. By holding out baits, he keeps him on the march; then with a body of picked men he lies in wait for him.[86]

21. The clever combatant looks to the effect of combined energy, and does not require too much from individuals.[87] Hence his ability to pick out the right men and utilize combined energy.

22. When he utilizes combined energy, his fighting men become as it were like unto rolling logs or stones. For it is the nature of a log or stone to remain motionless on level ground, and to move when on a slope; if four-cornered, to come to a standstill, but if round-shaped, to go rolling down.[88]

23. Thus the energy developed by good fighting men is as the momentum of a round stone rolled down a mountain thousands of feet in height. So much on the subject of energy.[89]

---

the border into Wei territory, he gave orders to show 100,000 fires on the first night, 50,000 on the next, and the night after only 20,000. P'ang Chuan pursued them hotly, saying to himself: "I knew these men of Ch'i were cowards: their numbers have already fallen away by more than half." In his retreat, Sun Pin came to a narrow defile, which he calculated that his pursuers would reach after dark. Here he had a tree stripped of its bark, and inscribed upon it the words: "Under this tree shall P'ang Chuan die." Then, as night began to fall, he placed a strong body of archers in ambush near by, with orders to shoot directly if they saw a light. Later on, P'ang Chuan arrived at the spot, and noticing the tree, struck a light in order to read what was written on it. His body was immediately riddled by a volley of arrows, and his whole army thrown into confusion. [The above is Tu Mu's version of the story; the *Shih Chi*, less dramatically but probably with more historical truth, makes P'ang Chuan cut his own throat with an exclamation of despair, after the rout of his army.]

86   With an emendation suggested by Li Ching, this then reads, "He lies in wait with the main body of his troops."

87   Tu Mu says: "He first of all considers the power of his army in the bulk; afterwards he takes individual talent into account, and uses each men according to his capabilities. He does not demand perfection from the untalented."

88   Ts'au Kung calls this "the use of natural or inherent power."

89   The chief lesson of this chapter, in Tu Mu's opinion, is the paramount importance in war of rapid evolutions and sudden rushes. "Great results," he adds, "can thus be achieved with small forces."

CHAPTER SIX

Weak Points and Strong[90]

1. Sun Tzu said: Whoever is first in the field and awaits the coming of the enemy, will be fresh for the fight; whoever is second in the field and has to hasten to battle will arrive exhausted.

2. Therefore the clever combatant imposes his will on the enemy, but does not allow the enemy's will to be imposed on him.[91]

3. By holding out advantages to him, he can cause the enemy to approach of his own accord; or, by inflicting damage, he can make it impossible for the enemy to draw near.[92]

4. If the enemy is taking his ease, he can harass him; if well supplied with food, he can starve him out; if quietly encamped, he can force him to move.

5. Appear at points which the enemy must hasten to defend; march swiftly to places where you are not expected.

90 Chang Yu attempts to explain the sequence of chapters as follows: "Chapter IV, on Tactical Dispositions, treated of the offensive and the defensive; chapter V, on Energy, dealt with direct and indirect methods. The good general acquaints himself first with the theory of attack and defense, and then turns his attention to direct and indirect methods. He studies the art of varying and combining these two methods before proceeding to the subject of weak and strong points. For the use of direct or indirect methods arises out of attack and defense, and the perception of weak and strong points depends again on the above methods. Hence the present chapter comes immediately after the chapter on Energy."
91 One mark of a great soldier is that he fight on his own terms or fights not at all.
92 In the first case, he will entice him with a bait; in the second, he will strike at some important point which the enemy will have to defend.

6. An army may march great distances without distress, if it marches through country where the enemy is not.[93]

7. You can be sure of succeeding in your attacks if you only attack places which are undefended.[94] You can ensure the safety of your defense if you only hold positions that cannot be attacked.[95]

8. Hence that general is skillful in attack whose opponent does not know what to defend; and he is skillful in defense whose opponent does not know what to attack.[96]

9. O divine art of subtlety and secrecy! Through you we learn to be invisible, through you inaudible;[97] and hence we can hold the enemy's fate in our hands.

10. You may advance and be absolutely irresistible, if you make for the enemy's weak points; you may retire and be safe from pursuit if your movements are more rapid than those of the enemy.

11. If we wish to fight, the enemy can be forced to an engagement even though he be sheltered behind a high rampart and a deep ditch. All we need do is attack some other place that he will be obliged to relieve.[98]

93　Ts`ao Kung sums up very well: "Emerge from the void [q.d. like "a bolt from the blue"], strike at vulnerable points, shun places that are defended, attack in unexpected quarters."
94　Wang Hsi explains "undefended places" as "weak points; that is to say, where the general is lacking in capacity, or the soldiers in spirit; where the walls are not strong enough, or the precautions not strict enough; where relief comes too late, or provisions are too scanty, or the defenders are variance amongst themselves."
95　I.e., where there are none of the weak points mentioned above. There is rather a nice point involved in the interpretation of this later clause. Tu Mu, Ch`en Hao, and Mei Yao-ch`en assume the meaning to be: "In order to make your defense quite safe, you must defend *even* those places that are not likely to be attacked;" and Tu Mu adds: "How much more, then, those that will be attacked." Taken thus, however, the clause balances less well with the preceding – always a consideration in the highly antithetical style which is natural to the Chinese. Chang Yu, therefore, seems to come nearer the mark in saying: "He who is skilled in attack flashes forth from the topmost heights of heaven [see IV. ss. 7], making it impossible for the enemy to guard against him. This being so, the places that I shall attack are precisely those that the enemy cannot defend…. He who is skilled in defense hides in the most secret recesses of the earth, making it impossible for the enemy to estimate his whereabouts. This being so, the places that I shall hold are precisely those that the enemy cannot attack."
96　An aphorism which puts the whole art of war in a nutshell.
97　Literally, "without form or sound," but it is said of course with reference to the enemy.
98　Tu Mu says: "If the enemy is the invading party, we can cut his line of communications and occupy the roads by which he will have to return; if we are the

12. If we do not wish to fight, we can prevent the enemy from engaging us even though the lines of our encampment be merely traced out on the ground. All we need do is to throw something odd and unaccountable in his way.[99]

13. By discovering the enemy's dispositions and remaining invisible ourselves, we can keep our forces concentrated, while the enemy's must be divided.[100]

14. We can form a single united body, while the enemy must split up into fractions. Hence there will be a whole pitted against separate parts of a whole, which means that we shall be many to the enemy's few.

15. And if we are able thus to attack an inferior force with a superior one, our opponents will be in dire straits.

16. The spot where we intend to fight must not be made known; for then the enemy will have to prepare against a possible attack at several different points;[101] and his forces being thus distributed in many directions, the numbers we shall have to face at any given point will be proportionately few.

17. For should the enemy strengthen his van, he will weaken his rear; should he strengthen his rear, he will weaken his van; should he

---

invaders, we may direct our attack against the sovereign himself." It is clear that Sun Tzu, unlike certain generals in the late Boer war, was no believer in frontal attacks.

99   This extremely concise expression is intelligibly paraphrased by Chia Lin: "even though we have constructed neither wall nor ditch." Li Ch`uan says: "we puzzle him by strange and unusual dispositions;" and Tu Mu finally clinches the meaning by three illustrative anecdotes – one of Chu-ko Liang, who when occupying Yang-p`ing and about to be attacked by Ssu-ma I, suddenly struck his colors, stopped the beating of the drums, and flung open the city gates, showing only a few men engaged in sweeping and sprinkling the ground. This unexpected proceeding had the intended effect; for Ssu-ma I, suspecting an ambush, actually drew off his army and retreated. What Sun Tzu is advocating here, therefore, is nothing more nor less than the timely use of "bluff."

100   The conclusion is perhaps not very obvious, but Chang Yu (after Mei Yao-ch`en) rightly explains it thus: "If the enemy's dispositions are visible, we can make for him in one body; whereas, our own dispositions being kept secret, the enemy will be obliged to divide his forces in order to guard against attack from every quarter."

101   Sheridan once explained the reason of General Grant's victories by saying that "while his opponents were kept fully employed wondering what he was going to do, HE was thinking most of what he was going to do himself."

strengthen his left, he will weaken his right; should he strengthen his right, he will weaken his left. If he sends reinforcements every-where, he will everywhere be weak.[102]

18. Numerical weakness comes from having to prepare against pos-sible attacks; numerical strength, from compelling our adversary to make these preparations against us.[103]

19. Knowing the place and the time of the coming battle, we may con-centrate from the greatest distances in order to fight.[104]

20. But if neither time nor place be known, then the left wing will be impotent to succor the right, the right equally impotent to succor the left, the van unable to relieve the rear, or the rear to support the van. How much more so if the furthest portions of the army are anything under a hundred *li* apart, and even the nearest are sepa-rated by several *li*![105]

102   In Frederick the Great's *Instructions to His Generals* we read: "A defensive war is apt to betray us into too frequent detachment. Those generals who have had but little experience attempt to protect every point, while those who are better acquainted with their profession, having only the capital object in view, guard against a decisive blow, and acquiesce in small misfortunes to avoid greater."

103   The highest generalship, in Col. Henderson's words, is "to compel the enemy to disperse his army, and then to concentrate superior force against each fraction in turn."

104   What Sun Tzu evidently has in mind is that nice calculation of distances and that masterly employment of strategy which enable a general to divide his army for the purpose of a long and rapid march, and afterwards to effect a junction at precisely the right spot and the right hour in order to confront the enemy in overwhelming strength. Among many such successful junctions which military history records, one of the most dramatic and decisive was the appearance of Blucher just at the critical moment on the field of Waterloo.

105   The Chinese of this last sentence is a little lacking in precision, but the mental picture we are required to draw is probably that of an army advancing towards a given rendezvous in separate columns, each of which has orders to be there on a fixed date. If the general allows the various detachments to proceed at haphazard, without precise instructions as to the time and place of meeting, the enemy will be able to annihilate the army in detail. Chang Yu's note may be worth quoting here: "If we do not know the place where our opponents mean to concentrate or the day on which they will join battle, our unity will be forfeited through our preparations for defense, and the positions we hold will be insecure. Suddenly happening upon a powerful foe, we shall be brought to battle in a flurried condition, and no mutual support will be possible between wings, vanguard or rear, especially if there is any great distance between the foremost and hindmost divisions of the army."

21. Though according to my estimate the soldiers of Yueh exceed our own in number, that shall advantage them nothing in the matter of victory. I say then that victory can be achieved.[106]

22. Though the enemy be stronger in numbers, we may prevent him from fighting. Scheme so as to discover his plans and the likelihood of their success.[107]

23. Rouse him, and learn the principle of his activity or inactivity.[108] Force him to reveal himself, so as to find out his vulnerable spots.

24. Carefully compare the opposing army with your own, so that you may know where strength is superabundant and where it is deficient.

25. In making tactical dispositions, the highest pitch you can attain is to conceal them;[109] conceal your dispositions, and you will be safe from the prying of the subtlest spies, from the machinations of the wisest brains.[110]

26. How victory may be produced for them out of the enemy's own tactics – that is what the multitude cannot comprehend.

106 Alas for these brave words! The long feud between the two states ended in 473 B.C. with the total defeat of Wu by Kou Chien and its incorporation in Yueh. This was doubtless long after Sun Tzu's death. With his present assertion compare IV. ss. 4. Chang Yu is the only one to point out the seeming discrepancy, which he thus goes on to explain: "In the chapter on Tactical Dispositions it is said, 'One may *know* how to conquer without being able to *do* it,' whereas here we have the statement that 'victory' can be achieved.' The explanation is, that in the former chapter, where the offensive and defensive are under discussion, it is said that if the enemy is fully prepared, one cannot make certain of beating him. But the present passage refers particularly to the soldiers of Yueh who, according to Sun Tzu's calculations, will be kept in ignorance of the time and place of the impending struggle. That is why he says here that victory can be achieved."
107 An alternative reading offered by Chia Lin is: "Know beforehand all plans conducive to our success and to the enemy's failure."
108 Chang Yu tells us that by noting the joy or anger shown by the enemy on being thus disturbed, we shall be able to conclude whether his policy is to lie low or the reverse. He instances the action of Cho-ku Liang, who sent the scornful present of a woman's head-dress to Ssu-ma I, in order to goad him out of his Fabian tactics.
109 The piquancy of the paradox evaporates in translation. Concealment is perhaps not so much actual invisibility (see supra ss. 9) as "showing no sign" of what you mean to do, of the plans that are formed in your brain.
110 Tu Mu explains: "Though the enemy may have clever and capable officers, they will not be able to lay any plans against us."

27. All men can see the tactics whereby I conquer, but what none can see is the strategy out of which victory is evolved.[111]

28. Do not repeat the tactics which have gained you one victory, but let your methods be regulated by the infinite variety of circumstances.[112]

29. Military tactics are like unto water; for water in its natural course runs away from high places and hastens downwards.

30. So in war, the way is to avoid what is strong and to strike at what is weak.[113]

31. Water shapes its course according to the nature of the ground over which it flows; the soldier works out his victory in relation to the foe whom he is facing.

32. Therefore, just as water retains no constant shape, so in warfare there are no constant conditions.

33. He who can modify his tactics in relation to his opponent and thereby succeed in winning, may be called a heaven-born captain.

34. The five elements (water, fire, wood, metal, earth) are not always equally predominant;[114] the four seasons make way for each other in turn.[115] There are short days and long; the moon has its periods of waning and waxing.[116]

111 I.e., everybody can see superficially how a battle is won; what they cannot see is the long series of plans and combinations which has preceded the battle.
112 As Wang Hsi sagely remarks: "There is but one root- principle underlying victory, but the tactics which lead up to it are infinite in number." With this compare Col. Henderson: "The rules of strategy are few and simple. They may be learned in a week. They may be taught by familiar illustrations or a dozen diagrams. But such knowledge will no more teach a man to lead an army like Napoleon than a knowledge of grammar will teach him to write like Gibbon."
113 Like water, taking the line of least resistance.
114 That is, as Wang Hsi says: "they predominate alternately."
115 Literally, "have no invariable seat."
116 Confer with chapter 5, section 6. The purport of the passage is simply to illustrate the want of fixity in war by the changes constantly taking place in Nature. The comparison is not very happy, however, because the regularity of the phenomena which Sun Tzu mentions is by no means paralleled in war.

CHAPTER SEVEN

Maneuvering

1. Sun Tzu said: In war, the general receives his commands from the sovereign.

2. Having collected an army and concentrated his forces, he must blend and harmonize the different elements thereof before pitching his camp.[117]

3. After that, comes tactical maneuvering, than which there is nothing more difficult.[118] The difficulty of tactical maneuvering consists in turning the devious into the direct, and misfortune into gain.[119]

117   "Chang Yu says: "the establishment of harmony and confidence between the higher and lower ranks before venturing into the field;" and he quotes a saying of Wu Tzu (chap. 1 ad init.): "Without harmony in the State, no military expedition can be undertaken; without harmony in the army, no battle array can be formed." In an historical romance Sun Tzu is represented as saying to Wu Yuan: "As a general rule, those who are waging war should get rid of all the domestic troubles before proceeding to attack the external foe."
118   I have departed slightly from the traditional interpretation of Ts`ao Kung, who says: "From the time of receiving the sovereign's instructions until our encampment over against the enemy, the tactics to be pursued are most difficult." It seems to me that the tactics or maneuvers can hardly be said to begin until the army has sallied forth and encamped, and Ch`ien Hao's note gives color to this view: "For levying, concentrating, harmonizing and entrenching an army, there are plenty of old rules which will serve. The real difficulty comes when we engage in tactical operations." Tu Yu also observes that "the great difficulty is to be beforehand with the enemy in seizing favorable position."
119   This sentence contains one of those highly condensed and somewhat enigmatical expressions of which Sun Tzu is so fond. This is how it is explained by Ts`ao Kung: "Make it appear that you are a long way off, then cover the distance rapidly and arrive on the scene before your opponent." Tu Mu says: "Hoodwink the enemy, so that he may be remiss and leisurely while you are dashing along with utmost speed." Ho Shih gives a slightly different turn: "Although you may have difficult ground to traverse and natural

4. Thus, to take a long and circuitous route, after enticing the enemy out of the way, and though starting after him, to contrive to reach the goal before him, shows knowledge of the artifice of *deviation*.[120]

5. Maneuvering with an army is advantageous; with an undisciplined multitude, most dangerous.[121]

6. If you set a fully equipped army in march in order to snatch an advantage, the chances are that you will be too late. On the other hand, to detach a flying column for the purpose involves the sacrifice of its baggage and stores.[122]

7. Thus, if you order your men to roll up their buff-coats, and make forced marches without halting day or night, covering double the usual distance at a stretch,[123] doing a hundred *li* in order to wrest an advantage, the leaders of all your three divisions will fall into the hands of the enemy.

---

obstacles to encounter this is a drawback which can be turned into actual advantage by celerity of movement." Signal examples of this saying are afforded by the two famous passages across the Alps – that of Hannibal, which laid Italy at his mercy, and that of Napoleon two thousand years later, which resulted in the great victory of Marengo.

120 Tu Mu cites the famous march of Chao She in 270 B.C. to relieve the town of O-yu, which was closely invested by a Ch`in army. The King of Chao first consulted Lien P`o on the advisability of attempting a relief, but the latter thought the distance too great, and the intervening country too rugged and difficult. His Majesty then turned to Chao She, who fully admitted the hazardous nature of the march, but finally said: "We shall be like two rats fighting in a whole – and the pluckier one will win!" So he left the capital with his army, but had only gone a distance of 30 LI when he stopped and began throwing up entrenchments. For 28 days he continued strengthening his fortifications, and took care that spies should carry the intelligence to the enemy. The Ch`in general was overjoyed, and attributed his adversary's tardiness to the fact that the beleaguered city was in the Han State, and thus not actually part of Chao territory. But the spies had no sooner departed than Chao She began a forced march lasting for two days and one night, and arrive on the scene of action with such astonishing rapidity that he was able to occupy a commanding position on the "North hill" before the enemy had got wind of his movements. A crushing defeat followed for the Ch`in forces, who were obliged to raise the siege of O-yu in all haste and retreat across the border.

121 I adopt the reading of the *T`Ung Tien*, Cheng Yu-hsien and the *T`U Shu*, since they appear to apply the exact nuance required in order to make sense. The commentators using the standard text take this line to mean that maneuvers may be profitable, or they may be dangerous: it all depends on the ability of the general.

122 Some of the Chinese text is unintelligible to the Chinese commentators, who paraphrase the sentence. I submit my own rendering without much enthusiasm, being convinced that there is some deep-seated corruption in the text. On the whole, it is clear that Sun Tzu does not approve of a lengthy march being undertaken without supplies.

123 The ordinary day's march, according to Tu Mu, was 30 *li*; but on one occasion, when pursuing Liu Pei, Ts`ao Ts`ao is said to have covered the incredible distance of 300 *li* within twenty-four hours.

8. The stronger men will be in front, the jaded ones will fall behind, and on this plan only one-tenth of your army will reach its destination.[124]

9. If you march fifty *li* in order to outmaneuver the enemy, you will lose the leader of your first division, and only half your force will reach the goal.[125]

10. If you march thirty *li* with the same object, two-thirds of your army will arrive.[126]

11. We may take it then that an army without its baggage-train is lost; without provisions it is lost; without bases of supply it is lost.[127]

12. We cannot enter into alliances until we are acquainted with the designs of our neighbors.

13. We are not fit to lead an army on the march unless we are familiar with the face of the country – its mountains and forests, its pitfalls and precipices, its marshes and swamps.

14. We shall be unable to turn natural advantage to account unless we make use of local guides.[128]

15. In war, practice dissimulation, and you will succeed.[129]

16. Whether to concentrate or to divide your troops, must be decided by circumstances.

124 The moral is, as Ts`ao Kung and others point out: Don't march a hundred *li* to gain a tactical advantage, either with or without impedimenta. Maneuvers of this description should be confined to short distances. Stonewall Jackson said: "The hardships of forced marches are often more painful than the dangers of battle." He did not often call upon his troops for extraordinary exertions. It was only when he intended a surprise, or when a rapid retreat was imperative, that he sacrificed everything for speed.
125 Literally, "the leader of the first division will be *torn away*."
126 In the *T`Ung Tien* is added: "From this we may know the difficulty of maneuvering."
127 I think Sun Tzu meant "stores accumulated in depots." But Tu Yu says "fodder and the like," Chang Yu says "Goods in general," and Wang Hsi says "fuel, salt, foodstuffs, etc."
128 Lines 12-14 are repeated in chapter eleven.
129 In the tactics of Turenne, deception of the enemy, especially as to the numerical strength of his troops, took a very prominent position.

17. Let your rapidity be that of the wind,[130] your compactness that of the forest.[131]

18. In raiding and plundering be like fire,[132] in immovability like a mountain.[133]

19. Let your plans be dark and impenetrable as night, and when you move, fall like a thunderbolt.[134]

20. When you plunder a countryside, let the spoil be divided amongst your men;[135] when you capture new territory, cut it up into allotments for the benefit of the soldiery.[136]

21. Ponder and deliberate before you make a move.[137]

22. He will conquer who has learnt the artifice of deviation. Such is the art of maneuvering.[138]

---

130   The simile is doubly appropriate, because the wind is not only swift but, as Mei Yao-ch`en points out, "invisible and leaves no tracks."

131   Meng Shih comes nearer to the mark in his note: "When slowly marching, order and ranks must be preserved" – so as to guard against surprise attacks. But natural forest do not grow in rows, whereas they do generally possess the quality of density or compactness.

132   The *Shih Ching* reads "Fierce as a blazing fire which no man can check."

133   That is, when holding a position from which the enemy is trying to dislodge you, or perhaps, as Tu Yu says, when he is trying to entice you into a trap.

134   Tu Yu quotes a saying of T`ai Kung which has passed into a proverb: "You cannot shut your ears to the thunder or your eyes to the lighting – so rapid are they." Likewise, an attack should be made so quickly that it cannot be parried.

135   Sun Tzu wishes to lessen the abuses of indiscriminate plundering by insisting that all booty shall be thrown into a common stock, which may afterwards be fairly divided amongst all.

136   Ch`en Hao says "quarter your soldiers on the land, and let them sow and plant it." It is by acting on this principle, and harvesting the lands they invaded, that the Chinese have succeeded in carrying out some of their most memorable and triumphant expeditions, such as that of Pan Ch`ao who penetrated to the Caspian, and in more recent years, those of Fu-k`ang-an and Tso Tsung-t`ang.

137   Chang Yu quotes Wei Liao Tzu as saying that we must not break camp until we have gained the resisting power of the enemy and the cleverness of the opposing general.

138   With these words, the chapter would naturally come to an end. But there now follows a long appendix in the shape of an extract from an earlier book on War, now lost, but apparently extant at the time when Sun Tzu wrote. The style of this fragment is not noticeably different from that of Sun Tzu himself, but no commentator raises a doubt as to its genuineness.

23. The Book of Army Management says:[139] On the field of battle,[140] the spoken word does not carry far enough: hence the institution of gongs and drums. Nor can ordinary objects be seen clearly enough: hence the institution of banners and flags.

24. Gongs and drums, banners and flags, are means whereby the ears and eyes of the host may be focused on one particular point.[141]

25. The host thus forming a single united body, is it impossible either for the brave to advance alone, or for the cowardly to retreat alone.[142] This is the art of handling large masses of men.

26. In night-fighting, then, make much use of signal-fires and drums, and in fighting by day, of flags and banners, as a means of influencing the ears and eyes of your army.[143]

27. A whole army may be robbed of its spirit;[144] a commander-in-chief

139   It is perhaps significant that none of the earlier commentators give us any information about this work. Mei Yao- Ch`en calls it "an ancient military classic," and Wang Hsi, "an old book on war." Considering the enormous amount of fighting that had gone on for centuries before Sun Tzu's time between the various kingdoms and principalities of China, it is not in itself improbable that a collection of military maxims should have been made and written down at some earlier period.

140   Implied, though not actually in the Chinese.

141   Chang Yu says: "If sight and hearing converge simultaneously on the same object, the evolutions of as many as a million soldiers will be like those of a single man."!

142   Chuang Yu quotes a saying: "Equally guilty are those who advance against orders and those who retreat against orders." Tu Mu tells a story in this connection of Wu Ch`i, when he was fighting against the Ch`in State. Before the battle had begun, one of his soldiers, a man of matchless daring, sallied forth by himself, captured two heads from the enemy, and returned to camp. Wu Ch`i had the man instantly executed, whereupon an officer ventured to remonstrate, saying: "This man was a good soldier, and ought not to have been beheaded." Wu Ch`i replied: "I fully believe he was a good soldier, but I had him beheaded because he acted without orders."

143   Ch`en Hao alludes to Li Kuang-pi's night ride to Ho-yang at the head of 500 mounted men; they made such an imposing display with torches, that though the rebel leader Shih Ssu-ming had a large army, he did not dare to dispute their passage.

144   "In war," says Chang Yu, "if a spirit of anger can be made to pervade all ranks of an army at one and the same time, its onset will be irresistible. Now the spirit of the enemy's soldiers will be keenest when they have newly arrived on the scene, and it is therefore our cue not to fight at once, but to wait until their ardor and enthusiasm have worn off, and then strike. It is in this way that they may be robbed of their keen spirit." Li Ch`uan and others tell an anecdote (to be found in the *Tso Chuan*, year 10, ss. 1) of Ts`ao Kuei, a protege of Duke Chuang of Lu. The latter State was attacked by Ch`i, and the duke was about to join battle at Ch`ang-cho, after the first roll of the enemy's drums, when Ts`ao said: "Not just yet." Only after their drums had beaten for the third time, did he give the word for attack. Then they fought, and the men of Ch`i were utterly defeated. Questioned

may be robbed of his presence of mind.[145]

28. Now a soldier's spirit is keenest in the morning;[146] by noonday it has begun to flag; and in the evening, his mind is bent only on returning to camp.

29. A clever general, therefore, avoids an army when its spirit is keen, but attacks it when it is sluggish and inclined to return. This is the art of studying moods.

30. Disciplined and calm, to await the appearance of disorder and hubbub amongst the enemy: – this is the art of retaining self-possession.

31. To be near the goal while the enemy is still far from it, to wait at ease while the enemy is toiling and struggling, to be well-fed while the enemy is famished: – this is the art of husbanding one's strength.

32. To refrain from intercepting an enemy whose banners are in perfect order, to refrain from attacking an army drawn up in calm and confident array: – this is the art of studying circumstances.

33. It is a military axiom not to advance uphill against the enemy, nor to oppose him when he comes downhill.

34. Do not pursue an enemy who simulates flight; do not attack soldiers whose temper is keen.

---

afterwards by the Duke as to the meaning of his delay, Ts'ao Kuei replied: "In battle, a courageous spirit is everything. Now the first roll of the drum tends to create this spirit, but with the second it is already on the wane, and after the third it is gone altogether. I attacked when their spirit was gone and ours was at its height. Hence our victory." Wu Tzu (chap. 4) puts "spirit" first among the "four important influences" in war, and continues: "The value of a whole army – a mighty host of a million men – is dependent on one man alone: such is the influence of spirit!"

145   Chang Yu says: "Presence of mind is the general's most important asset. It is the quality which enables him to discipline disorder and to inspire courage into the panic-stricken." The great general Li Ching (A.D. 571-649) has a saying: "Attacking does not merely consist in assaulting walled cities or striking at an army in battle array; it must include the art of assailing the enemy's mental equilibrium."

146   Always provided, I suppose, that he has had breakfast. At the battle of the Trebia, the Romans were foolishly allowed to fight fasting, whereas Hannibal's men had breakfasted at their leisure.

35. Do not swallow bait offered by the enemy.[147] Do not interfere with an army that is returning home.[148]

36. When you surround an army, leave an outlet free.[149] Do not press a desperate foe too hard.[150]

37. Such is the art of warfare.

147   Li Ch`uan and Tu Mu, with extraordinary inability to see a metaphor, take these words quite literally of food and drink that have been poisoned by the enemy. Ch`en Hao and Chang Yu carefully point out that the saying has a wider application.

148   The commentators explain this rather singular piece of advice by saying that a man whose heart is set on returning home will fight to the death against any attempt to bar his way, and is therefore too dangerous an opponent to be tackled. Chang Yu quotes the words of Han Hsin: "Invincible is the soldier who hath his desire and returneth homewards." A marvelous tale is told of Ts`ao Ts`ao's courage and resource in ch. 1 of the *San Kuo Chi*: In 198 A.D., he was besieging Chang Hsiu in Jang, when Liu Piao sent reinforcements with a view to cutting off Ts`ao's retreat. The latter was obliged to draw off his troops, only to find himself hemmed in between two enemies, who were guarding each outlet of a narrow pass in which he had engaged himself. In this desperate plight Ts`ao waited until nightfall, when he bored a tunnel into the mountain side and laid an ambush in it. As soon as the whole army had passed by, the hidden troops fell on his rear, while Ts`ao himself turned and met his pursuers in front, so that they were thrown into confusion and annihilated. Ts`ao Ts`ao said afterwards: "The brigands tried to check my army in its retreat and brought me to battle in a desperate position: hence I knew how to overcome them."

149   This does not mean that the enemy is to be allowed to escape. The object, as Tu Mu puts it, is "to make him believe that there is a road to safety, and thus prevent his fighting with the courage of despair." Tu Mu adds pleasantly: "After that, you may crush him."

150   Ch`en Hao quotes the saying: "Birds and beasts when brought to bay will use their claws and teeth." Chang Yu says: "If your adversary has burned his boats and destroyed his cooking-pots, and is ready to stake all on the issue of a battle, he must not be pushed to extremities." Ho Shih illustrates the meaning by a story taken from the life of Yen-ch`ing. That general, together with his colleague Tu Chung-wei was surrounded by a vastly superior army of Khitans in the year 945 A.D. The country was bare and desert-like, and the little Chinese force was soon in dire straits for want of water. The wells they bored ran dry, and the men were reduced to squeezing lumps of mud and sucking out the moisture. Their ranks thinned rapidly, until at last Fu Yen-ch`ing exclaimed: "We are desperate men. Far better to die for our country than to go with fettered hands into captivity!" A strong gale happened to be blowing from the northeast and darkening the air with dense clouds of sandy dust. To Chung-wei was for waiting until this had abated before deciding on a final attack; but luckily another officer, Li Shou-cheng by name, was quicker to see an opportunity, and said: "They are many and we are few, but in the midst of this sandstorm our numbers will not be discernible; victory will go to the strenuous fighter, and the wind will be our best ally." Accordingly, Fu Yen-ch`ing made a sudden and wholly unexpected onslaught with his cavalry, routed the barbarians and succeeded in breaking through to safety.

CHAPTER EIGHT

Variation in Tactics[151]

1. Sun Tzu said: In war, the general receives his commands from the sovereign, collects his army and concentrates his forces.[152]

2. When in difficult country, do not encamp. In country where high roads intersect, join hands with your allies. Do not linger in dangerously isolated positions.[153] In hemmed-in situations, you must resort to stratagem. In desperate position, you must fight.

3. There are roads which must not be followed,[154] armies which must

---

151 The heading means literally "The Nine Variations," but as Sun Tzu does not appear to enumerate these, and as, indeed, he has already told us (V SS. 6-11) that such deflections from the ordinary course are practically innumerable, we have little option but to follow Wang Hsi, who says that "Nine" stands for an indefinitely large number. "All it means is that in warfare we ought to vary our tactics to the utmost degree.... I do not know what Ts`ao Kung makes these Nine Variations out to be, but it has been suggested that they are connected with the Nine Situations" - of chapter eleven. This is the view adopted by Chang Yu. The only other alternative is to suppose that something has been lost – a supposition to which the unusual shortness of the chapter lends some weight.
152 Repeated from chapter seven, where it is certainly more in place. It may have been interpolated here merely in order to supply a beginning to the chapter.
153 The last situation is not one of the Nine Situations as given in the beginning of chapter eleven, but occurs later on (ibid. ss. 43. q.v.). Chang Yu defines this situation as being situated across the frontier, in hostile territory. Li Ch`uan says it is "country in which there are no springs or wells, flocks or herds, vegetables or firewood;" Chia Lin, "one of gorges, chasms and precipices, without a road by which to advance."
154 "Especially those leading through narrow defiles," says Li Ch`uan, "where an ambush is to be feared."

be not attacked,[155] towns which must not be besieged,[156] positions which must not be contested, commands of the sovereign which must not be obeyed.[157]

4. The general who thoroughly understands the advantages that accompany variation of tactics knows how to handle his troops.

5. The general who does not understand these, may be well acquainted with the configuration of the country, yet he will not be able to turn his knowledge to practical account.[158]

6. So, the student of war who is unversed in the art of war of varying his plans, even though he be acquainted with the Five Advantages, will fail to make the best use of his men.[159]

155   More correctly, perhaps, "there are times when an army must not be attacked." Ch`en Hao says: "When you see your way to obtain a rival advantage, but are powerless to inflict a real defeat, refrain from attacking, for fear of overtaxing your men's strength."

156   Ts`ao Kung gives an interesting illustration from his own experience. When invading the territory of Hsu-chou, he ignored the city of Hua-pi, which lay directly in his path, and pressed on into the heart of the country. This excellent strategy was rewarded by the subsequent capture of no fewer than fourteen important district cities. Chang Yu says: "No town should be attacked which, if taken, cannot be held, or if left alone, will not cause any trouble." Hsun Ying, when urged to attack Pi-yang, replied: "The city is small and well-fortified; even if I succeed intaking it, it will be no great feat of arms; whereas if I fail, I shall make myself a laughing-stock." In the seventeenth century, sieges still formed a large proportion of war. It was Turenne who directed attention to the importance of marches, countermarches and maneuvers. He said: "It is a great mistake to waste men in taking a town when the same expenditure of soldiers will gain a province."

157   This is a hard saying for the Chinese, with their reverence for authority, and Wei Liao Tzu (quoted by Tu Mu) is moved to exclaim: "Weapons are baleful instruments, strife is antagonistic to virtue, a military commander is the negation of civil order!" The unpalatable fact remains, however, that even Imperial wishes must be subordinated to military necessity.

158   Literally, "get the advantage of the ground," which means not only securing good positions, but availing oneself of natural advantages in every possible way. Chang Yu says: "Every kind of ground is characterized by certain natural features, and also gives scope for a certain variability of plan. How it is possible to turn these natural features to account unless topographical knowledge is supplemented by versatility of mind?"

159   Chia Lin tells us that these imply five obvious and generally advantageous lines of action, namely: "if a certain road is short, it must be followed; if an army is isolated, it must be attacked; if a town is in a parlous condition, it must be besieged; if a position can be stormed, it must be attempted; and if consistent with military operations, the ruler's commands must be obeyed." But there are circumstances which sometimes forbid a general to use these advantages. For instance, "a certain road may be the shortest way for him, but if he knows that it abounds in natural obstacles, or that the enemy has laid an ambush on it, he will not follow that road. A hostile force may be open to attack, but if he knows that it is hard-pressed and likely to fight with desperation, he will refrain from striking," and so on.

7. Hence in the wise leader's plans, considerations of advantage and of disadvantage will be blended together.[160]

8. If our expectation of advantage be tempered in this way, we may succeed in accomplishing the essential part of our schemes.[161]

9. If, on the other hand, in the midst of difficulties we are always ready to seize an advantage, we may extricate ourselves from misfortune.[162]

10. Reduce the hostile chiefs by inflicting damage on them;[163] and make trouble for them,[164] and keep them constantly engaged;[165] hold out specious allurements, and make them rush to any given point.[166]

160   "Whether in an advantageous position or a disadvantageous one," says Ts`ao Kung, "the opposite state should be always present to your mind."

161   Tu Mu says: "If we wish to wrest an advantage from the enemy, we must not fix our minds on that alone, but allow for the possibility of the enemy also doing some harm to us, and let this enter as a factor into our calculations."

162   Tu Mu says: "If I wish to extricate myself from a dangerous position, I must consider not only the enemy's ability to injure me, but also my own ability to gain an advantage over the enemy. If in my counsels these two considerations are properly blended, I shall succeed in liberating myself.... For instance; if I am surrounded by the enemy and only think of effecting an escape, the nervelessness of my policy will incite my adversary to pursue and crush me; it would be far better to encourage my men to deliver a bold counter-attack, and use the advantage thus gained to free myself from the enemy's toils."

163   Chia Lin enumerates several ways of inflicting this injury, some of which would only occur to the Oriental mind: – "Entice away the enemy's best and wisest men, so that he may be left without counselors. Introduce traitors into his country, that the government policy may be rendered futile. Foment intrigue and deceit, and thus sow dissension between the ruler and his ministers. By means of every artful contrivance, cause deterioration amongst his men and waste of his treasure. Corrupt his morals by insidious gifts leading him into excess. Disturb and unsettle his mind by presenting him with lovely women." Chang Yu (after Wang Hsi) makes a different interpretation of Sun Tzu here: "Get the enemy into a position where he must suffer injury, and he will submit of his own accord."

164   Tu Mu, in this phrase, in his interpretation indicates that trouble should be made for the enemy affecting their "possessions," or, as we might say, "assets," which he considers to be "a large army, a rich exchequer, harmony amongst the soldiers, punctual fulfillment of commands." These give us a whip-hand over the enemy.

165   Literally, "make servants of them." Tu Yu says "prevent the from having any rest."

166   Meng Shih's note contains an excellent example of the idiomatic use of: "cause them to forget *pien* (the reasons for acting otherwise than on their first impulse), and hasten in our direction."

11. The art of war teaches us to rely not on the likelihood of the enemy's not coming, but on our own readiness to receive him; not on the chance of his not attacking, but rather on the fact that we have made our position unassailable.

12. There are five dangerous faults which may affect a general:
    (1) Recklessness, which leads to destruction;[167]
    (2) Cowardice, which leads to capture;[168]
    (3) A hasty temper, which can be provoked by insults;[169]
    (4) A delicacy of honor which is sensitive to shame;[170]

167   "Bravery without forethought," as Ts'ao Kung analyzes it, which causes a man to fight blindly and desperately like a mad bull. Such an opponent, says Chang Yu, "must not be encountered with brute force, but may be lured into an ambush and slain." Cf. Wu Tzu, chap. IV. ad init.: "In estimating the character of a general, men are wont to pay exclusive attention to his courage, forgetting that courage is only one out of many qualities which a general should possess. The merely brave man is prone to fight recklessly; and he who fights recklessly, without any perception of what is expedient, must be condemned." Ssu-ma Fa, too, make the incisive remark: "Simply going to one's death does not bring about victory."

168   Ts'ao Kung defines the Chinese word translated here as "cowardice" as being of the man "whom timidity prevents from advancing to seize an advantage," and Wang Hsi adds "who is quick to flee at the sight of danger." Meng Shih gives the closer paraphrase "he who is bent on returning alive," this is, the man who will never take a risk. But, as Sun Tzu knew, nothing is to be achieved in war unless you are willing to take risks. T'ai Kung said: "He who lets an advantage slip will subsequently bring upon himself real disaster." In 404 A.D., Liu Yu pursued the rebel Huan Hsuan up the Yangtsze and fought a naval battle with him at the island of Ch'eng-hung. The loyal troops numbered only a few thousands, while their opponents were in great force. But Huan Hsuan, fearing the fate which was in store for him should be be overcome, had a light boat made fast to the side of his war-junk, so that he might escape, if necessary, at a moment's notice. The natural result was that the fighting spirit of his soldiers was utterly quenched, and when the loyalists made an attack from windward with fireships, all striving with the utmost ardor to be first in the fray, Huan Hsuan's forces were routed, had to burn all their baggage and fled for two days and nights without stopping. Chang Yu tells a somewhat similar story of Chao Ying-ch'i, a general of the Chin State who during a battle with the army of Ch'u in 597 B.C. had a boat kept in readiness for him on the river, wishing in case of defeat to be the first to get across.

169   Tu Mu tells us that Yao Hsing, when opposed in 357 A.D. by Huang Mei, Teng Ch'iang and others shut himself up behind his walls and refused to fight. Teng Ch'iang said: "Our adversary is of a choleric temper and easily provoked; let us make constant sallies and break down his walls, then he will grow angry and come out. Once we can bring his force to battle, it is doomed to be our prey." This plan was acted upon, Yao Hsiang came out to fight, was lured as far as San-yuan by the enemy's pretended flight, and finally attacked and slain.

170   This need not be taken to mean that a sense of honor is really a defect in a general. What Sun Tzu condemns is rather an exaggerated sensitiveness to slanderous reports, the thin-skinned man who is stung by opprobrium, however undeserved. Mei Yao-ch'en truly observes, though somewhat paradoxically: "The seek after glory should be careless of public opinion."

(5) Over-solicitude for his men, which exposes him to worry and trouble.[171]

13. These are the five besetting sins of a general, ruinous to the conduct of war.

14. When an army is overthrown and its leader slain, the cause will surely be found among these five dangerous faults. Let them be a subject of meditation.

171   Here again, Sun Tzu does not mean that the general is to be careless of the welfare of his troops. All he wishes to emphasize is the danger of sacrificing any important military advantage to the immediate comfort of his men. This is a shortsighted policy, because in the long run the troops will suffer more from the defeat, or, at best, the prolongation of the war, which will be the consequence. A mistaken feeling of pity will often induce a general to relieve a beleaguered city, or to reinforce a hard-pressed detachment, contrary to his military instincts. It is now generally admitted that our repeated efforts to relieve Ladysmith in the South African War were so many strategical blunders which defeated their own purpose. And in the end, relief came through the very man who started out with the distinct resolve no longer to subordinate the interests of the whole to sentiment in favor of a part. An old soldier of one of our generals who failed most conspicuously in this war, tried once, I remember, to defend him to me on the ground that he was always "so good to his men." By this plea, had he but known it, he was only condemning him out of Sun Tzu's mouth.

CHAPTER NINE

The Army on the March[172]

1. Sun Tzu said: We come now to the question of encamping the army, and observing signs of the enemy. Pass quickly over mountains, and keep in the neighborhood of valleys.[173]

2. Camp in high places,[174] facing the sun.[175] Do not climb heights in order to fight. So much for mountain warfare.

3. After crossing a river, you should get far away from it.[176]

4. When an invading force crosses a river in its onward march, do not advance to meet it in mid-stream. It will be best to let half the army get across, and then deliver your attack.[177]

172 The contents of this interesting chapter are better indicated in section 1 of this chapter, than by this heading.
173 The idea is, not to linger among barren uplands, but to keep close to supplies of water and grass. Wu Tzu writes "Abide not in natural ovens," i.e. "the openings of valleys." Chang Yu tells the following anecdote: Wu-tu Ch`iang was a robber captain in the time of the Later Han, and Ma Yuan was sent to exterminate his gang. Ch`iang having found a refuge in the hills, Ma Yuan made no attempt to force a battle, but seized all the favorable positions commanding supplies of water and forage. Ch`iang was soon in such a desperate plight for want of provisions that he was forced to make a total surrender. He did not know the advantage of keeping in the neighborhood of valleys."
174 Not on high hills, but on knolls or hillocks elevated above the surrounding country.
175 Tu Mu takes this to mean "facing south," and Ch`en Hao "facing east."
176 "In order to tempt the enemy to cross after you," according to Ts`ao Kung, and also, says Chang Yu, "in order not to be impeded in your evolutions." The T`ung Tien reads, "if the enemy crosses a river," etc. But in view of the next sentence, this is almost certainly an interpolation.
177 Li Ch`uan alludes to the great victory won by Han Hsin over Lung Chu at the Wei

5. If you are anxious to fight, you should not go to meet the invader near a river which he has to cross.[178]

6. Moor your craft higher up than the enemy, and facing the sun.[179] Do not move up-stream to meet the enemy.[180] So much for river warfare.

7. In crossing salt-marshes, your sole concern should be to get over them quickly, without any delay.[181]

8. If forced to fight in a salt-marsh, you should have water and grass near you, and get your back to a clump of trees.[182] So much for operations in salt-marches.

9. In dry, level country, take up an easily accessible position with rising ground to your right and on your rear,[183] so that the danger may be in front, and safety lie behind. So much for campaigning in flat country.

River. Turning to the *Ch'Ien Han Shu*, ch. 34, fol. 6 verso, we find the battle described as follows: "The two armies were drawn up on opposite sides of the river. In the night, Han Hsin ordered his men to take some ten thousand sacks filled with sand and construct a dam higher up. Then, leading half his army across, he attacked Lung Chu; but after a time, pretending to have failed in his attempt, he hastily withdrew to the other bank. Lung Chu was much elated by this unlooked-for success, and exclaiming: "I felt sure that Han Hsin was really a coward!" he pursued him and began crossing the river in his turn. Han Hsin now sent a party to cut open the sandbags, thus releasing a great volume of water, which swept down and prevented the greater portion of Lung Chu's army from getting across. He then turned upon the force which had been cut off, and annihilated it, Lung Chu himself being amongst the slain. The rest of the army, on the further bank, also scattered and fled in all directions.

178   For fear of preventing his crossing.
179   The repetition of these words in connection with water is very awkward. Chang Yu has the note: "Said either of troops marshaled on the river-bank, or of boats anchored in the stream itself; in either case it is essential to be higher than the enemy and facing the sun." The other commentators are not at all explicit.
180   Tu Mu says: "As water flows downwards, we must not pitch our camp on the lower reaches of a river, for fear the enemy should open the sluices and sweep us away in a flood. Chu-ko Wu- hou has remarked that 'in river warfare we must not advance against the stream,' which is as much as to say that our fleet must not be anchored below that of the enemy, for then they would be able to take advantage of the current and make short work of us." There is also the danger, noted by other commentators, that the enemy may throw poison on the water to be carried down to us.
181   Because of the lack of fresh water, the poor quality of the herbage, and last but not least, because they are low, flat, and exposed to attack.
182   Li Ch'uan remarks that the ground is less likely to be treacherous where there are trees, while Tu Mu says that they will serve to protect the rear.
183   Tu Mu quotes T'ai Kung as saying: "An army should have a stream or a marsh on its left, and a hill or tumulus on its right."

10. These are the four useful branches of military knowledge[184] which enabled the Yellow Emperor to vanquish four several sovereigns.[185]

11. All armies prefer high ground to low[186] and sunny places to dark.

12. If you are careful of your men,[187] and camp on hard ground, the army will be free from disease of every kind,[188] and this will spell victory.

13. When you come to a hill or a bank, occupy the sunny side, with the slope on your right rear. Thus you will at once act for the benefit of your soldiers and utilize the natural advantages of the ground.

14. When, in consequence of heavy rains up-country, a river which you wish to ford is swollen and flecked with foam, you must wait until it subsides.

15. Country in which there are precipitous cliffs with torrents running between, deep natural hollows,[189] confined places,[190] tangled

---

184 Those, namely, concerned with (1) mountains, (2) rivers, (3) marshes, and (4) plains. Compare Napoleon's "Military Maxims," no. 1.

185 Regarding the "Yellow Emperor": Mei Yao-ch`en asks, with some plausibility, whether there is an error in the text as nothing is known of Huang Ti having conquered four other Emperors. The *Shih Chi* (ch. 1 ad init.) speaks only of his victories over Yen Ti and Ch`ih Yu. In the *Liu T`Ao* it is mentioned that he "fought seventy battles and pacified the Empire." Ts`ao Kung's explanation is, that the Yellow Emperor was the first to institute the feudal system of vassals princes, each of whom (to the number of four) originally bore the title of Emperor. Li Ch`uan tells us that the art of war originated under Huang Ti, who received it from his Minister Feng Hou.

186 "High Ground," says Mei Yao-ch`en, "is not only more agreeable and salubrious, but more convenient from a military point of view; low ground is not only damp and unhealthy, but also disadvantageous for fighting."

187 Ts`ao Kung says: "Make for fresh water and pasture, where you can turn out your animals to graze."

188 Chang Yu says: "The dryness of the climate will prevent the outbreak of illness."

189 The latter defined as "places enclosed on every side by steep banks, with pools of water at the bottom.

190 Defined as "natural pens or prisons" or "places surrounded by precipices on three sides – easy to get into, but hard to get out of."

thickets,[191] quagmires[192] and crevasses,[193] should be left with all possible speed and not approached.

16. While we keep away from such places, we should get the enemy to approach them; while we face them, we should let the enemy have them on his rear.

17. If in the neighborhood of your camp there should be any hilly country, ponds surrounded by aquatic grass, hollow basins filled with reeds, or woods with thick undergrowth, they must be carefully routed out and searched; for these are places where men in ambush or insidious spies are likely to be lurking.[194]

18. When the enemy is close at hand and remains quiet, he is relying on the natural strength of his position.[195]

19. When he keeps aloof and tries to provoke a battle, he is anxious for the other side to advance.[196]

20. If his place of encampment is easy of access, he is tendering a bait.

21. Movement amongst the trees of a forest shows that the enemy is advancing.[197] The appearance of a number of screens in the midst

191 Defined as "places covered with such dense undergrowth that spears cannot be used."
192 Defined as "low-lying places, so heavy with mud as to be impassable for chariots and horsemen."
193 Defined by Mei Yao-ch`en as "a narrow difficult way between beetling cliffs." Tu Mu's note is "ground covered with trees and rocks, and intersected by numerous ravines and pitfalls." This is very vague, but Chia Lin explains it clearly enough as a defile or narrow pass, and Chang Yu takes much the same view. On the whole, the weight of the commentators certainly inclines to the rendering "defile." But the ordinary meaning of the Chinese in one place is "a crack or fissure" and the fact that the meaning of the Chinese elsewhere in the sentence indicates something in the nature of a defile, make me think that Sun Tzu is here speaking of crevasses.
194 Chang Yu has the note: "We must also be on our guard against traitors who may lie in close covert, secretly spying out our weaknesses and overhearing our instructions."
195 Here begin Sun Tzu's remarks on the reading of signs, much of which is so good that it could almost be included in a modern manual like Gen. Baden-Powell's "Aids to Scouting."
196 Probably because we are in a strong position from which he wishes to dislodge us. "If he came close up to us, says Tu Mu, "and tried to force a battle, he would seem to despise us, and there would be less probability of our responding to the challenge."
197 Ts`ao Kung explains this as "felling trees to clear a passage," and Chang Yu says: "Every man sends out scouts to climb high places and observe the enemy. If a scout sees that the trees of a forest are moving and shaking, he may know that they are being cut down to clear a passage for the enemy's march."

of thick grass means that the enemy wants to make us suspicious.[198]

22. The rising of birds in their flight is the sign of an ambuscade.[199] Startled beasts indicate that a sudden attack is coming.

23. When there is dust rising in a high column, it is the sign of chariots advancing; when the dust is low, but spread over a wide area, it betokens the approach of infantry.[200] When it branches out in different directions, it shows that parties have been sent to collect firewood. A few clouds of dust moving to and fro signify that the army is encamping.[201]

24. Humble words and increased preparations are signs that the enemy is about to advance.[202] Violent language and driving forward as if to

198 Tu Yu's explanation, borrowed from Ts'ao Kung's, is as follows: "The presence of a number of screens or sheds in the midst of thick vegetation is a sure sign that the enemy has fled and, fearing pursuit, has constructed these hiding-places in order to make us suspect an ambush." It appears that these "screens" were hastily knotted together out of any long grass which the retreating enemy happened to come across.
199 Chang Yu's explanation is doubtless right: "When birds that are flying along in a straight line suddenly shoot upwards, it means that soldiers are in ambush at the spot beneath."
200 "High and sharp," or rising to a peak, is of course somewhat exaggerated as applied to dust. The commentators explain the phenomenon by saying that horses and chariots, being heavier than men, raise more dust, and also follow one another in the same wheel-track, whereas foot-soldiers would be marching in ranks, many abreast. According to Chang Yu, "every army on the march must have scouts some way in advance, who on sighting dust raised by the enemy, will gallop back and report it to the commander-in-chief." Cf. Gen. Baden-Powell: "As you move along, say, in a hostile country, your eyes should be looking afar for the enemy or any signs of him: figures, dust rising, birds getting up, glitter of arms, etc."
201 Chang Yu says: "In apportioning the defenses for a cantonment, light horse will be sent out to survey the position and ascertain the weak and strong points all along its circumference. Hence the small quantity of dust and its motion."
202 "As though they stood in great fear of us," says Tu Mu. "Their object is to make us contemptuous and careless, after which they will attack us." Chang Yu alludes to the story of T'ien Tan of the Ch'i-mo against the Yen forces, led by Ch'i Chieh. In ch. 82 of the *Shih Chi* we read: "T'ien Tan openly said: 'My only fear is that the Yen army may cut off the noses of their Ch'i prisoners and place them in the front rank to fight against us; that would be the undoing of our city.' The other side being informed of this speech, at once acted on the suggestion; but those within the city were enraged at seeing their fellow-countrymen thus mutilated, and fearing only lest they should fall into the enemy's hands, were nerved to defend themselves more obstinately than ever. Once again T'ien Tan sent back converted spies who reported these words to the enemy: "What I dread most is that the men of Yen may dig up the ancestral tombs outside the town, and by inflicting this indignity on our forefathers cause us to become faint-hearted." Forthwith the besiegers dug up all the graves and burned the corpses lying in them. And the inhabitants of Chi-mo, witnessing the outrage from the city-walls, wept passionately and were all

the attack are signs that he will retreat.

25. When the light chariots come out first and take up a position on the wings, it is a sign that the enemy is forming for battle.

26. Peace proposals unaccompanied by a sworn covenant indicate a plot.[203]

27. When there is much running about[204] and the soldiers fall into rank, it means that the critical moment has come.

28. When some are seen advancing and some retreating, it is a lure.

29. When the soldiers stand leaning on their spears, they are faint from want of food.

---

impatient to go out and fight, their fury being increased tenfold. T`ien Tan knew then that his soldiers were ready for any enterprise. But instead of a sword, he himself took a mattock in his hands, and ordered others to be distributed amongst his best warriors, while the ranks were filled up with their wives and concubines. He then served out all the remaining rations and bade his men eat their fill. The regular soldiers were told to keep out of sight, and the walls were manned with the old and weaker men and with women. This done, envoys were dispatched to the enemy's camp to arrange terms of surrender, whereupon the Yen army began shouting for joy. T`ien Tan also collected 20,000 ounces of silver from the people, and got the wealthy citizens of Chi-mo to send it to the Yen general with the prayer that, when the town capitulated, he would allow their homes to be plundered or their women to be maltreated. Ch`i Chieh, in high good humor, granted their prayer; but his army now became increasingly slack and careless. Meanwhile, T`ien Tan got together a thousand oxen, decked them with pieces of red silk, painted their bodies, dragon-like, with colored stripes, and fastened sharp blades on their horns and well-greased rushes on their tails. When night came on, he lighted the ends of the rushes, and drove the oxen through a number of holes which he had pierced in the walls, backing them up with a force of 5000 picked warriors. The animals, maddened with pain, dashed furiously into the enemy's camp where they caused the utmost confusion and dismay; for their tails acted as torches, showing up the hideous pattern on their bodies, and the weapons on their horns killed or wounded any with whom they came into contact. In the meantime, the band of 5000 had crept up with gags in their mouths, and now threw themselves on the enemy. At the same moment a frightful din arose in the city itself, all those that remained behind making as much noise as possible by banging drums and hammering on bronze vessels, until heaven and earth were convulsed by the uproar. Terror-stricken, the Yen army fled in disorder, hotly pursued by the men of Ch`i, who succeeded in slaying their general Ch`i Chien.... The result of the battle was the ultimate recovery of some seventy cities which had belonged to the Ch`i State."

203   The reading here is uncertain. Li Ch`uan indicates "a treaty confirmed by oaths and hostages." Wang Hsi and Chang Yu, on the other hand, simply say "without reason," "on a frivolous pretext."

204   Every man hastening to his proper place under his own regimental banner.

30. If those who are sent to draw water begin by drinking themselves, the army is suffering from thirst.[205]

31. If the enemy sees an advantage to be gained and makes no effort to secure it, the soldiers are exhausted.

32. If birds gather on any spot, it is unoccupied.[206] Clamor by night betokens nervousness.

33. If there is disturbance in the camp, the general's authority is weak. If the banners and flags are shifted about, sedition is afoot. If the officers are angry, it means that the men are weary.[207]

34. When an army feeds its horses with grain and kills its cattle for food,[208] and when the men do not hang their cooking-pots over the camp-fires, showing that they will not return to their tents, you may know that they are determined to fight to the death.[209]

35. The sight of men whispering together in small knots or speaking in subdued tones points to disaffection amongst the rank and file.

36. Too frequent rewards signify that the enemy is at the end of his

---

205 As Tu Mu remarks: "One may know the condition of a whole army from the behavior of a single man."

206 A useful fact to bear in mind when, for instance, as Ch'en Hao says, the enemy has secretly abandoned his camp.

207 Tu Mu understands the sentence differently: "If all the officers of an army are angry with their general, it means that they are broken with fatigue" owing to the exertions which he has demanded from them.

208 In the ordinary course of things, the men would be fed on grain and the horses chiefly on grass.

209 I may quote here the illustrative passage from the *Hou Han Shu*, ch. 71, given in abbreviated form by the *P'Ei Wen Yun Fu*: "The rebel Wang Kuo of Liang was besieging the town of Ch'en-ts'ang, and Huang-fu Sung, who was in supreme command, and Tung Cho were sent out against him. The latter pressed for hasty measures, but Sung turned a deaf ear to his counsel. At last the rebels were utterly worn out, and began to throw down their weapons of their own accord. Sung was not advancing to the attack, but Cho said: 'It is a principle of war not to pursue desperate men and not to press a retreating host.' Sung answered: 'That does not apply here. What I am about to attack is a jaded army, not a retreating host; with disciplined troops I am falling on a disorganized multitude, not a band of desperate men.' Thereupon he advances to the attack unsupported by his colleague, and routed the enemy, Wang Kuo being slain."

resources;[210] too many punishments betray a condition of dire distress.[211]

37. To begin by bluster, but afterwards to take fright at the enemy's numbers, shows a supreme lack of intelligence.[212]

38. When envoys are sent with compliments in their mouths, it is a sign that the enemy wishes for a truce.[213]

39. If the enemy's troops march up angrily and remain facing ours for a long time without either joining battle or taking themselves off again, the situation is one that demands great vigilance and circumspection.[214]

40. If our troops are no more in number than the enemy, that is amply sufficient; it only means that no direct attack can be made.[215] What we can do is simply to concentrate all our available strength, keep a close watch on the enemy, and obtain reinforcements.[216]

41. He who exercises no forethought but makes light of his opponents

210 Because, when an army is hard pressed, as Tu Mu says, there is always a fear of mutiny, and lavish rewards are given to keep the men in good temper.
211 Because in such case discipline becomes relaxed, and unwonted severity is necessary to keep the men to their duty.
212 I follow the interpretation of Ts'ao Kung, also adopted by Li Ch'uan, Tu Mu, and Chang Yu. Another possible meaning set forth by Tu Yu, Chia Lin, Mei Tao-ch'en and Wang Hsi, is: "The general who is first tyrannical towards his men, and then in terror lest they should mutiny, etc." This would connect the sentence with what went before about rewards and punishments.
213 Tu Mu says: "If the enemy open friendly relations be sending hostages, it is a sign that they are anxious for an armistice, either because their strength is exhausted or for some other reason." But it hardly needs a Sun Tzu to draw such an obvious inference.
214 Ts'ao Kung says a maneuver of this sort may be only a ruse to gain time for an unexpected flank attack or the laying of an ambush.
215 Literally, "no martial advance." That is to say, *cheng* tactics and frontal attacks must be eschewed, and stratagem resorted to instead.
216 This is an obscure sentence, and none of the commentators succeed in squeezing very good sense out of it. I follow Li Ch'uan, who appears to offer the simplest explanation: "Only the side that gets more men will win." Fortunately we have Chang Yu to expound its meaning to us in language which is lucidity itself: "When the numbers are even, and no favorable opening presents itself, although we may not be strong enough to deliver a sustained attack, we can find additional recruits amongst our sutlers and camp-followers, and then, concentrating our forces and keeping a close watch on the enemy, contrive to snatch the victory. But we must avoid borrowing foreign soldiers to help us." He then quotes from Wei Liao Tzu, ch. 3: "The nominal strength of mercenary troops may be 100,000, but their real value will be not more than half that figure."

is sure to be captured by them.[217]

42. If soldiers are punished before they have grown attached to you, they will not prove submissive; and, unless submissive, then will be practically useless. If, when the soldiers have become attached to you, punishments are not enforced, they will still be useless.

43. Therefore soldiers must be treated in the first instance with humanity, but kept under control by means of iron discipline.[218] This is a certain road to victory.

44. If in training soldiers commands are habitually enforced, the army will be well-disciplined; if not, its discipline will be bad.

45. If a general shows confidence in his men but always insists on his orders being obeyed,[219] the gain will be mutual.[220]

---

217 Ch'en Hao, quoting from the *Tso Chuan*, says: "If bees and scorpions carry poison, how much more will a hostile state! Even a puny opponent, then, should not be treated with contempt."

218 Yen Tzu [B.C. 493] said of Ssu-ma Jang-chu: "His civil virtues endeared him to the people; his martial prowess kept his enemies in awe." Cf. Wu Tzu, ch. 4 init.: "The ideal commander unites culture with a warlike temper; the profession of arms requires a combination of hardness and tenderness."

219 Tu Mu says: "A general ought in time of peace to show kindly confidence in his men and also make his authority respected, so that when they come to face the enemy, orders may be executed and discipline maintained, because they all trust and look up to him." What Sun Tzu has said in ss. 44, however, would lead one rather to expect something like this: "If a general is always confident that his orders will be carried out," etc."

220 Chang Yu says: "The general has confidence in the men under his command, and the men are docile, having confidence in him. Thus the gain is mutual." He quotes a pregnant sentence from Wei Liao Tzu, ch. 4: "The art of giving orders is not to try to rectify minor blunders and not to be swayed by petty doubts." Vacillation and fussiness are the surest means of sapping the confidence of an army.

CHAPTER TEN

Terrain[221]

1. Sun Tzu said: We may distinguish six kinds of terrain, to wit: (1) Accessible ground;[222] (2) entangling ground;[223] (3) temporizing ground; [224](4) narrow passes; (5) precipitous heights; (6) positions at a great distance from the enemy.[225]

2. Ground which can be freely traversed by both sides is called *accessible*.

3. With regard to ground of this nature, be before the enemy in occupying the raised and sunny spots, and carefully guard your line of supplies.[226] Then you will be able to fight with advantage.

221 Only about a third of the chapter, comprising sections 1-13, deals with "terrain," the subject being more fully treated in chapter eleven. The "six calamities" are discussed in sections 14-20, and the rest of the chapter is again a mere string of desultory remarks, though not less interesting, perhaps, on that account.
222 Mei Yao-ch`en says: "plentifully provided with roads and means of communications."
223 The same commentator says: "Net-like country, venturing into which you become entangled."
224 Ground which allows you to "stave off" or "delay."
225 It is hardly necessary to point out the faultiness of this classification. A strange lack of logical perception is shown in the Chinaman's unquestioning acceptance of glaring cross- divisions such as the above.
226 The general meaning of the last phrase is doubtlessly, as Tu Yu says, "not to allow the enemy to cut your communications." In view of Napoleon's dictum, "the secret of war lies in the communications," we could wish that Sun Tzu had done more than skirt the edge of this important subject here and in chapter 1 section 10, chapter 7 section 11. Col. Henderson says: "The line of supply may be said to be as vital to the existence of an army as the heart to the life of a human being. Just as the duelist who finds his adversary's point menacing him with certain death, and his own guard astray, is compelled to conform to his adversary's movements, and to content himself with warding off his thrusts, so the

4. Ground which can be abandoned but is hard to re-occupy is called *entangling*.

5. From a position of this sort, if the enemy is unprepared, you may sally forth and defeat him. But if the enemy is prepared for your coming, and you fail to defeat him, then, return being impossible, disaster will ensue.

6. When the position is such that neither side will gain by making the first move, it is called *temporizing* ground.[227]

7. In a position of this sort, even though the enemy should offer us an attractive bait,[228] it will be advisable not to stir forth, but rather to retreat, thus enticing the enemy in his turn; then, when part of his army has come out, we may deliver our attack with advantage.

8. With regard to *narrow passes*, if you can occupy them first, let them be strongly garrisoned and await the advent of the enemy.[229]

9. Should the army forestall you in occupying a pass, do not go after him if the pass is fully garrisoned, but only if it is weakly garrisoned.

10. With regard to *precipitous heights*, if you are beforehand with your adversary, you should occupy the raised and sunny spots, and there wait for him to come up.[230]

---

commander whose communications are suddenly threatened finds himself in a false position, and he will be fortunate if he has not to change all his plans, to split up his force into more or less isolated detachments, and to fight with inferior numbers on ground which he has not had time to prepare, and where defeat will not be an ordinary failure, but will entail the ruin or surrender of his whole army."

227   Tu Mu says: "Each side finds it inconvenient to move, and the situation remains at a deadlock."

228   Tu Yu says, "turning their backs on us and pretending to flee." But this is only one of the lures which might induce us to quit our position.

229   Because then, as Tu Yu observes, "the initiative will lie with us, and by making sudden and unexpected attacks we shall have the enemy at our mercy."

230   Ts'ao Kung says: "The particular advantage of securing heights and defiles is that your actions cannot then be dictated by the enemy." [For the enunciation of the grand principle alluded to, see chapter 6 section 2]. Chang Yu tells the following anecdote of P'ei Hsing-chien (A.D. 619-682), who was sent on a punitive expedition against the Turkic tribes. "At night he pitched his camp as usual, and it had already been completely fortified by wall and ditch, when suddenly he gave orders that the army should shift its quarters to a hill near by. This was highly displeasing to his officers, who protested loudly

11. If the enemy has occupied them before you, do not follow him, but retreat and try to entice him away.[231]

12. If you are situated at a great distance from the enemy, and the strength of the two armies is equal, it is not easy to provoke a battle,[232] and fighting will be to your disadvantage.

13. These six are the principles connected with Earth.[233] The general who has attained a responsible post must be careful to study them.

14. Now an army is exposed to six several calamities, not arising from natural causes, but from faults for which the general is responsible. These are: (1) Flight; (2) insubordination; (3) collapse; (4) ruin; (5) disorganization; (6) rout.

15. Other conditions being equal, if one force is hurled against another ten times its size, the result will be the *flight* of the former.

16. When the common soldiers are too strong and their officers too weak, the result is *insubordination*.[234] When the officers are too strong and the common soldiers too weak, the result is *collapse*.[235]

---

against the extra fatigue which it would entail on the men. P`ei Hsing- chien, however, paid no heed to their remonstrances and had the camp moved as quickly as possible. The same night, a terrific storm came on, which flooded their former place of encampment to the depth of over twelve feet. The recalcitrant officers were amazed at the sight, and owned that they had been in the wrong. 'How did you know what was going to happen?' they asked. P`ei Hsing-chien replied: 'From this time forward be content to obey orders without asking unnecessary questions.' From this it may be seen," Chang Yu continues, "that high and sunny places are advantageous not only for fighting, but also because they are immune from disastrous floods."

231 The turning point of Li Shih-min's campaign in 621 A.D. against the two rebels, Tou Chien-te, King of Hsia, and Wang Shih-ch`ung, Prince of Cheng, was his seizure of the heights of Wu-lao, in spite of which Tou Chien-te persisted in his attempt to relieve his ally in Lo-yang, was defeated and taken prisoner. See *Chiu T`Ang*, ch. 2, fol. 5 verso, and also ch. 54.

232 The point is that we must not think of undertaking a long and wearisome march, at the end of which, as Tu Yu says, "we should be exhausted and our adversary fresh and keen."

233 Or perhaps, "the principles relating to ground." See, however, Chapter 1, section 8.

234 Tu Mu cites the unhappy case of T`ien Pu [*Hsin T`Ang Shu*, ch. 148], who was sent to Wei in 821 A.D. with orders to lead an army against Wang T`ing-ts`ou. But the whole time he was in command, his soldiers treated him with the utmost contempt, and openly flouted his authority by riding about the camp on donkeys, several thousands at a time. T`ien Pu was powerless to put a stop to this conduct, and when, after some months had passed, he made an attempt to engage the enemy, his troops turned tail and dispersed in every direction. After that, the unfortunate man committed suicide by cutting his throat.

235 Ts`ao Kung says: "The officers are energetic and want to press on, the common soldiers are feeble and suddenly collapse."

17. When the higher officers are angry and insubordinate, and on meeting the enemy give battle on their own account from a feeling of resentment, before the commander-in-chief can tell whether or not he is in a position to fight, the result is *ruin*.[236]

18. When the general is weak and without authority; when his orders are not clear and distinct;[237] when there are no fixes duties assigned to officers and men,[238] and the ranks are formed in a slovenly haphazard manner, the result is utter *disorganization*.

19. When a general, unable to estimate the enemy's strength, allows an inferior force to engage a larger one, or hurls a weak detachment against a powerful one, and neglects to place picked soldiers in the front rank, the result must be *rout*.[239]

20. These are six ways of courting defeat, which must be carefully noted by the general who has attained a responsible post.

21. The natural formation of the country is the soldier's best ally;[240] but a power of estimating the adversary, of controlling the forces of victory, and of shrewdly calculating difficulties, dangers and distances, constitutes the test of a great general.

22. He who knows these things, and in fighting puts his knowledge into practice, will win his battles. He who knows them not, nor practices them, will surely be defeated.

236 Wang Hsi`s note is: "This means, the general is angry without cause, and at the same time does not appreciate the ability of his subordinate officers; thus he arouses fierce resentment and brings an avalanche of ruin upon his head."
237 *Wei Liao Tzu* (ch. 4) says: "If the commander gives his orders with decision, the soldiers will not wait to hear them twice; if his moves are made without vacillation, the soldiers will not be in two minds about doing their duty." General Baden- Powell says, italicizing the words: "The secret of getting successful work out of your trained men lies in one nutshell – in the clearness of the instructions they receive." See also *Wu Tzu* ch. 3: "the most fatal defect in a military leader is difference; the worst calamities that befall an army arise from hesitation."
238 Tu Mu says: "Neither officers nor men have any regular routine."
239 Chang Yu paraphrases the latter part of the sentence and continues: "Whenever there is fighting to be done, the keenest spirits should be appointed to serve in the front ranks, both in order to strengthen the resolution of our own men and to demoralize the enemy." See the primi ordines of Caesar ("*De Bello Gallico*," V. 28, 44, et al.).
240 Ch`en Hao says: "The advantages of weather and season are not equal to those connected with ground."

23. If fighting is sure to result in victory, then you must fight, even though the ruler forbid it; if fighting will not result in victory, then you must not fight even at the ruler's bidding.[241]

24. The general who advances without coveting fame and retreats without fearing disgrace,[242] whose only thought is to protect his country and do good service for his sovereign, is the jewel of the kingdom.[243]

25. Regard your soldiers as your children, and they will follow you into the deepest valleys; look upon them as your own beloved sons, and they will stand by you even unto death.[244]

26. If, however, you are indulgent, but unable to make your authority felt; kind-hearted, but unable to enforce your commands; and incapable, moreover, of quelling disorder: then your soldiers must be likened to spoilt children; they are useless for any practical purpose.[245]

241 See chapter 8 section 3. Huang Shih-kung of the Ch'in dynasty, who is said to have been the patron of Chang Liang and to have written the *San Lueh*, has these words attributed to him: "The responsibility of setting an army in motion must devolve on the general alone; if advance and retreat are controlled from the Palace, brilliant results will hardly be achieved. Hence the god-like ruler and the enlightened monarch are content to play a humble part in furthering their country's cause [lit., kneel down to push the chariot wheel]." This means that "in matters lying outside the zenana, the decision of the military commander must be absolute." Chang Yu also quote the saying: "Decrees from the Son of Heaven do not penetrate the walls of a camp."
242 It was Wellington, I think, who said that the hardest thing of all for a soldier is to retreat.
243 A noble presentiment, in few words, of the Chinese "happy warrior." Such a man, says Ho Shih, "even if he had to suffer punishment, would not regret his conduct."
244 See chapter 1 section 6. In this connection, Tu Mu draws for us an engaging picture of the famous general Wu Ch'i, from whose treatise on war I have frequently had occasion to quote: "He wore the same clothes and ate the same food as the meanest of his soldiers, refused to have either a horse to ride or a mat to sleep on, carried his own surplus rations wrapped in a parcel, and shared every hardship with his men. One of his soldiers was suffering from an abscess, and Wu Ch'i himself sucked out the virus. The soldier's mother, hearing this, began wailing and lamenting. Somebody asked her, saying: 'Why do you cry? Your son is only a common soldier, and yet the commander-in-chief himself has sucked the poison from his sore.' The woman replied, 'Many years ago, Lord Wu performed a similar service for my husband, who never left him afterwards, and finally met his death at the hands of the enemy. And now that he has done the same for my son, he too will fall fighting I know not where.'" Li Ch'uan mentions the Viscount of Ch'u, who invaded the small state of Hsiao during the winter. The Duke of Shen said to him: "Many of the soldiers are suffering severely from the cold." So he made a round of the whole army, comforting and encouraging the men; and straightway they felt as if they were clothed in garments lined with floss silk.
245 Li Ching once said that if you could make your soldiers afraid of you, they would not be afraid of the enemy. Tu Mu recalls an instance of stern military discipline which occurred in 219 A.D., when Lu Meng was occupying the town of Chiang-ling. He had

27. If we know that our own men are in a condition to attack, but are unaware that the enemy is not open to attack, we have gone only halfway towards victory.[246]

28. If we know that the enemy is open to attack, but are unaware that our own men are not in a condition to attack, we have gone only halfway towards victory.

29. If we know that the enemy is open to attack, and also know that our men are in a condition to attack, but are unaware that the nature of the ground makes fighting impracticable, we have still gone only halfway towards victory.

30. Hence the experienced soldier, once in motion, is never bewildered; once he has broken camp, he is never at a loss.[247]

31. Hence the saying: If you know the enemy and know yourself, your victory will not stand in doubt; if you know Heaven and know Earth, you may make your victory complete.[248]

---

given stringent orders to his army not to molest the inhabitants nor take anything from them by force. Nevertheless, a certain officer serving under his banner, who happened to be a fellow-townsman, ventured to appropriate a bamboo hat belonging to one of the people, in order to wear it over his regulation helmet as a protection against the rain. Lu Meng considered that the fact of his being also a native of Ju-nan should not be allowed to palliate a clear breach of discipline, and accordingly he ordered his summary execution, the tears rolling down his face, however, as he did so. This act of severity filled the army with wholesome awe, and from that time forth even articles dropped in the highway were not picked up.

246   That is, Ts'ao Kung says, "the issue in this case is uncertain."

247   The reason being, according to Tu Mu, that he has taken his measures so thoroughly as to ensure victory beforehand. "He does not move recklessly," says Chang Yu, "so that when he does move, he makes no mistakes."

248   Li Ch'uan sums up as follows: "Given a knowledge of three things – the affairs of men, the seasons of heaven and the natural advantages of earth –, victory will invariably crown your battles."

CHAPTER ELEVEN

The Nine Situations

1. Sun Tzu said: The art of war recognizes nine varieties of ground: (1) Dispersive ground; (2) facile ground; (3) contentious ground; (4) open ground; (5) ground of intersecting highways; (6) serious ground; (7) difficult ground; (8) hemmed-in ground; (9) desperate ground.

2. When a chieftain is fighting in his own territory, it is *dispersive* ground.[249]

3. When he has penetrated into hostile territory, but to no great distance, it is *facile* ground.[250]

4. Ground the possession of which imports great advantage to either side, is *contentious* ground.[251]

---

249   So called because the soldiers, being near to their homes and anxious to see their wives and children, are likely to seize the opportunity afforded by a battle and scatter in every direction. "In their advance," observes Tu Mu, "they will lack the valor of desperation, and when they retreat, they will find harbors of refuge."

250   Li Ch'uan and Ho Shih say "because of the facility for retreating," and the other commentators give similar explanations. Tu Mu remarks: "When your army has crossed the border, you should burn your boats and bridges, in order to make it clear to everybody that you have no hankering after home."

251   Tu Mu defines the ground as ground "to be contended for." Ts'ao Kung says: "ground on which the few and the weak can defeat the many and the strong," such as "the neck of a pass," instanced by Li Ch'uan. Thus, Thermopylae was of this classification because the possession of it, even for a few days only, meant holding the entire invading army in check and thus gaining invaluable time. See *Wu Tzu*, chapter 5. ad init.: "For those who have to fight in the ratio of one to ten, there is nothing better than a narrow

5. Ground on which each side has liberty of movement is *open* ground.²⁵²

6. Ground which forms the key to three contiguous states,²⁵³ so that he who occupies it first has most of the Empire at his command,²⁵⁴ is a ground of *intersecting highways.*

7. When an army has penetrated into the heart of a hostile country, leaving a number of fortified cities in its rear, it is *serious* ground.²⁵⁵

8. Mountain forests,²⁵⁶ rugged steeps, marshes and fens – all country that is hard to traverse: this is *difficult* ground.

9. Ground which is reached through narrow gorges, and from which we can only retire by tortuous paths, so that a small number of the enemy would suffice to crush a large body of our men: this is *hemmed in* ground.

10. Ground on which we can only be saved from destruction by fighting without delay, is *desperate* ground.²⁵⁷

---

pass." When Lu Kuang was returning from his triumphant expedition to Turkestan in 385 A.D., and had got as far as I-ho, laden with spoils, Liang Hsi, administrator of Liang-chou, taking advantage of the death of Fu Chien, King of Ch'in, plotted against him and was for barring his way into the province. Yang Han, governor of Kao-ch'ang, counseled him, saying: "Lu Kuang is fresh from his victories in the west, and his soldiers are vigorous and mettlesome. If we oppose him in the shifting sands of the desert, we shall be no match for him, and we must therefore try a different plan. Let us hasten to occupy the defile at the mouth of the Kao-wu pass, thus cutting him off from supplies of water, and when his troops are prostrated with thirst, we can dictate our own terms without moving. Or if you think that the pass I mention is too far off, we could make a stand against him at the I-wu pass, which is nearer. The cunning and resource of Tzu-fang himself would be expended in vain against the enormous strength of these two positions." Liang Hsi, refusing to act on this advice, was overwhelmed and swept away by the invader.
252 There are various interpretations of the Chinese adjective for this type of ground. Ts'ao Kung says it means "ground covered with a network of roads," like a chessboard. Ho Shih suggested: "ground on which intercommunication is easy."
253 Ts'au Kung defines this as: "Our country adjoining the enemy's and a third country conterminous with both." Meng Shih instances the small principality of Cheng, which was bounded on the north-east by Ch'i, on the west by Chin, and on the south by Ch'u.
254 The belligerent who holds this dominating position can constrain most of them to become his allies.
255 Wang Hsi explains the name by saying that "when an army has reached such a point, its situation is serious."
256 Or simply "forests."
257 The situation, as pictured by Ts'ao Kung, is very similar to the "hemmed-in ground" except that here escape is no longer possible: "A lofty mountain in front, a large river

11. On dispersive ground, therefore, fight not. On facile ground, halt not. On contentious ground, attack not.[258]

12. On open ground, do not try to block the enemy's way.[259] On the ground of intersecting highways, join hands with your allies.[260]

13. On serious ground, gather in plunder.[261] In difficult ground, keep

---

behind, advance impossible, retreat blocked." Ch`en Hao says: "to be on 'desperate ground' is like sitting in a leaking boat or crouching in a burning house." Tu Mu quotes from Li Ching a vivid description of the plight of an army thus entrapped: "Suppose an army invading hostile territory without the aid of local guides: – it falls into a fatal snare and is at the enemy's mercy. A ravine on the left, a mountain on the right, a pathway so perilous that the horses have to be roped together and the chariots carried in slings, no passage open in front, retreat cut off behind, no choice but to proceed in single file. Then, before there is time to range our soldiers in order of battle, the enemy is overwhelming strength suddenly appears on the scene. Advancing, we can nowhere take a breathing-space; retreating, we have no haven of refuge. We seek a pitched battle, but in vain; yet standing on the defensive, none of us has a moment's respite. If we simply maintain our ground, whole days and months will crawl by; the moment we make a move, we have to sustain the enemy's attacks on front and rear. The country is wild, destitute of water and plants; the army is lacking in the necessaries of life, the horses are jaded and the men worn-out, all the resources of strength and skill unavailing, the pass so narrow that a single man defending it can check the onset of ten thousand; all means of offense in the hands of the enemy, all points of vantage already forfeited by ourselves: – in this terrible plight, even though we had the most valiant soldiers and the keenest of weapons, how could they be employed with the slightest effect?" Students of Greek history may be reminded of the awful close to the Sicilian expedition, and the agony of the Athenians under Nicias and Demonsthenes. [See *Thucydides*, VII. 78 sqq.].

258   But rather let all your energies be bent on occupying the advantageous position first. So Ts`ao Kung. Li Ch`uan and others, however, suppose the meaning to be that the enemy has already forestalled us, sot that it would be sheer madness to attack. In the *Sun Tzu Hsu Lu,* when the King of Wu inquires what should be done in this case, Sun Tzu replies: "The rule with regard to contentious ground is that those in possession have the advantage over the other side. If a position of this kind is secured first by the enemy, beware of attacking him. Lure him away by pretending to flee – show your banners and sound your drums – make a dash for other places that he cannot afford to lose – trail brushwood and raise a dust – confound his ears and eyes – detach a body of your best troops, and place it secretly in ambuscade. Then your opponent will sally forth to the rescue."

259   Because the attempt would be futile, and would expose the blocking force itself to serious risks. There are two interpretations available here. I follow that of Chang Yu. The other is indicated in Ts`ao Kung's brief note: "Draw closer together" – i.e., see that a portion of your own army is not cut off.

260   Or perhaps, "form alliances with neighboring states."

261   On this, Li Ch`uan has the following delicious note: "When an army penetrates far into the enemy's country, care must be taken not to alienate the people by unjust treatment. Follow the example of the Han Emperor Kao Tsu, whose march into Ch`in territory was marked by no violation of women or looting of valuables. [Nota bene: this was in 207 B.C., and may well cause us to blush for the Christian armies that entered Peking in 1900 A.D.] Thus he won the hearts of all. In the present passage, then, I think

steadily on the march.[262]

14. On hemmed-in ground, resort to stratagem.[263] On desperate ground, fight.[264]

15. Those who were called skillful leaders of old knew how to drive a wedge between the enemy's front and rear;[265] to prevent co-operation between his large and small divisions; to hinder the good troops from rescuing the bad, the officers from rallying their men.

16. When the enemy's men were united, they managed to keep them in disorder.

17. When it was to their advantage, they made a forward move; when otherwise, they stopped still.[266]

18. If asked how to cope with a great host of the enemy in orderly array and on the point of marching to the attack, I should say: "Begin by seizing something which your opponent holds dear; then he will be

---

that the true reading must be, not 'plunder,' but 'do not plunder.'" Alas, I fear that in this instance the worthy commentator's feelings outran his judgment. Tu Mu, at least, has no such illusions. He says: "When encamped on 'serious ground,' there being no inducement as yet to advance further, and no possibility of retreat, one ought to take measures for a protracted resistance by bringing in provisions from all sides, and keep a close watch on the enemy."

262 Or, in the words of Chapter 8, Section 2, "do not encamp."

263 Ts`au Kung says: "Try the effect of some unusual artifice;" and Tu Yu amplifies this by saying: "In such a position, some scheme must be devised which will suit the circumstances, and if we can succeed in deluding the enemy, the peril may be escaped." This is exactly what happened on the famous occasion when Hannibal was hemmed in among the mountains on the road to Casilinum, and to all appearances entrapped by the dictator Fabius. The stratagem which Hannibal devised to baffle his foes was remarkably like that which T`ien Tan had also employed with success exactly 62 years before. [See chapter 9, Section 24, note.] When night came on, bundles of twigs were fastened to the horns of some 2000 oxen and set on fire, the terrified animals being then quickly driven along the mountain side towards the passes which were beset by the enemy. The strange spectacle of these rapidly moving lights so alarmed and discomfited the Romans that they withdrew from their position, and Hannibal's army passed safely through the defile. [See Polybius, III. 93, 94; Livy, XXII. 16 17.]

264 For, as Chia Lin remarks: "if you fight with all your might, there is a chance of life; where as death is certain if you cling to your corner."

265 More literally, "cause the front and rear to lose touch with each other."

266 Mei Yao-ch`en connects this with the foregoing: "Having succeeded in thus dislocating the enemy, they would push forward in order to secure any advantage to be gained; if there was no advantage to be gained, they would remain where they were."

amenable to your will."[267]

19. Rapidity is the essence of war:[268] take advantage of the enemy's unreadiness, make your way by unexpected routes, and attack unguarded spots.

267 Opinions differ as to what Sun Tzu had in mind. Ts`ao Kung thinks it is "some strategical advantage on which the enemy is depending." Tu Mu says: "The three things which an enemy is anxious to do, and on the accomplishment of which his success depends, are: (1) to capture our favorable positions; (2) to ravage our cultivated land; (3) to guard his own communications." Our object then must be to thwart his plans in these three directions and thus render him helpless. [See chapter 3, section 3.] By boldly seizing the initiative in this way, you at once throw the other side on the defensive.

268 According to Tu Mu, "this is a summary of leading principles in warfare," and he adds: "These are the profoundest truths of military science, and the chief business of the general." The following anecdotes, told by Ho Shih, shows the importance attached to speed by two of China's greatest generals. In 227 A.D., Meng Ta, governor of Hsin-ch`eng under the Wei Emperor Wen Ti, was meditating defection to the House of Shu, and had entered into correspondence with Chu-ko Liang, Prime Minister of that State. The Wei general Ssu-ma I was then military governor of Wan, and getting wind of Meng Ta's treachery, he at once set off with an army to anticipate his revolt, having previously cajoled him by a specious message of friendly import. Ssu-ma's officers came to him and said: "If Meng Ta has leagued himself with Wu and Shu, the matter should be thoroughly investigated before we make a move." Ssu-ma I replied: "Meng Ta is an unprincipled man, and we ought to go and punish him at once, while he is still wavering and before he has thrown off the mask." Then, by a series of forced marches, be brought his army under the walls of Hsin-ch`eng with in a space of eight days. Now Meng Ta had previously said in a letter to Chu-ko Liang: "Wan is 1200 LI from here. When the news of my revolt reaches Ssu-ma I, he will at once inform his imperial master, but it will be a whole month before any steps can be taken, and by that time my city will be well fortified. Besides, Ssu-ma I is sure not to come himself, and the generals that will be sent against us are not worth troubling about." The next letter, however, was filled with consternation: "Though only eight days have passed since I threw off my allegiance, an army is already at the city-gates. What miraculous rapidity is this!" A fortnight later, Hsin- ch`eng had fallen and Meng Ta had lost his head. [See *Chin Shu*, ch. 1, f. 3.] In 621 A.D., Li Ching was sent from K`uei-chou in Ssu-ch`uan to reduce the successful rebel Hsiao Hsien, who had set up as Emperor at the modern Ching-chou Fu in Hupeh. It was autumn, and the Yangtsze being then in flood, Hsiao Hsien never dreamt that his adversary would venture to come down through the gorges, and consequently made no preparations. But Li Ching embarked his army without loss of time, and was just about to start when the other generals implored him to postpone his departure until the river was in a less dangerous state for navigation. Li Ching replied: "To the soldier, overwhelming speed is of paramount importance, and he must never miss opportunities. Now is the time to strike, before Hsiao Hsien even knows that we have got an army together. If we seize the present moment when the river is in flood, we shall appear before his capital with startling suddenness, like the thunder which is heard before you have time to stop your ears against it. [See chapter 7, section 19, note.] This is the great principle in war. Even if he gets to know of our approach, he will have to levy his soldiers in such a hurry that they will not be fit to oppose us. Thus the full fruits of victory will be ours." All came about as he predicted, and Hsiao Hsien was obliged to surrender, nobly stipulating that his people should be spared and he alone suffer the penalty of death.

20. The following are the principles to be observed by an invading force: The further you penetrate into a country, the greater will be the solidarity of your troops, and thus the defenders will not prevail against you.

21. Make forays in fertile country in order to supply your army with food.

22. Carefully study the well-being of your men,[269] and do not overtax them. Concentrate your energy and hoard your strength.[270] Keep your army continually on the move,[271] and devise unfathomable plans.

23. Throw your soldiers into positions whence there is no escape, and they will prefer death to flight. If they will face death, there is nothing they may not achieve.[272] Officers and men alike will put forth their uttermost strength.[273]

---

269 For "well-being", Wang Hsi means, "Pet them, humor them, give them plenty of food and drink, and look after them generally."

270 Ch`en recalls the line of action adopted in 224 B.C. by the famous general Wang Chien, whose military genius largely contributed to the success of the First Emperor. He had invaded the Ch`u State, where a universal levy was made to oppose him. But, being doubtful of the temper of his troops, he declined all invitations to fight and remained strictly on the defensive. In vain did the Ch`u general try to force a battle: day after day Wang Chien kept inside his walls and would not come out, but devoted his whole time and energy to winning the affection and confidence of his men. He took care that they should be well fed, sharing his own meals with them, provided facilities for bathing, and employed every method of judicious indulgence to weld them into a loyal and homogenous body. After some time had elapsed, he told off certain persons to find out how the men were amusing themselves. The answer was, that they were contending with one another in putting the weight and long-jumping. When Wang Chien heard that they were engaged in these athletic pursuits, he knew that their spirits had been strung up to the required pitch and that they were now ready for fighting. By this time the Ch`u army, after repeating their challenge again and again, had marched away eastwards in disgust. The Ch`in general immediately broke up his camp and followed them, and in the battle that ensued they were routed with great slaughter. Shortly afterwards, the whole of Ch`u was conquered by Ch`in, and the king Fu-ch`u led into captivity.

271 In order that the enemy may never know exactly where you are. It has struck me, however, that the true reading might be "link your army together."

272 Chang Yu quotes his favorite Wei Liao Tzu (ch. 3): "If one man were to run amok with a sword in the market-place, and everybody else tried to get out of his way, I should not allow that this man alone had courage and that all the rest were contemptible cowards. The truth is, that a desperado and a man who sets some value on his life do not meet on even terms."

273 Chang Yu says: "If they are in an awkward place together, they will surely exert their united strength to get out of it."

24. Soldiers when in desperate straits lose the sense of fear. If there is no place of refuge, they will stand firm. If they are in hostile country, they will show a stubborn front. If there is no help for it, they will fight hard.

25. Thus, without waiting to be marshaled, the soldiers will be constantly on the qui vive; without waiting to be asked, they will do your will;[274] without restrictions, they will be faithful; without giving orders, they can be trusted.

26. Prohibit the taking of omens, and do away with superstitious doubts. Then, until death itself comes, no calamity need be feared.[275]

27. If our soldiers are not overburdened with money, it is not because they have a distaste for riches; if their lives are not unduly long, it is not because they are disinclined to longevity.[276]

28. On the day they are ordered out to battle, your soldiers may weep, [277]those sitting up bedewing their garments, and those lying down letting the tears run down their cheeks.[278] But let them once be brought to bay, and they will display the courage of a Chu or a Kuei.[279]

274 Literally, "without asking, you will get."
275 The superstitious, "bound in to saucy doubts and fears," degenerate into cowards and "die many times before their deaths." Tu Mu quotes Huang Shih-kung: "'Spells and incantations should be strictly forbidden, and no officer allowed to inquire by divination into the fortunes of an army, for fear the soldiers' minds should be seriously perturbed.' The meaning is," he continues, "that if all doubts and scruples are discarded, your men will never falter in their resolution until they die."
276 Chang Yu has the best note on this passage: "Wealth and long life are things for which all men have a natural inclination. Hence, if they burn or fling away valuables, and sacrifice their own lives, it is not that they dislike them, but simply that they have no choice." Sun Tzu is slyly insinuating that, as soldiers are but human, it is for the general to see that temptations to shirk fighting and grow rich are not thrown in their way.
277 The word in the Chinese is "snivel." This is taken to indicate more genuine grief than tears alone.
278 Not because they are afraid, but because, as Ts'ao Kung says, "all have embraced the firm resolution to do or die." We may remember that the heroes of the Iliad were equally childlike in showing their emotion. Chang Yu alludes to the mournful parting at the I River between Ching K'o and his friends, when the former was sent to attempt the life of the King of Ch'in (afterwards First Emperor) in 227 B.C. The tears of all flowed down like rain as he bade them farewell and uttered the following lines: "The shrill blast is blowing, Chilly the burn; Your champion is going – Not to return."
279 Chu was the personal name of Chuan Chu, a native of the Wu State and contemporary with Sun Tzu himself, who was employed by Kung-tzu Kuang, better

29. The skillful tactician may be likened to the *shuai-jan*. Now the *shuai-jan* is a snake that is found in the Ch`ang mountains.[280] Strike at its head, and you will be attacked by its tail; strike at its tail, and you will be attacked by its head; strike at its middle, and you will be attacked by head and tail both.

30. Asked if an army can be made to imitate the *shuai-jan*,[281] I should answer, Yes. For the men of Wu and the men of Yueh are enemies;[282] yet if they are crossing a river in the same boat and are caught by a storm, they will come to each other's assistance just as the left hand helps the right.[283]

31. Hence it is not enough to put one's trust in the tethering of horses, and the burying of chariot wheels in the ground.[284]

---

known as Ho Lu Wang, to assassinate his sovereign Wang Liao with a dagger which he secreted in the belly of a fish served up at a banquet. He succeeded in his attempt, but was immediately hacked to pieced by the king's bodyguard. This was in 515 B.C. The other hero referred to, Ts`ao Kuei (or Ts`ao Mo), performed the exploit which has made his name famous 166 years earlier, in 681 B.C. Lu had been thrice defeated by Ch`i, and was just about to conclude a treaty surrendering a large slice of territory, when Ts`ao Kuei suddenly seized Huan Kung, the Duke of Ch`i, as he stood on the altar steps and held a dagger against his chest. None of the duke's retainers dared to move a muscle, and Ts`ao Kuei proceeded to demand full restitution, declaring the Lu was being unjustly treated because she was a smaller and a weaker state. Huan Kung, in peril of his life, was obliged to consent, whereupon Ts`ao Kuei flung away his dagger and quietly resumed his place amid the terrified assemblage without having so much as changed color. As was to be expected, the Duke wanted afterwards to repudiate the bargain, but his wise old counselor Kuan Chung pointed out to him the impolicy of breaking his word, and the upshot was that this bold stroke regained for Lu the whole of what she had lost in three pitched battles.

280 "Shuai-jan" means "suddenly" or "rapidly," and the snake in question was doubtless so called owing to the rapidity of its movements. Through this passage, the term in the Chinese has now come to be used in the sense of "military maneuvers."

281 That is, as Mei Yao-ch`en says, "Is it possible to make the front and rear of an army each swiftly responsive to attack on the other, just as though they were part of a single living body?"

282 See chapter 6, section 21.

283 The meaning is: If two enemies will help each other in a time of common peril, how much more should two parts of the same army, bound together as they are by every tie of interest and fellow-feeling. Yet it is notorious that many a campaign has been ruined through lack of cooperation, especially in the case of allied armies.

284 These quaint devices to prevent one's army from running away recall the Athenian hero Sophanes, who carried the anchor with him at the battle of Plataea, by means of which he fastened himself firmly to one spot. [See *Herodotus*, IX. 74.] It is not enough, says Sun Tzu, to render flight impossible by such mechanical means. You will not succeed unless your men have tenacity and unity of purpose, and, above all, a spirit of sympathetic cooperation. This is the lesson which can be learned from the *Shuai-Jan*.

32. The principle on which to manage an army is to set up one standard of courage which all must reach.[285]

33. How to make the best of both strong and weak – that is a question involving the proper use of ground.[286]

34. Thus the skillful general conducts his army just as though he were leading a single man, willy-nilly, by the hand.[287]

35. It is the business of a general to be quiet and thus ensure secrecy; upright and just, and thus maintain order.

36. He must be able to mystify his officers and men by false reports and appearances,[288] and thus keep them in total ignorance.[289]

285   Literally, "level the courage [of all] as though [it were that of] one." If the ideal army is to form a single organic whole, then it follows that the resolution and spirit of its component parts must be of the same quality, or at any rate must not fall below a certain standard. Wellington's seemingly ungrateful description of his army at Waterloo as "the worst he had ever commanded" meant no more than that it was deficient in this important particular – unity of spirit and courage. Had he not foreseen the Belgian defections and carefully kept those troops in the background, he would almost certainly have lost the day.

286   Mei Yao-ch`en's paraphrase is: "The way to eliminate the differences of strong and weak and to make both serviceable is to utilize accidental features of the ground." Less reliable troops, if posted in strong positions, will hold out as long as better troops on more exposed terrain. The advantage of position neutralizes the inferiority in stamina and courage. Col. Henderson says: "With all respect to the text books, and to the ordinary tactical teaching, I am inclined to think that the study of ground is often overlooked, and that by no means sufficient importance is attached to the selection of positions… and to the immense advantages that are to be derived, whether you are defending or attacking, from the proper utilization of natural features."

287   Tu Mu says: "The simile has reference to the ease with which he does it."

288   Literally, "to deceive their eyes and ears."

289   Ts`ao Kung gives us one of his excellent apophthegms: "The troops must not be allowed to share your schemes in the beginning; they may only rejoice with you over their happy outcome." "To mystify, mislead, and surprise the enemy," is one of the first principles in war, as had been frequently pointed out. But how about the other process – the mystification of one's own men? Those who may think that Sun Tzu is over-emphatic on this point would do well to read Col. Henderson's remarks on Stonewall Jackson's Valley campaign: "The infinite pains," he says, "with which Jackson sought to conceal, even from his most trusted staff officers, his movements, his intentions, and his thoughts, a commander less thorough would have pronounced useless" – etc. etc. In the year 88 A.D., as we read in ch. 47 of the *Hou Han Shu*, "Pan Ch`ao took the field with 25,000 men from Khotan and other Central Asian states with the object of crushing Yarkand. The King of Kutcha replied by dispatching his chief commander to succor the place with an army drawn from the kingdoms of Wen-su, Ku-mo, and Wei-t`ou, totaling 50,000 men. Pan Ch`ao summoned his officers and also the King of Khotan to a council of war, and said: 'Our forces are now outnumbered and unable to make head against the enemy. The

37. By altering his arrangements and changing his plans,[290] he keeps the enemy without definite knowledge.[291] By shifting his camp and taking circuitous routes, he prevents the enemy from anticipating his purpose.

38. At the critical moment, the leader of an army acts like one who has climbed up a height and then kicks away the ladder behind him. He carries his men deep into hostile territory before he shows his hand.[292]

39. He burns his boats and breaks his cooking-pots; like a shepherd driving a flock of sheep, he drives his men this way and that, and nothing knows whither he is going.[293]

40. To muster his host and bring it into danger: – this may be termed the business of the general.[294]

---

best plan, then, is for us to separate and disperse, each in a different direction. The King of Khotan will march away by the easterly route, and I will then return myself towards the west. Let us wait until the evening drum has sounded and then start.' Pan Ch'ao now secretly released the prisoners whom he had taken alive, and the King of Kutcha was thus informed of his plans. Much elated by the news, the latter set off at once at the head of 10,000 horsemen to bar Pan Ch'ao's retreat in the west, while the King of Wen-su rode eastward with 8000 horse in order to intercept the King of Khotan. As soon as Pan Ch'ao knew that the two chieftains had gone, he called his divisions together, got them well in hand, and at cock-crow hurled them against the army of Yarkand, as it lay encamped. The barbarians, panic-stricken, fled in confusion, and were closely pursued by Pan Ch'ao. Over 5000 heads were brought back as trophies, besides immense spoils in the shape of horses and cattle and valuables of every description. Yarkand then capitulating, Kutcha and the other kingdoms drew off their respective forces. From that time forward, Pan Ch'ao's prestige completely overawed the countries of the west." In this case, we see that the Chinese general not only kept his own officers in ignorance of his real plans, but actually took the bold step of dividing his army in order to deceive the enemy.

290   Wang Hsi thinks that this means not using the same stratagem twice.

291   Chang Yu, in a quotation from another work, says: "The axiom, that war is based on deception, does not apply only to deception of the enemy. You must deceive even your own soldiers. Make them follow you, but without letting them know why."

292   Literally, "releases the spring" (see chapter 5, section 15), that is, takes some decisive step which makes it impossible for the army to return – like Hsiang Yu, who sunk his ships after crossing a river. Ch'en Hao, followed by Chia Lin, understands the words less well as "puts forth every artifice at his command."

293   Tu Mu says: "The army is only cognizant of orders to advance or retreat; it is ignorant of the ulterior ends of attacking and conquering."

294   Sun Tzu means that after mobilization there should be no delay in aiming a blow at the enemy's heart. Note how he returns again and again to this point. Among the warring states of ancient China, desertion was no doubt a much more present fear and serious evil than it is in the armies of today.

41. The different measures suited to the nine varieties of ground;[295] the expediency of aggressive or defensive tactics; and the fundamental laws of human nature: these are things that must most certainly be studied.

42. When invading hostile territory, the general principle is, that penetrating deeply brings cohesion; penetrating but a short way means dispersion.

43. When you leave your own country behind, and take your army across neighborhood territory, you find yourself on critical ground. [296]When there are means of communication on all four sides, the ground is one of intersecting highways.

44. When you penetrate deeply into a country, it is serious ground. When you penetrate but a little way, it is facile ground.

45. When you have the enemy's strongholds on your rear, and narrow passes in front, it is hemmed-in ground. When there is no place of refuge at all, it is desperate ground.

46. Therefore, on dispersive ground, I would inspire my men with unity of purpose.[297] On facile ground, I would see that there is close connection between all parts of my army.[298]

47. On contentious ground, I would hurry up my rear.[299]

295 Chang Yu says: "One must not be hide-bound in interpreting the rules for the nine varieties of ground.
296 This "ground" is curiously mentioned in chapter 8, section 2, but it does not figure among the Nine Situations or the Six Calamities in chapter 10. One's first impulse would be to translate it distant ground," but this, if we can trust the commentators, is precisely what is not meant here. Mei Yao-ch`en says it is "a position not far enough advanced to be called 'facile,' and not near enough to home to be 'dispersive,' but something between the two." Wang Hsi says: "It is ground separated from home by an interjacent state, whose territory we have had to cross in order to reach it. Hence, it is incumbent on us to settle our business there quickly." He adds that this position is of rare occurrence, which is the reason why it is not included among the Nine Situations.
297 This end, according to Tu Mu, is best attained by remaining on the defensive, and avoiding battle.
298 As Tu Mu says, the object is to guard against two possible contingencies: "(1) the desertion of our own troops; (2) a sudden attack on the part of the enemy." See chapter 7, section 17. Mei Yao-ch`en says: "On the march, the regiments should be in close touch; in an encampment, there should be continuity between the fortifications."
299 This is Ts`ao Kung's interpretation. Chang Yu adopts it, saying: "We must quickly

48. On open ground, I would keep a vigilant eye on my defenses. On ground of intersecting highways, I would consolidate my alliances.

49. On serious ground, I would try to ensure a continuous stream of supplies.[300] On difficult ground, I would keep pushing on along the road.

50. On hemmed-in ground, I would block any way of retreat.[301] On desperate ground, I would proclaim to my soldiers the hopelessness of saving their lives.[302]

---

bring up our rear, so that head and tail may both reach the goal." That is, they must not be allowed to straggle up a long way apart. Mei Yao-ch`en offers another equally plausible explanation: "Supposing the enemy has not yet reached the coveted position, and we are behind him, we should advance with all speed in order to dispute its possession." Ch`en Hao, on the other hand, assuming that the enemy has had time to select his own ground, quotes chapter 6, section 1, where Sun Tzu warns us against coming exhausted to the attack. His own idea of the situation is rather vaguely expressed: "If there is a favorable position lying in front of you, detach a picked body of troops to occupy it, then if the enemy, relying on their numbers, come up to make a fight for it, you may fall quickly on their rear with your main body, and victory will be assured." It was thus, he adds, that Chao She beat the army of Ch`in.

300 The commentators take this as referring to forage and plunder, not, as one might expect, to an unbroken communication with a home base.

301 Meng Shih says: "To make it seem that I meant to defend the position, whereas my real intention is to burst suddenly through the enemy's lines." Mei Yao-ch`en says: "in order to make my soldiers fight with desperation." Wang Hsi says, "fearing lest my men be tempted to run away." Tu Mu points out that this is the converse of chapter 7, section 36, where it is the enemy who is surrounded. In 532 A.D., Kao Huan, afterwards Emperor and canonized as Shen-wu, was surrounded by a great army under Erh-chu Chao and others. His own force was comparatively small, consisting only of 2000 horse and something under 30,000 foot. The lines of investment had not been drawn very closely together, gaps being left at certain points. But Kao Huan, instead of trying to escape, actually made a shift to block all the remaining outlets himself by driving into them a number of oxen and donkeys roped together. As soon as his officers and men saw that there was nothing for it but to conquer or die, their spirits rose to an extraordinary pitch of exaltation, and they charged with such desperate ferocity that the opposing ranks broke and crumbled under their onslaught.

302 Tu Yu says: "Burn your baggage and impedimenta, throw away your stores and provisions, choke up the wells, destroy your cooking-stoves, and make it plain to your men that they cannot survive, but must fight to the death." Mei Yao-ch`en says: "The only chance of life lies in giving up all hope of it." This concludes what Sun Tzu has to say about "grounds" and the "variations" corresponding to them. Reviewing the passages which bear on this important subject, we cannot fail to be struck by the desultory and unmethodical fashion in which it is treated. Sun Tzu begins abruptly in chapter 8, section 2 to enumerate "variations" before touching on "grounds" at all, but only mentions five, namely nos. 7, 5, 8 and 9 of the subsequent list, and one that is not included in it. A few varieties of ground are dealt with in the earlier portion of chap. nine, and then chapter ten sets forth six new grounds, with six variations of plan to match. None of these is mentioned again, though the first is hardly to be distinguished from ground no. 4 in the

51. For it is the soldier's disposition to offer an obstinate resistance when surrounded, to fight hard when he cannot help himself, and to obey promptly when he has fallen into danger.[303]

52. We cannot enter into alliance with neighboring princes until we are acquainted with their designs. We are not fit to lead an army on the march unless we are familiar with the face of the country – its mountains and forests, its pitfalls and precipices, its marshes and swamps. We shall be unable to turn natural advantages to account

---

next chapter. At last, in chapter eleven, we come to the Nine Grounds par excellence, immediately followed by the variations. This takes us down to chapter 14. In sections 43-45, fresh definitions are provided for nos. 5, 6, 2, 8 and 9 (in the order given), as well as for the tenth ground noticed in chapter eight; and finally, the nine variations are enumerated once more from beginning to end, all, with the exception of 5, 6 and 7, being different from those previously given. Though it is impossible to account for the present state of Sun Tzu's text, a few suggestive facts maybe brought into prominence: (1) Chapter eight, according to the title, should deal with nine variations, whereas only five appear. (2) It is an abnormally short chapter. (3) Chapter eleven is entitled The Nine Grounds. Several of these are defined twice over, besides which there are two distinct lists of the corresponding variations. (4) The length of the chapter is disproportionate, being double that of any other except nine. I do not propose to draw any inferences from these facts, beyond the general conclusion that Sun Tzu's work cannot have come down to us in the shape in which it left his hands: chapter eight is obviously defective and probably out of place, while nine seems to contain matter that has either been added by a later hand or ought to appear elsewhere.

303   Chang Yu alludes to the conduct of Pan Ch`ao's devoted followers in 73 A.D. The story runs thus in the *Hou Han Shu*, chapter 47: "When Pan Ch`ao arrived at Shan-shan, Kuang, the King of the country, received him at first with great politeness and respect; but shortly afterwards his behavior underwent a sudden change, and he became remiss and negligent. Pan Ch`ao spoke about this to the officers of his suite: 'Have you noticed,' he said, 'that Kuang's polite intentions are on the wane? This must signify that envoys have come from the Northern barbarians, and that consequently he is in a state of indecision, not knowing with which side to throw in his lot. That surely is the reason. The truly wise man, we are told, can perceive things before they have come to pass; how much more, then, those that are already manifest!' Thereupon he called one of the natives who had been assigned to his service, and set a trap for him, saying: 'Where are those envoys from the Hsiung-nu who arrived some day ago?' The man was so taken aback that between surprise and fear he presently blurted out the whole truth. Pan Ch`ao, keeping his informant carefully under lock and key, then summoned a general gathering of his officers, thirty-six in all, and began drinking with them. When the wine had mounted into their heads a little, he tried to rouse their spirit still further by addressing them thus: 'Gentlemen, here we are in the heart of an isolated region, anxious to achieve riches and honor by some great exploit. Now it happens that an ambassador from the Hsiung-no arrived in this kingdom only a few days ago, and the result is that the respectful courtesy extended towards us by our royal host has disappeared. Should this envoy prevail upon him to seize our party and hand us over to the Hsiung-no, our bones will become food for the wolves of the desert. What are we to do?' With one accord, the officers replied: 'Standing as we do in peril of our lives, we will follow our commander through life and death.' For the sequel of this adventure, see chapter twelve, section 1, note.

unless we make use of local guides.[304]

53. To be ignored of any one of the following four or five principles does not befit a warlike prince.

54. When a warlike prince attacks a powerful state, his generalship shows itself in preventing the concentration of the enemy's forces. He overawes his opponents, and their allies are prevented from joining against him.[305]

55. Hence he does not strive to ally himself with all and sundry, nor does he foster the power of other states. He carries out his own secret designs, keeping his antagonists in awe.[306] Thus he is able to capture their cities and overthrow their kingdoms.[307]

304   These three sentences are repeated from chapter 7, sections 12-14 – in order to emphasize their importance, the commentators seem to think. I prefer to regard them as interpolated here in order to form an antecedent to the following words. With regard to local guides, Sun Tzu might have added that there is always the risk of going wrong, either through their treachery or some misunderstanding such as Livy records (XXII. 13): Hannibal, we are told, ordered a guide to lead him into the neighborhood of Casinum, where there was an important pass to be occupied; but his Carthaginian accent, unsuited to the pronunciation of Latin names, caused the guide to understand Casilinum instead of Casinum, and turning from his proper route, he took the army in that direction, the mistake not being discovered until they had almost arrived.

305   Mei Tao-ch`en constructs one of the chains of reasoning that are so much affected by the Chinese: "In attacking a powerful state, if you can divide her forces, you will have a superiority in strength; if you have a superiority in strength, you will overawe the enemy; if you overawe the enemy, the neighboring states will be frightened; and if the neighboring states are frightened, the enemy's allies will be prevented from joining her." The following gives a stronger meaning: "If the great state has once been defeated (before she has had time to summon her allies), then the lesser states will hold aloof and refrain from massing their forces." Ch`en Hao and Chang Yu take the sentence in quite another way. The former says: "Powerful though a prince may be, if he attacks a large state, he will be unable to raise enough troops, and must rely to some extent on external aid; if he dispenses with this, and with overweening confidence in his own strength, simply tries to intimidate the enemy, he will surely be defeated." Chang Yu puts his view thus: "If we recklessly attack a large state, our own people will be discontented and hang back. But if (as will then be the case) our display of military force is inferior by half to that of the enemy, the other chieftains will take fright and refuse to join us."

306   The train of thought, as said by Li Ch`uan, appears to be this: Secure against a combination of his enemies, "he can afford to reject entangling alliances and simply pursue his own secret designs, his prestige enable him to dispense with external friendships."

307   This paragraph, though written many years before the Ch`in State became a serious menace, is not a bad summary of the policy by which the famous Six Chancellors gradually paved the way for her final triumph under Shih Huang Ti. Chang Yu, following up his previous note, thinks that Sun Tzu is condemning this attitude of cold-blooded selfishness and haughty isolation.

56. Bestow rewards without regard to rule,[308] issue orders[309] without regard to previous arrangements;[310] and you will be able to handle a whole army as though you had to do with but a single man.

57. Confront your soldiers with the deed itself; never let them know your design.[311] When the outlook is bright, bring it before their eyes; but tell them nothing when the situation is gloomy.

58. Place your army in deadly peril, and it will survive; plunge it into desperate straits, and it will come off in safety.[312]

308 Wu Tzu (ch. 3) less wisely says: "Let advance be richly rewarded and retreat be heavily punished."

309 Literally, "hang" or post up."

310 "In order to prevent treachery," says Wang Hsi. The general meaning is made clear by Ts'ao Kung's quotation from the *Ssu-Ma Fa*: "Give instructions only on sighting the enemy; give rewards when you see deserving deeds." Ts'ao Kung's paraphrase: "The final instructions you give to your army should not correspond with those that have been previously posted up." Chang Yu simplifies this into "your arrangements should not be divulged beforehand." And Chia Lin says: "there should be no fixity in your rules and arrangements." Not only is there danger in letting your plans be known, but war often necessitates the entire reversal of them at the last moment.

311 Literally, "do not tell them words;" i.e. do not give your reasons for any order. Lord Mansfield once told a junior colleague to "give no reasons" for his decisions, and the maxim is even more applicable to a general than to a judge.

312 These words of Sun Tzu were once quoted by Han Hsin in explanation of the tactics he employed in one of his most brilliant battles. In 204 B.C., he was sent against the army of Chao, and halted ten miles from the mouth of the Ching-hsing pass, where the enemy had mustered in full force. Here, at midnight, he detached a body of 2000 light cavalry, every man of which was furnished with a red flag. Their instructions were to make their way through narrow defiles and keep a secret watch on the enemy. "When the men of Chao see me in full flight," Han Hsin said, "they will abandon their fortifications and give chase. This must be the sign for you to rush in, pluck down the Chao standards and set up the red banners of Han in their stead." Turning then to his other officers, he remarked: "Our adversary holds a strong position, and is not likely to come out and attack us until he sees the standard and drums of the commander-in-chief, for fear I should turn back and escape through the mountains." So saying, he first of all sent out a division consisting of 10,000 men, and ordered them to form in line of battle with their backs to the River Ti. Seeing this maneuver, the whole army of Chao broke into loud laughter. By this time it was broad daylight, and Han Hsin, displaying the generalissimo's flag, marched out of the pass with drums beating, and was immediately engaged by the enemy. A great battle followed, lasting for some time; until at length Han Hsin and his colleague Chang Ni, leaving drums and banner on the field, fled to the division on the river bank, where another fierce battle was raging. The enemy rushed out to pursue them and to secure the trophies, thus denuding their ramparts of men; but the two generals succeeded in joining the other army, which was fighting with the utmost desperation. The time had now come for the 2000 horsemen to play their part. As soon as they saw the men of Chao following up their advantage, they galloped behind the deserted walls, tore up the enemy's flags and replaced them by those of Han. When the Chao army looked back from the pursuit, the sight of these red flags struck them with terror. Convinced that the Hans had got in and

59. For it is precisely when a force has fallen into harm's way that is capable of striking a blow for victory.[313]

60. Success in warfare is gained by carefully accommodating ourselves to the enemy's purpose.[314]

61. By persistently hanging on the enemy's flank,[315] we shall succeed in the long run[316] in killing the commander-in-chief.[317]

62. This is called ability to accomplish a thing by sheer cunning.

63. On the day that you take up your command, block the frontier passes, destroy the official tallies,[318] and stop the passage of all emissaries.[319]

---

overpowered their king, they broke up in wild disorder, every effort of their leader to stay the panic being in vain. Then the Han army fell on them from both sides and completed the rout, killing a number and capturing the rest, amongst whom was King Ya himself.... After the battle, some of Han Hsin's officers came to him and said: "In the *Art of War* we are told to have a hill or tumulus on the right rear, and a river or marsh on the left front. [This appears to be a blend of Sun Tzu and T'ai Kung. See chapter nine, section 9, and note.] You, on the contrary, ordered us to draw up our troops with the river at our back. Under these conditions, how did you manage to gain the victory?" The general replied: "I fear you gentlemen have not studied the *Art of War* with sufficient care. Is it not written there: 'Plunge your army into desperate straits and it will come off in safety; place it in deadly peril and it will survive'? Had I taken the usual course, I should never have been able to bring my colleague round. What says the Military Classic – 'Swoop down on the market-place and drive the men off to fight.' [This passage does not occur in the present text of Sun Tzu.] If I had not placed my troops in a position where they were obliged to fight for their lives, but had allowed each man to follow his own discretion, there would have been a general debandade, and it would have been impossible to do anything with them." The officers admitted the force of his argument, and said: "These are higher tactics than we should have been capable of." [See *Ch'Ien Han Shu*, ch. 34, ff. 4, 5.]

313 Danger has a bracing effect.

314 Ts'ao Kung says: "Feign stupidity" – by an appearance of yielding and falling in with the enemy's wishes. Chang Yu's note makes the meaning clear: "If the enemy shows an inclination to advance, lure him on to do so; if he is anxious to retreat, delay on purpose that he may carry out his intention." The object is to make him remiss and contemptuous before we deliver our attack.

315 I understand the first four words to mean "accompanying the enemy in one direction." Ts'ao Kung says: "unite the soldiers and make for the enemy." But such a violent displacement of characters is quite indefensible.

316 Literally, "after a thousand *li*."

317 Always a great point with the Chinese.

318 These were tablets of bamboo or wood, one half of which was issued as a permit or passport by the official in charge of a gate. Cf. the "border-warden" of *Lun Yu* III. 24, who may have had similar duties. When this half was returned to him, within a fixed period, he was authorized to open the gate and let the traveler through.

319 Either to or from the enemy's country.

64. Be stern in the council-chamber,[320] so that you may control the situation.[321]

65. If the enemy leaves a door open, you must rush in.

66. Forestall your opponent by seizing what he holds dear, and subtly contrive to time his arrival on the ground.[322]

67. Walk in the path defined by rule,[323] and accommodate yourself to the enemy until you can fight a decisive battle.[324]

68. At first, then, exhibit the coyness of a maiden, until the enemy gives you an opening; afterwards emulate the rapidity of a running hare, and it will be too late for the enemy to oppose you.[325]

320 Show no weakness, and insist on your plans being ratified by the sovereign.
321 Mei Yao-ch`en understands the whole sentence to mean: Take the strictest precautions to ensure secrecy in your deliberations.
322 Ch`en Hao`s explanation: "If I manage to seize a favorable position, but the enemy does not appear on the scene, the advantage thus obtained cannot be turned to any practical account. He who intends therefore, to occupy a position of importance to the enemy, must begin by making an artful appointment, so to speak, with his antagonist, and cajole him into going there as well." Mei Yao-ch`en explains that this "artful appointment" is to be made through the medium of the enemy's own spies, who will carry back just the amount of information that we choose to give them. Then, having cunningly disclosed our intentions, "we must manage, though starting after the enemy, to arrive before him (chapter 7, section 4). We must start after him in order to ensure his marching thither; we must arrive before him in order to capture the place without trouble. Taken thus, the present passage lends some support to Mei Yao-ch`en's interpretation of section 47.
323 Chia Lin says: "Victory is the only thing that matters, and this cannot be achieved by adhering to conventional canons." It is unfortunate that this variant rests on very slight authority, for the sense yielded is certainly much more satisfactory. Napoleon, as we know, according to the veterans of the old school whom he defeated, won his battles by violating every accepted canon of warfare.
324 Tu Mu says: "Conform to the enemy's tactics until a favorable opportunity offers; then come forth and engage in a battle that shall prove decisive."
325 As the hare is noted for its extreme timidity, the comparison hardly appears felicitous. But of course Sun Tzu was thinking only of its speed. The words have been taken to mean: You must flee from the enemy as quickly as an escaping hare; but this is rightly rejected by Tu Mu.

CHAPTER TWELVE

The Attack by Fire [326]

1. Sun Tzu said: There are five ways of attacking with fire. The first is to burn soldiers in their camp;[327] the second is to burn

326   Rather more than half the chapter (sections 1-13) is devoted to the subject of fire, after which the author branches off into other topics.

327   So Tu Mu. Li Ch`uan says: "Set fire to the camp, and kill the soldiers" (when they try to escape from the flames). Pan Ch`ao, sent on a diplomatic mission to the King of Shan-shan [see chapter 9, section 51, note], found himself placed in extreme peril by the unexpected arrival of an envoy from the Hsiung-nu [the mortal enemies of the Chinese]. In consultation with his officers, he exclaimed: "Never venture, never win! The only course open to us now is to make an assault by fire on the barbarians under cover of night, when they will not be able to discern our numbers. Profiting by their panic, we shall exterminate them completely; this will cool the King's courage and cover us with glory, besides ensuring the success of our mission." the officers all replied that it would be necessary to discuss the matter first with the Intendant. Pan Ch`ao then fell into a passion: 'It is today,' he cried, 'that our fortunes must be decided! The Intendant is only a humdrum civilian, who on hearing of our project will certainly be afraid, and everything will be brought to light. An inglorious death is no worthy fate for valiant warriors.' All then agreed to do as he wished. Accordingly, as soon as night came on, he and his little band quickly made their way to the barbarian camp. A strong gale was blowing at the time. Pan Ch`ao ordered ten of the party to take drums and hide behind the enemy's barracks, it being arranged that when they saw flames shoot up, they should begin drumming and yelling with all their might. The rest of his men, armed with bows and crossbows, he posted in ambuscade at the gate of the camp. He then set fire to the place from the windward side, whereupon a deafening noise of drums and shouting arose on the front and rear of the Hsiung-nu, who rushed out pell-mell in frantic disorder. Pan Ch`ao slew three of them with his own hand, while his companions cut off the heads of the envoy and thirty of his suite. The remainder, more than a hundred in all, perished in the flames. On the following day, Pan Ch`ao, divining his thoughts, said with uplifted hand: 'Although you did not go with us last night, I should not think, Sir, of taking sole credit for our exploit.' This satisfied Kuo Hsun, and Pan Ch`ao, having sent for Kuang, King of Shan-shan, showed him the head of the barbarian envoy. The whole kingdom was seized with fear and trembling, which Pan Ch`ao took steps to allay by issuing a public

stores;[328] the third is to burn baggage trains;[329] the fourth is to burn arsenals and magazines;[330] the fifth is to hurl dropping fire amongst the enemy.[331]

2. In order to carry out an attack, we must have means available.[332] The material for raising fire should always be kept in readiness.[333]

3. There is a proper season for making attacks with fire, and special days for starting a conflagration.

4. The proper season is when the weather is very dry; the special days are those when the moon is in the constellations of the Sieve, the Wall, the Wing or the Cross-bar;[334] for these four are all days of rising wind.

5. In attacking with fire, one should be prepared to meet five possible developments:

6. (1) When fire breaks out inside to enemy's camp, respond at once with an attack from without.

7. (2) If there is an outbreak of fire, but the enemy's soldiers remain quiet, bide your time and do not attack.[335]

---

proclamation. Then, taking the king's sons as hostage, he returned to make his report to Tou Ku." *Hou Han Shu*, ch. 47, ff. 1, 2.]

328   Tu Mu says: "Provisions, fuel and fodder." In order to subdue the rebellious population of Kiangnan, Kao Keng recommended Wen Ti of the Sui dynasty to make periodical raids and burn their stores of grain, a policy which in the long run proved entirely successful.

329   An example given is the destruction of Yuan Shao's wagons and impedimenta by Ts'ao Ts'ao in 200 A.D.

330   Tu Mu says that the things contained in "arsenals" and "magazines" are the same. He specifies weapons and other implements, bullion and clothing.

331   Tu Yu says in the *T'Ung Tien*: "To drop fire into the enemy's camp. The method by which this may be done is to set the tips of arrows alight by dipping them into a brazier, and then shoot them from powerful crossbows into the enemy's lines."

332   T'sao Kung thinks that "traitors in the enemy's camp" are referred to. But Ch'en Hao is more likely to be right in saying: "We must have favorable circumstances in general, not merely traitors to help us." Chia Lin says: "We must avail ourselves of wind and dry weather."

333   Tu Mu suggests as material for making fire: "dry vegetable matter, reeds, brushwood, straw, grease, oil, etc." Here we have the material cause. Chang Yu says: "vessels for hoarding fire, stuff for lighting fires."

334   These are, respectively, the 7th, 14th, 27th, and 28th of the Twenty-eight Stellar Mansions, corresponding roughly to Sagittarius, Pegasus, Crater and Corvus.

335   The prime object of attacking with fire is to throw the enemy into confusion. If this

8. (3) When the force of the flames has reached its height, follow it up with an attack, if that is practicable; if not, stay where you are.[336]

9. (4) If it is possible to make an assault with fire from without, do not wait for it to break out within, but deliver your attack at a favorable moment.[337]

10. (5) When you start a fire, be to windward of it. Do not attack from the leeward.[338]

11. A wind that rises in the daytime lasts long, but a night breeze soon falls.[339]

---

effect is not produced, it means that the enemy is ready to receive us. Hence the necessity for caution.

336 Ts'ao Kung says: "If you see a possible way, advance; but if you find the difficulties too great, retire."

337 Tu Mu says that the previous paragraphs had reference to the fire breaking out (either accidentally, we may suppose, or by the agency of incendiaries) inside the enemy's camp. "But," he continues, "if the enemy is settled in a waste place littered with quantities of grass, or if he has pitched his camp in a position which can be burnt out, we must carry our fire against him at any seasonable opportunity, and not await on in hopes of an outbreak occurring within, for fear our opponents should themselves burn up the surrounding vegetation, and thus render our own attempts fruitless." The famous Li Ling once baffled the leader of the Hsiung-nu in this way. The latter, taking advantage of a favorable wind, tried to set fire to the Chinese general's camp, but found that every scrap of combustible vegetation in the neighborhood had already been burnt down. On the other hand, Po-ts'ai, a general of the Yellow Turban rebels, was badly defeated in 184 A.D. through his neglect of this simple precaution. "At the head of a large army he was besieging Ch'ang-she, which was held by Huang-fu Sung. The garrison was very small, and a general feeling of nervousness pervaded the ranks; so Huang-fu Sung called his officers together and said: "In war, there are various indirect methods of attack, and numbers do not count for everything. [The commentator here quotes Sun Tzu, V. SS. 5, 6 and 10.] Now the rebels have pitched their camp in the midst of thick grass which will easily burn when the wind blows. If we set fire to it at night, they will be thrown into a panic, and we can make a sortie and attack them on all sides at once, thus emulating the achievement of T'ien Tan.' That same evening, a strong breeze sprang up; so Huang-fu Sung instructed his soldiers to bind reeds together into torches and mount guard on the city walls, after which he sent out a band of daring men, who stealthily made their way through the lines and started the fire with loud shouts and yells. Simultaneously, a glare of light shot up from the city walls, and Huang-fu Sung, sounding his drums, led a rapid charge, which threw the rebels into confusion and put them to headlong flight." [Hou Han Shu, ch. 71.]

338 Chang Yu, following Tu Yu, says: "When you make a fire, the enemy will retreat away from it; if you oppose his retreat and attack him then, he will fight desperately, which will not conduce to your success." A rather more obvious explanation is given by Tu Mu: "If the wind is in the east, begin burning to the east of the enemy, and follow up the attack yourself from that side. If you start the fire on the east side, and then attack from the west, you will suffer in the same way as your enemy."

339 Cf. Lao Tzu's saying: "A violent wind does not last the space of a morning." (Tao Te

12. In every army, the five developments connected with fire must be known, the movements of the stars calculated, and a watch kept for the proper days.[340]

13. Hence those who use fire as an aid to the attack show intelligence; those who use water as an aid to the attack gain an accession of strength.

14. By means of water, an enemy may be intercepted, but not robbed of all his belongings.[341]

15. Unhappy is the fate of one who tries to win his battles and succeed in his attacks without cultivating the spirit of enterprise; for the result is waste of time and general stagnation.[342]

16. Hence the saying: The enlightened ruler lays his plans well ahead; the good general cultivates his resources.[343]

Ching, chap. 23.) Mei Yao-ch`en and Wang Hsi say: "A day breeze dies down at nightfall, and a night breeze at daybreak. This is what happens as a general rule." The phenomenon observed may be correct enough, but how this sense is to be obtained is not apparent.

340 Tu Mu says: "We must make calculations as to the paths of the stars, and watch for the days on which wind will rise, before making our attack with fire." Chang Yu seems to interpret the text differently: "We must not only know how to assail our opponents with fire, but also be on our guard against similar attacks from them."

341 Ts`ao Kung's note is: "We can merely obstruct the enemy's road or divide his army, but not sweep away all his accumulated stores." Water can do useful service, but it lacks the terrible destructive power of fire. This is the reason, Chang Yu concludes, why the former is dismissed in a couple of sentences, whereas the attack by fire is discussed in detail. Wu Tzu (ch. 4) speaks thus of the two elements: "If an army is encamped on low-lying marshy ground, from which the water cannot run off, and where the rainfall is heavy, it may be submerged by a flood. If an army is encamped in wild marsh lands thickly overgrown with weeds and brambles, and visited by frequent gales, it may be exterminated by fire."

342 This is one of the most perplexing passages in Sun Tzu. Ts`ao Kung says: "Rewards for good service should not be deferred a single day." And Tu Mu: "If you do not take opportunity to advance and reward the deserving, your subordinates will not carry out your commands, and disaster will ensue." For several reasons, however, and in spite of the formidable array of scholars on the other side, I prefer the interpretation suggested by Mei Yao-ch`en alone, whose words I will quote: "Those who want to make sure of succeeding in their battles and assaults must seize the favorable moments when they come and not shrink on occasion from heroic measures: that is to say, they must resort to such means of attack of fire, water and the like. What they must not do, and what will prove fatal, is to sit still and simply hold to the advantages they have got."

343 Tu Mu quotes the following from the *San Lueh*, ch. 2: "The warlike prince controls his soldiers by his authority, kits them together by good faith, and by rewards makes them serviceable. If faith decays, there will be disruption; if rewards are deficient, commands will not be respected."

17. Move not unless you see an advantage; use not your troops unless there is something to be gained; fight not unless the position is critical.[344]

18. No ruler should put troops into the field merely to gratify his own spleen; no general should fight a battle simply out of pique.

19. If it is to your advantage, make a forward move; if not, stay where you are.[345]

20. Anger may in time change to gladness; vexation may be succeeded by content.

21. But a kingdom that has once been destroyed can never come again into being;[346] nor can the dead ever be brought back to life.

22. Hence the enlightened ruler is heedful, and the good general full of caution. This is the way to keep a country at peace and an army intact.

344 Sun Tzu may at times appear to be over-cautious, but he never goes so far in that direction as the remarkable passage in the *Tao Te Ching*, ch. 69. "I dare not take the initiative, but prefer to act on the defensive; I dare not advance an inch, but prefer to retreat a foot."
345 This is repeated from chapter 11, section 17. Here I feel convinced that it is an interpolation, for it is evident that section 20 ought to follow immediately on section 18.
346 The Wu State was destined to be a melancholy example of this saying.

CHAPTER THIRTEEN

The Use of Spies

1. Sun Tzu said: Raising a host of a hundred thousand men and marching them great distances entails heavy loss on the people and a drain on the resources of the State. The daily expenditure will amount to a thousand ounces of silver.[347] There will be commotion at home and abroad, and men will drop down exhausted on the highways.[348] As many as seven hundred thousand families will be impeded in their labor.[349]

2. Hostile armies may face each other for years, striving for the victory which is decided in a single day. This being so, to remain in ignorance of the enemy's condition simply because one grudges the

---

347   Confer with chapter 2, sections 1, 13, 14.

348   Confer with the *Tao Te Ching*, ch. 30: "Where troops have been quartered, brambles and thorns spring up. Chang Yu has the note: "We may be reminded of the saying: 'On serious ground, gather in plunder.' Why then should carriage and transportation cause exhaustion on the highways? – The answer is, that not victuals alone, but all sorts of munitions of war have to be conveyed to the army. Besides, the injunction to 'forage on the enemy' only means that when an army is deeply engaged in hostile territory, scarcity of food must be provided against. Hence, without being solely dependent on the enemy for corn, we must forage in order that there may be an uninterrupted flow of supplies. Then, again, there are places like salt deserts where provisions being unobtainable, supplies from home cannot be dispensed with."

349   Mei Yao-ch`en says: "Men will be lacking at the plough- tail." The allusion is to the system of dividing land into nine parts, each consisting of about 15 acres, the plot in the center being cultivated on behalf of the State by the tenants of the other eight. It was here also, so Tu Mu tells us, that their cottages were built and a well sunk, to be used by all in common. [See chapter 2, section 12, note.] In time of war, one of the families had to serve in the army, while the other seven contributed to its support. Thus, by a levy of 100,000 men (reckoning one able- bodied soldier to each family) the husbandry of 700,000 families would be affected.

outlay of a hundred ounces of silver in honors and emoluments,[350] is the height of inhumanity.[351]

3. One who acts thus is no leader of men, no present help to his sovereign, no master of victory.[352]

4. Thus, what enables the wise sovereign and the good general to strike and conquer, and achieve things beyond the reach of ordinary men, is *foreknowledge*.[353]

5. Now this foreknowledge cannot be elicited from spirits; it cannot be obtained inductively from experience,[354] nor by any deductive calculation.[355]

6. Knowledge of the enemy's dispositions can only be obtained from other men.[356]

7. Hence the use of spies, of whom there are five classes:
(1) Local spies;

350 "For spies" is of course the meaning, though it would spoil the effect of this curiously elaborate exordium if spies were actually mentioned at this point.
351 Sun Tzu's agreement is certainly ingenious. He begins by adverting to the frightful misery and vast expenditure of blood and treasure which war always brings in its train. Now, unless you are kept informed of the enemy's condition, and are ready to strike at the right moment, a war may drag on for years. The only way to get this information is to employ spies, and it is impossible to obtain trustworthy spies unless they are properly paid for their services. But it is surely false economy to grudge a comparatively trifling amount for this purpose, when every day that the war lasts eats up an incalculably greater sum. This grievous burden falls on the shoulders of the poor, and hence Sun Tzu concludes that to neglect the use of spies is nothing less than a crime against humanity.
352 This idea, that the true object of war is peace, has its root in the national temperament of the Chinese. Even so far back as 597 B.C., these memorable words were uttered by Prince Chuang of the Ch`u State: "The [Chinese] character for 'prowess' is made up of [the characters for] 'to stay' and 'a spear' (cessation of hostilities). Military prowess is seen in the repression of cruelty, the calling in of weapons, the preservation of the appointment of Heaven, the firm establishment of merit, the bestowal of happiness on the people, putting harmony between the princes, the diffusion of wealth."
353 That is, knowledge of the enemy's dispositions, and what he means to do.
354 Tu Mu's note is: "[knowledge of the enemy] cannot be gained by reasoning from other analogous cases."
355 Li Ch`uan says: "Quantities like length, breadth, distance and magnitude, are susceptible of exact mathematical determination; human actions cannot be so calculated."
356 Mei Yao-ch`en has rather an interesting note: "Knowledge of the spirit-world is to be obtained by divination; information in natural science may be sought by inductive reasoning; the laws of the universe can be verified by mathematical calculation: but the dispositions of an enemy are ascertainable through spies and spies alone."

(2) inward spies;

(3) converted spies;

(4) doomed spies;

(5) surviving spies.

8. When these five kinds of spy are all at work, none can discover the secret system. This is called "divine manipulation of the threads." It is the sovereign's most precious faculty.[357]

9. Having *local spies* means employing the services of the inhabitants of a district.[358]

10. Having *inward spies*, making use of officials of the enemy.[359]

357 Cromwell, one of the greatest and most practical of all cavalry leaders, had officers styled 'scout masters,' whose business it was to collect all possible information regarding the enemy, through scouts and spies, etc., and much of his success in war was traceable to the previous knowledge of the enemy's moves thus gained."

358 Tu Mu says: "In the enemy's country, win people over by kind treatment, and use them as spies."

359 Tu Mu enumerates the following classes as likely to do good service in this respect: "Worthy men who have been degraded from office, criminals who have undergone punishment; also, favorite concubines who are greedy for gold, men who are aggrieved at being in subordinate positions, or who have been passed over in the distribution of posts, others who are anxious that their side should be defeated in order that they may have a chance of displaying their ability and talents, fickle turncoats who always want to have a foot in each boat. Officials of these several kinds," he continues, "should be secretly approached and bound to one's interests by means of rich presents. In this way you will be able to find out the state of affairs in the enemy's country, ascertain the plans that are being formed against you, and moreover disturb the harmony and create a breach between the sovereign and his ministers." The necessity for extreme caution, however, in dealing with "inward spies," appears from an historical incident related by Ho Shih: "Lo Shang, Governor of I-Chou, sent his general Wei Po to attack the rebel Li Hsiung of Shu in his stronghold at P`i. After each side had experienced a number of victories and defeats, Li Hsiung had recourse to the services of a certain P`o-t`ai, a native of Wu-tu. He began to have him whipped until the blood came, and then sent him off to Lo Shang, whom he was to delude by offering to cooperate with him from inside the city, and to give a fire signal at the right moment for making a general assault. Lo Shang, confiding in these promises, march out all his best troops, and placed Wei Po and others at their head with orders to attack at P`o-t`ai's bidding. Meanwhile, Li Hsiung's general, Li Hsiang, had prepared an ambuscade on their line of march; and P`o-t`ai, having reared long scaling-ladders against the city walls, now lighted the beacon-fire. Wei Po's men raced up on seeing the signal and began climbing the ladders as fast as they could, while others were drawn up by ropes lowered from above. More than a hundred of Lo Shang's soldiers entered the city in this way, every one of whom was forthwith beheaded. Li Hsiung then charged with all his forces, both inside and outside the city, and routed the enemy completely." [This happened in 303 A.D. I do not know where Ho Shih got the story from. It is not given in the biography of Li Hsiung or that of his father Li T`e, *Chin Shu*, ch. 120, 121.]

11. Having *converted spies*, getting hold of the enemy's spies and using them for our own purposes.[360]

12. Having *doomed spies*, doing certain things openly for purposes of deception, and allowing our spies to know of them and report them to the enemy.[361]

360   By means of heavy bribes and liberal promises detaching them from the enemy's service, and inducing them to carry back false information as well as to spy in turn on their own countrymen. On the other hand, Hsiao Shih-hsien says that we pretend not to have detected him, but contrive to let him carry away a false impression of what is going on. Several of the commentators accept this as an alternative definition; but that it is not what Sun Tzu meant is conclusively proved by his subsequent remarks about treating the converted spy generously (See section 21). Ho Shih notes three occasions on which converted spies were used with conspicuous success: (1) by T'ien Tan in his defense of Chi-mo; (2) by Chao She on his march to O-yu; and by the wily Fan Chu in 260 B.C., when Lien P'o was conducting a defensive campaign against Ch'in. The King of Chao strongly disapproved of Lien P'o's cautious and dilatory methods, which had been unable to avert a series of minor disasters, and therefore lent a ready ear to the reports of his spies, who had secretly gone over to the enemy and were already in Fan Chu's pay. They said: "The only thing which causes Ch'in anxiety is lest Chao Kua should be made general. Lien P'o they consider an easy opponent, who is sure to be vanquished in the long run." Now this Chao Kua was a son of the famous Chao She. From his boyhood, he had been wholly engrossed in the study of war and military matters, until at last he came to believe that there was no commander in the whole Empire who could stand against him. His father was much disquieted by this overweening conceit, and the flippancy with which he spoke of such a serious thing as war, and solemnly declared that if ever Kua was appointed general, he would bring ruin on the armies of Chao. This was the man who, in spite of earnest protests from his own mother and the veteran statesman Lin Hsiang-ju, was now sent to succeed Lien P'o. Needless to say, he proved no match for the redoubtable Po Ch'i and the great military power of Ch'in. He fell into a trap by which his army was divided into two and his communications cut; and after a desperate resistance lasting 46 days, during which the famished soldiers devoured one another, he was himself killed by an arrow, and his whole force, amounting, it is said, to 400,000 men, ruthlessly put to the sword.
361   Tu Yu gives the best exposition of the meaning: "We ostentatiously do thing calculated to deceive our own spies, who must be led to believe that they have been unwittingly disclosed. Then, when these spies are captured in the enemy's lines, they will make an entirely false report, and the enemy will take measures accordingly, only to find that we do something quite different. The spies will thereupon be put to death." As an example of doomed spies, Ho Shih mentions the prisoners released by Pan Ch'ao in his campaign against Yarkand. He also refers to T'ang Chien, who in 630 A.D. was sent by T'ai Tsung to lull the Turkish Kahn Chieh-li into fancied security, until Li Ching was able to deliver a crushing blow against him. Chang Yu says that the Turks revenged themselves by killing T'ang Chien, but this is a mistake, for we read in both the old and the *New T'ang History* (ch. 58, fol. 2 and ch. 89, fol. 8 respectively) that he escaped and lived on until 656. Li I-chi played a somewhat similar part in 203 B.C., when sent by the King of Han to open peaceful negotiations with Ch'i. He has certainly more claim to be described a "doomed spy", for the king of Ch'i, being subsequently attacked without warning by Han Hsin, and infuriated by what he considered the treachery of Li I-chi, ordered the unfortunate envoy to be boiled alive.

13. *Surviving spies*, finally, are those who bring back news from the enemy's camp.[362]

14. Hence it is that which none in the whole army are more intimate relations to be maintained than with spies.[363] None should be more liberally rewarded. In no other business should greater secrecy be preserved.[364]

15. Spies cannot be usefully employed without a certain intuitive sagacity.[365]

16. They cannot be properly managed without benevolence and straightforwardness.[366]

362   This is the ordinary class of spies, properly so called, forming a regular part of the army. Tu Mu says: "Your surviving spy must be a man of keen intellect, though in outward appearance a fool; of shabby exterior, but with a will of iron. He must be active, robust, endowed with physical strength and courage; thoroughly accustomed to all sorts of dirty work, able to endure hunger and cold, and to put up with shame and ignominy." Ho Shih tells the following story of Ta`hsi Wu of the Sui dynasty: "When he was governor of Eastern Ch`in, Shen-wu of Ch`i made a hostile movement upon Sha-yuan. The Emperor T`ai Tsu [? Kao Tsu] sent Ta-hsi Wu to spy upon the enemy. He was accompanied by two other men. All three were on horseback and wore the enemy's uniform. When it was dark, they dismounted a few hundred feet away from the enemy's camp and stealthily crept up to listen, until they succeeded in catching the passwords used in the army. Then they got on their horses again and boldly passed through the camp under the guise of night-watchmen; and more than once, happening to come across a soldier who was committing some breach of discipline, they actually stopped to give the culprit a sound cudgeling! Thus they managed to return with the fullest possible information about the enemy's dispositions, and received warm commendation from the Emperor, who in consequence of their report was able to inflict a severe defeat on his adversary."
363   Tu Mu and Mei Yao-ch`en point out that the spy is privileged to enter even the general's private sleeping-tent.
364   Tu Mu gives a graphic touch: all communication with spies should be carried "mouth-to-ear." The following remarks on spies may be quoted from Turenne, who made perhaps larger use of them than any previous commander: "Spies are attached to those who give them most, he who pays them ill is never served. They should never be known to anybody; nor should they know one another. When they propose anything very material, secure their persons, or have in your possession their wives and children as hostages for their fidelity. Never communicate anything to them but what is absolutely necessary that they should know.
365   Mei Yao-ch`en says: "In order to use them, one must know fact from falsehood, and be able to discriminate between honesty and double-dealing." Wang Hsi in a different interpretation thinks more along the lines of "intuitive perception" and "practical intelligence." Tu Mu strangely refers these attributes to the spies themselves: "Before using spies we must assure ourselves as to their integrity of character and the extent of their experience and skill." But he continues: "A brazen face and a crafty disposition are more dangerous than mountains or rivers; it takes a man of genius to penetrate such." So that we are left in some doubt as to his real opinion on the passage."
366   Chang Yu says: "When you have attracted them by substantial offers, you must treat

17. Without subtle ingenuity of mind, one cannot make certain of the truth of their reports.[367]

18. Be subtle! be subtle! and use your spies for every kind of business.[368]

19. If a secret piece of news is divulged by a spy before the time is ripe, he must be put to death together with the man to whom the secret was told.[369]

20. Whether the object be to crush an army, to storm a city, or to assassinate an individual, it is always necessary to begin by finding out the names of the attendants, the aides-de-camp,[370] and door-keepers and sentries of the general in command. Our spies must be commissioned to ascertain these.[371]

21. The enemy's spies who have come to spy on us must be sought out, tempted with bribes, led away and comfortably housed. Thus they will become converted spies and available for our service.

22. It is through the information brought by the converted spy that we are able to acquire and employ local and inward spies.[372]

23. It is owing to his information, again, that we can cause the doomed spy to carry false tidings to the enemy.[373]

---

them with absolute sincerity; then they will work for you with all their might."
367 Mei Yao-ch`en says: "Be on your guard against the possibility of spies going over to the service of the enemy."
368 Confer with chapter 6, section 9.
369 Word for word, the translation here is: "If spy matters are heard before [our plans] are carried out," etc. Sun Tzu's main point in this passage is: Whereas you kill the spy himself "as a punishment for letting out the secret," the object of killing the other man is only, as Ch`en Hao puts it, "to stop his mouth" and prevent news leaking any further. If it had already been repeated to others, this object would not be gained. Either way, Sun Tzu lays himself open to the charge of inhumanity, though Tu Mu tries to defend him by saying that the man deserves to be put to death, for the spy would certainly not have told the secret unless the other had been at pains to worm it out of him."
370 Literally "visitors", is equivalent, as Tu Yu says, to "those whose duty it is to keep the general supplied with information," which naturally necessitates frequent interviews with him.
371 As the first step, no doubt towards finding out if any of these important functionaries can be won over by bribery.
372 Tu Yu says: "through conversion of the enemy's spies we learn the enemy's condition." And Chang Yu says: "We must tempt the converted spy into our service, because it is he that knows which of the local inhabitants are greedy of gain, and which of the officials are open to corruption."
373 Chang Yu says, "because the converted spy knows how the enemy can best be deceived."

24. Lastly, it is by his information that the surviving spy can be used on appointed occasions.

25. The end and aim of spying in all its five varieties is knowledge of the enemy; and this knowledge can only be derived, in the first instance, from the converted spy.[374] Hence it is essential that the converted spy be treated with the utmost liberality.

26. Of old, the rise of the Yin dynasty[375] was due to I Chih[376] who had served under the Hsia. Likewise, the rise of the Chou dynasty was due to Lu Ya[377] who had served under the Yin.[378]

27. Hence it is only the enlightened ruler and the wise general who will use the highest intelligence of the army for purposes of spying and thereby they achieve great results.[379] Spies are a most important element in water, because on them depends an army's ability to move.[380]

---

374   As explained in sections 22-24. He not only brings information himself, but makes it possible to use the other kinds of spy to advantage.

375   Sun Tzu means the Shang dynasty, founded in 1766 B.C. Its name was changed to Yin by P`an Keng in 1401.

376   Better known as I Yin, the famous general and statesman who took part in Ch`eng T`ang's campaign against Chieh Kuei.

377   Lu Shang rose to high office under the tyrant Chou Hsin, whom he afterwards helped to overthrow. Popularly known as T`ai Kung, a title bestowed on him by Wen Wang, he is said to have composed a treatise on war, erroneously identified with the *Liu T`Ao*.

378   There is less precision in the Chinese than I have thought it well to introduce into my translation, and the commentaries on the passage are by no means explicit. But, having regard to the context, we can hardly doubt that Sun Tzu is holding up I Chih and Lu Ya as illustrious examples of the converted spy, or something closely analogous. His suggestion is, that the Hsia and Yin dynasties were upset owing to the intimate knowledge of their weaknesses and shortcoming which these former ministers were able to impart to the other side. Mei Yao-ch`en appears to resent any such aspersion on these historic names: "I Yin and Lu Ya," he says, "were not rebels against the Government. Hsia could not employ the former, hence Yin employed him. Yin could not employ the latter, hence Hou employed him. Their great achievements were all for the good of the people." Ho Shih is also indignant: "How should two divinely inspired men such as I and Lu have acted as common spies? Sun Tzu's mention of them simply means that the proper use of the five classes of spies is a matter which requires men of the highest mental caliber like I and Lu, whose wisdom and capacity qualified them for the task. The above words only emphasize this point." Ho Shih believes then that the two heroes are mentioned on account of their supposed skill in the use of spies. But this is very weak.

379   Tu Mu closes with a note of warning: "Just as water, which carries a boat from bank to bank, may also be the means of sinking it, so reliance on spies, while production of great results, is oft-times the cause of utter destruction."

380   Chia Lin says that an army without spies is like a man without ears or eyes.

THE COMMENTATORS

Sᴜɴ Tᴢᴜ can boast an exceptionally long distinguished roll of commentators, which would do honor to any classic. Ou-yang Hsiu remarks on this fact, though he wrote before the tale was complete, and rather ingeniously explains it by saying that the artifices of war, being inexhaustible, must therefore be susceptible of treatment in a great variety of ways.

1. *Ts'Ao Ts'Ao* or Ts'ao Kung, afterwards known as Wei Wu Ti [A.D. 155-220]. There is hardly any room for doubt that the earliest commentary on Sun Tzu actually came from the pen of this extraordinary man, whose biography in the *San Kuo Chih* reads like a romance. One of the greatest military geniuses that the world has seen, and Napoleonic in the scale of his operations, he was especially famed for the marvelous rapidity of his marches, which has found expression in the line "Talk of Ts'ao Ts'ao, and Ts'ao Ts'ao will appear." Ou-yang Hsiu says of him that he was a great captain who "measured his strength against Tung Cho, Lu Pu and the two Yuan, father and son, and vanquished them all; whereupon he divided the Empire of Han with Wu and Shu, and made himself king. It is recorded that whenever a council of war was held by Wei on the eve of a far-reaching campaign, he had all his calculations ready; those generals who made use of them did not lose one battle in ten; those who ran counter to them in any particular saw their armies incontinently beaten and put to flight." Ts'ao Kung's notes on Sun Tzu, models of austere brevity, are so thoroughly characteristic of the stern commander known to history, that it is hard indeed to conceive of them as the work of a mere *litterateur*. Sometimes, indeed, owing to extreme compression, they are scarcely intelligible and stand no less in need of a commentary than the text itself.

2. *Meng Shih*. The commentary which has come down to us under this name is comparatively meager, and nothing about the author is known. Even his personal name has not been recorded. Chi T`ien-pao's edition places him after Chia Lin,and Ch`ao Kung- wu also assigns him to the T`ang dynasty, but this is a mistake. In Sun Hsing-yen's preface, he appears as Meng Shih of the Liang dynasty [502-557]. Others would identify him with Meng K`ang of the 3rd century. He is named in one work as the last of the "Five Commentators," the others being Wei Wu Ti, Tu Mu, Ch`en Hao and Chia Lin.

3. *Li Ch`Uan* of the 8th century was a well-known writer on military tactics. One of his works has been in constant use down to the present day. The *T`Ung Chih* mentions "Lives of famous generals from the Chou to the T`ang dynasty" as written by him. According to Ch`ao Kung-wu and the *T`Ien-I-Ko* catalogue, he followed a variant of the text of Sun Tzu which differs considerably from those now extant. His notes are mostly short and to the point, and he frequently illustrates his remarks by anecdotes from Chinese history.

4. *Tu Yu* (died 812) did not publish a separate commentary on Sun Tzu, his notes being taken from the *T`Ung Tien*, the encyclopedic treatise on the Constitution which was his life- work. They are largely repetitions of Ts`ao Kung and Meng Shih, besides which it is believed that he drew on the ancient commentaries of Wang Ling and others. Owing to the peculiar arrangement of *T`Ung Tien*, he has to explain each passage on its merits, apart from the context, and sometimes his own explanation does not agree with that of Ts`ao Kung, whom he always quotes first. Though not strictly to be reckoned as one of the "Ten Commentators," he was added to their number by Chi T`ien-pao, being wrongly placed after his grandson Tu Mu.

5. *Tu Mu* (803-852) is perhaps the best known as a poet – a bright star even in the glorious galaxy of the T`ang period. We learn from Ch`ao Kung-wu that although he had no practical experience of war, he was extremely fond of discussing the subject, and was moreover well read in the military history of the *Ch`Un Ch`Iu* and *Chan Kuo* eras. His notes, therefore, are well worth attention. They are very copious, and replete with historical parallels. The gist of Sun Tzu's work is thus summarized by him: "Practice benevolence and justice, but on the other hand make full use of artifice and measures of expediency." He further declared that all the military tri-

umphs and disasters of the thousand years which had elapsed since Sun Tzu's death would, upon examination, be found to uphold and corroborate, in every particular, the maxims contained in his book. Tu Mu's somewhat spiteful charge against Ts`ao Kung has already been considered elsewhere.

6. *Ch`En Hao* appears to have been a contemporary of Tu Mu. Ch`ao Kung-wu says that he was impelled to write a new commentary on Sun Tzu because Ts`ao Kung's on the one hand was too obscure and subtle, and that of Tu Mu on the other too long-winded and diffuse. Ou-yang Hsiu, writing in the middle of the 11th century, calls Ts`ao Kung, Tu Mu and Ch`en Hao the three chief commentators on Sun Tzu, and observes that Ch`en Hao is continually attacking Tu Mu's shortcomings. His commentary, though not lacking in merit, must rank below those of his predecessors.

7. *Chia Lin* is known to have lived under the T`ang dynasty, for his commentary on Sun Tzu is mentioned in the T`ang Shu and was afterwards republished by Chi Hsieh of the same dynasty together with those of Meng Shih and Tu Yu. It is of somewhat scanty texture, and in point of quality, too, perhaps the least valuable of the eleven.

8. *Mei Yao-Ch`En* (1002-1060), commonly known by his "style" as Mei Sheng-yu, was, like Tu Mu, a poet of distinction. His commentary was published with a laudatory preface by the great Ou-yang Hsiu, from which we may cull the following: −

Later scholars have misread Sun Tzu, distorting his words and trying to make them square with their own one-sided views. Thus, though commentators have not been lacking, only a few have proved equal to the task. My friend Sheng-yu has not fallen into this mistake. In attempting to provide a critical commentary for Sun Tzu's work, he does not lose sight of the fact that these sayings were intended for states engaged in internecine warfare; that the author is not concerned with the military conditions prevailing under the sovereigns of the three ancient dynasties, nor with the nine punitive measures prescribed to the Minister of War. Again, Sun Wu loved brevity of diction, but his meaning is always deep. Whether the subject be marching an army, or handling soldiers, or estimating the enemy, or controlling the forces of victory, it is always systematically treated; the sayings are bound together in strict logical sequence, though this has been obscured by commentators who have probably failed to grasp their meaning. In his own commentary, Mei Sheng-yu has brushed aside all the obstinate prejudices of these critics, and has tried to bring out the true meaning of Sun Tzu himself. In this way, the clouds of confusion have been dispersed and the sayings made clear. I am convinced that the present work deserves to be handed down side by side with the three great commentaries; and for a great deal that they find in the sayings, coming generations will have constant reason to thank my friend Sheng-yu.

Making some allowance for the exuberance of friendship, I am inclined to endorse this favorable judgment, and would certainly place him above Ch'en Hao in order of merit.

9. *Wang Hsi*, also of the Sung dynasty, is decidedly original in some of his interpretations, but much less judicious than Mei Yao-ch'en, and on the whole not a very trustworthy guide. He is fond of comparing his own commentary with that of Ts'ao Kung, but the comparison is not often flattering to him. We learn from Ch'ao Kung-wu that Wang Hsi revised the ancient text of Sun Tzu, filling up lacunae and correcting mistakes.

10. *Ho Yen-Hsi* of the Sung dynasty. The personal name of this commentator is given as above by Cheng Ch'iao in the *Tung Chih*, written about the middle of the twelfth century, but he appears simply as Ho Shih in the *Yu Hai*, and Ma Tuan-lin quotes Ch'ao Kung-wu as saying that his personal name is unknown. There seems to be no reason to doubt Cheng Ch'iao's statement, otherwise I should have been inclined to hazard a guess and identify him with one Ho Ch'u-fei, the author of a short treatise on war, who lived in the latter part of the 11th century. Ho Shih's commentary, in the words of the *T'Ien-I-Ko* catalogue, "contains helpful additions" here and there, but is chiefly remarkable for the copious extracts taken, in adapted form, from the dynastic histories and other sources.

11. *Chang Yu*. The list closes with a commentator of no great originality perhaps, but gifted with admirable powers of lucid exposition. His commentator is based on that of Ts'ao Kung, whose terse sentences he contrives to expand and develop in masterly fashion. Without Chang Yu, it is safe to say that much of Ts'ao Kung's com-

mentary would have remained cloaked in its pristine obscurity and therefore valueless. His work is not mentioned in the Sung history, the *T'Ung K'Ao*, or the *Yu Hai*, but it finds a niche in the *T'Ung Chih*, which also names him as the author of the "Lives of Famous Generals." It is rather remarkable that the last-named four should all have flourished within so short a space of time. Ch'ao Kung-wu accounts for it by saying: "During the early years of the Sung dynasty the Empire enjoyed a long spell of peace, and men ceased to practice the art of war. but when [Chao] Yuan-hao's rebellion came [1038-42] and the frontier generals were defeated time after time, the Court made strenuous inquiry for men skilled in war, and military topics became the vogue amongst all the high officials. Hence it is that the commentators of Sun Tzu in our dynasty belong mainly to that period."

Besides these eleven commentators, there are several others whose work has not come down to us. The Sui Shu mentions four, namely Wang Ling (often quoted by Tu Yu as Wang Tzu); Chang Tzu-shang; Chia Hsu of Wei; and Shen Yu of Wu. The T'Ang Shu adds Sun Hao, and the T'Ung Chih Hsiao Chi, while the T'U Shu mentions a Ming commentator, Huang Jun-yu. It is possible that some of these may have been merely collectors and editors of other commentaries, like Chi T'ien-pao and Chi Hsieh, mentioned above.

THE
PRINCE

CONTENTS

THE PRINCE

INTRODUCTION

Niccolò Machiavelli was born at Florence on 3rd May 1469. He was the second son of Bernardo di Niccolò Machiavelli, a lawyer of some repute, and of Bartolommea di Stefano Nelli, his wife. Both parents were members of the old Florentine nobility.

His life falls naturally into three periods, each of which singularly enough constitutes a distinct and important era in the history of Florence. His youth was concurrent with the greatness of Florence as an Italian power under the guidance of Lorenzo de' Medici, Il Magnifico. The downfall of the Medici in Florence occurred in 1494, in which year Machiavelli entered the public service. During his official career Florence was free under the government of a Republic, which lasted until 1512, when the Medici returned to power, and Machiavelli lost his office. The Medici again ruled Florence from 1512 until 1527, when they were once more driven out. This was the period of Machiavelli's literary activity and increasing influence; but he died, within a few weeks of the expulsion of the Medici, on 22nd June 1527, in his fifty-eighth year, without having regained office.

YOUTH – AGE 1-25 – 1469-94

ALTHOUGH THERE IS LITTLE RECORDED of the youth of Machiavelli, the Florence of those days is so well known that the early environment of this representative citizen may be easily imagined. Florence has been described as a city with two opposite currents of life, one directed by the fervent and austere Savonarola, the other by the splendour-loving Lorenzo. Savonarola's influence upon the young Machiavelli must have been slight, for although at one time he wielded immense power over the fortunes of Florence, he only furnished Machiavelli with a subject of a gibe in *The Prince*, where he is cited as an example of an unarmed prophet who came to a bad end. Whereas the magnificence of the Medicean rule during the life of Lorenzo appeared to have impressed Machiavelli strongly, for he frequently recurs to it in his writings, and it is to Lorenzo's grandson that he dedicates *The Prince*.

Machiavelli, in his *History of Florence*, gives us a picture of the young men among whom his youth was passed. He writes: "They were freer than their forefathers in dress and living, and spent more in other kinds of excesses, consuming their time and money in idleness, gaming, and women; their chief aim was to appear well dressed and to speak with wit and acuteness, whilst he who could wound others the most cleverly was thought the wisest." In a letter to his son Guido, Machiavelli shows why youth should avail itself of its opportunities for study, and leads us to infer that his own youth had been so occupied. He writes: "I have received your letter, which has given me the greatest pleasure, especially because you tell me you are quite restored in health, than which I could have no better news; for if God grant life to you, and to me, I hope to make a good man of you if you are willing to do your share." Then, writing of a new patron, he continues: "This will turn out well for you, but it is necessary for you to study; since, then, you have no longer the excuse of illness, take pains to study letters and music, for you see what honour is done to me for the little skill I have. Therefore, my son, if you wish to please me, and to bring success and honour to yourself, do right and study, because others will help you if you help yourself."

OFFICE – AGE 25-43 – 1494-1512

THE SECOND PERIOD of Machiavelli's life was spent in the service of the free Republic of Florence, which flourished, as stated above, from the expulsion of the Medici in 1494 until their return in 1512. After serving four years in one of the public offices he was appointed Chancellor and Secretary to the Second Chancery, the Ten of Liberty and Peace. Here we are on firm ground when dealing with the events of Machiavelli's life, for during this time he took a leading part in the affairs of the Republic, and we have its decrees, records, and dispatches to guide us, as well as his own writings. A mere recapitulation of a few of his transactions with the statesmen and soldiers of his time gives a fair indication of his activities, and supplies the sources from which he drew the experiences and characters which illustrate *The Prince*.

His first mission was in 1499 to Catherina Sforza, "my lady of Forli" of *The Prince*, from whose conduct and fate he drew the moral that it is far better to earn the confidence of the people than to rely on fortresses. This is a very noticeable principle in Machiavelli, and is urged by him in many ways as a matter of vital importance to princes.

In 1500 he was sent to France to obtain terms from Louis XII for continuing the war against Pisa: this king it was who, in his conduct of affairs in Italy, committed the five capital errors in statecraft summarized in *The Prince*, and was consequently driven out. He, also, it was who made the dissolution of his marriage a condition of support to Pope Alexander VI; which leads Machiavelli to refer those who urge that such promises should be kept to what he has written concerning the faith of princes.

Machiavelli's public life was largely occupied with events arising out of the ambitions of Pope Alexander VI and his son, Cesare Borgia, the Duke Valentino, and these characters fill a large space of *The Prince*. Machiavelli never hesitates to cite the actions of the duke for the benefit of usurpers who wish to keep the states they have seized; he can, indeed, find no precepts to offer so good as the pattern of Cesare Borgia's conduct, insomuch that Cesare is acclaimed by some critics as the "hero" of *The Prince*. Yet in *The Prince* the duke is in point of fact cited as a type of man who rises on the fortune of others, and falls with them; who takes every course that might be expected from a prudent man but the course which will save him; who is prepared for all eventualities but the one which happens; and who, when all his abilities fail to carry him through, exclaims that it was not his fault, but an extraordinary and unforeseen fatality.

On the death of Pius III, in 1503, Machiavelli was sent to Rome to watch the election of his successor, and there he saw Cesare Borgia cheated into allowing the choice of the College to fall on Giuliano delle Rovere (Julius II), who was one of the cardinals that had most reason to fear the duke. Machiavelli, when commenting on this election, says that he who thinks new favours will cause great personages to forget old injuries deceives himself. Julius did not rest until he had ruined Cesare.

It was to Julius II that Machiavelli was sent in 1506, when that pontiff was commencing his enterprise against Bologna; which he brought to a successful issue, as he did many of his other adventures, owing chiefly to his impetuous character. It is in reference to Pope Julius that Machiavelli moralizes on the resemblance between Fortune and women, and concludes that it is the bold rather than the cautious man that will win and hold them both.

It is impossible to follow here the varying fortunes of the Italian states, which in 1507 were controlled by France, Spain, and Germany, with results that have lasted to our day; we are concerned with those events, and with the three great actors in them, so far only as they impinge on the personality of Machiavelli. He had several meetings with Louis XII of France, and his estimate of that monarch's character has already been alluded to. Machiavelli has painted Ferdinand of Aragon as the man who accomplished great things under the cloak of religion, but who in reality had no mercy, faith, humanity, or integrity; and who, had he allowed himself to be influenced by such motives, would have been ruined. The Emperor Maximilian was one of the most interesting men of the age, and his character has been drawn by many hands; but Machiavelli, who was an envoy at his court in 1507-8, reveals the secret of his many failures when he describes him as a secretive man, without force of character – ignoring the human agencies necessary to carry his schemes into effect, and never insisting on the fulfilment of his wishes.

The remaining years of Machiavelli's official career were filled with events arising out of the League of Cambrai, made in 1508 between the three great European powers already mentioned and the pope, with the object of crushing the Venetian Republic. This result was attained in the battle of Vaila, when Venice lost in one day all that she had won in eight hundred years. Florence had a difficult part to play during these events, complicated as they were by the feud which broke out between the pope and the French, because friendship with France had dictated the entire policy of the Republic. When, in 1511, Julius II finally formed the Holy League against France, and with the assistance of the Swiss drove the French out of Italy, Florence lay at the mercy of the Pope, and had to submit to his terms, one of which was that the Medici should be restored. The return of the Medici to Florence on 1st September 1512, and the consequent fall of the Republic, was the signal for the dismissal of Machiavelli and his friends, and thus put an end to his public career, for, as we have seen, he died without regaining office.

ON THE RETURN OF THE MEDICI, Machiavelli, who for a few weeks had vainly hoped to retain his office under the new masters of Florence, was dismissed by decree dated 7th November 1512. Shortly after this he was accused of complicity in an abortive conspiracy against the Medici, imprisoned, and put to the question by torture. The new Medicean people, Leo X, procured his release, and he retired to his small property at San Casciano, near Florence, where he devoted himself to literature. In a letter to Francesco Vettori, dated 13th December 1513, he has left a very interesting description of his life at this period, which elucidates his methods and his motives in writing "The Prince." After describing his daily occupations with his family and neighbours, he writes: "The evening being come, I return home and go to my study; at the entrance I pull off my peasant-clothes, covered with dust and dirt, and put on my noble court dress, and thus becomingly re-clothed I pass into the ancient courts of the men of old, where, being lovingly received by them, I am fed with that food which is mine alone; where I do not hesitate to speak with them, and to ask for the reason of their actions, and they in their benignity answer me; and for four hours I feel no weariness, I forget every trouble, poverty does not dismay, death does not terrify me; I am possessed entirely by those great men. And because Dante says:

> *Knowledge doth come of learning well retained,*
> *Unfruitful else,*

I have noted down what I have gained from their conversation, and have composed a small work on 'Principalities,' where I pour myself out as fully as I can in meditation on the subject, discussing what a principality is, what kinds there are, how they can be acquired, how they can be kept, why they are lost: and if any of my fancies ever pleased you, this ought not to displease you: and to a prince, especially to a new one, it should be welcome: therefore I dedicate it to his Magnificence Giuliano. Filippo Casavecchio has seen it; he will be able to tell you what is in it, and of the discourses I have had with him; nevertheless, I am still enriching and polishing it."

The "little book" suffered many vicissitudes before attaining the form in which it has reached us. Various mental influences were at work during its composition; its title and patron were changed; and for some unknown reason it was finally dedicated to Lorenzo de' Medici. Although Machiavelli discussed with Casavecchio whether it should be sent or presented in person to the patron, there is no evidence that Lorenzo ever received or even read it: he certainly never gave Machiavelli any employment. Although it was plagiarized during Machiavelli's lifetime, *The Prince* was never published by him, and its text is still disputable.

Machiavelli concludes his letter to Vettori thus: "And as to this little thing [his book], when it has been read it will be seen that during the fifteen years I have given to the study of statecraft I have neither slept nor idled; and men ought ever to desire to be served by one who has reaped experience at the expense of others. And of my loyalty none could doubt, because having always kept faith I could not now learn how to break it; for he who has been faithful and honest, as I have, cannot change his nature; and my poverty is a witness to my honesty."

Before Machiavelli had got *The Prince* off his hands he commenced his *Discourse on the First Decade of Titus Livius*, which should be read concurrently with *The Prince*. These and several minor works occupied him until the year 1518, when he accepted a small commission to look after the affairs of some Florentine merchants at Genoa. In 1519 the Medicean rulers of Florence granted a few political concessions to her citizens, and Machiavelli with others was consulted upon a new constitution under which the Great Council was to be restored; but on one pretext or another it was not promulgated.

In 1520 the Florentine merchants again had recourse to Machiavelli to settle their difficulties with Lucca, but this year was chiefly remarkable for his re-entry into Florentine literary society, where he was much sought after, and also for the production of his *Art of War*. It was in the same year that he received a commission at the instance of Cardinal de' Medici to write the *History of Florence*, a task which occupied him until 1525. His return to popular favour may have determined the Medici to give him this employment, for an old writer observes that "an able statesman out of work, like a huge whale, will endeavour to overturn the ship unless he has an empty cask to play with."

When the *History of Florence* was finished, Machiavelli took it to Rome for presentation to his patron, Giuliano de' Medici, who had in the meanwhile become pope under the title of Clement VII. It is somewhat remarkable that, as, in 1513, Machiavelli had written *The Prince* for the instruction of the Medici after they had just regained power in Florence, so, in 1525, he dedicated the *History of Florence* to the head of the family when its ruin was now at hand. In that year the battle of Pavia destroyed the French rule in Italy, and left Francis I a prisoner in the hands of his great rival, Charles V. This was followed by the sack of Rome, upon the news of which the popular party at Florence threw off the yoke of the Medici, who were once more banished.

Machiavelli was absent from Florence at this time, but hastened his return, hoping to secure his former office of secretary to the "Ten of Liberty and Peace." Unhappily he was taken ill soon after he reached Florence, where he died on 22nd June 1527.

THE MAN AND HIS WORKS

No one can say where the bones of Machiavelli rest, but modern Florence has decreed him a stately cenotaph in Santa Croce, by the side of her most famous sons; recognizing that, whatever other nations may have found in his works, Italy found in them the idea of her unity and the germs of her renaissance among the nations of Europe. Whilst it is idle to protest against the world-wide and evil signification of his name, it may be pointed out that the harsh construction of his doctrine which this sinister reputation implies was unknown to his own day, and that the researches of recent times have enabled us to interpret him more reasonably. It is due to these inquiries that the shape of an "unholy necromancer," which so long haunted men's vision, has begun to fade.

Machiavelli was undoubtedly a man of great observation, acuteness, and industry; noting with appreciative eye whatever passed before him, and with his supreme literary gift turning it to account in his enforced retirement from affairs. He does not present himself, nor is he depicted by his contemporaries, as a type of that rare combination, the successful statesman and author, for he appears to have been only moderately prosperous in his several embassies and political employments. He was misled by Catherina Sforza, ignored by Louis XII, overawed by Cesare Borgia; several of his embassies were quite barren of results; his attempts to fortify Florence failed, and the soldiery that he raised astonished everybody by their cowardice. In the conduct of his own affairs he was timid and time-serving; he dared not appear by the side of Soderini, to whom he owed so much, for fear of compromising himself; his connection with the Medici was open to suspicion, and Giuliano appears to have recognized his real forte when he set him to write the *History of Florence*, rather than employ him in the state. And it is on the literary side of his character, and there alone, that we find no weakness and no failure.

Although the light of almost four centuries has been focused on *The Prince*, its problems are still debatable and interesting, because they are the eternal problems between the ruled and their rulers. Such as they are, its ethics are those of Machiavelli's contemporaries; yet they cannot be said to be out of date so long as the governments of Europe rely on material rather than on moral forces. Its historical incidents and personages become interesting by reason of the uses which Machiavelli makes of them to illustrate his theories of government and conduct.

Leaving out of consideration those maxims of state which still furnish some European and eastern statesmen with principles of action, *The Prince* is bestrewn with truths that can be proved at every turn. Men are still the dupes of their simplicity and greed, as they were in the days of Alexander VI. The cloak of religion still conceals the vices which Machiavelli laid bare in the character of Ferdinand of Aragon. Men will not look at things as they really are, but as they wish them to be – and are ruined. In politics there are no perfectly safe courses; prudence consists in choosing the least dangerous ones. Then – to pass to a higher plane – Machiavelli reiterates that, although crimes may win an empire, they do not win glory. Necessary wars are just wars, and the arms of a nation are hallowed when it has no other resource but to fight.

It is the cry of a far later day than Machiavelli's that government should be elevated into a living moral force, capable of inspiring the people with a just recognition of the fundamental principles of society; to this "high argument" *The Prince* contributes but little. Machiavelli always refused to write either of men or of governments otherwise than as he found them, and he writes with such skill and insight that his work is of abiding value. But what invests *The Prince* with more than a merely artistic or historical interest is the incontrovertible truth that it deals with the great principles which still guide nations and rulers in their relationship with each other and their neighbours.

In translating *The Prince* my aim has been to achieve at all costs an exact literal rendering of the original, rather than a fluent paraphrase adapted to the modern notions of style and expression. Machiavelli was no facile phrasemonger; the conditions under which he wrote obliged him to weigh every word; his themes were lofty, his substance grave, his manner nobly plain and serious. "Quis eo fuit unquam in partiundis rebus, in definiendis, in explanandis pressior?" In *The Prince*, it may be truly said, there is reason assignable, not only for every word, but for the position of every word. To an Englishman of Shakespeare's time the translation of such a treatise was in some ways a comparatively easy task, for in those times the genius of the English more nearly resembled that of the Italian language; to the Englishman of today it is not so simple. To take a single example: the word "intrattenere," employed by Machiavelli to indicate the policy adopted by the Roman Senate towards the weaker states of Greece, would by an Elizabethan be correctly rendered "entertain," and every contemporary reader would understand what was meant by saying that "Rome entertained the Aetolians and the Achaeans without augmenting their power." But today such a phrase would seem obsolete and ambiguous, if not unmeaning: we are compelled to say that "Rome maintained friendly relations with the Aetolians," etc., using four words to do the work of one. I have tried to preserve the pithy brevity of the Italian so far as was consistent with an absolute fidelity to the sense. If the result be an occasional asperity I can only hope that the reader, in his eagerness to reach the author's meaning, may overlook the roughness of the road that leads him to it.

The following is a list of the works of Machiavelli:

Principal works. Discorso sopra le cose di Pisa, 1499; Del modo di trattare i popoli della Valdichiana ribellati, 1502; Del modo tenuto dal duca Valentino nell' ammazzare Vitellozzo Vitelli, Oliverotto da Fermo, etc., 1502; Discorso sopra la provisione del danaro, 1502; Decennale primo (poem in terza rima), 1506; Ritratti delle cose dell' Alemagna, 1508-12; Decennale secondo, 1509; Ritratti delle cose di Francia, 1510; Discorsi sopra la prima deca di T. Livio, 3 vols., 1512-17; Il Principe, 1513; Andria, comedy translated from Terence, 1513 (?); Mandragola, prose comedy in five acts, with prologue in verse, 1513; Della lingua (dialogue), 1514; Clizia, comedy in prose, 1515 (?); Belfagor arcidiavolo (novel), 1515; Asino d'oro (poem in terza rima), 1517; Dell' arte della guerra, 1519-20; Discorso sopra il riformare lo stato di Firenze, 1520; Sommario delle cose della citta di Lucca, 1520; Vita di Castruccio Castracani da Lucca, 1520; Istorie fiorentine, 8 books, 1521-5; Frammenti storici, 1525.

Other poems include Sonetti, Canzoni, Ottave, and Canti carnascialeschi.

Editions. Aldo, Venice, 1546; della Tertina, 1550; Cambiagi, Florence, 6 vols., 1782-5; dei Classici, Milan, 10 1813; Silvestri, 9 vols., 1820-2; Passerini, Fanfani, Milanesi, 6 vols. only published, 1873-7.

Minor works. Ed. F. L. Polidori, 1852; Lettere familiari, ed. E. Alvisi, 1883, 2 editions, one with excisions; Credited Writings, ed. G. Canestrini, 1857; Letters to F. Vettori, see A. Ridolfi, Pensieri intorno allo scopo di N. Machiavelli nel libro Il Principe, etc.; D. Ferrara, The Private Correspondence of Nicolo Machiavelli, 1929.

DEDICATION

To the Magnificent Lorenzo Di Piero De' Medici:

Those who strive to obtain the good graces of a prince are accustomed to come before him with such things as they hold most precious, or in which they see him take most delight; whence one often sees horses, arms, cloth of gold, precious stones, and similar ornaments presented to princes, worthy of their greatness.

Desiring therefore to present myself to your Magnificence with some testimony of my devotion towards you, I have not found among my possessions anything which I hold more dear than, or value so much as, the knowledge of the actions of great men, acquired by long experience in contemporary affairs, and a continual study of antiquity; which, having reflected upon it with great and prolonged diligence, I now send, digested into a little volume, to your Magnificence.

And although I may consider this work unworthy of your countenance, nevertheless I trust much to your benignity that it may be acceptable, seeing that it is not possible for me to make a better gift than to offer you the opportunity of understanding in the shortest time all that I have learnt in so many years, and with so many troubles and dangers; which work I have not embellished with swelling or magnificent words, nor stuffed with rounded periods, nor with any extrinsic allurements or adornments whatever, with which so many are accustomed to embellish their works; for I have wished either that no honour should be given it, or else that the truth of the matter and the weightiness of the theme shall make it acceptable.

Nor do I hold with those who regard it as a presumption if a man of low and humble condition dare to discuss and settle the concerns of princes; because, just as those who draw landscapes place themselves below in the plain to contemplate the nature of the mountains and of lofty places, and in order to contemplate the plains place themselves upon high mountains, even so to understand the nature of the people it needs to be a prince, and to understand that of princes it needs to be of the people.

Take then, your Magnificence, this little gift in the spirit in which I send it; wherein, if it be diligently read and considered by you, you will learn my extreme desire that you should attain that greatness which fortune and your other attributes promise.

And if your Magnificence from the summit of your greatness will sometimes turn your eyes to these lower regions, you will see how un-meritedly I suffer a great and continued malignity of fortune.

CHAPTER ONE

How Many Kinds of Principalities there are, and by what Means they are Acquired

ALL STATES, ALL POWERS, that have held and hold rule over men have been and are either republics or principalities.

Principalities are either hereditary, in which the family has been long established; or they are new.

The new are either entirely new, as was Milan to Francesco Sforza, or they are, as it were, members annexed to the hereditary state of the prince who has acquired them, as was the kingdom of Naples to that of the King of Spain.

Such dominions thus acquired are either accustomed to live under a prince, or to live in freedom; and are acquired either by the arms of the prince himself, or of others, or else by fortune or by ability.

CHAPTER TWO

Concerning Hereditary Principalities

I WILL LEAVE OUT ALL DISCUSSION on republics, inasmuch as in another place I have written of them at length, and will address myself only to principalities. In doing so I will keep to the order indicated above, and discuss how such principalities are to be ruled and preserved.

I say at once there are fewer difficulties in holding hereditary states, and those long accustomed to the family of their prince, than new ones; for it is sufficient only not to transgress the customs of his ancestors, and to deal prudently with circumstances as they arise, for a prince of average powers to maintain himself in his state, unless he be deprived of it by some extraordinary and excessive force; and if he should be so deprived of it, whenever anything sinister happens to the usurper, he will regain it.

We have in Italy, for example, the Duke of Ferrara, who could not have withstood the attacks of the Venetians in '84, nor those of Pope Julius in '10, unless he had been long established in his dominions. For the hereditary prince has less cause and less necessity to offend; hence it happens that he will be more loved; and unless extraordinary vices cause him to be hated, it is reasonable to expect that his subjects will be naturally well disposed towards him; and in the antiquity and duration of his rule the memories and motives that make for change are lost, for one change always leaves the toothing for another.

CHAPTER THREE

Concerning Mixed Principalities

BUT THE DIFFICULTIES OCCUR in a new principality. And firstly, if it be not entirely new, but is, as it were, a member of a state which, taken collectively, may be called composite, the changes arise chiefly from an inherent difficulty which there is in all new principalities; for men change their rulers willingly, hoping to better themselves, and this hope induces them to take up arms against him who rules: wherein they are deceived, because they afterwards find by experience they have gone from bad to worse. This follows also on another natural and common necessity, which always causes a new prince to burden those who have submitted to him with his soldiery and with infinite other hardships which he must put upon his new acquisition.

In this way you have enemies in all those whom you have injured in seizing that principality, and you are not able to keep those friends who put you there because of your not being able to satisfy them in the way they expected, and you cannot take strong measures against them, feeling bound to them. For, although one may be very strong in armed forces, yet in entering a province one has always need of the goodwill of the natives.

For these reasons Louis the Twelfth, King of France, quickly occupied Milan, and as quickly lost it; and to turn him out the first time it only needed Lodovico's own forces; because those who had opened the gates to him, finding themselves deceived in their hopes of future benefit, would not endure the ill-treatment of the new prince. It is very true that, after acquiring rebellious provinces a second time, they are not so lightly lost afterwards, because the prince, with little reluctance, takes the opportunity of the rebellion to punish the delinquents, to clear out the suspects, and to strengthen himself in the weakest places. Thus to cause France to lose Milan the first time it was enough for the Duke Lodovico[1] to raise insurrections on the borders; but to cause him to lose it a second time it was necessary to bring the whole world against him, and that his armies should be defeated and driven out of Italy; which followed from the causes above mentioned.

Nevertheless Milan was taken from France both the first and the second time. The general reasons for the first have been discussed; it remains to name those for the second, and to see what resources he had, and what any one in his situation would have had for maintaining himself more securely in his acquisition than did the King of France.

Now I say that those dominions which, when acquired, are added to an ancient state by him who acquires them, are either of the same country and language, or they are not. When they are, it is easier to hold them, especially when they have not been accustomed to self-government; and to hold them securely it is enough to have destroyed the family of the prince who was ruling them; because the two peoples, preserving in other things the old conditions, and not being unlike in customs, will live quietly together, as one has seen in Brittany, Burgundy, Gascony, and Normandy, which have been bound to France for so long a time: and, although there may be some difference in language, nevertheless the customs are alike, and the people will easily be able to get on amongst themselves. He who has annexed them, if he wishes to hold them, has only to bear in mind two considerations: the one, that the family of their former lord is extinguished; the other, that neither their laws nor their taxes are altered, so that in a very short time they will become entirely one body with the old principality.

But when states are acquired in a country differing in language, customs, or laws, there are difficulties, and good fortune and great energy are needed to hold them, and one of the greatest and most real helps would be that he who has acquired them should go and reside there. This would make his position more secure and durable, as it has made that of the Turk in Greece, who, notwithstanding all the other measures taken by him for holding that state, if he had not settled there, would not have been able to keep it. Because, if one is on the spot, disorders are seen as they spring up, and one can quickly remedy them; but if one is not at hand, they are heard of only when they are great, and then one can no longer remedy them. Besides this, the country is not pillaged

---

1   Duke Lodovico was Lodovico Moro, a son of Francesco Sforza, who married Beatrice d'Este. He ruled over Milan from 1494 to 1500, and died in 1510.

by your officials; the subjects are satisfied by prompt recourse to the prince; thus, wishing to be good, they have more cause to love him, and wishing to be otherwise, to fear him. He who would attack that state from the outside must have the utmost caution; as long as the prince resides there it can only be wrested from him with the greatest difficulty.

The other and better course is to send colonies to one or two places, which may be as keys to that state, for it is necessary either to do this or else to keep there a great number of cavalry and infantry. A prince does not spend much on colonies, for with little or no expense he can send them out and keep them there, and he offends a minority only of the citizens from whom he takes lands and houses to give them to the new inhabitants; and those whom he offends, remaining poor and scattered, are never able to injure him; whilst the rest being uninjured are easily kept quiet, and at the same time are anxious not to err for fear it should happen to them as it has to those who have been despoiled. In conclusion, I say that these colonies are not costly, they are more faithful, they injure less, and the injured, as has been said, being poor and scattered, cannot hurt. Upon this, one has to remark that men ought either to be well treated or crushed, because they can avenge themselves of lighter injuries, of more serious ones they cannot; therefore the injury that is to be done to a man ought to be of such a kind that one does not stand in fear of revenge.

But in maintaining armed men there in place of colonies one spends much more, having to consume on the garrison all the income from the state, so that the acquisition turns into a loss, and many more are exasperated, because the whole state is injured; through the shifting of the garrison up and down all become acquainted with hardship, and all become hostile, and they are enemies who, whilst beaten on their own ground, are yet able to do hurt. For every reason, therefore, such guards are as useless as a colony is useful.

Again, the prince who holds a country differing in the above respects ought to make himself the head and defender of his less powerful neighbours, and to weaken the more powerful amongst them, taking care that no foreigner as powerful as himself shall, by any accident, get a footing there; for it will always happen that such a one will be introduced by those who are discontented, either through excess of ambition or through fear, as one has seen already. The Romans were brought into Greece by the Aetolians; and in every other country where they obtained a footing they were brought in by the inhabitants. And the usual course of affairs is that, as soon as a powerful foreigner enters a country, all the subject states are drawn to him, moved by the hatred which they feel against the ruling power. So that in respect to those subject states he has not to take any trouble to gain them over to himself, for the whole of them quickly rally to the state which he has acquired there. He has only to take care that they do not get hold of too much power and too much authority, and then with his own forces, and with their goodwill, he can easily keep down the more powerful of them, so as to remain entirely master in the country. And he who does not properly manage this business will soon lose what he has acquired, and whilst he does hold it he will have endless difficulties and troubles.

The Romans, in the countries which they annexed, observed closely these measures; they sent colonies and maintained friendly relations with[2] the minor powers, without increasing their strength; they kept down the greater, and did not allow any strong foreign powers to gain authority. Greece appears to me sufficient for an example. The Achaeans and Aetolians were kept friendly by them, the kingdom of Macedonia was humbled, Antiochus was driven out; yet the merits of the Achaeans and Aetolians never secured for them permission to increase their power, nor did the persuasions of Philip ever induce the Romans to be his friends without first humbling him, nor did the influence of Antiochus make them agree that he should retain any lordship over the country. Because the Romans did in these instances what all prudent princes ought to do, who have to regard not only present troubles, but also future ones, for which they must prepare with every energy, because, when foreseen, it is easy to remedy them; but if you wait until they approach, the medicine is no longer in time because the malady has become incurable; for it happens in this, as the physicians say it happens in hectic fever, that in the beginning of the malady it is easy to cure but difficult to detect, but in the course of time, not having been either detected or treated in the beginning, it becomes easy to detect but difficult to cure. This it happens in affairs of state, for when the evils that arise have been foreseen (which it is only given to a wise man to see), they can be quickly redressed, but when, through not having been foreseen, they have been permitted to grow in a way that every one can see them, there is no longer a remedy. Therefore, the Romans, foreseeing troubles, dealt with them at once, and, even to avoid a war, would not let them come to a head, for they knew that war is not to be avoided, but is only to be put off to the advantage of others; moreover they wished to fight with Philip and Antiochus in Greece so as not to

2   See remark in the introduction on the word "intrattenere."

have to do it in Italy; they could have avoided both, but this they did not wish; nor did that ever please them which is for ever in the mouths of the wise ones of our time: – Let us enjoy the benefits of the time – but rather the benefits of their own valour and prudence, for time drives everything before it, and is able to bring with it good as well as evil, and evil as well as good.

But let us turn to France and inquire whether she has done any of the things mentioned. I will speak of Louis[3] (and not of Charles)[4] as the one whose conduct is the better to be observed, he having held possession of Italy for the longest period; and you will see that he has done the opposite to those things which ought to be done to retain a state composed of divers elements.

King Louis was brought into Italy by the ambition of the Venetians, who desired to obtain half the state of Lombardy by his intervention. I will not blame the course taken by the king, because, wishing to get a foothold in Italy, and having no friends there – seeing rather that every door was shut to him owing to the conduct of Charles – he was forced to accept those friendships which he could get, and he would have succeeded very quickly in his design if in other matters he had not made some mistakes. The king, however, having acquired Lombardy, regained at once the authority which Charles had lost: Genoa yielded; the Florentines became his friends; the Marquess of Mantua, the Duke of Ferrara, the Bentivogli, my lady of Forli, the Lords of Faenza, of Pesaro, of Rimini, of Camerino, of Piombino, the Lucchese, the Pisans, the Sienese – everybody made advances to him to become his friend. Then could the Venetians realize the rashness of the course taken by them, which, in order that they might secure two towns in Lombardy, had made the king master of two-thirds of Italy.

Let any one now consider with what little difficulty the king could have maintained his position in Italy had he observed the rules above laid down, and kept all his friends secure and protected; for although they were numerous they were both weak and timid, some afraid of the Church, some of the Venetians, and thus they would always have been forced to stand in with him, and by their means he could easily have made himself secure against those who remained powerful. But he was no sooner in Milan than he did the contrary by assisting Pope Alexander to occupy the Romagna. It never occurred to him that by this action he was weakening himself, depriving himself of friends and

3   Louis XII, King of France, "The Father of the People," born 1462, died 1515.

4   Charles VIII, King of France, born 1470, died 1498.

of those who had thrown themselves into his lap, whilst he aggrandized the Church by adding much temporal power to the spiritual, thus giving it greater authority. And having committed this prime error, he was obliged to follow it up, so much so that, to put an end to the ambition of Alexander, and to prevent his becoming the master of Tuscany, he was himself forced to come into Italy.

And as if it were not enough to have aggrandized the Church, and deprived himself of friends, he, wishing to have the kingdom of Naples, divides it with the King of Spain, and where he was the prime arbiter in Italy he takes an associate, so that the ambitious of that country and the malcontents of his own should have somewhere to shelter; and whereas he could have left in the kingdom his own pensioner as king, he drove him out, to put one there who was able to drive him, Louis, out in turn.

The wish to acquire is in truth very natural and common, and men always do so when they can, and for this they will be praised not blamed; but when they cannot do so, yet wish to do so by any means, then there is folly and blame. Therefore, if France could have attacked Naples with her own forces she ought to have done so; if she could not, then she ought not to have divided it. And if the partition which she made with the Venetians in Lombardy was justified by the excuse that by it she got a foothold in Italy, this other partition merited blame, for it had not the excuse of that necessity.

Therefore Louis made these five errors: he destroyed the minor powers, he increased the strength of one of the greater powers in Italy, he brought in a foreign power, he did not settle in the country, he did not send colonies. Which errors, had he lived, were not enough to injure him had he not made a sixth by taking away their dominions from the Venetians; because, had he not aggrandized the Church, nor brought Spain into Italy, it would have been very reasonable and necessary to humble them; but having first taken these steps, he ought never to have consented to their ruin, for they, being powerful, would always have kept off others from designs on Lombardy, to which the Venetians would never have consented except to become masters themselves there; also because the others would not wish to take Lombardy from France in order to give it to the Venetians, and to run counter to both they would not have had the courage.

And if any one should say: "King Louis yielded the Romagna to Alexander and the kingdom to Spain to avoid war," I answer for the reasons given above that a blunder ought never to be perpetrated to avoid war, because it is not to be avoided, but is only deferred to your disadvantage. And if another should allege the pledge which the king had given to the Pope that he would assist him in the enterprise, in exchange for the dissolution of his marriage[5] and for the cap to Rouen,[6] to that I reply what I shall write later on concerning the faith of princes, and how it ought to be kept.

Thus King Louis lost Lombardy by not having followed any of the conditions observed by those who have taken possession of countries and wished to retain them. Nor is there any miracle in this, but much that is reasonable and quite natural. And on these matters I spoke at Nantes with Rouen, when Valentino, as Cesare Borgia, the son of Pope Alexander, was usually called, occupied the Romagna, and on Cardinal Rouen observing to me that the Italians did not understand war, I replied to him that the French did not understand statecraft, meaning that otherwise they would not have allowed the Church to reach such greatness. And in fact it has been seen that the greatness of the Church and of Spain in Italy has been caused by France, and her ruin may be attributed to them. From this a general rule is drawn which never or rarely fails: that he who is the cause of another becoming powerful is ruined; because that predominancy has been brought about either by astuteness or else by force, and both are distrusted by him who has been raised to power.

5   Louis XII divorced his wife, Jeanne, daughter of Louis XI, and married in 1499 Anne of Brittany, widow of Charles VIII, in order to retain the Duchy of Brittany for the crown.

6   The Archbishop of Rouen. He was Georges d'Amboise, created a cardinal by Alexander VI. Born 1460, died 1510.

CHAPTER FOUR

Why the Kingdom of Darius, Conquered by Alexander, Did Not Rebel Against the Successors of Alexander at his Death

CONSIDERING THE DIFFICULTIES which men have had to hold to a newly acquired state, some might wonder how, seeing that Alexander the Great became the master of Asia in a few years, and died whilst it was scarcely settled (whence it might appear reasonable that the whole empire would have rebelled), nevertheless his successors maintained themselves, and had to meet no other difficulty than that which arose among themselves from their own ambitions.

I answer that the principalities of which one has record are found to be governed in two different ways; either by a prince, with a body of servants, who assist him to govern the kingdom as ministers by his favour and permission; or by a prince and barons, who hold that dignity by antiquity of blood and not by the grace of the prince. Such barons have states and their own subjects, who recognize them as lords and hold them in natural affection. Those states that are governed by a prince and his servants hold their prince in more consideration, because in all the country there is no one who is recognized as superior to him, and if they yield obedience to another they do it as to a minister and official, and they do not bear him any particular affection.

The examples of these two governments in our time are the Turk and the King of France. The entire monarchy of the Turk is governed by one lord, the others are his servants; and, dividing his kingdom into sanjaks, he sends there different administrators, and shifts and changes them as he chooses. But the King of France is placed in the midst of an ancient body of lords, acknowledged by their own subjects, and beloved by them; they have their own prerogatives, nor can the king take these away except at his peril. Therefore, he who considers both of these states will recognize great difficulties in seizing the state of the Turk, but, once it is conquered, great ease in holding it. The causes of the difficulties in seizing the kingdom of the Turk are that the usurper cannot be called in by the princes of the kingdom, nor can he hope to be assisted in his designs by the revolt of those whom the lord has around him. This arises from the reasons given above; for his ministers, being all slaves and bondmen, can only be corrupted with great difficulty, and one can expect little advantage from them when they have been corrupted, as they cannot carry the people with them, for the reasons assigned. Hence, he who attacks the Turk must bear in mind that he will find him united, and he will have to rely more on his own strength than on the revolt of others; but, if once the Turk has been conquered, and routed in the field in such a way that he cannot replace his armies, there is nothing to fear but the family of this prince, and, this being exterminated, there remains no one to fear, the others having no credit with the people; and as the conqueror did not rely on them before his victory, so he ought not to fear them after it.

The contrary happens in kingdoms governed like that of France, because one can easily enter there by gaining over some baron of the kingdom, for one always finds malcontents and such as desire a change. Such men, for the reasons given, can open the way into the state and render the victory easy; but if you wish to hold it afterwards, you meet with infinite difficulties, both from those who have assisted you and from those you have crushed. Nor is it enough for you to have exterminated the family of the prince, because the lords that remain make themselves the heads of fresh movements against you, and as you are unable either to satisfy or exterminate them, that state is lost whenever time brings the opportunity.

Now if you will consider what was the nature of the government of Darius, you will find it similar to the kingdom of the Turk, and therefore it was only necessary for Alexander, first to overthrow him in the field, and then to take the country from him. After which victory, Darius being killed, the state remained secure to Alexander, for the above reasons. And if his successors had been united they would have enjoyed it securely and at their ease, for there were no tumults raised in the kingdom except those they provoked themselves.

But it is impossible to hold with such tranquillity states constituted like that of France. Hence arose those frequent rebellions against the Romans in Spain, France, and Greece, owing to the many principalities there were in these states, of which, as long as the memory of them endured, the Romans always held an insecure possession; but with the power and long continuance of the empire the memory of them passed away, and the Romans then became secure possessors. And when fighting afterwards amongst themselves, each one was able to attach to himself his own parts of the country, according to the authority he had assumed there; and the family of the former lord being exterminated, none other than the Romans were acknowledged.

When these things are remembered no one will marvel at the ease with which Alexander held the Empire of Asia, or at the difficulties which others have had to keep an acquisition, such as Pyrrhus and many more; this is not occasioned by the little or abundance of ability in the conqueror, but by the want of uniformity in the subject state.

Concerning the Way to Govern Cities or Principalities which Lived Under their own Laws Before they were Annexed

WHENEVER THOSE STATES which have been acquired as stated have been accustomed to live under their own laws and in freedom, there are three courses for those who wish to hold them: the first is to ruin them, the next is to reside there in person, the third is to permit them to live under their own laws, drawing a tribute, and establishing within it an oligarchy which will keep it friendly to you. Because such a government, being created by the prince, knows that it cannot stand without his friendship and interest, and does it utmost to support him; and therefore he who would keep a city accustomed to freedom will hold it more easily by the means of its own citizens than in any other way.

There are, for example, the Spartans and the Romans. The Spartans held Athens and Thebes, establishing there an oligarchy, nevertheless they lost them. The Romans, in order to hold Capua, Carthage, and Numantia, dismantled them, and did not lose them. They wished to hold Greece as the Spartans held it, making it free and permitting its laws, and did not succeed. So to hold it they were compelled to dismantle many cities in the country, for in truth there is no safe way to retain them otherwise than by ruining them. And he who becomes master of a city accustomed to freedom and does not destroy it, may expect to be destroyed by it, for in rebellion it has always the watchword of liberty and its ancient privileges as a rallying point, which neither time nor benefits will ever cause it to forget. And whatever you may do or provide against, they never forget that name or their privileges unless they are disunited or dispersed, but at every chance they immediately rally to them, as Pisa after the hundred years she had been held in bondage by the Florentines.

But when cities or countries are accustomed to live under a prince, and his family is exterminated, they, being on the one hand accustomed to obey and on the other hand not having the old prince, cannot agree in making one from amongst themselves, and they do not know how to govern themselves. For this reason they are very slow to take up arms, and a prince can gain them to himself and secure them much more easily. But in republics there is more vitality, greater hatred, and more desire for vengeance, which will never permit them to allow the memory of their former liberty to rest; so that the safest way is to destroy them or to reside there.

CHAPTER SIX

Concerning New Principalities which are Acquired by One's Own Arms and Ability

LET NO ONE BE SURPRISED if, in speaking of entirely new principalities as I shall do, I adduce the highest examples both of prince and of state; because men, walking almost always in paths beaten by others, and following by imitation their deeds, are yet unable to keep entirely to the ways of others or attain to the power of those they imitate. A wise man ought always to follow the paths beaten by great men, and to imitate those who have been supreme, so that if his ability does not equal theirs, at least it will savour of it. Let him act like the clever archers who, designing to hit the mark which yet appears too far distant, and knowing the limits to which the strength of their bow attains, take aim much higher than the mark, not to reach by their strength or arrow to so great a height, but to be able with the aid of so high an aim to hit the mark they wish to reach.

I say, therefore, that in entirely new principalities, where there is a new prince, more or less difficulty is found in keeping them, accordingly as there is more or less ability in him who has acquired the state. Now, as the fact of becoming a prince from a private station presupposes either ability or fortune, it is clear that one or other of these things will mitigate in some degree many difficulties. Nevertheless, he who has relied least on fortune is established the strongest. Further, it facilitates matters when the prince, having no other state, is compelled to reside there in person.

But to come to those who, by their own ability and not through fortune, have risen to be princes, I say that Moses, Cyrus, Romulus, Theseus, and such like are the most excellent examples. And although one may not discuss Moses, he having been a mere executor of the will of God, yet he ought to be admired, if only for that favour which made him worthy to speak with God. But in considering Cyrus and others who have acquired or founded kingdoms, all will be found admirable; and if their particular deeds and conduct shall be considered, they will not be found inferior to those of Moses, although he had so great a preceptor. And in examining their actions and lives one cannot see that they owed anything to fortune beyond opportunity, which brought them the material to mould into the form which seemed best to them. Without that opportunity their powers of mind would have been extinguished, and without those powers the opportunity would have come in vain.

It was necessary, therefore, to Moses that he should find the people of Israel in Egypt enslaved and oppressed by the Egyptians, in order that they should be disposed to follow him so as to be delivered out of bondage. It was necessary that Romulus should not remain in Alba, and that he should be abandoned at his birth, in order that he should become King of Rome and founder of the fatherland. It was necessary that Cyrus should find the Persians discontented with the government of the Medes, and the Medes soft and effeminate through their long peace. Theseus could not have shown his ability had he not found the Athenians dispersed. These opportunities, therefore, made those men fortunate, and their high ability enabled them to recognize the opportunity whereby their country was ennobled and made famous.

Those who by valorous ways become princes, like these men, acquire a principality with difficulty, but they keep it with ease. The difficulties they have in acquiring it rise in part from the new rules and methods which they are forced to introduce to establish their government and its security. And it ought to be remembered that there is nothing more difficult to take in hand, more perilous to conduct, or more uncertain in its success, then to take the lead in the introduction of a new order of things. Because the innovator has for enemies all those who have done well under the old conditions, and lukewarm defenders in those who may do well under the new. This coolness arises partly from fear of the opponents, who have the laws on their side, and partly from the incredulity of men, who do not readily believe in new things until they have had a long experience of them. Thus it happens that whenever those who are hostile have the opportunity to attack they do it like partisans, whilst the others defend lukewarmly, in such wise that the prince is endangered along with them.

It is necessary, therefore, if we desire to discuss this matter thoroughly, to inquire whether these innovators can rely on themselves or have to depend on others: that is to say, whether, to consummate their enterprise, have they to use prayers or can they use force? In the first instance they always succeed badly, and never compass anything; but when they can rely on themselves and use force, then they are rarely endangered. Hence it is that all armed prophets have conquered, and the unarmed ones have been destroyed. Besides the reasons mentioned, the nature of the people is variable, and whilst it is easy to persuade them, it is difficult to fix them in that persuasion. And thus it is necessary to take such measures that, when they believe no longer, it may be possible to make them believe by force.

If Moses, Cyrus, Theseus, and Romulus had been unarmed they could not have enforced their constitutions for long – as happened in our time to Fra Girolamo Savonarola, who was ruined with his new order of things immediately the multitude believed in him no longer, and he had no means of keeping steadfast those who believed or of making the unbelievers to believe. Therefore such as these have great difficulties in consummating their enterprise, for all their dangers are in the ascent, yet with ability they will overcome them; but when these are overcome, and those who envied them their success are exterminated, they will begin to be respected, and they will continue afterwards powerful, secure, honoured, and happy.

To these great examples I wish to add a lesser one; still it bears some resemblance to them, and I wish it to suffice me for all of a like kind: it is Hiero the Syracusan.[7] This man rose from a private station to be Prince of Syracuse, nor did he, either, owe anything to fortune but opportunity; for the Syracusans, being oppressed, chose him for their captain, afterwards he was rewarded by being made their prince. He was of so great ability, even as a private citizen, that one who writes of him says he wanted nothing but a kingdom to be a king. This man abolished the old soldiery, organized the new, gave up old alliances, made new ones; and as he had his own soldiers and allies, on such foundations he was able to build any edifice: thus, whilst he had endured much trouble in acquiring, he had but little in keeping.

---

7   Hiero II, born about 307 B.C., died 216 B.C.

Concerning New Principalities which are Acquired Either by the Arms of Others or by Good Fortune

THOSE WHO SOLELY BY GOOD FORTUNE become princes from being private citizens have little trouble in rising, but much in keeping atop; they have not any difficulties on the way up, because they fly, but they have many when they reach the summit. Such are those to whom some state is given either for money or by the favour of him who bestows it; as happened to many in Greece, in the cities of Ionia and of the Hellespont, where princes were made by Darius, in order that they might hold the cities both for his security and his glory; as also were those emperors who, by the corruption of the soldiers, from being citizens came to empire. Such stand simply elevated upon the goodwill and the fortune of him who has elevated them – two most inconstant and unstable things. Neither have they the knowledge requisite for the position; because, unless they are men of great worth and ability, it is not reasonable to expect that they should know how to command, having always lived in a private condition; besides, they cannot hold it because they have not forces which they can keep friendly and faithful.

States that rise unexpectedly, then, like all other things in nature which are born and grow rapidly, cannot leave their foundations and correspondencies[8] fixed in such a way that the first storm will not overthrow them; unless, as is said, those who unexpectedly become princes are men of so much ability that they know they have to be prepared at once to hold that which fortune has thrown into their laps, and that those foundations, which others have laid *before* they became princes, they must lay *afterwards*.

---

8   "Le radici e corrispondenze," their roots (i.e. foundations) and correspondencies or relations with other states – a common meaning of "correspondence" and "correspondency" in the sixteenth and seventeenth centuries.

Concerning these two methods of rising to be a prince by ability or fortune, I wish to adduce two examples within our own recollection, and these are Francesco Sforza[9] and Cesare Borgia. Francesco, by proper means and with great ability, from being a private person rose to be Duke of Milan, and that which he had acquired with a thousand anxieties he kept with little trouble. On the other hand, Cesare Borgia, called by the people Duke Valentino, acquired his state during the ascendancy of his father, and on its decline he lost it, notwithstanding that he had taken every measure and done all that ought to be done by a wise and able man to fix firmly his roots in the states which the arms and fortunes of others had bestowed on him.

Because, as is stated above, he who has not first laid his foundations may be able with great ability to lay them afterwards, but they will be laid with trouble to the architect and danger to the building. If, therefore, all the steps taken by the duke be considered, it will be seen that he laid solid foundations for his future power, and I do not consider it superfluous to discuss them, because I do not know what better precepts to give a new prince than the example of his actions; and if his dispositions were of no avail, that was not his fault, but the extraordinary and extreme malignity of fortune.

Alexander the Sixth, in wishing to aggrandize the duke, his son, had many immediate and prospective difficulties. Firstly, he did not see his way to make him master of any state that was not a state of the Church; and if he was willing to rob the Church he knew that the Duke of Milan and the Venetians would not consent, because Faenza and Rimini were already under the protection of the Venetians. Besides this, he saw the arms of Italy, especially those by which he might have been assisted, in hands that would fear the aggrandizement of the Pope, namely, the Orsini and the Colonnesi and their following. It behoved him, therefore, to upset this state of affairs and embroil the powers, so as to make himself securely master of part of their states. This was easy for him to do, because he found the Venetians, moved by other reasons, inclined to bring back the French into Italy; he would not only not oppose this, but he would render it more easy by dissolving the former marriage of King

---

9   Francesco Sforza, born 1401, died 1466. He married Bianca Maria Visconti, a natural daughter of Filippo Visconti, the Duke of Milan, on whose death he procured his own elevation to the duchy. Machiavelli was the accredited agent of the Florentine Republic to Cesare Borgia (1478-1507) during the transactions which led up to the assassinations of the Orsini and Vitelli at Sinigalia, and along with his letters to his chiefs in Florence he has left an account, written ten years before *The Prince*, of the proceedings of the duke in his "Descritione del modo tenuto dal duca Valentino nello ammazzare Vitellozzo Vitelli."

Louis. Therefore the king came into Italy with the assistance of the Venetians and the consent of Alexander. He was no sooner in Milan than the Pope had soldiers from him for the attempt on the Romagna, which yielded to him on the reputation of the king. The duke, therefore, having acquired the Romagna and beaten the Colonnesi, while wishing to hold that and to advance further, was hindered by two things: the one, his forces did not appear loyal to him, the other, the goodwill of France: that is to say, he feared that the forces of the Orsini, which he was using, would not stand to him, that not only might they hinder him from winning more, but might themselves seize what he had won, and that the king might also do the same. Of the Orsini he had a warning when, after taking Faenza and attacking Bologna, he saw them go very unwillingly to that attack. And as to the king, he learned his mind when he himself, after taking the Duchy of Urbino, attacked Tuscany, and the king made him desist from that undertaking; hence the duke decided to depend no more upon the arms and the luck of others.

For the first thing he weakened the Orsini and Colonnesi parties in Rome, by gaining to himself all their adherents who were gentlemen, making them his gentlemen, giving them good pay, and, according to their rank, honouring them with office and command in such a way that in a few months all attachment to the factions was destroyed and turned entirely to the duke. After this he awaited an opportunity to crush the Orsini, having scattered the adherents of the Colonna house. This came to him soon and he used it well; for the Orsini, perceiving at length that the aggrandizement of the duke and the Church was ruin to them, called a meeting of the Magione in Perugia. From this sprung the rebellion at Urbino and the tumults in the Romagna, with endless dangers to the duke, all of which he overcame with the help of the French. Having restored his authority, not to leave it at risk by trusting either to the French or other outside forces, he had recourse to his wiles, and he knew so well how to conceal his mind that, by the mediation of Signor Pagolo – whom the duke did not fail to secure with all kinds of attention, giving him money, apparel, and horses – the Orsini were reconciled, so that their simplicity brought them into his power at Sinigalia.[10] Having exterminated the leaders, and turned their partisans into his friends, the duke laid sufficiently good foundations to his power, having all the Romagna and the Duchy of Urbino; and the people now beginning to appreciate their prosperity, he gained them all over to himself. And as this point is worthy of notice, and to be imitated by others, I am not willing to leave it out.

---

10   Sinigalia, 31st December 1502.

When the duke occupied the Romagna he found it under the rule of weak masters, who rather plundered their subjects than ruled them, and gave them more cause for disunion than for union, so that the country was full of robbery, quarrels, and every kind of violence; and so, wishing to bring back peace and obedience to authority, he considered it necessary to give it a good governor. Thereupon he promoted Messer Ramiro d'Orco,[11] a swift and cruel man, to whom he gave the fullest power. This man in a short time restored peace and unity with the greatest success. Afterwards the duke considered that it was not advisable to confer such excessive authority, for he had no doubt but that he would become odious, so he set up a court of judgment in the country, under a most excellent president, wherein all cities had their advocates. And because he knew that the past severity had caused some hatred against himself, so, to clear himself in the minds of the people, and gain them entirely to himself, he desired to show that, if any cruelty had been practised, it had not originated with him, but in the natural sternness of the minister. Under this pretence he took Ramiro, and one morning caused him to be executed and left on the piazza at Cesena with the block and a bloody knife at his side. The barbarity of this spectacle caused the people to be at once satisfied and dismayed.

But let us return whence we started. I say that the duke, finding himself now sufficiently powerful and partly secured from immediate dangers by having armed himself in his own way, and having in a great measure crushed those forces in his vicinity that could injure him if he wished to proceed with his conquest, had next to consider France, for he knew that the king, who too late was aware of his mistake, would not support him. And from this time he began to seek new alliances and to temporize with France in the expedition which she was making towards the kingdom of Naples against the Spaniards who were besieging Gaeta. It was his intention to secure himself against them, and this he would have quickly accomplished had Alexander lived.

Such was his line of action as to present affairs. But as to the future he had to fear, in the first place, that a new successor to the Church might not be friendly to him and might seek to take from him that which Alexander had given him, so he decided to act in four ways. Firstly, by exterminating the families of those lords whom he had despoiled, so as to take away that pretext from the Pope. Secondly, by winning to himself all the gentlemen of Rome, so as to be able to curb the Pope with their aid,

11   Ramiro d'Orco. Ramiro de Lorqua.

as has been observed. Thirdly, by converting the college more to himself. Fourthly, by acquiring so much power before the Pope should die that he could by his own measures resist the first shock. Of these four things, at the death of Alexander, he had accomplished three. For he had killed as many of the dispossessed lords as he could lay hands on, and few had escaped; he had won over the Roman gentlemen, and he had the most numerous party in the college. And as to any fresh acquisition, he intended to become master of Tuscany, for he already possessed Perugia and Piombino, and Pisa was under his protection. And as he had no longer to study France (for the French were already driven out of the kingdom of Naples by the Spaniards, and in this way both were compelled to buy his goodwill), he pounced down upon Pisa. After this, Lucca and Siena yielded at once, partly through hatred and partly through fear of the Florentines; and the Florentines would have had no remedy had he continued to prosper, as he was prospering the year that Alexander died, for he had acquired so much power and reputation that he would have stood by himself, and no longer have depended on the luck and the forces of others, but solely on his own power and ability.

But Alexander died five years after he had first drawn the sword. He left the duke with the state of Romagna alone consolidated, with the rest in the air, between two most powerful hostile armies, and sick unto death. Yet there were in the duke such boldness and ability, and he knew so well how men are to be won or lost, and so firm were the foundations which in so short a time he had laid, that if he had not had those armies on his back, or if he had been in good health, he would have overcome all difficulties. And it is seen that his foundations were good, for the Romagna awaited him for more than a month. In Rome, although but half alive, he remained secure; and whilst the Baglioni, the Vitelli, and the Orsini might come to Rome, they could not effect anything against him. If he could not have made Pope him whom he wished, at least the one whom he did not wish would not have been elected. But if he had been in sound health at the death of Alexander,[12] everything would have been different to him. On the day that Julius the Second[13] was elected, he told me that he had thought of everything that might occur at the death of his father, and had provided a remedy for all, except that he had never anticipated that, when the death did happen, he himself would be on the point to die.

---

12   Alexander VI died of fever, 18th August 1503.

13   Julius II was Giuliano della Rovere, Cardinal of San Pietro ad Vincula, born 1443, died 1513.

When all the actions of the duke are recalled, I do not know how to blame him, but rather it appears to be, as I have said, that I ought to offer him for imitation to all those who, by the fortune or the arms of others, are raised to government. Because he, having a lofty spirit and far-reaching aims, could not have regulated his conduct otherwise, and only the shortness of the life of Alexander and his own sickness frustrated his designs. Therefore, he who considers it necessary to secure himself in his new principality, to win friends, to overcome either by force or fraud, to make himself beloved and feared by the people, to be followed and revered by the soldiers, to exterminate those who have power or reason to hurt him, to change the old order of things for new, to be severe and gracious, magnanimous and liberal, to destroy a disloyal soldiery and to create new, to maintain friendship with kings and princes in such a way that they must help him with zeal and offend with caution, cannot find a more lively example than the actions of this man.

Only can he be blamed for the election of Julius the Second, in whom he made a bad choice, because, as is said, not being able to elect a Pope to his own mind, he could have hindered any other from being elected Pope; and he ought never to have consented to the election of any cardinal whom he had injured or who had cause to fear him if they became pontiffs. For men injure either from fear or hatred. Those whom he had injured, amongst others, were San Pietro ad Vincula, Colonna, San Giorgio, and Ascanio.[14] The rest, in becoming Pope, had to fear him, Rouen and the Spaniards excepted; the latter from their relationship and obligations, the former from his influence, the kingdom of France having relations with him. Therefore, above everything, the duke ought to have created a Spaniard Pope, and, failing him, he ought to have consented to Rouen and not San Pietro ad Vincula. He who believes that new benefits will cause great personages to forget old injuries is deceived. Therefore, the duke erred in his choice, and it was the cause of his ultimate ruin.

---

14   San Giorgio is Raffaello Riario. Ascanio is Ascanio Sforza.

CHAPTER EIGHT

Concerning Those who have Obtained a Principality by Wikedness

ALTHOUGH A PRINCE MAY RISE from a private station in two ways, neither of which can be entirely attributed to fortune or genius, yet it is manifest to me that I must not be silent on them, although one could be more copiously treated when I discuss republics. These methods are when, either by some wicked or nefarious ways, one ascends to the principality, or when by the favour of his fellow-citizens a private person becomes the prince of his country. And speaking of the first method, it will be illustrated by two examples – one ancient, the other modern – and without entering further into the subject, I consider these two examples will suffice those who may be compelled to follow them.

Agathocles, the Sicilian[15] became King of Syracuse not only from a private but from a low and abject position. This man, the son of a potter, through all the changes in his fortunes always led an infamous life. Nevertheless, he accompanied his infamies with so much ability of mind and body that, having devoted himself to the military profession, he rose through its ranks to be Praetor of Syracuse. Being established in that position, and having deliberately resolved to make himself prince and to seize by violence, without obligation to others, that which had been conceded to him by assent, he came to an understanding for this purpose with Amilcar, the Carthaginian, who, with his army, was fighting in Sicily. One morning he assembled the people and the senate of Syracuse, as if he had to discuss with them things relating to the Republic, and at a given signal the soldiers killed all the senators and the richest of the people; these dead, he seized and held the princedom of that city without any civil

---

15   Agathocles the Sicilian, born 361 B.C., died 289 B.C.

commotion. And although he was twice routed by the Carthaginians, and ultimately besieged, yet not only was he able to defend his city, but leaving part of his men for its defence, with the others he attacked Africa, and in a short time raised the siege of Syracuse. The Carthaginians, reduced to extreme necessity, were compelled to come to terms with Agathocles, and, leaving Sicily to him, had to be content with the possession of Africa.

Therefore, he who considers the actions and the genius of this man will see nothing, or little, which can be attributed to fortune, inasmuch as he attained pre-eminence, as is shown above, not by the favour of any one, but step by step in the military profession, which steps were gained with a thousand troubles and perils, and were afterwards boldly held by him with many hazardous dangers. Yet it cannot be called talent to slay fellow-citizens, to deceive friends, to be without faith, without mercy, without religion; such methods may gain empire, but not glory. Still, if the courage of Agathocles in entering into and extricating himself from dangers be considered, together with his greatness of mind in enduring and overcoming hardships, it cannot be seen why he should be esteemed less than the most notable captain. Nevertheless, his barbarous cruelty and inhumanity with infinite wickedness do not permit him to be celebrated among the most excellent men. What he achieved cannot be attributed either to fortune or genius.

In our times, during the rule of Alexander the Sixth, Oliverotto da Fermo, having been left an orphan many years before, was brought up by his maternal uncle, Giovanni Fogliani, and in the early days of his youth sent to fight under Pagolo Vitelli, that, being trained under his discipline, he might attain some high position in the military profession. After Pagolo died, he fought under his brother Vitellozzo, and in a very short time, being endowed with wit and a vigorous body and mind, he became the first man in his profession. But it appearing a paltry thing to serve under others, he resolved, with the aid of some citizens of Fermo, to whom the slavery of their country was dearer than its liberty, and with the help of the Vitelleschi, to seize Fermo. So he wrote to Giovanni Fogliani that, having been away from home for many years, he wished to visit him and his city, and in some measure to look upon his patrimony; and although he had not laboured to acquire anything except honour, yet, in order that the citizens should see he had not spent his time in vain, he desired to come honourably, so would be accompanied by one hundred horsemen, his friends and retainers; and he entreated Giovanni to arrange that he should be received honourably by the Fermians, all of which would be not only to his honour, but also to that of Giovanni himself, who had brought him up.

Giovanni, therefore, did not fail in any attentions due to his nephew, and he caused him to be honourably received by the Fermians, and he lodged him in his own house, where, having passed some days, and having arranged what was necessary for his wicked designs, Oliverotto gave a solemn banquet to which he invited Giovanni Fogliani and the chiefs of Fermo. When the viands and all the other entertainments that are usual in such banquets were finished, Oliverotto artfully began certain grave discourses, speaking of the greatness of Pope Alexander and his son Cesare, and of their enterprises, to which discourse Giovanni and others answered; but he rose at once, saying that such matters ought to be discussed in a more private place, and he betook himself to a chamber, whither Giovanni and the rest of the citizens went in after him. No sooner were they seated than soldiers issued from secret places and slaughtered Giovanni and the rest. After these murders Oliverotto, mounted on horseback, rode up and down the town and besieged the chief magistrate in the palace, so that in fear the people were forced to obey him, and to form a government, of which he made himself the prince. He killed all the malcontents who were able to injure him, and strengthened himself with new civil and military ordinances, in such a way that, in the year during which he held the principality, not only was he secure in the city of Fermo, but he had become formidable to all his neighbours. And his destruction would have been as difficult as that of Agathocles if he had not allowed himself to be overreached by Cesare Borgia, who took him with the Orsini and Vitelli at Sinigalia, as was stated above. Thus one year after he had committed this parricide, he was strangled, together with Vitellozzo, whom he had made his leader in valour and wickedness.

Some may wonder how it can happen that Agathocles, and his like, after infinite treacheries and cruelties, should live for long secure in his country, and defend himself from external enemies, and never be conspired against by his own citizens; seeing that many others, by means of cruelty, have never been able even in peaceful times to hold the state, still less in the doubtful times of war. I believe that this follows from severities[16] being badly or properly used. Those may be called properly used, if of evil it is possible to speak well, that are applied at one blow and are necessary to one's security, and that are not persisted in afterwards unless they can be turned to the advantage of the subjects. The badly employed are those which, notwithstanding they may be few in

---

16   This word probably comes near the modern equivalent of Machiavelli's thought when he speaks of "crudelta" than the more obvious "cruelties."

the commencement, multiply with time rather than decrease. Those who practise the first system are able, by aid of God or man, to mitigate in some degree their rule, as Agathocles did. It is impossible for those who follow the other to maintain themselves.

Hence it is to be remarked that, in seizing a state, the usurper ought to examine closely into all those injuries which it is necessary for him to inflict, and to do them all at one stroke so as not to have to repeat them daily; and thus by not unsettling men he will be able to reassure them, and win them to himself by benefits. He who does otherwise, either from timidity or evil advice, is always compelled to keep the knife in his hand; neither can he rely on his subjects, nor can they attach themselves to him, owing to their continued and repeated wrongs. For injuries ought to be done all at one time, so that, being tasted less, they offend less; benefits ought to be given little by little, so that the flavour of them may last longer.

And above all things, a prince ought to live amongst his people in such a way that no unexpected circumstances, whether of good or evil, shall make him change; because if the necessity for this comes in troubled times, you are too late for harsh measures; and mild ones will not help you, for they will be considered as forced from you, and no one will be under any obligation to you for them.

CHAPTER NINE

Concerning a Civil Principality

BUT COMING TO THE OTHER POINT – where a leading citizen becomes the prince of his country, not by wickedness or any intolerable violence, but by the favour of his fellow citizens – this may be called a civil principality: nor is genius or fortune altogether necessary to attain to it, but rather a happy shrewdness. I say then that such a principality is obtained either by the favour of the people or by the favour of the nobles. Because in all cities these two distinct parties are found, and from this it arises that the people do not wish to be ruled nor oppressed by the nobles, and the nobles wish to rule and oppress the people; and from these two opposite desires there arises in cities one of three results, either a principality, self-government, or anarchy.

A principality is created either by the people or by the nobles, accordingly as one or other of them has the opportunity; for the nobles, seeing they cannot withstand the people, begin to cry up the reputation of one of themselves, and they make him a prince, so that under his shadow they can give vent to their ambitions. The people, finding they cannot resist the nobles, also cry up the reputation of one of themselves, and make him a prince so as to be defended by his authority. He who obtains sovereignty by the assistance of the nobles maintains himself with more difficulty than he who comes to it by the aid of the people, because the former finds himself with many around him who consider themselves his equals, and because of this he can neither rule nor manage them to his liking. But he who reaches sovereignty by popular favour finds himself alone, and has none around him, or few, who are not prepared to obey him.

Besides this, one cannot by fair dealing, and without injury to others, satisfy the nobles, but you can satisfy the people, for their object is more righteous than that of the nobles, the latter wishing to oppress, while the former only desire not to be oppressed. It is to be added also that a prince can never secure himself against a hostile people, because of their being too many, whilst from the nobles he can secure himself, as they are few in number. The worst that a prince may expect from a hostile people is to be abandoned by them; but from hostile nobles he has not only to fear abandonment, but also that they will rise against him; for they, being in these affairs more far-seeing and astute, always come forward in time to save themselves, and to obtain favours from him whom they expect to prevail. Further, the prince is compelled to live always with the same people, but he can do well without the same nobles, being able to make and unmake them daily, and to give or take away authority when it pleases him.

Therefore, to make this point clearer, I say that the nobles ought to be looked at mainly in two ways: that is to say, they either shape their course in such a way as binds them entirely to your fortune, or they do not. Those who so bind themselves, and are not rapacious, ought to be honoured and loved; those who do not bind themselves may be dealt with in two ways; they may fail to do this through pusillanimity and a natural want of courage, in which case you ought to make use of them, especially of those who are of good counsel; and thus, whilst in prosperity you honour them, in adversity you do not have to fear them. But when for their own ambitious ends they shun binding themselves, it is a token that they are giving more thought to themselves than to you, and a prince ought to guard against such, and to fear them as if they were open enemies, because in adversity they always help to ruin him.

Therefore, one who becomes a prince through the favour of the people ought to keep them friendly, and this he can easily do seeing they only ask not to be oppressed by him. But one who, in opposition to the people, becomes a prince by the favour of the nobles, ought, above everything, to seek to win the people over to himself, and this he may easily do if he takes them under his protection. Because men, when they receive good from him of whom they were expecting evil, are bound more closely to their benefactor; thus the people quickly become more devoted to him than if he had been raised to the principality by their favours; and the prince can win their affections in many ways, but as these vary according to the circumstances one cannot give fixed rules, so I omit them; but, I repeat, it is necessary for a prince to have the people friendly, otherwise he has no security in adversity.

Nabis,[17] Prince of the Spartans, sustained the attack of all Greece, and of a victorious Roman army, and against them he defended his country and his government; and for the overcoming of this peril it was only necessary for him to make himself secure against a few, but this would not have been sufficient had the people been hostile. And do not let any one impugn this statement with the trite proverb that "He who builds on the people, builds on the mud," for this is true when a private citizen makes a foundation there, and persuades himself that the people will free him when he is oppressed by his enemies or by the magistrates; wherein he would find himself very often deceived, as happened to the Gracchi in Rome and to Messer Giorgio Scali[18] in Florence. But granted a prince who has established himself as above, who can command, and is a man of courage, undismayed in adversity, who does not fail in other qualifications, and who, by his resolution and energy, keeps the whole people encouraged – such a one will never find himself deceived in them, and it will be shown that he has laid his foundations well.

These principalities are liable to danger when they are passing from the civil to the absolute order of government, for such princes either rule personally or through magistrates. In the latter case their government is weaker and more insecure, because it rests entirely on the goodwill of those citizens who are raised to the magistracy, and who, especially in troubled times, can destroy the government with great ease, either by intrigue or open defiance; and the prince has not the chance amid tumults to exercise absolute authority, because the citizens and subjects, accustomed to receive orders from magistrates, are not of a mind to obey him amid these confusions, and there will always be in doubtful times a scarcity of men whom he can trust. For such a prince cannot rely upon what he observes in quiet times, when citizens have need of the state, because then every one agrees with him; they all promise, and when death is far distant they all wish to die for him; but in troubled times, when the state has need of its citizens, then he finds but few. And so much the more is this experiment dangerous, inasmuch as it can only be tried once. Therefore a wise prince ought to adopt such a course that his citizens will always in every sort and kind of circumstance have need of the state and of him, and then he will always find them faithful.

---

17 Nabis, tyrant of Sparta, conquered by the Romans under Flamininus in 195 B.C.; killed 192 B.C.

18 Messer Giorgio Scali. This event is to be found in Machiavelli's "Florentine History," Book III.

CHAPTER TEN

Concerning the Way in which the Strength of all Principalities Ought to be Measured

IT IS NECESSARY TO CONSIDER another point in examining the character of these principalities: that is, whether a prince has such power that, in case of need, he can support himself with his own resources, or whether he has always need of the assistance of others. And to make this quite clear I say that I consider those who are able to support themselves by their own resources who can, either by abundance of men or money, raise a sufficient army to join battle against any one who comes to attack them; and I consider those always to have need of others who cannot show themselves against the enemy in the field, but are forced to defend themselves by sheltering behind walls. The first case has been discussed, but we will speak of it again should it recur. In the second case one can say nothing except to encourage such princes to provision and fortify their towns, and not on any account to defend the country. And whoever shall fortify his town well, and shall have managed the other concerns of his subjects in the way stated above, and to be often repeated, will never be attacked without great caution, for men are always adverse to enterprises where difficulties can be seen, and it will be seen not to be an easy thing to attack one who has his town well fortified, and is not hated by his people.

The cities of Germany are absolutely free, they own but little country around them, and they yield obedience to the emperor when it suits them, nor do they fear this or any other power they may have near them, because they are fortified in such a way that every one thinks the taking of them by assault would be tedious and difficult, seeing they have proper ditches and walls, they have sufficient artillery, and they always keep in public depots enough for one year's eating, drinking, and firing. And beyond this, to keep the people quiet and without loss to the state, they always have the means of giving work to the community in those labours that are the life and strength of the city, and on the pursuit of which the people are supported; they also hold military exercises in repute, and moreover have many ordinances to uphold them.

Therefore, a prince who has a strong city, and had not made himself odious, will not be attacked, or if any one should attack he will only be driven off with disgrace; again, because that the affairs of this world are so changeable, it is almost impossible to keep an army a whole year in the field without being interfered with. And whoever should reply: If the people have property outside the city, and see it burnt, they will not remain patient, and the long siege and self-interest will make them forget their prince; to this I answer that a powerful and courageous prince will overcome all such difficulties by giving at one time hope to his subjects that the evil will not be for long, at another time fear of the cruelty of the enemy, then preserving himself adroitly from those subjects who seem to him to be too bold.

Further, the enemy would naturally on his arrival at once burn and ruin the country at the time when the spirits of the people are still hot and ready for the defence; and, therefore, so much the less ought the prince to hesitate; because after a time, when spirits have cooled, the damage is already done, the ills are incurred, and there is no longer any remedy; and therefore they are so much the more ready to unite with their prince, he appearing to be under obligations to them now that their houses have been burnt and their possessions ruined in his defence. For it is the nature of men to be bound by the benefits they confer as much as by those they receive. Therefore, if everything is well considered, it will not be difficult for a wise prince to keep the minds of his citizens steadfast from first to last, when he does not fail to support and defend them.

CHAPTER ELEVEN

Concerning Ecclesiastical Principalities

IT ONLY REMAINS NOW TO SPEAK of ecclesiastical principalities, touching which all difficulties are prior to getting possession, because they are acquired either by capacity or good fortune, and they can be held without either; for they are sustained by the ancient ordinances of religion, which are so all-powerful, and of such a character that the principalities may be held no matter how their princes behave and live. These princes alone have states and do not defend them; and they have subjects and do not rule them; and the states, although unguarded, are not taken from them, and the subjects, although not ruled, do not care, and they have neither the desire nor the ability to alienate themselves. Such principalities only are secure and happy. But being upheld by powers, to which the human mind cannot reach, I shall speak no more of them, because, being exalted and maintained by God, it would be the act of a presumptuous and rash man to discuss them.

Nevertheless, if any one should ask of me how comes it that the Church has attained such greatness in temporal power, seeing that from Alexander backwards the Italian potentates (not only those who have been called potentates, but every baron and lord, though the smallest) have valued the temporal power very slightly – yet now a king of France trembles before it, and it has been able to drive him from Italy, and to ruin the Venetians – although this may be very manifest, it does not appear to me superfluous to recall it in some measure to memory.

Before Charles, King of France, passed into Italy,[19] this country was under the dominion of the Pope, the Venetians, the King of Naples, the

---

19   Charles VIII invaded Italy in 1494.

Duke of Milan, and the Florentines. These potentates had two principal anxieties: the one, that no foreigner should enter Italy under arms; the other, that none of themselves should seize more territory. Those about whom there was the most anxiety were the Pope and the Venetians. To restrain the Venetians the union of all the others was necessary, as it was for the defence of Ferrara; and to keep down the Pope they made use of the barons of Rome, who, being divided into two factions, Orsini and Colonnesi, had always a pretext for disorder, and, standing with arms in their hands under the eyes of the Pontiff, kept the pontificate weak and powerless. And although there might arise sometimes a courageous pope, such as Sixtus, yet neither fortune nor wisdom could rid him of these annoyances. And the short life of a pope is also a cause of weakness; for in the ten years, which is the average life of a pope, he can with difficulty lower one of the factions; and if, so to speak, one people should almost destroy the Colonnesi, another would arise hostile to the Orsini, who would support their opponents, and yet would not have time to ruin the Orsini. This was the reason why the temporal powers of the pope were little esteemed in Italy.

Alexander the Sixth arose afterwards, who of all the pontiffs that have ever been showed how a pope with both money and arms was able to prevail; and through the instrumentality of the Duke Valentino, and by reason of the entry of the French, he brought about all those things which I have discussed above in the actions of the duke. And although his intention was not to aggrandize the Church, but the duke, nevertheless, what he did contributed to the greatness of the Church, which, after his death and the ruin of the duke, became the heir to all his labours.

Pope Julius came afterwards and found the Church strong, possessing all the Romagna, the barons of Rome reduced to impotence, and, through the chastisements of Alexander, the factions wiped out; he also found the way open to accumulate money in a manner such as had never been practised before Alexander's time. Such things Julius not only followed, but improved upon, and he intended to gain Bologna, to ruin the Venetians, and to drive the French out of Italy. All of these enterprises prospered with him, and so much the more to his credit, inasmuch as he did everything to strengthen the Church and not any private person. He kept also the Orsini and Colonnesi factions within the bounds in which he found them; and although there was among them some mind to make disturbance, nevertheless he held two things firm: the one, the greatness of the Church, with which he terrified them; and the other, not allowing them to have their own cardinals, who caused the disorders among them. For whenever these factions have their cardinals they do not remain quiet for long, because cardinals foster the factions in Rome and out of it, and the barons are compelled to support them, and thus from the ambitions of prelates arise disorders and tumults among the barons. For these reasons his Holiness Pope Leo[20] found the pontificate most powerful, and it is to be hoped that, if others made it great in arms, he will make it still greater and more venerated by his goodness and infinite other virtues.

20   Pope Leo X was the Cardinal de' Medici.

CHAPTER TWELVE

How Many Kinds of Soldiery there are, and Concerning Mercenaries

HAVING DISCOURSED PARTICULARLY on the characteristics of such principalities as in the beginning I proposed to discuss, and having considered in some degree the causes of their being good or bad, and having shown the methods by which many have sought to acquire them and to hold them, it now remains for me to discuss generally the means of offence and defence which belong to each of them.

We have seen above how necessary it is for a prince to have his foundations well laid, otherwise it follows of necessity he will go to ruin. The chief foundations of all states, new as well as old or composite, are good laws and good arms; and as there cannot be good laws where the state is not well armed, it follows that where they are well armed they have good laws. I shall leave the laws out of the discussion and shall speak of the arms.

I say, therefore, that the arms with which a prince defends his state are either his own, or they are mercenaries, auxiliaries, or mixed. Mercenaries and auxiliaries are useless and dangerous; and if one holds his state based on these arms, he will stand neither firm nor safe; for they are disunited, ambitious, and without discipline, unfaithful, valiant before friends, cowardly before enemies; they have neither the fear of God nor fidelity to men, and destruction is deferred only so long as the attack is; for in peace one is robbed by them, and in war by the enemy. The fact is, they have no other attraction or reason for keeping the field than a trifle of stipend, which is not sufficient to make them willing to die for you. They are ready enough to be your soldiers whilst you do not make war, but if war comes they take themselves off or run from the foe; which I should have little trouble to prove, for the ruin of Italy has been caused by nothing else than by resting all her hopes for many years on mercenaries, and although they formerly made some display and appeared valiant amongst themselves, yet when the foreigners came they showed what they were. Thus it was that Charles, King of France, was allowed to seize Italy with chalk in hand;[21] and he who told us that our sins were the cause of it told the truth, but they were not the sins he imagined, but those which I have related. And as they were the sins of princes, it is the princes who have also suffered the penalty.

I wish to demonstrate further the infelicity of these arms. The mercenary captains are either capable men or they are not; if they are, you cannot trust them, because they always aspire to their own greatness, either by oppressing you, who are their master, or others contrary to your intentions; but if the captain is not skilful, you are ruined in the usual way.

And if it be urged that whoever is armed will act in the same way, whether mercenary or not, I reply that when arms have to be resorted to, either by a prince or a republic, then the prince ought to go in person and perform the duty of a captain; the republic has to send its citizens, and when one is sent who does not turn out satisfactorily, it ought to recall him, and when one is worthy, to hold him by the laws so that he does not leave the command. And experience has shown princes and republics, single-handed, making the greatest progress, and mercenaries doing nothing except damage; and it is more difficult to bring a republic, armed with its own arms, under the sway of one of its citizens than it is to bring one armed with foreign arms. Rome and Sparta stood for many ages armed and free. The Switzers are completely armed and quite free.

Of ancient mercenaries, for example, there are the Carthaginians, who were oppressed by their mercenary soldiers after the first war with the Romans, although the Carthaginians had their own citizens for captains. After the death of Epaminondas, Philip of Macedon was made captain of their soldiers by the Thebans, and after victory he took away their liberty.

---

21   "With chalk in hand," "col gesso." This is one of the bons mots of Alexander VI, and refers to the ease with which Charles VIII seized Italy, implying that it was only necessary for him to send his quartermasters to chalk up the billets for his soldiers to conquer the country. Cf. "The History of Henry VII," by Lord Bacon: "King Charles had conquered the realm of Naples, and lost it again, in a kind of a felicity of a dream. He passed the whole length of Italy without resistance: so that it was true what Pope Alexander was wont to say: That the Frenchmen came into Italy with chalk in their hands, to mark up their lodgings, rather than with swords to fight."

Duke Filippo being dead, the Milanese enlisted Francesco Sforza against the Venetians, and he, having overcome the enemy at Caravaggio,[22] allied himself with them to crush the Milanese, his masters. His father, Sforza, having been engaged by Queen Johanna[23] of Naples, left her unprotected, so that she was forced to throw herself into the arms of the King of Aragon, in order to save her kingdom. And if the Venetians and Florentines formerly extended their dominions by these arms, and yet their captains did not make themselves princes, but have defended them, I reply that the Florentines in this case have been favoured by chance, for of the able captains, of whom they might have stood in fear, some have not conquered, some have been opposed, and others have turned their ambitions elsewhere. One who did not conquer was Giovanni Acuto,[24] and since he did not conquer his fidelity cannot be proved; but every one will acknowledge that, had he conquered, the Florentines would have stood at his discretion. Sforza had the Bracceschi always against him, so they watched each other. Francesco turned his ambition to Lombardy; Braccio against the Church and the kingdom of Naples. But let us come to that which happened a short while ago. The Florentines appointed as their captain Pagolo Vitelli, a most prudent man, who from a private position had risen to the greatest renown. If this man had taken Pisa, nobody can deny that it would have been proper for the Florentines to keep in with him, for if he became the soldier of their enemies they had no means of resisting, and if they held to him they must obey him. The Venetians, if their achievements are considered, will be seen to have acted safely and gloriously so long as they sent to war their own men, when with armed gentlemen and plebians they did valiantly. This was before they turned to enterprises on land, but when they began to fight on land they forsook this virtue and followed the custom of Italy. And in the beginning of their expansion on land, through not having much territory, and because of their great reputation, they had not much to fear from their captains; but when they expanded, as under Carmignuola,[25] they had a taste of this

---

22 Battle of Caravaggio, 15th September 1448.

23 Johanna II of Naples, the widow of Ladislao, King of Naples.

24 Giovanni Acuto. An English knight whose name was Sir John Hawkwood. He fought in the English wars in France, and was knighted by Edward III; afterwards he collected a body of troops and went into Italy. These became the famous "White Company." He took part in many wars, and died in Florence in 1394. He was born about 1320 at Sible Hedingham, a village in Essex. He married Domnia, a daughter of Bernabo Visconti.

25 Carmignuola. Francesco Bussone, born at Carmagnola about 1390, executed at Venice, 5th May 1432.

mistake; for, having found him a most valiant man (they beat the Duke of Milan under his leadership), and, on the other hand, knowing how lukewarm he was in the war, they feared they would no longer conquer under him, and for this reason they were not willing, nor were they able, to let him go; and so, not to lose again that which they had acquired, they were compelled, in order to secure themselves, to murder him. They had afterwards for their captains Bartolomeo da Bergamo, Roberto da San Severino, the count of Pitigliano,[26] and the like, under whom they had to dread loss and not gain, as happened afterwards at Vaila,[27] where in one battle they lost that which in eight hundred years they had acquired with so much trouble. Because from such arms conquests come but slowly, long delayed and inconsiderable, but the losses sudden and portentous.

And as with these examples I have reached Italy, which has been ruled for many years by mercenaries, I wish to discuss them more seriously, in order that, having seen their rise and progress, one may be better prepared to counteract them. You must understand that the empire has recently come to be repudiated in Italy, that the Pope has acquired more temporal power, and that Italy has been divided up into more states, for the reason that many of the great cities took up arms against their nobles, who, formerly favoured by the emperor, were oppressing them, whilst the Church was favouring them so as to gain authority in temporal power: in many others their citizens became princes. From this it came to pass that Italy fell partly into the hands of the Church and of republics, and, the Church consisting of priests and the republic of citizens unaccustomed to arms, both commenced to enlist foreigners.

The first who gave renown to this soldiery was Alberigo da Conio,[28] the Romagnian. From the school of this man sprang, among others, Braccio and Sforza, who in their time were the arbiters of Italy. After these came all the other captains who till now have directed the arms of Italy; and the end of all their valour has been, that she has been overrun by Charles, robbed by Louis, ravaged by Ferdinand, and insulted by the Switzers. The principle that has guided them has been, first, to lower the credit of infantry so that they might increase their own. They did this

26   Bartolomeo Colleoni of Bergamo; died 1457. Roberto of San Severino; died fighting for Venice against Sigismund, Duke of Austria, in 1487. "Primo capitano in Italia." – Machiavelli. Count of Pitigliano; Nicolo Orsini, born 1442, died 1510.

27   Battle of Vaila in 1509.

28   Alberigo da Conio. Alberico da Barbiano, Count of Cunio in Romagna. He was the leader of the famous "Company of St George," composed entirely of Italian soldiers. He died in 1409.

because, subsisting on their pay and without territory, they were unable to support many soldiers, and a few infantry did not give them any authority; so they were led to employ cavalry, with a moderate force of which they were maintained and honoured; and affairs were brought to such a pass that, in an army of twenty thousand soldiers, there were not to be found two thousand foot soldiers. They had, besides this, used every art to lessen fatigue and danger to themselves and their soldiers, not killing in the fray, but taking prisoners and liberating without ransom. They did not attack towns at night, nor did the garrisons of the towns attack encampments at night; they did not surround the camp either with stockade or ditch, nor did they campaign in the winter. All these things were permitted by their military rules, and devised by them to avoid, as I have said, both fatigue and dangers; thus they have brought Italy to slavery and contempt.

CHAPTER THIRTEEN

Concerning Auxiliaries, Mixed Soldiery, and One's Own

AUXILIARIES, WHICH ARE THE OTHER USELESS ARM, are employed when a prince is called in with his forces to aid and defend, as was done by Pope Julius in the most recent times; for he, having, in the enterprise against Ferrara, had poor proof of his mercenaries, turned to auxiliaries, and stipulated with Ferdinand, King of Spain,[29] for his assistance with men and arms. These arms may be useful and good in themselves, but for him who calls them in they are always disadvantageous; for losing, one is undone, and winning, one is their captive.

And although ancient histories may be full of examples, I do not wish to leave this recent one of Pope Julius the Second, the peril of which cannot fail to be perceived; for he, wishing to get Ferrara, threw himself entirely into the hands of the foreigner. But his good fortune brought about a third event, so that he did not reap the fruit of his rash choice; because, having his auxiliaries routed at Ravenna, and the Switzers having risen and driven out the conquerors (against all expectation, both his and others), it so came to pass that he did not become prisoner to his enemies, they having fled, nor to his auxiliaries, he having conquered by other arms than theirs.

The Florentines, being entirely without arms, sent ten thousand Frenchmen to take Pisa, whereby they ran more danger than at any other time of their troubles.

---

29   Ferdinand V (F. II of Aragon and Sicily, F. III of Naples), surnamed "The Catholic," born 1542, died 1516.

The Emperor of Constantinople,[30] to oppose his neighbours, sent ten thousand Turks into Greece, who, on the war being finished, were not willing to quit; this was the beginning of the servitude of Greece to the infidels.

Therefore, let him who has no desire to conquer make use of these arms, for they are much more hazardous than mercenaries, because with them the ruin is ready made; they are all united, all yield obedience to others; but with mercenaries, when they have conquered, more time and better opportunities are needed to injure you; they are not all of one community, they are found and paid by you, and a third party, which you have made their head, is not able all at once to assume enough authority to injure you. In conclusion, in mercenaries dastardy is most dangerous; in auxiliaries, valour. The wise prince, therefore, has always avoided these arms and turned to his own; and has been willing rather to lose with them than to conquer with the others, not deeming that a real victory which is gained with the arms of others.

I shall never hesitate to cite Cesare Borgia and his actions. This duke entered the Romagna with auxiliaries, taking there only French soldiers, and with them he captured Imola and Forli; but afterwards, such forces not appearing to him reliable, he turned to mercenaries, discerning less danger in them, and enlisted the Orsini and Vitelli; whom presently, on handling and finding them doubtful, unfaithful, and dangerous, he destroyed and turned to his own men. And the difference between one and the other of these forces can easily be seen when one considers the difference there was in the reputation of the duke, when he had the French, when he had the Orsini and Vitelli, and when he relied on his own soldiers, on whose fidelity he could always count and found it ever increasing; he was never esteemed more highly than when every one saw that he was complete master of his own forces.

I was not intending to go beyond Italian and recent examples, but I am unwilling to leave out Hiero, the Syracusan, he being one of those I have named above. This man, as I have said, made head of the army by the Syracusans, soon found out that a mercenary soldiery, constituted like our Italian condottieri, was of no use; and it appearing to him that he could neither keep them not let them go, he had them all cut to pieces, and afterwards made war with his own forces and not with aliens.

I wish also to recall to memory an instance from the Old Testament applicable to this subject. David offered himself to Saul to fight with Goliath, the Philistine champion, and, to give him courage, Saul armed him with

30   Joannes Cantacuzenus, born 1300, died 1383.

his own weapons; which David rejected as soon as he had them on his back, saying he could make no use of them, and that he wished to meet the enemy with his sling and his knife. In conclusion, the arms of others either fall from your back, or they weigh you down, or they bind you fast.

Charles the Seventh,[31] the father of King Louis the Eleventh,[32] having by good fortune and valour liberated France from the English, recognized the necessity of being armed with forces of his own, and he established in his kingdom ordinances concerning men-at-arms and infantry. Afterwards his son, King Louis, abolished the infantry and began to enlist the Switzers, which mistake, followed by others, is, as is now seen, a source of peril to that kingdom; because, having raised the reputation of the Switzers, he has entirely diminished the value of his own arms, for he has destroyed the infantry altogether; and his men-at-arms he has subordinated to others, for, being as they are so accustomed to fight along with Switzers, it does not appear that they can now conquer without them. Hence it arises that the French cannot stand against the Switzers, and without the Switzers they do not come off well against others. The armies of the French have thus become mixed, partly mercenary and partly national, both of which arms together are much better than mercenaries alone or auxiliaries alone, but much inferior to one's own forces. And this example proves it, for the kingdom of France would be unconquerable if the ordinance of Charles had been enlarged or maintained.

But the scanty wisdom of man, on entering into an affair which looks well at first, cannot discern the poison that is hidden in it, as I have said above of hectic fevers. Therefore, if he who rules a principality cannot recognize evils until they are upon him, he is not truly wise; and this insight is given to few. And if the first disaster to the Roman Empire[33] should be examined, it will be found to have commenced only with the enlisting of the Goths; because from that time the vigour of the Roman Empire began to decline, and all that valour which had raised it passed away to others.

---

31   Charles VII of France, surnamed "The Victorious," born 1403, died 1461.

32   Louis XI, son of the above, born 1423, died 1483.

33   "Many speakers to the House the other night in the debate on the reduction of armaments seemed to show a most lamentable ignorance of the conditions under which the British Empire maintains its existence. When Mr Balfour replied to the allegations that the Roman Empire sank under the weight of its military obligations, he said that this was 'wholly unhistorical.' He might well have added that the Roman power was at its zenith when every citizen acknowledged his liability to fight for the State, but that it began to decline as soon as this obligation was no longer recognized." – Pall Mall Gazette, 15th May 1906.

I conclude, therefore, that no principality is secure without having its own forces; on the contrary, it is entirely dependent on good fortune, not having the valour which in adversity would defend it. And it has always been the opinion and judgment of wise men that nothing can be so uncertain or unstable as fame or power not founded on its own strength. And one's own forces are those which are composed either of subjects, citizens, or dependents; all others are mercenaries or auxiliaries. And the way to make ready one's own forces will be easily found if the rules suggested by me shall be reflected upon, and if one will consider how Philip, the father of Alexander the Great, and many republics and princes have armed and organized themselves, to which rules I entirely commit myself.

CHAPTER FOURTEEN

That which Concerns a Prince on the Subject of the Art of War

A PRINCE OUGHT TO HAVE no other aim or thought, nor select anything else for his study, than war and its rules and discipline; for this is the sole art that belongs to him who rules, and it is of such force that it not only upholds those who are born princes, but it often enables men to rise from a private station to that rank. And, on the contrary, it is seen that when princes have thought more of ease than of arms they have lost their states. And the first cause of your losing it is to neglect this art; and what enables you to acquire a state is to be master of the art. Francesco Sforza, through being martial, from a private person became Duke of Milan; and the sons, through avoiding the hardships and troubles of arms, from dukes became private persons. For among other evils which being un-armed brings you, it causes you to be despised, and this is one of those ignominies against which a prince ought to guard himself, as is shown later on. Because there is nothing proportionate between the armed and the unarmed; and it is not reasonable that he who is armed should yield obedience willingly to him who is unarmed, or that the unarmed man should be secure among armed servants. Because, there being in the one disdain and in the other suspicion, it is not possible for them to work well together. And therefore a prince who does not understand the art of war, over and above the other misfortunes already mentioned, cannot be respected by his soldiers, nor can he rely on them. He ought never, therefore, to have out of his thoughts this subject of war, and in peace he should addict himself more to its exercise than in war; this he can do in two ways, the one by action, the other by study.

As regards action, he ought above all things to keep his men well orga-nized and drilled, to follow incessantly the chase, by which he accustoms his body to hardships, and learns something of the nature of localities, and gets to find out how the mountains rise, how the valleys open out, how the plains lie, and to understand the nature of rivers and marshes, and in all this to take the greatest care. Which knowledge is useful in two ways. Firstly, he learns to know his country, and is better able to undertake its defence; afterwards, by means of the knowledge and observation of that locality, he understands with ease any other which it may be necessary for him to study hereafter; because the hills, valleys, and plains, and rivers and marshes that are, for instance, in Tuscany, have a certain resemblance to those of other countries, so that with a knowledge of the aspect of one country one can easily arrive at a knowledge of others. And the prince that lacks this skill lacks the essential which it is desirable that a captain should possess, for it teaches him to surprise his enemy, to select quarters, to lead armies, to array the battle, to besiege towns to advantage.

Philopoemen,[34] Prince of the Achaeans, among other praises which writers have bestowed on him, is commended because in time of peace he never had anything in his mind but the rules of war; and when he was in the country with friends, he often stopped and reasoned with them: "If the enemy should be upon that hill, and we should find ourselves here with our army, with whom would be the advantage? How should one best advance to meet him, keeping the ranks? If we should wish to retreat, how ought we to pursue?" And he would set forth to them, as he went, all the chances that could befall an army; he would listen to their opinion and state his, confirming it with reasons, so that by these continual discussions there could never arise, in time of war, any unexpected circumstances that he could not deal with.

But to exercise the intellect the prince should read histories, and study there the actions of illustrious men, to see how they have borne themselves in war, to examine the causes of their victories and defeat, so as to avoid the latter and imitate the former; and above all do as an illustrious man did, who took as an exemplar one who had been praised and famous before him, and whose achievements and deeds he always kept in his mind, as it is said Alexander the Great imitated Achilles, Caesar Alexander, Scipio Cyrus. And whoever reads the life of Cyrus, written by Xenophon, will recognize afterwards in the life of Scipio how that imitation was his glory, and how in chastity, affability, humanity, and liberality Scipio conformed to those things which have been written of Cyrus by Xenophon. A wise prince ought to observe some such rules, and never in peaceful times stand idle, but increase his resources with industry in such a way that they may be available to him in adversity, so that if fortune chances it may find him prepared to resist her blows.

34 Philopoemen, "the last of the Greeks," born 252 B.C., died 183 B.C.

CHAPTER FIFTEEN

Concerning Things for which Men, and Especially Princes, are Praised or Blamed

It REMAINS NOW TO SEE what ought to be the rules of conduct for a prince towards subject and friends. And as I know that many have written on this point, I expect I shall be considered presumptuous in mentioning it again, especially as in discussing it I shall depart from the methods of other people. But, it being my intention to write a thing which shall be useful to him who apprehends it, it appears to me more appropriate to follow up the real truth of the matter than the imagination of it; for many have pictured republics and principalities which in fact have never been known or seen, because how one lives is so far distant from how one ought to live, that he who neglects what is done for what ought to be done, sooner effects his ruin than his preservation; for a man who wishes to act entirely up to his professions of virtue soon meets with what destroys him among so much that is evil.

Hence it is necessary for a prince wishing to hold his own to know how to do wrong, and to make use of it or not according to necessity. Therefore, putting on one side imaginary things concerning a prince, and discussing those which are real, I say that all men when they are spoken of, and chiefly princes for being more highly placed, are remarkable for some of those qualities which bring them either blame or praise; and thus it is that one is reputed liberal, another miserly, using a Tuscan term (because an avaricious person in our language is still he who desires to possess by robbery, whilst we call one miserly who deprives himself too much of the use of his own); one is reputed generous, one rapacious; one cruel, one compassionate; one faithless, another faithful; one effeminate and cowardly, another bold and brave; one affable, another haughty; one lascivious, another chaste; one sincere, another cunning; one hard, another easy; one grave, another frivolous; one religious, another unbelieving, and the like. And I know that every one will confess that it would be most praiseworthy in a prince to exhibit all the above qualities that are considered good; but because they can neither be entirely possessed nor observed, for human conditions do not permit it, it is necessary for him to be sufficiently prudent that he may know how to avoid the reproach of those vices which would lose him his state; and also to keep himself, if it be possible, from those which would not lose him it; but this not being possible, he may with less hesitation abandon himself to them. And again, he need not make himself uneasy at incurring a reproach for those vices without which the state can only be saved with difficulty, for if everything is considered carefully, it will be found that something which looks like virtue, if followed, would be his ruin; whilst something else, which looks like vice, yet followed brings him security and prosperity.

CHAPTER SIXTEEN

Concerning Liberality and Meanness

COMMENCING THEN WITH THE FIRST of the above-named character-istics, I say that it would be well to be reputed liberal. Nevertheless, liberality exercised in a way that does not bring you the reputation for it, injures you; for if one exercises it honestly and as it should be exercised, it may not become known, and you will not avoid the reproach of its opposite. Therefore, any one wishing to maintain among men the name of liberal is obliged to avoid no attribute of magnificence; so that a prince thus inclined will consume in such acts all his property, and will be compelled in the end, if he wish to maintain the name of liberal, to unduly weigh down his people, and tax them, and do everything he can to get money. This will soon make him odious to his subjects, and becoming poor he will be little valued by any one; thus, with his liberality, having offended many and rewarded few, he is affected by the very first trouble and imperilled by whatever may be the first danger; recognizing this himself, and wishing to draw back from it, he runs at once into the reproach of being miserly.

Therefore, a prince, not being able to exercise this virtue of liberality in such a way that it is recognized, except to his cost, if he is wise he ought not to fear the reputation of being mean, for in time he will come to be more considered than if liberal, seeing that with his economy his revenues are enough, that he can defend himself against all attacks, and is able to engage in enterprises without burdening his people; thus it comes to pass that he exercises liberality towards all from whom he does not take, who are numberless, and meanness towards those to whom he does not give, who are few.

We have not seen great things done in our time except by those who have been considered mean; the rest have failed. Pope Julius the Second was assisted in reaching the papacy by a reputation for liberality, yet he did not strive afterwards to keep it up, when he made war on the King of France; and he made many wars without imposing any extraordinary tax on his subjects, for he supplied his additional expenses out of his long thriftiness. The present King of Spain would not have undertaken or conquered in so many enterprises if he had been reputed liberal. A prince, therefore, provided that he has not to rob his subjects, that he can defend himself, that he does not become poor and abject, that he is not forced to become rapacious, ought to hold of little account a reputation for being mean, for it is one of those vices which will enable him to govern.

And if any one should say: Caesar obtained empire by liberality, and many others have reached the highest positions by having been liberal, and by being considered so, I answer: Either you are a prince in fact, or in a way to become one. In the first case this liberality is dangerous, in the second it is very necessary to be considered liberal; and Caesar was one of those who wished to become pre-eminent in Rome; but if he had survived after becoming so, and had not moderated his expenses, he would have destroyed his government. And if any one should reply: Many have been princes, and have done great things with armies, who have been considered very liberal, I reply: Either a prince spends that which is his own or his subjects' or else that of others. In the first case he ought to be sparing, in the second he ought not to neglect any opportunity for liberality. And to the prince who goes forth with his army, supporting it by pillage, sack, and extortion, handling that which belongs to others, this liberality is necessary, otherwise he would not be followed by soldiers. And of that which is neither yours nor your subjects' you can be a ready giver, as were Cyrus, Caesar, and Alexander; because it does not take away your reputation if you squander that of others, but adds to it; it is only squandering your own that injures you.

And there is nothing wastes so rapidly as liberality, for even whilst you exercise it you lose the power to do so, and so become either poor or despised, or else, in avoiding poverty, rapacious and hated. And a prince should guard himself, above all things, against being despised and hated; and liberality leads you to both. Therefore it is wiser to have a reputation for meanness which brings reproach without hatred, than to be compelled through seeking a reputation for liberality to incur a name for rapacity which begets reproach with hatred.

CHAPTER SEVENTEEN

Concerning Cruelty and Clemency, and Whether it is Better to be Loved than Feared

COMING NOW TO THE OTHER QUALITIES mentioned above, I say that every prince ought to desire to be considered clement and not cruel. Nevertheless he ought to take care not to misuse this clemency. Cesare Borgia was considered cruel; notwithstanding, his cruelty reconciled the Romagna, unified it, and restored it to peace and loyalty. And if this be rightly considered, he will be seen to have been much more merciful than the Florentine people, who, to avoid a reputation for cruelty, permitted Pistoia to be destroyed.[35] Therefore a prince, so long as he keeps his subjects united and loyal, ought not to mind the reproach of cruelty; because with a few examples he will be more merciful than those who, through too much mercy, allow disorders to arise, from which follow murders or robberies; for these are wont to injure the whole people, whilst those executions which originate with a prince offend the individual only.

And of all princes, it is impossible for the new prince to avoid the imputation of cruelty, owing to new states being full of dangers. Hence Virgil, through the mouth of Dido, excuses the inhumanity of her reign owing to its being new, saying:

"*Res dura, et regni novitas me talia cogunt*
Moliri, et late fines custode tueri."[36]

35   During the rioting between the Cancellieri and Panciatichi factions in 1502 and 1503.

36   ... *against my will, my fate*
A throne unsettled, and an infant state,
Bid me defend my realms with all my pow'rs,
And guard with these severities my shores.
Christopher Pitt.

Nevertheless he ought to be slow to believe and to act, nor should he himself show fear, but proceed in a temperate manner with prudence and humanity, so that too much confidence may not make him incautious and too much distrust render him intolerable.

Upon this a question arises: whether it be better to be loved than feared or feared than loved? It may be answered that one should wish to be both, but, because it is difficult to unite them in one person, it is much safer to be feared than loved, when, of the two, either must be dispensed with. Because this is to be asserted in general of men, that they are ungrateful, fickle, false, cowardly, covetous, and as long as you succeed they are yours entirely; they will offer you their blood, property, life, and children, as is said above, when the need is far distant; but when it approaches they turn against you. And that prince who, relying entirely on their promises, has neglected other precautions, is ruined; because friendships that are obtained by payments, and not by greatness or nobility of mind, may indeed be earned, but they are not secured, and in time of need cannot be relied upon; and men have less scruple in offending one who is beloved than one who is feared, for love is preserved by the link of obligation which, owing to the baseness of men, is broken at every opportunity for their advantage; but fear preserves you by a dread of punishment which never fails.

Nevertheless a prince ought to inspire fear in such a way that, if he does not win love, he avoids hatred; because he can endure very well being feared whilst he is not hated, which will always be as long as he abstains from the property of his citizens and subjects and from their women. But when it is necessary for him to proceed against the life of someone, he must do it on proper justification and for manifest cause, but above all things he must keep his hands off the property of others, because men more quickly forget the death of their father than the loss of their patrimony. Besides, pretexts for taking away the property are never wanting; for he who has once begun to live by robbery will always find pretexts for seizing what belongs to others; but reasons for taking life, on the contrary, are more difficult to find and sooner lapse. But when a prince is with his army, and has under control a multitude of soldiers, then it is quite necessary for him to disregard the reputation of cruelty, for without it he would never hold his army united or disposed to its duties.

Among the wonderful deeds of Hannibal this one is enumerated: that having led an enormous army, composed of many various races of men, to fight in foreign lands, no dissensions arose either among them or against the prince, whether in his bad or in his good fortune.

This arose from nothing else than his inhuman cruelty, which, with his boundless valour, made him revered and terrible in the sight of his soldiers, but without that cruelty, his other virtues were not sufficient to produce this effect. And short-sighted writers admire his deeds from one point of view and from another condemn the principal cause of them. That it is true his other virtues would not have been sufficient for him may be proved by the case of Scipio, that most excellent man, not only of his own times but within the memory of man, against whom, nevertheless, his army rebelled in Spain; this arose from nothing but his too great forbearance, which gave his soldiers more license than is consistent with military discipline. For this he was upbraided in the Senate by Fabius Maximus, and called the corrupter of the Roman soldiery. The Locrians were laid waste by a legate of Scipio, yet they were not avenged by him, nor was the insolence of the legate punished, owing entirely to his easy nature. Insomuch that someone in the Senate, wishing to excuse him, said there were many men who knew much better how not to err than to correct the errors of others. This disposition, if he had been continued in the command, would have destroyed in time the fame and glory of Scipio; but, he being under the control of the Senate, this injurious characteristic not only concealed itself, but contributed to his glory.

Returning to the question of being feared or loved, I come to the conclusion that, men loving according to their own will and fearing according to that of the prince, a wise prince should establish himself on that which is in his own control and not in that of others; he must endeavour only to avoid hatred, as is noted.

Concerning the Way in which Princes Should Keep Faith

EVERY ONE ADMITS HOW PRAISEWORTHY it is in a prince to keep faith, and to live with integrity and not with craft. Nevertheless our experience has been that those princes who have done great things have held good faith of little account, and have known how to circumvent the intellect of men by craft, and in the end have overcome those who have relied on their word. You must know there are two ways of contesting,[38] the one by the law, the other by force; the first method is proper to men, the second to beasts; but because the first is frequently not sufficient, it is necessary to have recourse to the second. Therefore it is necessary for a prince to understand how to avail himself of the beast and the man. This has been figuratively taught to princes by ancient writers, who describe how Achilles and many other princes of old were given to the Centaur Chiron to nurse, who brought them up in his discipline; which means solely that, as they had for a teacher one who was half beast and half man, so it is necessary for a prince to know how to make use of both natures, and that one without the other is not durable. A prince, therefore, being compelled knowingly to adopt the beast, ought to choose the fox and the lion; because the lion cannot defend himself against snares and the fox cannot defend himself against wolves. Therefore, it is necessary to be a fox to discover the snares and a lion to terrify

---

37   The present chapter has given greater offence than any other portion of Machiavelli's writings.

38   "Contesting," i.e. "striving for mastery." This passage is imitated directly from Cicero's "De Officiis": "Nam cum sint duo genera decertandi, unum per disceptationem, alterum per vim; cumque illud proprium sit hominis, hoc beluarum; confugiendum est ad posterius, si uti non licet superiore."

the wolves. Those who rely simply on the lion do not understand what they are about. Therefore a wise lord cannot, nor ought he to, keep faith when such observance may be turned against him, and when the reasons that caused him to pledge it exist no longer. If men were entirely good this precept would not hold, but because they are bad, and will not keep faith with you, you too are not bound to observe it with them. Nor will there ever be wanting to a prince legitimate reasons to excuse this non-observance. Of this endless modern examples could be given, showing how many treaties and engagements have been made void and of no effect through the faithlessness of princes; and he who has known best how to employ the fox has succeeded best.

But it is necessary to know well how to disguise this characteristic, and to be a great pretender and dissembler; and men are so simple, and so subject to present necessities, that he who seeks to deceive will always find someone who will allow himself to be deceived. One recent example I cannot pass over in silence. Alexander the Sixth did nothing else but deceive men, nor ever thought of doing otherwise, and he always found victims; for there never was a man who had greater power in asserting, or who with greater oaths would affirm a thing, yet would observe it less; nevertheless his deceits always succeeded according to his wishes,[39] because he well understood this side of mankind.

> *Alexander never did what he said,*
> *Cesare never said what he did.*
> Italian Proverb.

Therefore it is unnecessary for a prince to have all the good qualities I have enumerated, but it is very necessary to appear to have them. And I shall dare to say this also, that to have them and always to observe them is injurious, and that to appear to have them is useful; to appear merciful, faithful, humane, religious, upright, and to be so, but with a mind so framed that should you require not to be so, you may be able and know how to change to the opposite.

And you have to understand this, that a prince, especially a new one, cannot observe all those things for which men are esteemed, being often forced, in order to maintain the state, to act contrary to fidelity,[40]

39   "Nondimanco sempre gli succederono gli inganni (ad votum)." The words "ad votum" are omitted in the Testina addition, 1550.

40   "Contrary to fidelity" or "faith," "contro alla fede," and "tutto fede," "altogether faithful," in the next paragraph. It is noteworthy that these two phrases, "contro alla fede" and "tutto fede," were omitted in the Testina edition, which was published with the

friendship, humanity, and religion. Therefore it is necessary for him to have a mind ready to turn itself accordingly as the winds and variations of fortune force it, yet, as I have said above, not to diverge from the good if he can avoid doing so, but, if compelled, then to know how to set about it.

For this reason a prince ought to take care that he never lets anything slip from his lips that is not replete with the above-named five qualities, that he may appear to him who sees and hears him altogether merciful, faithful, humane, upright, and religious. There is nothing more necessary to appear to have than this last quality, inasmuch as men judge generally more by the eye than by the hand, because it belongs to everybody to see you, to few to come in touch with you. Every one sees what you appear to be, few really know what you are, and those few dare not oppose themselves to the opinion of the many, who have the majesty of the state to defend them; and in the actions of all men, and especially of princes, which it is not prudent to challenge, one judges by the result.

For that reason, let a prince have the credit of conquering and holding his state, the means will always be considered honest, and he will be praised by everybody; because the vulgar are always taken by what a thing seems to be and by what comes of it; and in the world there are only the vulgar, for the few find a place there only when the many have no ground to rest on.

One prince[41] of the present time, whom it is not well to name, never preaches anything else but peace and good faith, and to both he is most hostile, and either, if he had kept it, would have deprived him of reputation and kingdom many a time.

sanction of the papal authorities. It may be that the meaning attached to the word "fede" was "the faith," i.e. the Catholic creed, and not as rendered here "fidelity" and "faithful." Observe that the word "religione" was suffered to stand in the text of the Testina, being used to signify indifferently every shade of belief, as witness "the religion," a phrase inevitably employed to designate the Huguenot heresy. South in his Sermon IX, p. 69, ed. 1843, comments on this passage as follows: "That great patron and Coryphaeus of this tribe, Nicolo Machiavel, laid down this for a master rule in his political scheme: 'That the show of religion was helpful to the politician, but the reality of it hurtful and pernicious.'"

41   Ferdinand of Aragon. "When Machiavelli was writing *The Prince* it would have been clearly impossible to mention Ferdinand's name here without giving offence.

CHAPTER NINETEEN

That One Should Avoid Being Despised and Hated

NOW, CONCERNING THE CHARACTERISTICS of which mention is made above, I have spoken of the more important ones, the others I wish to discuss briefly under this generality, that the prince must consider, as has been in part said before, how to avoid those things which will make him hated or contemptible; and as often as he shall have succeeded he will have fulfilled his part, and he need not fear any danger in other reproaches.

It makes him hated above all things, as I have said, to be rapacious, and to be a violator of the property and women of his subjects, from both of which he must abstain. And when neither their property nor their honor is touched, the majority of men live content, and he has only to contend with the ambition of a few, whom he can curb with ease in many ways.

It makes him contemptible to be considered fickle, frivolous, effeminate, mean-spirited, irresolute, from all of which a prince should guard himself as from a rock; and he should endeavour to show in his actions greatness, courage, gravity, and fortitude; and in his private dealings with his subjects let him show that his judgments are irrevocable, and maintain himself in such reputation that no one can hope either to deceive him or to get round him.

That prince is highly esteemed who conveys this impression of himself, and he who is highly esteemed is not easily conspired against; for, provided it is well known that he is an excellent man and revered by his people, he can only be attacked with difficulty. For this reason a prince ought to have two fears, one from within, on account of his subjects, the other from without, on account of external powers. From the latter he is defended by being well armed and having good allies, and if he is well armed he will have good friends, and affairs will always remain quiet within when they are quiet without, unless they should have been already disturbed by conspiracy; and even should affairs outside be disturbed, if he has carried out his preparations and has lived as I have said, as long as he does not despair, he will resist every attack, as I said Nabis the Spartan did.

But concerning his subjects, when affairs outside are disturbed he has only to fear that they will conspire secretly, from which a prince can easily secure himself by avoiding being hated and despised, and by keeping the people satisfied with him, which it is most necessary for him to accomplish, as I said above at length. And one of the most efficacious remedies that a prince can have against conspiracies is not to be hated and despised by the people, for he who conspires against a prince always expects to please them by his removal; but when the conspirator can only look forward to offending them, he will not have the courage to take such a course, for the difficulties that confront a conspirator are infinite. And as experience shows, many have been the conspiracies, but few have been successful; because he who conspires cannot act alone, nor can he take a companion except from those whom he believes to be malcontents, and as soon as you have opened your mind to a malcontent you have given him the material with which to content himself, for by denouncing you he can look for every advantage; so that, seeing the gain from this course to be assured, and seeing the other to be doubtful and full of dangers, he must be a very rare friend, or a thoroughly obstinate enemy of the prince, to keep faith with you.

And, to reduce the matter into a small compass, I say that, on the side of the conspirator, there is nothing but fear, jealousy, prospect of punishment to terrify him; but on the side of the prince there is the majesty of the principality, the laws, the protection of friends and the state to defend him; so that, adding to all these things the popular goodwill, it is impossible that any one should be so rash as to conspire. For whereas in general the conspirator has to fear before the execution of his plot, in this case he has also to fear the sequel to the crime; because on account of it he has the people for an enemy, and thus cannot hope for any escape.

Endless examples could be given on this subject, but I will be content with one, brought to pass within the memory of our fathers. Messer Annibale Bentivogli, who was prince in Bologna (grandfather of the present Annibale), having been murdered by the Canneschi, who had conspired against him, not one of his family survived but Messer Giovanni,[42] who was in childhood: immediately after his assassination the people rose and murdered all the Canneschi. This sprung from the popular goodwill which the house of Bentivogli enjoyed in those days in Bologna; which was so great that, although none remained there after the death of Annibale who was able to rule the state, the Bolognese, having information that there was one of the Bentivogli family in Florence, who up to that time had been considered the son of a blacksmith, sent to Florence for him and gave him the government of their city, and it was ruled by him until Messer Giovanni came in due course to the government.

For this reason I consider that a prince ought to reckon conspiracies of little account when his people hold him in esteem; but when it is hostile to him, and bears hatred towards him, he ought to fear everything and everybody. And well-ordered states and wise princes have taken every care not to drive the nobles to desperation, and to keep the people satisfied and contented, for this is one of the most important objects a prince can have.

Among the best ordered and governed kingdoms of our times is France, and in it are found many good institutions on which depend the liberty and security of the king; of these the first is the parliament and its authority, because he who founded the kingdom, knowing the ambition of the nobility and their boldness, considered that a bit to their mouths would be necessary to hold them in; and, on the other side, knowing the hatred of the people, founded in fear, against the nobles, he wished to protect them, yet he was not anxious for this to be the particular care of the king; therefore, to take away the reproach which he would be liable to from the nobles for favouring the people, and from the people for favouring the nobles, he set up an arbiter, who should be one who could beat down the great and favour the lesser without reproach to the king. Neither could you have a better or a more prudent arrangement, or a greater source of security to the king and kingdom. From this one can draw another important conclusion, that princes ought to leave affairs of reproach to the management of others, and keep those of grace in their own hands. And further, I consider that a prince ought to cherish the nobles, but not so as to make himself hated by the people.

---

42   Giovanni Bentivogli, born in Bologna 1438, died at Milan 1508. He ruled Bologna from 1462 to 1506. Machiavelli's strong condemnation of conspiracies may get its edge from his own very recent experience (February 1513), when he had been arrested and tortured for his alleged complicity in the Boscoli conspiracy.

It may appear, perhaps, to some who have examined the lives and deaths of the Roman emperors that many of them would be an example contrary to my opinion, seeing that some of them lived nobly and showed great qualities of soul, nevertheless they have lost their empire or have been killed by subjects who have conspired against them. Wishing, therefore, to answer these objections, I will recall the characters of some of the emperors, and will show that the causes of their ruin were not different to those alleged by me; at the same time I will only submit for consideration those things that are noteworthy to him who studies the affairs of those times.

It seems to me sufficient to take all those emperors who succeeded to the empire from Marcus the philosopher down to Maximinus; they were Marcus and his son Commodus, Pertinax, Julian, Severus and his son Antoninus Caracalla, Macrinus, Heliogabalus, Alexander, and Maximinus.

There is first to note that, whereas in other principalities the ambition of the nobles and the insolence of the people only have to be contended with, the Roman emperors had a third difficulty in having to put up with the cruelty and avarice of their soldiers, a matter so beset with difficulties that it was the ruin of many; for it was a hard thing to give satisfaction both to soldiers and people; because the people loved peace, and for this reason they loved the unaspiring prince, whilst the soldiers loved the warlike prince who was bold, cruel, and rapacious, which qualities they were quite willing he should exercise upon the people, so that they could get double pay and give vent to their own greed and cruelty. Hence it arose that those emperors were always overthrown who, either by birth or training, had no great authority, and most of them, especially those who came new to the principality, recognizing the difficulty of these two opposing humours, were inclined to give satisfaction to the soldiers, caring little about injuring the people. Which course was necessary, because, as princes cannot help being hated by someone, they ought, in the first place, to avoid being hated by every one, and when they cannot compass this, they ought to endeavour with the utmost diligence to avoid the hatred of the most powerful. Therefore, those emperors who through inexperience had need of special favour adhered more readily to the soldiers than to the people; a course which turned out advantageous to them or not, accordingly as the prince knew how to maintain authority over them.

From these causes it arose that Marcus, Pertinax, and Alexander, being all men of modest life, lovers of justice, enemies to cruelty, humane, and benignant, came to a sad end except Marcus; he alone lived and died honoured, because he had succeeded to the throne by hereditary title, and owed nothing either to the soldiers or the people; and afterwards, being possessed of many virtues which made him respected, he always kept both orders in their places whilst he lived, and was neither hated nor despised.

But Pertinax was created emperor against the wishes of the soldiers, who, being accustomed to live licentiously under Commodus, could not endure the honest life to which Pertinax wished to reduce them; thus, having given cause for hatred, to which hatred there was added contempt for his old age, he was overthrown at the very beginning of his administration. And here it should be noted that hatred is acquired as much by good works as by bad ones, therefore, as I said before, a prince wishing to keep his state is very often forced to do evil; for when that body is corrupt whom you think you have need of to maintain yourself – it may be either the people or the soldiers or the nobles – you have to submit to its humours and to gratify them, and then good works will do you harm.

But let us come to Alexander, who was a man of such great goodness, that among the other praises which are accorded him is this, that in the fourteen years he held the empire no one was ever put to death by him unjudged; nevertheless, being considered effeminate and a man who allowed himself to be governed by his mother, he became despised, the army conspired against him, and murdered him.

Turning now to the opposite characters of Commodus, Severus, Antoninus Caracalla, and Maximinus, you will find them all cruel and rapacious-men who, to satisfy their soldiers, did not hesitate to commit every kind of iniquity against the people; and all, except Severus, came to a bad end; but in Severus there was so much valour that, keeping the soldiers friendly, although the people were oppressed by him, he reigned successfully; for his valour made him so much admired in the sight of the soldiers and people that the latter were kept in a way astonished and awed and the former respectful and satisfied. And because the actions of this man, as a new prince, were great, I wish to show briefly that he knew well how to counterfeit the fox and the lion, which natures, as I said above, it is necessary for a prince to imitate.

Knowing the sloth of the Emperor Julian, he persuaded the army in Sclavonia, of which he was captain, that it would be right to go to Rome and avenge the death of Pertinax, who had been killed by the praetorian soldiers; and under this pretext, without appearing to aspire to the throne, he moved the army on Rome, and reached Italy before it was known that he had started. On his arrival at Rome, the Senate, through fear, elected him emperor and killed Julian. After this there remained for Severus, who wished to make himself master of the whole empire, two difficulties; one in Asia, where Niger, head of the Asiatic army, had caused himself to be proclaimed emperor; the other in the west where Albinus was, who also aspired to the throne. And as he considered it dangerous to declare himself hostile to both, he decided to attack Niger and to deceive Albinus. To the latter he wrote that, being elected emperor by the Senate, he was willing to share that dignity with him and sent him the title of Caesar; and, moreover, that the Senate had made Albinus his colleague; which things were accepted by Albinus as true. But after Severus had conquered and killed Niger, and settled oriental affairs, he returned to Rome and complained to the Senate that Albinus, little recognizing the benefits that he had received from him, had by treachery sought to murder him, and for this ingratitude he was compelled to punish him. Afterwards he sought him out in France, and took from him his government and life. He who will, therefore, carefully examine the actions of this man will find him a most valiant lion and a most cunning fox; he will find him feared and respected by every one, and not hated by the army; and it need not be wondered at that he, a new man, was able to hold the empire so well, because his supreme renown always protected him from that hatred which the people might have conceived against him for his violence.

But his son Antoninus was a most eminent man, and had very excellent qualities, which made him admirable in the sight of the people and acceptable to the soldiers, for he was a warlike man, most enduring of fatigue, a despiser of all delicate food and other luxuries, which caused him to be beloved by the armies. Nevertheless, his ferocity and cruelties were so great and so unheard of that, after endless single murders, he killed a large number of the people of Rome and all those of Alexandria. He became hated by the whole world, and also feared by those he had around him, to such an extent that he was murdered in the midst of his army by a centurion. And here it must be noted that such-like deaths, which are deliberately inflicted with a resolved and desperate courage, cannot be avoided by princes, because any one who does not fear to die can inflict them; but a prince may fear them the less because they are very rare; he has only to be careful not to do any grave injury to those whom he employs or has around him in the service of the state. Antoninus had not taken this care, but had contumeliously killed a brother of that centurion, whom also he daily threatened, yet retained in his bodyguard; which, as it turned out, was a rash thing to do, and proved the emperor's ruin.

But let us come to Commodus, to whom it should have been very easy to hold the empire, for, being the son of Marcus, he had inherited it, and he had only to follow in the footsteps of his father to please his people and soldiers; but, being by nature cruel and brutal, he gave himself up to amusing the soldiers and corrupting them, so that he might indulge his rapacity upon the people; on the other hand, not maintaining his dignity, often descending to the theatre to compete with gladiators, and doing other vile things, little worthy of the imperial majesty, he fell into contempt with the soldiers, and being hated by one party and despised by the other, he was conspired against and was killed.

It remains to discuss the character of Maximinus. He was a very warlike man, and the armies, being disgusted with the effeminacy of Alexander, of whom I have already spoken, killed him and elected Maximinus to the throne. This he did not possess for long, for two things made him hated and despised; the one, his having kept sheep in Thrace, which brought him into contempt (it being well known to all, and considered a great indignity by every one), and the other, his having at the accession to his dominions deferred going to Rome and taking possession of the imperial seat; he had also gained a reputation for the utmost ferocity by having, through his prefects in Rome and elsewhere in the empire, practised many cruelties, so that the whole world was moved to anger at the meanness of his birth and to fear at his barbarity. First Africa rebelled, then the Senate with all the people of Rome, and all Italy conspired against him, to which may be added his own army; this latter, besieging Aquileia and meeting with difficulties in taking it, were disgusted with his cruelties, and fearing him less when they found so many against him, murdered him.

I do not wish to discuss Heliogabalus, Macrinus, or Julian, who, being thoroughly contemptible, were quickly wiped out; but I will bring this discourse to a conclusion by saying that princes in our times have this difficulty of giving inordinate satisfaction to their soldiers in a far less degree, because, notwithstanding one has to give them some indulgence, that is soon done; none of these princes have armies that are veterans in the governance and administration of provinces, as were the armies of the Roman Empire; and whereas it was then more necessary to give satisfaction to the soldiers than to the people, it is now more necessary to all princes, except the Turk and the Soldan, to satisfy the people rather the soldiers, because the people are the more powerful.

From the above I have excepted the Turk, who always keeps round him twelve thousand infantry and fifteen thousand cavalry on which depend the security and strength of the kingdom, and it is necessary that, putting aside every consideration for the people, he should keep them his friends. The kingdom of the Soldan is similar; being entirely in the hands of soldiers, it follows again that, without regard to the people, he must keep them his friends. But you must note that the state of the Soldan is unlike all other principalities, for the reason that it is like the Christian pontificate, which cannot be called either an hereditary or a newly formed principality; because the sons of the old prince are not the heirs, but he who is elected to that position by those who have authority, and the sons remain only noblemen. And this being an ancient custom, it cannot be called a new principality, because there are none of those difficulties in it that are met with in new ones; for although the prince is new, the constitution of the state is old, and it is framed so as to receive him as if he were its hereditary lord.

But returning to the subject of our discourse, I say that whoever will consider it will acknowledge that either hatred or contempt has been fatal to the above-named emperors, and it will be recognized also how it happened that, a number of them acting in one way and a number in another, only one in each way came to a happy end and the rest to unhappy ones. Because it would have been useless and dangerous for Pertinax and Alexander, being new princes, to imitate Marcus, who was heir to the principality; and likewise it would have been utterly destructive to Caracalla, Commodus, and Maximinus to have imitated Severus, they not having sufficient valour to enable them to tread in his footsteps. Therefore a prince, new to the principality, cannot imitate the actions of Marcus, nor, again, is it necessary to follow those of Severus, but he ought to take from Severus those parts which are necessary to found his state, and from Marcus those which are proper and glorious to keep a state that may already be stable and firm.

CHAPTER TWENTY

Are Fortresses, and Many other things to which Princes Often Resort, Advantageous or Hurtful?

1. SOME PRINCES, so as to hold securely the state, have disarmed their subjects; others have kept their subject towns distracted by factions; others have fostered enmities against themselves; others have laid themselves out to gain over those whom they distrusted in the beginning of their governments; some have built fortresses; some have overthrown and destroyed them. And although one cannot give a final judgment on all of these things unless one possesses the particulars of those states in which a decision has to be made, nevertheless I will speak as comprehensively as the matter of itself will admit.

2. There never was a new prince who has disarmed his subjects; rather when he has found them disarmed he has always armed them, because, by arming them, those arms become yours, those men who were distrusted become faithful, and those who were faithful are kept so, and your subjects become your adherents. And whereas all subjects cannot be armed, yet when those whom you do arm are benefited, the others can be handled more freely, and this difference in their treatment, which they quite understand, makes the former your dependents, and the latter, considering it to be necessary that those who have the most danger and service should have the most reward, excuse you. But when you disarm them, you at once offend them by showing that you distrust them, either for cowardice or for want of loyalty, and either of these opinions breeds hatred against you. And because you cannot remain unarmed, it follows that you turn to mercenaries, which are of the character already shown; even if they should be good they would not be sufficient to defend you against powerful enemies and distrusted subjects. Therefore, as I have said, a new prince in a new principality

has always distributed arms. Histories are full of examples. But when a prince acquires a new state, which he adds as a province to his old one, then it is necessary to disarm the men of that state, except those who have been his adherents in acquiring it; and these again, with time and opportunity, should be rendered soft and effeminate; and matters should be managed in such a way that all the armed men in the state shall be your own soldiers who in your old state were living near you.

3. Our forefathers, and those who were reckoned wise, were accustomed to say that it was necessary to hold Pistoia by factions and Pisa by fortresses; and with this idea they fostered quarrels in some of their tributary towns so as to keep possession of them the more easily. This may have been well enough in those times when Italy was in a way balanced, but I do not believe that it can be accepted as a precept for today, because I do not believe that factions can ever be of use; rather it is certain that when the enemy comes upon you in divided cities you are quickly lost, because the weakest party will always assist the outside forces and the other will not be able to resist. The Venetians, moved, as I believe, by the above reasons, fostered the Guelph and Ghibelline factions in their tributary cities; and although they never allowed them to come to bloodshed, yet they nursed these disputes amongst them, so that the citizens, distracted by their differences, should not unite against them. Which, as we saw, did not afterwards turn out as expected, because, after the rout at Vaila, one party at once took courage and seized the state. Such methods argue, therefore, weakness in the prince, because these factions will never be permitted in a vigorous principality; such methods for enabling one the more easily to manage subjects are only useful in times of peace, but if war comes this policy proves fallacious.

4. Without doubt princes become great when they overcome the difficulties and obstacles by which they are confronted, and therefore fortune, especially when she desires to make a new prince great, who has a greater necessity to earn renown than an hereditary one, causes enemies to arise and form designs against him, in order that he may have the opportunity of overcoming them, and by them to mount higher, as by a ladder which his enemies have raised. For this reason many consider that a wise prince, when he has the opportunity, ought with craft to foster some animosity against himself, so that, having crushed it, his renown may rise higher.

5. Princes, especially new ones, have found more fidelity and assistance in those men who in the beginning of their rule were distrusted than among those who in the beginning were trusted. Pandolfo Pe-

trucci, Prince of Siena, ruled his state more by those who had been distrusted than by others. But on this question one cannot speak generally, for it varies so much with the individual; I will only say this, that those men who at the commencement of a princedom have been hostile, if they are of a description to need assistance to support themselves, can always be gained over with the greatest ease, and they will be tightly held to serve the prince with fidelity, inasmuch as they know it to be very necessary for them to cancel by deeds the bad impression which he had formed of them; and thus the prince always extracts more profit from them than from those who, serving him in too much security, may neglect his affairs. And since the matter demands it, I must not fail to warn a prince, who by means of secret favours has acquired a new state, that he must well consider the reasons which induced those to favour him who did so; and if it be not a natural affection towards him, but only discontent with their government, then he will only keep them friendly with great trouble and difficulty, for it will be impossible to satisfy them. And weighing well the reasons for this in those examples which can be taken from ancient and modern affairs, we shall find that it is easier for the prince to make friends of those men who were contented under the former government, and are therefore his enemies, than of those who, being discontented with it, were favourable to him and encouraged him to seize it.

6. It has been a custom with princes, in order to hold their states more securely, to build fortresses that may serve as a bridle and bit to those who might design to work against them, and as a place of refuge from a first attack. I praise this system because it has been made use of formerly. Notwithstanding that, Messer Nicolo Vitelli in our times has been seen to demolish two fortresses in Citta di Castello so that he might keep that state; Guido Ubaldo, Duke of Urbino, on returning to his dominion, whence he had been driven by Cesare Borgia, razed to the foundations all the fortresses in that province, and considered that without them it would be more difficult to lose it; the Bentivogli returning to Bologna came to a similar decision. Fortresses, therefore, are useful or not according to circumstances; if they do you good in one way they injure you in another. And this question can be reasoned thus: the prince who has more to fear from the people than from foreigners ought to build fortresses, but he who has more to fear from foreigners than from the people ought to leave them alone. The castle of Milan, built by Francesco Sforza, has made, and will make, more trouble for the house of Sforza than any other disorder in the state. For this reason the best possible fortress is – not to be hated by the people, because,

although you may hold the fortresses, yet they will not save you if the people hate you, for there will never be wanting foreigners to assist a people who have taken arms against you. It has not been seen in our times that such fortresses have been of use to any prince, unless to the Countess of Forli,[43] when the Count Girolamo, her consort, was killed; for by that means she was able to withstand the popular attack and wait for assistance from Milan, and thus recover her state; and the posture of affairs was such at that time that the foreigners could not assist the people. But fortresses were of little value to her afterwards when Cesare Borgia attacked her, and when the people, her enemy, were allied with foreigners. Therefore, it would have been safer for her, both then and before, not to have been hated by the people than to have had the fortresses. All these things considered then, I shall praise him who builds fortresses as well as him who does not, and I shall blame whoever, trusting in them, cares little about being hated by the people.

---

43   Catherine Sforza, a daughter of Galeazzo Sforza and Lucrezia Landriani, born 1463, died 1509. It was to the Countess of Forli that Machiavelli was sent as envy on 1499. A letter from Fortunati to the countess announces the appointment: "I have been with the signori," wrote Fortunati, "to learn whom they would send and when. They tell me that Nicolo Machiavelli, a learned young Florentine noble, secretary to my Lords of the Ten, is to leave with me at once." Cf. "Catherine Sforza," by Count Pasolini, translated by P. Sylvester, 1898.

CHAPTER TWENTY ONE

How a Prince Should Conduct Himself so as to Gain Renown

NOTHING MAKES A PRINCE so much esteemed as great enterprises and set-ting a fine example. We have in our time Ferdinand of Aragon, the present King of Spain. He can almost be called a new prince, because he has risen, by fame and glory, from being an insignificant king to be the foremost king in Christendom; and if you will consider his deeds you will find them all great and some of them extraordinary. In the beginning of his reign he attacked Granada, and this enterprise was the foundation of his domin-ions. He did this quietly at first and without any fear of hindrance, for he held the minds of the barons of Castile occupied in thinking of the war and not anticipating any innovations; thus they did not perceive that by these means he was acquiring power and authority over them. He was able with the money of the Church and of the people to sustain his armies, and by that long war to lay the foundation for the military skill which has since distinguished him. Further, always using religion as a plea, so as to undertake greater schemes, he devoted himself with pious cruelty to driv-ing out and clearing his kingdom of the Moors; nor could there be a more admirable example, nor one more rare. Under this same cloak he assailed Africa, he came down on Italy, he has finally attacked France; and thus his achievements and designs have always been great, and have kept the minds of his people in suspense and admiration and occupied with the issue of them. And his actions have arisen in such a way, one out of the other, that men have never been given time to work steadily against him.

Again, it much assists a prince to set unusual examples in internal affairs, similar to those which are related of Messer Bernabo da Milano, who, when he had the opportunity, by any one in civil life doing some extraordinary thing, either good or bad, would take some method of rewarding or punishing him, which would be much spoken about. And a prince ought, above all things, always endeavour in every action to gain for himself the reputation of being a great and remarkable man.

A prince is also respected when he is either a true friend or a downright enemy, that is to say, when, without any reservation, he declares himself in favour of one party against the other; which course will always be more advantageous than standing neutral; because if two of your powerful neighbours come to blows, they are of such a character that, if one of them conquers, you have either to fear him or not. In either case it will always be more advantageous for you to declare yourself and to make war strenuously; because, in the first case, if you do not declare yourself, you will invariably fall a prey to the conqueror, to the pleasure and satisfaction of him who has been conquered, and you will have no reasons to offer, nor anything to protect or to shelter you. Because he who conquers does not want doubtful friends who will not aid him in the time of trial; and he who loses will not harbour you because you did not willingly, sword in hand, court his fate.

Antiochus went into Greece, being sent for by the Aetolians to drive out the Romans. He sent envoys to the Achaeans, who were friends of the Romans, exhorting them to remain neutral; and on the other hand the Romans urged them to take up arms. This question came to be discussed in the council of the Achaeans, where the legate of Antiochus urged them to stand neutral. To this the Roman legate answered: "As for that which has been said, that it is better and more advantageous for your state not to interfere in our war, nothing can be more erroneous; because by not interfering you will be left, without favour or consideration, the guerdon of the conqueror." Thus it will always happen that he who is not your friend will demand your neutrality, whilst he who is your friend will entreat you to declare yourself with arms. And irresolute princes, to avoid present dangers, generally follow the neutral path, and are generally ruined. But when a prince declares himself gallantly in favour of one side, if the party with whom he allies himself conquers, although the victor may be powerful and may have him at his mercy, yet he is indebted to him, and there is established a bond of amity; and men are never so shameless as to become a monument of ingratitude by oppressing you. Victories after all are never so complete that the victor must not show some regard, especially to justice. But if he with whom you ally yourself loses, you may be sheltered by him, and whilst he is able he may aid you, and you become companions on a fortune that may rise again.

In the second case, when those who fight are of such a character that you have no anxiety as to who may conquer, so much the more is it greater prudence to be allied, because you assist at the destruction of one by the aid of another who, if he had been wise, would have saved him; and conquering, as it is impossible that he should not do with your assistance, he remains at your discretion. And here it is to be noted that a prince ought to take care never to make an alliance with one more powerful than himself for the purposes of attacking others, unless necessity compels him, as is said above; because if he conquers you are at his discretion, and princes ought to avoid as much as possible being at the discretion of any one. The Venetians joined with France against the Duke of Milan, and this alliance, which caused their ruin, could have been avoided. But when it cannot be avoided, as happened to the Florentines when the Pope and Spain sent armies to attack Lombardy, then in such a case, for the above reasons, the prince ought to favour one of the parties.

Never let any Government imagine that it can choose perfectly safe courses; rather let it expect to have to take very doubtful ones, because it is found in ordinary affairs that one never seeks to avoid one trouble without running into another; but prudence consists in knowing how to distinguish the character of troubles, and for choice to take the lesser evil.

A prince ought also to show himself a patron of ability, and to honour the proficient in every art. At the same time he should encourage his citizens to practise their callings peaceably, both in commerce and agriculture, and in every other following, so that the one should not be deterred from improving his possessions for fear lest they be taken away from him or another from opening up trade for fear of taxes; but the prince ought to offer rewards to whoever wishes to do these things and designs in any way to honour his city or state.

Further, he ought to entertain the people with festivals and spectacles at convenient seasons of the year; and as every city is divided into guilds or into societies,[44] he ought to hold such bodies in esteem, and associate with them sometimes, and show himself an example of courtesy and liberality; nevertheless, always maintaining the majesty of his rank, for this he must never consent to abate in anything.

---

44 "Guilds or societies," "in arti o in tribu." "Arti" were craft or trade guilds, cf. Florio: "Arte . . . a whole company of any trade in any city or corporation town." The guilds of Florence are most admirably described by Mr Edgcumbe Staley in his work on the subject (Methuen, 1906). Institutions of a somewhat similar character, called "artel," exist in Russia today, cf. Sir Mackenzie Wallace's "Russia," ed. 1905: "The sons . . . were always during the working season members of an artel. In some of the larger towns there are artels of a much more complex kind – permanent associations, possessing large capital, and pecuniarily responsible for the acts of the individual members." The word "artel," despite its apparent similarity, has, Mr Aylmer Maude assures me, no connection with "ars" or "arte." Its root is that of the verb "rotisya," to bind oneself by an oath; and it is generally admitted to be only another form of "rota," which now signifies a "regimental company." In both words the underlying idea is that of a body of men united by an oath. "Tribu" were possibly gentile groups, united by common descent, and included individuals connected by marriage. Perhaps our words "sects" or "clans" would be most appropriate.

Concerning the Secretaries of Princes

THE CHOICE OF SERVANTS is of no little importance to a prince, and they are good or not according to the discrimination of the prince. And the first opinion which one forms of a prince, and of his understanding, is by observing the men he has around him; and when they are capable and faithful he may always be considered wise, because he has known how to recognize the capable and to keep them faithful. But when they are otherwise one cannot form a good opinion of him, for the prime error which he made was in choosing them.

There were none who knew Messer Antonio da Venafro as the servant of Pandolfo Petrucci, Prince of Siena, who would not consider Pandolfo to be a very clever man in having Venafro for his servant. Because there are three classes of intellects: one which comprehends by itself; another which appreciates what others comprehended; and a third which neither comprehends by itself nor by the showing of others; the first is the most excellent, the second is good, the third is useless. Therefore, it follows necessarily that, if Pandolfo was not in the first rank, he was in the second, for whenever one has judgment to know good and bad when it is said and done, although he himself may not have the initiative, yet he can recognize the good and the bad in his servant, and the one he can praise and the other correct; thus the servant cannot hope to deceive him, and is kept honest.

But to enable a prince to form an opinion of his servant there is one test which never fails; when you see the servant thinking more of his own interests than of yours, and seeking inwardly his own profit in everything, such a man will never make a good servant, nor will you ever be able to trust him; because he who has the state of another in his hands ought never to think of himself, but always of his prince, and never pay any attention to matters in which the prince is not concerned.

On the other hand, to keep his servant honest the prince ought to study him, honouring him, enriching him, doing him kindnesses, sharing with him the honours and cares; and at the same time let him see that he cannot stand alone, so that many honours may not make him desire more, many riches make him wish for more, and that many cares may make him dread chances. When, therefore, servants, and princes towards servants, are thus disposed, they can trust each other, but when it is otherwise, the end will always be disastrous for either one or the other.

CHAPTER TWENTY THREE

How Flatterers Should be Avoided

I DO NOT WISH TO LEAVE OUT an important branch of this subject, for it is a danger from which princes are with difficulty preserved, unless they are very careful and discriminating. It is that of flatterers, of whom courts are full, because men are so self-complacent in their own affairs, and in a way so deceived in them, that they are preserved with difficulty from this pest, and if they wish to defend themselves they run the danger of falling into contempt. Because there is no other way of guarding oneself from flatterers except letting men understand that to tell you the truth does not offend you; but when every one may tell you the truth, respect for you abates.

Therefore a wise prince ought to hold a third course by choosing the wise men in his state, and giving to them only the liberty of speaking the truth to him, and then only of those things of which he inquires, and of none others; but he ought to question them upon everything, and listen to their opinions, and afterwards form his own conclusions. With these councillors, separately and collectively, he ought to carry himself in such a way that each of them should know that, the more freely he shall speak, the more he shall be preferred; outside of these, he should listen to no one, pursue the thing resolved on, and be steadfast in his resolutions. He who does otherwise is either overthrown by flatterers, or is so often changed by varying opinions that he falls into contempt.

I wish on this subject to adduce a modern example. Fra Luca, the man of affairs to Maximilian,[45] the present emperor, speaking of his

---

45   Maximilian I, born in 1459, died 1519, Emperor of the Holy Roman Empire. He married, first, Mary, daughter of Charles the Bold; after her death, Bianca Sforza; and thus became involved in Italian politics.

majesty, said: He consulted with no one, yet never got his own way in anything. This arose because of his following a practice the opposite to the above; for the emperor is a secretive man – he does not communicate his designs to any one, nor does he receive opinions on them. But as in carrying them into effect they become revealed and known, they are at once obstructed by those men whom he has around him, and he, being pliant, is diverted from them. Hence it follows that those things he does one day he undoes the next, and no one ever understands what he wishes or intends to do, and no one can rely on his resolutions.

A prince, therefore, ought always to take counsel, but only when he wishes and not when others wish; he ought rather to discourage every one from offering advice unless he asks it; but, however, he ought to be a constant inquirer, and afterwards a patient listener concerning the things of which he inquired; also, on learning that any one, on any consideration, has not told him the truth, he should let his anger be felt.

And if there are some who think that a prince who conveys an impression of his wisdom is not so through his own ability, but through the good advisers that he has around him, beyond doubt they are deceived, because this is an axiom which never fails: that a prince who is not wise himself will never take good advice, unless by chance he has yielded his affairs entirely to one person who happens to be a very prudent man. In this case indeed he may be well governed, but it would not be for long, because such a governor would in a short time take away his state from him.

But if a prince who is not inexperienced should take counsel from more than one he will never get united counsels, nor will he know how to unite them. Each of the counsellors will think of his own interests, and the prince will not know how to control them or to see through them. And they are not to found otherwise, because men will always prove untrue to you unless they are kept honest by constraint. Therefore it must be inferred that good counsels, whencesoever they come, are born of the wisdom of the prince, and not the wisdom of the prince from good counsels.

CHAPTER TWENTY FOUR

Why the Princes of Italy have Lost their States

THE PREVIOUS SUGGESTIONS, carefully observed, will enable a new prince to appear well established, and render him at once more secure and fixed in the state than if he had been long seated there. For the actions of a new prince are more narrowly observed than those of an hereditary one, and when they are seen to be able they gain more men and bind far tighter than ancient blood; because men are attracted more by the present than by the past, and when they find the present good they enjoy it and seek no further; they will also make the utmost defence of a prince if he fails them not in other things. Thus it will be a double glory for him to have established a new principality, and adorned and strengthened it with good laws, good arms, good allies, and with a good example; so will it be a double disgrace to him who, born a prince, shall lose his state by want of wisdom.

And if those seigniors are considered who have lost their states in Italy in our times, such as the King of Naples, the Duke of Milan, and others, there will be found in them, firstly, one common defect in regard to arms from the causes which have been discussed at length; in the next place, some one of them will be seen, either to have had the people hostile, or if he has had the people friendly, he has not known how to secure the nobles. In the absence of these defects states that have power enough to keep an army in the field cannot be lost.

Philip of Macedon, not the father of Alexander the Great, but he who was conquered by Titus Quintius, had not much territory compared to the greatness of the Romans and of Greece who attacked him, yet being a warlike man who knew how to attract the people and secure the nobles, he sustained the war against his enemies for many years, and if in the end he lost the dominion of some cities, nevertheless he retained the kingdom.

Therefore, do not let our princes accuse fortune for the loss of their principalities after so many years' possession, but rather their own sloth, because in quiet times they never thought there could be a change (it is a common defect in man not to make any provision in the calm against the tempest), and when afterwards the bad times came they thought of flight and not of defending themselves, and they hoped that the people, disgusted with the insolence of the conquerors, would recall them. This course, when others fail, may be good, but it is very bad to have neglected all other expedients for that, since you would never wish to fall because you trusted to be able to find someone later on to restore you. This again either does not happen, or, if it does, it will not be for your security, because that deliverance is of no avail which does not depend upon yourself; those only are reliable, certain, and durable that depend on yourself and your valour.

CHAPTER TWENTY FIVE

What Fortune Can Effect in Human Affairs and how to Withstand Her

It is not unknown to me how many men have had, and still have, the opinion that the affairs of the world are in such wise governed by fortune and by God that men with their wisdom cannot direct them and that no one can even help them; and because of this they would have us believe that it is not necessary to labour much in affairs, but to let chance govern them. This opinion has been more credited in our times because of the great changes in affairs which have been seen, and may still be seen, every day, beyond all human conjecture. Sometimes pondering over this, I am in some degree inclined to their opinion. Nevertheless, not to extinguish our free will, I hold it to be true that Fortune is the arbiter of one-half of our actions,[46] but that she still leaves us to direct the other half, or perhaps a little less.

I compare her to one of those raging rivers, which when in flood overflows the plains, sweeping away trees and buildings, bearing away the soil from place to place; everything flies before it, all yield to its violence, without being able in any way to withstand it; and yet, though its nature be such, it does not follow therefore that men, when the weather becomes fair, shall not make provision, both with defences and barriers, in such a manner that, rising again, the waters may pass away by canal, and their force be neither so unrestrained nor so dangerous. So it happens with fortune, who shows her power where valour has not prepared to resist her, and thither she turns her forces where she knows that barriers and defences have not been raised to constrain her.

46   Frederick the Great was accustomed to say: "The older one gets the more convinced one becomes that his Majesty King Chance does three-quarters of the business of this miserable universe." Sorel's "Eastern Question."

And if you will consider Italy, which is the seat of these changes, and which has given to them their impulse, you will see it to be an open country without barriers and without any defence. For if it had been defended by proper valour, as are Germany, Spain, and France, either this invasion would not have made the great changes it has made or it would not have come at all. And this I consider enough to say concerning resistance to fortune in general.

But confining myself more to the particular, I say that a prince may be seen happy today and ruined tomorrow without having shown any change of disposition or character. This, I believe, arises firstly from causes that have already been discussed at length, namely, that the prince who relies entirely on fortune is lost when it changes. I believe also that he will be successful who directs his actions according to the spirit of the times, and that he whose actions do not accord with the times will not be successful. Because men are seen, in affairs that lead to the end which every man has before him, namely, glory and riches, to get there by various methods; one with caution, another with haste; one by force, another by skill; one by patience, another by its opposite; and each one succeeds in reaching the goal by a different method. One can also see of two cautious men the one attain his end, the other fail; and similarly, two men by different observances are equally successful, the one being cautious, the other impetuous; all this arises from nothing else than whether or not they conform in their methods to the spirit of the times. This follows from what I have said, that two men working differently bring about the same effect, and of two working similarly, one attains his object and the other does not.

Changes in estate also issue from this, for if, to one who governs himself with caution and patience, times and affairs converge in such a way that his administration is successful, his fortune is made; but if times and affairs change, he is ruined if he does not change his course of action. But a man is not often found sufficiently circumspect to know how to accommodate himself to the change, both because he cannot deviate from what nature inclines him to do, and also because, having always prospered by acting in one way, he cannot be persuaded that it is well to leave it; and, therefore, the cautious man, when it is time to turn adventurous, does not know how to do it, hence he is ruined; but had he changed his conduct with the times fortune would not have changed.

Pope Julius the Second went to work impetuously in all his affairs, and found the times and circumstances conform so well to that line of action that he always met with success. Consider his first enterprise against Bologna, Messer Giovanni Bentivogli being still alive. The Venetians were not agreeable to it, nor was the King of Spain, and he had the enterprise still under discussion with the King of France; nevertheless he personally entered upon the expedition with his accustomed boldness and energy, a move which made Spain and the Venetians stand irresolute and passive, the latter from fear, the former from desire to recover the kingdom of Naples; on the other hand, he drew after him the King of France, because that king, having observed the movement, and desiring to make the Pope his friend so as to humble the Venetians, found it impossible to refuse him. Therefore Julius with his impetuous action accomplished what no other pontiff with simple human wisdom could have done; for if he had waited in Rome until he could get away, with his plans arranged and everything fixed, as any other pontiff would have done, he would never have succeeded. Because the King of France would have made a thousand excuses, and the others would have raised a thousand fears.

I will leave his other actions alone, as they were all alike, and they all succeeded, for the shortness of his life did not let him experience the contrary; but if circumstances had arisen which required him to go cautiously, his ruin would have followed, because he would never have deviated from those ways to which nature inclined him.

I conclude, therefore that, fortune being changeful and mankind steadfast in their ways, so long as the two are in agreement men are successful, but unsuccessful when they fall out. For my part I consider that it is better to be adventurous than cautious, because fortune is a woman, and if you wish to keep her under it is necessary to beat and ill-use her; and it is seen that she allows herself to be mastered by the adventurous rather than by those who go to work more coldly. She is, therefore, always, woman-like, a lover of young men, because they are less cautious, more violent, and with more audacity command her.

CHAPTER TWENTY SIX

An Exhortation to Liberate Italy from the Barbarians

HAVING CAREFULLY CONSIDERED THE SUBJECT of the above discourses, and wondering within myself whether the present times were propitious to a new prince, and whether there were elements that would give an opportunity to a wise and virtuous one to introduce a new order of things which would do honour to him and good to the people of this country, it appears to me that so many things concur to favour a new prince that I never knew a time more fit than the present.

And if, as I said, it was necessary that the people of Israel should be captive so as to make manifest the ability of Moses; that the Persians should be oppressed by the Medes so as to discover the greatness of the soul of Cyrus; and that the Athenians should be dispersed to illustrate the capabilities of Theseus: then at the present time, in order to discover the virtue of an Italian spirit, it was necessary that Italy should be reduced to the extremity that she is now in, that she should be more enslaved than the Hebrews, more oppressed than the Persians, more scattered than the Athenians; without head, without order, beaten, despoiled, torn, overrun; and to have endured every kind of desolation.

Although lately some spark may have been shown by one, which made us think he was ordained by God for our redemption, nevertheless it was afterwards seen, in the height of his career, that fortune rejected him; so that Italy, left as without life, waits for him who shall yet heal her wounds and put an end to the ravaging and plundering of Lombardy, to the swindling and taxing of the kingdom and of Tuscany, and cleanse those sores that for long have festered. It is seen how she entreats God to send someone who shall deliver her from these wrongs and barbarous insolencies. It is seen also that she is ready and willing to follow a banner if only someone will raise it.

Nor is there to be seen at present one in whom she can place more hope than in your illustrious house,[47] with its valour and fortune, favoured by God and by the Church of which it is now the chief, and which could be made the head of this redemption. This will not be difficult if you will recall to yourself the actions and lives of the men I have named. And although they were great and wonderful men, yet they were men, and each one of them had no more opportunity than the present offers, for their enterprises were neither more just nor easier than this, nor was God more their friend than He is yours.

With us there is great justice, because that war is just which is necessary, and arms are hallowed when there is no other hope but in them. Here there is the greatest willingness, and where the willingness is great the difficulties cannot be great if you will only follow those men to whom I have directed your attention. Further than this, how extraordinarily the ways of God have been manifested beyond example: the sea is divided, a cloud has led the way, the rock has poured forth water, it has rained manna, everything has contributed to your greatness; you ought to do the rest. God is not willing to do everything, and thus take away our free will and that share of glory which belongs to us.

And it is not to be wondered at if none of the above-named Italians have been able to accomplish all that is expected from your illustrious house; and if in so many revolutions in Italy, and in so many campaigns, it has always appeared as if military virtue were exhausted, this has happened because the old order of things was not good, and none of us have known how to find a new one. And nothing honours a man more than to establish new laws and new ordinances when he himself was newly risen. Such things when they are well founded and dignified will make him revered and admired, and in Italy there are not wanting opportunities to bring such into use in every form.

Here there is great valour in the limbs whilst it fails in the head. Look attentively at the duels and the hand-to-hand combats, how superior the Italians are in strength, dexterity, and subtlety. But when it comes to armies they do not bear comparison, and this springs entirely from the insufficiency of the leaders, since those who are capable are not obedient, and each one seems to himself to know, there having never been any one so distinguished above the rest, either by valour or fortune,

---

47   Giuliano de Medici. He had just been created a cardinal by Leo X. In 1523 Giuliano was elected Pope, and took the title of Clement VII.

that others would yield to him. Hence it is that for so long a time, and during so much fighting in the past twenty years, whenever there has been an army wholly Italian, it has always given a poor account of itself; the first witness to this is Il Taro, afterwards Allesandria, Capua, Genoa, Vaila, Bologna, Mestri.[48]

If, therefore, your illustrious house wishes to follow these remarkable men who have redeemed their country, it is necessary before all things, as a true foundation for every enterprise, to be provided with your own forces, because there can be no more faithful, truer, or better soldiers. And although singly they are good, altogether they will be much better when they find themselves commanded by their prince, honoured by him, and maintained at his expense. Therefore it is necessary to be prepared with such arms, so that you can be defended against foreigners by Italian valour.

And although Swiss and Spanish infantry may be considered very formidable, nevertheless there is a defect in both, by reason of which a third order would not only be able to oppose them, but might be relied upon to overthrow them. For the Spaniards cannot resist cavalry, and the Switzers are afraid of infantry whenever they encounter them in close combat. Owing to this, as has been and may again be seen, the Spaniards are unable to resist French cavalry, and the Switzers are overthrown by Spanish infantry. And although a complete proof of this latter cannot be shown, nevertheless there was some evidence of it at the battle of Ravenna, when the Spanish infantry were confronted by German battalions, who follow the same tactics as the Swiss; when the Spaniards, by agility of body and with the aid of their shields, got in under the pikes of the Germans and stood out of danger, able to attack, while the Germans stood helpless, and, if the cavalry had not dashed up, all would have been over with them. It is possible, therefore, knowing the defects of both these infantries, to invent a new one, which will resist cavalry and not be afraid of infantry; this need not create a new order of arms, but a variation upon the old. And these are the kind of improvements which confer reputation and power upon a new prince.

This opportunity, therefore, ought not to be allowed to pass for letting Italy at last see her liberator appear. Nor can one express the love with which he would be received in all those provinces which have suffered so much from these foreign scourings, with what thirst for revenge, with what stubborn faith, with what devotion, with what tears.

48   The battles of Il Taro, 1495; Alessandria, 1499; Capua, 1501; Genoa, 1507; Vaila, 1509; Bologna, 1511; Mestri, 1513.

What door would be closed to him? Who would refuse obedience to him? What envy would hinder him? What Italian would refuse him homage? To all of us this barbarous dominion stinks. Let, therefore, your illustrious house take up this charge with that courage and hope with which all just enterprises are undertaken, so that under its standard our native country may be ennobled, and under its auspices may be verified that saying of Petrarch:

Virtu contro al Furore
Prendera l'arme, e fia il combatter corto:
Che l'antico valore
Negli italici cuor non e ancor morto.

Virtue against fury shall advance the fight,
And it i' th' combat soon shall put to flight:
For the old Roman valour is not dead,
Nor in th' Italians' brests extinguished.

Edward Dacre, 1640.

ON WAR

CONTENTS

BOOK SIX. Defence

INTRODUCTION

THE GERMANS interpret their new national colours – black, red, and white – by the saying, "Durch Nacht und Blut zur licht." ("Through night and blood to light"), and no work yet written conveys to the thinker a clearer conception of all that the red streak in their flag stands for than this deep and philosophical analysis of "War" by Clausewitz.

It reveals "War," stripped of all accessories, as the exercise of force for the attainment of a political object, unrestrained by any law save that of expediency, and thus gives the key to the interpretation of German political aims, past, present, and future, which is unconditionally necessary for every student of the modern conditions of Europe. Step by step, every event since Waterloo follows with logical consistency from the teachings of Napoleon, formulated for the first time, some twenty years afterwards, by this remarkable thinker.

What Darwin accomplished for Biology generally Clausewitz did for the Life-History of Nations nearly half a century before him, for both have proved the existence of the same law in each case, viz., "The survival of the fittest" – the "fittest," as Huxley long since pointed out, not being necessarily synonymous with the ethically "best." Neither of these thinkers was concerned with the ethics of the struggle which each studied so exhaustively, but to both men the phase or condition presented itself neither as moral nor immoral, any more than are famine, disease, or other natural phenomena, but as emanating from a force inherent in all living organisms which can only be mastered by understanding its nature. It is in that spirit that, one after the other, all the Nations of the Continent, taught by such drastic lessons as Koniggrätz and Sedan, have accepted the lesson, with the result that to-day Europe is an armed camp, and peace is maintained by the equilibrium of forces, and will continue just as long as this equilibrium exists, and no longer.

Whether this state of equilibrium is in itself a good or desirable thing may be open to argument. I have discussed it at length in my "War and the World's Life"; but I venture to suggest that to no one would a renewal of the era of warfare be a change for the better, as far as existing humanity is concerned. Meanwhile, however, with every year that elapses the forces at present in equilibrium are changing in magnitude – the pressure of populations which have to be fed is rising, and an explosion along the line of least resistance is, sooner or later, inevitable.

As I read the teaching of the recent Hague Conference, no responsible Government on the Continent is anxious to form in themselves that line of least resistance; they know only too well what War would mean; and we alone, absolutely unconscious of the trend of the dominant thought of Europe, are pulling down the dam which may at any moment let in on us the flood of invasion.

Now no responsible man in Europe, perhaps least of all in Germany, thanks us for this voluntary destruction of our defences, for all who are of any importance would very much rather end their days in peace than incur the burden of responsibility which War would entail. But they realise that the gradual dissemination of the principles taught by Clausewitz has created a condition of molecular tension in the minds of the Nations they govern analogous to the "critical temperature of water heated above boiling-point under pressure," which may at any moment bring about an explosion which they will be powerless to control.

The case is identical with that of an ordinary steam boiler, delivering so and so many pounds of steam to its engines as long as the envelope can contain the pressure; but let a breach in its continuity arise – relieving the boiling water of all restraint – and in a moment the whole mass flashes into vapour, developing a power no work of man can oppose.

The ultimate consequences of defeat no man can foretell. The only way to avert them is to ensure victory; and, again following out the principles of Clausewitz, victory can only be ensured by the creation in peace of an organisation which will bring every available man, horse, and gun (or ship and gun, if the war be on the sea) in the shortest possible time, and with the utmost possible momentum, upon the decisive field of action – which in turn leads to the final doctrine formulated by Von der Goltz in excuse for the action of the late President Kruger in 1899:

"The Statesman who, knowing his instrument to be ready, and seeing War inevitable, hesitates to strike first is guilty of a crime against his country."

It is because this sequence of cause and effect is absolutely unknown to our Members of Parliament, elected by popular representation, that all our efforts to ensure a lasting peace by securing efficiency with economy in our National Defences have been rendered nugatory.

This estimate of the influence of Clausewitz's sentiments on contemporary thought in Continental Europe may appear exaggerated to those who have not familiarised themselves with M. Gustav de Bon's exposition of the laws governing the formation and conduct of crowds I do not wish for one minute to be understood as asserting that Clausewitz has been conscientiously studied and understood in any Army, not even in the Prussian, but his work has been the ultimate foundation on which every drill regulation in Europe, except our own, has been reared. It is this ceaseless repetition of his fundamental ideas to which one-half of the male population of every Continental Nation has been subjected for two to three years of their lives, which has tuned their minds to vibrate in harmony with his precepts, and those who know and appreciate this fact at its true value have only to strike the necessary chords in order to evoke a response sufficient to overpower any other ethical conception which those who have not organised their forces beforehand can appeal to.

The recent set-back experienced by the Socialists in Germany is an illustration of my position. The Socialist leaders of that country are far behind the responsible Governors in their knowledge of the management of crowds. The latter had long before (in 1893, in fact) made their arrangements to prevent the spread of Socialistic propaganda beyond certain useful limits. As long as the Socialists only threatened capital they were not seriously interfered with, for the Government knew quite well that the undisputed sway of the employer was not for the ultimate good of the State. The standard of comfort must not be pitched too low if men are to be ready to die for their country. But the moment the Socialists began to interfere seriously with the discipline of the Army the word went round, and the Socialists lost heavily at the polls.

If this power of predetermined reaction to acquired ideas can be evoked successfully in a matter of internal interest only, in which the "obvious interest" of the vast majority of the population is so clearly on the side of the Socialist, it must be evident how enormously greater it will prove when set in motion against an external enemy, where the "obvious interest" of the people is, from the very nature of things, as manifestly on the side of the Government; and the Statesman who failed to take into account the force of the "resultant thought wave" of a crowd of some seven million men, all trained to respond to their ruler's call, would be guilty of treachery as grave as one who failed to strike when he knew the Army to be ready for immediate action.

As already pointed out, it is to the spread of Clausewitz's ideas that the present state of more or less immediate readiness for war of all European Armies is due, and since the organisation of these forces is uniform this "more or less" of readiness exists in precise proportion to the sense of duty which animates the several Armies. Where the spirit of duty and self-sacrifice is low the troops are unready and inefficient; where, as in Prussia, these qualities, by the training of a whole century, have become instinctive, troops really are ready to the last button, and might be poured down upon any one of her neighbours with such rapidity that the very first collision must suffice to ensure ultimate success – a success by no means certain if the enemy, whoever he may be, is allowed breathing-time in which to set his house in order.

An example will make this clearer. In 1887 Germany was on the very verge of War with France and Russia. At that moment her superior efficiency, the consequence of this inborn sense of duty – surely one of the highest qualities of humanity – was so great that it is more than probable that less than six weeks would have sufficed to bring the French to their knees. Indeed, after the first fortnight it would have been possible to begin transferring troops from the Rhine to the Niemen; and the same case may arise again. But if France and Russia had been allowed even ten days' warning the German plan would have been completely defeated. France alone might then have claimed all the efforts that Germany could have put forth to defeat her.

Yet there are politicians in England so grossly ignorant of the German reading of the Napoleonic lessons that they expect that Nation to sacrifice the enormous advantage they have prepared by a whole century of self-sacrifice and practical patriotism by an appeal to a Court of Arbitration, and the further delays which must arise by going through the medieaeval formalities of recalling Ambassadors and exchanging ultimatums.

Most of our present-day politicians have made their money in business – a "form of human competition greatly resembling War," to paraphrase Clausewitz. Did they, when in the throes of such competition, send formal notice to their rivals of their plans to get the better of them in commerce? Did Mr. Carnegie, the arch-priest of Peace at any price, when he built up the Steel Trust, notify his competitors when and how he proposed to strike the blows which successively made him master of millions? Surely the Directors of a Great Nation may consider the interests of their shareholders – i.e., the people they govern – as sufficiently serious not to be endangered by the deliberate sacrifice of the preponderant position of readiness which generations of self-devotion, patriotism and wise forethought have won for them?

As regards the strictly military side of this work, though the recent researches of the French General Staff into the records and documents of the Napoleonic period have shown conclusively that Clausewitz had never grasped the essential point of the Great Emperor's strategic method, yet it is admitted that he has completely fathomed the spirit which gave life to the form; and notwithstandingthe variations in application which have resulted from the progress of invention in every field of national activity (not in the technical improvements in armament alone), this spirit still remains the essential factor in the whole matter. Indeed, if anything, modern appliances have intensified its importance, for though, with equal armaments on both sides, the form of battles must always remain the same, the facility and certainty of combination which better methods of communicating orders and intelligence have conferred upon the Commanders has rendered the control of great masses immeasurably more certain than it was in the past.

Men kill each other at greater distances, it is true – but killing is a constant factor in all battles. The difference between "now and then" lies in this, that, thanks to the enormous increase in range (the essential feature in modern armaments), it is possible to concentrate by surprise, on any chosen spot, a man-killing power fully twentyfold greater than was conceivable in the days of Waterloo; and whereas in Napoleon's time this concentration of man-killing power (which in his hands took the form of the great case-shot attack) depended almost entirely on the shape and condition of the ground, which might or might not be favourable, nowadays such concentration of fire-power is almost independent of the country altogether.

Thus, at Waterloo, Napoleon was compelled to wait till the ground became firm enough for his guns to gallop over; nowadays every gun at his disposal, and five times that number had he possessed them, might have opened on any point in the British position he had selected, as soon as it became light enough to see.

Or, to take a more modern instance, viz., the battle of St. Privat-Gravelotte, August 18, 1870, where the Germans were able to concentrate on both wings batteries of two hundred guns and upwards, it would have been practically impossible, owing to the section of the slopes of the French position, to carry out the old-fashioned case-shot attack at all. Nowadays there would be no difficulty in turning on the fire of two thousand guns on any point of the position, and switching this fire up and down the line like water from a fire-engine hose, if the occasion demanded such concentration.

But these alterations in method make no difference in the truth of the picture of War which Clausewitz presents, with which every soldier, and above all every Leader, should be saturated.

Death, wounds, suffering, and privation remain the same, whatever the weapons employed, and their reaction on the ultimate nature of man is the same now as in the struggle a century ago. It is this reaction that the Great Commander has to understand and prepare himself to control; and the task becomes ever greater as, fortunately for humanity, the opportunities for gathering experience become more rare.

In the end, and with every improvement in science, the result depends more and more on the character of the Leader and his power of resisting "the sensuous impressions of the battlefield." Finally, for those who would fit themselves in advance for such responsibility, I know of no more inspiring advice than that given by Krishna to Arjuna ages ago, when the latter trembled before the awful responsibility of launching his Army against the hosts of the Pandav's:

> This Life within all living things, my Prince,
> Hides beyond harm. Scorn thou to suffer, then,
> For that which cannot suffer. Do thy part!
> Be mindful of thy name, and tremble not.
> Nought better can betide a martial soul
> Than lawful war. Happy the warrior
> To whom comes joy of battle....
> ... But if thou shunn'st
> This honourable field – a Kshittriya –
> If, knowing thy duty and thy task, thou bidd'st
> Duty and task go by – that shall be sin!
> And those to come shall speak thee infamy
> From age to age. But infamy is worse
> For men of noble blood to bear than death!
>
> . . . . . .
>
> Therefore arise, thou Son of Kunti! Brace
> Thine arm for conflict; nerve thy heart to meet,
> As things alike to thee, pleasure or pain,
> Profit or ruin, victory or defeat.
> So minded, gird thee to the fight, for so
> Thou shalt not sin!

Col. F. N. Maude, C.B., late R.E.

PREFACE TO THE FIRST EDITION

IT WILL NATURALLY excite surprise that a preface by a female hand
should accompany a work on such a subject as the present. For my
friends no explanation of the circumstance is required; but I hope by
a simple relation of the cause to clear myself of the appearance of presumption in the eyes also of those to whom I am not known.

The work to which these lines serve as a preface occupied almost
entirely the last twelve years of the life of my inexpressibly beloved husband, who has unfortunately been torn too soon from myself and his
country. To complete it was his most earnest desire; but it was not his
intention that it should be published during his life; and if I tried to
persuade him to alter that intention, he often answered, half in jest, but
also, perhaps, half in a foreboding of early death: "Thou shalt publish
it." These words (which in those happy days often drew tears from me,
little as I was inclined to attach a serious meaning to them) make it now,
in the opinion of my friends, a duty incumbent on me to introduce the
posthumous works of my beloved husband, with a few prefatory lines
from myself; and although here may be a difference of opinion on this
point, still I am sure there will be no mistake as to the feeling which has
prompted me to overcome the timidity which makes any such appearance, even in a subordinate part, so difficult for a woman.

It will be understood, as a matter of course, that I cannot have the most
remote intention of considering myself as the real editress of a work which
is far above the scope of my capacity: I only stand at its side as an affec-
tionate companion on its entrance into the world. This position I may well
claim, as a similar one was allowed me during its formation and progress.
Those who are acquainted with our happy married life, and know how
we shared everything with each other – not only joy and sorrow, but also
every occupation, every interest of daily life – will understand that my
beloved husband could not be occupied on a work of this kind without

its being known to me. Therefore, no one can like me bear testimony to
the zeal, to the love with which he laboured on it, to the hopes which he
bound up with it, as well as the manner and time of its elaboration. His
richly gifted mind had from his early youth longed for light and truth,
and, varied as were his talents, still he had chiefly directed his reflections
to the science of war, to which the duties of his profession called him,
and which are of such importance for the benefit of States. Scharnhorst
was the first to lead him into the right road, and his subsequent appointment in 1810 as Instructor at the General War School, as well as the honour conferred on him at the same time of giving military instruction to
H.R.H. the Crown Prince, tended further to give his investigations and
studies that direction, and to lead him to put down in writing whatever
conclusions he arrived at. A paper with which he finished the instruction
of H.R.H. the Crown Prince contains the germ of his subsequent works.
But it was in the year 1816, at Coblentz, that he first devoted himself again
to scientific labours, and to collecting the fruits which his rich experience
in those four eventful years had brought to maturity. He wrote down his
views, in the first place, in short essays, only loosely connected with each
other. The following, without date, which has been found amongst his
papers, seems to belong to those early days.

"In the principles here committed to paper, in my opinion, the chief
things which compose Strategy, as it is called, are touched upon. I
looked upon them only as materials, and had just got to such a length
towards the moulding them into a whole.

"These materials have been amassed without any regularly preconceived plan. My view was at first, without regard to system and strict
connection, to put down the results of my reflections upon the most important points in quite brief, precise, compact propositions. The manner
in which Montesquieu has treated his subject floated before me in idea. I
thought that concise, sententious chapters, which I proposed at first to call
grains, would attract the attention of the intelligent just as much by that
which was to be developed from them, as by that which they contained in
themselves. I had, therefore, before me in idea, intelligent readers already
acquainted with the subject. But my nature, which always impels me to
development and systematising, at last worked its way out also in this instance. For some time I was able to confine myself to extracting only the
most important results from the essays, which, to attain clearness and conviction in my own mind, I wrote upon different subjects, to concentrating
in that manner their spirit in a small compass; but afterwards my peculiarity gained ascendency completely – I have developed what I could, and
thus naturally have supposed a reader not yet acquainted with the subject.

"The more I advanced with the work, and the more I yielded to the spirit of investigation, so much the more I was also led to system; and thus, then, chapter after chapter has been inserted.

"My ultimate view has now been to go through the whole once more, to establish by further explanation much of the earlier treatises, and perhaps to condense into results many analyses on the later ones, and thus to make a moderate whole out of it, forming a small octavo volume. But it was my wish also in this to avoid everything common, everything that is plain of itself, that has been said a hundred times, and is generally accepted; for my ambition was to write a book that would not be forgotten in two or three years, and which any one interested in the subject would at all events take up more than once."

In Coblentz, where he was much occupied with duty, he could only give occasional hours to his private studies. It was not until 1818, after his appointment as Director of the General Academy of War at Berlin, that he had the leisure to expand his work, and enrich it from the history of modern wars. This leisure also reconciled him to his new avocation, which, in other respects, was not satisfactory to him, as, according to the existing organisation of the Academy, the scientific part of the course is not under the Director, but conducted by a Board of Studies. Free as he was from all petty vanity, from every feeling of restless, egotistical ambition, still he felt a desire to be really useful, and not to leave inactive the abilities with which God had endowed him. In active life he was not in a position in which this longing could be satisfied, and he had little hope of attaining to any such position: his whole energies were therefore directed upon the domain of science, and the benefit which he hoped to lay the foundation of by his work was the object of his life. That, notwithstanding this, the resolution not to let the work appear until after his death became more confirmed is the best proof that no vain, paltry longing for praise and distinction, no particle of egotistical views, was mixed up with this noble aspiration for great and lasting usefulness.

Thus he worked diligently on, until, in the spring of 1830, he was appointed to the artillery, and his energies were called into activity in such a different sphere, and to such a high degree, that he was obliged, for the moment at least, to give up all literary work. He then put his papers in order, sealed up the separate packets, labelled them, and took sorrowful leave of this employment which he loved so much. He was sent to Breslau in August of the same year, as Chief of the Second Artillery District, but in December recalled to Berlin, and appointed Chief of the Staff to Field-Marshal Count Gneisenau (for the term of his command). In March 1831, he accompanied his revered Commander to Posen. When he returned from there to Breslau in November after the melancholy event which had taken place, he hoped to resume his work and perhaps complete it in the course of the winter. The Almighty has willed it should be otherwise. On the 7th November he returned to Breslau; on the 16th he was no more; and the packets sealed by himself were not opened until after his death.

The papers thus left are those now made public in the following volumes, exactly in the condition in which they were found, without a word being added or erased. Still, however, there was much to do before publication, in the way of putting them in order and consulting about them; and I am deeply indebted to several sincere friends for the assistance they have afforded me, particularly Major O'Etzel, who kindly undertook the correction of the Press, as well as the preparation of the maps to accompany the historical parts of the work. I must also mention my much-loved brother, who was my support in the hour of my misfortune, and who has also done much for me in respect of these papers; amongst other things, by carefully examining and putting them in order, he found the commencement of the revision which my dear husband wrote in the year 1827, and mentions in the Notice hereafter annexed as a work he had in view. This revision has been inserted in the place intended for it in the first book (for it does not go any further).

There are still many other friends to whom I might offer my thanks for their advice, for the sympathy and friendship which they have shown me; but if I do not name them all, they will, I am sure, not have any doubts of my sincere gratitude. It is all the greater, from my firm conviction that all they have done was not only on my own account, but for the friend whom God has thus called away from them so soon.

If I have been highly blessed as the wife of such a man during one and twenty years, so am I still, notwithstanding my irreparable loss, by the treasure of my recollections and of my hopes, by the rich legacy of sympathy and friendship which I owe the beloved departed, by the elevating feeling which I experience at seeing his rare worth so generally and honourably acknowledged.

The trust confided to me by a Royal Couple is a fresh benefit for which I have to thank the Almighty, as it opens to me an honourable occupation, to which I devote myself. May this occupation be blessed, and may the dear little Prince who is now entrusted to my care, some day read this book, and be animated by it to deeds like those of his glorious ancestors.

Written at the Marble Palace, Potsdam, 30th June, 1832.

Marie Von Clausewitz, Born Countess Bruhl, Oberhofmeisterinn to H.R.H. the Princess William.

NOTICE

I LOOK UPON the first six books, of which a fair copy has now been made, as only a mass which is still in a manner without form, and which has yet to be again revised. In this revision the two kinds of War will be everywhere kept more distinctly in view, by which all ideas will acquire a clearer meaning, a more precise direction, and a closer application. The two kinds of War are, first, those in which the object is the *overthrow of the enemy*, whether it be that we aim at his destruction, politically, or merely at disarming him and forcing him to conclude peace on our terms; and next, those in which our object is *merely to make some conquests on the frontiers of his country*, either for the purpose of retaining them permanently, or of turning them to account as matter of exchange in the settlement of a peace. Transition from one kind to the other must certainly continue to exist, but the completely different nature of the tendencies of the two must everywhere appear, and must separate from each other things which are incompatible.

Besides establishing this real difference in Wars, another practically necessary point of view must at the same time be established, which is, that *war is only a continuation of state policy by other means.* This point of view being adhered to everywhere, will introduce much more unity into the consideration of the subject, and things will be more easily disentangled from each other. Although the chief application of this point of view does not commence until we get to the eighth book, still it must be completely developed in the first book, and also lend assistance throughout the revision of the first six books. Through such a revision the first six books will get rid of a good deal of dross, many rents and chasms will be closed up, and much that is of a general nature will be transformed into distinct conceptions and forms.

The seventh book – on attack – for the different chapters of which sketches are already made, is to be considered as a reflection of the sixth, and must be completed at once, according to the above-mentioned more distinct points of view, so that it will require no fresh revision, but rather may serve as a model in the revision of the first six books.

For the eighth book – on the Plan of a War, that is, of the organisation of a whole War in general – several chapters are designed, but they are not at all to be regarded as real materials, they are merely a track, roughly cleared, as it were, through the mass, in order by that means to ascertain the points of most importance. They have answered this object, and I propose, on finishing the seventh book, to proceed at once to the working out of the eighth, where the two points of view above mentioned will be chiefly affirmed, by which everything will be simplified, and at the same time have a spirit breathed into it. I hope in this book to iron out many creases in the heads of strategists and statesmen, and at least to show the object of action, and the real point to be considered in War.

Now, when I have brought my ideas clearly out by finishing this eighth book, and have properly established the leading features of War, it will be easier for me to carry the spirit of these ideas in to the first six books, and to make these same features show themselves everywhere. Therefore I shall defer till then the revision of the first six books.

Should the work be interrupted by my death, then what is found can only be called a mass of conceptions not brought into form; but as these are open to endless misconceptions, they will doubtless give rise to a number of crude criticisms: for in these things, every one thinks, when he takes up his pen, that whatever comes into his head is worth saying and printing, and quite as incontrovertible as that twice two make four. If such a one would take the pains, as I have done, to think over the subject, for years, and to compare his ideas with military history, he would certainly be a little more guarded in his criticism.

Still, notwithstanding this imperfect form, I believe that an impartial reader thirsting for truth and conviction will rightly appreciate in the first six books the fruits of several years' reflection and a diligent study of War, and that, perhaps, he will find in them some leading ideas which may bring about a revolution in the theory of War.

Berlin, 10th July, 1827.

Besides this notice, amongst the papers left the following unfinished memorandum was found, which appears of very recent date:

The manuscript on the conduct of the Grande Guerre, which will be found after my death, in its present state can only be regarded as a collection of materials from which it is intended to construct a theory of War. With the greater part I am not yet satisfied; and the sixth book is to be looked at as a mere essay: I should have completely remodelled it, and have tried a different line.

But the ruling principles which pervade these materials I hold to be the right ones: they are the result of a very varied reflection, keeping always in view the reality, and always bearing in mind what I have learnt by experience and by my intercourse with distinguished soldiers.

The seventh book is to contain the attack, the subjects of which are thrown together in a hasty manner: the eighth, the plan for a War, in which I would have examined War more especially in its political and human aspects.

The first chapter of the first book is the only one which I consider as completed; it will at least serve to show the manner in which I proposed to treat the subject throughout.

The theory of the Grande Guerre, or Strategy, as it is called, is beset with extraordinary difficulties, and we may affirm that very few men have clear conceptions of the separate subjects, that is, conceptions carried up to their full logical conclusions. In real action most men are guided merely by the tact of judgment which hits the object more or less accurately, according as they possess more or less genius.

This is the way in which all great Generals have acted, and therein partly lay their greatness and their genius, that they always hit upon what was right by this tact. Thus also it will always be in action, and so far this tact is amply sufficient. But when it is a question, not of acting oneself, but of convincing others in a consultation, then all depends on clear conceptions and demonstration of the inherent relations, and so little progress has been made in this respect that most deliberations are merely a contention of words, resting on no firm basis, and ending either in every one retaining his own opinion, or in a compromise from mutual considerations of respect, a middle course really without any value.[1]

Clear ideas on these matters are therefore not wholly useless; besides, the human mind has a general tendency to clearness, and always wants to be consistent with the necessary order of things.

---

1   Herr Clausewitz evidently had before his mind the endless consultations at the Headquarters of the Bohemian Army in the Leipsic Campaign 1813.

Owing to the great difficulties attending a philosophical construction of the Art of War, and the many attempts at it that have failed, most people have come to the conclusion that such a theory is impossible, because it concerns things which no standing law can embrace. We should also join in this opinion and give up any attempt at a theory, were it not that a great number of propositions make themselves evident without any difficulty, as, for instance, that the defensive form, with a negative object, is the stronger form, the attack, with the positive object, the weaker – that great results carry the little ones with them – that, therefore, strategic effects may be referred to certain centres of gravity – that a demonstration is a weaker application of force than a real attack, that, therefore, there must be some special reason for resorting to the former – that victory consists not merely in the conquest on the field of battle, but in the destruction of armed forces, physically and morally, which can in general only be effected by a pursuit after the battle is gained – that successes are always greatest at the point where the victory has been gained, that, therefore, the change from one line and object to another can only be regarded as a necessary evil – that a turning movement is only justified by a superiority of numbers generally or by the advantage of our lines of communication and retreat over those of the enemy – that flank positions are only justifiable on similar grounds – that every attack becomes weaker as it progresses.

THE INTRODUCTION OF THE AUTHOR

THAT THE CONCEPTION of the scientific does not consist alone, or chiefly, in system, and its finished theoretical constructions, requires nowadays no exposition. System in this treatise is not to be found on the surface, and instead of a finished building of theory, there are only materials.

The scientific form lies here in the endeavour to explore the nature of military phenomena to show their affinity with the nature of the things of which they are composed. Nowhere has the philosophical argument been evaded, but where it runs out into too thin a thread the Author has preferred to cut it short, and fall back upon the corresponding results of experience; for in the same way as many plants only bear fruit when they do not shoot too high, so in the practical arts the theoretical leaves and flowers must not be made to sprout too far, but kept near to experience, which is their proper soil.

Unquestionably it would be a mistake to try to discover from the chemical ingredients of a grain of corn the form of the ear of corn which it bears, as we have only to go to the field to see the ears ripe. Investigation and observation, philosophy and experience, must neither despise nor exclude one another; they mutually afford each other the rights of citizenship. Consequently, the propositions of this book, with their arch of inherent necessity, are supported either by experience or by the conception of War itself as external points, so that they are not without abutments.[2]

It is, perhaps, not impossible to write a systematic theory of War full of spirit and substance, but ours hitherto, have been very much the reverse. To say nothing of their unscientific spirit, in their striving after

2   That this is not the case in the works of many military writers especially of those who have aimed at treating of War itself in a scientific manner, is shown in many instances, in which by their reasoning, the pro and contra swallow each other up so effectually that there is no   vestige of the tails even which were left in the case of the two lions.

coherence and completeness of system, they overflow with common-places, truisms, and twaddle of every kind. If we want a striking picture of them we have only to read Lichtenberg's extract from a code of regulations in case of fire.

If a house takes fire, we must seek, above all things, to protect the right side of the house standing on the left, and, on the other hand, the left side of the house on the right; for if we, for example, should protect the left side of the house on the left, then the right side of the house lies to the right of the left, and consequently as the fire lies to the right of this side, and of the right side (for we have assumed that the house is situated to the left of the fire), therefore the right side is situated nearer to the fire than the left, and the right side of the house might catch fire if it was not protected before it came to the left, which is protected. Consequently, something might be burnt that is not protected, and that sooner than something else would be burnt, even if it was not protected; consequently we must let alone the latter and protect the former. In order to impress the thing on one's mind, we have only to note if the house is situated to the right of the fire, then it is the left side, and if the house is to the left it is the right side.

In order not to frighten the intelligent reader by such common-places, and to make the little good that there is distasteful by pouring water upon it, the Author has preferred to give in small ingots of fine metal his impressions and convictions, the result of many years' reflection on War, of his intercourse with men of ability, and of much personal experience. Thus the seemingly weakly bound-together chapters of this book have arisen, but it is hoped they will not be found wanting in logical connection. Perhaps soon a greater head may appear, and instead of these single grains, give the whole in a casting of pure metal without dross.

BRIEF MEMOIR OF GENERAL CLAUSEWITZ

THE AUTHOR of the work here translated, General Carl Von Clausewitz, was born at Burg, near Magdeburg, in 1780, and entered the Prussian Army as Fahnenjunker (i.e., ensign) in 1792. He served in the campaigns of 1793-94 on the Rhine, after which he seems to have devoted some time to the study of the scientific branches of his profession. In 1801 he entered the Military School at Berlin, and remained there till 1803. During his residence there he attracted the notice of General Scharnhorst, then at the head of the establishment; and the patronage of this distinguished officer had immense influence on his future career, and we may gather from his writings that he ever afterwards continued to entertain a high esteem for Scharnhorst. In the campaign of 1806 he served as Aide-de-camp to Prince Augustus of Prussia; and being wounded and taken prisoner, he was sent into France until the close of that war. On his return, he was placed on General Scharnhorst's Staff, and employed in the work then going on for the reorganisation of the Army. He was also at this time selected as military instructor to the late King of Prussia, then Crown Prince. In 1812 Clausewitz, with several other Prussian officers, having entered the Russian service, his first appointment was as Aide-de-camp to General Phul. Afterwards, while serving with Wittgenstein's army, he assisted in negotiating the famous convention of Tauroggen with York. Of the part he took in that affair he has left an interesting account in his work on the "Russian Campaign." It is there stated that, in order to bring the correspondence which had been carried on with York to a termination in one way or another, the Author was despatched to York's headquarters with two letters, one was from General d'Auvray, the Chief of the Staff of Wittgenstein's army, to General Diebitsch, showing the arrangements made to cut off York's corps from Macdonald (this was necessary in order to give York a plausible excuse for seceding from the French); the other was an intercepted letter from Macdonald to the Duke of Bassano. With regard to the former of these, the Author says, "it would not have had weight with a man like York, but for a military justification, if the Prussian Court should require one as against the French, it was important."

The second letter was calculated at the least to call up in General York's mind all the feelings of bitterness which perhaps for some days past had been diminished by the consciousness of his own behaviour towards the writer.

As the Author entered General York's chamber, the latter called out to him, "Keep off from me; I will have nothing more to do with you; your d – – d Cossacks have let a letter of Macdonald's pass through them, which brings me an order to march on Piktrepohnen, in order there to effect our junction. All doubt is now at an end; your troops do not come up; you are too weak; march I must, and I must excuse myself from further negotiation, which may cost me my head." The Author said that be would make no opposition to all this, but begged for a candle, as he had letters to show the General, and, as the latter seemed still to hesitate, the Author added, "Your Excellency will not surely place me in the embarrassment of departing without having executed my commission." The General ordered candles, and called in Colonel von Roeder, the chief of his staff, from the ante-chamber. The letters were read. After a pause of an instant, the General said, "Clausewitz, you are a Prussian, do you believe that the letter of General d'Auvray is sincere, and that Wittgenstein's troops will really be at the points he mentioned on the 31st?" The Author replied, "I pledge myself for the sincerity of this letter upon the knowledge I have of General d'Auvray and the other men of Wittgenstein's headquarters; whether the dispositions he announces can be accomplished as he lays down I certainly cannot pledge myself; for your Excellency knows that in war we must often fall short of the line we have drawn for ourselves." The General was silent for a few minutes of earnest reflection; then he held out his hand to the Author, and said, "You have me. Tell General Diebitsch that we must confer early tomorrow at the mill of Poschenen, and that I am now firmly determined to separate myself from the French and their cause." The hour was fixed for 8 A.M. After this was settled, the General added, "But I will not do the thing by halves, I will get you Massenbach also." He called in an officer who was of Massenbach's cavalry, and who had just left them. Much like Schiller's Wallenstein, he asked, walking up and down the room the while, "What say your regiments?" The officer broke out with enthusiasm at the idea of a riddance from the French alliance, and said that every man of the troops in question felt the same.

"You young ones may talk; but my older head is shaking on my shoulders," replied the General.[3]

After the close of the Russian campaign Clausewitz remained in the service of that country, but was attached as a Russian staff officer to Blucher's headquarters till the Armistice in 1813.

In 1814, he became Chief of the Staff of General Walmoden's Russo-German Corps, which formed part of the Army of the North under Bernadotte. His name is frequently mentioned with distinction in that campaign, particularly in connection with the affair of Goehrde.

Clausewitz re-entered the Prussian service in 1815, and served as Chief of the Staff to Thielman's corps, which was engaged with Grouchy at Wavre, on the 18th of June.

After the Peace, he was employed in a command on the Rhine. In 1818, he became Major-General, and Director of the Military School at which he had been previously educated.

In 1830, he was appointed Inspector of Artillery at Breslau, but soon after nominated Chief of the Staff to the Army of Observation, under Marshal Gneisenau on the Polish frontier.

The latest notices of his life and services are probably to be found in the memoirs of General Brandt, who, from being on the staff of Gneisenau's army, was brought into daily intercourse with Clausewitz in matters of duty, and also frequently met him at the table of Marshal Gneisenau, at Posen.

Amongst other anecdotes, General Brandt relates that, upon one occasion, the conversation at the Marshal's table turned upon a sermon preached by a priest, in which some great absurdities were introduced, and a discussion arose as to whether the Bishop should not be made responsible for what the priest had said. This led to the topic of theology in general, when General Brandt, speaking of himself, says, "I expressed an opinion that theology is only to be regarded as an historical process, as a *moment* in the gradual development of the human race. This brought upon me an attack from all quarters, but more especially from Clausewitz, who ought to have been on my side, he having been an adherent and pupil of Kiesewetter's, who had indoctrinated him in the philosophy of Kant, certainly diluted – I might even say in homoeopathic doses." This anecdote is only interesting as the mention of Kiesewetter points to a circumstance in the life of Clausewitz that may have had an influence in forming those habits of thought which distinguish his writings.

---

3   "Campaign in Russia in 1812"; translated from the German   of General Von Clausewitz (by Lord Ellesmere).

"The way," says General Brandt, "in which General Clausewitz judged of things, drew conclusions from movements and marches, calculated the times of the marches, and the points where decisions would take place, was extremely interesting. Fate has unfortunately denied him an opportunity of showing his talents in high command, but I have a firm persuasion that as a strategist he would have greatly distinguished himself. As a leader on the field of battle, on the other hand, he would not have been so much in his right place, from a manque d'habitude du commandement, he wanted the art d'enlever les troupes."

After the Prussian Army of Observation was dissolved, Clausewitz returned to Breslau, and a few days after his arrival was seized with cholera, the seeds of which he must have brought with him from the army on the Polish frontier. His death took place in November 1831.

His writings are contained in nine volumes, published after his death, but his fame rests most upon the three volumes forming his treatise on "War." In the present attempt to render into English this portion of the works of Clausewitz, the translator is sensible of many deficiencies, but he hopes at all events to succeed in making this celebrated treatise better known in England, believing, as he does, that so far as the work concerns the interests of this country, it has lost none of the importance it possessed at the time of its first publication.

J. J. Graham (Col.)

BOOK ONE
On the Nature of War

CHAPTER ONE

What is War?

1. *Introduction.*

WE PROPOSE to consider first the single elements of our subject, then each branch or part, and, last of all, the whole, in all its relations – therefore to advance from the simple to the complex. But it is necessary for us to commence with a glance at the nature of the whole, because it is particularly necessary that in the consideration of any of the parts their relation to the whole should be kept constantly in view.

2. *Definition.*

We shall not enter into any of the abstruse definitions of War used by publicists. We shall keep to the element of the thing itself, to a duel. War is nothing but a duel on an extensive scale. If we would conceive as a unit the countless number of duels which make up a War, we shall do so best by supposing to ourselves two wrestlers. Each strives by physical force to compel the other to submit to his will: each endeavours to throw his adversary, and thus render him incapable of further resistance.

War therefore is an act of violence intended to compel our opponent to fulfil our will.

Violence arms itself with the inventions of Art and Science in order to contend against violence. Self-imposed restrictions, almost imperceptible and hardly worth mentioning, termed usages of International Law, accompany it without essentially impairing its power. Violence, that is to say, physical force (for there is no moral force without the conception of States and Law), is therefore the *means*; the compulsory submission of the enemy to our will is the ultimate object. In order to attain this object fully, the enemy must be disarmed, and disarmament becomes therefore the immediate *object* of hostilities in theory. It takes the place of the final object, and puts it aside as something we can eliminate from our calculations.

3. *Utmost use of force.*

Now, philanthropists may easily imagine there is a skilful method of disarming and overcoming an enemy without great bloodshed, and that this is the proper tendency of the Art of War. However plausible this may appear, still it is an error which must be extirpated; for in such dangerous things as War, the errors which proceed from a spirit of benevolence are the worst. As the use of physical power to the utmost extent by no means excludes the co-operation of the intelligence, it follows that he who uses force unsparingly, without reference to the bloodshed involved, must obtain a superiority if his adversary uses less vigour in its application. The former then dictates the law to the latter, and both proceed to extremities to which the only limitations are those imposed by the amount of counter-acting force on each side.

This is the way in which the matter must be viewed and it is to no purpose, it is even against one's own interest, to turn away from the consideration of the real nature of the affair because the horror of its elements excites repugnance.

If the Wars of civilised people are less cruel and destructive than those of savages, the difference arises from the social condition both of States in themselves and in their relations to each other. Out of this social condition and its relations War arises, and by it War is subjected to conditions, is controlled and modified. But these things do not belong to War itself; they are only given conditions; and to introduce into the philosophy of War itself a principle of moderation would be an absurdity.

Two motives lead men to War: instinctive hostility and hostile intention. In our definition of War, we have chosen as its characteristic the latter of these elements, because it is the most general. It is impossible to conceive the passion of hatred of the wildest description, bordering on mere instinct, without combining with it the idea of a hostile intention. On the other hand, hostile intentions may often exist without being accompanied by any, or at all events by any extreme, hostility of feeling. Amongst savages views emanating from the feelings, amongst civilised nations those emanating from the understanding, have the predominance; but this difference arises from attendant circumstances, existing institutions, &c., and, therefore, is not to be found necessarily in all cases, although it prevails in the majority. In short, even the most civilised nations may burn with passionate hatred of each other.

We may see from this what a fallacy it would be to refer the War of a civilised nation entirely to an intelligent act on the part of the Government, and to imagine it as continually freeing itself more and more from all feeling of passion in such a way that at last the physical masses of combatants would no longer be required; in reality, their mere relations would suffice – a kind of algebraic action.

Theory was beginning to drift in this direction until the facts of the last War[4] taught it better. If War is an *act* of force, it belongs necessarily also to the feelings. If it does not originate in the feelings, it *reacts*, more or less, upon them, and the extent of this reaction depends not on the degree of civilisation, but upon the importance and duration of the interests involved.

Therefore, if we find civilised nations do not put their prisoners to death, do not devastate towns and countries, this is because their intelligence exercises greater influence on their mode of carrying on War, and has taught them more effectual means of applying force than these rude acts of mere instinct. The invention of gunpowder, the constant progress of improvements in the construction of firearms, are sufficient proofs that the tendency to destroy the adversary which lies at the bottom of the conception of War is in no way changed or modified through the progress of civilisation.

We therefore repeat our proposition, that War is an act of violence pushed to its utmost bounds; as one side dictates the law to the other, there arises a sort of reciprocal action, which logically must lead to an extreme. This is the first reciprocal action, and the first extreme with which we meet (*first reciprocal action*).

4. *The aim is to disarm the enemy.*

We have already said that the aim of all action in War is to disarm the enemy, and we shall now show that this, theoretically at least, is indispensable.

If our opponent is to be made to comply with our will, we must place him in a situation which is more oppressive to him than the sacrifice which we demand; but the disadvantages of this position must naturally not be of a transitory nature, at least in appearance, otherwise the enemy, instead of yielding, will hold out, in the prospect of a change for the better. Every change in this position which is produced by a continuation of the War should therefore be a change for the worse. The worst condition in which a belligerent can be placed is that of being completely disarmed. If, therefore, the enemy is to be reduced to submission by an act of War, he must either be positively disarmed or placed in such a position that he is threatened with it. From this it follows that the disarming or overthrow of the enemy, whichever we call

4   Clausewitz alludes here to the "Wars of Liberation," 1813,14,15.

it, must always be the aim of Warfare. Now War is always the shock of two hostile bodies in collision, not the action of a living power upon an inanimate mass, because an absolute state of endurance would not be making War; therefore, what we have just said as to the aim of action in War applies to both parties. Here, then, is another case of reciprocal action. As long as the enemy is not defeated, he may defeat me; then I shall be no longer my own master; he will dictate the law to me as I did to him. This is the second reciprocal action, and leads to a second extreme (*second reciprocal action*).

5. *Utmost exertion of powers.*

If we desire to defeat the enemy, we must proportion our efforts to his powers of resistance. This is expressed by the product of two factors which cannot be separated, namely, the sum of available means and the strength of the Will. The sum of the available means may be estimated in a measure, as it depends (although not entirely) upon numbers; but the strength of volition is more difficult to determine, and can only be estimated to a certain extent by the strength of the motives. Granted we have obtained in this way an approximation to the strength of the power to be contended with, we can then take of our own means, and either increase them so as to obtain a preponderance, or, in case we have not the resources to effect this, then do our best by increasing our means as far as possible. But the adversary does the same; therefore, there is a new mutual enhancement, which, in pure conception, must create a fresh effort towards an extreme. This is the third case of reciprocal action, and a third extreme with which we meet (*third reciprocal action*).

6. *Modification in the reality.*

Thus reasoning in the abstract, the mind cannot stop short of an extreme, because it has to deal with an extreme, with a conflict of forces left to themselves, and obeying no other but their own inner laws. If we should seek to deduce from the pure conception of War an absolute point for the aim which we shall propose and for the means which we shall apply, this constant reciprocal action would involve us in extremes, which would be nothing but a play of ideas produced by an almost invisible train of logical subtleties. If, adhering closely to the absolute, we try to avoid all difficulties by a stroke of the pen, and insist with logical strictness that in every case the extreme must be the object, and the utmost effort must be exerted in that direction, such a stroke of the pen would be a mere paper law, not by any means adapted to the real world.

Even supposing this extreme tension of forces was an absolute which could easily be ascertained, still we must admit that the human mind would hardly submit itself to this kind of logical chimera. There would be in many cases an unnecessary waste of power, which would be in opposition to other principles of statecraft; an effort of Will would be required disproportioned to the proposed object, which therefore it would be impossible to realise, for the human will does not derive its impulse from logical subtleties.

But everything takes a different shape when we pass from abstractions to reality. In the former, everything must be subject to optimism, and we must imagine the one side as well as the other striving after perfection and even attaining it. Will this ever take place in reality? It will if,

(1) War becomes a completely isolated act, which arises suddenly, and is in no way connected with the previous history of the combatant States.

(2) If it is limited to a single solution, or to several simultaneous solutions.

(3) If it contains within itself the solution perfect and complete, free from any reaction upon it, through a calculation beforehand of the political situation which will follow from it.

7. *War is never an isolated act.*

With regard to the first point, neither of the two opponents is an abstract person to the other, not even as regards that factor in the sum of resistance which does not depend on objective things, viz., the Will. This Will is not an entirely unknown quantity; it indicates what it will be to-morrow by what it is to-day. War does not spring up quite suddenly, it does not spread to the full in a moment; each of the two opponents can, therefore, form an opinion of the other, in a great measure, from what he is and what he does, instead of judging of him according to what he, strictly speaking, should be or should do. But, now, man with his incomplete organisation is always below the line of absolute perfection, and thus these deficiencies, having an influence on both sides, become a modifying principle.

8. *War does not consist of a single instantaneous blow.*

The second point gives rise to the following considerations: –

If War ended in a single solution, or a number of simultaneous ones, then naturally all the preparations for the same would have a tendency to the extreme, for an omission could not in any way be repaired; the utmost, then, that the world of reality could furnish as a guide for us would be the preparations of the enemy, as far as they are known to us; all the rest would fall into the domain of the abstract. But if the result is made up from several successive acts, then naturally that which precedes with all its phases may be taken as a measure for that which will follow, and in this manner the world of reality again takes the place of the abstract, and thus modifies the effort towards the extreme.

Yet every War would necessarily resolve itself into a single solution, or a sum of simultaneous results, if all the means required for the struggle were raised at once, or could be at once raised; for as one adverse result necessarily diminishes the means, then if all the means have been applied in the first, a second cannot properly be supposed. All hostile acts which might follow would belong essentially to the first, and form, in reality only its duration.

But we have already seen that even in the preparation for War the real world steps into the place of mere abstract conception – a material standard into the place of the hypotheses of an extreme: that therefore in that way both parties, by the influence of the mutual reaction, remain below the line of extreme effort, and therefore all forces are not at once brought forward.

It lies also in the nature of these forces and their application that they cannot all be brought into activity at the same time. These forces are *the armies actually on foot, the country*, with its superficial extent and its population, *and the allies*.

In point of fact, the country, with its superficial area and the population, besides being the source of all military force, constitutes in itself an integral part of the efficient quantities in War, providing either the theatre of war or exercising a considerable influence on the same.

Now, it is possible to bring all the movable military forces of a country into operation at once, but not all fortresses, rivers, mountains, people, &c. – in short, not the whole country, unless it is so small that it may be completely embraced by the first act of the War. Further, the co-operation of allies does not depend on the Will of the belligerents; and from the nature of the political relations of states to each other, this co-operation is frequently not afforded until after the War has commenced, or it may be increased to restore the balance of power.

That this part of the means of resistance, which cannot at once be brought into activity, in many cases, is a much greater part of the whole than might at first be supposed, and that it often restores the balance of power, seriously affected by the great force of the first decision, will be more fully shown hereafter. Here it is sufficient to show that a complete concentration of all available means in a moment of time is contradictory to the nature of War.

Now this, in itself, furnishes no ground for relaxing our efforts to accumulate strength to gain the first result, because an unfavourable issue is always a disadvantage to which no one would purposely expose himself, and also because the first decision, although not the only one, still will have the more influence on subsequent events, the greater it is in itself.

But the possibility of gaining a later result causes men to take refuge in that expectation, owing to the repugnance in the human mind to making excessive efforts; and therefore forces are not concentrated and measures are not taken for the first decision with that energy which would otherwise be used. Whatever one belligerent omits from weakness, becomes to the other a real objective ground for limiting his own efforts, and thus again, through this reciprocal action, extreme tendencies are brought down to efforts on a limited scale.

9. *The result in war is never absolute.*

Lastly, even the final decision of a whole War is not always to be regarded as absolute. The conquered State often sees in it only a passing evil, which may be repaired in after times by means of political combinations. How much this must modify the degree of tension, and the vigour of the efforts made, is evident in itself.

10. *The probabilities of real life take the place of the conceptions of the extreme and the absolute.*

In this manner, the whole act of War is removed from the rigorous law of forces exerted to the utmost. If the extreme is no longer to be apprehended, and no longer to be sought for, it is left to the judgment to determine the limits for the efforts to be made in place of it, and this can only be done on the data furnished by the facts of the real world by the *laws of probability*. Once the belligerents are no longer mere conceptions, but individual States and Governments, once the War is no longer an ideal, but a definite substantial procedure, then the reality will furnish the data to compute the unknown quantities which are required to be found.

From the character, the measures, the situation of the adversary, and the relations with which he is surrounded, each side will draw conclusions by the law of probability as to the designs of the other, and act accordingly.

11. *The political object now reappears.*

Here the question which we had laid aside forces itself again into consideration (see No. 2), viz., the political object of the War. The law of the extreme, the view to disarm the adversary, to overthrow him, has hitherto to a certain extent usurped the place of this end or object. Just as this law loses its force, the political must again come forward. If the whole consideration is a calculation of probability based on definite persons and relations, then the political object, being the original motive, must be an essential factor in the product. The smaller the sacrifice we demand from ours, the smaller, it may be expected, will be the means of resistance which he will employ; but the smaller his prepara-

tion, the smaller will ours require to be. Further, the smaller our political object, the less value shall we set upon it, and the more easily shall
we be induced to give it up altogether.

Thus, therefore, the political object, as the original motive of the War,
will be the standard for determining both the aim of the military force
and also the amount of effort to be made. This it cannot be in itself, but
it is so in relation to both the belligerent States, because we are concerned with realities, not with mere abstractions. One and the same political object may produce totally different effects upon different people,
or even upon the same people at different times; we can, therefore, only
admit the political object as the measure, by considering it in its effects
upon those masses which it is to move, and consequently the nature of
those masses also comes into consideration. It is easy to see that thus
the result may be very different according as these masses are animated
with a spirit which will infuse vigour into the action or otherwise. It
is quite possible for such a state of feeling to exist between two States
that a very trifling political motive for War may produce an effect quite
disproportionate – in fact, a perfect explosion.

This applies to the efforts which the political object will call forth
in the two States, and to the aim which the military action shall prescribe for itself. At times it may itself be that aim, as, for example,
the conquest of a province. At other times the political object itself is
not suitable for the aim of military action; then such a one must be
chosen as will be an equivalent for it, and stand in its place as regards
the conclusion of peace. But also, in this, due attention to the peculiar
character of the States concerned is always supposed. There are circumstances in which the equivalent must be much greater than the
political object, in order to secure the latter. The political object will
be so much the more the standard of aim and effort, and have more
influence in itself, the more the masses are indifferent, the less that
any mutual feeling of hostility prevails in the two States from other
causes, and therefore there are cases where the political object almost
alone will be decisive.

If the aim of the military action is an equivalent for the political object, that action will in general diminish as the political object diminishes, and in a greater degree the more the political object dominates.
Thus it is explained how, without any contradiction in itself, there may
be Wars of all degrees of importance and energy, from a War of exter-
mination down to the mere use of an army of observation. This, however, leads to a question of another kind which we have hereafter to
develop and answer.

12. *A suspension in the action of war unexplained by anything said as yet.*

However insignificant the political claims mutually advanced, however weak the means put forth, however small the aim to which military action is directed, can this action be suspended even for a moment? This is a question which penetrates deeply into the nature of the subject.

Every transaction requires for its accomplishment a certain time which we call its duration. This may be longer or shorter, according as the person acting throws more or less despatch into his movements.

About this more or less we shall not trouble ourselves here. Each person acts in his own fashion; but the slow person does not protract the thing because he wishes to spend more time about it, but because by his nature he requires more time, and if he made more haste would not do the thing so well. This time, therefore, depends on subjective causes, and belongs to the length, so called, of the action.

If we allow now to every action in War this, its length, then we must assume, at first sight at least, that any expenditure of time beyond this length, that is, every suspension of hostile action, appears an absurdity; with respect to this it must not be forgotten that we now speak not of the progress of one or other of the two opponents, but of the general progress of the whole action of the War.

13. *There is only one cause which can suspend the action, and this seems to be only possible on one side in any case.*

If two parties have armed themselves for strife, then a feeling of animosity must have moved them to it; as long now as they continue armed, that is, do not come to terms of peace, this feeling must exist; and it can only be brought to a standstill by either side by one single motive alone, which is, *that he waits for a more favourable moment for action.* Now, at first sight, it appears that this motive can never exist except on one side, because it, eo ipso, must be prejudicial to the other. If the one has an interest in acting, then the other must have an interest in waiting.

A complete equilibrium of forces can never produce a suspension of action, for during this suspension he who has the positive object (that is, the assailant) must continue progressing; for if we should imagine an equilibrium in this way, that he who has the positive object, therefore the strongest motive, can at the same time only command the lesser means, so that the equation is made up by the product of the motive and the power, then we must say, if no alteration in this condition of equilibrium is to be expected, the two parties must make peace; but if an alteration is to be expected, then it can only be favourable to one side, and therefore the other has a manifest interest to act without delay. We see that the conception of an equilibrium cannot explain a suspension of arms, but that it ends in the question of the *expectation of a more favourable moment.*

Let us suppose, therefore, that one of two States has a positive object, as, for instance, the conquest of one of the enemy's provinces – which is to be utilised in the settlement of peace. After this conquest, his political object is accomplished, the necessity for action ceases, and for him a pause ensues. If the adversary is also contented with this solution, he will make peace; if not, he must act. Now, if we suppose that in four weeks he will be in a better condition to act, then he has sufficient grounds for putting off the time of action.

But from that moment the logical course for the enemy appears to be to act that he may not give the conquered party *the desired* time. Of course, in this mode of reasoning a complete insight into the state of circumstances on both sides is supposed.

14. *Thus a continuance of action will ensue which will advance towards a climax.*

If this unbroken continuity of hostile operations really existed, the effect would be that everything would again be driven towards the extreme; for, irrespective of the effect of such incessant activity in inflaming the feelings, and infusing into the whole a greater degree of passion, a greater elementary force, there would also follow from this continuance of action a stricter continuity, a closer connection between cause and effect, and thus every single action would become of more importance, and consequently more replete with danger.

But we know that the course of action in War has seldom or never this unbroken continuity, and that there have been many Wars in which action occupied by far the smallest portion of time employed, the whole of the rest being consumed in inaction. It is impossible that this should be always an anomaly; suspension of action in War must therefore be possible, that is no contradiction in itself. We now proceed to show how this is.

15. *Here, therefore, the principle of polarity is brought into requisition.*

As we have supposed the interests of one Commander to be always antagonistic to those of the other, we have assumed a true *polarity*. We reserve a fuller explanation of this for another chapter, merely making the following observation on it at present.

The principle of polarity is only valid when it can be conceived in one and the same thing, where the positive and its opposite the negative completely destroy each other. In a battle both sides strive to conquer; that is true polarity, for the victory of the one side destroys that of the other. But when we speak of two different things which have a common relation external to themselves, then it is not the things but their relations which have the polarity.

16. *Attack and defence are things differing in kind and of unequal force. polarity is, therefore, not applicable to them.*

If there was only one form of War, to wit, the attack of the enemy, therefore no defence; or, in other words, if the attack was distinguished from the defence merely by the positive motive, which the one has and the other has not, but the methods of each were precisely one and the same: then in this sort of fight every advantage gained on the one side would be a corresponding disadvantage on the other, and true polarity would exist.

But action in War is divided into two forms, attack and defence, which, as we shall hereafter explain more particularly, are very different and of unequal strength. Polarity therefore lies in that to which both bear a relation, in the decision, but not in the attack or defence itself.

If the one Commander wishes the solution put off, the other must wish to hasten it, but only by the same form of action. If it is A's interest not to attack his enemy at present, but four weeks hence, then it is B's interest to be attacked, not four weeks hence, but at the present moment. This is the direct antagonism of interests, but it by no means follows that it would be for B's interest to attack A at once. That is plainly something totally different.

17. *The effect of polarity is often destroyed by the superiority of the defence over the attack, and thus the suspension of action in war is explained.*

If the form of defence is stronger than that of offence, as we shall hereafter show, the question arises, Is the advantage of a deferred decision as great on the one side as the advantage of the defensive form on the other? If it is not, then it cannot by its counter-weight over-balance the latter, and thus influence the progress of the action of the War. We see, therefore, that the impulsive force existing in the polarity of interests may be lost in the difference between the strength of the offensive and the defensive, and thereby become ineffectual.

If, therefore, that side for which the present is favourable, is too weak to be able to dispense with the advantage of the defensive, he must put up with the unfavourable prospects which the future holds out; for it may still be better to fight a defensive battle in the unpromising future than to assume the offensive or make peace at present. Now, being convinced that the superiority of the defensive[5] (rightly understood) is very great,

---

5   It must be remembered that all this antedates by some   years the introduction of long-range weapons.

and much greater than may appear at first sight, we conceive that the greater number of those periods of inaction which occur in war are thus explained without involving any contradiction. The weaker the motives to action are, the more will those motives be absorbed and neutralised by this difference between attack and defence, the more frequently, therefore, will action in warfare be stopped, as indeed experience teaches.

18 *A second ground consists in the imperfect knowledge of circumstances.*

But there is still another cause which may stop action in War, viz., an incomplete view of the situation. Each Commander can only fully know his own position; that of his opponent can only be known to him by reports, which are uncertain; he may, therefore, form a wrong judgment with respect to it upon data of this description, and, in consequence of that error, he may suppose that the power of taking the initiative rests with his adversary when it lies really with himself. This want of perfect insight might certainly just as often occasion an untimely action as untimely inaction, and hence it would in itself no more contribute to delay than to accelerate action in War. Still, it must always be regarded as one of the natural causes which may bring action in War to a standstill without involving a contradiction. But if we reflect how much more we are inclined and induced to estimate the power of our opponents too high than too low, because it lies in human nature to do so, we shall admit that our imperfect insight into facts in general must contribute very much to delay action in War, and to modify the application of the principles pending our conduct.

The possibility of a standstill brings into the action of War a new modification, inasmuch as it dilutes that action with the element of time, checks the influence or sense of danger in its course, and increases the means of reinstating a lost balance of force. The greater the tension of feelings from which the War springs, the greater therefore the energy with which it is carried on, so much the shorter will be the periods of inaction; on the other hand, the weaker the principle of warlike activity, the longer will be these periods: for powerful motives increase the force of the will, and this, as we know, is always a factor in the product of force.

19. *Frequent periods of inaction in war remove it further from the absolute, and make it still more a calculation of probabilities.*

But the slower the action proceeds in War, the more frequent and longer the periods of inaction, so much the more easily can an error be repaired; therefore, so much the bolder a General will be in his calculations, so much the more readily will he keep them below the line of the absolute, and build everything upon probabilities and conjecture. Thus, according as the course of the War is more or less slow, more or less time will be allowed for that which the nature of a concrete case particularly requires, calculation of probability based on given circumstances.

20. *Therefore, the element of chance only is wanting to make of war a game, and in that element it is least of all deficient.*

We see from the foregoing how much the objective nature of War makes it a calculation of probabilities; now there is only one single element still wanting to make it a game, and that element it certainly is not without: it is chance. There is no human affair which stands so constantly and so generally in close connection with chance as War. But together with chance, the accidental, and along with it good luck, occupy a great place in War.

21. *War is a game both objectively and subjectively.*

If we now take a look at the subjective nature of War, that is to say, at those conditions under which it is carried on, it will appear to us still more like a game. Primarily the element in which the operations of War are carried on is danger; but which of all the moral qualities is the first in danger? *Courage.* Now certainly courage is quite compatible with prudent calculation, but still they are things of quite a different kind, essentially different qualities of the mind; on the other hand, daring reliance on good fortune, boldness, rashness, are only expressions of courage, and all these propensities of the mind look for the fortuitous (or accidental), because it is their element.

We see, therefore, how, from the commencement, the absolute, the mathematical as it is called, nowhere finds any sure basis in the calculations in the Art of War; and that from the outset there is a play of possibilities, probabilities, good and bad luck, which spreads about with all the coarse and fine threads of its web, and makes War of all branches of human activity the most like a gambling game.

22. *How this accords best with the human mind in general.*

Although our intellect always feels itself urged towards clearness and certainty, still our mind often feels itself attracted by uncertainty. Instead of threading its way with the understanding along the narrow path of philosophical investigations and logical conclusions, in order, almost unconscious of itself, to arrive in spaces where it feels itself a stranger, and where it seems to part from all well-known objects, it prefers to remain with the imagination in the realms of chance and luck. Instead of living yonder on poor necessity, it revels here in the wealth of possibilities; animated thereby, courage then takes wings to itself, and daring and danger make the element into which it launches itself as a fearless swimmer plunges into the stream.

Shall theory leave it here, and move on, self-satisfied with absolute conclusions and rules? Then it is of no practical use. Theory must also take
into account the human element; it must accord a place to courage, to
boldness, even to rashness. The Art of War has to deal with living and
with moral forces, the consequence of which is that it can never attain
the absolute and positive. There is therefore everywhere a margin for the
accidental, and just as much in the greatest things as in the smallest. As
there is room for this accidental on the one hand, so on the other there
must be courage and self-reliance in proportion to the room available.
If these qualities are forthcoming in a high degree, the margin left may
likewise be great. Courage and self-reliance are, therefore, principles quite
essential to War; consequently, theory must only set up such rules as allow
ample scope for all degrees and varieties of these necessary and noblest
of military virtues. In daring there may still be wisdom, and prudence as
well, only they are estimated by a different standard of value.

23. *War is always a serious means for a serious object. its more particular definition.*

Such is War; such the Commander who conducts it; such the theory
which rules it. But War is no pastime; no mere passion for venturing
and winning; no work of a free enthusiasm: it is a serious means for
a serious object. All that appearance which it wears from the varying
hues of fortune, all that it assimilates into itself of the oscillations of
passion, of courage, of imagination, of enthusiasm, are only particular
properties of this means.

The War of a community – of whole Nations, and particularly of civilised Nations – always starts from a political condition, and is called
forth by a political motive. It is, therefore, a political act. Now if it was
a perfect, unrestrained, and absolute expression of force, as we had to
deduct it from its mere conception, then the moment it is called forth
by policy it would step into the place of policy, and as something quite
independent of it would set it aside, and only follow its own laws, just
as a mine at the moment of explosion cannot be guided into any other
direction than that which has been given to it by preparatory arrangements. This is how the thing has really been viewed hitherto, whenever
a want of harmony between policy and the conduct of a War has led
to theoretical distinctions of the kind. But it is not so, and the idea is
radically false. War in the real world, as we have already seen, is not an
extreme thing which expends itself at one single discharge; it is the operation of powers which do not develop themselves completely in the
same manner and in the same measure, but which at one time expand
sufficiently to overcome the resistance opposed by inertia or friction,

while at another they are too weak to produce an effect; it is therefore, in a certain measure, a pulsation of violent force more or less vehement, consequently making its discharges and exhausting its powers more or less quickly – in other words, conducting more or less quickly to the aim, but always lasting long enough to admit of influence being exerted on it in its course, so as to give it this or that direction, in short, to be subject to the will of a guiding intelligence., if we reflect that War has its root in a political object, then naturally this original motive which called it into existence should also continue the first and highest consideration in its conduct. Still, the political object is no despotic lawgiver on that account; it must accommodate itself to the nature of the means, and though changes in these means may involve modification in the political objective, the latter always retains a prior right to consideration. Policy, therefore, is interwoven with the whole action of War, and must exercise a continuous influence upon it, as far as the nature of the forces liberated by it will permit.

24. *War is a mere continuation of policy by other means.*

We see, therefore, that War is not merely a political act, but also a real political instrument, a continuation of political commerce, a carrying out of the same by other means. All beyond this which is strictly peculiar to War relates merely to the peculiar nature of the means which it uses. That the tendencies and views of policy shall not be incompatible with these means, the Art of War in general and the Commander in each particular case may demand, and this claim is truly not a trifling one. But however powerfully this may react on political views in particular cases, still it must always be regarded as only a modification of them; for the political view is the object, War is the means, and the means must always include the object in our conception.

25. *Diversity in the nature of wars.*

The greater and the more powerful the motives of a War, the more it affects the whole existence of a people. The more violent the excitement which precedes the War, by so much the nearer will the War approach to its abstract form, so much the more will it be directed to the destruction of the enemy, so much the nearer will the military and political ends coincide, so much the more purely military and less political the War appears to be; but the weaker the motives and the tensions, so much the less will the natural direction of the military element – that is, force – be coincident with the direction which the political element indicates; so much the more must, therefore, the War become diverted from its natural direction, the political object diverge from the aim of an ideal War, and the War appear to become political.

But, that the reader may not form any false conceptions, we must here observe that by this natural tendency of War we only mean the philosophical, the strictly logical, and by no means the tendency of forces actually engaged in conflict, by which would be supposed to be included all the emotions and passions of the combatants. No doubt in some cases these also might be excited to such a degree as to be with difficulty restrained and confined to the political road; but in most cases such a contradiction will not arise, because by the existence of such strenuous exertions a great plan in harmony therewith would be implied. If the plan is directed only upon a small object, then the impulses of feeling amongst the masses will be also so weak that these masses will require to be stimulated rather than repressed.

26. *They may all be regarded as political acts.*

Returning now to the main subject, although it is true that in one kind of War the political element seems almost to disappear, whilst in another kind it occupies a very prominent place, we may still affirm that the one is as political as the other; for if we regard the State policy as the intelligence of the personified State, then amongst all the constellations in the political sky whose movements it has to compute, those must be included which arise when the nature of its relations imposes the necessity of a great War. It is only if we understand by policy not a true appreciation of affairs in general, but the conventional conception of a cautious, subtle, also dishonest craftiness, averse from violence, that the latter kind of War may belong more to policy than the first.

27. *Influence of this view on the right understanding of military history, and on the foundations of theory.*

We see, therefore, in the first place, that under all circumstances War is to be regarded not as an independent thing, but as a political instrument; and it is only by taking this point of view that we can avoid finding ourselves in opposition to all military history. This is the only means of unlocking the great book and making it intelligible. Secondly, this view shows us how Wars must differ in character according to the nature of the motives and circumstances from which they proceed.

Now, the first, the grandest, and most decisive act of judgment which the Statesman and General exercises is rightly to understand in this respect the War in which he engages, not to take it for something, or to wish to make of it something, which by the nature of its relations it is impossible for it to be. This is, therefore, the first, the most comprehensive, of all strategical questions. We shall enter into this more fully in treating of the plan of a War.

For the present we content ourselves with having brought the subject up to this point, and having thereby fixed the chief point of view from which War and its theory are to be studied.

28. *Result for theory.*

War is, therefore, not only chameleon-like in character, because it changes its colour in some degree in each particular case, but it is also, as a whole, in relation to the predominant tendencies which are in it, a wonderful trinity, composed of the original violence of its elements, hatred and animosity, which may be looked upon as blind instinct; of the play of probabilities and chance, which make it a free activity of the soul; and of the subordinate nature of a political instrument, by which it belongs purely to the reason.

The first of these three phases concerns more the people the second, more the General and his Army; the third, more the Government. The passions which break forth in War must already have a latent existence in the peoples. The range which the display of courage and talents shall get in the realm of probabilities and of chance depends on the particular characteristics of the General and his Army, but the political objects belong to the Government alone.

These three tendencies, which appear like so many different law-givers, are deeply rooted in the nature of the subject, and at the same time variable in degree. A theory which would leave any one of them out of account, or set up any arbitrary relation between them, would immediately become involved in such a contradiction with the reality, that it might be regarded as destroyed at once by that alone.

The problem is, therefore, that theory shall keep itself poised in a manner between these three tendencies, as between three points of attraction.

The way in which alone this difficult problem can be solved we shall examine in the book on the "Theory of War." In every case the conception of War, as here defined, will be the first ray of light which shows us the true foundation of theory, and which first separates the great masses and allows us to distinguish them from one another.

CHAPTER TWO
End and Means in War

HAVING IN THE foregoing chapter ascertained the complicated and variable nature of War, we shall now occupy ourselves in examining into the influence which this nature has upon the end and means in War.

If we ask, first of all, for the object upon which the whole effort of War is to be directed, in order that it may suffice for the attainment of the political object, we shall find that it is just as variable as are the political object and the particular circumstances of the War.

If, in the next place, we keep once more to the pure conception of War, then we must say that the political object properly lies out of its province, for if War is an act of violence to compel the enemy to fulfil our will, then in every case all depends on our overthrowing the enemy, that is, disarming him, and on that alone. This object, developed from abstract conceptions, but which is also the one aimed at in a great many cases in reality, we shall, in the first place, examine in this reality.

In connection with the plan of a campaign we shall hereafter examine more closely into the meaning of disarming a nation, but here we must at once draw a distinction between three things, which, as three general objects, comprise everything else within them. They are the *military power, the country,* and *the will of the enemy.*

The military power must be destroyed, that is, reduced to such a state as not to be able to prosecute the War. This is the sense in which we wish to be understood hereafter, whenever we use the expression "destruction of the enemy's military power."

The country must be conquered, for out of the country a new military force may be formed.

But even when both these things are done, still the War, that is, the hostile feeling and action of hostile agencies, cannot be considered as at an end as long as the will of the enemy is not subdued also; that is, its Government and its Allies must be forced into signing a peace, or the people into submission; for whilst we are in full occupation of the country, the War may break out afresh, either in the interior or through assistance given by Allies. No doubt, this may also take place after a peace, but that shows nothing more than that every War does not carry in itself the elements for a complete decision and final settlement.

But even if this is the case, still with the conclusion of peace a number of sparks are always extinguished which would have smouldered on quietly, and the excitement of the passions abates, because all those whose minds are disposed to peace, of which in all nations and under all circumstances there is always a great number, turn themselves away completely from the road to resistance. Whatever may take place subsequently, we must always look upon the object as attained, and the business of War as ended, by a peace.

As protection of the country is the primary object for which the military force exists, therefore the natural order is, that first of all this force should be destroyed, then the country subdued; and through the effect of these two results, as well as the position we then hold, the enemy should be forced to make peace. Generally the destruction of the enemy's force is done by degrees, and in just the same measure the conquest of the country follows immediately. The two likewise usually react upon each other, because the loss of provinces occasions a diminution of military force. But this order is by no means necessary, and on that account it also does not always take place. The enemy's Army, before it is sensibly weakened, may retreat to the opposite side of the country, or even quite outside of it. In this case, therefore, the greater part or the whole of the country is conquered.

But this object of War in the abstract, this final means of attaining the political object in which all others are combined, the *disarming the enemy*, is rarely attained in practice and is not a condition necessary to peace. Therefore it can in no wise be set up in theory as a law. There are innumerable instances of treaties in which peace has been settled before either party could be looked upon as disarmed; indeed, even before the balance of power had undergone any sensible alteration. Nay, further, if we look at the case in the concrete, then we must say that in a whole class of cases, the idea of a complete defeat of the enemy would be a mere imaginative flight, especially when the enemy is considerably superior.

The reason why the object deduced from the conception of War is not adapted in general to real War lies in the difference between the two, which is discussed in the preceding chapter. If it was as pure theory gives it, then a War between two States of very unequal military strength would appear an absurdity; therefore impossible. At most, the inequality between the physical forces might be such that it could be balanced by the moral forces, and that would not go far with our present social condition in Europe. Therefore, if we have seen Wars take place between States of very unequal power, that has been the case because there is a wide difference between War in reality and its original conception.

There are two considerations which as motives may practically take the place of inability to continue the contest. The first is the improbability, the second is the excessive price, of success.

According to what we have seen in the foregoing chapter, War must always set itself free from the strict law of logical necessity, and seek aid from the calculation of probabilities; and as this is so much the more the case, the more the War has a bias that way, from the circumstances out of which it has arisen – the smaller its motives are, and the excitement it has raised – so it is also conceivable how out of this calculation of probabilities even motives to peace may arise. War does not, therefore, always require to be fought out until one party is overthrown; and we may suppose that, when the motives and passions are slight, a weak probability will suffice to move that side to which it is unfavourable to give way. Now, were the other side convinced of this beforehand, it is natural that he would strive for this probability only, instead of first wasting time and effort in the attempt to achieve the total destruction of the enemy's Army.

Still more general in its influence on the resolution to peace is the consideration of the expenditure of force already made, and further required. As War is no act of blind passion, but is dominated by the political object, therefore the value of that object determines the measure of the sacrifices by which it is to be purchased. This will be the case, not only as regards extent, but also as regards duration. As soon, therefore, as the required outlay becomes so great that the political object is no longer equal in value, the object must be given up, and peace will be the result.

We see, therefore, that in Wars where one side cannot completely disarm the other, the motives to peace on both sides will rise or fall on each side according to the probability of future success and the required outlay. If these motives were equally strong on both sides, they would meet in the centre of their political difference. Where they are strong on one side, they might be weak on the other. If their amount is only sufficient, peace will follow, but naturally to the advantage of that side which has the weakest motive for its conclusion. We purposely

pass over here the difference which the *positive* and *negative* character
of the political end must necessarily produce practically; for although
that is, as we shall hereafter show, of the highest importance, still we
are obliged to keep here to a more general point of view, because the
original political views in the course of the War change very much, and
at last may become totally different, *just because they are determined by
results and probable events.*

Now comes the question how to influence the probability of success.
In the first place, naturally by the same means which we use when the
object is the subjugation of the enemy, by the destruction of his military
force and the conquest of his provinces; but these two means are not
exactly of the same import here as they would be in reference to that
object. If we attack the enemy's Army, it is a very different thing whether
we intend to follow up the first blow with a succession of others, until
the whole force is destroyed, or whether we mean to content ourselves
with a victory to shake the enemy's feeling of security, to convince him
of our superiority, and to instil into him a feeling of apprehension about
the future. If this is our object, we only go so far in the destruction of
his forces as is sufficient. In like manner, the conquest, of the enemy's
provinces is quite a different measure if the object is not the destruction
of the enemy's Army. In the latter case the destruction of the Army is the
real effectual action, and the taking of the provinces only a consequence
of it; to take them before the Army had been defeated would always be
looked upon only as a necessary evil. On the other hand, if our views are
not directed upon the complete destruction of the enemy's force, and if
we are sure that the enemy does not seek but fears to bring matters to a
bloody decision, the taking possession of a weak or defenceless province
is an advantage in itself, and if this advantage is of sufficient importance
to make the enemy apprehensive about the general result, then it may
also be regarded as a shorter road to peace.

But now we come upon a peculiar means of influencing the probability of the result without destroying the enemy's Army, namely, upon
the expeditions which have a direct connection with political views. If
there are any enterprises which are particularly likely to break up the
enemy's alliances or make them inoperative, to gain new alliances for
ourselves, to raise political powers in our own favour, &c. &c., then
it is easy to conceive how much these may increase the probability of
success, and become a shorter way towards our object than the routing
of the enemy's forces.

The second question is how to act upon the enemy's expenditure in
strength, that is, to raise the price of success.

The enemy's outlay in strength lies in the *wear and tear* of his forces, consequently in the *destruction* of them on our part, and in the *loss of provinces*, consequently the *conquest* of them by us.

Here, again, on account of the various significations of these means, so likewise it will be found that neither of them will be identical in its signification in all cases if the objects are different. The smallness in general of this difference must not cause us perplexity, for in reality the weakest motives, the finest shades of difference, often decide in favour of this or that method of applying force. Our only business here is to show that, certain conditions being supposed, the possibility of attaining our purpose in different ways is no contradiction, absurdity, nor even error.

Besides these two means, there are three other peculiar ways of directly increasing the waste of the enemy's force. The first is *invasion*, that is *the occupation of the enemy's territory, not with a view to keeping it*, but in order to levy contributions upon it, or to devastate it.

The immediate object here is neither the conquest of the enemy's territory nor the defeat of his armed force, but merely to *do him damage in a general way*. The second way is to select for the object of our enterprises those points at which we can do the enemy most harm. Nothing is easier to conceive than two different directions in which our force may be employed, the first of which is to be preferred if our object is to defeat the enemy's Army, while the other is more advantageous if the defeat of the enemy is out of the question. According to the usual mode of speaking, we should say that the first is primarily military, the other more political. But if we take our view from the highest point, both are equally military, and neither the one nor the other can be eligible unless it suits the circumstances of the case. The third, by far the most important, from the great number of cases which it embraces, is the *wearing out* of the enemy. We choose this expression not only to explain our meaning in few words, but because it represents the thing exactly, and is not so figurative as may at first appear. The idea of wearing out in a struggle amounts in practice to *a gradual exhaustion of the physical powers and of the will by the long continuance of exertion.*

Now, if we want to overcome the enemy by the duration of the contest, we must content ourselves with as small objects as possible, for it is in the nature of the thing that a great end requires a greater expenditure of force than a small one; but the smallest object that we can propose to ourselves is simple passive resistance, that is a combat without any positive view. In this way, therefore, our means attain their greatest relative value, and therefore the result is best secured. How far now can this negative mode of proceeding be carried? Plainly not to absolute passivity, for mere endurance would not be fighting; and the defensive is an activity by which so much of the enemy's power must be destroyed that he must give up his object. That alone is what we aim at in each single act, and therein consists the negative nature of our object.

No doubt this negative object in its single act is not so effective as the positive object in the same direction would be, supposing it successful; but there is this difference in its favour, that it succeeds more easily than the positive, and therefore it holds out greater certainty of success; what is wanting in the efficacy of its single act must be gained through time, that is, through the duration of the contest, and therefore this negative intention, which constitutes the principle of the pure defensive, is also the natural means of overcoming the enemy by the duration of the combat, that is of wearing him out.

Here lies the origin of that difference of *offensive* and *defensive*, the influence of which prevails throughout the whole province of War. We cannot at present pursue this subject further than to observe that from this negative intention are to be deduced all the advantages and all the stronger forms of combat which are on the side of the Defensive, and in which that philosophical-dynamic law which exists between the greatness and the certainty of success is realised. We shall resume the consideration of all this hereafter.

If then the negative purpose, that is the concentration of all the means into a state of pure resistance, affords a superiority in the contest, and if this advantage is sufficient to *balance* whatever superiority in numbers the adversary may have, then the mere *duration* of the contest will suffice gradually to bring the loss of force on the part of the adversary to a point at which the political object can no longer be an equivalent, a point at which, therefore, he must give up the contest. We see then that this class of means, the wearing out of the enemy, includes the great number of cases in which the weaker resists the stronger.

Frederick the Great, during the Seven Years' War, was never strong enough to overthrow the Austrian monarchy; and if he had tried to do so after the fashion of Charles the Twelfth, he would inevitably have had to succumb himself. But after his skilful application of the system of husbanding his resources had shown the powers allied against him, through a seven years' struggle, that the actual expenditure of strength far exceeded what they had at first anticipated, they made peace.

We see then that there are many ways to one's object in War; that the complete subjugation of the enemy is not essential in every case; that the destruction of the enemy's military force, the conquest of the enemy's provinces, the mere occupation of them, the mere invasion of them –

enterprises which are aimed directly at political objects – lastly, a passive expectation of the enemy's blow, are all means which, each in itself, may be used to force the enemy's will according as the peculiar circumstances of the case lead us to expect more from the one or the other. We could still add to these a whole category of shorter methods of gaining the end, which might be called arguments ad hominem. What branch of human affairs is there in which these sparks of individual spirit have not made their appearance, surmounting all formal considerations? And least of all can they fail to appear in War, where the personal character of the combatants plays such an important part, both in the cabinet and in the field. We limit ourselves to pointing this out, as it would be pedantry to attempt to reduce such influences into classes. Including these, we may say that the number of possible ways of reaching the object rises to infinity.

To avoid under-estimating these different short roads to one's purpose, either estimating them only as rare exceptions, or holding the difference which they cause in the conduct of War as insignificant, we must bear in mind the diversity of political objects which may cause a War – measure at a glance the distance which there is between a death struggle for political existence and a War which a forced or tottering alliance makes a matter of disagreeable duty. Between the two innumerable gradations occur in practice. If we reject one of these gradations in theory, we might with equal right reject the whole, which would be tantamount to shutting the real world completely out of sight.

These are the circumstances in general connected with the aim which we have to pursue in War; let us now turn to the means.

There is only one single means, it is the *fight*. However diversified this may be in form, however widely it may differ from a rough vent of hatred and animosity in a hand-to-hand encounter, whatever number of things may introduce themselves which are not actual fighting, still it is always implied in the conception of War that all the effects manifested have their roots in the combat.

That this must always be so in the greatest diversity and complication of the reality is proved in a very simple manner. All that takes place in War takes place through armed forces, but where the forces of War, i.e., armed men, are applied, there the idea of fighting must of necessity be at the foundation.

All, therefore, that relates to forces of War – all that is connected with their creation, maintenance, and application – belongs to military activity.

Creation and maintenance are obviously only the means, whilst application is the object.

The contest in War is not a contest of individual against individual, but an organised whole, consisting of manifold parts; in this great whole we may distinguish units of two kinds, the one determined by the subject, the other by the object. In an Army the mass of combatants ranges itself always into an order of new units, which again form members of a higher order. The combat of each of these members forms, therefore, also a more or less distinct unit. Further, the motive of the fight; therefore its object forms its unit.

Now, to each of these units which we distinguish in the contest we attach the name of combat.

If the idea of combat lies at the foundation of every application of armed power, then also the application of armed force in general is nothing more than the determining and arranging a certain number of combats.

Every activity in War, therefore, necessarily relates to the combat either directly or indirectly. The soldier is levied, clothed, armed, exercised, he sleeps, eats, drinks, and marches, all *merely to fight at the right time and place.*

If, therefore, all the threads of military activity terminate in the combat, we shall grasp them all when we settle the order of the combats. Only from this order and its execution proceed the effects, never directly from the conditions preceding them. Now, in the combat all the action is directed to the *destruction* of the enemy, or rather of *his fighting powers*, for this lies in the conception of combat. The destruction of the enemy's fighting power is, therefore, always the means to attain the object of the combat.

This object may likewise be the mere destruction of the enemy's armed force; but that is not by any means necessary, and it may be something quite different. Whenever, for instance, as we have shown, the defeat of the enemy is not the only means to attain the political object, whenever there are other objects which may be pursued as the aim in a War, then it follows of itself that such other objects may become the object of particular acts of Warfare, and therefore also the object of combats.

But even those combats which, as subordinate acts, are in the strict sense devoted to the destruction of the enemy's fighting force need not have that destruction itself as their first object.

If we think of the manifold parts of a great armed force, of the number of circumstances which come into activity when it is employed, then it is clear that the combat of such a force must also require a manifold organisation, a subordinating of parts and formation. There may and must naturally arise for particular parts a number of objects which are not themselves the destruction of the enemy's armed force, and which, while they certainly contribute to increase that destruction, do so only in an indirect manner. If a battalion is ordered to drive the enemy from a rising ground, or a bridge, &c., then properly the occupation of any such locality is the real object, the destruction of the enemy's armed force which takes place only the means or secondary matter. If the enemy can be driven away merely by a demonstration, the object is attained all the same; but this hill or bridge is, in point of fact, only required as a means of increasing the gross amount of loss inflicted on the enemy's armed force. It is the case on the field of battle, much more must it be so on the whole theatre of war, where not only one Army is opposed to another, but one State, one Nation, one whole country to another. Here the number of possible relations, and consequently possible combinations, is much greater, the diversity of measures increased, and by the gradation of objects, each subordinate to another the first means employed is further apart from the ultimate object.

It is therefore for many reasons possible that the object of a combat is not the destruction of the enemy's force, that is, of the force immediately opposed to us, but that this only appears as a means. But in all such cases it is no longer a question of complete destruction, for the combat is here nothing else but a measure of strength – has in itself no value except only that of the present result, that is, of its decision.

But a measuring of strength may be effected in cases where the opposing sides are very unequal by a mere comparative estimate. In such cases no fighting will take place, and the weaker will immediately give way.

If the object of a combat is not always the destruction of the enemy's forces therein engaged – and if its object can often be attained as well without the combat taking place at all, by merely making a resolve to fight, and by the circumstances to which this resolution gives rise – then that explains how a whole campaign may be carried on with great activity without the actual combat playing any notable part in it.

That this may be so military history proves by a hundred examples. How many of those cases can be justified, that is, without involving a contradiction and whether some of the celebrities who rose out of them would stand criticism, we shall leave undecided, for all we have to do with the matter is to show the possibility of such a course of events in War.

We have only one means in War – the battle; but this means, by the infinite variety of paths in which it may be applied, leads us into all the different ways which the multiplicity of objects allows of, so that we seem to have gained nothing; but that is not the case, for from this unity of means proceeds a thread which assists the study of the subject, as it runs through the whole web of military activity and holds it together.

But we have considered the destruction of the enemy's force as one of the objects which maybe pursued in War, and left undecided what relative importance should be given to it amongst other objects. In certain cases it will depend on circumstances, and as a general question we have left its value undetermined. We are once more brought back upon it, and we shall be able to get an insight into the value which must necessarily be accorded to it.

The combat is the single activity in War; in the combat the destruction of the enemy opposed to us is the means to the end; it is so even when the combat does not actually take place, because in that case there lies at the root of the decision the supposition at all events that this destruction is to be regarded as beyond doubt. It follows, therefore, that the destruction of the enemy's military force is the foundation-stone of all action in War, the great support of all combinations, which rest upon it like the arch on its abutments. All action, therefore, takes place on the supposition that if the solution by force of arms which lies at its foundation should be realised, it will be a favourable one. The decision by arms is, for all operations in War, great and small, what cash payment is in bill transactions. However remote from each other these relations, however seldom the realisation may take place, still it can never entirely fail to occur.

If the decision by arms lies at the foundation of all combinations, then it follows that the enemy can defeat each of them by gaining a victory on the field, not merely in the one on which our combination directly depends, but also in any other encounter, if it is only important enough; for every important decision by arms – that is, destruction of the enemy's forces – reacts upon all preceding it, because, like a liquid element, they tend to bring themselves to a level.

Thus, the destruction of the enemy's armed force appears, therefore, always as the superior and more effectual means, to which all others must give way.

It is, however, only when there is a supposed equality in all other conditions that we can ascribe to the destruction of the enemy's armed force the greater efficacy. It would, therefore, be a great mistake to draw the conclusion that a blind dash must always gain the victory over skill and caution. An unskilful attack would lead to the destruction of our own and not of the enemy's force, and therefore is not what is here meant. The superior efficacy belongs not to the *means* but to the *end*, and we are only comparing the effect of one realised purpose with the other.

If we speak of the destruction of the enemy's armed force, we must expressly point out that nothing obliges us to confine this idea to the mere physical force; on the contrary, the moral is necessarily implied as well, because both in fact are interwoven with each other, even in the most minute details, and therefore cannot be separated. But it is just in connection with the inevitable effect which has been referred to, of a great act of destruction (a great victory) upon all other decisions by arms, that this moral element is most fluid, if we may use that expression, and therefore distributes itself the most easily through all the parts.

Against the far superior worth which the destruction of the enemy's armed force has over all other means stands the expense and risk of this means, and it is only to avoid these that any other means are taken. That these must be costly stands to reason, for the waste of our own military forces must, ceteris paribus, always be greater the more our aim is directed upon the destruction of the enemy's power.

The danger lies in this, that the greater efficacy which we seek recoils on ourselves, and therefore has worse consequences in case we fail of success.

Other methods are, therefore, less costly when they succeed, less dangerous when they fail; but in this is necessarily lodged the condition that they are only opposed to similar ones, that is, that the enemy acts on the same principle; for if the enemy should choose the way of a great decision by arms, *our means must on that account be changed against our will, in order to correspond with his.* Then all depends on the issue of the act of destruction; but of course it is evident that, ceteris paribus, in this act we must be at a disadvantage in all respects because our views and our means had been directed in part upon other objects, which is not the case with the enemy. Two different objects of which one is not part, the other exclude each other, and therefore a force which may be applicable for the one may not serve for the other. If, therefore, one of two belligerents is determined to seek the great decision by arms, then he has a high probability of success, as soon as he is certain his opponent will not take that way, but follows a different object; and every one who sets before himself any such other aim only does so in a reasonable manner, provided he acts on the supposition that his adversary has as little intention as he has of resorting to the great decision by arms.

But what we have here said of another direction of views and forces relates only to other *positive objects*, which we may propose to ourselves in War, besides the destruction of the enemy's force, not by any means to the pure defensive, which may be adopted with a view thereby to exhaust the enemy's forces. In the pure defensive the positive object is wanting, and therefore, while on the defensive, our forces cannot at the same time be directed on other objects; they can only be employed to defeat the intentions of the enemy.

We have now to consider the opposite of the destruction of the enemy's armed force, that is to say, the preservation of our own. These two efforts always go together, as they mutually act and react on each other; they are integral parts of one and the same view, and we have only to ascertain what effect is produced when one or the other has the predominance. The endeavour to destroy the enemy's force has a positive object, and leads to positive results, of which the final aim is the conquest of the enemy. The preservation of our own forces has a negative object, leads therefore to the defeat of the enemy's intentions, that is to pure resistance, of which the final aim can be nothing more than to prolong the duration of the contest, so that the enemy shall exhaust himself in it.

The effort with a positive object calls into existence the act of destruction; the effort with the negative object awaits it.

How far this state of expectation should and may be carried we shall enter into more particularly in the theory of attack and defence, at the origin of which we again find ourselves. Here we shall content ourselves with saying that the awaiting must be no absolute endurance, and that in the action bound up with it the destruction of the enemy's armed force engaged in this conflict may be the aim just as well as anything else. It would therefore be a great error in the fundamental idea to suppose that the consequence of the negative course is that we are precluded from choosing the destruction of the enemy's military force as our object, and must prefer a bloodless solution. The advantage which the negative effort gives may certainly lead to that, but only at the risk of its not being the most advisable method, as that question is dependent on totally different conditions, resting not with ourselves but with our opponents. This other bloodless way cannot, therefore, be looked upon at all as the natural means of satisfying our great anxiety to spare our forces; on the contrary, when circumstances are not favourable, it would be the means of completely ruining them. Very many Generals have fallen into this error, and been ruined by it. The only necessary effect resulting from the superiority of the negative effort is the delay of the decision, so that the party acting takes refuge in that way, as it were, in the expectation of the decisive moment. The consequence of that is generally *the postponement of the action* as much as possible in time, and also in space, in so far as space is in connection with it. If the moment has arrived in which this can no longer be done without ruinous disadvantage, then the advantage of the negative must be considered as exhausted, and then comes forward unchanged the effort for the destruction of the enemy's force, which was kept back by a counterpoise, but never discarded.

We have seen, therefore, in the foregoing reflections, that there are many ways to the aim, that is, to the attainment of the political object; but that the only means is the combat, and that consequently everything is subject to a supreme law: which is the *decision by arms*; that where this is really demanded by one, it is a redress which cannot be refused by the other; that, therefore, a belligerent who takes any other way must make sure that his opponent will not take this means of redress, or his cause may be lost in that supreme court; hence therefore the destruction of the enemy's armed force, amongst all the objects which can be pursued in War, appears always as the one which overrules all others.

What may be achieved by combinations of another kind in War we shall only learn in the sequel, and naturally only by degrees. We content ourselves here with acknowledging in general their possibility, as something pointing to the difference between the reality and the conception, and to the influence of particular circumstances. But we could not avoid showing at once that the *bloody solution of the crisis*, the effort for the destruction of the enemy's force, is the firstborn son of War. If when political objects are unimportant, motives weak, the excitement of forces small, a cautious commander tries in all kinds of ways, without great crises and bloody solutions, to twist himself skilfully into a peace through the characteristic weaknesses of his enemy in the field and in the Cabinet, we have no right to find fault with him, if the premises on which he acts are well founded and justified by success; still we must require him to remember that he only travels on forbidden tracks, where the God of War may surprise him; that he ought always to keep his eye on the enemy, in order that he may not have to defend himself with a dress rapier if the enemy takes up a sharp sword.

The consequences of the nature of War, how ends and means act in it, how in the modifications of reality it deviates sometimes more, sometimes less, from its strict original conception, fluctuating backwards and forwards, yet always remaining under that strict conception as under a supreme law: all this we must retain before us, and bear constantly in mind in the consideration of each of the succeeding subjects, if we would rightly comprehend their true relations and proper importance, and not become involved incessantly in the most glaring contradictions with the reality, and at last with our own selves.

CHAPTER THREE

The Genius for War

EVERY SPECIAL calling in life, if it is to be followed with success, requires peculiar qualifications of understanding and soul. Where these are of a high order, and manifest themselves by extraordinary achievements, the mind to which they belong is termed *genius*.

We know very well that this word is used in many significations which are very different both in extent and nature, and that with many of these significations it is a very difficult task to define the essence of Genius; but as we neither profess to be philosopher nor grammarian, we must be allowed to keep to the meaning usual in ordinary language, and to understand by "genius" a very high mental capacity for certain employments.

We wish to stop for a moment over this faculty and dignity of the mind, in order to vindicate its title, and to explain more fully the meaning of the conception. But we shall not dwell on that (genius) which has obtained its title through a very great talent, on genius properly so called, that is a conception which has no defined limits. What we have to do is to bring under consideration every common tendency of the powers of the mind and soul towards the business of War, the whole of which common tendencies we may look upon as the *essence of military genius*. We say "common," for just therein consists military genius, that it is not one single quality bearing upon War, as, for instance, courage, while other qualities of mind and soul are wanting or have a direction which is unserviceable for War, but that it is *an harmonious association of powers*, in which one or other may predominate, but none must be in opposition.

If every combatant required to be more or less endowed with military genius, then our armies would be very weak; for as it implies a peculiar bent of the intelligent powers, therefore it can only rarely be found where the mental powers of a people are called into requisition and trained in many different ways. The fewer the employments followed by a Nation, the more that of arms predominates, so much the more prevalent will military genius also be found. But this merely applies to its prevalence, by no means to its degree, for that depends on the general state of intellectual culture in the country. If we look at a wild, warlike race, then we find a warlike spirit in individuals much more common than in a civilised people; for in the former almost every warrior possesses it, whilst in the civilised whole, masses are only carried away by it from necessity, never by inclination. But amongst uncivilised people we never find a really great General, and very seldom what we can properly call a military genius, because that requires a development of the intelligent powers which cannot be found in an uncivilised state. That a civilised people may also have a warlike tendency and development is a matter of course; and the more this is general, the more frequently also will military spirit be found in individuals in their armies. Now as this coincides in such case with the higher degree of civilisation, therefore from such nations have issued forth the most brilliant military exploits, as the Romans and the French have exemplified. The greatest names in these and in all other nations that have been renowned in War belong strictly to epochs of higher culture.

From this we may infer how great a share the intelligent powers have in superior military genius. We shall now look more closely into this point.

War is the province of danger, and therefore courage above all things is the first quality of a warrior.

Courage is of two kinds: first, physical courage, or courage in presence of danger to the person; and next, moral courage, or courage before responsibility, whether it be before the judgment-seat of external authority, or of the inner power, the conscience. We only speak here of the first.

Courage before danger to the person, again, is of two kinds. First, it may be indifference to danger, whether proceeding from the organism of the individual, contempt of death, or habit: in any of these cases it is to be regarded as a permanent condition.

Secondly, courage may proceed from positive motives, such as personal pride, patriotism, enthusiasm of any kind. In this case courage is not so much a normal condition as an impulse.

We may conceive that the two kinds act differently. The first kind is more certain, because it has become a second nature, never forsakes the man; the second often leads him farther. In the first there is more of firmness, in the second, of boldness. The first leaves the judgment cooler, the second raises its power at times, but often bewilders it. The two combined make up the most perfect kind of courage.

War is the province of physical exertion and suffering. In order not to be completely overcome by them, a certain strength of body and mind is required, which, either natural or acquired, produces indifference to them. With these qualifications, under the guidance of simply a sound understanding, a man is at once a proper instrument for War; and these are the qualifications so generally to be met with amongst wild and half-civilised tribes. If we go further in the demands which War makes on it, then we find the powers of the understanding predominating. War is the province of uncertainty: three-fourths of those things upon which action in War must be calculated, are hidden more or less in the clouds of great uncertainty. Here, then, above all a fine and penetrating mind is called for, to search out the truth by the tact of its judgment.

An average intellect may, at one time, perhaps hit upon this truth by accident; an extraordinary courage, at another, may compensate for the want of this tact; but in the majority of cases the average result will always bring to light the deficient understanding.

War is the province of chance. In no sphere of human activity is such a margin to be left for this intruder, because none is so much in constant contact with him on all sides. He increases the uncertainty of every circumstance, and deranges the course of events.

From this uncertainty of all intelligence and suppositions, this continual interposition of chance, the actor in War constantly finds things different from his expectations; and this cannot fail to have an influence on his plans, or at least on the presumptions connected with these plans. If this influence is so great as to render the pre-determined plan completely nugatory, then, as a rule, a new one must be substituted in its place; but at the moment the necessary data are often wanting for this, because in the course of action circumstances press for immediate decision, and allow no time to look about for fresh data, often not enough for mature consideration.

But it more often happens that the correction of one premise, and the knowledge of chance events which have arisen, are not sufficient to overthrow our plans completely, but only suffice to produce hesitation. Our knowledge of circumstances has increased, but our uncertainty, instead of having diminished, has only increased. The reason of this is, that we do not gain all our experience at once, but by degrees; thus our determinations continue to be assailed incessantly by fresh experience; and the mind, if we may use the expression, must always be "under arms."

Now, if it is to get safely through this perpetual conflict with the unexpected, two qualities are indispensable: in the first place an intellect which, even in the midst of this intense obscurity, is not without some traces of inner light, which lead to the truth, and then the courage to follow this faint light. The first is figuratively expressed by the French phrase coup d'oeil. The other is resolution. As the battle is the feature in War to which attention was originally chiefly directed, and as time and space are important elements in it, more particularly when cavalry with their rapid decisions were the chief arm, the idea of rapid and correct decision related in the first instance to the estimation of these two elements, and to denote the idea an expression was adopted which actually only points to a correct judgment by eye. Many teachers of the Art of War then gave this limited signification as the definition of coup d'oeil. But it is undeniable that all able decisions formed in the moment of action soon came to be understood by the expression, as, for instance, the hitting upon the right point of attack, &c. It is, therefore, not only the physical, but more frequently the mental eye which is meant in coup d'oeil. Naturally, the expression, like the thing, is always more in its place in the field of tactics: still, it must not be wanting in strategy, inasmuch as in it rapid decisions are often necessary. If we strip this conception of that which the expression has given it of the over-figurative and restricted, then it amounts simply to the rapid discovery of a truth which to the ordinary mind is either not visible at all or only becomes so after long examination and reflection.

Resolution is an act of courage in single instances, and if it becomes a characteristic trait, it is a habit of the mind. But here we do not mean courage in face of bodily danger, but in face of responsibility, therefore, to a certain extent against moral danger. This has been often called courage d'esprit, on the ground that it springs from the understanding; nevertheless, it is no act of the understanding on that account; it is an act of feeling. Mere intelligence is still not courage, for we often see the cleverest people devoid of resolution. The mind must, therefore, first awaken the feeling of courage, and then be guided and supported by it, because in momentary emergencies the man is swayed more by his feelings than his thoughts.

We have assigned to resolution the office of removing the torments of doubt, and the dangers of delay, when there are no sufficient motives for guidance. Through the unscrupulous use of language which is prevalent, this term is often applied to the mere propensity to daring, to bravery, boldness, or temerity. But, when there are *sufficient motives* in the man, let them be objective or subjective, true or false, we have no right to speak of his resolution; for, when we do so, we put ourselves in his place, and we throw into the scale doubts which did not exist with him.

Here there is no question of anything but of strength and weakness. We are not pedantic enough to dispute with the use of language about this little misapplication, our observation is only intended to remove wrong objections.

This resolution now, which overcomes the state of doubting, can only be called forth by the intellect, and, in fact, by a peculiar tendency of the same. We maintain that the mere union of a superior understanding and the necessary feelings are not sufficient to make up resolution. There are persons who possess the keenest perception for the most difficult problems, who are also not fearful of responsibility, and yet in cases of difficulty cannot come to a resolution. Their courage and their sagacity operate independently of each other, do not give each other a hand, and on that account do not produce resolution as a result. The forerunner of resolution is an act of the mind making evident the necessity of venturing, and thus influencing the will. This quite peculiar direction of the mind, which conquers every other fear in man by the fear of wavering or doubting, is what makes up resolution in strong minds; therefore, in our opinion, men who have little intelligence can never be resolute. They may act without hesitation under perplexing circumstances, but then they act without reflection. Now, of course, when a man acts without reflection he cannot be at variance with himself by doubts, and such a mode of action may now and then lead to the right point; but we say now as before, it is the average result which indicates the existence of military genius. Should our assertion appear extraordinary to any one, because he knows many a resolute hussar officer who is no deep thinker, we must remind him that the question here is about a peculiar direction of the mind, and not about great thinking powers.

We believe, therefore, that resolution is indebted to a special direction of the mind for its existence, a direction which belongs to a strong head rather than to a brilliant one. In corroboration of this genealogy of resolution we may add that there have been many instances of men who have shown the greatest resolution in an inferior rank, and have lost it in a higher position. While, on the one hand, they are obliged to resolve, on the other they see the dangers of a wrong decision, and as they are surrounded with things new to them, their understanding loses its original force, and they become only the more timid the more they become aware of the danger of the irresolution into which they have fallen, and the more they have formerly been in the habit of acting on the spur of the moment.

From the coup d'oeil and resolution we are naturally to speak of its kindred quality, *presence of mind*, which in a region of the unexpected like War must act a great part, for it is indeed nothing but a great conquest over the unexpected. As we admire presence of mind in a pithy answer to anything said unexpectedly, so we admire it in a ready expedient on sudden danger. Neither the answer nor the expedient need be in themselves extraordinary, if they only hit the point; for that which as the result of mature reflection would be nothing unusual, therefore insignificant in its impression on us, may as an instantaneous act of the mind produce a pleasing impression. The expression "presence of mind" certainly denotes very fitly the readiness and rapidity of the help rendered by the mind.

Whether this noble quality of a man is to be ascribed more to the peculiarity of his mind or to the equanimity of his feelings, depends on the nature of the case, although neither of the two can be entirely wanting. A telling repartee bespeaks rather a ready wit, a ready expedient on sudden danger implies more particularly a well-balanced mind.

If we take a general view of the four elements composing the atmosphere in which War moves, of *danger, physical effort, uncertainty,* and *chance,* it is easy to conceive that a great force of mind and understanding is requisite to be able to make way with safety and success amongst such opposing elements, a force which, according to the different modifications arising out of circumstances, we find termed by military writers and annalists as *energy, firmness, staunchness, strength of mind and character.* All these manifestations of the heroic nature might be regarded as one and the same power of volition, modified according to circumstances; but nearly related as these things are to each other, still they are not one and the same, and it is desirable for us to distinguish here a little more closely at least the action of the powers of the soul in relation to them.

In the first place, to make the conception clear, it is essential to observe that the weight, burden, resistance, or whatever it may be called, by which that force of the soul in the General is brought to light, is only in a very small measure the enemy's activity, the enemy's resistance, the enemy's action directly. The enemy's activity only affects the General directly in the first place in relation to his person, without disturbing his action as Commander. If the enemy, instead of two hours, resists for four, the Commander instead of two hours is four hours in danger; this is a quantity which plainly diminishes the higher the rank of the Commander. What is it for one in the post of Commander-in-Chief? It is nothing.

Secondly, although the opposition offered by the enemy has a direct effect on the Commander through the loss of means arising from prolonged resistance, and the responsibility connected with that loss, and his force of will is first tested and called forth by these anxious considerations, still we maintain that this is not the heaviest burden by far which he has to bear, because he has only himself to settle with. All the other effects of the enemy's resistance act directly upon the combatants under his command, and through them react upon him.

As long as his men full of good courage fight with zeal and spirit, it is seldom necessary for the Chief to show great energy of purpose in the pursuit of his object. But as soon as difficulties arise – and that must always happen when great results are at stake – then things no longer move on of themselves like a well-oiled machine, the machine itself then begins to offer resistance, and to overcome this the Commander must have a great force of will. By this resistance we must not exactly suppose disobedience and murmurs, although these are frequent enough with particular individuals; it is the whole feeling of the dissolution of all physical and moral power, it is the heartrending sight of the bloody sacrifice which the Commander has to contend with in himself, and then in all others who directly or indirectly transfer to him their impressions, feelings, anxieties, and desires. As the forces in one individual after another become prostrated, and can no longer be excited and supported by an effort of his own will, the whole inertia of the mass gradually rests its weight on the Will of the Commander: by the spark in his breast, by the light of his spirit, the spark of purpose, the light of hope, must be kindled afresh in others: in so far only as he is equal to this, he stands above the masses and continues to be their master; whenever that influence ceases, and his own spirit is no longer strong enough to revive the spirit of all others, the masses drawing him down with them sink into the lower region of animal nature, which shrinks from danger and knows not shame. These are the weights which the courage and intelligent faculties of the military Commander have to overcome if he is to make his name illustrious. They increase with the masses, and therefore, if the forces in question are to continue equal to the burden, they must rise in proportion to the height of the station.

Energy in action expresses the strength of the motive through which the action is excited, let the motive have its origin in a conviction of the understanding, or in an impulse. But the latter can hardly ever be wanting where great force is to show itself.

Of all the noble feelings which fill the human heart in the exciting tumult of battle, none, we must admit, are so powerful and constant as the soul's thirst for honour and renown, which the German language treats so unfairly and tends to depreciate by the unworthy associations in the words Ehrgeiz (greed of honour) and Ruhmsucht (hankering after glory). No doubt it is just in War that the abuse of these proud aspirations of the soul must bring upon the human race the most shocking outrages, but by their origin they are certainly to be counted amongst the noblest feelings which belong to human nature, and in War they are the vivifying principle which gives the enormous body a spirit. Although other feelings may be more general in their influence, and many of them – such as love of country, fanaticism, revenge, enthusiasm of every kind – may seem to stand higher, the thirst for honour and renown still remains indispensable. Those other feelings may rouse the great masses in general, and excite them more powerfully, but they do not give the Leader a desire to will more than others, which is an essential requisite in his position if he is to make himself distinguished in it. They do not, like a thirst for honour, make the military act specially the property of the Leader, which he strives to turn to the best account; where he ploughs with toil, sows with care, that he may reap plentifully. It is through these aspirations we have been speaking of in Commanders, from the highest to the lowest, this sort of energy, this spirit of emulation, these incentives, that the action of armies is chiefly animated and made successful. And now as to that which specially concerns the head of all, we ask, Has there ever been a great Commander destitute of the love of honour, or is such a character even conceivable?

Firmness denotes the resistance of the will in relation to the force of a single blow, *staunchness* in relation to a continuance of blows. Close as is the analogy between the two, and often as the one is used in place of the other, still there is a notable difference between them which cannot be mistaken, inasmuch as firmness against a single powerful impression may have its root in the mere strength of a feeling, but staunchness must be supported rather by the understanding, for the greater the duration of an action the more systematic deliberation is connected with it, and from this staunchness partly derives its power.

If we now turn to *strength of mind or soul*, then the first question is, What are we to understand thereby?

Plainly it is not vehement expressions of feeling, nor easily excited passions, for that would be contrary to all the usage of language, but the power of listening to reason in the midst of the most intense excitement, in the storm of the most violent passions. Should this power depend on strength of understanding alone? We doubt it. The fact that there are men of the greatest intellect who cannot command themselves certainly proves nothing to the contrary, for we might say that it perhaps requires an understanding of a powerful rather than of a comprehensive nature; but we believe we shall be nearer the truth if we assume that the power of submitting oneself to the control of the understanding, even in moments of the most violent excitement of the feelings, that power which we call *self-command*, has its root in the heart itself. It is, in point of fact, another feeling, which in strong minds balances the excited passions without destroying them; and it is only through this equilibrium that the mastery of the understanding is secured. This counterpoise is nothing but a sense of the dignity of man, that noblest pride, that deeply-seated desire of the soul always to act as a being endued with understanding and reason. We may therefore say that a strong mind is one which does not lose its balance even under the most violent excitement.

If we cast a glance at the variety to be observed in the human character in respect to feeling, we find, first, some people who have very little excitability, who are called phlegmatic or indolent.

Secondly, some very excitable, but whose feelings still never overstep certain limits, and who are therefore known as men full of feeling, but sober-minded.

Thirdly, those who are very easily roused, whose feelings blaze up quickly and violently like gunpowder, but do not last.

Fourthly, and lastly, those who cannot be moved by slight causes, and who generally are not to be roused suddenly, but only gradually; but whose feelings become very powerful and are much more lasting. These are men with strong passions, lying deep and latent.

This difference of character lies probably close on the confines of the physical powers which move the human organism, and belongs to that amphibious organisation which we call the nervous system, which appears to be partly material, partly spiritual. With our weak philosophy, we shall not proceed further in this mysterious field. But it is important for us to spend a moment over the effects which these different natures have on, action in War, and to see how far a great strength of mind is to be expected from them.

Indolent men cannot easily be thrown out of their equanimity, but we cannot certainly say there is strength of mind where there is a want of all manifestation of power.

At the same time, it is not to be denied that such men have a certain peculiar aptitude for War, on account of their constant equanimity. They often want the positive motive to action, impulse, and consequently activity, but they are not apt to throw things into disorder.

The peculiarity of the second class is that they are easily excited to act on trifling grounds, but in great matters they are easily overwhelmed. Men of this kind show great activity in helping an unfortunate individual, but by the distress of a whole Nation they are only inclined to despond, not roused to action.

Such people are not deficient in either activity or equanimity in War; but they will never accomplish anything great unless a great intellectual force furnishes the motive, and it is very seldom that a strong, independent mind is combined with such a character.

Excitable, inflammable feelings are in themselves little suited for practical life, and therefore they are not very fit for War. They have certainly the advantage of strong impulses, but that cannot long sustain them. At the same time, if the excitability in such men takes the direction of courage, or a sense of honour, they may often be very useful in inferior positions in War, because the action in War over which commanders in inferior positions have control is generally of shorter duration. Here one courageous resolution, one effervescence of the forces of the soul, will often suffice. A brave attack, a soul-stirring hurrah, is the work of a few moments, whilst a brave contest on the battle-field is the work of a day, and a campaign the work of a year.

Owing to the rapid movement of their feelings, it is doubly difficult for men of this description to preserve equilibrium of the mind; therefore they frequently lose head, and that is the worst phase in their nature as respects the conduct of War. But it would be contrary to experience to maintain that very excitable spirits can never preserve a steady equilibrium – that is to say, that they cannot do so even under the strongest excitement. Why should they not have the sentiment of self-respect, for, as a rule, they are men of a noble nature? This feeling is seldom wanting in them, but it has not time to produce an effect. After an outburst they suffer most from a feeling of inward humiliation. If through education, self-observance, and experience of life, they have learned, sooner or later, the means of being on their guard, so that at the moment of powerful excitement they are conscious betimes of the counteracting force within their own breasts, then even such men may have great strength of mind.

Lastly, those who are difficult to move, but on that account susceptible of very deep feelings, men who stand in the same relation to the preceding as red heat to a flame, are the best adapted by means of their Titanic strength to roll away the enormous masses by which we may figuratively represent the difficulties which beset command in War. The effect of their feelings is like the movement of a great body, slower, but more irresistible.

Although such men are not so likely to be suddenly surprised by their feelings and carried away so as to be afterwards ashamed of themselves, like the preceding, still it would be contrary to experience to believe that they can never lose their equanimity, or be overcome by blind passion; on the contrary, this must always happen whenever the noble pride of self-control is wanting, or as often as it has not sufficient weight. We see examples of this most frequently in men of noble minds belonging to savage nations, where the low degree of mental cultivation favours always the dominance of the passions. But even amongst the most civilised classes in civilised States, life is full of examples of this kind – of men carried away by the violence of their passions, like the poacher of old chained to the stag in the forest.

We therefore say once more a strong mind is not one that is merely susceptible of strong excitement, but one which can maintain its serenity under the most powerful excitement, so that, in spite of the storm in the breast, the perception and judgment can act with perfect freedom, like the needle of the compass in the storm-tossed ship.

By the term *strength of character*, or simply *character*, is denoted tenacity of conviction, let it be the result of our own or of others' views, and whether they are principles, opinions, momentary inspirations, or any kind of emanations of the understanding; but this kind of firmness certainly cannot manifest itself if the views themselves are subject to frequent change. This frequent change need not be the consequence of external influences; it may proceed from the continuous activity of our own mind, in which case it indicates a characteristic unsteadiness of mind. Evidently we should not say of a man who changes his views every moment, however much the motives of change may originate with himself, that he has character. Only those men, therefore, can be said to have this quality whose conviction is very constant, either because it is deeply rooted and clear in itself, little liable to alteration, or because, as in the case of indolent men, there is a want of mental activity, and therefore a want of motives to change; or lastly, because an explicit act of the will, derived from an imperative maxim of the understanding, refuses any change of opinion up to a certain point.

Now in War, owing to the many and powerful impressions to which the mind is exposed, and in the uncertainty of all knowledge and of all science, more things occur to distract a man from the road he has entered upon, to make him doubt himself and others, than in any other human activity.

The harrowing sight of danger and suffering easily leads to the feelings gaining ascendency over the conviction of the understanding; and in the twilight which surrounds everything a deep clear view is so difficult that a change of opinion is more conceivable and more pardonable. It is, at all times, only conjecture or guesses at truth which we have to act upon. This is why differences of opinion are nowhere so great as in War, and the stream of impressions acting counter to one's own convictions never ceases to flow. Even the greatest impassibility of mind is hardly proof against them, because the impressions are powerful in their nature, and always act at the same time upon the feelings.

When the discernment is clear and deep, none but general principles and views of action from a high standpoint can be the result; and on these principles the opinion in each particular case immediately under consideration lies, as it were, at anchor. But to keep to these results of bygone reflection, in opposition to the stream of opinions and phenomena which the present brings with it, is just the difficulty. Between the particular case and the principle there is often a wide space which cannot always be traversed on a visible chain of conclusions, and where a certain faith in self is necessary and a certain amount of scepticism is serviceable. Here often nothing else will help us but an imperative maxim which, independent of reflection, at once controls it: that maxim is, in all doubtful cases to adhere to the first opinion, and not to give it up until a clear conviction forces us to do so. We must firmly believe in the superior authority of well-tried maxims, and under the dazzling influence of momentary events not forget that their value is of an inferior stamp. By this preference which in doubtful cases we give to first convictions, by adherence to the same our actions acquire that stability and consistency which make up what is called character.

It is easy to see how essential a well-balanced mind is to strength of character; therefore men of strong minds generally have a great deal of character.

Force of character leads us to a spurious variety of it – *obstinacy*.

It is often very difficult in concrete cases to say where the one ends and the other begins; on the other hand, it does not seem difficult to determine the difference in idea.

Obstinacy is no fault of the understanding; we use the term as denoting a resistance against our better judgment, and it would be inconsistent to charge that to the understanding, as the understanding is the power of judgment. Obstinacy is *a fault of the feelings* or heart. This inflexibility of will, this impatience of contradiction, have their origin only in a particular kind of egotism, which sets above every other pleasure that of governing both self and others by its own mind alone. We should call it a kind of vanity, were it not decidedly something better. Vanity is satisfied with mere show, but obstinacy rests upon the enjoyment of the thing.

We say, therefore, force of character degenerates into obstinacy whenever the resistance to opposing judgments proceeds not from better convictions or a reliance upon a trustworthy maxim, but from a feeling of opposition. If this definition, as we have already admitted, is of little assistance practically, still it will prevent obstinacy from being considered merely force of character intensified, whilst it is something essentially different – something which certainly lies close to it and is cognate to it, but is at the same time so little an intensification of it that there are very obstinate men who from want of understanding have very little force of character.

Having in these high attributes of a great military Commander made ourselves acquainted with those qualities in which heart and head co-operate, we now come to a speciality of military activity which perhaps may be looked upon as the most marked if it is not the most important, and which only makes a demand on the power of the mind without regard to the forces of feelings. It is the connection which exists between War and country or ground.

This connection is, in the first place, a permanent condition of War, for it is impossible to imagine our organised Armies effecting any operation otherwise than in some given space; it is, secondly, of the most decisive importance, because it modifies, at times completely alters, the action of all forces; thirdly, while on the one hand it often concerns the most minute features of locality, on the other it may apply to immense tracts of country.

In this manner a great peculiarity is given to the effect of this connection of War with country and ground. If we think of other occupations of man which have a relation to these objects, on horticulture, agriculture, on building houses and hydraulic works, on mining, on the chase, and forestry, they are all confined within very limited spaces which may be soon explored with sufficient exactness. But the Commander in War must commit the business he has in hand to a corresponding space which his eye cannot survey, which the keenest zeal cannot always explore, and with which, owing to the constant changes taking place, he can also seldom become properly acquainted. Certainly the enemy generally is in the same situation; still, in the first place, the difficulty, although common to both, is not the less a difficulty, and he who by talent and practice overcomes it will have a great advantage on his side; secondly, this equality of the difficulty on both sides is merely an abstract supposition which is rarely realised in the particular case, as one of the two opponents (the defensive) usually knows much more of the locality than his adversary.

This very peculiar difficulty must be overcome by a natural mental gift of a special kind which is known by the – too restricted – term of Orisinn sense of locality. It is the power of quickly forming a correct geometrical idea of any portion of country, and consequently of being able to find one's place in it exactly at any time. This is plainly an act of the imagination. The perception no doubt is formed partly by means of the physical eye, partly by the mind, which fills up what is wanting with ideas derived from knowledge and experience, and out of the fragments visible to the physical eye forms a whole; but that this whole should present itself vividly to the reason, should become a picture, a mentally drawn map, that this picture should be fixed, that the details should never again separate themselves – all that can only be effected by the mental faculty which we call imagination. If some great poet or painter should feel hurt that we require from his goddess such an office; if he shrugs his shoulders at the notion that a sharp gamekeeper must necessarily excel in imagination, we readily grant that we only speak here of imagination in a limited sense, of its service in a really menial capacity. But, however slight this service, still it must be the work of that natural gift, for if that gift is wanting, it would be difficult to imagine things plainly in all the completeness of the visible. That a good memory is a great assistance we freely allow, but whether memory is to be considered as an independent faculty of the mind in this case, or whether it is just that power of imagination which here fixes these things better on the memory, we leave undecided, as in many respects it seems difficult upon the whole to conceive these two mental powers apart from each other.

That practice and mental acuteness have much to do with it is not to be denied. Puysegur, the celebrated Quartermaster-General of the famous Luxemburg, used to say that he had very little confidence in himself in this respect at first, because if he had to fetch the parole from a distance he always lost his way.

It is natural that scope for the exercise of this talent should increase along with rank. If the hussar and rifleman in command of a patrol must know well all the highways and byways, and if for that a few marks, a few limited powers of observation, are sufficient, the Chief of an Army must make himself familiar with the general geographical features of a province and of a country; must always have vividly before his eyes the direction of the roads, rivers, and hills, without at the same time being able to dispense with the narrower "sense of locality" Orisinn. No doubt, information of various kinds as to objects in general, maps, books, memoirs, and for details the assistance of his Staff, are a great help to him; but it is nevertheless certain that if he has himself a talent for forming an ideal picture of a country quickly and distinctly, it lends to his action an easier and firmer step, saves him from a certain mental helplessness, and makes him less dependent on others.

If this talent then is to be ascribed to imagination, it is also almost the only service which military activity requires from that erratic goddess, whose influence is more hurtful than useful in other respects.

We think we have now passed in review those manifestations of the powers of mind and soul which military activity requires from human nature. Everywhere intellect appears as an essential co-operative force; and thus we can understand how the work of War, although so plain and simple in its effects, can never be conducted with distinguished success by people without distinguished powers of the understanding.

When we have reached this view, then we need no longer look upon such a natural idea as the turning an enemy's position, which has been done a thousand times, and a hundred other similar conceptions, as the result of a great effort of genius.

Certainly one is accustomed to regard the plain honest soldier as the very opposite of the man of reflection, full of inventions and ideas, or of the brilliant spirit shining in the ornaments of refined education of every kind. This antithesis is also by no means devoid of truth; but it does not show that the efficiency of the soldier consists only in his courage, and that there is no particular energy and capacity of the brain required in addition to make a man merely what is called a true soldier. We must again repeat that there is nothing more common than to hear of men losing their energy on being raised to a higher position, to which they do not feel themselves equal; but we must also remind our readers that we are speaking of pre-eminent services, of such as give renown in the branch of activity to which they belong. Each grade of command in War therefore forms its own stratum of requisite capacity of fame and honour.

An immense space lies between a General – that is, one at the head of a whole War, or of a theatre of War – and his Second in Command, for the simple reason that the latter is in more immediate subordination to a superior authority and supervision, consequently is restricted to a more limited sphere of independent thought. This is why common opinion sees no room for the exercise of high talent except in high places, and looks upon an ordinary capacity as sufficient for all beneath: this is why people are rather inclined to look upon a subordinate General grown grey in the service, and in whom constant discharge of routine duties has produced a decided poverty of mind, as a man of failing intellect, and, with all respect for his bravery, to laugh at his simplicity. It is not our object to gain for these brave men a better lot – that would contribute nothing to their efficiency, and little to their happiness; we only wish to represent things as they are, and to expose the error of believing that a mere bravo without intellect can make himself distinguished in War.

As we consider distinguished talents requisite for those who are to attain distinction, even in inferior positions, it naturally follows that we think highly of those who fill with renown the place of Second in Command of an Army; and their seeming simplicity of character as compared with a polyhistor, with ready men of business, or with councillors of state, must not lead us astray as to the superior nature of their intellectual activity. It happens sometimes that men import the fame gained in an inferior position into a higher one, without in reality deserving it in the new position; and then if they are not much employed, and therefore not much exposed to the risk of showing their weak points, the judgment does not distinguish very exactly what degree of fame is really due to them; and thus such men are often the occasion of too low an estimate being formed of the characteristics required to shine in certain situations.

For each station, from the lowest upwards, to render distinguished services in War, there must be a particular genius. But the title of genius, history and the judgment of posterity only confer, in general, on those minds which have shone in the highest rank, that of Commanders-in-Chief. The reason is that here, in point of fact, the demand on the reasoning and intellectual powers generally is much greater.

To conduct a whole War, or its great acts, which we call campaigns, to a successful termination, there must be an intimate knowledge of State policy in its higher relations. The conduct of the War and the policy of the State here coincide, and the General becomes at the same time the Statesman.

We do not give Charles XII. the name of a great genius, because he could not make the power of his sword subservient to a higher judgment and philosophy – could not attain by it to a glorious object. We do not give that title to Henry IV. (of France), because he did not live long enough to set at rest the relations of different States by his military activity, and to occupy himself in that higher field where noble feelings and a chivalrous disposition have less to do in mastering the enemy than in overcoming internal dissension.

In order that the reader may appreciate all that must be comprehended and judged of correctly at a glance by a General, we refer to the first chapter. We say the General becomes a Statesman, but he must not cease to be the General. He takes into view all the relations of the State on the one hand; on the other, he must know exactly what he can do with the means at his disposal.

As the diversity, and undefined limits, of all the circumstances bring a great number of factors into consideration in War, as the most of these factors can only be estimated according to probability, therefore, if the Chief of an Army does not bring to bear upon them a mind with an intuitive perception of the truth, a confusion of ideas and views must take place, in the midst of which the judgment will become bewildered. In this sense, Buonaparte was right when he said that many of the questions which come before a General for decision would make problems for a mathematical calculation not unworthy of the powers of Newton or Euler.

What is here required from the higher powers of the mind is a sense of unity, and a judgment raised to such a compass as to give the mind an extraordinary faculty of vision which in its range allays and sets aside a thousand dim notions which an ordinary understanding could only bring to light with great effort, and over which it would exhaust itself. But this higher activity of the mind, this glance of genius, would still not become matter of history if the qualities of temperament and character of which we have treated did not give it their support.

Truth alone is but a weak motive of action with men, and hence there is always a great difference between knowing and action, between science and art. The man receives the strongest impulse to action through the feelings, and the most powerful succour, if we may use the expression, through those faculties of heart and mind which we have considered under the terms of resolution, firmness, perseverance, and force of character.

If, however, this elevated condition of heart and mind in the General did not manifest itself in the general effects resulting from it, and could only be accepted on trust and faith, then it would rarely become matter of history.

All that becomes known of the course of events in War is usually very simple, and has a great sameness in appearance; no one on the mere relation of such events perceives the difficulties connected with them which had to be overcome. It is only now and again, in the memoirs of Generals or of those in their confidence, or by reason of some special historical inquiry directed to a particular circumstance, that a portion of the many threads composing the whole web is brought to light. The reflections, mental doubts, and conflicts which precede the execution of great acts are purposely concealed because they affect political interests, or the recollection of them is accidentally lost because they have been looked upon as mere scaffolding which had to be removed on the completion of the building.

If, now, in conclusion, without venturing upon a closer definition of the higher powers of the soul, we should admit a distinction in the intelligent faculties themselves according to the common ideas established by language, and ask ourselves what kind of mind comes closest to military genius, then a look at the subject as well as at experience will tell us that searching rather than inventive minds, comprehensive minds rather than such as have a special bent, cool rather than fiery heads, are those to which in time of War we should prefer to trust the welfare of our women and children, the honour and the safety of our fatherland.

CHAPTER FOUR
Of Danger in War

USUALLY BEFORE we have learnt what danger really is, we form an idea of it which is rather attractive than repulsive. In the intoxication of enthusiasm, to fall upon the enemy at the charge – who cares then about bullets and men falling? To throw oneself, blinded by excitement for a moment, against cold death, uncertain whether we or another shall escape him, and all this close to the golden gate of victory, close to the rich fruit which ambition thirsts for – can this be difficult? It will not be difficult, and still less will it appear so. But such moments, which, however, are not the work of a single pulse-beat, as is supposed, but rather like doctors' draughts, must be taken diluted and spoilt by mixture with time – such moments, we say, are but few.

Let us accompany the novice to the battle-field. As we approach, the thunder of the cannon becoming plainer and plainer is soon followed by the howling of shot, which attracts the attention of the inexperienced. Balls begin to strike the ground close to us, before and behind. We hasten to the hill where stands the General and his numerous Staff. Here the close striking of the cannon balls and the bursting of shells is so frequent that the seriousness of life makes itself visible through the youthful picture of imagination. Suddenly some one known to us falls – a shell strikes amongst the crowd and causes some involuntary movements – we begin to feel that we are no longer perfectly at ease and collected; even the bravest is at least to some degree confused. Now, a step farther into the battle which is raging before us like a scene in a theatre, we get to the nearest General of Division; here ball follows ball, and the noise of our own guns increases the confusion. From the General of Division to the Brigadier. He, a man of acknowledged bravery, keeps carefully behind a rising ground, a house, or a tree – a sure sign of increasing danger. Grape rattles on the roofs of the houses and in the fields; cannon balls howl over us, and plough the air in all directions, and soon there is a frequent whistling of musket balls. A step farther towards the troops, to that sturdy infantry which for hours has maintained its firmness under this heavy fire; here the air is filled with the hissing of balls which announce their proximity by a short sharp noise as they pass within an inch of the ear, the head, or the breast.

To add to all this, compassion strikes the beating heart with pity at the sight of the maimed and fallen. The young soldier cannot reach any of these different strata of danger without feeling that the light of reason does not move here in the same medium, that it is not refracted in the same manner as in speculative contemplation. Indeed, he must be a very extraordinary man who, under these impressions for the first time, does not lose the power of making any instantaneous decisions. It is true that habit soon blunts such impressions; in half in hour we begin to be more or less indifferent to all that is going on around us: but an ordinary character never attains to complete coolness and the natural elasticity of mind; and so we perceive that here again ordinary qualities will not suffice – a thing which gains truth, the wider the sphere of activity which is to be filled. Enthusiastic, stoical, natural bravery, great ambition, or also long familiarity with danger – much of all this there must be if all the effects produced in this resistant medium are not to fall far short of that which in the student's chamber may appear only the ordinary standard.

Danger in War belongs to its friction; a correct idea of its influence is necessary for truth of perception, and therefore it is brought under notice here.

CHAPTER FIVE

Of Bodily Exertion in War

IF NO ONE were allowed to pass an opinion on the events of War, except at a moment when he is benumbed by frost, sinking from heat and thirst, or dying with hunger and fatigue, we should certainly have fewer judgments correct *objectively; but they would be so, *subjectively*, at least; that is, they would contain in themselves the exact relation between the person giving the judgment and the object. We can perceive this by observing how modestly subdued, even spiritless and desponding, is the opinion passed upon the results of untoward events by those who have been eye-witnesses, but especially if they have been parties concerned. This is, according to our view, a criterion of the influence which bodily fatigue exercises, and of the allowance to be made for it in matters of opinion.

Amongst the many things in War for which no tariff can be fixed, bodily effort may be specially reckoned. Provided there is no waste, it is a coefficient of all the forces, and no one can tell exactly to what extent it may be carried. But what is remarkable is, that just as only a strong arm enables the archer to stretch the bowstring to the utmost extent, so also in War it is only by means of a great directing spirit that we can expect the full power latent in the troops to be developed. For it is one thing if an Army, in consequence of great misfortunes, surrounded with danger, falls all to pieces like a wall that has been thrown down, and can only find safety in the utmost exertion of its bodily strength; it is another thing entirely when a victorious Army, drawn on by proud feelings only, is conducted at the will of its Chief. The same effort which in the one case might at most excite our pity must in the other call forth our admiration, because it is much more difficult to sustain.

By this comes to light for the inexperienced eye one of those things which put fetters in the dark, as it were, on the action of the mind, and wear out in secret the powers of the soul.

Although here the question is strictly only respecting the extreme effort required by a Commander from his Army, by a leader from his followers, therefore of the spirit to demand it and of the art of getting it, still the personal physical exertion of Generals and of the Chief Commander must not be overlooked. Having brought the analysis of War conscientiously up to this point, we could not but take account also of the weight of this small remaining residue.

We have spoken here of bodily effort, chiefly because, like danger, it belongs to the fundamental causes of friction, and because its indefinite quantity makes it like an elastic body, the friction of which is well known to be difficult to calculate.

To check the abuse of these considerations, of such a survey of things which aggravate the difficulties of War, nature has given our judgment a guide in our sensibilities, just as an individual cannot with advantage refer to his personal deficiencies if he is insulted and ill-treated, but may well do so if he has successfully repelled the affront, or has fully revenged it, so no Commander or Army will lessen the impression of a disgraceful defeat by depicting the danger, the distress, the exertions, things which would immensely enhance the glory of a victory. Thus our feeling, which after all is only a higher kind of judgment, forbids us to do what seems an act of justice to which our judgment would be inclined.

CHAPTER SIX

Information in War

By THE WORD "information" we denote all the knowledge which we have of the enemy and his country; therefore, in fact, the foundation of all our ideas and actions. Let us just consider the nature of this foundation, its want of trustworthiness, its changefulness, and we shall soon feel what a dangerous edifice War is, how easily it may fall to pieces and bury us in its ruins. For although it is a maxim in all books that we should trust only certain information, that we must be always suspicious, that is only a miserable book comfort, belonging to that description of knowledge in which writers of systems and compendiums take refuge for want of anything better to say.

Great part of the information obtained in War is contradictory, a still greater part is false, and by far the greatest part is of a doubtful character. What is required of an officer is a certain power of discrimination, which only knowledge of men and things and good judgment can give. The law of probability must be his guide. This is not a trifling difficulty even in respect of the first plans, which can be formed in the chamber outside the real sphere of War, but it is enormously increased when in the thick of War itself one report follows hard upon the heels of another; it is then fortunate if these reports in contradicting each other show a certain balance of probability, and thus themselves call forth a scrutiny. It is much worse for the inexperienced when accident does not render him this service, but one report supports another, confirms it, magnifies it, finishes off the picture with fresh touches of colour, until necessity in urgent haste forces from us a resolution which will soon be discovered to be folly, all those reports having been lies, exaggerations, errors, &c. &c. In a few words, most reports are false, and the timidity of men acts as a multiplier of lies and untruths. As a general rule, every one is more inclined to lend credence to the bad than the good. Every one is inclined to magnify the bad in some measure, and although the alarms which are thus propagated like the waves of the sea subside into themselves, still, like them, without any apparent cause they rise again. Firm in reliance on his own better convictions, the Chief must stand like a rock against which the sea breaks its fury in vain. The role is not easy; he who is not by nature of a buoyant disposition, or trained by experience in War, and matured in judgment, may let it be his rule to do violence to his own natural conviction by inclining from the side of fear to that of hope; only by that means will he be able to preserve his balance. This difficulty of seeing things correctly, which is one of the greatest sources of friction in War, makes things appear quite different from what was expected. The impression of the senses is stronger than the force of the ideas resulting from methodical reflection, and this goes so far that no important undertaking was ever yet carried out without the Commander having to subdue new doubts in himself at the time of commencing the execution of his work. Ordinary men who follow the suggestions of others become, therefore, generally undecided on the spot; they think that they have found circumstances different from what they had expected, and this view gains strength by their again yielding to the suggestions of others. But even the man who has made his own plans, when he comes to see things with his own eyes will often think he has done wrong. Firm reliance on self must make him proof against the seeming pressure of the moment; his first conviction will in the end prove true, when the foreground scenery which fate has pushed on to the stage of War, with its accompaniments of terrific objects, is drawn aside and the horizon extended. This is one of the great chasms which separate *conception* from *execution*.

CHAPTER SEVEN
Friction in War

As LONG AS we have no personal knowledge of War, we cannot conceive where those difficulties lie of which so much is said, and what that genius and those extraordinary mental powers required in a General have really to do. All appears so simple, all the requisite branches of knowledge appear so plain, all the combinations so unimportant, that in comparison with them the easiest problem in higher mathematics impresses us with a certain scientific dignity. But if we have seen War, all becomes intelligible; and still, after all, it is extremely difficult to describe what it is which brings about this change, to specify this invisible and completely efficient factor.

Everything is very simple in War, but the simplest thing is difficult. These difficulties accumulate and produce a friction which no man can imagine exactly who has not seen War, Suppose now a traveller, who towards evening expects to accomplish the two stages at the end of his day's journey, four or five leagues, with post-horses, on the high road – it is nothing. He arrives now at the last station but one, finds no horses, or very bad ones; then a hilly country, bad roads; it is a dark night, and he is glad when, after a great deal of trouble, he reaches the next station, and finds there some miserable accommodation. So in War, through the influence of an infinity of petty circumstances, which cannot properly be described on paper, things disappoint us, and we fall short of the mark. A powerful iron will overcomes this friction; it crushes the obstacles, but certainly the machine along with them. We shall often meet with this result. Like an obelisk towards which the principal streets of a town converge, the strong will of a proud spirit stands prominent and commanding in the middle of the Art of War.

Friction is the only conception which in a general way corresponds to that which distinguishes real War from War on paper. The military machine, the Army and all belonging to it, is in fact simple, and appears on this account easy to manage. But let us reflect that no part of it is in one piece, that it is composed entirely of individuals, each of which keeps up its own friction in all directions. Theoretically all sounds very well: the commander of a battalion is responsible for the execution of the order given; and as the battalion by its discipline is glued together into one piece, and the chief must be a man of acknowledged zeal, the beam turns on an iron pin with little friction. But it is not so in reality, and all that is exaggerated and false in such a conception manifests itself at once in War. The battalion always remains composed of a number of men, of whom, if chance so wills, the most insignificant is able to occasion delay and even irregularity. The danger which War brings with it, the bodily exertions which it requires, augment this evil so much that they may be regarded as the greatest causes of it.

This enormous friction, which is not concentrated, as in mechanics, at a few points, is therefore everywhere brought into contact with chance, and thus incidents take place upon which it was impossible to calculate, their chief origin being chance. As an instance of one such chance: the weather. Here the fog prevents the enemy from being discovered in time, a battery from firing at the right moment, a report from reaching the General; there the rain prevents a battalion from arriving at the right time, because instead of for three it had to march perhaps eight hours; the cavalry from charging effectively because it is stuck fast in heavy ground.

These are only a few incidents of detail by way of elucidation, that the reader may be able to follow the author, for whole volumes might be written on these difficulties. To avoid this, and still to give a clear conception of the host of small difficulties to be contended with in War, we might go on heaping up illustrations, if we were not afraid of being tiresome. But those who have already comprehended us will permit us to add a few more.

Activity in War is movement in a resistant medium. Just as a man immersed in water is unable to perform with ease and regularity the most natural and simplest movement, that of walking, so in War, with ordinary powers, one cannot keep even the line of mediocrity. This is the reason that the correct theorist is like a swimming master, who teaches on dry land movements which are required in the water, which must appear grotesque and ludicrous to those who forget about the water. This is also why theorists, who have never plunged in them-selves, or who cannot deduce any generalities from their experience, are unpractical and even absurd, because they only teach what every one knows – how to walk.

Further, every War is rich in particular facts, while at the same time each is an unexplored sea, full of rocks which the General may have a suspicion of, but which he has never seen with his eye, and round which, moreover, he must steer in the night. If a contrary wind also springs up, that is, if any great accidental event declares itself adverse to him, then the most consummate skill, presence of mind, and energy are required, whilst to those who only look on from a distance all seems to proceed with the utmost ease. The knowledge of this friction is a chief part of that so often talked of, experience in War, which is required in a good General. Certainly he is not the best General in whose mind it assumes the greatest dimensions, who is the most over-awed by it (this includes that class of over-anxious Generals, of whom there are so many amongst the experienced); but a General must be aware of it that he may overcome it, where that is possible, and that he may not expect a degree of precision in results which is impossible on account of this very friction. Besides, it can never be learnt theoretically; and if it could, there would still be wanting that experience of judgment which is called tact, and which is always more necessary in a field full of innumerable small and diversified objects than in great and decisive cases, when one's own judgment may be aided by consultation with others. Just as the man of the world, through tact of judgment which has become habit, speaks, acts, and moves only as suits the occasion, so the officer experienced in War will always, in great and small matters, at every pulsation of War as we may say, decide and determine suitably to the occasion. Through this experience and practice the idea comes to his mind of itself that so and so will not suit. And thus he will not easily place himself in a position by which he is compromised, which, if it often occurs in War, shakes all the foundations of confidence and becomes extremely dangerous.

It is therefore this friction, or what is so termed here, which makes that which appears easy in War difficult in reality. As we proceed, we shall often meet with this subject again, and it will hereafter become plain that besides experience and a strong will, there are still many other rare qualities of the mind required to make a man a consum-mate General.

CHAPTER EIGHT
Concluding Remarks, Book One

THOSE THINGS which as elements meet together in the atmosphere of War and make it a resistant medium for every activity we have designated under the terms danger, bodily effort (exertion), information, and friction. In their impedient effects they may therefore be comprehended again in the collective notion of a general friction. Now is there, then, no kind of oil which is capable of diminishing this friction? Only one, and that one is not always available at the will of the Commander or his Army. It is the habituation of an Army to War.

Habit gives strength to the body in great exertion, to the mind in great danger, to the judgment against first impressions. By it a valuable circumspection is generally gained throughout every rank, from the hussar and rifleman up to the General of Division, which facilitates the work of the Chief Commander.

As the human eye in a dark room dilates its pupil, draws in the little light that there is, partially distinguishes objects by degrees, and at last knows them quite well, so it is in War with the experienced soldier, whilst the novice is only met by pitch dark night.

Habituation to War no General can give his Army at once, and the camps of manoeuvre (peace exercises) furnish but a weak substitute for it, weak in comparison with real experience in War, but not weak in relation to other Armies in which the training is limited to mere mechanical exercises of routine. So to regulate the exercises in peace time as to include some of these causes of friction, that the judgment, circumspection, even resolution of the separate leaders may be brought into exercise, is of much greater consequence than those believe who do not know the thing by experience. It is of immense importance that the soldier, high or low, whatever rank he has, should not have to encounter in War those things which, when seen for the first time, set him in astonishment and perplexity; if he has only met with them one single time before, even by that he is half acquainted with them. This relates even to bodily fatigues. They should be practised less to accustom the body to them than the mind. In War the young soldier is very apt to regard unusual fatigues as the consequence of faults, mistakes, and embarrassment in the conduct of the whole, and to become distressed and despondent as a consequence. This would not happen if he had been prepared for this beforehand by exercises in peace.

Another less comprehensive but still very important means of gaining habituation to War in time of peace is to invite into the service officers of foreign armies who have had experience in War. Peace seldom reigns over all Europe, and never in all quarters of the world. A State which has been long at peace should, therefore, always seek to procure some officers who have done good service at the different scenes of Warfare, or to send there some of its own, that they may get a lesson in War.

However small the number of officers of this description may appear in proportion to the mass, still their influence is very sensibly felt.[6] Their experience, the bent of their genius, the stamp of their character, influence their subordinates and comrades; and besides that, if they cannot be placed in positions of superior command, they may always be regarded as men acquainted with the country, who may be questioned on many special occasions.

---

6   The War of 1870 furnishes a marked illustration. Von   Moltke and von Goeben, not to mention many others, had both   seen service in this manner, the former in Turkey and Syria,   the latter in Spain – *Editor*.

BOOK TWO

On the Theory of War

CHAPTER ONE

Branches of the Art of War

WAR IN ITS LITERAL meaning is fighting, for fighting alone is the efficient principle in the manifold activity which in a wide sense is called War. But fighting is a trial of strength of the moral and physical forces by means of the latter. That the moral cannot be omitted is evident of itself, for the condition of the mind has always the most decisive influence on the forces employed in War.

The necessity of fighting very soon led men to special inventions to turn the advantage in it in their own favour: in consequence of these the mode of fighting has undergone great alterations; but in whatever way it is conducted its conception remains unaltered, and fighting is that which constitutes War.

The inventions have been from the first weapons and equipments for the individual combatants. These have to be provided and the use of them learnt before the War begins. They are made suitable to the nature of the fighting, consequently are ruled by it; but plainly the activity engaged in these appliances is a different thing from the fight itself; it is only the preparation for the combat, not the conduct of the same. That arming and equipping are not essential to the conception of fighting is plain, because mere wrestling is also fighting.

Fighting has determined everything appertaining to arms and equipment, and these in turn modify the mode of fighting; there is, therefore, a reciprocity of action between the two.

Nevertheless, the fight itself remains still an entirely special activity, more particularly because it moves in an entirely special element, namely, in the element of danger.

If, then, there is anywhere a necessity for drawing a line between two different activities, it is here; and in order to see clearly the importance of this idea, we need only just to call to mind how often eminent personal fitness in one field has turned out nothing but the most useless pedantry in the other.

It is also in no way difficult to separate in idea the one activity from the other, if we look at the combatant forces fully armed and equipped as a given means, the profitable use of which requires nothing more than a knowledge of their general results.

The Art of War is therefore, in its proper sense, the art of making use of the given means in fighting, and we cannot give it a better name than the "Conduct of War." On the other hand, in a wider sense all activities which have their existence on account of War, therefore the whole creation of troops, that is levying them, arming, equipping, and exercising them, belong to the Art of War.

To make a sound theory it is most essential to separate these two activities, for it is easy to see that if every act of War is to begin with the preparation of military forces, and to presuppose forces so organised as a primary condition for conducting War, that theory will only be applicable in the few cases to which the force available happens to be exactly suited. If, on the other hand, we wish to have a theory which shall suit most cases, and will not be wholly useless in any case, it must be founded on those means which are in most general use, and in respect to these only on the actual results springing from them.

The conduct of War is, therefore, the formation and conduct of the fighting. If this fighting was a single act, there would be no necessity for any further subdivision, but the fight is composed of a greater or less number of single acts, complete in themselves, which we call combats, as we have shown in the first chapter of the first book, and which form new units. From this arises the totally different activities, that of the *formation* and *conduct* of these single combats in themselves, and the *combination* of them with one another, with a view to the ultimate object of the War. The first is called *tactics*, the other *strategy*.

This division into tactics and strategy is now in almost general use, and every one knows tolerably well under which head to place any single fact, without knowing very distinctly the grounds on which the classification is founded. But when such divisions are blindly adhered to in practice, they must have some deep root. We have searched for this root, and we might say that it is just the usage of the majority which has brought us to it. On the other hand, we look upon the arbitrary, unnatural definitions of these conceptions sought to be established by some writers as not in accordance with the general usage of the terms.

According to our classification, therefore, tactics *is the theory of the use of military forces in combat.* Strategy *is the theory of the use of combats for the object of the war.*

The way in which the conception of a single, or independent combat, is more closely determined, the conditions to which this unit is attached, we shall only be able to explain clearly when we consider the combat; we must content ourselves for the present with saying that in relation to space, therefore in combats taking place at the same time, the unit reaches just as far as *personal command* reaches; but in regard to time, and therefore in relation to combats which follow each other in close succession, it reaches to the moment when the crisis which takes place in every combat is entirely passed.

That doubtful cases may occur, cases, for instance, in which several combats may perhaps be regarded also as a single one, will not overthrow the ground of distinction we have adopted, for the same is the case with all grounds of distinction of real things which are differentiated by a gradually diminishing scale. There may, therefore, certainly be acts of activity in War which, without any alteration in the point of view, may just as well be counted strategic as tactical; for example, very extended positions resembling a chain of posts, the preparations for the passage of a river at several points, &c.

Our classification reaches and covers only the *use of the military force.* But now there are in War a number of activities which are subservient to it, and still are quite different from it; sometimes closely allied, sometimes less near in their affinity. All these activities relate to the *maintenance of the military force.* In the same way as its creation and training precede its use, so its maintenance is always a necessary condition. But, strictly viewed, all activities thus connected with it are always to be regarded only as preparations for fighting; they are certainly nothing more than activities which are very close to the action, so that they run through the hostile act alternate in importance with the use of the forces. We have therefore a right to exclude them as well as the other preparatory activities from the Art of War in its restricted sense, from the conduct of War properly so called; and we are obliged to do so if we would comply with the first principle of all theory, the elimination of all heterogeneous elements. Who would include in the real "conduct of War" the whole litany of subsistence and administration, because it is admitted to stand in constant reciprocal action with the use of the troops, but is something essentially different from it?

We have said, in the third chapter of our first book, that as the fight or combat is the only directly effective activity, therefore the threads of all others, as they end in it, are included in it. By this we meant to say that to all others an object was thereby appointed which, in accordance with the laws peculiar to themselves, they must seek to attain. Here we must go a little closer into this subject.

The subjects which constitute the activities outside of the combat are of various kinds.

The one part belongs, in one respect, to the combat itself, is identical with it, whilst it serves in another respect for the maintenance of the military force. The other part belongs purely to the subsistence, and has only, in consequence of the reciprocal action, a limited influence on the combats by its results. The subjects which in one respect belong to the fighting itself are *marches, camps*, and *cantonments*, for they suppose so many different situations of troops, and where troops are supposed there the idea of the combat must always be present.

The other subjects, which only belong to the maintenance, are *subsistence, care of the sick*, the *supply and repair of arms and equipment*.

Marches are quite identical with the use of the troops. The act of marching in the combat, generally called manoeuvring, certainly does not necessarily include the use of weapons, but it is so completely and necessarily combined with it that it forms an integral part of that which we call a combat. But the march outside the combat is nothing but the execution of a strategic measure. By the strategic plan is settled *when, where*, and *with what forces* a battle is to be delivered – and to carry that into execution the march is the only means.

The march outside of the combat is therefore an instrument of strategy, but not on that account exclusively a subject of strategy, for as the armed force which executes it may be involved in a possible combat at any moment, therefore its execution stands also under tactical as well as strategic rules. If we prescribe to a column its route on a particular side of a river or of a branch of a mountain, then that is a strategic measure, for it contains the intention of fighting on that particular side of the hill or river in preference to the other, in case a combat should be necessary during the march.

But if a column, instead of following the road through a valley, marches along the parallel ridge of heights, or for the convenience of marching divides itself into several columns, then these are tactical arrangements, for they relate to the manner in which we shall use the troops in the anticipated combat.

The particular order of march is in constant relation with readiness for combat, is therefore tactical in its nature, for it is nothing more than the first or preliminary disposition for the battle which may possibly take place.

As the march is the instrument by which strategy apportions its active elements, the combats, but these last often only appear by their results and not in the details of their real course, it could not fail to happen that in theory the instrument has often been substituted for the efficient principle. Thus we hear of a decisive skilful march, allusion being thereby made to those combat-combinations to which these marches led. This substitution of ideas is too natural and conciseness of expression too desirable to call for alteration, but still it is only a condensed chain of ideas in regard to which we must never omit to bear in mind the full meaning, if we would avoid falling into error.

We fall into an error of this description if we attribute to strategical combinations a power independent of tactical results. We read of marches and manoeuvres combined, the object attained, and at the same time not a word about combat, from which the conclusion is drawn that there are means in War of conquering an enemy without fighting. The prolific nature of this error we cannot show until hereafter.

But although a march can be regarded absolutely as an integral part of the combat, still there are in it certain relations which do not belong to the combat, and therefore are neither tactical nor strategic. To these belong all arrangements which concern only the accommodation of the troops, the construction of bridges, roads, &c. These are only conditions; under many circumstances they are in very close connection, and may almost identify themselves with the troops, as in building a bridge in presence of the enemy; but in themselves they are always activities, the theory of which does not form part of the theory of the conduct of War.

Camps, by which we mean every disposition of troops in concentrated, therefore in battle order, in contradistinction to cantonments or quarters, are a state of rest, therefore of restoration; but they are at the same time also the strategic appointment of a battle on the spot, chosen; and by the manner in which they are taken up they contain the fundamental lines of the battle, a condition from which every defensive battle starts; they are therefore essential parts of both strategy and tactics.

Cantonments take the place of camps for the better refreshment of the troops. They are therefore, like camps, strategic subjects as regards position and extent; tactical subjects as regards internal organisation, with a view to readiness to fight.

The occupation of camps and cantonments no doubt usually combines with the recuperation of the troops another object also, for example, the covering a district of country, the holding a position; but it can very well be only the first. We remind our readers that strategy may follow a great diversity of objects, for everything which appears an advantage may be the object of a combat, and the preservation of the instrument with which War is made must necessarily very often become the object of its partial combinations.

If, therefore, in such a case strategy ministers only to the maintenance of the troops, we are not on that account out of the field of strategy, for we are still engaged with the use of the military force, because every disposition of that force upon any point Whatever of the theatre of War is such a use.

But if the maintenance of the troops in camp or quarters calls forth activities which are no employment of the armed force, such as the construction of huts, pitching of tents, subsistence and sanitary services in camps or quarters, then such belong neither to strategy nor tactics.

Even entrenchments, the site and preparation of which are plainly part of the order of battle, therefore tactical subjects, do not belong to the theory of the conduct of War so far as respects the execution of their construction the knowledge and skill required for such work being, in point of fact, qualities inherent in the nature of an organised Army; the theory of the combat takes them for granted.

Amongst the subjects which belong to the mere keeping up of an armed force, because none of the parts are identified with the combat, the victualling of the troops themselves comes first, as it must be done almost daily and for each individual. Thus it is that it completely permeates military action in the parts constituting strategy – we say parts constituting strategy, because during a battle the subsistence of troops will rarely have any influence in modifying the plan, although the thing is conceivable enough. The care for the subsistence of the troops comes therefore into reciprocal action chiefly with strategy, and there is nothing more common than for the leading strategic features of a campaign and War to be traced out in connection with a view to this supply. But however frequent and however important these views of supply may be, the subsistence of the troops always remains a completely different activity from the use of the troops, and the former has only an influence on the latter by its results.

The other branches of administrative activity which we have mentioned stand much farther apart from the use of the troops. The care of sick and wounded, highly important as it is for the good of an Army, directly affects it only in a small portion of the individuals composing it, and therefore has only a weak and indirect influence upon the use of the rest. The completing and replacing articles of arms and equipment, except so far as by the organism of the forces it constitutes a continuous activity inherent in them – takes place only periodically, and therefore seldom affects strategic plans.

We must, however, here guard ourselves against a mistake. In certain cases these subjects may be really of decisive importance. The distance of hospitals and depôts of munitions may very easily be imagined as the sole cause of very important strategic decisions. We do not wish either to contest that point or to throw it into the shade. But we are at present occupied not with the particular facts of a concrete case, but with abstract theory; and our assertion therefore is that such an influence is too rare to give the theory of sanitary measures and the supply of munitions and arms an importance in theory of the conduct of War such as to make it worth while to include in the theory of the conduct of War the consideration of the different ways and systems which the above theories may furnish, in the same way as is certainly necessary in regard to victualling troops.

If we have clearly understood the results of our reflections, then the activities belonging to War divide themselves into two principal classes, into such as are only "preparations for War" and into the "War itself." This division must therefore also be made in theory.

The knowledge and applications of skill in the preparations for War are engaged in the creation, discipline, and maintenance of all the military forces; what general names should be given to them we do not enter into, but we see that artillery, fortification, elementary tactics, as they are called, the whole organisation and administration of the various armed forces, and all such things are included. But the theory of War itself occupies itself with the use of these prepared means for the object of the war. It needs of the first only the results, that is, the knowledge of the principal properties of the means taken in hand for use. This we call "The Art of War" in a limited sense, or "Theory of the Conduct of War," or "Theory of the Employment of Armed Forces," all of them denoting for us the same thing.

The present theory will therefore treat the combat as the real contest, marches, camps, and cantonments as circumstances which are more or less identical with it. The subsistence of the troops will only come into consideration like *other given circumstances* in respect of its results, not as an activity belonging to the combat.

The Art of War thus viewed in its limited sense divides itself again into tactics and strategy. The former occupies itself with the form of the separate combat, the latter with its use. Both connect themselves with the circumstances of marches, camps, cantonments only through the combat, and these circumstances are tactical or strategic according as they relate to the form or to the signification of the battle.

No doubt there will be many readers who will consider superfluous this careful separation of two things lying so close together as tactics and strategy, because it has no direct effect on the conduct itself of War. We admit, certainly that it would be pedantry to look for direct effects on the field of battle from a theoretical distinction.

But the first business of every theory is to clear up conceptions and ideas which have been jumbled together, and, we may say, entangled and confused; and only when a right understanding is established, as to names and conceptions, can we hope to progress with clearness and facility, and be certain that author and reader will always see things from the same point of view. Tactics and strategy are two activities mutually permeating each other in time and space, at the same time essentially different activities, the inner laws and mutual relations of which cannot be intelligible at all to the mind until a clear conception of the nature of each activity is established.

He to whom all this is nothing, must either repudiate all theoretical consideration, *or his understanding has not as yet been pained* by the confused and perplexing ideas resting on no fixed point of view, leading to no satisfactory result, sometimes dull, sometimes fantastic, sometimes floating in vague generalities, which we are often obliged to hear and read on the conduct of War, owing to the spirit of scientific investigation having hitherto been little directed to these subjects.

CHAPTER TWO

On the Theory of War

1. *The first conception of the "art of war" was merely the preparation of the armed forces.*

FORMERLY by the term "Art of War," or "Science of War," nothing was understood but the totality of those branches of knowledge and those appliances of skill occupied with material things. The pattern and preparation and the mode of using arms, the construction of fortifications and entrenchments, the organism of an army and the mechanism of its movements, were the subject; these branches of knowledge and skill above referred to, and the end and aim of them all was the establishment of an armed force fit for use in War. All this concerned merely things belonging to the material world and a one-sided activity only, and it was in fact nothing but an activity advancing by gradations from the lower occupations to a finer kind of mechanical art. The relation of all this to War itself was very much the same as the relation of the art of the sword cutler to the art of using the sword. The employment in the moment of danger and in a state of constant reciprocal action of the particular energies of mind and spirit in the direction proposed to them was not yet even mooted.

2. *True war first appears in the art of sieges.*

In the art of sieges we first perceive a certain degree of guidance of the combat, something of the action of the intellectual faculties upon the material forces placed under their control, but generally only so far that it very soon embodied itself again in new material forms, such as approaches, trenches, counter-approaches, batteries, &c., and every step which this action of the higher faculties took was marked by some such result; it was only the thread that was required on which to string these material inventions in order. As the intellect can hardly manifest itself in this kind of War, except in such things, so therefore nearly all that was necessary was done in that way.

3. *Then tactics tried to find its way in the same direction.*

Afterwards tactics attempted to give to the mechanism of its joints the character of a general disposition, built upon the peculiar properties of the instrument, which character leads indeed to the battle-field, but instead of leading to the free activity of mind, leads to an Army made like an automaton by its rigid formations and orders of battle, which, movable only by the word of command, is intended to unwind its activities like a piece of clockwork.

4. *The real conduct of war only made its appearance incidentally and incognito.*

The conduct of War properly so called, that is, a use of the prepared means adapted to the most special requirements, was not considered as any suitable subject for theory, but one which should be left to natural talents alone. By degrees, as War passed from the hand-to-hand encounters of the middle ages into a more regular and systematic form, stray reflections on this point also forced themselves into men's minds, but they mostly appeared only incidentally in memoirs and narratives, and in a certain measure incognito.

5. *Reflections on military events brought about the want of a theory.*

As contemplation on War continually increased, and its history every day assumed more of a critical character, the urgent want appeared of the support of fixed maxims and rules, in order that in the controversies naturally arising about military events the war of opinions might be brought to some one point. This whirl of opinions, which neither revolved on any central pivot nor according to any appreciable laws, could not but be very distasteful to people's minds.

6. *Endeavours to establish a positive theory.*

There arose, therefore, an endeavour to establish maxims, rules, and even systems for the conduct of War. By this the attainment of a positive object was proposed, without taking into view the endless difficulties which the conduct of War presents in that respect. The conduct of War, as we have shown, has no definite limits in any direction, while every system has the circumscribing nature of a synthesis, from which results an irreconcileable opposition between such a theory and practice.

7. *Limitation to material objects.*

Writers on theory felt the difficulty of the subject soon enough, and thought themselves entitled to get rid of it by directing their maxims and systems only upon material things and a one-sided activity. Their aim was to reach results, as in the science for the preparation for War, entirely certain and positive, and therefore only to take into consideration that which could be made matter of calculation.

8. *Superiority of numbers.*

The superiority in numbers being a material condition, it was chosen from amongst all the factors required to produce victory, because it could be brought under mathematical laws through combinations of time and space. It was thought possible to leave out of sight all other circumstances, by supposing them to be equal on each side, and therefore to neutralise one another. This would have been very well if it had been done to gain a preliminary knowledge of this one factor, according to its relations, but to make it a rule for ever to consider superiority of numbers as the sole law; to see the whole secret of the Art of War in the formula, *in a certain time, at a certain point, to bring up superior masses* – was a restriction overruled by the force of realities.

9. *Victualling of troops.*

By one theoretical school an attempt was made to systematise another material element also, by making the subsistence of troops, according to a previously established organism of the Army, the supreme legislator in the higher conduct of War. In this way certainly they arrived at definite figures, but at figures which rested on a number of arbitrary calculations, and which therefore could not stand the test of practical application.

10. *Base.*

An ingenious author tried to concentrate in a single conception, that of a *base*, a whole host of objects amongst which sundry relations even with immaterial forces found their way in as well. The list comprised the subsistence of the troops, the keeping them complete in numbers and equipment, the security of communications with the home country, lastly, the security of retreat in case it became necessary; and, first of all, he proposed to substitute this conception of a base for all these things; then for the base itself to substitute its own length (extent); and, last of all, to substitute the angle formed by the army with this base: all this was done to obtain a pure geometrical result utterly useless. This last is, in fact, unavoidable, if we reflect that none of these substitutions could be made without violating truth and leaving out some of the things contained in the original conception. The idea of a base is a real necessity for strategy, and to have conceived it is meritorious; but to make such a use of it as we have depicted is completely inadmissible, and could not but lead to partial conclusions which have forced these theorists into a direction opposed to common sense, namely, to a belief in the decisive effect of the enveloping form of attack.

11. *Interior lines.*

As a reaction against this false direction, another geometrical principle, that of the so-called interior lines, was then elevated to the throne. Although this principle rests on a sound foundation, on the truth that the combat is the only effectual means in War, still it is, just on account of its purely geometrical nature, nothing but another case of one-sided theory which can never gain ascendency in the real world.

12. *All these attempts are open to objection.*

All these attempts at theory are only to be considered in their analytical part as progress in the province of truth, but in their synthetical part, in their precepts and rules, they are quite unserviceable.

They strive after determinate quantities, whilst in War all is undetermined, and the calculation has always to be made with varying quantities.

They direct the attention only upon material forces, while the whole military action is penetrated throughout by intelligent forces and their effects.

They only pay regard to activity on one side, whilst War is a constant state of reciprocal action, the effects of which are mutual.

13. *As a rule they exclude genius.*

All that was not attainable by such miserable philosophy, the offspring of partial views, lay outside the precincts of science – and was the field of genius, which *raises itself above rules.*

Pity the warrior who is contented to crawl about in this beggardom of rules, which are too bad for genius, over which it can set itself superior, over which it can perchance make merry! What genius does must be the best of all rules, and theory cannot do better than to show how and why it is so.

Pity the theory which sets itself in opposition to the mind! It cannot repair this contradiction by any humility, and the humbler it is so much the sooner will ridicule and contempt drive it out of real life.

14. *The difficulty of theory as soon as moral quantities come into consideration.*

Every theory becomes infinitely more difficult from the moment that it touches on the province of moral quantities. Architecture and painting know quite well what they are about as long as they have only to do with matter; there is no dispute about mechanical or optical construction. But as soon as the moral activities begin their work, as soon as moral impressions and feelings are produced, the whole set of rules dissolves into vague ideas.

The science of medicine is chiefly engaged with bodily phenomena only; its business is with the animal organism, which, liable to perpetual change, is never exactly the same for two moments. This makes its practice very difficult, and places the judgment of the physician above his science; but how much more difficult is the case if a moral effect is added, and how much higher must we place the physician of the mind?

15. *The moral quantities must not be excluded in war.*

But now the activity in War is never directed solely against matter; it is always at the same time directed against the intelligent force which gives life to this matter, and to separate the two from each other is impossible.

But the intelligent forces are only visible to the inner eye, and this is different in each person, and often different in the same person at different times.

As danger is the general element in which everything moves in War, it is also chiefly by courage, the feeling of one's own power, that the judgment is differently influenced. It is to a certain extent the crystalline lens through which all appearances pass before reaching the understanding.

And yet we cannot doubt that these things acquire a certain objective value simply through experience.

Every one knows the moral effect of a surprise, of an attack in flank or rear. Every one thinks less of the enemy's courage as soon as he turns his back, and ventures much more in pursuit than when pursued. Every one judges of the enemy's General by his reputed talents, by his age and experience, and shapes his course accordingly. Every one casts a scrutinising glance at the spirit and feeling of his own and the enemy's troops. All these and similar effects in the province of the moral nature of man have established themselves by experience, are perpetually recurring, and therefore warrant our reckoning them as real quantities of their kind. What could we do with any theory which should leave them out of consideration?

Certainly experience is an indispensable title for these truths. With psychological and philosophical sophistries no theory, no General, should meddle.

16. *Principal difficulty of a theory for the conduct of war.*

In order to comprehend clearly the difficulty of the proposition which is contained in a theory for the conduct of War, and thence to deduce the necessary characteristics of such a theory, we must take a closer view of the chief particulars which make up the nature of activity in War.

17. *First speciality. – moral forces and their effects. (hostile feeling.)*

The first of these specialities consists in the moral forces and effects.

The combat is, in its origin, the expression of *hostile feeling*, but in our great combats, which we call Wars, the hostile feeling frequently resolves itself into merely a hostile *view*, and there is usually no innate hostile feeling residing in individual against individual. Nevertheless, the combat never passes off without such feelings being brought into activity. National hatred, which is seldom wanting in our Wars, is a substitute for personal hostility in the breast of individual opposed to individual. But where this also is wanting, and at first no animosity of feeling subsists, a hostile feeling is kindled by the combat itself; for an act of violence which any one commits upon us by order of his superior, will excite in us a desire to retaliate and be revenged on him, sooner than on the superior power at whose command the act was done. This is human, or animal if we will; still it is so. We are very apt to regard the combat in theory as an abstract trial of strength, without any participation on the part of the feelings, and that is one of the thousand errors which theorists deliberately commit, because they do not see its consequences.

Besides that excitation of feelings naturally arising from the combat itself, there are others also which do not essentially belong to it, but which, on account of their relationship, easily unite with it – ambition, love of power, enthusiasm of every kind, &c. &c.

18. *The impressions of danger. (courage.)*

Finally, the combat begets the element of danger, in which all the activities of War must live and move, like the bird in the air or the fish in the water. But the influences of danger all pass into the feelings, either directly – that is, instinctively – or through the medium of the understanding. The effect in the first case would be a desire to escape from the danger, and, if that cannot be done, fright and anxiety. If this effect does not take place, then it is *courage*, which is a counterpoise to that instinct. Courage is, however, by no means an act of the understanding, but likewise a feeling, like fear; the latter looks to the physical preservation, courage to the moral preservation. Courage, then, is a nobler instinct. But because it is so, it will not allow itself to be used as a lifeless instrument, which produces its effects exactly according to prescribed measure. Courage is therefore no mere counterpoise to danger in order to neutralise the latter in its effects, but a peculiar power in itself.

19. *Extent of the influence of danger.*

But to estimate exactly the influence of danger upon the principal actors in War, we must not limit its sphere to the physical danger of the moment. It dominates over the actor, not only by threatening him, but also by threatening all entrusted to him, not only at the moment in which it is actually present, but also through the imagination at all other moments, which have a connection with the present; lastly, not only directly by itself, but also indirectly by the responsibility which makes it bear with tenfold weight on the mind of the chief actor. Who could advise, or resolve upon a great battle, without feeling his mind more or less wrought up, or perplexed by, the danger and responsibility which such a great act of decision carries in itself? We may say that action in War, in so far as it is real action, not a mere condition, is never out of the sphere of danger.

20. *Other powers of feeling.*

If we look upon these affections which are excited by hostility and danger as peculiarly belonging to War, we do not, therefore, exclude from it all others accompanying man in his life's journey. They will also find room here frequently enough. Certainly we may say that many a petty action of the passions is silenced in this serious business of life; but that holds good only in respect to those acting in a lower sphere, who, hurried on from one state of danger and exertion to another, lose sight of the rest of the things of life, *become unused to deceit,* because it is of no avail with death, and so attain to that soldierly simplicity of character which has always been the best representative of the military profession. In higher regions it is otherwise, for the higher a man's rank, the more he must look around him; then arise interests on every side, and a manifold activity of the passions of good and bad. Envy and generosity, pride and humility, fierceness and tenderness, all may appear as active powers in this great drama.

21. *Peculiarity of mind.*

The peculiar characteristics of mind in the chief actor have, as well as those of the feelings, a high importance. From an imaginative, flighty, inexperienced head, and from a calm, sagacious understanding, different things are to be expected.

22. *From the diversity in mental individualities arises the diversity of ways leading to the end.*

It is this great diversity in mental individuality, the influence of which is to be supposed as chiefly felt in the higher ranks, because it increases as we progress upwards, which chiefly produces the diversity of ways leading to the end noticed by us in the first book, and which gives, to the play of probabilities and chance, such an unequal share in determining the course of events.

23. *Second peculiarity. – living reaction.*

The second peculiarity in War is the living reaction, and the reciprocal action resulting therefrom. We do not here speak of the difficulty of estimating that reaction, for that is included in the difficulty before mentioned, of treating the moral powers as quantities; but of this, that reciprocal action, by its nature, opposes anything like a regular plan. The effect which any measure produces upon the enemy is the most distinct of all the data which action affords; but every theory must keep to classes (or groups) of phenomena, and can never take up the really individual case in itself: that must everywhere be left to judgment and talent. It is therefore natural that in a business such as War, which in its plan – built upon general circumstances – is so often thwarted by unexpected and singular accidents, more must generally be left to talent; and less use can be made of a *theoretical guide* than in any other.

24. *Third peculiarity. – uncertainty of all data.*

Lastly, the great uncertainty of all data in War is a peculiar difficulty, because all action must, to a certain extent, be planned in a mere twilight, which in addition not unfrequently – like the effect of a fog or moonshine – gives to things exaggerated dimensions and an unnatural appearance.

What this feeble light leaves indistinct to the sight talent must discover, or must be left to chance. It is therefore again talent, or the favour of fortune, on which reliance must be placed, for want of objective knowledge.

25. *Positive theory is impossible.*

With materials of this kind we can only say to ourselves that it is a sheer impossibility to construct for the Art of War a theory which, like a scaffolding, shall ensure to the chief actor an external support on all sides. In all those cases in which he is thrown upon his talent he would find himself away from this scaffolding of theory and in opposition to it, and, however many-sided it might be framed, the same result would ensue of which we spoke when we said that talent and genius act beyond the law, and theory is in opposition to reality.

26. *Means left by which a theory is possible (the difficulties are not everywhere equally great).*

Two means present themselves of getting out of this difficulty. In the first place, what we have said of the nature of military action in general does not apply in the same manner to the action of every one, whatever may be his standing. In the lower ranks the spirit of self-sacrifice is called more into request, but the difficulties which the understanding and judgment meet with are infinitely less. The field of occurrences is more confined. Ends and means are fewer in number. Data more distinct; mostly also contained in the actually visible. But the higher we ascend the more the difficulties increase, until in the Commander-in-Chief they reach their climax, so that with him almost everything must be left to genius.

Further, according to a division of the subject in *agreement with its nature*, the difficulties are not everywhere the same, but diminish the more results manifest themselves in the material world, and increase the more they pass into the moral, and become motives which influence the will. Therefore it is easier to determine, by theoretical rules, the order and conduct of a battle, than the use to be made of the battle itself. Yonder physical weapons clash with each other, and although mind is not wanting therein, matter must have its rights. But in the effects to be produced by battles when the material results become motives, we have only to do with the moral nature. In a word, it is easier to make a theory for *tactics* than for *strategy*.

27. *Theory must be of the nature of observations not of doctrine.*

The second opening for the possibility of a theory lies in the point of view that it does not necessarily require to be a *direction* for action. As a general rule, whenever an *activity* is for the most part occupied with the same objects over and over again, with the same ends and means, although there may be trifling alterations and a corresponding number of varieties of combination, such things are capable of becoming a subject of study for the reasoning faculties. But such study is just the most essential part of every *theory*, and has a peculiar title to that name. It is an analytical investigation of the subject that leads to an exact knowledge; and if brought to bear on the results of experience, which in our case would be military history, to a thorough familiarity with it. The nearer theory attains the latter object, so much the more it passes over from the objective form of knowledge into the subjective one of skill in action; and so much the more, therefore, it will prove itself effective when circumstances allow of no other decision but that of personal talents; it will show its effects in that talent itself. If theory investigates the subjects which constitute War; if it separates more distinctly that which at first sight seems amalgamated; if it explains fully the properties of the means; if it shows their probable effects; if it makes evident the nature of objects; if it brings to bear all over the field of War the light of essentially critical investigation – then it has fulfilled the chief duties of its province. It becomes then a guide to him who wishes to make himself acquainted with War from books; it lights up the whole road for him, facilitates his progress, educates his judgment, and shields him from error.

If a man of expertness spends half his life in the endeavour to clear up an obscure subject thoroughly, he will probably know more about it than a person who seeks to master it in a short time. Theory is instituted that each person in succession may not have to go through the same labour of clearing the ground and toiling through his subject, but may find the thing in order, and light admitted on it. It should educate the mind of the future leader in War, or rather guide him in his self-instruction, but not accompany him to the field of battle; just as a sensible tutor forms and enlightens the opening mind of a youth without, therefore, keeping him in leading strings all through his life.

If maxims and rules result of themselves from the considerations which theory institutes, if the truth accretes itself into that form of crystal, then theory will not oppose this natural law of the mind; it will rather, if the arch ends in such a keystone, bring it prominently out; but so does this, only in order to satisfy the philosophical law of reason, in order to show distinctly the point to which the lines all converge, not in order to form out of it an algebraical formula for use upon the battle-field; for even these maxims and rules serve more to determine in the reflecting mind the leading outline of its habitual movements than as landmarks indicating to it the way in the act of execution.

28. *By this point of view theory becomes possible, and ceases to be in contradiction to practice.*

Taking this point of view, there is a possibility afforded of a satisfactory, that is, of a useful, theory of the conduct of War, never coming into opposition with the reality, and it will only depend on rational treatment to bring it so far into harmony with action that between theory and practice there shall no longer be that absurd difference which an unreasonable theory, in defiance of common sense, has often produced, but which, just as often, narrow-mindedness and ignorance have used as a pretext for giving way to their natural incapacity.

29. *Theory therefore considers the nature of ends and means – ends and means in tactics.*

Theory has therefore to consider the nature of the means and ends.

In tactics the means are the disciplined armed forces which are to carry on the contest. The object is victory. The precise definition of this conception can be better explained hereafter in the consideration of the combat. Here we content ourselves by denoting the retirement of the enemy from the field of battle as the sign of victory. By means of this victory strategy gains the object for which it appointed the combat, and which constitutes its special signification. This signification has certainly some influence on the nature of the victory. A victory which is intended to weaken the enemy's armed forces is a different thing from one which is designed only to put us in possession of a position. The signification of a combat may therefore have a sensible influence on the preparation and conduct of it, consequently will be also a subject of consideration in tactics.

30. *Circumstances which always attend the application of the means.*

As there are certain circumstances which attend the combat through-out, and have more or less influence upon its result, therefore these must be taken into consideration in the application of the armed forces.

These circumstances are the locality of the combat (ground), the time of day, and the weather.

31. *Locality.*

The locality, which we prefer leaving for solution, under the head of "Country and Ground," might, strictly speaking, be without any influ-ence at all if the combat took place on a completely level and unculti-vated plain.

In a country of steppes such a case may occur, but in the cultivated countries of Europe it is almost an imaginary idea. Therefore a combat between civilised nations, in which country and ground have no influ-ence, is hardly conceivable.

32. *Time of day.*

The time of day influences the combat by the difference between day and night; but the influence naturally extends further than merely to the limits of these divisions, as every combat has a certain duration, and great battles last for several hours. In the preparations for a great battle, it makes an essential difference whether it begins in the morning or the evening. At the same time, certainly many battles may be fought in which the question of the time of day is quite immaterial, and in the generality of cases its influence is only trifling.

33. *Weather.*

Still more rarely has the weather any decisive influence, and it is mostly only by fogs that it plays a part.

34. *End and means in strategy.*

Strategy has in the first instance only the victory, that is, the tactical re-sult, as a means to its object, and ultimately those things which lead direct-ly to peace. The application of its means to this object is at the same time attended by circumstances which have an influence thereon more or less.

35. *Circumstances which attend the application of the means of strategy.*

These circumstances are country and ground, the former including the territory and inhabitants of the whole theatre of war; next the time of the day, and the time of the year as well; lastly, the weather, particu-larly any unusual state of the same, severe frost, &c.

36. *These form new means.*

By bringing these things into combination with the results of a com-bat, strategy gives this result – and therefore the combat – a special signification, places before it a particular object. But when this object is not that which leads directly to peace, therefore a subordinate one, it is only to be looked upon as a means; and therefore in strategy we may look upon the results of combats or victories, in all their different significations, as means. The conquest of a position is such a result of a combat applied to ground. But not only are the different combats with special objects to be considered as means, but also every higher aim which we may have in view in the combination of battles directed on a common object is to be regarded as a means. A winter campaign is a combination of this kind applied to the season.

There remain, therefore, as objects, only those things which may be supposed as leading *directly* to peace, Theory investigates all these ends and means according to the nature of their effects and their mutual relations.

37. *Strategy deduces only from experience the ends and means to be examined.*

The first question is, How does strategy arrive at a complete list of these things? If there is to be a philosophical inquiry leading to an absolute result, it would become entangled in all those difficulties which the logical necessity of the conduct of War and its theory exclude. It therefore turns to experience, and directs its attention on those combinations which military history can furnish. In this manner, no doubt, nothing more than a limited theory can be obtained, which only suits circumstances such as are presented in history. But this incompleteness is unavoidable, because in any case theory must either have deduced from, or have compared with, history what it advances with respect to things. Besides, this incompleteness in every case is more theoretical than real.

One great advantage of this method is that theory cannot lose itself in abstruse disquisitions, subtleties, and chimeras, but must always remain practical.

38. *How far the analysis of the means should be carried.*

Another question is, How far should theory go in its analysis of the means? Evidently only so far as the elements in a separate form present themselves for consideration in practice. The range and effect of different weapons is very important to tactics; their construction, although these effects result from it, is a matter of indifference; for the conduct of War is not making powder and cannon out of a given quantity of charcoal, sulphur, and saltpetre, of copper and tin: the given quantities for the conduct of War are arms in a finished state and their effects. Strategy makes use of maps without troubling itself about triangulations; it does not inquire how the country is subdivided into departments and provinces, and how the people are educated and governed, in order to attain the best military results; but it takes things as it finds them in the community of European States, and observes where very different conditions have a notable influence on War.

39. *Great simplification of the knowledge required.*

That in this manner the number of subjects for theory is much simplified, and the knowledge requisite for the conduct of War much reduced, is easy to perceive. The very great mass of knowledge and appliances of skill which minister to the action of War in general, and which are necessary before an army fully equipped can take the field, unite in a few great results before they are able to reach, in actual War, the final goal of their activity; just as the streams of a country unite themselves in rivers before they fall into the sea. Only those activities emptying themselves directly into the sea of War have to be studied by him who is to conduct its operations.

40. *This explains the rapid growth of great generals, and why a general is not a man of learning.*

This result of our considerations is in fact so necessary, any other would have made us distrustful of their accuracy. Only thus is explained how so often men have made their appearance with great success in War, and indeed in the higher ranks even in supreme Command, whose pursuits had been previously of a totally different nature; indeed how, as a rule, the most distinguished Generals have never risen from the very learned or really erudite class of officers, but have been mostly men who, from the circumstances of their position, could not have attained to any great amount of knowledge. On that account those who have considered it necessary or even beneficial to commence the education of a future General by instruction in all details have always been ridiculed as absurd pedants. It would be easy to show the injurious tendency of such a course, because the human mind is trained by the knowledge imparted to it and the direction given to its ideas. Only what is great can make it great; the little can only make it little, if the mind itself does not reject it as something repugnant.

41. *Former contradictions.*

Because this simplicity of knowledge requisite in War was not attended to, but that knowledge was always jumbled up with the whole impedimenta of subordinate sciences and arts, therefore the palpable opposition to the events of real life which resulted could not be solved otherwise than by ascribing it all to genius, which requires no theory and for which no theory could be prescribed.

42. *On this account all use of knowledge was denied, and everything ascribed to natural talents.*

People with whom common sense had the upper hand felt sensible of the immense distance remaining to be filled up between a genius of the highest order and a learned pedant; and they became in a manner free-thinkers, rejected all belief in theory, and affirmed the conduct of War to be a natural function of man, which he performs more or less well according as he has brought with him into the world more or less talent in that direction. It cannot be denied that these were nearer to the truth than those who placed a value on false knowledge: at the same time it may easily be seen that such a view is itself but an exaggeration. No activity of the human understanding is possible without a certain stock of ideas; but these are, for the greater part at least, not innate but acquired, and constitute his knowledge. The only question therefore is, of what kind should these ideas be; and we think we have answered it if we say that they should be directed on those things which man has directly to deal with in War.

43. *The knowledge must be made suitable to the position.*

Inside this field itself of military activity, the knowledge required must be different according to the station of the Commander. It will be directed on smaller and more circumscribed objects if he holds an inferior, upon greater and more comprehensive ones if he holds a higher situation. There are Field Marshals who would not have shone at the head of a cavalry regiment, and vice versa.

44. *The knowledge in war is very simple, but not, at the same time, very easy.*

But although the knowledge in War is simple, that is to say directed to so few subjects, and taking up those only in their final results, the art of execution is not, on that account, easy. Of the difficulties to which activity in War is subject generally, we have already spoken in the first book; we here omit those things which can only be overcome by courage, and maintain also that the activity of mind, is only simple, and easy in inferior stations, but increases in difficulty with increase of rank, and in the highest position, in that of Commander-in-Chief, is to be reckoned among the most difficult which there is for the human mind.

45. *Of the nature of this knowledge.*

The Commander of an Army neither requires to be a learned explorer of history nor a publicist, but he must be well versed in the higher affairs of State; he must know, and be able to judge correctly of traditional tendencies, interests at stake, the immediate questions at issue, and the characters of leading persons; he need not be a close observer of men, a sharp dissector of human character, but he must know the character, the feelings, the habits, the peculiar faults and inclinations of those whom he is to command. He need not understand anything about the make of a carriage, or the harness of a battery horse, but he must know how to calculate exactly the march of a column, under different circumstances, according to the time it requires. These are matters the knowledge of which cannot be forced out by an apparatus of scientific formula and machinery: they are only to be gained by the exercise of an accurate judgment in the observation of things and of men, aided by a special talent for the apprehension of both.

The necessary knowledge for a high position in military action is therefore distinguished by this, that by observation, therefore by study and reflection, it is only to be attained through a special talent which as an intellectual instinct understands how to extract from the phenomena of life only the essence or spirit, as bees do the honey from the flowers; and that it is also to be gained by experience of life as well as by study and reflection. Life will never bring forth a Newton or an Euler by its rich teachings, but it may bring forth great calculators in War, such as Conde' or Frederick.

It is therefore not necessary that, in order to vindicate the intellectual dignity of military activity, we should resort to untruth and silly pedantry. There never has been a great and distinguished Commander of contracted mind, but very numerous are the instances of men who, after serving with the greatest distinction in inferior positions, remained below mediocrity in the highest, from insufficiency of intellectual capacity. That even amongst those holding the post of Commander-in-Chief there may be a difference according to the degree of their plenitude of power is a matter of course.

46. *Science must become art.*

Now we have yet to consider one condition which is more necessary for the knowledge of the conduct of War than for any other, which is, that it must pass completely into the mind and almost completely cease to be something objective. In almost all other arts and occupations of life the active agent can make use of truths which he has only learnt once, and in the spirit and sense of which he no longer lives, and which he extracts from dusty books. Even truths which he has in hand and uses daily may continue something external to himself, If the architect takes up a pen to settle the strength of a pier by a complicated calculation, the truth found as a result is no emanation from his own mind. He had first to find the data with labour, and then to submit these to an operation of the mind, the rule for which he did not discover, the necessity of which he is perhaps at the moment only partly conscious of, but which he applies, for the most part, as if by mechanical dexterity. But it is never so in War. The moral reaction, the ever-changeful form of things, makes it necessary for the chief actor to carry in himself the whole mental apparatus of his knowledge, that anywhere and at every pulse-beat he may be capable of giving the requisite decision from himself. Knowledge must, by this complete assimilation with his own mind and life, be converted into real power. This is the reason why everything seems so easy with men distinguished in War, and why everything is ascribed to natural talent. We say natural talent, in order thereby to distinguish it from that which is formed and matured by observation and study.

We think that by these reflections we have explained the problem of a theory of the conduct of War; and pointed out the way to its solution.

Of the two fields into which we have divided the conduct of War, tactics and strategy, the theory of the latter contains unquestionably, as before observed, the greatest difficulties, because the first is almost limited to a circumscribed field of objects, but the latter, in the direction of objects leading directly to peace, opens to itself an unlimited field of possibilities. Since for the most part the Commander-in-Chief has only to keep these objects steadily in view, therefore the part of strategy in which he moves is also that which is particularly subject to this difficulty.

Theory, therefore, especially where it comprehends the highest services, will stop much sooner in strategy than in tactics at the simple consideration of things, and content itself to assist the Commander to that insight into things which, blended with his whole thought, makes his course easier and surer, never forces him into opposition with himself in order to obey an objective truth.

CHAPTER THREE

Art or Science of War

1. – *Usage still unsettled*
*(Power and knowledge. science when mere knowing; art, when doing,
is the object.)*

THE CHOICE BETWEEN these terms seems to be still unsettled, and no
one seems to know rightly on what grounds it should be decided, and
yet the thing is simple. We have already said elsewhere that "knowing"
is something different from "doing." The two are so different that they
should not easily be mistaken the one for the other. The "doing" cannot
properly stand in any book, and therefore also Art should never be the
title of a book. But because we have once accustomed ourselves to combine in conception, under the name of theory of Art, or simply Art, the
branches of knowledge (which may be separately pure sciences) necessary for the practice of an Art, therefore it is consistent to continue
this ground of distinction, and to call everything Art when the object
is to carry out the "doing" (being able), as for example, Art of building;
Science, when merely knowledge is the object; as Science of mathematics, of astronomy. That in every Art certain complete sciences may be
included is intelligible of itself, and should not perplex us. But still it is
worth observing that there is also no science without a mixture of Art.
In mathematics, for instance, the use of figures and of algebra is an Art,
but that is only one amongst many instances. The reason is, that however plain and palpable the difference is between knowledge and power
in the composite results of human knowledge, yet it is difficult to trace
out their line of separation in man himself.

2. *Difficulty of separating perception from judgment. (art of war.)*
All thinking is indeed Art. Where the logician draws the line, where
the premises stop which are the result of cognition – where judgment

begins, there Art begins. But more than this even the perception of the mind is judgment again, and consequently Art; and at last, even the perception by the senses as well. In a word, if it is impossible to imagine a human being possessing merely the faculty of cognition, devoid of judgment or the reverse, so also Art and Science can never be completely separated from each other. The more these subtle elements of light embody themselves in the outward forms of the world, so much the more separate appear their domains; and now once more, where the object is creation and production, there is the province of Art; where the object is investigation and knowledge Science holds sway. – After all this it results of itself that it is more fitting to say Art of War than Science of War.

So much for this, because we cannot do without these conceptions. But now we come forward with the assertion that War is neither an Art nor a Science in the real signification, and that it is just the setting out from that starting-point of ideas which has led to a wrong direction being taken, which has caused War to be put on a par with other arts and sciences, and has led to a number of erroneous analogies.

This has indeed been felt before now, and on that it was maintained that War is a handicraft; but there was more lost than gained by that, for a handicraft is only an inferior art, and as such is also subject to definite and rigid laws. In reality the Art of War did go on for some time in the spirit of a handicraft – we allude to the times of the Condottieri – but then it received that direction, not from intrinsic but from external causes; and military history shows how little it was at that time in accordance with the nature of the thing.

3. *War is part of the intercourse of the human race.*

We say therefore War belongs not to the province of Arts and Sciences, but to the province of social life. It is a conflict of great interests which is settled by bloodshed, and only in that is it different from others. It would be better, instead of comparing it with any Art, to liken it to business competition, which is also a conflict of human interests and activities; and it is still more like State policy, which again, on its part, may be looked upon as a kind of business competition on a great scale. Besides, State policy is the womb in which War is developed, in which its outlines lie hidden in a rudimentary state, like the qualities of living creatures in their germs.[7]

7 The analogy has become much closer since Clausewitz's time. Now that the first business of the State is regarded as the development of facilities for trade, War between great nations is only a question of time. No Hague Conferences can avert it – *Editor.*

4. *Difference.*

The essential difference consists in this, that War is no activity of the will, which exerts itself upon inanimate matter like the mechanical Arts; or upon a living but still passive and yielding subject, like the human mind and the human feelings in the ideal Arts, but against a living and re-acting force. How little the categories of Arts and Sciences are applicable to such an activity strikes us at once; and we can understand at the same time how that constant seeking and striving after laws like those which may be developed out of the dead material world could not but lead to constant errors. And yet it is just the mechanical Arts that some people would imitate in the Art of War. The imitation of the ideal Arts was quite out of the question, because these themselves dispense too much with laws and rules, and those hitherto tried, always acknowledged as insuf-ficient and one-sided, are perpetually undermined and washed away by the current of opinions, feelings, and customs.

Whether such a conflict of the living, as takes place and is settled in War, is subject to general laws, and whether these are capable of indi-cating a useful line of action, will be partly investigated in this book; but so much is evident in itself, that this, like every other subject which does not surpass our powers of understanding, may be lighted up, and be made more or less plain in its inner relations by an inquiring mind, and that alone is sufficient to realise the idea of a *theory*.

CHAPTER FOUR
Methodicism

IN ORDER TO EXPLAIN ourselves clearly as to the conception of method, and method of action, which play such an important part in War, we must be allowed to cast a hasty glance at the logical hierarchy through which, as through regularly constituted official functionaries, the world of action is governed.

Law, in the widest sense strictly applying to perception as well as action, has plainly something subjective and arbitrary in its literal meaning, and expresses just that on which we and those things external to us are dependent. As a subject of cognition, *law* is the relation of things and their effects to one another; as a subject of the will, it is a motive of action, and is then equivalent to *command* or *prohibition*.

Principle is likewise such a law for action, except that it has not the formal definite meaning, but is only the spirit and sense of law in order to leave the judgment more freedom of application when the diversity of the real world cannot be laid hold of under the definite form of a law. As the judgment must of itself suggest the cases in which the principle is not applicable, the latter therefore becomes in that way a real aid or guiding star for the person acting.

Principle is *objective* when it is the result of objective truth, and consequently of equal value for all men; it is *subjective*, and then generally called *maxim* if there are subjective relations in it, and if it therefore has a certain value only for the person himself who makes it.

Rule is frequently taken in the sense of *law*, and then means the same as Principle, for we say "no rule without exceptions," but we do not say "no law without exceptions," a sign that with *rule* we retain to ourselves more freedom of application.

In another meaning *rule* is the means used of discerning a recondite truth in a particular sign lying close at hand, in order to attach to this particular sign the law of action directed upon the whole truth. Of this kind are all the rules of games of play, all abridged processes in mathematics, &c.

Directions and *instructions* are determinations of action which have an influence upon a number of minor circumstances too numerous and unimportant for general laws.

Lastly, *method, mode of acting*, is an always recurring proceeding selected out of several possible ones; and *methodicism (methodismus)* is that which is determined by methods instead of by general principles or particular prescriptions. By this the cases which are placed under such methods must necessarily be supposed alike in their essential parts. As they cannot all be this, then the point is that at least as many as possible should be; in other words, that Method should be calculated on the most probable cases. Methodicism is therefore not founded on determined particular premises, but on the average probability of cases one with another; and its ultimate tendency is to set up an average truth, the constant and uniform, application of which soon acquires something of the nature of a mechanical appliance, which in the end does that which is right almost unwittingly.

The conception of law in relation to perception is not necessary for the conduct of War, because the complex phenomena of War are not so regular, and the regular are not so complex, that we should gain anything more by this conception than by the simple truth. And where a simple conception and language is sufficient, to resort to the complex becomes affected and pedantic. The conception of law in relation to action cannot be used in the theory of the conduct of War, because owing to the variableness and diversity of the phenomena there is in it no determination of such a general nature as to deserve the name of law.

But principles, rules, prescriptions, and methods are conceptions indispensable to a theory of the conduct of War, in so far as that theory leads to positive doctrines, because in doctrines the truth can only crystallise itself in such forms.

As tactics is the branch of the conduct of War in which theory can attain the nearest to positive doctrine, therefore these conceptions will appear in it most frequently.

Not to use cavalry against unbroken infantry except in some case of special emergency, only to use firearms within effective range in the combat, to spare the forces as much as possible for the final struggle – these are tactical principles. None of them can be applied absolutely in every case, but they must always be present to the mind of the Chief, in order that the benefit of the truth contained in them may not be lost in cases where that truth can be of advantage.

If from the unusual cooking by an enemy's camp his movement is inferred, if the intentional exposure of troops in a combat indicates a false attack, then this way of discerning the truth is called rule, because from a single visible circumstance that conclusion is drawn which corresponds with the same.

If it is a rule to attack the enemy with renewed vigour, as soon as he begins to limber up his artillery in the combat, then on this particular fact depends a course of action which is aimed at the general situation of the enemy as inferred from the above fact, namely, that he is about to give up the fight, that he is commencing to draw off his troops, and is neither capable of making a serious stand while thus drawing off nor of making his retreat gradually in good order.

Regulations and *methods* bring preparatory theories into the conduct of War, in so far as disciplined troops are inoculated with them as active principles. The whole body of instructions for formations, drill, and field service are regulations and methods: in the drill instructions the first predominate, in the field service instructions the latter. To these things the real conduct of War attaches itself; it takes them over, therefore, as given modes of proceeding, and as such they must appear in the theory of the conduct of War.

But for those activities retaining freedom in the employment of these forces there cannot be regulations, that is, definite instructions, because they would do away with freedom of action. Methods, on the other hand, as a general way of executing duties as they arise, calculated, as we have said, on an average of probability, or as a dominating influence of principles and rules carried through to application, may certainly appear in the theory of the conduct of War, provided only they are not represented as something different from what they are, not as the absolute and necessary modes of action (systems), but as the best of general forms which may be used as shorter ways in place of a particular disposition for the occasion, at discretion.

But the frequent application of methods will be seen to be most essential and unavoidable in the conduct of War, if we reflect how much action proceeds on mere conjecture, or in complete uncertainty, because one side is prevented from learning all the circumstances which influence the dispositions of the other, or because, even if these circumstances which influence the decisions of the one were really known, there is not, owing to their extent and the dispositions they would entail, sufficient time for the other to carry out all necessary counteracting measures – that therefore measures in War must always be calculated on a certain number of possibilities; if we reflect how numberless are the trifling things belonging to any single event, and which therefore should be taken into account along with it, and that therefore there is no other means to suppose the one counteracted by the other, and to base our arrangements only upon what is of a general nature and probable; if we reflect lastly that, owing to the increasing number of officers as we descend the scale of rank, less must be left to the true discernment and ripe judgment of individuals the lower the sphere of action, and that when we reach those ranks where we can look for no other notions but those which the regulations of the service and experience afford, we must help them with the methodic forms bordering on those regulations. This will serve both as a support to their judgment and a barrier against those extravagant and erroneous views which are so especially to be dreaded in a sphere where experience is so costly.

Besides this absolute need of method in action, we must also acknowledge that it has a positive advantage, which is that, through the constant repetition of a formal exercise, a readiness, precision, and firmness is attained in the movement of troops which diminishes the natural friction, and makes the machine move easier.

Method will therefore be the more generally used, become the more indispensable, the farther down the scale of rank the position of the active agent; and on the other hand, its use will diminish upwards, until in the highest position it quite disappears. For this reason it is more in its place in tactics than in strategy.

War in its highest aspects consists not of an infinite number of little events, the diversities in which compensate each other, and which therefore by a better or worse method are better or worse governed, but of separate great decisive events which must be dealt with separately. It is not like a field of stalks, which, without any regard to the particular form of each stalk, will be mowed better or worse, according as the mowing instrument is good or bad, but rather as a group of large trees, to which the axe must be laid with judgment, according to the particular form and inclination of each separate trunk.

How high up in military activity the admissibility of method in action reaches naturally determines itself, not according to actual rank, but according to things; and it affects the highest positions in a less degree, only because these positions have the most comprehensive subjects of activity. A constant order of battle, a constant formation of advance guards and outposts, are methods by which a General ties not only his subordinates' hands, but also his own in certain cases. Certainly they may have been devised by himself, and may be applied by him according to circumstances, but they may also be a subject of theory, in so far as they are based on the general properties of troops and weapons. On the other hand, any method by which definite plans for wars or campaigns are to be given out all ready made as if from a machine are absolutely worthless.

As long as there exists no theory which can be sustained, that is, no enlightened treatise on the conduct of War, method in action cannot but encroach beyond its proper limits in high places, for men employed in these spheres of activity have not always had the opportunity of educating themselves, through study and through contact with the higher interests. In the impracticable and inconsistent disquisitions of theorists and critics they cannot find their way, their sound common sense rejects them, and as they bring with them no knowledge but that derived from experience, therefore in those cases which admit of, and require, a free individual treatment they readily make use of the means which experience gives them – that is, an imitation of the particular methods practised by great Generals, by which a method of action then arises of itself. If we see Frederick the Great's Generals always making their appearance in the so-called oblique order of battle, the Generals of the French Revolution always using turning movements with a long, extended line of battle, and Buonaparte's lieutenants rushing to the attack with the bloody energy of concentrated masses, then we recognise in the recurrence of the mode of proceeding evidently an adopted method, and see therefore that method of action can reach up to regions bordering on the highest. Should an improved theory facilitate the study of the conduct of War, form the mind and judgment of men who are rising to the highest commands, then also method in action will no longer reach so far, and so much of it as is to be considered indispensable will then at least be formed from theory itself, and not take place out of mere imitation. However pre-eminently a great Commander does things, there is always something subjective in the way he does them; and if he has a certain manner, a large share of his individuality is contained in it which does not always accord with the individuality of the person who copies his manner.

At the same time, it would neither be possible nor right to banish subjective methodicism or manner completely from the conduct of War: it is rather to be regarded as a manifestation of that influence which the general character of a War has upon its separate events, and to which satisfaction can only be done in that way if theory is not able to foresee this general character and include it in its considerations. What is more natural than that the War of the French Revolution had its own way of doing things? and what theory could ever have included that peculiar method? The evil is only that such a manner originating in a special case easily outlives itself, because it continues whilst circumstances imperceptibly change. This is what theory should prevent by lucid and rational criticism. When in the year 1806 the Prussian Generals, Prince Louis at Saalfeld, Tauentzien on the Dornberg near Jena, Grawert before and Ruechel behind Kappellendorf, all threw themselves into the open jaws of destruction in the oblique order of Frederick the Great, and managed to ruin Hohenlohe's Army in a way that no Army was ever ruined, even on the field of battle, all this was done through a manner which had outlived its day, together with the most downright stupidity to which methodicism ever led.

CHAPTER FIVE

Criticism

THE INFLUENCE of theoretical principles upon real life is produced more through criticism than through doctrine, for as criticism is an application of abstract truth to real events, therefore it not only brings truth of this description nearer to life, but also accustoms the understanding more to such truths by the constant repetition of their application. We therefore think it necessary to fix the point of view for criticism next to that for theory.

From the simple narration of an historical occurrence which places events in chronological order, or at most only touches on their more immediate causes, we separate the *critical*.

In this *critical* three different operations of the mind may be observed.

First, the historical investigation and determining of doubtful facts. This is properly historical research, and has nothing in common with theory.

Secondly, the tracing of effects to causes. This is the *real critical inquiry*; it is indispensable to theory, for everything which in theory is to be established, supported, or even merely explained, by experience can only be settled in this way.

Thirdly, the testing of the means employed. This is criticism, properly speaking, in which praise and censure is contained. This is where theory helps history, or rather, the teaching to be derived from it.

In these two last strictly critical parts of historical study, all depends on tracing things to their primary elements, that is to say, up to undoubted truths, and not, as is so often done, resting half-way, that is, on some arbitrary assumption or supposition.

As respects the tracing of effect to cause, that is often attended with the insuperable difficulty that the real causes are not known. In none of the relations of life does this so frequently happen as in War, where events are seldom fully known, and still less motives, as the latter have been, perhaps purposely, concealed by the chief actor, or have been of such a transient and accidental character that they have been lost for history. For this reason critical narration must generally proceed hand in hand with historical investigation, and still such a want of connection between cause and effect will often present itself, that it does not seem justifiable to consider effects as the necessary results of known causes. Here, therefore must occur, that is, historical results which cannot be made use of for teaching. All that theory can demand is that the investigation should be rigidly conducted up to that point, and there leave off without drawing conclusions. A real evil springs up only if the known is made perforce to suffice as an explanation of effects, and thus a false importance is ascribed to it.

Besides this difficulty, critical inquiry also meets with another great and intrinsic one, which is that the progress of events in War seldom proceeds from one simple cause, but from several in common, and that it therefore is not sufficient to follow up a series of events to their origin in a candid and impartial spirit, but that it is then also necessary to apportion to each contributing cause its due weight. This leads, therefore, to a closer investigation of their nature, and thus a critical investigation may lead into what is the proper field of theory.

The critical *consideration*, that is, the testing of the means, leads to the question, Which are the effects peculiar to the means applied, and whether these effects were comprehended in the plans of the person directing?

The effects peculiar to the means lead to the investigation of their nature, and thus again into the field of theory.

We have already seen that in criticism all depends upon attaining to positive truth; therefore, that we must not stop at arbitrary propositions which are not allowed by others, and to which other perhaps equally arbitrary assertions may again be opposed, so that there is no end to pros and cons; the whole is without result, and therefore without instruction.

We have seen that both the search for causes and the examination of means lead into the field of theory; that is, into the field of universal truth, which does not proceed solely from the case immediately under examination. If there is a theory which can be used, then the critical consideration will appeal to the proofs there afforded, and the examination may there stop. But where no such theoretical truth is to be found, the inquiry must be pushed up to the original elements. If this necessity occurs often, it must lead the historian (according to a common expression) into a labyrinth of details. He then has his hands full, and it is impossible for him to stop to give the requisite attention everywhere; the consequence is, that in order to set bounds to his investigation, he adopts some arbitrary assumptions which, if they do not appear so to him, do so to others, as they are not evident in themselves or capable of proof.

A sound theory is therefore an essential foundation for criticism, and it is impossible for it, without the assistance of a sensible theory, to attain to that point at which it commences chiefly to be instructive, that is, where it becomes demonstration, both convincing and sans re'plique.

But it would be a visionary hope to believe in the possibility of a theory applicable to every abstract truth, leaving nothing for criticism to do but to place the case under its appropriate law: it would be ridiculous pedantry to lay down as a rule for criticism that it must always halt and turn round on reaching the boundaries of sacred theory. The same spirit of analytical inquiry which is the origin of theory must also guide the critic in his work; and it can and must therefore happen that he strays beyond the boundaries of the province of theory and elucidates those points with which he is more particularly concerned. It is more likely, on the contrary, that criticism would completely fail in its object if it degenerated into a mechanical application of theory. All positive results of theoretical inquiry, all principles, rules, and methods, are the more wanting in generality and positive truth the more they become positive doctrine. They exist to offer themselves for use as required, and it must always be left for judgment to decide whether they are suitable or not. Such results of theory must never be used in criticism as rules or norms for a standard, but in the same way as the person acting should use them, that is, merely as aids to judgment. If it is an acknowledged principle in tactics that in the usual order of battle cavalry should be placed behind infantry, not in line with it, still it would be folly on this account to condemn every deviation from this principle. Criticism must investigate the grounds of the deviation, and it is only in case these are insufficient that it has a right to appeal to principles laid down in theory. If it is further established in theory that a divided attack diminishes the probability of success, still it would be just as unreasonable, whenever there is a divided attack and an unsuccessful issue, to regard the latter as the result of the former, without further investigation into the connection between the two, as where a divided attack is successful to infer from it the fallacy of that theoretical principle. The spirit of investigation which belongs to criticism cannot allow either. Criticism therefore supports itself chiefly on the results of the analytical investigation of theory; what has been made out and determined by theory does not require to be demonstrated over again by criticism, and it is so determined by theory that criticism may find it ready demonstrated.

This office of criticism, of examining the effect produced by certain causes, and whether a means applied has answered its object, will be easy enough if cause and effect, means and end, are all near together.

If an Army is surprised, and therefore cannot make a regular and in-telligent use of its powers and resources, then the effect of the surprise is not doubtful. – If theory has determined that in a battle the con-vergent form of attack is calculated to produce greater but less certain results, then the question is whether he who employs that convergent form had in view chiefly that greatness of result as his object; if so, the proper means were chosen. But if by this form he intended to make the result more certain, and that expectation was founded not on some ex-ceptional circumstances (in this case), but on the general nature of the convergent form, as has happened a hundred times, then he mistook the nature of the means and committed an error.

Here the work of military investigation and criticism is easy, and it will always be so when confined to the immediate effects and objects. This can be done quite at option, if we abstract the connection of the parts with the whole, and only look at things in that relation.

But in War, as generally in the world, there is a connection between everything which belongs to a whole; and therefore, however small a cause may be in itself, its effects reach to the end of the act of warfare, and modify or influence the final result in some degree, let that degree be ever so small. In the same manner every means must be felt up to the ultimate object.

We can therefore trace the effects of a cause as long as events are worth noticing, and in the same way we must not stop at the testing of a means for the immediate object, but test also this object as a means to a higher one, and thus ascend the series of facts in succession, until we come to one so absolutely necessary in its nature as to require no ex-amination or proof. In many cases, particularly in what concerns great and decisive measures, the investigation must be carried to the final aim, to that which leads immediately to peace.

It is evident that in thus ascending, at every new station which we reach a new point of view for the judgment is attained, so that the same means which appeared advisable at one station, when looked at from the next above it may have to be rejected.

The search for the causes of events and the comparison of means with ends must always go hand in hand in the critical review of an act, for the investigation of causes leads us first to the discovery of those things which are worth examining.

This following of the clue up and down is attended with considerable difficulty, for the farther from an event the cause lies which we are looking for, the greater must be the number of other causes which must at the same time be kept in view and allowed for in reference to the share which they have in the course of events, and then eliminated, because the higher the importance of a fact the greater will be the number of separate forces and circumstances by which it is conditioned. If we have unravelled the causes of a battle being lost, we have certainly also ascertained a part of the causes of the consequences which this defeat has upon the whole War, but only a part, because the effects of other causes, more or less according to circumstances, will flow into the final result.

The same multiplicity of circumstances is presented also in the examination of the means the higher our point of view, for the higher the object is situated, the greater must be the number of means employed to reach it. The ultimate object of the War is the object aimed at by all the Armies simultaneously, and it is therefore necessary that the consideration should embrace all that each has done or could have done.

It is obvious that this may sometimes lead to a wide field of inquiry, in which it is easy to wander and lose the way, and in which this difficulty prevails – that a number of assumptions or suppositions must be made about a variety of things which do not actually appear, but which in all probability did take place, and therefore cannot possibly be left out of consideration.

When Buonaparte, in 1797,[8] at the head of the Army of Italy, advanced from the Tagliamento against the Archduke Charles, he did so with a view to force that General to a decisive action before the reinforcements expected from the Rhine had reached him. If we look, only at the immediate object, the means were well chosen and justified by the result, for the Archduke was so inferior in numbers that he only made a show of resistance on the Tagliamento, and when he saw his adversary so strong and resolute, yielded ground, and left open the passages, of the Norican Alps. Now to what use could Buonaparte turn this fortunate event? To penetrate into the heart of the Austrian empire itself, to facilitate the advance of the Rhine Armies under Moreau and Hoche, and open communication with them? This was

8 Compare Hinterlassene Werke, 2nd edition, vol. iv. p. 276 et seq.

the view taken by Buonaparte, and from this point of view he was right. But now, if criticism places itself at a higher point of view – namely, that of the French Directory, which body could see and know that the Armies on the Rhine could not commence the campaign for six weeks, then the advance of Buonaparte over the Norican Alps can only be regarded as an extremely hazardous measure; for if the Austrians had drawn largely on their Rhine Armies to reinforce their Army in Styria, so as to enable the Archduke to fall upon the Army of Italy, not only would that Army have been routed, but the whole campaign lost. This consideration, which attracted the serious attention of Buonaparte at Villach, no doubt induced him to sign the armistice of Leoben with so much readiness.

If criticism takes a still higher position, and if it knows that the Austrians had no reserves between the Army of the Archduke Charles and Vienna, then we see that Vienna became threatened by the advance of the Army of Italy.

Supposing that Buonaparte knew that the capital was thus uncovered, and knew that he still retained the same superiority in numbers over the Archduke as he had in Styria, then his advance against the heart of the Austrian States was no longer without purpose, and its value depended on the value which the Austrians might place on preserving their capital. If that was so great that, rather than lose it, they would accept the conditions of peace which Buonaparte was ready to offer them, it became an object of the first importance to threaten Vienna. If Buonaparte had any reason to know this, then criticism may stop there, but if this point was only problematical, then criticism must take a still higher position, and ask what would have followed if the Austrians had resolved to abandon Vienna and retire farther into the vast dominions still left to them. But it is easy to see that this question cannot be answered without bringing into the consideration the probable movements of the Rhine Armies on both sides. Through the decided superiority of numbers on the side of the French – 130,000 to 80,000 – there could be little doubt of the result; but then next arises the question, What use would the Directory make of a victory; whether they would follow up their success to the opposite frontiers of the Austrian monarchy, therefore to the complete breaking up or overthrow of that power, or whether they would be satisfied with the conquest of a considerable portion to serve as a security for peace? The probable result in each case must be estimated, in order to come to a conclusion as to the probable determination of the Directory. Supposing the result of these considerations to be that the French forces were much too weak for the complete subjugation of the Austrian monarchy, so that the attempt might completely reverse the respective positions of the contending Armies, and that even the conquest and occupation of a considerable district of country would place the French Army in strategic relations to which they were not equal, then that result must naturally influence the estimate of the position of the Army of Italy, and compel it to lower its expectations. And this, it was no doubt which influenced Buonaparte, although fully aware of the helpless condition of the Archduke, still to sign the peace of Campo Formio, which imposed no greater sacrifices on the Austrians than the loss of provinces which, even if the campaign took the most favourable turn for them, they could not have reconquered. But the French could not have reckoned on even the moderate treaty of Campo Formio, and therefore it could not have been their object in making their bold advance if two considerations had not presented themselves to their view, the first of which consisted in the question, what degree of value the Austrians would attach to each of the above-mentioned results; whether, notwithstanding the probability of a satisfactory result in either of these cases, would it be worth while to make the sacrifices inseparable from a continuance of the War, when they could be spared those sacrifices by a peace on terms not too humiliating? The second consideration is the question whether the Austrian Government, instead of seriously weighing the possible results of a resistance pushed to extremities, would not prove completely disheartened by the impression of their present reverses.

The consideration which forms the subject of the first is no idle piece of subtle argument, but a consideration of such decidedly practical importance that it comes up whenever the plan of pushing War to the utmost extremity is mooted, and by its weight in most cases restrains the execution of such plans.

The second consideration is of equal importance, for we do not make War with an abstraction but with a reality, which we must always keep in view, and we may be sure that it was not overlooked by the bold Buonaparte – that is, that he was keenly alive to the terror which the appearance of his sword inspired. It was reliance on that which led him to Moscow. There it led him into a scrape. The terror of him had been weakened by the gigantic struggles in which he had been engaged; in the year 1797 it was still fresh, and the secret of a resistance pushed to extremities had not been discovered; nevertheless even in 1797 his boldness might have led to a negative result if, as already said, he had not with a sort of presentiment avoided it by signing the moderate peace of Campo Formio.

We must now bring these considerations to a close – they will suffice to show the wide sphere, the diversity and embarrassing nature of the subjects embraced in a critical examination carried to the fullest extent, that is, to those measures of a great and decisive class which must necessarily be included. It follows from them that besides a theoretical acquaintance with the subject, natural talent must also have a great influence on the value of critical examinations, for it rests chiefly with the latter to throw the requisite light on the interrelations of things, and to distinguish from amongst the endless connections of events those which are really essential.

But talent is also called into requisition in another way. Critical examination is not merely the appreciation of those means which have been actually employed, but also of all possible means, which therefore must be suggested in the first place – that is, must be discovered; and the use of any particular means is not fairly open to censure until a better is pointed out. Now, however small the number of possible combinations may be in most cases, still it must be admitted that to point out those which have not been used is not a mere analysis of actual things, but a spontaneous creation which cannot be prescribed, and depends on the fertility of genius.

We are far from seeing a field for great genius in a case which admits only of the application of a few simple combinations, and we think it exceedingly ridiculous to hold up, as is often done, the turning of a position as an invention showing the highest genius; still nevertheless this creative self-activity on the part of the critic is necessary, and it is one of the points which essentially determine the value of critical examination.

When Buonaparte on 30th July, 1796,[9] determined to raise the siege of Mantua, in order to march with his whole force against the enemy, advancing in separate columns to the relief of the place, and to beat them in detail, this appeared the surest way to the attainment of brilliant victories. These victories actually followed, and were afterwards again repeated on a still more brilliant scale on the attempt to relieve the fortress being again renewed. We hear only one opinion on these achievements, that of unmixed admiration.

At the same time, Buonaparte could not have adopted this course on the 30th July without quite giving up the idea of the siege of Mantua, because it was impossible to save the siege train, and it could not be replaced by another in this campaign. In fact, the siege was converted

9 Compare Hinterlassene Werke, 2nd edition, vol. iv. p. 107 et seq.

into a blockade, and the town, which if the siege had continued must have very shortly fallen, held out for six months in spite of Buonaparte's victories in the open field.

Criticism has generally regarded this as an evil that was unavoidable, because critics have not been able to suggest any better course. Resistance to a relieving Army within lines of circumvallation had fallen into such disrepute and contempt that it appears to have entirely escaped consideration as a means. And yet in the reign of Louis XIV. that measure was so often used with success that we can only attribute to the force of fashion the fact that a hundred years later it never occurred to any one even to propose such a measure. If the practicability of such a plan had ever been entertained for a moment, a closer consideration of circumstances would have shown that 40,000 of the best infantry in the world under Buonaparte, behind strong lines of circumvallation round Mantua, had so little to fear from the 50,000 men coming to the relief under Wurmser, that it was very unlikely that any attempt even would be made upon their lines. We shall not seek here to establish this point, but we believe enough has been said to show that this means was one which had a right to a share of consideration. Whether Buonaparte himself ever thought of such a plan we leave undecided; neither in his memoirs nor in other sources is there any trace to be found of his having done so; in no critical works has it been touched upon, the measure being one which the mind had lost sight of. The merit of resuscitating the idea of this means is not great, for it suggests itself at once to any one who breaks loose from the trammels of fashion. Still it is necessary that it should suggest itself for us to bring it into consideration and compare it with the means which Buonaparte employed. Whatever may be the result of the comparison, it is one which should not be omitted by criticism.

When Buonaparte, in February, 1814,[10] after gaining the battles at Etoges, Champ-Aubert, and Montmirail, left Bluecher's Army, and turning upon Schwartzenberg, beat his troops at Montereau and Mormant, every one was filled with admiration, because Buonaparte, by thus throwing his concentrated force first upon one opponent, then upon another, made a brilliant use of the mistakes which his adversaries had committed in dividing their forces. If these brilliant strokes in different directions failed to save him, it was generally considered to be no fault of his, at least. No one has yet asked the question, What would have been the result if, instead of turning from Bluecher upon Schwart-

---

10   Compare Hinterlassene Werks, 2nd edition. vol. vii. p. 193 et seq.

zenberg, he had tried another blow at Bluecher, and pursued him to the Rhine? We are convinced that it would have completely changed the course of the campaign, and that the Army of the Allies, instead of marching to Paris, would have retired behind the Rhine. We do not ask others to share our conviction, but no one who understands the thing will doubt, at the mere mention of this alternative course, that it is one which should not be overlooked in criticism.

In this case the means of comparison lie much more on the surface than in the foregoing, but they have been equally overlooked, because one-sided views have prevailed, and there has been no freedom of judgment.

From the necessity of pointing out a better means which might have been used in place of those which are condemned has arisen the form of criticism almost exclusively in use, which contents itself with pointing out the better means without demonstrating in what the superiority consists. The consequence is that some are not convinced, that others start up and do the same thing, and that thus discussion arises which is without any fixed basis for the argument. Military literature abounds with matter of this sort.

The demonstration we require is always necessary when the superiority of the means propounded is not so evident as to leave no room for doubt, and it consists in the examination of each of the means on its own merits, and then of its comparison with the object desired. When once the thing is traced back to a simple truth, controversy must cease, or at all events a new result is obtained, whilst by the other plan the pros and cons go on for ever consuming each other.

Should we, for example, not rest content with assertion in the case before mentioned, and wish to prove that the persistent pursuit of Bluecher would have been more advantageous than the turning on Schwartzenberg, we should support the arguments on the following simple truths:

1. In general it is more advantageous to continue our blows in one and the same direction, because there is a loss of time in striking in different directions; and at a point where the moral power is already shaken by considerable losses there is the more reason to expect fresh successes, therefore in that way no part of the preponderance already gained is left idle.

2. Because Bluecher, although weaker than Schwartzenberg, was, on account of his enterprising spirit, the more important adversary; in him, therefore, lay the centre of attraction which drew the others along in the same direction.

3. Because the losses which Bluecher had sustained almost amounted to a defeat, which gave Buonaparte such a preponderance over him as to make his retreat to the Rhine almost certain, and at the same time no reserves of any consequence awaited him there.

4. Because there was no other result which would be so terrific in its aspects, would appear to the imagination in such gigantic proportions, an immense advantage in dealing with a Staff so weak and irresolute as that of Schwartzenberg notoriously was at this time. What had happened to the Crown Prince of Wartemberg at Montereau, and to Count Wittgenstein at Mormant, Prince Schwartzenberg must have known well enough; but all the untoward events on Bluecher's distant and separate line from the Marne to the Rhine would only reach him by the avalanche of rumour. The desperate movements which Buonaparte made upon Vitry at the end of March, to see what the Allies would do if he threatened to turn them strategically, were evidently done on the principle of working on their fears; but it was done under far different circumstances, in consequence of his defeat at Laon and Arcis, and because Bluecher, with 100,000 men, was then in communication with Schwartzenberg.

There are people, no doubt, who will not be convinced on these arguments, but at all events they cannot retort by saying, that "whilst Buonaparte threatened Schwartzenberg's base by advancing to the Rhine, Schwartzenberg at the same time threatened Buonaparte's communications with Paris," because we have shown by the reasons above given that Schwartzenberg would never have thought of marching on Paris.

With respect to the example quoted by us from the campaign of 1796, we should say: Buonaparte looked upon the plan he adopted as the surest means of beating the Austrians; but admitting that it was so, still the object to be attained was only an empty victory, which could have hardly any sensible influence on the fall of Mantua. The way which we should have chosen would, in our opinion, have been much more certain to prevent the relief of Mantua; but even if we place ourselves in the position of the French General and assume that it was not so, and look upon the certainty of success to have been less, the question then amounts to a choice between a more certain but less useful, and therefore less important, victory on the one hand, and a somewhat less probable but far more decisive and important victory, on the other hand. Presented in this form, boldness must have declared for the second solution, which is the reverse of what took place, when the thing was only superficially viewed. Buonaparte certainly was anything but deficient in boldness, and we may be sure that he did not see the whole case and its consequences as fully and clearly as we can at the present time.

Naturally the critic, in treating of the means, must often appeal to military history, as experience is of more value in the Art of War than all philosophical truth. But this exemplification from history is subject to certain conditions, of which we shall treat in a special chapter and unfortunately these conditions are so seldom regarded that reference to history generally only serves to increase the confusion of ideas.

We have still a most important subject to consider, which is, How far criticism in passing judgments on particular events is permitted, or in duty bound, to make use of its wider view of things, and therefore also of that which is shown by results; or when and where it should leave out of sight these things in order to place itself, as far as possible, in the exact position of the chief actor?

If criticism dispenses praise or censure, it should seek to place itself as nearly as possible at the same point of view as the person acting, that is to say, to collect all he knew and all the motives on which he acted, and, on the other hand, to leave out of the consideration all that the person acting could not or did not know, and above all, the result. But this is only an object to aim at, which can never be reached because the state of circumstances from which an event proceeded can never be placed before the eye of the critic exactly as it lay before the eye of the person acting. A number of inferior circumstances, which must have influenced the result, are completely lost to sight, and many a subjective motive has never come to light.

The latter can only be learnt from the memoirs of the chief actor, or from his intimate friends; and in such things of this kind are often treated of in a very desultory manner, or purposely misrepresented. Criticism must, therefore, always forego much which was present in the minds of those whose acts are criticised.

On the other hand, it is much more difficult to leave out of sight that which criticism knows in excess. This is only easy as regards accidental circumstances, that is, circumstances which have been mixed up, but are in no way necessarily related. But it is very difficult, and, in fact, can never be completely done with regard to things really essential.

Let us take first, the result. If it has not proceeded from accidental circumstances, it is almost impossible that the knowledge of it should not have an effect on the judgment passed on events which have pre-ceded it, for we see these things in the light of this result, and it is to a certain extent by it that we first become acquainted with them and appreciate them. Military history, with all its events, is a source of instruction for criticism itself, and it is only natural that criticism should throw that light on things which it has itself obtained from the consideration of the whole. If therefore it might wish in some cases to leave the result out of the consideration, it would be impossible to do so completely.

But it is not only in relation to the result, that is, with what takes place at the last, that this embarrassment arises; the same occurs in relation to preceding events, therefore with the data which furnished the motives to action. Criticism has before it, in most cases, more information on this point than the principal in the transaction. Now it may seem easy to dismiss from the consideration everything of this nature, but it is not so easy as we may think. The knowledge of preceding and concurrent events is founded not only on certain information, but on a number of conjectures and suppositions; indeed, there is hardly any of the information respecting things not purely accidental which has not been preceded by suppositions or conjectures destined to take the place of certain information in case such should never be supplied. Now is it conceivable that criticism in after times, which has before it as facts all the preceding and concurrent circumstances, should not allow itself to be thereby influenced when it asks itself the question, What portion of the circumstances, which at the moment of action were unknown, would it have held to be probable? We maintain that in this case, as in the case of the results, and for the same reason, it is impossible to disregard all these things completely.

If therefore the critic wishes to bestow praise or blame upon any single act, he can only succeed to a certain degree in placing himself in the position of the person whose act he has under review. In many cases he can do so sufficiently near for any practical purpose, but in many instances it is the very reverse, and this fact should never be overlooked.

But it is neither necessary nor desirable that criticism should completely identify itself with the person acting. In War, as in all matters of skill, there is a certain natural aptitude required which is called talent. This may be great or small. In the first case it may easily be superior to that of the critic, for what critic can pretend to the skill of a Frederick or a Buonaparte? Therefore, if criticism is not to abstain altogether from offering an opinion where eminent talent is concerned, it must be allowed to make use of the advantage which its enlarged horizon affords. Criticism must not, therefore, treat the solution of a problem by a great General like a sum in arithmetic; it is only through the results and through the exact coincidences of events that it can recognise with admiration how much is due to the exercise of genius, and that it first learns the essential combination which the glance of that genius devised.

But for every, even the smallest, act of genius it is necessary that criticism should take a higher point of view, so that, having at command many objective grounds of decision, it may be as little subjective as possible, and that the critic may not take the limited scope of his own mind as a standard.

This elevated position of criticism, its praise and blame pronounced with a full knowledge of all the circumstances, has in itself nothing which hurts our feelings; it only does so if the critic pushes himself forward, and speaks in a tone as if all the wisdom which he has obtained by an exhaustive examination of the event under consideration were really his own talent. Palpable as is this deception, it is one which people may easily fall into through vanity, and one which is naturally distasteful to others. It very often happens that although the critic has no such arrogant pretensions, they are imputed to him by the reader because he has not expressly disclaimed them, and then follows immediately a charge of a want of the power of critical judgment.

If therefore a critic points out an error made by a Frederick or a Buonaparte, that does not mean that he who makes the criticism would not have committed the same error; he may even be ready to grant that had he been in the place of these great Generals he might have made much greater mistakes; he merely sees this error from the chain of events, and he thinks that it should not have escaped the sagacity of the General.

This is, therefore, an opinion formed through the connection of events, and therefore through the *result*. But there is another quite different effect of the result itself upon the judgment, that is if it is used quite alone as an example for or against the soundness of a measure. This may be called *judgment according to the result*. Such a judgment appears at first sight inadmissible, and yet it is not.

When Buonaparte marched to Moscow in 1812, all depended upon whether the taking of the capital, and the events which preceded the capture, would force the Emperor Alexander to make peace, as he had been compelled to do after the battle of Friedland in 1807, and the Emperor Francis in 1805 and 1809 after Austerlitz and Wagram; for if Buonaparte did not obtain a peace at Moscow, there was no alternative but to return – that is, there was nothing for him but a strategic defeat. We shall leave out of the question what he did to get to Moscow, and whether in his advance he did not miss many opportunities of bringing the Emperor Alexander to peace; we shall also exclude all consideration of the disastrous circumstances which attended his retreat, and which perhaps had their origin in the general conduct of the campaign. Still the question remains the same, for however much more brilliant the course of the campaign up to Moscow might have been, still there was always an uncertainty whether the Emperor Alexander would be intimidated into making peace; and then, even if a retreat did not contain in itself the seeds of such disasters as did in fact occur, still it could never be anything else than a great strategic defeat. If the Emperor Alexander agreed to a peace which was disadvantageous to him, the campaign of 1812 would have ranked with those of Austerlitz, Friedland, and Wagram. But these campaigns also, if they had not led to peace, would in all probability have ended in similar catastrophes. Whatever, therefore, of genius, skill, and energy the Conqueror of the World applied to the task, this last question addressed to fate[11] remained always the same. Shall we then discard the campaigns of 1805, 1807, 1809, and say on account of the campaign of 1812 that they were acts of imprudence; that the results were against the nature of things, and that in 1812 strategic justice at last found vent for itself in opposition to blind chance? That would be an unwarrantable conclusion, a most arbitrary judgment, a case only half proved, because no human, eye can trace the thread of the necessary connection of events up to the determination of the conquered Princes.

Still less can we say the campaign of 1812 merited the same success as the others, and that the reason why it turned out otherwise lies in something unnatural, for we cannot regard the firmness of Alexander as something unpredictable.

What can be more natural than to say that in the years 1805, 1807, 1809, Buonaparte judged his opponents correctly, and that in 1812 he erred in that point? On the former occasions, therefore, he was right, in the latter wrong, and in both cases we judge by the *result*.

All action in War, as we have already said, is directed on probable, not on certain, results. Whatever is wanting in certainty must always be left to fate, or chance, call it which you will. We may demand that what is so left should be as little as possible, but only in relation to the particular case – that is, as little as is possible in this one case, but not that the case in which the least is left to chance is always to be preferred. That would be an enormous error, as follows from all our theoretical views. There are cases in which the greatest daring is the greatest wisdom.

Now in everything which is left to chance by the chief actor, his personal merit, and therefore his responsibility as well, seems to be completely set aside; nevertheless we cannot suppress an inward feeling of satisfaction whenever expectation realises itself, and if it dis-

---

11 "Frage an der Schicksal," a familiar quotation from Schiller. – *TR.*

appoints us our mind is dissatisfied; and more than this of right and wrong should not be meant by the judgment which we form from the mere result, or rather that we find there.

Nevertheless, it cannot be denied that the satisfaction which our mind experiences at success, the pain caused by failure, proceed from a sort of mysterious feeling; we suppose between that success ascribed to good fortune and the genius of the chief a fine connecting thread, invisible to the mind's eye, and the supposition gives pleasure. What tends to confirm this idea is that our sympathy increases, becomes more decided, if the successes and defeats of the principal actor are often repeated. Thus it becomes intelligible how good luck in War assumes a much nobler nature than good luck at play. In general, when a fortunate warrior does not otherwise lessen our interest in his behalf, we have a pleasure in accompanying him in his career.

Criticism, therefore, after having weighed all that comes within the sphere of human reason and conviction, will let the result speak for that part where the deep mysterious relations are not disclosed in any visible form, and will protect this silent sentence of a higher authority from the noise of crude opinions on the one hand, while on the other it prevents the gross abuse which might be made of this last tribunal.

This verdict of the result must therefore always bring forth that which human sagacity cannot discover; and it will be chiefly as regards the intellectual powers and operations that it will be called into requisition, partly because they can be estimated with the least certainty, partly because their close connection with the will is favourable to their exercising over it an important influence. When fear or bravery precipitates the decision, there is nothing objective intervening between them for our consideration, and consequently nothing by which sagacity and calculation might have met the probable result.

We must now be allowed to make a few observations on the instrument of criticism, that is, the language which it uses, because that is to a certain extent connected with the action in War; for the critical examination is nothing more than the deliberation which should precede action in War. We therefore think it very essential that the language used in criticism should have the same character as that which deliberation in War must have, for otherwise it would cease to be practical, and criticism could gain no admittance in actual life.

We have said in our observations on the theory of the conduct of War that it should educate the mind of the Commander for War, or that its teaching should guide his education; also that it is not intended to furnish him with positive doctrines and systems which he can use like mental appliances. But if the construction of scientific formulae is never required, or even allowable, in War to aid the decision on the case presented, if truth does not appear there in a systematic shape, if it is not found in an indirect way, but directly by the natural perception of the mind, then it must be the same also in a critical review.

It is true as we have seen that, wherever complete demonstration of the nature of things would be too tedious, criticism must support itself on those truths which theory has established on the point. But, just as in War the actor obeys these theoretical truths rather because his mind is imbued with them than because he regards them as objective inflexible laws, so criticism must also make use of them, not as an external law or an algebraic formula, of which fresh proof is not required each time they are applied, but it must always throw a light on this proof itself, leaving only to theory the more minute and circumstantial proof. Thus it avoids a mysterious, unintelligible phraseology, and makes its progress in plain language, that is, with a clear and always visible chain of ideas.

Certainly this cannot always be completely attained, but it must always be the aim in critical expositions. Such expositions must use complicated forms of science as sparingly as possible, and never resort to the construction of scientific aids as of a truth apparatus of its own, but always be guided by the natural and unbiassed impressions of the mind.

But this pious endeavour, if we may use the expression, has unfortunately seldom hitherto presided over critical examinations: the most of them have rather been emanations of a species of vanity – a wish to make a display of ideas.

The first evil which we constantly stumble upon is a lame, totally inadmissible application of certain one-sided systems as of a formal code of laws. But it is never difficult to show the one-sidedness of such systems, and this only requires to be done once to throw discredit for ever on critical judgments which are based on them. We have here to deal with a definite subject, and as the number of possible systems after all can be but small, therefore also they are themselves the lesser evil.

Much greater is the evil which lies in the pompous retinue of technical terms – scientific expressions and metaphors, which these systems carry in their train, and which like a rabble-like the baggage of an Army broken away from its Chief – hang about in all directions. Any critic who has not adopted a system, either because he has not found one to please him, or because he has not yet been able to make himself master of one, will at least occasionally make use of a piece of one, as one would use a ruler, to show the blunders committed by a General. The most of them are incapable of reasoning without using as a help here and there some shreds of scientific military theory. The smallest of these fragments, consisting in mere scientific words and metaphors, are often nothing more than ornamental flourishes of critical narration. Now it is in the nature of things that all technical and scientific expressions which belong to a system lose their propriety, if they ever had any, as soon as they are distorted, and used as general axioms, or as small crystalline talismans, which have more power of demonstration than simple speech.

Thus it has come to pass that our theoretical and critical books, instead of being straightforward, intelligible dissertations, in which the author always knows at least what he says and the reader what he reads, are brimful of these technical terms, which form dark points of interference where author and reader part company. But frequently they are something worse, being nothing but hollow shells without any kernel. The author himself has no clear perception of what he means, contents himself with vague ideas, which if expressed in plain language would be unsatisfactory even to himself.

A third fault in criticism is the *misuse* of *historical examples*, and a display of great reading or learning. What the history of the Art of War is we have already said, and we shall further explain our views on examples and on military history in general in special chapters. One fact merely touched upon in a very cursory manner may be used to support the most opposite views, and three or four such facts of the most heterogeneous description, brought together out of the most distant lands and remote times and heaped up, generally distract and bewilder the judgment and understanding without demonstrating anything; for when exposed to the light they turn out to be only trumpery rubbish, made use of to show off the author's learning.

But what can be gained for practical life by such obscure, partly false, confused arbitrary conceptions? So little is gained that theory on account of them has always been a true antithesis of practice, and frequently a subject of ridicule to those whose soldierly qualities in the field are above question.

But it is impossible that this could have been the case, if theory in simple language, and by natural treatment of those things which constitute the Art of making War, had merely sought to establish just so much as admits of being established; if, avoiding all false pretensions and irrelevant display of scientific forms and historical parallels, it had kept close to the subject, and gone hand in hand with those who must conduct affairs in the field by their own natural genius.

CHAPTER SIX

On Examples

EXAMPLES FROM HISTORY make everything clear, and furnish the best description of proof in the empirical sciences. This applies with more force to the Art of War than to any other. General Scharnhorst, whose handbook is the best ever written on actual War, pronounces historical examples to be of the first importance, and makes an admirable use of them himself. Had he survived the War in which he fell,[12] the fourth part of his revised treatise on artillery would have given a still greater proof of the observing and enlightened spirit in which he sifted matters of experience.

But such use of historical examples is rarely made by theoretical writers; the way in which they more commonly make use of them is rather calculated to leave the mind unsatisfied, as well as to offend the understanding. We therefore think it important to bring specially into view the use and abuse of historical examples.

Unquestionably the branches of knowledge which lie at the foundation of the Art of War come under the denomination of empirical sciences; for although they are derived in a great measure from the nature of things, still we can only learn this very nature itself for the most part from experience; and besides that, the practical application is modified by so many circumstances that the effects can never be completely learnt from the mere nature of the means.

The effects of gunpowder, that great agent in our military activity, were only learnt by experience, and up to this hour experiments are continually in progress in order to investigate them more fully. That an iron ball to which powder has given a velocity of 1000 feet in a second, smashes every

---

12 General Scharnhorst died in 1813, of a wound received in the battle of Bautzen or Grosz Gorchen – *Editor*.

living thing which it touches in its course is intelligible in itself; experience is not required to tell us that; but in producing this effect how many hundred circumstances are concerned, some of which can only be learnt by experience! And the physical is not the only effect which we have to study, it is the moral which we are in search of, and that can only be ascertained by experience; and there is no other way of learning and appreciating it but by experience. In the middle ages, when firearms were first invented, their effect, owing to their rude make, was materially but trifling compared to what it now is, but their effect morally was much greater. One must have witnessed the firmness of one of those masses taught and led by Buonaparte, under the heaviest and most unintermittent cannonade, in order to understand what troops, hardened by long practice in the field of danger, can do, when by a career of victory they have reached the noble principle of demanding from themselves their utmost efforts. In pure conception no one would believe it. On the other hand, it is well known that there are troops in the service of European Powers at the present moment who would easily be dispersed by a few cannon shots.

But no empirical science, consequently also no theory of the Art of War, can always corroborate its truths by historical proof; it would also be, in some measure, difficult to support experience by single facts. If any means is once found efficacious in War, it is repeated; one nation copies another, the thing becomes the fashion, and in this manner it comes into use, supported by experience, and takes its place in theory, which contents itself with appealing to experience in general in order to show its origin, but not as a verification of its truth.

But it is quite otherwise if experience is to be used in order to overthrow some means in use, to confirm what is doubtful, or introduce something new; then particular examples from history must be quoted as proofs.

Now, if we consider closely the use of historical proofs, four points of view readily present themselves for the purpose.

First, they may be used merely as an *explanation* of an idea. In every abstract consideration it is very easy to be misunderstood, or not to be intelligible at all: when an author is afraid of this, an exemplification from history serves to throw the light which is wanted on his idea, and to ensure his being intelligible to his reader.

Secondly, it may serve as an *application* of an idea, because by means of an example there is an opportunity of showing the action of those minor circumstances which cannot all be comprehended and explained in any general expression of an idea; for in that consists, indeed, the difference between theory and experience. Both these cases belong to examples properly speaking, the two following belong to historical proofs.

Thirdly, a historical fact may be referred to particularly, in order to support what one has advanced. This is in all cases sufficient, if we have *only* to prove the *possibility* of a fact or effect.

Lastly, in the fourth place, from the circumstantial detail of a historical event, and by collecting together several of them, we may deduce some theory, which therefore has its true *proof* in this testimony itself.

For the first of these purposes all that is generally required is a cursory notice of the case, as it is only used partially. Historical correctness is a secondary consideration; a case invented might also serve the purpose as well, only historical ones are always to be preferred, because they bring the idea which they illustrate nearer to practical life.

The second use supposes a more circumstantial relation of events, but historical authenticity is again of secondary importance, and in respect to this point the same is to be said as in the first case.

For the third purpose the mere quotation of an undoubted fact is generally sufficient. If it is asserted that fortified positions may fulfil their object under certain conditions, it is only necessary to mention the position of Bunzelwitz[13] in support of the assertion.

But if, through the narrative of a case in history, an abstract truth is to be demonstrated, then everything in the case bearing on the demonstration must be analysed in the most searching and complete manner; it must, to a certain extent, develop itself carefully before the eyes of the reader. The less effectually this is done the weaker will be the proof, and the more necessary it will be to supply the demonstrative proof which is wanting in the single case by a number of cases, because we have a right to suppose that the more minute details which we are unable to give neutralise each other in their effects in a certain number of cases.

If we want to show by example derived from experience that cavalry are better placed behind than in a line with infantry; that it is very hazardous without a decided preponderance of numbers to attempt an enveloping movement, with widely separated columns, either on a field of battle or in the theatre of war – that is, either tactically or strategically – then in the first of these cases it would not be sufficient to specify some lost battles in which the cavalry was on the flanks and some gained in which the cavalry was in rear of the infantry; and in the tatter of these cases it is not sufficient to refer to the battles of Rivoli and Wagram, to the attack of the Austrians on the theatre of war in Italy, in 1796, or of the French upon the German theatre of war in the same year. The way in which these orders of battle or plans of attack essentially contributed to disastrous issues in

---

13   Frederick the Great's celebrated entrenched camp in 1761.

those particular cases must be shown by closely tracing out circumstances and occurrences. Then it will appear how far such forms or measures are to be condemned, a point which it is very necessary to show, for a total condemnation would be inconsistent with truth.

It has been already said that when a circumstantial detail of facts is impossible, the demonstrative power which is deficient may to a certain extent be supplied by the number of cases quoted; but this is a very dangerous method of getting out of the difficulty, and one which has been much abused. Instead of one well-explained example, three or four are just touched upon, and thus a show is made of strong evidence. But there are matters where a whole dozen of cases brought forward would prove nothing, if, for instance, they are facts of frequent occurrence, and therefore a dozen other cases with an opposite result might just as easily be brought forward. If any one will instance a dozen lost battles in which the side beaten attacked in separate converging columns, we can instance a dozen that have been gained in which the same order was adopted. It is evident that in this way no result is to be obtained.

Upon carefully considering these different points, it will be seen how easily examples may be misapplied.

An occurrence which, instead of being carefully analysed in all its parts, is superficially noticed, is like an object seen at a great distance, presenting the same appearance on each side, and in which the details of its parts cannot be distinguished. Such examples have, in reality, served to support the most contradictory opinions. To some Daun's campaigns are models of prudence and skill. To others, they are nothing but examples of timidity and want of resolution. Buonaparte's passage across the Noric Alps in 1797 may be made to appear the noblest resolution, but also as an act of sheer temerity. His strategic defeat in 1812 may be represented as the consequence either of an excess, or of a deficiency, of energy. All these opinions have been broached, and it is easy to see that they might very well arise, because each person takes a different view of the connection of events. At the same time these antagonistic opinions cannot be reconciled with each other, and therefore one of the two must be wrong.

Much as we are obliged to the worthy Feuquieres for the numerous examples introduced in his memoirs – partly because a number of historical incidents have thus been preserved which might otherwise have been lost, and partly because he was one of the first to bring theoretical, that is, abstract, ideas into connection with the practical in war, in so far that the cases brought forward may be regarded as intended to exemplify and confirm what is theoretically asserted – yet, in the opinion of an impartial reader, he will hardly be allowed to have attained the object

he proposed to himself, that of proving theoretical principles by historical examples. For although he sometimes relates occurrences with great
minuteness, still he falls short very often of showing that the deductions
drawn necessarily proceed from the inner relations of these events.

Another evil which comes from the superficial notice of historical
events, is that some readers are either wholly ignorant of the events, or
cannot call them to remembrance sufficiently to be able to grasp the
author's meaning, so that there is no alternative between either accept-
ing blindly what is said, or remaining unconvinced.

It is extremely difficult to put together or unfold historical events before
the eyes of a reader in such a way as is necessary, in order to be able to use
them as proofs; for the writer very often wants the means, and can neither
afford the time nor the requisite space; but we maintain that, when the
object is to establish a new or doubtful opinion, one single example, thoroughly analysed, is far more instructive than ten which are superficially
treated. The great mischief of these superficial representations is not that
the writer puts his story forward as a proof when it has only a false title,
but that he has not made himself properly acquainted with the subject,
and that from this sort of slovenly, shallow treatment of history, a hundred
false views and attempts at the construction of theories arise, which would
never have made their appearance if the writer had looked upon it as his
duty to deduce from the strict connection of events everything new which
he brought to market, and sought to prove from history.

When we are convinced of these difficulties in the use of historical
examples, and at the same time of the necessity (of making use of such
examples), then we shall also come to the conclusion that the latest
military history is naturally the best field from which to draw them,
inasmuch as it alone is sufficiently authentic and detailed.

In ancient times, circumstances connected with War, as well as the
method of carrying it on, were different; therefore its events are of less use
to us either theoretically or practically; in addition to which, military history, like every other, naturally loses in the course of time a number of small
traits and lineaments originally to be seen, loses in colour and life, like a
worn-out or darkened picture; so that perhaps at last only the large masses
and leading features remain, which thus acquire undue proportions.

If we look at the present state of warfare, we should say that the Wars
since that of the Austrian succession are almost the only ones which, at
least as far as armament, have still a considerable similarity to the present, and which, notwithstanding the many important changes which have
taken place both great and small, are still capable of affording much instruction. It is quite otherwise with the War of the Spanish succession, as

the use of fire-arms had not then so far advanced towards perfection, and cavalry still continued the most important arm. The farther we go back, the less useful becomes military history, as it gets so much the more meagre and barren of detail. The most useless of all is that of the old world.

But this uselessness is not altogether absolute, it relates only to those subjects which depend on a knowledge of minute details, or on those things in which the method of conducting war has changed. Although we know very little about the tactics in the battles between the Swiss and the Austrians, the Burgundians and French, still we find in them unmistakable evidence that they were the first in which the superiority of a good infantry over the best cavalry was, displayed. A general glance at the time of the Condottieri teaches us how the whole method of conducting War is dependent on the instrument used; for at no period have the forces used in War had so much the characteristics of a special instrument, and been a class so totally distinct from the rest of the national community. The memorable way in which the Romans in the second Punic War attacked the Carthaginan possessions in Spain and Africa, while Hannibal still maintained himself in Italy, is a most instructive subject to study, as the general relations of the States and Armies concerned in this indirect act of defence are sufficiently well known.

But the more things descend into particulars and deviate in character from the most general relations, the less we can look for examples and lessons of experience from very remote periods, for we have neither the means of judging properly of corresponding events, nor can we apply them to our completely different method of War.

Unfortunately, however, it has always been the fashion with historical writers to talk about ancient times. We shall not say how far vanity and charlatanism may have had a share in this, but in general we fail to discover any honest intention and earnest endeavour to instruct and convince, and we can therefore only look upon such quotations and references as embellishments to fill up gaps and hide defects.

It would be an immense service to teach the Art of War entirely by historical examples, as Feuquieres proposed to do; but it would be full work for the whole life of a man, if we reflect that he who undertakes it must first qualify himself for the task by a long personal experience in actual War.

Whoever, stirred by ambition, undertakes such a task, let him prepare himself for his pious undertaking as for a long pilgrimage; let him give up his time, spare no sacrifice, fear no temporal rank or power, and rise above all feelings of personal vanity, of false shame, in order, according to the French code, to speak *the truth, the whole truth, and nothing but the truth.*

BOOK THREE

Of Strategy in General

CHAPTER ONE

Strategy

IN THE SECOND chapter of the second book, Strategy has been defined as "the employment of the battle as the means towards the attainment of the object of the War." Properly speaking it has to do with nothing but the battle, but its theory must include in this consideration the instrument of this real activity – the armed force – in itself and in its principal relations, for the battle is fought by it, and shows its effects upon it in turn. It must be well acquainted with the battle itself as far as relates to its possible results, and those mental and moral powers which are the most important in the use of the same.

Strategy is the employment of the battle to gain the end of the War; it must therefore give an aim to the whole military action, which must be in accordance with the object of the War; in other words, Strategy forms the plan of the War, and to this end it links together the series of acts which are to lead to the final decision, that, is to say, it makes the plans for the separate campaigns and regulates the combats to be fought in each. As these are all things which to a great extent can only be determined on conjectures some of which turn out incorrect, while a number of other arrangements pertaining to details cannot be made at all beforehand, it follows, as a matter of course, that Strategy must go with the Army to the field in order to arrange particulars on the spot, and to make the modifications in the general plan, which incessantly become necessary in War. Strategy can therefore never take its hand from the work for a moment.

That this, however, has not always been the view taken is evident from the former custom of keeping Strategy in the cabinet and not with the Army, a thing only allowable if the cabinet is so near to the Army that it can be taken for the chief head-quarters of the Army.

Theory will therefore attend on Strategy in the determination of its plans, or, as we may more properly say, it will throw a light on things in themselves, and on their relations to each other, and bring out prominently the little that there is of principle or rule.

If we recall to mind from the first chapter how many things of the highest importance War touches upon, we may conceive that a consideration of all requires a rare grasp of mind.

A Prince or General who knows exactly how to organise his War according to his object and means, who does neither too little nor too much, gives by that the greatest proof of his genius. But the effects of this talent are exhibited not so much by the invention of new modes of action, which might strike the eye immediately, as in the successful final result of the whole. It is the exact fulfilment of silent suppositions, it is the noiseless harmony of the whole action which we should admire, and which only makes itself known in the total result. Inquirer who, tracing back from the final result, does not perceive the signs of that harmony is one who is apt to seek for genius where it is not, and where it cannot be found.

The means and forms which Strategy uses are in fact so extremely simple, so well known by their constant repetition, that it only appears ridiculous to sound common sense when it hears critics so frequently speaking of them with high-flown emphasis. Turning a flank, which has been done a thousand times, is regarded here as a proof of the most brilliant genius, there as a proof of the most profound penetration, indeed even of the most comprehensive knowledge. Can there be in the book-world more absurd productions?[14]

It is still more ridiculous if, in addition to this, we reflect that the same critic, in accordance with prevalent opinion, excludes all moral forces from theory, and will not allow it to be concerned with anything but the material forces, so that all must be confined to a few mathematical relations of equilibrium and preponderance, of time and space, and a few lines and angles. If it were nothing more than this, then out of such a miserable business there would not be a scientific problem for even a schoolboy.

But let us admit: there is no question here about scientific formulas and problems; the relations of material things are all very simple; the right comprehension of the moral forces which come into play is more difficult. Still, even in respect to them, it is only in the highest branches of Strategy that moral complications and a great diversity of quantities and relations are to be looked for, only at that point where Strategy borders on political science, or rather where the two become one, and there, as we have before observed, they have more influence on the "how much" and "how little"

14   This paragraph refers to the works of Lloyd, Buelow, indeed to all the eighteenth-century writers, from whose influence we in England are not even yet free. – *ED.*

is to be done than on the form of execution. Where the latter is the principal question, as in the single acts both great and small in War, the moral quantities are already reduced to a very small number.

Thus, then, in Strategy everything is very simple, but not on that account very easy. Once it is determined from the relations of the State what should and may be done by War, then the way to it is easy to find; but to follow that way straightforward, to carry out the plan without being obliged to deviate from it a thousand times by a thousand varying influences, requires, besides great strength of character, great clearness and steadiness of mind, and out of a thousand men who are remarkable, some for mind, others for penetration, others again for boldness or strength of will, perhaps not one will combine in himself all those qualities which are required to raise a man above mediocrity in the career of a general.

It may sound strange, but for all who know War in this respect it is a fact beyond doubt, that much more strength of will is required to make an important decision in Strategy than in tactics. In the latter we are hurried on with the moment; a Commander feels himself borne along in a strong current, against which he durst not contend without the most destructive consequences, he suppresses the rising fears, and boldly ventures further. In Strategy, where all goes on at a slower rate, there is more room allowed for our own apprehensions and those of others, for objections and remonstrances, consequently also for unseasonable regrets; and as we do not see things in Strategy as we do at least half of them in tactics, with the living eye, but everything must be conjectured and assumed, the convictions produced are less powerful. The consequence is that most Generals, when they should act, remain stuck fast in bewildering doubts.

Now let us cast a glance at history – upon Frederick the Great's campaign of 1760, celebrated for its fine marches and manoeuvres: a perfect masterpiece of Strategic skill as critics tell us. Is there really anything to drive us out of our wits with admiration in the King's first trying to turn Daun's right flank, then his left, then again his right, &c.? Are we to see profound wisdom in this? No, that we cannot, if we are to decide naturally and without affectation. What we rather admire above all is the sagacity of the King in this respect, that while pursuing a great object with very limited means, he undertook nothing beyond his powers, and *just enough* to gain his object. This sagacity of the General is visible not only in this campaign, but throughout all the three Wars of the Great King!

To bring Silesia into the safe harbour of a well-guaranteed peace was his object.

At the head of a small State, which was like other States in most things, and only ahead of them in some branches of administration; he could not be an Alexander, and, as Charles XII, he would only, like him, have broken his head. We find, therefore, in the whole of his conduct of War, a controlled power, always well balanced, and never wanting in energy, which in the most critical moments rises to astonishing deeds, and the next moment oscillates quietly on again in subordination to the play of the most subtle political influences. Neither vanity, thirst for glory, nor vengeance could make him deviate from his course, and this course alone it is which brought him to a fortunate termination of the contest.

These few words do but scant justice to this phase of the genius of the great General; the eyes must be fixed carefully on the extraordinary issue of the struggle, and the causes which brought about that issue must be traced out, in order thoroughly to understand that nothing but the King's penetrating eye brought him safely out of all his dangers.

This is one feature in this great Commander which we admire in the campaign of 1760 – and in all others, but in this especially – because in none did he keep the balance even against such a superior hostile force, with such a small sacrifice.

Another feature relates to the difficulty of execution. Marches to turn a flank, right or left, are easily combined; the idea of keeping a small force always well concentrated to be able to meet the enemy on equal terms at any point, to multiply a force by rapid movement, is as easily conceived as expressed; the mere contrivance in these points, therefore, cannot excite our admiration, and with respect to such simple things, there is nothing further than to admit that they are simple.

But let a General try to do these things like Frederick the Great. Long afterwards authors, who were eyewitnesses, have spoken of the danger, indeed of the imprudence, of the King's camps, and doubtless, at the time he pitched them, the danger appeared three times as great as afterwards.

It was the same with his marches, under the eyes, nay, often under the cannon of the enemy's Army; these camps were taken up, these marches made, not from want of prudence, but because in Daun's system, in his mode of drawing up his Army, in the responsibility which pressed upon him, and in his character, Frederick found that security which justified his camps and marches. But it required the King's boldness, determination, and strength of will to see things in this light, and not to be led astray and intimidated by the danger of which thirty years after people still wrote and spoke. Few Generals in this situation would have believed these simple strategic means to be practicable.

Again, another difficulty in execution lay in this, that the King's Army in this campaign was constantly in motion. Twice it marched by wretched cross-roads, from the Elbe into Silesia, in rear of Daun and pursued by Lascy (beginning of July, beginning of August). It required to be always ready for battle, and its marches had to be organised with a degree of skill which necessarily called forth a proportionate amount of exertion. Although attended and delayed by thousands of waggons, still its subsistence was extremely difficult. In Silesia, for eight days before the battle of Leignitz, it had constantly to march, defiling alternately right and left in front of the enemy: – this costs great fatigue, and entails great privations.

Is it to be supposed that all this could have been done without producing great friction in the machine? Can the mind of a Commander elaborate such movements with the same ease as the hand of a land surveyor uses the astrolabe? Does not the sight of the sufferings of their hungry, thirsty comrades pierce the hearts of the Commander and his Generals a thousand times? Must not the murmurs and doubts which these cause reach his ear? Has an ordinary man the courage to demand such sacrifices, and would not such efforts most certainly demoralise the Army, break up the bands of discipline, and, in short, undermine its military virtue, if firm reliance on the greatness and infallibility of the Commander did not compensate for all? Here, therefore, it is that we should pay respect; it is these miracles of execution which we should admire. But it is impossible to realise all this in its full force without a foretaste of it by experience. He who only knows War from books or the drill-ground cannot realise the whole effect of this counterpoise in action; *we beg him, therefore, to accept from us on faith and trust all that he is unable to supply from any personal experiences of his own.*

This illustration is intended to give more clearness to the course of our ideas, and in closing this chapter we will only briefly observe that in our exposition of Strategy we shall describe those separate subjects which appear to us the most important, whether of a moral or material nature; then proceed from the simple to the complex, and conclude with the inner connection of the whole act of War, in other words, with the plan for a War or campaign.

Observation.

In an earlier manuscript of the second book are the following passages endorsed by the author himself to be used for the first Chapter of the second Book: the projected revision of that chapter not having been made, the passages referred to are introduced here in full.

By the mere assemblage of armed forces at a particular point, a battle there becomes possible, but does not always take place. Is that possibility now to be regarded as a reality and therefore an effective thing? Certainly, it is so by its results, and these effects, whatever they may be, can never fail.

1. *Possible combats are on account of their results to be looked upon as real ones.*

If a detachment is sent away to cut off the retreat of a flying enemy, and the enemy surrenders in consequence without further resistance, still it is through the combat which is offered to him by this detachment sent after him that he is brought to his decision.

If a part of our Army occupies an enemy's province which was undefended, and thus deprives the enemy of very considerable means of keeping up the strength of his Army, it is entirely through the battle which our detached body gives the enemy to expect, in case he seeks to recover the lost province, that we remain in possession of the same.

In both cases, therefore, the mere possibility of a battle has produced results, and is therefore to be classed amongst actual events. Suppose that in these cases the enemy has opposed our troops with others superior in force, and thus forced ours to give up their object without a combat, then certainly our plan has failed, but the battle which we offered at (either of) those points has not on that account been without effect, for it attracted the enemy's forces to that point. And in case our whole undertaking has done us harm, it cannot be said that these positions, these possible battles, have been attended with no results; their effects, then, are similar to those of a lost battle.

In this manner we see that the destruction of the enemy's military forces, the overthrow of the enemy's power, is only to be done through the effect of a battle, whether it be that it actually takes place, or that it is merely offered, and not accepted.

2. *Twofold object of the combat.*

But these effects are of two kinds, direct and indirect they are of the latter, if other things intrude themselves and become the object of the combat – things which cannot be regarded as the destruction of enemy's force, but only leading up to it, certainly by a circuitous road, but with so much the greater effect. The possession of provinces, towns, fortresses, roads, bridges, magazines, &c., may be the *immediate* object of a battle, but never the ultimate one. Things of this description can never be, looked upon otherwise than as means of gaining greater superiority, so as at last to offer battle to the enemy in such a way that it will be impossible for him to accept it. Therefore all these things must only be regarded as intermediate links, steps, as it were, leading up to the effectual principle, but never as that principle itself.

3. *Example.*

In 1814, by the capture of Buonaparte's capital the object of the War was attained. The political divisions which had their roots in Paris came into active operation, and an enormous split left the power of the Emperor to collapse of itself. Nevertheless the point of view from which we must look at all this is, that through these causes the forces and defensive means of Buonaparte were suddenly very much diminished, the superiority of the Allies, therefore, just in the same measure increased, and any further resistance then became *impossible*. It was this impossibility which produced the peace with France. If we suppose the forces of the Allies at that moment diminished to a like extent through external causes; – if the superiority vanishes, then at the same time vanishes also all the effect and importance of the taking of Paris.

We have gone through this chain of argument in order to show that this is the natural and only true view of the thing from which it derives its importance. It leads always back to the question, What at any given moment of the War or campaign will be the probable result of the great or small combats which the two sides might offer to each other? In the consideration of a plan for a campaign, this question only is decisive as to the measures which are to be taken all through from the very commencement.

4. *When this view is not taken, then a false value is given to other things.*

If we do not accustom ourselves to look upon War, and the single campaigns in a War, as a chain which is all composed of battles strung together, one of which always brings on another; if we adopt the idea that the taking of a certain geographical point, the occupation of an undefended province, is in itself anything; then we are very likely to regard it as an acquisition which we may retain; and if we look at it so, and not as a term in the whole series of events, we do not ask ourselves whether this possession may not lead to greater disadvantages hereafter. How often we find this mistake recurring in military history.

We might say that, just as in commerce the merchant cannot set apart and place in security gains from one single transaction by itself, so in War a single advantage cannot be separated from the result of the whole. Just as the former must always operate with the whole bulk of his means, just so in War, only the sum total will decide on the advantage or disadvantage of each item.

If the mind's eye is always directed upon the series of combats, so far as they can be seen beforehand, then it is always looking in the right direction, and thereby the motion of the force acquires that rapidity, that is to say, willing and doing acquire that energy which is suitable to the matter, and which is not to be thwarted or turned aside by extraneous influences.[15]

15 The whole of this chapter is directed against the theories of the Austrian Staff in 1814. It may be taken as the foundation of the modern teaching of the Prussian General Staff. See especially von Kammer. – *ED*.

CHAPTER TWO

Elements of Strategy

THE CAUSES which condition the use of the combat in Strategy may be easily divided into elements of different kinds, such as the moral, physical, mathematical, geographical and statistical elements.

The first class includes all that can be called forth by moral qualities and effects; to the second belong the whole mass of the military force, its organisation, the proportion of the three arms, &c. &c.; to the third, the angle of the lines of operation, the concentric and eccentric movements in as far as their geometrical nature has any value in the calculation; to the fourth, the influences of country, such as commanding points, hills, rivers, woods, roads, &c. &c.; lastly, to the fifth, all the means of supply. The separation of these things once for all in the mind does good in giving clearness and helping us to estimate at once, at a higher or lower value, the different classes as we pass onwards. For, in considering them separately, many lose of themselves their borrowed importance; one feels, for instance, quite plainly that the value of a base of operations, even if we look at nothing in it but its relative position to the line of operations, depends much less in that simple form on the geometrical element of the angle which they form with one another, than on the nature of the roads and the country through which they pass.

But to treat upon Strategy according to these elements would be the most unfortunate idea that could be conceived, for these elements are generally manifold, and intimately connected with each other in every single operation of War. We should lose ourselves in the most soulless analysis, and as if in a horrid dream, we should be for ever trying in vain to build up an arch to connect this base of abstractions with facts belonging to the real world. Heaven preserve every theorist from such an undertaking! We shall keep to the world of things in their totality, and not pursue our analysis further than is necessary from time to time to give distinctness to the idea which we wish to impart, and which has come to us, not by a speculative investigation, but through the impression made by the realities of War in their entirety.

Moral Forces

WE MUST RETURN again to this subject, which is touched upon in the third chapter of the second book, because the moral forces are amongst the most important subjects in War. They form the spirit which permeates the whole being of War. These forces fasten themselves soonest and with the greatest affinity on to the Will which puts in motion and guides the whole mass of powers, uniting with it as it were in one stream, because this is a moral force itself. Unfortunately they will escape from all book-analysis, for they will neither be brought into numbers nor into classes, and require to be both seen and felt.

The spirit and other moral qualities which animate an Army, a General, or Governments, public opinion in provinces in which a War is raging, the moral effect of a victory or of a defeat, are things which in themselves vary very much in their nature, and which also, according as they stand with regard to our object and our relations, may have an influence in different ways.

Although little or nothing can be said about these things in books, still they belong to the theory of the Art of War, as much as everything else which constitutes War. For I must here once more repeat that it is a miserable philosophy if, according to the old plan, we establish rules and principles wholly regardless of all moral forces, and then, as soon as these forces make their appearance, we begin to count exceptions which we thereby establish as it were theoretically, that is, make into rules; or if we resort to an appeal to genius, which is above all rules, thus giving out by implication, not only that rules were only made for fools, but also that they themselves are no better than folly.

Even if the theory of the Art of War does no more in reality than recall these things to remembrance, showing the necessity of allowing to the moral forces their full value, and of always taking them into consideration, by so doing it extends its borders over the region of immaterial forces, and by establishing that point of view, condemns beforehand every one who would endeavour to justify himself before its judgment seat by the mere physical relations of forces.

Further out of regard to all other so-called rules, theory cannot banish the moral forces beyond its frontier, because the effects of the physical forces and the moral are completely fused, and are not to be decomposed like a metal alloy by a chemical process. In every rule relating to the physical forces, theory must present to the mind at the same time the share which the moral powers will have in it, if it would not be led to categorical propositions, at one time too timid and contracted, at another too dogmatical and wide. Even the most matter-of-fact theories have, without knowing it, strayed over into this moral kingdom; for, as an example, the effects of a victory cannot in any way be explained without taking into consideration the moral impressions. And therefore the most of the subjects which we shall go through in this book are composed half of physical, half of moral causes and effects, and we might say the physical are almost no more than the wooden handle, whilst the moral are the noble metal, the real bright-polished weapon.

The value of the moral powers, and their frequently incredible influence, are best exemplified by history, and this is the most generous and the purest nourishment which the mind of the General can extract from it. – At the same time it is to be observed, that it is less demonstrations, critical examinations, and learned treatises, than sentiments, general impressions, and single flashing sparks of truth, which yield the seeds of knowledge that are to fertilise the mind.

We might go through the most important moral phenomena in War, and with all the care of a diligent professor try what we could impart about each, either good or bad. But as in such a method one slides too much into the commonplace and trite, whilst real mind quickly makes its escape in analysis, the end is that one gets imperceptibly to the relation of things which everybody knows. We prefer, therefore, to remain here more than usually incomplete and rhapsodical, content to have drawn attention to the importance of the subject in a general way, and to have pointed out the spirit in which the views given in this book have been conceived.

CHAPTER FOUR
The Chief Moral Powers

THESE ARE The Talents of the Commander; The Military Virtue of the Army; Its National feeling. Which of these is the most important no one can tell in a general way, for it is very difficult to say anything in general of their strength, and still more difficult to compare the strength of one with that of another. The best plan is not to undervalue any of them, a fault which human judgment is prone to, sometimes on one side, sometimes on another, in its whimsical oscillations. It is better to satisfy ourselves of the undeniable efficacy of these three things by sufficient evidence from history.

It is true, however, that in modern times the Armies of European states have arrived very much at a par as regards discipline and fitness for service, and that the conduct of War has – as philosophers would say – naturally developed itself, thereby become a method, common as it were to all Armies, so that even from Commanders there is nothing further to be expected in the way of application of special means of Art, in the limited sense (such as Frederick the Second's oblique order). Hence it cannot be denied that, as matters now stand, greater scope is afforded for the influence of National spirit and habituation of an army to War. A long peace may again alter all this.[16]

The national spirit of an Army (enthusiasm, fanatical zeal, faith, opinion) displays itself most in mountain warfare, where every one down to the common soldier is left to himself. On this account, a mountainous country is the best campaigning ground for popular levies.

---

16   Written shortly after the Great Napoleonic campaigns.

Expertness of an Army through training, and that well-tempered courage which holds the ranks together as if they had been cast in a mould, show their superiority in an open country.

The talent of a General has most room to display itself in a closely intersected, undulating country. In mountains he has too little command over the separate parts, and the direction of all is beyond his powers; in open plains it is simple and does not exceed those powers.

According to these undeniable elective affinities, plans should be regulated.

CHAPTER FIVE

Military Virtue of an Army

THIS IS DISTINGUISHED from mere bravery, and still more from enthusiasm for the business of War. The first is certainly a necessary constituent part of it, but in the same way as bravery, which is a natural gift in some men, may arise in a soldier as a part of an Army from habit and custom, so with him it must also have a different direction from that which it has with others. It must lose that impulse to unbridled activity and exercise of force which is its characteristic in the individual, and submit itself to demands of a higher kind, to obedience, order, rule, and method. Enthusiasm for the profession gives life and greater fire to the military virtue of an Army, but does not necessarily constitute a part of it.

War is a special business, and however general its relations may be, and even if all the male population of a country, capable of bearing arms, exercise this calling, still it always continues to be different and separate from the other pursuits which occupy the life of man. – To be imbued with a sense of the spirit and nature of this business, to make use of, to rouse, to assimilate into the system the powers which should be active in it, to penetrate completely into the nature of the business with the understanding, through exercise to gain confidence and expertness in it, to be completely given up to it, to pass out of the man into the part which it is assigned to us to play in War, that is the military virtue of an Army in the individual.

However much pains may be taken to combine the soldier and the citizen in one and the same individual, whatever may be done to nationalise Wars, and however much we may imagine times have changed since the days of the old Condottieri, never will it be possible to do away with the individuality of the business; and if that cannot be done, then those who belong to it, as long as they belong to it, will always look upon themselves as a kind of guild, in the regulations, laws and customs in which the "Spirit of War" by preference finds its expression. And so it is in fact. Even with the most decided inclination to look at War from the highest point of view, it would be very wrong to look down upon this corporate spirit (e'sprit de corps) which may and should exist more or less in every Army. This corporate spirit forms the bond of union between the natural forces which are active in that which we have called military virtue. The crystals of military virtue have a greater affinity for the spirit of a corporate body than for anything else.

An Army which preserves its usual formations under the heaviest fire, which is never shaken by imaginary fears, and in the face of real danger disputes the ground inch by inch, which, proud in the feeling of its victories, never loses its sense of obedience, its respect for and confidence in its leaders, even under the depressing effects of defeat; an Army with all its physical powers, inured to privations and fatigue by exercise, like the muscles of an athlete; an Army which looks upon all its toils as the means to victory, not as a curse which hovers over its standards, and which is always reminded of its duties and virtues by the short catechism of one idea, namely the *honour of its arms*; – Such an Army is imbued with the true military spirit.

Soldiers may fight bravely like the Vende'ans, and do great things like the Swiss, the Americans, or Spaniards, without displaying this military virtue. A Commander may also be successful at the head of standing Armies, like Eugene and Marlborough, without enjoying the benefit of its assistance; we must not, therefore, say that a successful War without it cannot be imagined; and we draw especial attention to that point, in order the more to individualise the conception which is here brought forward, that the idea may not dissolve into a generalisation and that it may not be thought that military virtue is in the end everything. It is not so. Military virtue in an Army is a definite moral power which may be supposed wanting, and the influence of which may therefore be estimated – like any instrument the power of which may be calculated.

Having thus characterised it, we proceed to consider what can be predicated of its influence, and what are the means of gaining its assistance.

Military virtue is for the parts, what the genius of the Commander is for the whole. The General can only guide the whole, not each separate part, and where he cannot guide the part, there military virtue must be its leader. A General is chosen by the reputation of his superior talents, the chief leaders of large masses after careful probation; but this probation diminishes as we descend the scale of rank, and in just the same measure we may reckon less and less upon individual talents; but what is wanting in this respect military virtue should supply. The natural qualities of a warlike people play just this part: *bravery, aptitude, powers of endurance and enthusiasm.*

These properties may therefore supply the place of military virtue, and vice versa, from which the following may be deduced:

1. Military virtue is a quality of standing Armies only, but they require it the most. In national risings its place is supplied by natural qualities, which develop themselves there more rapidly.

2. Standing Armies opposed to standing Armies, can more easily dispense with it, than a standing Army opposed to a national insurrection, for in that case, the troops are more scattered, and the divisions left more to themselves. But where an Army can be kept concentrated, the genius of the General takes a greater place, and supplies what is wanting in the spirit of the Army. Therefore generally military virtue becomes more necessary the more the theatre of operations and other circumstances make the War complicated, and cause the forces to be scattered.

From these truths the only lesson to be derived is this, that if an Army is deficient in this quality, every endeavour should be made to simplify the operations of the War as much as possible, or to introduce double efficiency in the organisation of the Army in some other respect, and not to expect from the mere name of a standing Army, that which only the veritable thing itself can give.

The military virtue of an Army is, therefore, one of the most important moral powers in War, and where it is wanting, we either see its place supplied by one of the others, such as the great superiority of generalship or popular enthusiasm, or we find the results not commensurate with the exertions made. – How much that is great, this spirit, this sterling worth of an army, this refining of ore into the polished metal, has already done, we see in the history of the Macedonians under Alexander, the Roman legions under Cesar, the Spanish infantry under Alexander Farnese, the Swedes under Gustavus Adolphus and Charles XII, the Prussians under Frederick the Great, and the French under Buonaparte. We must purposely shut our eyes against all historical proof, if we do not admit, that the astonishing successes of these Generals and their greatness in situations of extreme difficulty, were only possible with Armies possessing this virtue.

This spirit can only be generated from two sources, and only by these two conjointly; the first is a succession of campaigns and great victories; the other is, an activity of the Army carried sometimes to the highest pitch. Only by these, does the soldier learn to know his powers. The more a General is in the habit of demanding from his troops, the surer he will be that his demands will be answered. The soldier is as proud of overcoming toil, as he is of surmounting danger. Therefore it is only in the soil of incessant activity and exertion that the germ will thrive, but also only in the sunshine of victory. Once it becomes a *strong tree*, it will stand against the fiercest storms of misfortune and defeat, and even against the indolent inactivity of peace, at least for a time. It can therefore only be created in War, and under great Generals, but no doubt it may last at least for several generations, even under Generals of moderate capacity, and through considerable periods of peace.

With this generous and noble spirit of union in a line of veteran troops, covered with scars and thoroughly inured to War, we must not compare the self-esteem and vanity of a standing Army,[17] held together merely by the glue of service-regulations and a drill book; a certain plodding earnestness and strict discipline may keep up military virtue for a long time, but can never create it; these things therefore have a certain value, but must not be over-rated. Order, smartness, good will, also a certain degree of pride and high feeling, are qualities of an Army formed in time of peace which are to be prized, but cannot stand alone. The whole retains the whole, and as with glass too quickly cooled, a single crack breaks the whole mass. Above all, the highest spirit in the world changes only too easily at the first check into depression, and one might say into a kind of rhodomontade of alarm, the French sauve que peut. – Such an Army can only achieve something through its leader, never by itself. It must be led with double caution, until by degrees, in victory and hardships, the strength grows into the full armour. Beware then of confusing the *spirit* of an Army with its temper.

---

17 Clausewitz is, of course, thinking of the long-service standing armies of his own youth. Not of the short-service standing armies of to-day (*Editor*).

CHAPTER SIX

Boldness

THE PLACE AND PART which boldness takes in the dynamic system of powers, where it stands opposed to Foresight and prudence, has been stated in the chapter on the certainty of the result in order thereby to show, that theory has no right to restrict it by virtue of its legislative power.

But this noble impulse, with which the human soul raises itself above the most formidable dangers, is to be regarded as an active principle peculiarly belonging to War. In fact, in what branch of human activity should boldness have a right of citizenship if not in War?

From the transport-driver and the drummer up to the General, it is the noblest of virtues, the true steel which gives the weapon its edge and brilliancy.

Let us admit in fact it has in War even its own prerogatives. Over and above the result of the calculation of space, time, and quantity, we must allow a certain percentage which boldness derives from the weakness of others, whenever it gains the mastery. It is therefore, virtually, a creative power. This is not difficult to demonstrate philosophically. As often as boldness encounters hesitation, the probability of the result is of necessity in its favour, because the very state of hesitation implies a loss of equilibrium already. It is only when it encounters cautious foresight – which we may say is just as bold, at all events just as strong and powerful as itself – that it is at a disadvantage; such cases, however, rarely occur. Out of the whole multitude of prudent men in the world, the great majority are so from timidity.

Amongst large masses, boldness is a force, the special cultivation of which can never be to the detriment of other forces, because the great mass is bound to a higher will by the frame-work and joints of the order of battle and of the service, and therefore is guided by an intelligent power which is extraneous. Boldness is therefore here only like a spring held down until its action is required.

The higher the rank the more necessary it is that boldness should be accompanied by a reflective mind, that it may not be a mere blind outburst of passion to no purpose; for with increase of rank it becomes always less a matter of self-sacrifice and more a matter of the preservation of others, and the good of the whole. Where regulations of the service, as a kind of second nature, prescribe for the masses, reflection must be the guide of the General, and in his case individual boldness in action may easily become a fault. Still, at the same time, it is a fine failing, and must not be looked at in the same light as any other. Happy the Army in which an untimely boldness frequently manifests itself; it is an exuberant growth which shows a rich soil. Even foolhardiness, that is boldness without an object, is not to be despised; in point of fact it is the same energy of feeling, only exercised as a kind of passion without any co-operation of the intelligent faculties. It is only when it strikes at the root of obedience, when it treats with contempt the orders of superior authority, that it must be repressed as a dangerous evil, not on its own account but on account of the act of disobedience, for there is nothing in War which is of *greater importance than obedience.*

The reader will readily agree with us that, supposing an equal degree of discernment to be forthcoming in a certain number of cases, a thousand times as many of them will end in disaster through over-anxiety as through boldness.

One would suppose it natural that the interposition of a reasonable object should stimulate boldness, and therefore lessen its intrinsic merit, and yet the reverse is the case in reality.

The intervention of lucid thought or the general supremacy of mind deprives the emotional forces of a great part of their power. On that account *boldness becomes of rarer occurrence the higher we ascend the scale of rank,* for whether the discernment and the understanding do or do not increase with these ranks still the Commanders, in their several stations as they rise, are pressed upon more and more severely by objective things, by relations and claims from without, so that they become the more perplexed the lower the degree of their individual intelligence. This so far as regards War is the chief foundation of the truth of the French proverb: –

"Tel brille au second qui s' éclipse an premier."

Almost all the Generals who are represented in history as merely having attained to mediocrity, and as wanting in decision when in supreme command, are men celebrated in their antecedent career for their boldness and decision.[18]

In those motives to bold action which arise from the pressure of necessity we must make a distinction. Necessity has its degrees of intensity. If it lies near at hand, if the person acting is in the pursuit of his object driven into great dangers in order to escape others equally great, then we can only admire his resolution, which still has also its value. If a young man to show his skill in horsemanship leaps across a deep cleft, then he is bold; if he makes the same leap pursued by a troop of head-chopping Janissaries he is only resolute. But the farther off the necessity from the point of action, the greater the number of relations intervening which the mind has to traverse; in order to realise them, by so much the less does necessity take from boldness in action. If Frederick the Great, in the year 1756, saw that War was inevitable, and that he could only escape destruction by being beforehand with his enemies, it became necessary for him to commence the War himself, but at the same time it was certainly very bold: for few men in his position would have made up their minds to do so.

Although Strategy is only the province of Generals-in-Chief or Commanders in the higher positions, still boldness in all the other branches of an Army is as little a matter of indifference to it as their other military virtues. With an Army belonging to a bold race, and in which the spirit of boldness has been always nourished, very different things may be undertaken than with one in which this virtue, is unknown; for that reason we have considered it in connection with an Army. But our subject is specially the boldness of the General, and yet we have not much to say about it after having described this military virtue in a general way to the best of our ability.

The higher we rise in a position of command, the more of the mind, understanding, and penetration predominate in activity, the more therefore is boldness, which is a property of the feelings, kept in subjection, and for that reason we find it so rarely in the highest positions, but then, so much the more should it be admired. Boldness, directed by an overruling intelligence, is the stamp of the hero: this boldness does not consist in venturing directly against the nature of things, in a downright contempt of the laws of probability, but, if a choice is once made, in the rigorous adherence to that higher calculation which genius, the tact of judgment, has gone over with the speed of lightning. The more boldness

18   Beaulieu, Benedek, Bazaine, Buller, Melas, Mack. &c. &c.

lends wings to the mind and the discernment, so much the farther they will reach in their flight, so much the more comprehensive will be the view, the more exact the result, but certainly always only in the sense that with greater objects greater dangers are connected. The ordinary man, not to speak of the weak and irresolute, arrives at an exact result so far as such is possible without ocular demonstration, at most after diligent reflection in his chamber, at a distance from danger and responsibility. Let danger and responsibility draw close round him in every direction, then he loses the power of comprehensive vision, and if he retains this in any measure by the influence of others, still he will lose his power of *decision*, because in that point no one can help him.

We think then that it is impossible to imagine a distinguished General without boldness, that is to say, that no man can become one who is not born with this power of the soul, and we therefore look upon it as the first requisite for such a career. How much of this inborn power, developed and moderated through education and the circumstances of life, is left when the man has attained a high position, is the second question. The greater this power still is, the stronger will genius be on the wing, the higher will be its flight. The risks become always greater, but the purpose grows with them. Whether its lines proceed out of and get their direction from a distant necessity, or whether they converge to the keystone of a building which ambition has planned, whether Frederick or Alexander acts, is much the same as regards the critical view. If the one excites the imagination more because it is bolder, the other pleases the understanding most, because it has in it more absolute necessity.

We have still to advert to one very important circumstance.

The spirit of boldness can exist in an Army, either because it is in the people, or because it has been generated in a successful War conducted by able Generals. In the latter case it must of course be dispensed with at the commencement.

Now in our days there is hardly any other means of educating the spirit of a people in this respect, except by War, and that too under bold Generals. By it alone can that effeminacy of feeling be counteracted, that propensity to seek for the enjoyment of comfort, which cause degeneracy in a people rising in prosperity and immersed in an extremely busy commerce.

A Nation can hope to have a strong position in the political world only if its character and practice in actual War mutually support each other in constant reciprocal action.

CHAPTER SEVEN

Perseverance

THE READER EXPECTS to hear of angles and lines, and finds, instead of these citizens of the scientific world, only people out of common life, such as he meets with every day in the street. And yet the author cannot make up his mind to become a hair's breadth more mathematical than the subject seems to him to require, and he is not alarmed at the surprise which the reader may show.

In War more than anywhere else in the world things happen differently to what we had expected, and look differently when near, to what they did at a distance. With what serenity the architect can watch his work gradually rising and growing into his plan. The doctor although much more at the mercy of mysterious agencies and chances than the architect, still knows enough of the forms and effects of his means. In War, on the other hand, the Commander of an immense whole finds himself in a constant whirlpool of false and true information, of mistakes committed through fear, through negligence, through precipitation, of contraventions of his authority, either from mistaken or correct motives, from ill will, true or false sense of duty, indolence or exhaustion, of accidents which no mortal could have foreseen. In short, he is the victim of a hundred thousand impressions, of which the most have an intimidating, the fewest an encouraging tendency. By long experience in War, the tact is acquired of readily appreciating the value of these incidents; high courage and stability of character stand proof against them, as the rock resists the beating of the waves. He who would yield to these impressions would never carry out an undertaking, and on that account *perseverance* in the proposed object, as long as there is no decided reason against it, is a most necessary counterpoise. Further, there is hardly any celebrated enterprise in War which was not achieved by endless exertion, pains, and privations; and as here the weakness of the physical and moral man is ever disposed to yield, only an immense force of will, which manifests itself in perseverance admired by present and future generations, can conduct to our goal.

CHAPTER EIGHT
Superiority of Numbers

THIS IS IN TACTICS, as well as in Strategy, the most general principle of victory, and shall be examined by us first in its generality, for which we may be permitted the following exposition:

Strategy fixes the point where, the time when, and the numerical force with which the battle is to be fought. By this triple determination it has therefore a very essential influence on the issue of the combat. If tactics has fought the battle, if the result is over, let it be victory or defeat, Strategy makes such use of it as can be made in accordance with the great object of the War. This object is naturally often a very distant one, seldom does it lie quite close at hand. A series of other objects subordinate themselves to it as means. These objects, which are at the same time means to a higher purpose, may be practically of various kinds; even the ultimate aim of the whole War may be a different one in every case. We shall make ourselves acquainted with these things according as we come to know the separate objects which they come, in contact with; and it is not our intention here to embrace the whole subject by a complete enumeration of them, even if that were possible. We therefore let the employment of the battle stand over for the present.

Even those things through which Strategy has an influence on the issue of the combat, inasmuch as it establishes the same, to a certain extent decrees them, are not so simple that they can be embraced in one single view. For as Strategy appoints time, place and force, it can do so in practice in many ways, each of which influences in a different manner the result of the combat as well as its consequences. Therefore we shall only get acquainted with this also by degrees, that is, through the subjects which more closely determine the application.

If we strip the combat of all modifications which it may undergo according to its immediate purpose and the circumstances from which it proceeds, lastly if we set aside the valour of the troops, because that is a given quantity, then there remains only the bare conception of the combat, that is a combat without form, in which we distinguish nothing but the number of the combatants.

This number will therefore determine victory. Now from the number of things above deducted to get to this point, it is shown that the superiority in numbers in a battle is only one of the factors employed to produce victory that therefore so far from having with the superiority in number obtained all, or even only the principal thing, we have perhaps got very little by it, according as the other circumstances which co-operate happen to vary.

But this superiority has degrees, it may be imagined as twofold, threefold or fourfold, and every one sees, that by increasing in this way, it must (at last) overpower everything else.

In such an aspect we grant, that the superiority in numbers is the most important factor in the result of a combat, only it must be sufficiently great to be a counterpoise to all the other co-operating circumstances. The direct result of this is, that the greatest possible number of troops should be brought into action at the decisive point.

Whether the troops thus brought are sufficient or not, we have then done in this respect all that our means allowed. This is the first principle in Strategy, therefore in general as now stated, it is just as well suited for Greeks and Persians, or for Englishmen and Mahrattas, as for French and Germans. But we shall take a glance at our relations in Europe, as respects War, in order to arrive at some more definite idea on this subject.

Here we find Armies much more alike in equipment, organisation, and practical skill of every kind. There only remains a difference in the military virtue of Armies, and in the talent of Generals which may fluctuate with time from side to side. If we go through the military history of modern Europe, we find no example of a Marathon.

Frederick the Great beat 80,000 Austrians at Leuthen with about 30,000 men, and at Rosbach with 25,000 some 50,000 allies; these are however the only instances of victories gained against an enemy double, or more than double in numbers. Charles XII, in the battle of Narva, we cannot well quote, for the Russians were at that time hardly to be regarded as Europeans, also the principal circumstances, even of the battle, are too little known. Buonaparte had at Dresden 120,000 against 220,000, therefore not the double. At Kollin, Frederick the Great did not succeed, with 30,000 against 50,000 Austrians, neither did Buonaparte in the desperate battle of Leipsic, where he was 160,000 strong, against 280,000.

From this we may infer, that it is very difficult in the present state of Europe, for the most talented General to gain a victory over an enemy double his strength. Now if we see double numbers prove such a weight in the scale against the greatest Generals, we may be sure, that in ordinary cases, in small as well as great combats, an important superiority of numbers, but which need not be over two to one, will be sufficient to ensure the victory, however disadvantageous other circumstances may be. Certainly, we may imagine a defile which even tenfold would not suffice to force, but in such a case it can be no question of a battle at all.

We think, therefore, that under our conditions, as well as in all similar ones, the superiority at the decisive point is a matter of capital importance, and that this subject, in the generality of cases, is decidedly the most important of all. The strength at the decisive point depends on the absolute strength of the Army, and on skill in making use of it.

The first rule is therefore to enter the field with an Army as strong as possible. This sounds very like a commonplace, but still it is really not so.

In order to show that for a long time the strength of forces was by no means regarded as a chief point, we need only observe, that in most, and even in the most detailed histories of the Wars in the eighteenth century, the strength of the Armies is either not given at all, or only incidentally, and in no case is any special value laid upon it. Tempelhof in his history of the Seven Years' War is the earliest writer who gives it regularly, but at the same time he does it only very superficially.

Even Massenbach, in his manifold critical observations on the Prussian campaigns of 1793-94 in the Vosges, talks a great deal about hills and valleys, roads and footpaths, but does not say a syllable about mutual strength.

Another proof lies in a wonderful notion which haunted the heads of many critical historians, according to which there was a certain size of an Army which was the best, a normal strength, beyond which the forces in excess were burdensome rather than serviceable.[19]

Lastly, there are a number of instances to be found, in which all the available forces were not really brought into the battle,[20] or into the War, because the superiority of numbers was not considered to have that importance which in the nature of things belongs to it.

19 Tempelhof and Montalembert are the first we recollect as examples – the first in a passage of his first part, page 148; the other in his correspondence relative to the plan of operations of the Russians in 1759.
20 The Prussians at Jena, 1806. Wellington at Waterloo.

If we are thoroughly penetrated with the conviction that with a considerable superiority of numbers everything possible is to be effected, then it cannot fail that this clear conviction reacts on the preparations for the War, so as to make us appear in the field with as many troops as possible, and either to give us ourselves the superiority, or at least to guard against the enemy obtaining it. So much for what concerns the absolute force with which the War is to be conducted.

The measure of this absolute force is determined by the Government; and although with this determination the real action of War commences, and it forms an essential part of the Strategy of the War, still in most cases the General who is to command these forces in the War must regard their absolute strength as a given quantity, whether it be that he has had no voice in fixing it, or that circumstances prevented a sufficient expansion being given to it.

There remains nothing, therefore, where an absolute superiority is not attainable, but to produce a relative one at the decisive point, by making skilful use of what we have.

The calculation of space and time appears as the most essential thing to this end – and this has caused that subject to be regarded as one which embraces nearly the whole art of using military forces. Indeed, some have gone so far as to ascribe to great strategists and tacticians a mental organ peculiarly adapted to this point.

But the calculation of time and space, although it lies universally at the foundation of Strategy, and is to a certain extent its daily bread, is still neither the most difficult, nor the most decisive one.

If we take an unprejudiced glance at military history, we shall find that the instances in which mistakes in such a calculation have proved the cause of serious losses are very rare, at least in Strategy. But if the conception of a skilful combination of time and space is fully to account for every instance of a resolute and active Commander beating several separate opponents with one and the same army (Frederick the Great, Buonaparte), then we perplex ourselves unnecessarily with conventional language. For the sake of clearness and the profitable use of conceptions, it is necessary that things should always be called by their right names.

The right appreciation of their opponents (Daun, Schwartzenberg), the audacity to leave for a short space of time a small force only before them, energy in forced marches, boldness in sudden attacks, the intensified activity which great souls acquire in the moment of danger, these are the grounds of such victories; and what have these to do with the ability to make an exact calculation of two such simple things as time and space?

But even this ricochetting play of forces, "when the victories at Rosbach and Montmirail give the impulse to victories at Leuthen and Montereau," to which great Generals on the defensive have often trusted, is still, if we would be clear and exact, only a rare occurrence in history.

Much more frequently the relative superiority – that is, the skilful assemblage of superior forces at the decisive point – has its foundation in the right appreciation of those points, in the judicious direction which by that means has been given to the forces from the very first, and in the resolution required to sacrifice the unimportant to the advantage of the important – that is, to keep the forces concentrated in an overpowering mass. In this, Frederick the Great and Buonaparte are particularly characteristic.

We think we have now allotted to the superiority in numbers the importance which belongs to it; it is to be regarded as the fundamental idea, always to be aimed at before all and as far as possible.

But to regard it on this account as a necessary condition of victory would be a complete misconception of our exposition; in the conclusion to be drawn from it there lies nothing more than the value which should attach to numerical strength in the combat. If that strength is made as great as possible, then the maxim is satisfied; a review of the total relations must then decide whether or not the combat is to be avoided for want of sufficient force.[21]

---

21 Owing to our freedom from invasion, and to the condition   which arise in our Colonial Wars, we have not yet, in England, arrived at a correct appreciation of the value of superior numbers in War, and still adhere to the idea of an Army just "big enough," which Clausewitz has so unsparingly ridiculed. (*Editor.*)

CHAPTER NINE
The Surprise

FROM THE SUBJECT of the foregoing chapter, the general endeavour to attain a relative superiority, there follows another endeavour which must consequently be just as general in its nature: this is the *surprise* of the enemy. It lies more or less at the foundation of all undertakings, for without it the preponderance at the decisive point is not properly conceivable.

The surprise is, therefore, not only the means to the attainment of numerical superiority; but it is also to be regarded as a substantive principle in itself, on account of its moral effect. When it is successful in a high degree, confusion and broken courage in the enemy's ranks are the consequences; and of the degree to which these multiply a success, there are examples enough, great and small. We are not now speaking of the particular surprise which belongs to the attack, but of the endeavour by measures generally, and especially by the distribution of forces, to surprise the enemy, which can be imagined just as well in the defensive, and which in the tactical defence particularly is a chief point.

We say, surprise lies at the foundation of all undertakings without exception, only in very different degrees according to the nature of the undertaking and other circumstances.

This difference, indeed, originates in the properties or peculiarities of the Army and its Commander, in those even of the Government.

Secrecy and rapidity are the two factors in this product and these suppose in the Government and the Commander-in-Chief great energy, and on the part of the Army a high sense of military duty. With effeminacy and loose principles it is in vain to calculate upon a surprise. But so general, indeed so indispensable, as is this endeavour, and true as it is that it is never wholly unproductive of effect, still it is not the less true that it seldom succeeds to a *remarkable* degree, and this follows from the nature of the idea itself. We should form an erroneous conception if we believed that by this means chiefly there is much to be attained in War. In idea it promises a great deal; in the execution it generally sticks fast by the friction of the whole machine.

In tactics the surprise is much more at home, for the very natural reason that all times and spaces are on a smaller scale. It will, therefore, in Strategy be the more feasible in proportion as the measures lie nearer to the province of tactics, and more difficult the higher up they lie towards the province of policy.

The preparations for a War usually occupy several months; the assembly of an Army at its principal positions requires generally the formation of depôts and magazines, and long marches, the object of which can be guessed soon enough.

It therefore rarely happens that one State surprises another by a War, or by the direction which it gives the mass of its forces. In the seventeenth and eighteenth centuries, when War turned very much upon sieges, it was a frequent aim, and quite a peculiar and important chapter in the Art of War, to invest a strong place unexpectedly, but even that only rarely succeeded.[22]

On the other hand, with things which can be done in a day or two, a surprise is much more conceivable, and, therefore, also it is often not difficult thus to gain a march upon the enemy, and thereby a position, a point of country, a road, &c. But it is evident that what surprise gains in this way in easy execution, it loses in the efficacy, as the greater the efficacy the greater always the difficulty of execution. Whoever thinks that with such surprises on a small scale, he may connect great results – as, for example, the gain of a battle, the capture of an important magazine – believes in something which it is certainly very possible to imagine, but for which there is no warrant in history; for there are upon the whole very few instances where anything great has resulted from such surprises; from which we may justly conclude that inherent difficulties lie in the way of their success.

Certainly, whoever would consult history on such points must not depend on sundry battle steeds of historical critics, on their wise dicta and self-complacent terminology, but look at facts with his own eyes. There is, for instance, a certain day in the campaign in Silesia, 1761, which, in this respect, has attained a kind of notoriety. It is the 22nd

---

22 Railways, steamships, and telegraphs have, however, enormously modified the relative importance and practicability of surprise. (*Editor.*)

July, on which Frederick the Great gained on Laudon the march to Nossen, near Neisse, by which, as is said, the junction of the Austrian and Russian armies in Upper Silesia became impossible, and, therefore, a period of four weeks was gained by the King. Whoever reads over this occurrence carefully in the principal histories,[23] and considers it impartially, will, in the march of the 22nd July, never find this importance; and generally in the whole of the fashionable logic on this subject, he will see nothing but contradictions; but in the proceedings of Laudon, in this renowned period of manoeuvres, much that is unaccountable. How could one, with a thirst for truth, and clear conviction, accept such historical evidence?

When we promise ourselves great effects in a campaign from the principle of surprising, we think upon great activity, rapid resolutions, and forced marches, as the means of producing them; but that these things, even when forthcoming in a very high degree, will not always produce the desired effect, we see in examples given by Generals, who may be allowed to have had the greatest talent in the use of these means, Frederick the Great and Buonaparte. The first when he left Dresden so suddenly in July 1760, and falling upon Lascy, then turned against Dresden, gained nothing by the whole of that intermezzo, but rather placed his affairs in a condition notably worse, as the fortress Glatz fell in the meantime.

In 1813, Buonaparte turned suddenly from Dresden twice against Bluecher, to say nothing of his incursion into Bohemia from Upper Lusatia, and both times without in the least attaining his object. They were blows in the air which only cost him time and force, and might have placed him in a dangerous position in Dresden.

Therefore, even in this field, a surprise does not necessarily meet with great success through the mere activity, energy, and resolution of the Commander; it must be favoured by other circumstances. But we by no means deny that there can be success; we only connect with it a necessity of favourable circumstances, which, certainly do not occur very frequently, and which the Commander can seldom bring about himself.

Just those two Generals afford each a striking illustration of this. We take first Buonaparte in his famous enterprise against Bluecher's Army in February 1814, when it was separated from the Grand Army, and descending the Marne. It would not be easy to find a two days' march to surprise the enemy productive of greater results than this;

23 Tempelhof, The Veteran, Frederick the Great. Compare also (Clausewitz) "Hinterlassene Werke," vol. x., p. 158.

Bluecher's Army, extended over a distance of three days' march, was beaten in detail, and suffered a loss nearly equal to that of defeat in a great battle. This was completely the effect of a surprise, for if Bluecher had thought of such a near possibility of an attack from Buonaparte[24] he would have organised his march quite differently. To this mistake of Bluecher's the result is to be attributed. Buonaparte did not know all these circumstances, and so there was a piece of good fortune that mixed itself up in his favour.

It is the same with the battle of Liegnitz, 1760. Frederick the Great gained this fine victory through altering during the night a position which he had just before taken up. Laudon was through this completely surprised, and lost 70 pieces of artillery and 10,000 men. Although Frederick the Great had at this time adopted the principle of moving backwards and forwards in order to make a battle impossible, or at least to disconcert the enemy's plans, still the alteration of position on the night of the 14-15 was not made exactly with that intention, but as the King himself says, because the position of the 14th did not please him. Here, therefore, also chance was hard at work; without this happy conjunction of the attack and the change of position in the night, and the difficult nature of the country, the result would not have been the same.

Also in the higher and highest province of Strategy there are some instances of surprises fruitful in results. We shall only cite the brilliant marches of the Great Elector against the Swedes from Franconia to Pomerania and from the Mark (Brandenburg) to the Pregel in 1757, and the celebrated passage of the Alps by Buonaparte, 1800. In the latter case an Army gave up its whole theatre of war by a capitulation, and in 1757 another Army was very near giving up its theatre of war and itself as well. Lastly, as an instance of a War wholly unexpected, we may bring forward the invasion of Silesia by Frederick the Great. Great and powerful are here the results everywhere, but such events are not common in history if we do not confuse with them cases in which a State, for want of activity and energy (Saxony 1756, and Russia, 1812), has not completed its preparations in time.

Now there still remains an observation which concerns the essence of the thing. A surprise can only be effected by that party which gives the law to the other; and he who is in the right gives the law. If we surprise the adversary by a wrong measure, then instead of reaping good results, we may have to bear a sound blow in return; in any case the

24   Bluecher believed his march to be covered by Pahlen's Cossacks, but these had been withdrawn without warning to him by the Grand Army Headquarters under Schwartzenberg.

adversary need not trouble himself much about our surprise, he has in our mistake the means of turning off the evil. As the offensive includes in itself much more positive action than the defensive, so the surprise is certainly more in its place with the assailant, but by no means invariably, as we shall hereafter see. Mutual surprises by the offensive and defensive may therefore meet, and then that one will have the advantage who has hit the nail on the head the best.

So should it be, but practical life does not keep to this line so exactly, and that for a very simple reason. The moral effects which attend a surprise often convert the worst case into a good one for the side they favour, and do not allow the other to make any regular determination. We have here in view more than anywhere else not only the chief Commander, but each single one, because a surprise has the effect in particular of greatly loosening unity, so that the individuality of each separate leader easily comes to light.

Much depends here on the general relation in which the two parties stand to each other. If the one side through a general moral superiority can intimidate and outdo the other, then he can make use of the surprise with more success, and even reap good fruit where properly he should come to ruin.

CHAPTER TEN
Stratagem

STRATAGEM IMPLIES a concealed intention, and therefore is opposed to straightforward dealing, in the same way as wit is the opposite of direct proof. It has therefore nothing in common with means of persuasion, of self-interest, of force, but a great deal to do with deceit, because that likewise conceals its object. It is itself a deceit as well when it is done, but still it differs from what is commonly called deceit, in this respect that there is no direct breach of word. The deceiver by stratagem leaves it to the person himself whom he is deceiving to commit the errors of understanding which at last, flowing into *one* result, suddenly change the nature of things in his eyes. We may therefore say, as nit is a sleight of hand with ideas and conceptions, so stratagem is a sleight of hand with actions.

At first sight it appears as if Strategy had not improperly derived its name from stratagem; and that, with all the real and apparent changes which the whole character of War has undergone since the time of the Greeks, this term still points to its real nature.

If we leave to tactics the actual delivery of the blow, the battle itself, and look upon Strategy as the art of using this means with skill, then besides the forces of the character, such as burning ambition which always presses like a spring, a strong will which hardly bends &c. &c., there seems no subjective quality so suited to guide and inspire strategic activity as stratagem. The general tendency to surprise, treated of in the foregoing chapter, points to this conclusion, for there is a degree of stratagem, be it ever so small, which lies at the foundation of every attempt to surprise.

But however much we feel a desire to see the actors in War outdo each other in hidden activity, readiness, and stratagem, still we must admit that these qualities show themselves but little in history, and have rarely been able to work their way to the surface from amongst the mass of relations and circumstances.

The explanation of this is obvious, and it is almost identical with the subject matter of the preceding chapter.

Strategy knows no other activity than the regulating of combat with the measures which relate to it. It has no concern, like ordinary life, with transactions which consist merely of words – that is, in expressions, declarations, &c. But these, which are very inexpensive, are chiefly the means with which the wily one takes in those he practises upon.

That which there is like it in War, plans and orders given merely as make-believers, false reports sent on purpose to the enemy – is usually of so little effect in the strategic field that it is only resorted to in particular cases which offer of themselves, therefore cannot be regarded as spontaneous action which emanates from the leader.

But such measures as carrying out the arrangements for a battle, so far as to impose upon the enemy, require a considerable expenditure of time and power; of course, the greater the impression to be made, the greater the expenditure in these respects. And as this is usually not given for the purpose, very few demonstrations, so-called, in Strategy, effect the object for which they are designed. In fact, it is dangerous to detach large forces for any length of time merely for a trick, because there is always the risk of its being done in vain, and then these forces are wanted at the decisive point.

The chief actor in War is always thoroughly sensible of this sober truth, and therefore he has no desire to play at tricks of agility. The bitter earnestness of necessity presses so fully into direct action that there is no room for that game. In a word, the pieces on the strategical chess-board want that mobility which is the element of stratagem and subtility.

The conclusion which we draw, is that a correct and penetrating eye is a more necessary and more useful quality for a General than craftiness, although that also does no harm if it does not exist at the expense of necessary qualities of the heart, which is only too often the case.

But the weaker the forces become which are under the command of Strategy, so much the more they become adapted for stratagem, so that to the quite feeble and little, for whom no prudence, no sagacity is any longer sufficient at the point where all art seems to forsake him, stratagem offers itself as a last resource. The more helpless his situation, the more everything presses towards one single, desperate blow, the more readily stratagem comes to the aid of his boldness. Let loose from all further calculations, freed from all concern for the future, boldness and stratagem intensify each other, and thus collect at one point an infinitesimal glimmering of hope into a single ray, which may likewise serve to kindle a flame.

CHAPTER ELEVEN

Assembly of Forces in Space

THE BEST STRATEGY is *always to be very strong*, first generally then at the decisive point. Therefore, apart from the energy which creates the Army, a work which is not always done by the General, there is no more imperative and no simpler law for Strategy than to *keep the forces concentrated*. – No portion is to be separated from the main body unless called away by some urgent necessity. On this maxim we stand firm, and look upon it as a guide to be depended upon. What are the reasonable grounds on which a detachment of forces may be made we shall learn by degrees. Then we shall also see that this principle cannot have the same general effects in every War, but that these are different according to the means and end.

It seems incredible, and yet it has happened a hundred times, that troops have been divided and separated merely through a mysterious feeling of conventional manner, without any clear perception of the reason.

If the concentration of the whole force is acknowledged as the norm, and every division and separation as an exception which must be justified, then not only will that folly be completely avoided, but also many an erroneous ground for separating troops will be barred admission.

CHAPTER TWELVE

Assembly of Forces in Time

WE HAVE HERE to deal with a conception which in real life diffuses many kinds of illusory light. A clear definition and development of the idea is therefore necessary, and we hope to be allowed a short analysis.

War is the shock of two opposing forces in collision with each other, from which it follows as a matter of course that the stronger not only destroys the other, but carries it forward with it in its movement. This fundamentally admits of no successive action of powers, but makes the simultaneous application of all forces intended for the shock appear as a primordial law of War.

So it is in reality, but only so far as the struggle resembles also in practice a mechanical shock, but when it consists in a lasting, mutual action of destructive forces, then we can certainly imagine a successive action of forces. This is the case in tactics, principally because fire-arms form the basis of all tactics, but also for other reasons as well. If in a fire combat 1000 men are opposed to 500, then the gross loss is calculated from the amount of the enemy's force and our own; 1000 men fire twice as many shots as 500, but more shots will take effect on the 1000 than on the 500 because it is assumed that they stand in closer order than the other. If we were to suppose the number of hits to be double, then the losses on each side would be equal. From the 500 there would be for example 200 disabled, and out of the body of 1000 likewise the same; now if the 500 had kept another body of equal number quite out of fire, then both sides would have 800 effective men; but of these, on the one side there would be 500 men quite fresh, fully supplied with ammunition, and in their full vigour; on the other side only 800 all alike shaken in their order, in want of sufficient ammunition and weakened in physical force. The assumption that the 1000 men merely on account of their greater number would lose twice as many as 500 would have lost in their place, is certainly not correct; therefore the greater loss which the side suffers that has placed the half of its force in reserve, must be regarded as a disadvantage in that original formation; further it must be admitted, that in the generality of cases the 1000 men would have the advantage at the first commencement of being able to drive their opponent out of his position and force him to a retrograde movement; now, whether these two advantages are a counterpoise to the disadvantage of finding ourselves with 800 men to a certain extent disorganised by the combat, opposed to an enemy who is not materially weaker in numbers and who has 500 quite fresh troops, is one that cannot be decided by pursuing an analysis further, we must here rely upon experience, and there will scarcely be an officer experienced in War who will not in the generality of cases assign the advantage to that side which has the fresh troops.

In this way it becomes evident how the employment of too many forces in combat may be disadvantageous; for whatever advantages the superiority may give in the first moment, we may have to pay dearly for in the next.

But this danger only endures as long as the disorder, the state of confusion and weakness lasts, in a word, up to the crisis which every combat brings with it even for the conqueror. Within the duration of this relaxed state of exhaustion, the appearance of a proportionate number of fresh troops is decisive.

But when this disordering effect of victory stops, and therefore only the moral superiority remains which every victory gives, then it is no longer possible for fresh troops to restore the combat, they would only be carried along in the general movement; a beaten Army cannot be brought back to victory a day after by means of a strong reserve. Here we find ourselves at the source of a highly material difference between tactics and strategy.

The tactical results, the results within the four corners of the battle, and before its close, lie for the most part within the limits of that period of disorder and weakness. But the strategic result, that is to say, the result of the total combat, of the victories realised, let them be small or great, lies completely (beyond) outside of that period. It is only when the results of partial combats have bound themselves together into an independent whole, that the strategic result appears, but then, the state of crisis is over, the forces have resumed their original form, and are now only weakened to the extent of those actually destroyed (placed hors de combat).

The consequence of this difference is, that tactics can make a continued use of forces, Strategy only a simultaneous one.[25]

If I cannot, in tactics, decide all by the first success, if I have to fear the next moment, it follows of itself that I employ only so much of my force for the success of the first moment as appears sufficient for that object, and keep the rest beyond the reach of fire or conflict of any kind, in order to be able to oppose fresh troops to fresh, or with such to overcome those that are exhausted. But it is not so in Strategy. Partly, as we have just shown, it has not so much reason to fear a reaction after a success realised, because with that success the crisis stops; partly all the forces strategically employed are not necessarily weakened. Only so much of them as have been tactically in conflict with the enemy's force, that is, engaged in partial combat, are weakened by it; consequently, only so much as was unavoidably necessary, but by no means all which was strategically in conflict with the enemy, unless tactics has expended them unnecessarily. Corps which, on account of the general superiority in numbers, have either been little or not at all engaged, whose presence alone has assisted in the result, are after the decision the same as they were before, and for new enterprises as efficient as if they had been entirely inactive. How greatly such corps which thus constitute our excess may contribute to the total success is evident in itself; indeed, it is not difficult to see how they may even diminish considerably the loss of the forces engaged in tactical, conflict on our side.

If, therefore, in Strategy the loss does not increase with the number of the troops employed, but is often diminished by it, and if, as a natural consequence, the decision in our favor is, by that means, the more certain, then it follows naturally that in Strategy we can never employ too many forces, and consequently also that they must be applied simultaneously to the immediate purpose.

But we must vindicate this proposition upon another ground. We have hitherto only spoken of the combat itself; it is the real activity in War, but men, time, and space, which appear as the elements of this activity, must, at the same time, be kept in view, and the results of their influence brought into consideration also.

Fatigue, exertion, and privation constitute in War a special principle of destruction, not essentially belonging to contest, but more or less inseparably bound up with it, and certainly one which especially belongs to Strategy. They no doubt exist in tactics as well, and perhaps there in the highest degree; but as the duration of the tactical acts is shorter, therefore the small effects of exertion and privation on them can come but little

---

25 See chaps. xiii., and xiv., Book III and chap. xxix. Book V. – *TR.*

into consideration. But in Strategy on the other hand, where time and space, are on a larger scale, their influence is not only always very considerable, but often quite decisive. It is not at all uncommon for a victorious Army to lose many more by sickness than on the field of battle.

If, therefore, we look at this sphere of destruction in Strategy in the same manner as we have considered that of fire and close combat in tactics, then we may well imagine that everything which comes within its vortex will, at the end of the campaign or of any other strategic period, be reduced to a state of weakness, which makes the arrival of a fresh force decisive. We might therefore conclude that there is a motive in the one case as well as the other to strive for the first success with as few forces as possible, in order to keep up this fresh force for the last.

In order to estimate exactly this conclusion, which, in many cases in practice, will have a great appearance of truth, we must direct our attention to the separate ideas which it contains. In the first place, we must not confuse the notion of reinforcement with that of fresh unused troops. There are few campaigns at the end of which an increase of force is not earnestly desired by the conqueror as well as the conquered, and indeed should appear decisive; but that is not the point here, for that increase of force could not be necessary if the force had been so much larger at the first. But it would be contrary to all experience to suppose that an Army coming fresh into the field is to be esteemed higher in point of moral value than an Army already in the field, just as a tactical reserve is more to be esteemed than a body of troops which has been already severely handled in the fight. Just as much as an unfortunate campaign lowers the courage and moral powers of an Army, a successful one raises these elements in their value. In the generality of cases, therefore, these influences are compensated, and then there remains over and above as clear gain the habituation to War. We should besides look more here to successful than to unsuccessful campaigns, because when the greater probability of the latter may be seen beforehand, without doubt forces are wanted, and, therefore, the reserving a portion for future use is out of the question.

This point being settled, then the question is, Do the losses which a force sustains through fatigues and privations increase in proportion to the size of the force, as is the case in a combat? And to that we answer "No."

The fatigues of War result in a great measure from the dangers with which every moment of the act of War is more or less impregnated. To encounter these dangers at all points, to proceed onwards with security in the execution of one's plans, gives employment to a multitude of agencies which make up the tactical and strategic service of the Army.

This service is more difficult the weaker an Army is, and easier as its numerical superiority over that of the enemy increases. Who can doubt this? A campaign against a much weaker enemy will therefore cost smaller efforts than against one just as strong or stronger.

So much for the fatigues. It is somewhat different with the privations; they consist chiefly of two things, the want of food, and the want of shelter for the troops, either in quarters or in suitable camps. Both these wants will no doubt be greater in proportion as the number of men on one spot is greater. But does not the superiority in force afford also the best means of spreading out and finding more room, and therefore more means of subsistence and shelter?

If Buonaparte, in his invasion of Russia in 1812, concentrated his Army in great masses upon one single road in a manner never heard of before, and thus caused privations equally unparalleled, we must ascribe it to his maxim *that it is impossible to be too strong at the decisive point*. Whether in this instance he did not strain the principle too far is a question which would be out of place here; but it is certain that, if he had made a point of avoiding the distress which was by that means brought about, he had only to advance on a greater breadth of front. Room was not wanted for the purpose in Russia, and in very few cases can it be wanted. Therefore, from this no ground can be deduced to prove that the simultaneous employment of very superior forces must produce greater weakening. But now, supposing that in spite of the general relief afforded by setting apart a portion of the Army, wind and weather and the toils of War had produced a diminution even on the part which as a spare force had been reserved for later use, still we must take a comprehensive general view of the whole, and therefore ask, Will this diminution of force suffice to counterbalance the gain in forces, which we, through our superiority in numbers, may be able to make in more ways than one?

But there still remains a most important point to be noticed. In a partial combat, the force required to obtain a great result can be approximately estimated without much difficulty, and, consequently, we can form an idea of what is superfluous. In Strategy this may be said to be impossible, because the strategic result has no such well-defined object and no such circumscribed limits as the tactical. Thus what can be looked upon in tactics as an excess of power, must be regarded in Strategy as a means to give expansion to success, if opportunity offers for it; with the magnitude of the success the gain in force increases at the same time, and in this way the superiority of numbers may soon reach a point which the most careful economy of forces could never have attained.

By means of his enormous numerical superiority, Buonaparte was enabled to reach Moscow in 1812, and to take that central capital. Had he by means of this superiority succeeded in completely defeating the Russian Army, he would, in all probability, have concluded a peace in Moscow which in any other way was much less attainable. This example is used to explain the idea, not to prove it, which would require a circumstantial demonstration, for which this is not the place.[26]

All these reflections bear merely upon the idea of a successive employment of forces, and not upon the conception of a reserve properly so called, which they, no doubt, come in contact with throughout, but which, as we shall see in the following chapter, is connected with some other considerations.

What we desire to establish here is, that if in tactics the military force through the mere duration of actual employment suffers a diminution of power, if time, therefore, appears as a factor in the result, this is not the case in Strategy in a material degree. The destructive effects which are also produced upon the forces in Strategy by time, are partly diminished through their mass, partly made good in other ways, and, therefore, in Strategy it cannot be an object to make time an ally on its own account by bringing troops successively into action.

We say on "its own account," for the influence which time, on account of other circumstances which it brings about but which are different from itself can have, indeed must necessarily have, for one of the two parties, is quite another thing, is anything but indifferent or unimportant, and will be the subject of consideration hereafter.

The rule which we have been seeking to set forth is, therefore, that all forces which are available and destined for a strategic object should be *simultaneously* applied to it; and this application will be so much the more complete the more everything is compressed into one act and into one movement.

But still there is in Strategy a renewal of effort and a persistent action which, as a chief means towards the ultimate success, is more particularly not to be overlooked, it is the *continual development of new forces.* This is also the subject of another chapter, and we only refer to it here in order to prevent the reader from having something in view of which we have not been speaking.

We now turn to a subject very closely connected with our present considerations, which must be settled before full light can be thrown on the whole, we mean the *strategic reserve.*

26   Compare Book VII., second edition, p. 56.

CHAPTER THIRTEEN

Strategic Reserve

A RESERVE has two objects which are very distinct from each other, namely, first, the prolongation and renewal of the combat, and secondly, for use in case of unforeseen events. The first object implies the utility of a successive application of forces, and on that account cannot occur in Strategy. Cases in which a corps is sent to succour a point which is supposed to be about to fall are plainly to be placed in the category of the second object, as the resistance which has to be offered here could not have been sufficiently foreseen. But a corps which is destined expressly to prolong the combat, and with that object in view is placed in rear, would be only a corps placed out of reach of fire, but under the command and at the disposition of the General Commanding in the action, and accordingly would be a tactical and not a strategic reserve.

But the necessity for a force ready for unforeseen events may also take place in Strategy, and consequently there may also be a strategic reserve, but only where unforeseen events are imaginable. In tactics, where the enemy's measures are generally first ascertained by direct sight, and where they may be concealed by every wood, every fold of undulating ground, we must naturally always be alive, more or less, to the possibility of unforeseen events, in order to strengthen, subsequently, those points which appear too weak, and, in fact, to modify generally the disposition of our troops, so as to make it correspond better to that of the enemy.

Such cases must also happen in Strategy, because the strategic act is directly linked to the tactical. In Strategy also many a measure is first adopted in consequence of what is actually seen, or in consequence of uncertain reports arriving from day to day, or even from hour to hour, and lastly, from the actual results of the combats it is, therefore, an essential condition of strategic command that, according to the degree of uncertainty, forces must be kept in reserve against future contingencies.

In the defensive generally, but particularly in the defence of certain obstacles of ground, like rivers, hills, &c., such contingencies, as is well known, happen constantly.

But this uncertainty diminishes in proportion as the strategic activity has less of the tactical character, and ceases almost altogether in those regions where it borders on politics.

The direction in which the enemy leads his columns to the combat can be perceived by actual sight only; where he intends to pass a river is learnt from a few preparations which are made shortly before; the line by which he proposes to invade our country is usually announced by all the newspapers before a pistol shot has been fired. The greater the nature of the measure the less it will take the enemy by surprise. Time and space are so considerable, the circumstances out of which the action proceeds so public and little susceptible of alteration, that the coming event is either made known in good time, or can be discovered with reasonable certainty.

On the other hand the use of a reserve in this province of Strategy, even if one were available, will always be less efficacious the more the measure has a tendency towards being one of a general nature.

We have seen that the decision of a partial combat is nothing in itself, but that all partial combats only find their complete solution in the decision of the total combat.

But even this decision of the total combat has only a relative meaning of many different gradations, according as the force over which the victory has been gained forms a more or less great and important part of the whole. The lost battle of a corps may be repaired by the victory of the Army. Even the lost battle of an Army may not only be counterbalanced by the gain of a more important one, but converted into a fortunate event (the two days of Kulm, August 29 and 30, 1813[27]). No one can doubt this; but it is just as clear that the weight of each victory (the successful issue of each total combat) is so much the more substantial the more important the part conquered, and that therefore the possibility of repairing the loss by subsequent events diminishes in the same proportion. In another place we shall have to examine this more in detail; it suffices for the present to have drawn attention to the indubitable existence of this progression.

27   Refers to the destruction of Vandamme's column, which had been sent unsupported to intercept the retreat of the Austrians and Prussians from Dresden – but was forgotten by Napoleon. – *Editor.*

If we now add lastly to these two considerations the third, which is, that if the persistent use of forces in tactics always shifts the great result to the end of the whole act, law of the simultaneous use of the forces in Strategy, on the contrary, lets the principal result (which need not be the final one) take place almost always at the commencement of the great (or whole) act, then in these three results we have grounds sufficient to find strategic reserves always more superfluous, always more useless, always more dangerous, the more general their destination.

The point where the idea of a strategic reserve begins to become inconsistent is not difficult to determine: it lies in the *supreme decision*. Employment must be given to all the forces within the space of the supreme decision, and every reserve (active force available) which is only intended for use after that decision is opposed to common sense.

If, therefore, tactics has in its reserves the means of not only meeting unforeseen dispositions on the part of the enemy, but also of repairing that which never can be foreseen, the result of the combat, should that be unfortunate; Strategy on the other hand must, at least as far as relates to the capital result, renounce the use of these means. As A rule, it can only repair the losses sustained at one point by advantages gained at another, in a few cases by moving troops from one point to another; the idea of preparing for such reverses by placing forces in reserve beforehand, can never be entertained in Strategy.

We have pointed out as an absurdity the idea of a strategic reserve which is not to co-operate in the capital result, and as it is so beyond a doubt, we should not have been led into such an analysis as we have made in these two chapters, were it not that, in the disguise of other ideas, it looks like something better, and frequently makes its appearance. One person sees in it the acme of strategic sagacity and foresight; another rejects it, and with it the idea of any reserve, consequently even of a tactical one. This confusion of ideas is transferred to real life, and if we would see a memorable instance of it we have only to call to mind that Prussia in 1806 left a reserve of 20,000 men cantoned in the Mark, under Prince Eugene of Wurtemberg, which could not possibly reach the Saale in time to be of any use, and that another force Of 25,000 men belonging to this power remained in East and South Prussia, destined only to be put on a war-footing afterwards as a reserve.

After these examples we cannot be accused of having been fighting with windmills.

CHAPTER FOURTEEN

Economy of Forces

THE ROAD OF REASON, as we have said, seldom allows itself to be reduced to a mathematical line by principles and opinions. There remains always a certain margin. But it is the same in all the practical arts of life. For the lines of beauty there are no abscissae and ordinates; circles and ellipses are not described by means of their algebraical formulae. The actor in War therefore soon finds he must trust himself to the delicate tact of judgment which, founded on natural quickness of perception, and educated by reflection, almost unconsciously seizes upon the right; he soon finds that at one time he must simplify the law (by reducing it) to some prominent characteristic points which form his rules; that at another the adopted method must become the staff on which he leans.

As one of these simplified characteristic points as a mental appliance, we look upon the principle of watching continually over the co-operation of all forces, or in other words, of keeping constantly in view that no part of them should ever be idle. Whoever has forces where the enemy does not give them sufficient employment, whoever has part of his forces on the march – that is, allows them to lie dead – while the enemy's are fighting, he is a bad manager of his forces. In this sense there is a waste of forces, which is even worse than their employment to no purpose. If there must be action, then the first point is that all parts act, because the most purposeless activity still keeps employed and destroys a portion of the enemy's force, whilst troops completely inactive are for the moment quite neutralised. Unmistakably this idea is bound up with the principles contained in the last three chapters, it is the same truth, but seen from a somewhat more comprehensive point of view and condensed into a single conception.

CHAPTER FIFTEEN
Geometrical Element

THE LENGTH to which the geometrical element or form in the disposition of military force in War can become a predominant principle, we see in the art of fortification, where geometry looks after the great and the little. Also in tactics it plays a great part. It is the basis of elementary tactics, or of the theory of moving troops; but in field fortification, as well as in the theory of positions, and of their attack, its angles and lines rule like law givers who have to decide the contest. Many things here were at one time misapplied, and others were mere fribbles; still, however, in the tactics of the present day, in which in every combat the aim is to surround the enemy, the geometrical element has attained anew a great importance in a very simple, but constantly recurring application. Nevertheless, in tactics, where all is more movable, where the moral forces, individual traits, and chance are more influential than in a war of sieges, the geometrical element can never attain to the same degree of supremacy as in the latter. But less still is its influence in Strategy; certainly here, also, form in the disposition of troops, the shape of countries and states is of great importance; but the geometrical element is not decisive, as in fortification, and not nearly so important as in tactics. – The manner in which this influence exhibits itself, can only be shown by degrees at those places where it makes its appearance, and deserves notice. Here we wish more to direct attention to the difference which there is between tactics and Strategy in relation to it.

In tactics time and space quickly dwindle to their absolute minimum. If a body of troops is attacked in flank and rear by the enemy, it soon gets to a point where retreat no longer remains; such a position is very close to an absolute impossibility of continuing the fight; it must therefore extricate itself from it, or avoid getting into it. This gives to all combinations aiming at this from the first commencement a great efficiency, which chiefly consists in the disquietude which it causes the enemy as to consequences. This is why the geometrical disposition of the forces is such an important factor in the tactical product.

In Strategy this is only faintly reflected, on account of the greater space and time. We do not fire from one theatre of war upon another; and often weeks and months must pass before a strategic movement designed to surround the enemy can be executed. Further, the distances are so great that the probability of hitting the right point at last, even with the best arrangements, is but small.

In Strategy therefore the scope for such combinations, that is for those resting on the geometrical element, is much smaller, and for the same reason the effect of an advantage once actually gained at any point is much greater. Such advantage has time to bring all its effects to maturity before it is disturbed, or quite neutralised therein, by any counteracting apprehensions. We therefore do not hesitate to regard as an established truth, that in Strategy more depends on the number and the magnitude of the victorious combats, than on the form of the great lines by which they are connected.

A view just the reverse has been a favourite theme of modern theory, because a greater importance was supposed to be thus given to Strategy, and, as the higher functions of the mind were seen in Strategy, it was thought by that means to ennoble War, and, as it was said – through a new substitution of ideas – to make it more scientific. We hold it to be one of the principal uses of a complete theory openly to expose such vagaries, and as the geometrical element is the fundamental idea from which theory usually proceeds, therefore we have expressly brought out this point in strong relief.

CHAPTER SIXTEEN

On the Suspension of the
Act in Warfare

IF ONE CONSIDERS WAR as an act of mutual destruction, we must of necessity imagine both parties as making some progress; but at the same time, as regards the existing moment, we must almost as necessarily suppose the one party in a state of expectation, and only the other actually advancing, for circumstances can never be actually the same on both sides, or continue so. In time a change must ensue, from which it follows that the present moment is more favourable to one side than the other. Now if we suppose that both commanders have a full knowledge of this circumstance, then the one has a motive for action, which at the same time is a motive for the other to wait; therefore, according to this it cannot be for the interest of both at the same time to advance, nor can waiting be for the interest of both at the same time. This opposition of interest as regards the object is not deduced here from the principle of general polarity, and therefore is not in opposition to the argument in the fifth chapter of the second book; it depends on the fact that here in reality the same thing is at once an incentive or motive to both commanders, namely the probability of improving or impairing their position by future action.

But even if we suppose the possibility of a perfect equality of circumstances in this respect, or if we take into account that through imperfect knowledge of their mutual position such an equality may appear to the two Commanders to subsist, still the difference of political objects does away with this possibility of suspension. One of the parties must of necessity be assumed politically to be the aggressor, because no War could take place from defensive intentions on both sides. But the aggressor has the positive object, the defender merely a negative one. To the first then belongs the positive action, for it is only by that means that he can attain the positive object; therefore, in cases where both parties are in precisely similar circumstances, the aggressor is called upon to act by virtue of his positive object.

Therefore, from this point of view, a suspension in the act of Warfare, strictly speaking, is in contradiction with the nature of the thing; because two Armies, being two incompatible elements, should destroy one another unremittingly, just as fire and water can never put themselves in equilibrium, but act and react upon one another, until one quite disappears. What would be said of two wrestlers who remained clasped round each other for hours without making a movement. Action in War, therefore, like that of a clock which is wound up, should go on running down in regular motion. – But wild as is the nature of War it still wears the chains of human weakness, and the contradiction we see here, viz., that man seeks and creates dangers which he fears at the same time will astonish no one.

If we cast a glance at military history in general, we find so much the opposite of an incessant advance towards the aim, that *standing still* and *doing nothing* is quite plainly the *normal condition* of an Army in the midst of War, *acting*, the *exception*. This must almost raise a doubt as to the correctness of our conception. But if military history leads to this conclusion when viewed in the mass the latest series of campaigns redeems our position. The War of the French Revolution shows too plainly its reality, and only proves too clearly its necessity. In these operations, and especially in the campaigns of Buonaparte, the conduct of War attained to that unlimited degree of energy which we have represented as the natural law of the element. This degree is therefore possible, and if it is possible then it is necessary.

How could any one in fact justify in the eyes of reason the expenditure of forces in War, if acting was not the object? The baker only heats his oven if he has bread to put into it; the horse is only yoked to the carriage if we mean to drive; why then make the enormous effort of a War if we look for nothing else by it but like efforts on the part of the enemy?

So much in justification of the general principle; now as to its modifications, as far as they lie in the nature of the thing and are independent of special cases.

There are three causes to be noticed here, which appear as innate counterpoises and prevent the over-rapid or uncontrollable movement of the wheel-work.

The first, which produces a constant tendency to delay, and is thereby a retarding principle, is the natural timidity and want of resolution in the human mind, a kind of inertia in the moral world, but which is produced not by attractive, but by repellent forces, that is to say, by dread of danger and responsibility.

In the burning element of War, ordinary natures appear to become heavier; the impulsion given must therefore be stronger and more frequently repeated if the motion is to be a continuous one. The mere idea of the object for which arms have been taken up is seldom sufficient to overcome this resistant force, and if a warlike enterprising spirit is not at the head, who feels himself in War in his natural element, as much as a fish in the ocean, or if there is not the pressure from above of some great responsibility, then standing still will be the order of the day, and progress will be the exception.

The second cause is the imperfection of human perception and judgment, which is greater in War than anywhere, because a person hardly knows exactly his own position from one moment to another, and can only conjecture on slight grounds that of the enemy, which is purposely concealed; this often gives rise to the case of both parties looking upon one and the same object as advantageous for them, while in reality the interest of one must preponderate; thus then each may think he acts wisely by waiting another moment, as we have already said in the fifth chapter of the second book.

The third cause which catches hold, like a ratchet wheel in machinery, from time to time producing a complete standstill, is the greater strength of the defensive form. A may feel too weak to attack B, from which it does not follow that B is strong enough for an attack on A. The addition of strength, which the defensive gives is not merely lost by assuming the offensive, but also passes to the enemy just as, figuratively expressed, the difference of $a + b$ and $a - b$ is equal to $2b$. Therefore it may so happen that both parties, at one and the same time, not only feel themselves too weak to attack, but also are so in reality.

Thus even in the midst of the act of War itself, anxious sagacity and the apprehension of too great danger find vantage ground, by means of which they can exert their power, and tame the elementary impetuosity of War.

However, at the same time these causes without an exaggeration of their effect, would hardly explain the long states of inactivity which took place in military operations, in former times, in Wars undertaken about interests of no great importance, and in which inactivity consumed nine-tenths of the time that the troops remained under arms.

This feature in these Wars, is to be traced principally to the influence which the demands of the one party, and the condition, and feeling of the other, exercised over the conduct of the operations, as has been already observed in the chapter on the essence and object of War.

These things may obtain such a preponderating influence as to make of War a half-and-half affair. A War is often nothing more than an armed neutrality, or a menacing attitude to support negotiations or an attempt to gain some small advantage by small exertions, and then to wait the tide of circumstances, or a disagreeable treaty obligation, which is fulfilled in the most niggardly way possible.

In all these cases in which the impulse given by interest is slight, and the principle of hostility feeble, in which there is no desire to do much, and also not much to dread from the enemy; in short, where no powerful motives press and drive, cabinets will not risk much in the game; hence this tame mode of carrying on War, in which the hostile spirit of real War is laid in irons.

The more War becomes in this manner devitalised so much the more its theory becomes destitute of the necessary firm pivots and buttresses for its reasoning; the necessary is constantly diminishing, the accidental constantly increasing.

Nevertheless in this kind of Warfare, there is also a certain shrewdness, indeed, its action is perhaps more diversified, and more extensive than in the other. Hazard played with realeaux of gold seems changed into a game of commerce with groschen. And on this field, where the conduct of War spins out the time with a number of small flourishes, with skirmishes at outposts, half in earnest half in jest, with long dispositions which end in nothing with positions and marches, which afterwards are designated as skilful only because their infinitesimally small causes are lost, and common sense can make nothing of them, here on this very field many theorists find the real Art of War at home: in these feints, parades, half and quarter thrusts of former Wars, they find the aim of all theory, the supremacy of mind over matter, and modern Wars appear to them mere savage fisticuffs, from which nothing is to be learnt, and which must be regarded as mere retrograde steps towards barbarism. This opinion is as frivolous as the objects to which it relates. Where great forces and great passions are wanting, it is certainly easier for a practised dexterity to show its game; but is then the command of great forces, not in itself a higher exercise of the intelligent faculties? Is then that kind of conventional sword-exercise not comprised in and belonging to the other mode of conducting War? Does it not bear the same relation to it as the motions upon a ship to the motion of the ship itself? Truly it can take place only under the tacit condition that the adversary does no better. And can we tell, how long he may choose to respect those conditions? Has not then the French Revolution fallen upon us in the midst of the fancied security of our old system of War, and driven us from Chalons to Moscow? And did not Frederick the Great in like manner surprise the Austrians reposing in their ancient habits of War, and make their monarchy tremble? Woe to the cabinet which, with a shilly-shally policy, and a routine-ridden military system, meets with an adversary who, like the rude element, knows no other law than that of his intrinsic force. Every deficiency in energy and exertion is then a weight in the scales in favour of the enemy; it is not so easy then to change from the fencing posture into that of an athlete, and a slight blow is often sufficient to knock down the whole.

The result of all the causes now adduced is, that the hostile action of a campaign does not progress by a continuous, but by an intermittent movement, and that, therefore, between the separate bloody acts, there is a period of watching, during which both parties fall into the defensive, and also that usually a higher object causes the principle of aggression to predominate on one side, and thus leaves it in general in an advancing position, by which then its proceedings become modified in some degree.

CHAPTER SEVENTEEN
On the Character of Modern War

THE ATTENTION which must be paid to the character of War as it is now made, has a great influence upon all plans, especially on strategic ones.

Since all methods formerly usual were upset by Buonaparte's luck and boldness, and first-rate Powers almost wiped out at a blow; since the Spaniards by their stubborn resistance have shown what the general arming of a nation and insurgent measures on a great scale can effect, in spite of weakness and porousness of individual parts; since Russia, by the campaign of 1812 has taught us, first, that an Empire of great dimensions is not to be conquered (which might have been easily known before), secondly, that the probability of final success does not in all cases diminish in the same measure as battles, capitals, and provinces are lost (which was formerly an incontrovertible principle with all diplomatists, and therefore made them always ready to enter at once into some bad temporary peace), but that a nation is often strongest in the heart of its country, if the enemy's offensive power has exhausted itself, and with what enormous force the defensive then springs over to the offensive; further, since Prussia (1813) has shown that sudden efforts may add to an Army sixfold by means of the militia, and that this militia is just as fit for service abroad as in its own country; – since all these events have shown what an enormous factor the heart and sentiments of a Nation may be in the product of its political and military strength, in fine, since governments have found out all these additional aids, it is not to be expected that they will let them lie idle in future Wars, whether it be that danger threatens their own existence, or that restless ambition drives them on.

That a War which is waged with the whole weight of the national power on each side must be organised differently in principle to those where everything is calculated according to the relations of standing Armies to each other, it is easy to perceive. Standing Armies once resembled fleets, the land force the sea force in their relations to the remainder of the State, and from that the Art of War on shore had in it something of naval tactics, which it has now quite lost.

CHAPTER EIGHTEEN

Tension and Rest

The Dynamic Law of War

WE HAVE SEEN in the sixteenth chapter of this book, how, in most campaigns, much more time used to be spent in standing still and inaction than in activity.

Now, although, as observed in the preceding chapter we see quite a different character in the present form of War, still it is certain that real action will always be interrupted more or less by long pauses; and this leads to the necessity of our examining more closely the nature of these two phases of War.

If there is a suspension of action in War, that is, if neither party wills something positive, there is rest, and consequently equilibrium, but certainly an equilibrium in the largest signification, in which not only the moral and physical war-forces, but all relations and interests, come into calculation. As soon as ever one of the two parties proposes to himself a new positive object, and commences active steps towards it, even if it is only by preparations, and as soon as the adversary opposes this, there is a tension of powers; this lasts until the decision takes place – that is, until one party either gives up his object or the other has conceded it to him.

This decision – the foundation of which lies always in the combat – combinations which are made on each side – is followed by a movement in one or other direction.

When this movement has exhausted itself, either in the difficulties which had to be mastered, in overcoming its own internal friction, or through new resistant forces prepared by the acts of the enemy, then either a state of rest takes place or a new tension with a decision, and then a new movement, in most cases in the opposite direction.

This speculative distinction between equilibrium, tension, and motion is more essential for practical action than may at first sight appear.

In a state of rest and of equilibrium a varied kind of activity may prevail on one side that results from opportunity, and does not aim at a great alteration. Such an activity may contain important combats – even pitched battles – but yet it is still of quite a different nature, and on that account generally different in its effects.

If a state of tension exists, the effects of the decision are always greater partly because a greater force of will and a greater pressure of circumstances manifest themselves therein; partly because everything has been prepared and arranged for a great movement. The decision in such cases resembles the effect of a mine well closed and tamped, whilst an event in itself perhaps just as great, in a state of rest, is more or less like a mass of powder puffed away in the open air.

At the same time, as a matter of course, the state of tension must be imagined in different degrees of intensity, and it may therefore approach gradually by many steps towards the state of rest, so that at the last there is a very slight difference between them.

Now the real use which we derive from these reflections is the conclusion that every measure which is taken during a state of tension is more important and more prolific in results than the same measure could be in a state of equilibrium, and that this importance increases immensely in the highest degrees of tension.

The cannonade of Valmy, September 20, 1792, decided more than the battle of Hochkirch, October 14, 1758.

In a tract of country which the enemy abandons to us because he cannot defend it, we can settle ourselves differently from what we should do if the retreat of the enemy was only made with the view to a decision under more favourable circumstances. Again, a strategic attack in course of execution, a faulty position, a single false march, may be decisive in its consequence; whilst in a state of equilibrium such errors must be of a very glaring kind, even to excite the activity of the enemy in a general way.

Most bygone Wars, as we have already said, consisted, so far as regards the greater part of the time, in this state of equilibrium, or at least in such short tensions with long intervals between them, and weak in their effects, that the events to which they gave rise were seldom great successes, often they were theatrical exhibitions, got up in honour of a royal birthday (Hochkirch), often a mere satisfying of the honour of the arms (Kunersdorf), or the personal vanity of the commander (Freiberg).

That a Commander should thoroughly understand these states, that he should have the tact to act in the spirit of them, we hold to be a great requisite, and we have had experience in the campaign of 1806 how far it is sometimes wanting. In that tremendous tension, when everything pressed on towards a supreme decision, and that alone with all its consequences should have occupied the whole soul of the Commander, measures were proposed and even partly carried out (such as the reconnaissance towards Franconia), which at the most might have given a kind of gentle play of oscillation within a state of equilibrium. Over these blundering schemes and views, absorbing the activity of the Army, the really necessary means, which could alone save, were lost sight of.

But this speculative distinction which we have made is also necessary for our further progress in the construction of our theory, because all that we have to say on the relation of attack and defence, and on the completion of this double-sided act, concerns the state of the crisis in which the forces are placed during the tension and motion, and because all the activity which can take place during the condition of equilibrium can only be regarded and treated as a corollary; for that crisis is the real War and this state of equilibrium only its reflection.

BOOK FOUR

The Combat

CHAPTER ONE

Introductory

HAVING IN THE foregoing book examined the subjects which may be regarded as the efficient elements of War, we shall now turn our attention to the combat as the real activity in Warfare, which, by its physical and moral effects, embraces sometimes more simply, sometimes in a more complex manner, the object of the whole campaign. In this activity and in its effects these elements must therefore, reappear.

The formation of the combat is tactical in its nature; we only glance at it here in a general way in order to get acquainted with it in its aspect as a whole. In practice the minor or more immediate objects give every combat a characteristic form; these minor objects we shall not discuss until hereafter. But these peculiarities are in comparison to the general characteristics of a combat mostly only insignificant, so that most combats are very like one another, and, therefore, in order to avoid repeating that which is general at every stage, we are compelled to look into it here, before taking up the subject of its more special application.

In the first place, therefore, we shall give in the next chapter, in a few words, the characteristics of the modern battle in its tactical course, because that lies at the foundation of our conceptions of what the battle really is.

CHAPTER TWO

Character of the Modern Battle

ACCORDING TO THE notion we have formed of tactics and strategy, it follows, as a matter of course, that if the nature of the former is changed, that change must have an influence on the latter. If tactical facts in one case are entirely different from those in another, then the strategic, must be so also, if they are to continue consistent and reasonable. It is therefore important to characterise a general action in its modern form before we advance with the study of its employment in strategy.

What do we do now usually in a great battle? We place ourselves quietly in great masses arranged contiguous to and behind one another. We deploy relatively only a small portion of the whole, and let it wring itself out in a fire-combat which lasts for several hours, only interrupted now and again, and removed hither and thither by separate small shocks from charges with the bayonet and cavalry attacks. When this line has gradually exhausted part of its warlike ardour in this manner and there remains nothing more than the cinders, it is withdrawn[28] and replaced by another.

In this manner the battle on a modified principle burns slowly away like wet powder, and if the veil of night commands it to stop, because neither party can any longer see, and neither chooses to run the risk of blind chance, then an account is taken by each side respectively of the masses remaining, which can be called still effective, that is, which have not yet quite collapsed like extinct volcanoes; account is taken of the ground gained or lost, and of how stands the security of the rear;

---

28 The relief of the fighting line played a great part in the battles of the Smooth-Bore era; it was necessitated by the fouling of the muskets, physical fatigue of the men and consumption of ammunition, and was recognised as both necessary and advisable by Napoleon himself. – *Editor.*

these results with the special impressions as to bravery and cowardice, ability and stupidity, which are thought to have been observed in ourselves and in the enemy are collected into one single total impression, out of which there springs the resolution to quit the field or to renew the combat on the morrow.

This description, which is not intended as a finished picture of a modern battle, but only to give its general tone, suits for the offensive and defensive, and the special traits which are given, by the object proposed, the country, &c. &c., may be introduced into it, without materially altering the conception.

But modern battles are not so by accident; they are so because the parties find themselves nearly on a level as regards military organisation and the knowledge of the Art of War, and because the warlike element inflamed by great national interests has broken through artificial limits and now flows in its natural channel. Under these two conditions, battles will always preserve this character.

This general idea of the modern battle will be useful to us in the sequel in more places than one, if we want to estimate the value of the particular co-efficients of strength, country, &c. &c. It is only for general, great, and decisive combats, and such as come near to them that this description stands good; inferior ones have changed their character also in the same direction but less than great ones. The proof of this belongs to tactics; we shall, however, have an opportunity hereafter of making this subject plainer by giving a few particulars.

The Combat in General

THE COMBAT is the real warlike activity, everything else is only its auxiliary; let us therefore take an attentive look at its nature.

Combat means fighting, and in this the destruction or conquest of the enemy is the object, and the enemy, in the particular combat, is the armed force which stands opposed to us.

This is the simple idea; we shall return to it, but before we can do that we must insert a series of others.

If we suppose the State and its military force as a unit, then the most natural idea is to imagine the War also as one great combat, and in the simple relations of savage nations it is also not much otherwise. But our Wars are made up of a number of great and small simultaneous or consecutive combats, and this severance of the activity into so many separate actions is owing to the great multiplicity of the relations out of which War arises with us.

In point of fact, the ultimate object of our Wars, the political one, is not always quite a simple one; and even were it so, still the action is bound up with such a number of conditions and considerations to be taken into account, that the object can no longer be attained by one single great act but only through a number of greater or smaller acts which are bound up into a whole; each of these separate acts is therefore a part of a whole, and has consequently a special object by which it is bound to this whole.

We have already said that every strategic act can be referred to the idea of a combat, because it is an employment of the military force, and at the root of that there always lies the idea of fighting. We may therefore reduce every military activity in the province of Strategy to the unit of single combats, and occupy ourselves with the object of these only; we shall get acquainted with these special objects by degrees as we come to speak of the causes which produce them; here we content ourselves with saying that every combat, great or small, has its own peculiar object in subordination to the main object. If this is the case then, the destruction and conquest of the enemy is only to be regarded as the means of gaining this object; as it unquestionably is.

But this result is true only in its form, and important only on account of the connection which the ideas have between themselves, and we have only sought it out to get rid of it at once.

What is overcoming the enemy? Invariably the destruction of his military force, whether it be by death, or wounds, or any means; whether it be completely or only to such a degree that he can no longer continue the contest; therefore as long as we set aside all special objects of combats, we may look upon the complete or partial destruction of the enemy as the only object of all combats.

Now we maintain that in the majority of cases, and especially in great battles, the special object by which the battle is individualised and bound up with the great whole is only a weak modification of that general object, or an ancillary object bound up with it, important enough to individualise the battle, but always insignificant in comparison with that general object; so that if that ancillary object alone should be obtained, only an unimportant part of the purpose of the combat is fulfilled. If this assertion is correct, then we see that the idea, according to which the destruction of the enemy's force is only the means, and something else always the object, can only be true in form, but, that it would lead to false conclusions if we did not recollect that this destruction of the enemy's force is comprised in that object, and that this object is only a weak modification of it. Forgetfulness of this led to completely false views before the Wars of the last period, and created tendencies as well as fragments of systems, in which theory thought it raised itself so much the more above handicraft, the less it supposed itself to stand in need of the use of the real instrument, that is the destruction of the enemy's force.

Certainly such a system could not have arisen unless supported by other false suppositions, and unless in place of the destruction of the enemy, other things had been substituted to which an efficacy was ascribed which did not rightly belong to them. We shall attack these falsehoods whenever occasion requires, but we could not treat of the combat without claiming for it the real importance and value which belong to it, and giving warning against the errors to which merely formal truth might lead.

But now how shall we manage to show that in most cases, and in those of most importance, the destruction of the enemy's Army is the chief thing? How shall we manage to combat that extremely subtle idea, which supposes it possible, through the use of a special artificial form, to effect by a small direct destruction of the enemy's forces a much greater destruction indirectly, or by means of small but extremely well-directed blows to produce such paralysation of the enemy's forces, such a command over the enemy's will, that this mode of proceeding is to be viewed as a great shortening of the road? Undoubtedly a victory at one point may be of more value than at another. Undoubtedly there is a scientific arrangement of battles amongst themselves, even in Strategy, which is in fact nothing but the Art of thus arranging them. To deny that is not our intention, but we assert that the direct destruction of the enemy's forces is everywhere predominant; we contend here for the overruling importance of this destructive principle and nothing else.

We must, however, call to mind that we are now engaged with Strategy, not with tactics, therefore we do not speak of the means which the former may have of destroying at a small expense a large body of the enemy's forces, but under direct destruction we understand the tactical results, and that, therefore, our assertion is that only great tactical results can lead to great strategical ones, or, as we have already once before more distinctly expressed it, *the tactical successes* are of paramount importance in the conduct of War.

The proof of this assertion seems to us simple enough, it lies in the time which every complicated (artificial) combination requires. The question whether a simple attack, or one more carefully prepared, i.e., more artificial, will produce greater effects, may undoubtedly be decided in favour of the latter as long as the enemy is assumed to remain quite passive. But every carefully combined attack requires time for its preparation, and if a counter-stroke by the enemy intervenes, our whole design may be upset. Now if the enemy should decide upon some simple attack, which can be executed in a shorter time, then he gains the initiative, and destroys the effect of the great plan. Therefore, together with the expediency of a complicated attack we must consider all the dangers which we run during its preparation, and should only adopt it if there is no reason to fear that the enemy will disconcert our scheme. Whenever this is the case we must ourselves choose the simpler, i.e., quicker way, and lower our views in this sense as far as the character, the relations of the enemy, and other circumstances may render necessary. If we quit the weak impressions of abstract ideas and descend to the region of practical life, then it is evident that a bold, courageous, resolute enemy will not let us have time for wide-reaching skilful combinations, and it is just against such a one we should require skill the most. By this it appears to us that the advantage of simple and direct results over those that are complicated is conclusively shown.

Our opinion is not on that account that the simple blow is the best, but that we must not lift the arm too far for the time given to strike, and that this condition will always lead more to direct conflict the more warlike our opponent is. Therefore, far from making it our aim to gain upon the enemy by complicated plans, we must rather seek to be beforehand with him by greater simplicity in our designs.

If we seek for the lowest foundation-stones of these converse propositions we find that in the one it is ability, in the other, courage. Now, there is something very attractive in the notion that a moderate degree of courage joined to great ability will produce greater effects than moderate ability with great courage. But unless we suppose these elements in a disproportionate relation, not logical, we have no right to assign to ability this advantage over courage in a field which is called danger, and which must be regarded as the true domain of courage.

After this abstract view we shall only add that experience, very far from leading to a different conclusion, is rather the sole cause which has impelled us in this direction, and given rise to such reflections.

Whoever reads history with a mind free from prejudice cannot fail to arrive at a conviction that of all military virtues, energy in the conduct of operations has always contributed the most to the glory and success of arms.

How we make good our principle of regarding the destruction of the enemy's force as the principal object, not only in the War as a whole but also in each separate combat, and how that principle suits all the forms and conditions necessarily demanded by the relations out of which War springs, the sequel will show. For the present all that we desire is to uphold its general importance, and with this result we return again to the combat.

CHAPTER FOUR

The Combat in General
(Continuation)

IN THE LAST CHAPTER we showed the destruction of the enemy as the true object of the combat, and we have sought to prove by a special consideration of the point, that this is true in the majority of cases, and in respect to the most important battles, because the destruction of the enemy's Army is always the preponderating object in War. The other objects which may be mixed up with this destruction of the enemy's force, and may have more or less influence, we shall describe generally in the next chapter, and become better acquainted with by degrees afterwards; here we divest the combat of them entirely, and look upon the destruction of the enemy as the complete and sufficient object of any combat.

What are we now to understand by destruction of the enemy's Army? A diminution of it relatively greater than that on our own side. If we have a great superiority in numbers over the enemy, then naturally the same absolute amount of loss on both sides is for us a smaller one than for him, and consequently may be regarded in itself as an advantage. As we are here considering the combat as divested of all (other) objects, we must also exclude from our consideration the case in which the combat is used only indirectly for a greater destruction of the enemy's force; consequently also, only that direct gain which has been made in the mutual process of destruction, is to be regarded as the object, for this is an absolute gain, which runs through the whole campaign, and at the end of it will always appear as pure profit. But every other kind of victory over our opponent will either have its motive in other objects, which we have completely excluded here, or it will only yield a temporary relative advantage. An example will make this plain.

If by a skilful disposition we have reduced our opponent to such a dilemma, that he cannot continue the combat without danger, and after some resistance he retires, then we may say, that we have conquered him at that point; but if in this victory we have expended just as many forces as the enemy, then in closing the account of the campaign, there is no gain remaining from this victory, if such a result can be called a victory. Therefore the overcoming the enemy, that is, placing him in such a position that he must give up the fight, counts for nothing in itself, and for that reason cannot come under the definition of object. There remains, therefore, as we have said, nothing over except the direct gain which we have made in the process of destruction; but to this belong not only the losses which have taken place in the course of the combat, but also those which, after the withdrawal of the conquered part, take place as direct consequences of the same.

Now it is known by experience, that the losses in physical forces in the course of a battle seldom present a great difference between victor and vanquished respectively, often none at all, sometimes even one bearing an inverse relation to the result, and that the most decisive losses on the side of the vanquished only commence with the retreat, that is, those which the conqueror does not share with him. The weak remains of battalions already in disorder are cut down by cavalry, exhausted men strew the ground, disabled guns and broken caissons are abandoned, others in the bad state of the roads cannot be removed quickly enough, and are captured by the enemy's troops, during the night numbers lose their way, and fall defenceless into the enemy's hands, and thus the victory mostly gains bodily substance after it is already decided. Here would be a paradox, if it did not solve itself in the following manner.

The loss in physical force is not the only one which the two sides suffer in the course of the combat; the moral forces also are shaken, broken, and go to ruin. It is not only the loss in men, horses and guns, but in order, courage, confidence, cohesion and plan, which come into consideration when it is a question whether the fight can be still continued or not. It is principally the moral forces which decide here, and in all cases in which the conqueror has lost as heavily as the conquered, it is these alone.

The comparative relation of the physical losses is difficult to estimate in a battle, but not so the relation of the moral ones. Two things principally make it known. The one is the loss of the ground on which the fight has taken place, the other the superiority of the enemy's. The more our reserves have diminished as compared with those of the enemy, the more force we have used to maintain the equilibrium; in this at once, an evident proof of the moral superiority of the enemy is given which seldom fails to stir up in the soul of the Commander a certain bitterness of feeling, and a sort of contempt for his own troops. But the principal thing is, that men who have been engaged for a long continuance of time are more or less like burnt-out cinders; their ammunition is consumed; they have melted away to a certain extent; physical and moral energies are exhausted, perhaps their courage is broken as well. Such a force, irrespective of the diminution in its number, if viewed as an organic whole, is very different from what it was before the combat; and thus it is that the loss of moral force may be measured by the reserves that have been used as if it were on a foot-rule.

Lost ground and want of fresh reserves, are, therefore, usually the principal causes which determine a retreat; but at the same time we by no means exclude or desire to throw in the shade other reasons, which may lie in the interdependence of parts of the Army, in the general plan, &c.

Every combat is therefore the bloody and destructive measuring of the strength of forces, physical and moral; whoever at the close has the greatest amount of both left is the conqueror.

In the combat the loss of moral force is the chief cause of the decision; after that is given, this loss continues to increase until it reaches its culminating-point at the close of the whole act. This then is the opportunity the victor should seize to reap his harvest by the utmost possible restrictions of his enemy's forces, the real object of engaging in the combat. On the beaten side, the loss of all order and control often makes the prolongation of resistance by individual units, by the further punishment they are certain to suffer, more injurious than useful to the whole. The spirit of the mass is broken; the original excitement about losing or winning, through which danger was forgotten, is spent, and to the majority danger now appears no longer an appeal to their courage, but rather the endurance of a cruel punishment. Thus the instrument in the first moment of the enemy's victory is weakened and blunted, and therefore no longer fit to repay danger by danger.

This period, however, passes; the moral forces of the conquered will recover by degrees, order will be restored, courage will revive, and in the majority of cases there remains only a small part of the superiority obtained, often none at all. In some cases, even, although rarely, the spirit of revenge and intensified hostility may bring about an opposite result. On the other hand, whatever is gained in killed, wounded, prisoners, and guns captured can never disappear from the account.

The losses in a battle consist more in killed and wounded; those after the battle, more in artillery taken and prisoners. The first the conqueror shares with the conquered, more or less, but the second not; and for that reason they usually only take place on one side of the conflict, at least, they are considerably in excess on one side.

Artillery and prisoners are therefore at all times regarded as the true trophies of victory, as well as its measure, because through these things its extent is declared beyond a doubt. Even the degree of moral superiority may be better judged of by them than by any other relation, especially if the number of killed and wounded is compared therewith; and here arises a new power increasing the moral effects.

We have said that the moral forces, beaten to the ground in the battle and in the immediately succeeding movements, recover themselves gradually, and often bear no traces of injury; this is the case with small divisions of the whole, less frequently with large divisions; it may, however, also be the case with the main Army, but seldom or never in the State or Government to which the Army belongs. These estimate the situation more impartially, and from a more elevated point of view, and recognise in the number of trophies taken by the enemy, and their relation to the number of killed and wounded, only too easily and well, the measure of their own weakness and inefficiency.

In point of fact, the lost balance of moral power must not be treated lightly because it has no absolute value, and because it does not of necessity appear in all cases in the amount of the results at the final close; it may become of such excessive weight as to bring down everything with an irresistible force. On that account it may often become a great aim of the operations of which we shall speak elsewhere. Here we have still to examine some of its fundamental relations.

The moral effect of a victory increases, not merely in proportion to the extent of the forces engaged, but in a progressive ratio – that is to say, not only in extent, but also in its intensity. In a beaten detachment order is easily restored. As a single frozen limb is easily revived by the rest of the body, so the courage of a defeated detachment is easily raised again by the courage of the rest of the Army as soon as it rejoins it. If, therefore, the effects of a small victory are not completely done away with, still they are partly lost to the enemy. This is not the case if the Army itself sustains a great defeat; then one with the other fall together. A great fire attains quite a different heat from several small ones.

Another relation which determines the moral value of a victory is the numerical relation of the forces which have been in conflict with each other. To beat many with few is not only a double success, but shows also a greater, especially a more general superiority, which the conquered must always be fearful of encountering again. At the same time this influence is in reality hardly observable in such a case. In the moment of real action, the notions of the actual strength of the enemy are generally so uncertain, the estimate of our own commonly so incorrect, that the party superior in numbers either does not admit the disproportion, or is very far from admitting the full truth, owing to which, he evades almost entirely the moral disadvantages which would spring from it. It is only hereafter in history that the truth, long suppressed through ignorance, vanity, or a wise discretion, makes its appearance, and then it certainly casts a lustre on the Army and its Leader, but it can then do nothing more by its moral influence for events long past.

If prisoners and captured guns are those things by which the victory principally gains substance, its true crystallisations, then the plan of the battle should have those things specially in view; the destruction of the enemy by death and wounds appears here merely as a means to an end.

How far this may influence the dispositions in the battle is not an affair of Strategy, but the decision to fight the battle is in intimate connection with it, as is shown by the direction given to our forces, and their general grouping, whether we threaten the enemy's flank or rear, or he threatens ours. On this point, the number of prisoners and captured guns depends very much, and it is a point which, in many cases, tactics alone cannot satisfy, particularly if the strategic relations are too much in opposition to it.

The risk of having to fight on two sides, and the still more dangerous position of having no line of retreat left open, paralyse the movements and the power of resistance; further, in case of defeat, they increase the loss, often raising it to its extreme point, that is, to destruction. Therefore, the rear being endangered makes defeat more probable, and, at the same time, more decisive.

From this arises, in the whole conduct of the War, especially in great and small combats, a perfect instinct to secure our own line of retreat and to seize that of the enemy; this follows from the conception of victory, which, as we have seen, is something beyond mere slaughter.

In this effort we see, therefore, the first immediate purpose in the combat, and one which is quite universal. No combat is imaginable in which this effort, either in its double or single form, does not go hand in hand with the plain and simple stroke of force. Even the smallest troop will not throw itself upon its enemy without thinking of its line of retreat, and, in most cases, it will have an eye upon that of the enemy also.

We should have to digress to show how often this instinct is prevented from going the direct road, how often it must yield to the difficulties arising from more important considerations: we shall, therefore, rest contented with affirming it to be a general natural law of the combat.

It is, therefore, active; presses everywhere with its natural weight, and so becomes the pivot on which almost all tactical and strategic manoeuvres turn.

If we now take a look at the conception of victory as a whole, we find in it three elements: –

1. The greater loss of the enemy in physical power.
2. In moral power.
3. His open avowal of this by the relinquishment of his intentions.

The returns made up on each side of losses in killed and wounded, are never exact, seldom truthful, and in most cases, full of intentional misrepresentations. Even the statement of the number of trophies is seldom to be quite depended on; consequently, when it is not considerable it may also cast a doubt even on the reality of the victory. Of the loss in moral forces there is no reliable measure, except in the trophies: therefore, in many cases, the giving up the contest is the only real evidence of the victory. It is, therefore, to be regarded as a confession of inferiority – as the lowering of the flag, by which, in this particular instance, right and superiority are conceded to the enemy, and this degree of humiliation and disgrace, which, however, must be distinguished from all the other moral consequences of the loss of equilibrium, is an essential part of the victory. It is this part alone which acts upon the public opinion outside the Army, upon the people and the Government in both belligerent States, and upon all others in any way concerned.

But renouncement of the general object is not quite identical with quitting the field of battle, even when the battle has been very obstinate and long kept up; no one says of advanced posts, when they retire after an obstinate combat, that they have given up their object; even in combats aimed at the destruction of the enemy's Army, the retreat from the battlefield is not always to be regarded as a relinquishment of this aim, as for instance, in retreats planned beforehand, in which the ground is disputed foot by foot; all this belongs to that part of our subject where we shall speak of the separate object of the combat; here we only wish to draw attention to the fact that in most cases the giving up of the object is very difficult to distinguish from the retirement from the battlefield, and that the impression produced by the latter, both in and out of the Army, is not to be treated lightly.

For Generals and Armies whose reputation is not made, this is in it-self one of the difficulties in many operations, justified by circumstances when a succession of combats, each ending in retreat, may appear as a succession of defeats, without being so in reality, and when that appear-ance may exercise a very depressing influence. It is impossible for the retreating General by making known his real intentions to prevent the moral effect spreading to the public and his troops, for to do that with effect he must disclose his plans completely, which of course would run counter to his principal interests to too great a degree.

In order to draw attention to the special importance of this con-ception of victory we shall only refer to the battle of Soor,[29] the tro-phies from which were not important (a few thousand prisoners and twenty guns), and where Frederick proclaimed his victory by remain-ing for five days after on the field of battle, although his retreat into Silesia had been previously determined on, and was a measure natural to his whole situation. According to his own account, he thought he would hasten a peace by the moral effect of his victory. Now although a couple of other successes were likewise required, namely, the battle at Katholisch Hennersdorf, in Lusatia, and the battle of Kesseldorf, before this peace took place, still we cannot say that the moral effect of the battle of Soor was nil.

If it is chiefly the moral force which is shaken by defeat, and if the number of trophies reaped by the enemy mounts up to an unusual height, then the lost combat becomes a rout, but this is not the neces-sary consequence of every victory. A rout only sets in when the moral force of the defeated is very severely shaken then there often ensues a complete incapability of further resistance, and the whole action con-sists of giving way, that is of flight.

Jena and Belle Alliance were routs, but not so Borodino.

Although without pedantry we can here give no single line of sepa-ration, because the difference between the things is one of degrees, yet still the retention of the conception is essential as a central point to give clearness to our theoretical ideas and it is a want in our terminology that for a victory over the enemy tantamount to a rout, and a conquest of the enemy only tantamount to a simple victory, there is only one and the same word to use.

29 Soor, or Sohr, Sept. 30, 1745; Hennersdorf, Nov. 23, 1745; Kealteldorf, Dec. 15, 1745, all in the Second Silesian War.

CHAPTER FIVE

On the Signification of the Combat

HAVING IN THE preceding chapter examined the combat in its absolute form, as the miniature picture of the whole War, we now turn to the relations which it bears to the other parts of the great whole. First we inquire what is more precisely the signification of a combat.

As War is nothing else but a mutual process of destruction, then the most natural answer in conception, and perhaps also in reality, appears to be that all the powers of each party unite in one great volume and all results in one great shock of these masses. There is certainly much truth in this idea, and it seems to be very advisable that we should adhere to it and should on that account look upon small combats at first only as necessary loss, like the shavings from a carpenter's plane. Still, however, the thing cannot be settled so easily.

That a multiplication of combats should arise from a fractioning of forces is a matter of course, and the more immediate objects of separate combats will therefore come before us in the subject of a fractioning of forces; but these objects, and together with them, the whole mass of combats may in a general way be brought under certain classes, and the knowledge of these classes will contribute to make our observations more intelligible.

Destruction of the enemy's military forces is in reality the object of all combats; but other objects may be joined thereto, and these other objects may be at the same time predominant; we must therefore draw a distinction between those in which the destruction of the enemy's forces is the principal object, and those in which it is more the means. The destruction of the enemy's force, the possession of a place or the possession of some object may be the general motive for a combat, and it may be either one of these alone or several together, in which case however usually one is the principal motive. Now the two principal forms of War, the offensive and defensive, of which we shall shortly speak, do not modify the first of these motives, but they certainly do modify the other two, and therefore if we arrange them in a scheme they would appear thus: –

Offensive.	*Defensive.*
1. Destruction of enemy's force	1. Destruction of enemy's force.
2. Conquest of a place.	2. Defence of a place.
3. Conquest of some object.	3. Defence of some object.

These motives, however, do not seem to embrace completely the whole of the subject, if we recollect that there are reconnaissances and demonstrations, in which plainly none of these three points is the object of the combat. In reality we must, therefore, on this account be allowed a fourth class. Strictly speaking, in reconnaissances in which we wish the enemy to show himself, in alarms by which we wish to wear him out, in demonstrations by which we wish to prevent his leaving some point or to draw him off to another, the objects are all such as can only be attained indirectly and *under the pretext of one of the three objects specified in the table*, usually of the second; for the enemy whose aim is to reconnoitre must draw up his force as if he really intended to attack and defeat us, or drive us off, &c. &c. But this pretended object is not the real one, and our present question is only as to the latter; therefore, we must to the above three objects of the offensive further add a fourth, which is to lead the enemy to make a false conclusion. That offensive means are conceivable in connection with this object, lies in the nature of the thing.

On the other hand we must observe that the defence of a place may be of two kinds, either absolute, if as a general question the point is not to be given up, or relative if it is only required for a certain time. The latter happens perpetually in the combats of advanced posts and rear guards.

That the nature of these different intentions of a combat must have an essential influence on the dispositions which are its preliminaries, is a thing clear in itself. We act differently if our object is merely to drive an enemy's post out of its place from what we should if our object was to beat him completely; differently, if we mean to defend a place to the last extremity from what we should do if our design is only to detain the enemy for a certain time. In the first case we trouble ourselves little about the line of retreat, in the latter it is the principal point, &c.

But these reflections belong properly to tactics, and are only intro-duced here by way of example for the sake of greater clearness. What Strategy has to say on the different objects of the combat will appear in the chapters which touch upon these objects. Here we have only a few general observations to make, first, that the importance of the object decreases nearly in the order as they stand above, therefore, that the first of these objects must always predominate in the great battle; lastly, that the two last in a defensive battle are in reality such as yield no fruit, they are, that is to say, purely negative, and can, therefore, only be serviceable, indirectly, by facilitating something else which is positive. *it is, therefore, a bad sign of the strategic situation if battles of this kind become too frequent.*

CHAPTER SIX

Duration of the Combat

IF WE CONSIDER the combat no longer in itself but in relation to the other forces of War, then its duration acquires a special importance.

This duration is to be regarded to a certain extent as a second subordinate success. For the conqueror the combat can never be finished too quickly, for the vanquished it can never last too long. A speedy victory indicates a higher power of victory, a tardy decision is, on the side of the defeated, some compensation for the loss.

This is in general true, but it acquires a practical importance in its application to those combats, the object of which is a relative defence.

Here the whole success often lies in the mere duration. This is the reason why we have included it amongst the strategic elements.

The duration of a combat is necessarily bound up with its essential relations. These relations are, absolute magnitude of force, relation of force and of the different arms mutually, and nature of the country. Twenty thousand men do not wear themselves out upon one another as quickly as two thousand: we cannot resist an enemy double or three times our strength as long as one of the same strength; a cavalry combat is decided sooner than an infantry combat; and a combat between infantry only, quicker than if there is artillery[30] as well; in hills and forests we cannot advance as quickly as on a level country; all this is clear enough.

From this it follows, therefore, that strength, relation of the three arms, and position, must be considered if the combat is to fulfil an object by its duration; but to set up this rule was of less importance to us

---

30 The increase in the relative range of artillery and the introduction of shrapnel has altogether modified this conclusion.

in our present considerations than to connect with it at once the chief results which experience gives us on the subject.

Even the resistance of an ordinary Division of 8000 to 10,000 men of all arms even opposed to an enemy considerably superior in numbers, will last several hours, if the advantages of country are not too preponderating, and if the enemy is only a little, or not at all, superior in numbers, the combat will last half a day. A Corps of three or four Divisions will prolong it to double the time; an Army of 80,000 or 100,000 to three or four times. Therefore the masses may be left to themselves for that length of time, and no separate combat takes place if within that time other forces can be brought up, whose co-operation mingles then at once into one stream with the results of the combat which has taken place.

These calculations are the result of experience; but it is important to us at the same time to characterise more particularly the moment of the decision, and consequently the termination.

CHAPTER SEVEN

Decision of the Combat

No BATTLE IS DECIDED in a single moment, although in every battle there arise moments of crisis, on which the result depends. The loss of a battle is, therefore, a gradual falling of the scale. But there is in every combat a point of time[31] when it may be regarded as decided, in such a way that the renewal of the fight would be a new battle, not a continuation of the old one. To have a clear notion on this point of time, is very important, in order to be able to decide whether, with the prompt assistance of reinforcements, the combat can again be resumed with advantage.

Often in combats which are beyond restoration new forces are sacrificed in vain; often through neglect the decision has not been seized when it might easily have been secured. Here are two examples, which could not be more to the point:

When the Prince of Hohenlohe, in 1806, at Jena,[32] with 35,000 men opposed to from 60,000 to 70,000, under Buonaparte, had accepted battle, and lost it – but lost it in such a way that the 35,000 might be regarded as dissolved – General Ruchel undertook to renew the fight with about 12,000; the consequence was that in a moment his force was scattered in like manner.

On the other hand, on the same day at Auerstadt, the Prussians maintained a combat with 25,000, against Davoust, who had 28,000, until mid-day, without success, it is true, but still without the force being re-

---

31 Under the then existing conditions of armament understood. This point is of supreme importance, as practically the whole conduct of a great battle depends on a correct solution of this question – viz., How long can a given command prolong its resistance? If this is incorrectly answered in practice – the whole manoeuvre depending on it may collapse – e.g., Kouroupatkin at Liao-Yang, September 1904.
32 October 14, 1806.

duced to a state of dissolution without even greater loss than the enemy, who was very deficient in cavalry; – but they neglected to use the reserve of 18,000, under General Kalkreuth, to restore the battle which, under these circumstances, it would have been impossible to lose.

Each combat is a whole in which the partial combats combine themselves into one total result. In this total result lies the decision of the combat. This success need not be exactly a victory such as we have denoted in the sixth chapter, for often the preparations for that have not been made, often there is no opportunity if the enemy gives way too soon, and in most cases the decision, even when the resistance has been obstinate, takes place before such a degree of success is attained as would completely satisfy the idea of a victory.

We therefore ask, Which is commonly the moment of the decision, that is to say, that moment when a fresh, effective, of course not disproportionate, force, can no longer turn a disadvantageous battle?

If we pass over false attacks, which in accordance with their nature are properly without decision, then,

1. If the possession of a movable object was the object of the combat, the loss of the same is always the decision.

2. If the possession of ground was the object of the combat, then the decision generally lies in its loss. Still not always, only if this ground is of peculiar strength, ground which is easy to pass over, however important it may be in other respects, can be re-taken without much danger.

3. But in all other cases, when these two circumstances have not already decided the combat, therefore, particularly in case the destruction of the enemy's force is the principal object, the decision is reached at that moment when the conqueror ceases to feel himself in a state of disintegration, that is, of unserviceableness to a certain extent, when therefore, there is no further advantage in using the successive efforts spoken of in the twelfth chapter of the third book. On this ground we have given the strategic unity of the battle its place here.

A battle, therefore, in which the assailant has not lost his condition of order and perfect efficiency at all, or, at least, only in a small part of his force, whilst the opposing forces are, more or less, disorganised throughout, is also not to be retrieved; and just as little if the enemy has recovered his efficiency.

The smaller, therefore, that part of a force is which has really been engaged, the greater that portion which as reserve has contributed to the result only by its presence. So much the less will any new force of the enemy wrest again the victory from our hands, and that Commander who carries out to the furthest with his Army the principle of conducting the combat with the greatest economy of forces, and making the most of the moral effect of strong reserves, goes the surest way to victory. We must allow that the French, in modern times, especially when led by Buonaparte, have shown a thorough mastery in this.

Further, the moment when the crisis-stage of the combat ceases with the conqueror, and his original state of order is restored, takes place sooner the smaller the unit he controls. A picket of cavalry pursuing an enemy at full gallop will in a few minutes resume its proper order, and the crisis ceases. A whole regiment of cavalry requires a longer time. It lasts still longer with infantry, if extended in single lines of skirmishers, and longer again with Divisions of all arms, when it happens by chance that one part has taken one direction and another part another direction, and the combat has therefore caused a loss of the order of formation, which usually becomes still worse from no part knowing exactly where the other is. Thus, therefore, the point of time when the conqueror has collected the instruments he has been using, and which are mixed up and partly out of order, the moment when he has in some measure rearranged them and put them in their proper places, and thus brought the battle-workshop into a little order, this moment, we say, is always later, the greater the total force.

Again, this moment comes later if night overtakes the conqueror in the crisis, and, lastly, it comes later still if the country is broken and thickly wooded. But with regard to these two points, we must observe that night is also a great means of protection, and it is only seldom that circumstances favour the expectation of a successful result from a night attack, as on March 10, 1814, at Laon,[33] where York against Marmont gives us an example completely in place here. In the same way a wooded and broken country will afford protection against a reaction to those who are engaged in the long crisis of victory. Both, therefore, the night as well as the wooded and broken country are obstacles which make the renewal of the same battle more difficult instead of facilitating it.

Hitherto, we have considered assistance arriving for the losing side as a mere increase of force, therefore, as a reinforcement coming up directly from the rear, which is the most usual case. But the case is quite different if these fresh forces come upon the enemy in flank or rear.

On the effect of flank or rear attacks so far as they belong to Strategy, we shall speak in another place: such a one as we have here in view, intended for the restoration of the combat, belongs chiefly to tactics, and is only mentioned because we are here speaking of tactical results, our ideas, therefore, must trench upon the province of tactics.

33 The celebrated charge at night upon Marmont's Corps.

By directing a force against the enemy's flank and rear its efficacy may be much intensified; but this is so far from being a necessary result always that the efficacy may, on the other hand, be just as much weakened. The circumstances under which the combat has taken place decide upon this part of the plan as well as upon every other, without our being able to enter thereupon here. But, at the same time, there are in it two things of importance for our subject: first, *flank and rear attacks have, as a rule, a more favourable effect on the consequences of the decision than upon the decision itself.* Now as concerns the retrieving a battle, the first thing to be arrived at above all is a favourable decision and not magnitude of success. In this view one would therefore think that a force which comes to re-establish our combat is of less assistance if it falls upon the enemy in flank and rear, therefore separated from us, than if it joins itself to us directly; certainly, cases are not wanting where it is so, but we must say that the majority are on the other side, and they are so on account of the second point which is here important to us.

This second point *is the moral effect of the surprise, which, as a rule, a reinforcement coming up to re-establish a combat has generally in its favour.* Now the effect of a surprise is always heightened if it takes place in the flank or rear, and an enemy completely engaged in the crisis of victory in his extended and scattered order, is less in a state to counteract it. Who does not feel that an attack in flank or rear, which at the commencement of the battle, when the forces are concentrated and prepared for such an event would be of little importance, gains quite another weight in the last moment of the combat.

We must, therefore, at once admit that in most cases a reinforcement coming up on the flank or rear of the enemy will be more efficacious, will be like the same weight at the end of a longer lever, and therefore that under these circumstances, we may undertake to restore the battle with the same force which employed in a direct attack would be quite insufficient. Here results almost defy calculation, because the moral forces gain completely the ascendency. This is therefore the right field for boldness and daring.

The eye must, therefore, be directed on all these objects, all these moments of co-operating forces must be taken into consideration, when we have to decide in doubtful cases whether or not it is still possible to restore a combat which has taken an unfavourable turn.

If the combat is to be regarded as not yet ended, then the new contest which is opened by the arrival of assistance fuses into the former; therefore they flow together into one common result, and the first disadvantage vanishes completely out of the calculation. But this is not the case if the combat was already decided; then there are two results separate from each other. Now if the assistance which arrives is only of a relative strength, that is, if it is not in itself alone a match for the enemy, then a favourable result is hardly to be expected from this second combat: but if it is so strong that it can undertake the second combat without regard to the first, then it may be able by a favourable issue to compensate or even overbalance the first combat, but never to make it disappear altogether from the account.

At the battle of Kunersdorf,[34] Frederick the Great at the first onset carried the left of the Russian position, and took seventy pieces of artillery; at the end of the battle both were lost again, and the whole result of the first combat was wiped out of the account. Had it been possible to stop at the first success, and to put off the second part of the battle to the coming day, then, even if the King had lost it, the advantages of the first would always have been a set off to the second.

But when a battle proceeding disadvantageously is arrested and turned before its conclusion, its minus result on our side not only disappears from the account, but also becomes the foundation of a greater victory. If, for instance, we picture to ourselves exactly the tactical course of the battle, we may easily see that until it is finally concluded all successes in partial combats are only decisions in suspense, which by the capital decision may not only be destroyed, but changed into the opposite. The more our forces have suffered, the more the enemy will have expended on his side; the greater, therefore, will be the crisis for the enemy, and the more the superiority of our fresh troops will tell. If now the total result turns in our favour, if we wrest from the enemy the field of battle and recover all the trophies again, then all the forces which he has sacrificed in obtaining them become sheer gain for us, and our former defeat becomes a stepping-stone to a greater triumph. The most brilliant feats which with victory the enemy would have so highly prized that the loss of forces which they cost would have been disregarded, leave nothing now behind but regret at the sacrifice entailed. Such is the alteration which the magic of victory and the curse of defeat produces in the specific weight of the same elements.

Therefore, even if we are decidedly superior in strength, and are able to repay the enemy his victory by a greater still, it is always better to forestall the conclusion of a disadvantageous combat, if it is of proportionate importance, so as to turn its course rather than to deliver a second battle.

34 August 12, 1759.

Field-Marshal Daun attempted in the year 1760 to come to the assistance of General Laudon at Leignitz, whilst the battle lasted; but when he failed, he did not attack the King next day, although he did not want for means to do so.

For these reasons serious combats of advance guards which precede a battle are to be looked upon only as necessary evils, and when not necessary they are to be avoided.[35]

We have still another conclusion to examine.

If on a regular pitched battle, the decision has gone against one, this does not constitute a motive for determining on a new one. The determination for this new one must proceed from other relations. This conclusion, however, is opposed by a moral force, which we must take into account: it is the feeling of rage and revenge. From the oldest Field-Marshal to the youngest drummer-boy this feeling is general, and, therefore, troops are never in better spirits for fighting than when they have to wipe out a stain. This is, however, only on the supposition that the beaten portion is not too great in proportion to the whole, because otherwise the above feeling is lost in that of powerlessness.

There is therefore a very natural tendency to use this moral force to repair the disaster on the spot, and on that account chiefly to seek another battle if other circumstances permit. It then lies in the nature of the case that this second battle must be an offensive one.

In the catalogue of battles of second-rate importance there are many examples to be found of such retaliatory battles; but great battles have generally too many other determining causes to be brought on by this weaker motive.

Such a feeling must undoubtedly have led the noble Bluecher with his third Corps to the field of battle on February 14, 1814, when the other two had been beaten three days before at Montmirail. Had he known that he would have come upon Buonaparte in person, then, naturally, preponderating reasons would have determined him to put off his revenge to another day: but he hoped to revenge himself on Marmont, and instead of gaining the reward of his desire for honourable satisfaction, he suffered the penalty of his erroneous calculation.

---

35 This, however, was not Napoleon's view. A vigorous attack of his advance guard he held to be necessary always, to fix the enemy's attention and "paralyse his independent will-power." It was the failure to make this point which, in August 1870, led von Moltke repeatedly into the very jaws of defeat, from which only the lethargy of Bazaine on the one hand and the initiative of his subordinates, notably of von Alvensleben, rescued him. This is the essence of the new Strategic Doctrine of the French General Staff. See the works of Bonnal, Foch, &C. – *Editor*

On the duration of the combat and the moment of its decision depend the distances from each other at which those masses should be placed which are intended to fight *in conjunction with* each other. This disposition would be a tactical arrangement in so far as it relates to one and the same battle; it can, however, only be regarded as such, provided the position of the troops is so compact that two separate combats cannot be imagined, and consequently that the space which the whole occupies can be regarded strategically as a mere point. But in War, cases frequently occur where even those forces intended to fight *in unison* must be so far separated from each other that while their union for one common combat certainly remains the principal object, still the occurrence of separate combats remains possible. Such a disposition is therefore strategic.

Dispositions of this kind are: marches in separate masses and columns, the formation of advance guards, and flanking columns, also the grouping of reserves intended to serve as supports for more than one strategic point; the concentration of several Corps from widely extended cantonments, &c. &c. We can see that the necessity for these arrangements may constantly arise, and may consider them something like the small change in the strategic economy, whilst the capital battles, and all that rank with them are the gold and silver pieces.

CHAPTER EIGHT

Mutual Understanding as to a Battle

No BATTLE CAN take place unless by mutual consent; and in this idea, which constitutes the whole basis of a duel, is the root of a certain phraseology used by historical writers, which leads to many indefinite and false conceptions.

According to the view of the writers to whom we refer, it has frequently happened that one Commander has offered battle to the other, and the latter has not accepted it.

But the battle is a very modified duel, and its foundation is not merely in the mutual wish to fight, that is in consent, but in the objects which are bound up with the battle: these belong always to a greater whole, and that so much the more, as even the whole war considered as a "combat-unit" has political objects and conditions which belong to a higher standpoint. The mere desire to conquer each other therefore falls into quite a subordinate relation, or rather it ceases completely to be anything of itself, and only becomes the nerve which conveys the impulse of action from the higher will.

Amongst the ancients, and then again during the early period of standing Armies, the expression that we had offered battle to the enemy in vain, had more sense in it than it has now. By the ancients everything was constituted with a view to measuring each other's strength in the open field free from anything in the nature of a hindrance,[36] and the whole Art of War consisted in the organisation, and formation of the Army, that is in the order of battle.

---

36 Note the custom of sending formal challenges, fix time and place for action, and "enhazelug" the battlefield in Anglo-Saxon times. – *ED.*

Now as their Armies regularly entrenched themselves in their camps, therefore the position in a camp was regarded as something unassailable, and a battle did not become possible until the enemy left his camp, and placed himself in a practicable country, as it were entered the lists.

If therefore we hear about Hannibal having offered battle to Fabius in vain, that tells us nothing more as regards the latter than that a battle was not part of his plan, and in itself neither proves the physical nor moral superiority of Hannibal; but with respect to him the expression is still correct enough in the sense that Hannibal really wished a battle.

In the early period of modern Armies, the relations were similar in great combats and battles. That is to say, great masses were brought into action, and managed throughout it by means of an order of battle, which like a great helpless whole required a more or less level plain and was neither suited to attack, nor yet to defence in a broken, close or even mountainous country. The defender therefore had here also to some extent the means of avoiding battle. These relations although gradually becoming modified, continued until the first Silesian War, and it was not until the Seven Years' War that attacks on an enemy posted in a difficult country gradually became feasible, and of ordinary occurrence: ground did not certainly cease to be a principle of strength to those making use of its aid, but it was no longer a charmed circle, which shut out the natural forces of War.

During the past thirty years War has perfected itself much more in this respect, and there is no longer anything which stands in the way of a General who is in earnest about a decision by means of battle; he can seek out his enemy, and attack him: if he does not do so he cannot take credit for having wished to fight, and the expression he offered a battle which his opponent did not accept, therefore now means nothing more than that he did not find circumstances advantageous enough for a battle, an admission which the above expression does not suit, but which it only strives to throw a veil over.

It is true the defensive side can no longer refuse a battle, yet he may still avoid it by giving up his position, and the role with which that position was connected: this is however half a victory for the offensive side, and an acknowledgment of his superiority for the present.

This idea in connection with the cartel of defiance can therefore no longer be made use of in order by such rhodomontade to qualify the inaction of him whose part it is to advance, that is, the offensive. The defender who as long as he does not give way, must have the credit of willing the battle, may certainly say, he has offered it if he is not attacked, if that is not understood of itself.

But on the other hand, he who now wishes to, and can retreat cannot easily be forced to give battle. Now as the advantages to the aggressor from this retreat are often not sufficient, and a substantial victory is a matter of urgent necessity for him, in that way the few means which there are to compel such an opponent also to give battle are often sought for and applied with particular skill.

The principal means for this are – first *surrounding* the enemy so as to make his retreat impossible, or at least so difficult that it is better for him to accept battle; and, secondly, *surprising* him. This last way, for which there was a motive formerly in the extreme difficulty of all movements, has become in modern times very inefficacious.

From the pliability and manoeuvring capabilities of troops in the present day, one does not hesitate to commence a retreat even in sight of the enemy, and only some special obstacles in the nature of the country can cause serious difficulties in the operation.

As an example of this kind the battle of Neresheim may be given, fought by the Archduke Charles with Moreau in the Rauhe Alp, August 11, 1796, merely with a view to facilitate his retreat, although we freely confess we have never been able quite to understand the argument of the renowned general and author himself in this case.

The battle of Rosbach[37] is another example, if we suppose the commander of the allied army had not really the intention of attacking Frederick the Great.

Of the battle of Soor,[38] the King himself says that it was only fought because a retreat in the presence of the enemy appeared to him a critical operation; at the same time the King has also given other reasons for the battle.

On the whole, regular night surprises excepted, such cases will always be of rare occurrence, and those in which an enemy is compelled to fight by being practically surrounded, will happen mostly to single corps only, like Mortier's at Durrenstein 1809, and Vandamme at Kulm, 1813.

37 November 5, 1757.
38 Or Sohr, September 30, 1745.

CHAPTER NINE

The Battle[39]

Its decision

WHAT IS A BATTLE? A conflict of the main body, but not an unimportant one about a secondary object, not a mere attempt which is given up when we see betimes that our object is hardly within our reach: it is a conflict waged with all our forces for the attainment of a decisive victory.

Minor objects may also be mixed up with the principal object, and it will take many different tones of colour from the circumstances out of which it originates, for a battle belongs also to a greater whole of which it is only a part, but because the essence of War is conflict, and the battle is the conflict of the main Armies, it is always to be regarded as the real centre of gravity of the War, and therefore its distinguishing character is, that unlike all other encounters, it is arranged for, and undertaken with the sole purpose of obtaining a decisive victory.

This has an influence on the *manner of its decision*, on the *effect of the victory contained in it*, and determines *the value which theory is to assign to it as a means to an end.*

On that account we make it the subject of our special consideration, and at this stage before we enter upon the special ends which may be bound up with it, but which do not essentially alter its character if it really deserves to be termed a battle.

39 Clausewitz still uses the word "die Hauptschlacht" but modern usage employs only the word "die Schlacht" to designate the decisive act of a whole campaign – encounters arising from the collision or troops marching towards the strategic culmination of each portion or the campaign are spoken of either as "Treffen," i.e., "engagements" or "Gefecht," i.e., "combat" or "action." Thus technically, Gravelotte was a "Schlacht," i.e., "battle," but Spicheren, Woerth, Borny, even Vionville were only "Treffen."

If a battle takes place principally on its own account, the elements of its decision must be contained in itself; in other words, victory must be striven for as long as a possibility or hope remains. It must not, therefore, be given up on account of secondary circumstances, but only and alone in the event of the forces appearing completely insufficient.

Now how is that precise moment to be described?

If a certain artificial formation and cohesion of an Army is the principal condition under which the bravery of the troops can gain a victory, as was the case during a great part of the period of the modern Art of War, *then the breaking up of this formation* is the decision. A beaten wing which is put out of joint decides the fate of all that was connected with it. If as was the case at another time the essence of the defence consists in an intimate alliance of the Army with the ground on which it fights and its obstacles, so that Army and position are only one, then the *conquest* of *an essential point* in this position is the decision. It is said the key of the position is lost, it cannot therefore be defended any further; the battle cannot be continued. In both cases the beaten Armies are very much like the broken strings of an instrument which cannot do their work.

That geometrical as well as this geographical principle which had a tendency to place an Army in a state of crystallising tension which did not allow of the available powers being made use of up to the last man, have at least so far lost their influence that they no longer predominate. Armies are still led into battle in a certain order, but that order is no longer of decisive importance; obstacles of ground are also still turned to account to strengthen a position, but they are no longer the only support.

We attempted in the second chapter of this book to take a general view of the nature of the modern battle. According to our conception of it, the order of battle is only a disposition of the forces suitable to the convenient use of them, and the course of the battle a mutual slow wearing away of these forces upon one another, to see which will have soonest exhausted his adversary.

The resolution therefore to give up the fight arises, in a battle more than in any other combat, from the relation of the fresh reserves remaining available; for only these still retain all their moral vigour, and the cinders of the battered, knocked-about battalions, already burnt out in the destroying element, must not be placed on a level with them; also lost ground as we have elsewhere said, is a standard of lost moral force; it therefore comes also into account, but more as a sign of loss suffered than for the loss itself, and the number of fresh reserves is always the chief point to be looked at by both Commanders.

In general, an action inclines in one direction from the very commencement, but in a manner little observable. This direction is also frequently given in a very decided manner by the arrangements which have been made previously, and then it shows a want of discernment in that General who commences battle under these unfavourable circumstances without being aware of them. Even when this does not occur it lies in the nature of things that the course of a battle resembles rather a slow disturbance of equilibrium which commences soon, but as we have said almost imperceptibly at first, and then with each moment of time becomes stronger and more visible, than an oscillating to and fro, as those who are misled by mendacious descriptions usually suppose.

But whether it happens that the balance is for a long time little disturbed, or that even after it has been lost on one side it rights itself again, and is then lost on the other side, it is certain at all events that in most instances the defeated General foresees his fate long before he retreats, and that cases in which some critical event acts with unexpected force upon the course of the whole have their existence mostly in the colouring with which every one depicts his lost battle.

We can only here appeal to the decision of unprejudiced men of experience, who will, we are sure, assent to what we have said, and answer for us to such of our readers as do not know War from their own experience. To develop the necessity of this course from the nature of the thing would lead us too far into the province of tactics, to which this branch of the subject belongs; we are here only concerned with its results.

If we say that the defeated General foresees the unfavourable result usually some time before he makes up his mind to give up the battle, we admit that there are also instances to the contrary, because otherwise we should maintain a proposition contradictory in itself. If at the moment of each decisive tendency of a battle it should be considered as lost, then also no further forces should be used to give it a turn, and consequently this decisive tendency could not precede the retreat by any length of time. Certainly there are instances of battles which after having taken a decided turn to one side have still ended in favour of the other; but they are rare, not usual; these exceptional cases, however, are reckoned upon by every General against whom fortune declares itself, and he must reckon upon them as long as there remains a possibility of a turn of fortune. He hopes by stronger efforts, by raising the remaining moral forces, by surpassing himself, or also by some fortunate chance that the next moment will bring a change, and pursues this as far as his courage and his judgment can agree. We shall have something more to say on this subject, but before that we must show what are the signs of the scales turning.

The result of the whole combat consists in the sum total of the results of all partial combats; but these results of separate combats are settled by different considerations.

First by the pure moral power in the mind of the leading officers. If a General of Division has seen his battalions forced to succumb, it will have an influence on his demeanour and his reports, and these again will have an influence on the measures of the Commander-in-Chief; therefore even those unsuccessful partial combats which to all appearance are retrieved, are not lost in their results, and the impressions from them sum themselves up in the mind of the Commander without much trouble, and even against his will.

Secondly, by the quicker melting away of our troops, which can be easily estimated in the slow and relatively[40] little tumultuary course of our battles.

Thirdly, by lost ground.

All these things serve for the eye of the General as a compass to tell the course of the battle in which he is embarked. If whole batteries have been lost and none of the enemy's taken; if battalions have been overthrown by the enemy's cavalry, whilst those of the enemy everywhere present impenetrable masses; if the line of fire from his order of battle wavers involuntarily from one point to another; if fruitless efforts have been made to gain certain points, and the assaulting battalions each, time been scattered by well-directed volleys of grape and case; – if our artillery begins to reply feebly to that of the enemy – if the battalions under fire diminish unusually, fast, because with the wounded crowds of unwounded men go to the rear; – if single Divisions have been cut off and made prisoners through the disruption of the plan of the battle; – if the line of retreat begins to be endangered: the Commander may tell very well in which direction he is going with his battle. The longer this direction continues, the more decided it becomes, so much the more difficult will be the turning, so much the nearer the moment when he must give up the battle. We shall now make some observations on this moment.

We have already said more than once that the final decision is ruled mostly by the relative number of the fresh reserves remaining at the last; that Commander who sees his adversary is decidedly superior to him in this respect makes up his mind to retreat. It is the characteristic of modern battles that all mischances and losses which take place in the course of the same can be retrieved by fresh forces, because

---

40   Relatively, that is say to the shock of former days.

the arrangement of the modern order of battle, and the way in which troops are brought into action, allow of their use almost generally, and in each position. So long, therefore, as that Commander against whom the issue seems to declare itself still retains a superiority in reserve force, he will not give up the day. But from the moment that his reserves begin to become weaker than his enemy's, the decision may be regarded as settled, and what he now does depends partly on special circumstances, partly on the degree of courage and perseverance which he personally possesses, and which may degenerate into foolish obstinacy. How a Commander can attain to the power of estimating correctly the still remaining reserves on both sides is an affair of skilful practical genius, which does not in any way belong to this place; we keep ourselves to the result as it forms itself in his mind. But this conclusion is still not the moment of decision properly, for a motive which only arises gradually does not answer to that, but is only a general motive towards resolution, and the resolution itself requires still some special immediate causes. Of these there are two chief ones which constantly recur, that is, the danger of retreat, and the arrival of night.

If the retreat with every new step which the battle takes in its course becomes constantly in greater danger, and if the reserves are so much diminished that they are no longer adequate to get breathing room, then there is nothing left but to submit to fate, and by a well-conducted retreat to save what, by a longer delay ending in flight and disaster, would be lost.

But night as a rule puts an end to all battles, because a night combat holds out no hope of advantage except under particular circumstances; and as night is better suited for a retreat than the day, so, therefore, the Commander who must look at the retreat as a thing inevitable, or as most probable, will prefer to make use of the night for his purpose.

That there are, besides the above two usual and chief causes, yet many others also, which are less or more individual and not to be overlooked, is a matter of course; for the more a battle tends towards a complete upset of equilibrium the more sensible is the influence of each partial result in hastening the turn. Thus the loss of a battery, a successful charge of a couple of regiments of cavalry, may call into life the resolution to retreat already ripening.

As a conclusion to this subject, we must dwell for a moment on the point at which the courage of the Commander engages in a sort of conflict with his reason.

If, on the one hand the overbearing pride of a victorious conqueror, if the inflexible will of a naturally obstinate spirit, if the strenuous resistance of noble feelings will not yield the battlefield, where they must leave their honour, yet on the other hand, reason counsels not to give up everything, not to risk the last upon the game, but to retain as much over as is necessary for an orderly retreat. However highly we must esteem courage and firmness in War, and however little prospect there is of victory to him who cannot resolve to seek it by the exertion of all his power, still there is a point beyond which perseverance can only be termed desperate folly, and therefore can meet with no approbation from any critic. In the most celebrated of all battles, that of Belle-Alliance, Buonaparte used his last reserve in an effort to retrieve a battle which was past being retrieved. He spent his last farthing, and then, as a beggar, abandoned both the battle-field and his crown.

CHAPTER TEN
Effects of Victory

ACCORDING TO THE point from which our view is taken, we may feel as much astonished at the extraordinary results of some great battles as at the want of results in others. We shall dwell for a moment on the nature of the effect of a great victory.

Three things may easily be distinguished here: the effect upon the instrument itself, that is, upon the Generals and their Armies; the effect upon the States interested in the War; and the particular result of these effects as manifested in the subsequent course of the campaign.

If we only think of the trifling difference which there usually is between victor and vanquished in killed, wounded, prisoners, and artillery lost on the field of battle itself, the consequences which are developed out of this insignificant point seem often quite incomprehensible, and yet, usually, everything only happens quite naturally.

We have already said in the seventh chapter that the magnitude of a victory increases not merely in the same measure as the vanquished forces increase in number, but in a higher ratio. The moral effects resulting from the issue of a great battle are greater on the side of the conquered than on that of the conqueror: they lead to greater losses in physical force, which then in turn react on the moral element, and so they go on mutually supporting and intensifying each other. On this moral effect we must therefore lay special weight. It takes an opposite direction on the one side from that on the other; as it undermines the energies of the conquered so it elevates the powers and energy of the conqueror. But its chief effect is upon the vanquished, because here it is the direct cause of fresh losses, and besides it is homogeneous in nature with danger, with the fatigues, the hardships, and generally with all those embarrassing circumstances by which War is surrounded, therefore enters into league with them and increases by their help, whilst with the conqueror all these things are like weights which give a higher swing to his courage. It is therefore found, that the vanquished sinks much further below the original line of equilibrium than the conqueror raises himself above it; on this account, if we speak of the effects of victory we allude more particularly to those which manifest themselves in the army. If this effect is more powerful in an important combat than in a smaller one, so again it is much more powerful in a great battle than in a minor one. The great battle takes place for the sake of itself, for the sake of the victory which it is to give, and which is sought for with the utmost effort. Here on this spot, in this very hour, to conquer the enemy is the purpose in which the plan of the War with all its threads converges, in which all distant hopes, all dim glimmerings of the future meet, fate steps in before us to give an answer to the bold question. – This is the state of mental tension not only of the Commander but of his whole Army down to the lowest waggon-driver, no doubt in decreasing strength but also in decreasing importance.

According to the nature of the thing, a great battle has never at any time been an unprepared, unexpected, blind routine service, but a grand act, which, partly of itself and partly from the aim of the Commander, stands out from amongst the mass of ordinary efforts, sufficiently to raise the tension of all minds to a higher degree. But the higher this tension with respect to the issue, the more powerful must be the effect of that issue.

Again, the moral effect of victory in our battles is greater than it was in the earlier ones of modern military history. If the former are as we have depicted them, a real struggle of forces to the utmost, then the sum total of all these forces, of the physical as well as the moral, must decide more than certain special dispositions or mere chance.

A single fault committed may be repaired next time; from good fortune and chance we can hope for more favour on another occasion; but the sum total of moral and physical powers cannot be so quickly altered, and, therefore, what the award of a victory has decided appears of much greater importance for all futurity. Very probably, of all concerned in battles, whether in or out of the Army, very few have given a thought to this difference, but the course of the battle itself impresses on the minds of all present in it such a conviction, and the relation of this course in public documents, however much it may be coloured by twisting particular circumstances, shows also, more or less, to the world at large that the causes were more of a general than of a particular nature.

He who has not been present at the loss of a great battle will have difficulty in forming for himself a living or quite true idea of it, and the abstract notions of this or that small untoward affair will never come up to the perfect conception of a lost battle. Let us stop a moment at the picture.

The first thing which overpowers the imagination – and we may indeed say, also the understanding – is the diminution of the masses; then the loss of ground, which takes place always, more or less, and, therefore, on the side of the assailant also, if he is not fortunate; then the rupture of the original formation, the jumbling together of troops, the risks of retreat, which, with few exceptions may always be seen sometimes in a less sometimes in a greater degree; next the retreat, the most part of which commences at night, or, at least, goes on throughout the night. On this first march we must at once leave behind, a number of men completely worn out and scattered about, often just the bravest, who have been foremost in the fight who held out the longest: the feeling of being conquered, which only seized the superior officers on the battlefield, now spreads through all ranks, even down to the common soldiers, aggravated by the horrible idea of being obliged to leave in the enemy's hands so many brave comrades, who but a moment since were of such value to us in the battle, and aggravated by a rising distrust of the chief, to whom, more or less, every subordinate attributes as a fault the fruitless efforts he has made; and this feeling of being conquered is no ideal picture over which one might become master; it is an evident truth that the enemy is superior to us; a truth of which the causes might have been so latent before that they were not to be discovered, but which, in the issue, comes out clear and palpable, or which was also, perhaps, before suspected, but which in the want of any certainty, we had to oppose by the hope of chance, reliance on good fortune, Providence or a bold attitude. Now, all this has proved insufficient, and the bitter truth meets us harsh and imperious.

All these feelings are widely different from a panic, which in an army fortified by military virtue never, and in any other, only exceptionally, follows the loss of a battle. They must arise even in the best of Armies, and although long habituation to War and victory together with great confidence in a Commander may modify them a little here and there, they are never entirely wanting in the first moment. They are not the pure consequences of lost trophies; these are usually lost at a later period, and the loss of them does not become generally known so quickly; they will therefore not fail to appear even when the scale turns in the slowest and most gradual manner, and they constitute that effect of a victory upon which we can always count in every case.

We have already said that the number of trophies intensifies this effect.

It is evident that an Army in this condition, looked at as an instrument, is weakened! How can we expect that when reduced to such a degree that, as we said before, it finds new enemies in all the ordinary difficulties of making War, it will be able to recover by fresh efforts what has been lost! Before the battle there was a real or assumed equilibrium between the two sides; this is lost, and, therefore, some external assistance is requisite to restore it; every new effort without such external support can only lead to fresh losses.

Thus, therefore, the most moderate victory of the chief Army must tend to cause a constant sinking of the scale on the opponent's side, until new external circumstances bring about a change. If these are not near, if the conqueror is an eager opponent, who, thirsting for glory, pursues great aims, then a first-rate Commander, and in the beaten Army a true military spirit, hardened by many campaigns are required, in order to stop the swollen stream of prosperity from bursting all bounds, and to moderate its course by small but reiterated acts of resistance, until the force of victory has spent itself at the goal of its career.

And now as to the effect of defeat beyond the Army, upon the Nation and Government! It is the sudden collapse of hopes stretched to the utmost, the downfall of all self-reliance. In place of these extinct forces, fear, with its destructive properties of expansion, rushes into the vacuum left, and completes the prostration. It is a real shock upon the nerves, which one of the two athletes receives from the electric spark of victory. And that effect, however different in its degrees, is never completely wanting. Instead of every one hastening with a spirit of determination to aid in repairing the disaster, every one fears that his efforts will only be in vain, and stops, hesitating with himself, when he should rush forward; or in despondency he lets his arm drop, leaving everything to fate.

The consequence which this effect of victory brings forth in the course of the War itself depend in part on the character and talent of the victorious General, but more on the circumstances from which the victory proceeds, and to which it leads. Without boldness and an enterprising spirit on the part of the leader, the most brilliant victory will lead to no great success, and its force exhausts itself all the sooner on circumstances, if these offer a strong and stubborn opposition to it. How very differently from Daun, Frederick the Great would have used the victory at Kollin; and what different consequences France, in place of Prussia, might have given a battle of Leuthen!

The conditions which allow us to expect great results from a great victory we shall learn when we come to the subjects with which they are connected; then it will be possible to explain the disproportion which appears at first sight between the magnitude of a victory and its results, and which is only too readily attributed to a want of energy on the part of the conqueror. Here, where we have to do with the great battle in itself, we shall merely say that the effects now depicted never fail to attend a victory, that they mount up with the intensive strength of the victory – mount up more the more the whole strength of the Army has been concentrated in it, the more the whole military power of the Nation is contained in that Army, and the State in that military power.

But then the question may be asked, Can theory accept this effect of victory as absolutely necessary? – must it not rather endeavour to find out counteracting means capable of neutralising these effects? It seems quite natural to answer this question in the affirmative; but heaven defend us from taking that wrong course of most theories, out of which is begotten a mutually devouring Pro et Contra.

Certainly that effect is perfectly necessary, for it has its foundation in the nature of things, and it exists, even if we find means to struggle against it; just as the motion of a cannon ball is always in the direction of the terrestrial, although when fired from east to west part of the general velocity is destroyed by this opposite motion.

All War supposes human weakness, and against that it is directed.

Therefore, if hereafter in another place we examine what is to be done after the loss of a great battle, if we bring under review the resources which still remain, even in the most desperate cases, if we should express a belief in the possibility of retrieving all, even in such a case; it must not be supposed we mean thereby that the effects of such a defeat can by degrees be completely wiped out, for the forces and means used to repair the disaster might have been applied to the realisation of some positive object; and this applies both to the moral and physical forces.

Another question is, whether, through the loss of a great battle, forces are not perhaps roused into existence, which otherwise would never have come to life. This case is certainly conceivable, and it is what has actually occurred with many Nations. But to produce this intensified reaction is beyond the province of military art, which can only take account of it where it might be assumed as a possibility.

If there are cases in which the fruits of a victory appear rather of a destructive nature in consequence of the reaction of the forces which it had the effect of rousing into activity – cases which certainly are very exceptional – then it must the more surely be granted, that there is a difference in the effects which one and the same victory may produce according to the character of the people or state, which has been conquered.

CHAPTER ELEVEN

The Use of the Battle

WHATEVER FORM the conduct of War may take in particular cases, and whatever we may have to admit in the sequel as necessary respecting it: we have only to refer to the conception of War to be convinced of what follows:

1. The destruction of the enemy's military force, is the leading principle of War, and for the whole chapter of positive action the direct way to the object.

2. This destruction of the enemy's force, must be principally effected by means of battle.

3. Only great and general battles can produce great results.

4. The results will be greatest when combats unite themselves in one great battle.

5. It is only in a great battle that the General-in-Chief commands in person, and it is in the nature of things, that he should place more confidence in himself than in his subordinates.

From these truths a double law follows, the parts of which mutually support each other; namely, that the destruction of the enemy's military force is to be sought for principally by great battles, and their results; and that the chief object of great battles must be the destruction of the enemy's military force.

No doubt the annihilation-principle is to be found more or less in other means – granted there are instances in which through favourable circumstances in a minor combat, the destruction of the enemy's forces has been disproportionately great (Maxen), and on the other hand in a battle, the taking or holding a single post may be predominant in importance as an object – but as a general rule it remains a paramount truth, that battles are only fought with a view to the destruction of the enemy's Army, and that this destruction can only be effected by their means.

The battle may therefore be regarded as War concentrated, as the centre of effort of the whole War or campaign. As the sun's rays unite in the focus of the concave mirror in a perfect image, and in the fulness of their heat; to the forces and circumstances of War, unite in a focus in the great battle for one concentrated utmost effort.

The very assemblage of forces in one great whole, which takes place more or less in all Wars, indicates an intention to strike a decisive blow with this whole, either voluntarily as assailant, or constrained by the opposite party as defender. When this great blow does not follow, then some modifying, and retarding motives have attached themselves to the original motive of hostility, and have weakened, altered or completely checked the movement. But also, even in this condition of mutual inaction which has been the key-note in so many Wars, the idea of a possible battle serves always for both parties as a point of direction, a distant focus in the construction of their plans. The more War is War in earnest, the more it is a venting of animosity and hostility, a mutual struggle to overpower, so much the more will all activities join deadly contest, and also the more prominent in importance becomes the battle.

In general, when the object aimed at is of a great and positive nature, one therefore in which the interests of the enemy are deeply concerned, the battle offers itself as the most natural means; it is, therefore, also the best as we shall show more plainly hereafter: and, as a rule, when it is evaded from aversion to the great decision, punishment follows.

The positive object belong to the offensive, and therefore the battle is also more particularly his means. But without examining the conception of offensive and defensive more minutely here, we must still observe that, even for the defender in most cases, there is no other effectual means with which to meet the exigencies of his situation, to solve the problem presented to him.

The battle is the bloodiest way of solution. True, it is not merely reciprocal slaughter, and its effect is more a killing of the enemy's courage than of the enemy's soldiers, as we shall see more plainly in the next chapter – but still blood is always its price, and slaughter its character as well as name;[41] from this the humanity in the General's mind recoils with horror.

But the soul of the man trembles still more at the thought of the decision to be given with one single blow. *In one point* of space and time all action is here pressed together, and at such a moment there is stirred up

41 "Schlacht", from schlachten = to slaughter.

within us a dim feeling as if in this narrow space all our forces could not develop themselves and come into activity, as if we had already gained much by mere time, although this time owes us nothing at all. This is all mere illusion, but even as illusion it is something, and the same weakness which seizes upon the man in every other momentous decision may well be felt more powerfully by the General, when he must stake interests of such enormous weight upon one venture.

Thus, then, Statesmen and Generals have at all times endeavoured to avoid the decisive battle, seeking either to attain their aim without it, or dropping that aim unperceived. Writers on history and theory have then busied themselves to discover in some other feature in these campaigns not only an equivalent for the decision by battle which has been avoided, but even a higher art. In this way, in the present age, it came very near to this, that a battle in the economy of War was looked upon as an evil, rendered necessary through some error committed, a morbid paroxysm to which a regular prudent system of War would never lead: only those Generals were to deserve laurels who knew how to carry on War without spilling blood, and the theory of War – a real business for Brahmins – was to be specially directed to teaching this.

Contemporary history has destroyed this illusion,[42] but no one can guarantee that it will not sooner or later reproduce itself, and lead those at the head of affairs to perversities which please man's weakness, and therefore have the greater affinity for his nature. Perhaps, by-and-by, Buonaparte's campaigns and battles will be looked upon as mere acts of barbarism and stupidity, and we shall once more turn with satisfaction and confidence to the dress-sword of obsolete and musty institutions and forms. If theory gives a caution against this, then it renders a real service to those who listen to its warning voice. *May we succeed in lending a hand to those who in our dear native land are called upon to speak with authority on these matters, that we may be their guide into this field of inquiry, and excite them to make a candid examination of the subject.*[43]

Not only the conception of War but experience also leads us to look for a great decision only in a great battle. From time immemorial, only great victories have led to great successes on the offensive side in the absolute form, on the defensive side in a manner more or less satisfactory. Even Buonaparte would not have seen the day of Ulm, unique in its kind, if he had shrunk from shedding blood; it is rather to be regarded as only a second crop from the victorious events in his preceding

42 On the Continent only, it still preserves full vitality in the minds of British politicians and pressmen. – *Editor.*
43 This prayer was abundantly granted – vide the German victories of 1870. – *Editor.*

campaigns. It is not only bold, rash, and presumptuous Generals who have sought to complete their work by the great venture of a decisive battle, but also fortunate ones as well; and we may rest satisfied with the answer which they have thus given to this vast question.

Let us not hear of Generals who conquer without bloodshed. If a bloody slaughter is a horrible sight, then that is a ground for paying more respect to War, but not for making the sword we wear blunter and blunter by degrees from feelings of humanity, until some one steps in with one that is sharp and lops off the arm from our body.

We look upon a great battle as a principal decision, but certainly not as the only one necessary for a War or a campaign. Instances of a great battle deciding a whole campaign, have been frequent only in modern times, those which have decided a whole War, belong to the class of rare exceptions.

A decision which is brought about by a great battle depends naturally not on the battle itself, that is on the mass of combatants engaged in it, and on the intensity of the victory, but also on a number of other relations between the military forces opposed to each other, and between the States to which these forces belong. But at the same time that the principal mass of the force available is brought to the great duel, a great decision is also brought on, the extent of which may perhaps be foreseen in many respects, though not in all, and which although not the only one, still is the *first* decision, and as such, has an influence on those which succeed. Therefore a deliberately planned great battle, according to its relations, is more or less, but always in some degree, to be regarded as the leading means and central point of the whole system. The more a General takes the field in the true spirit of War as well as of every contest, with the feeling and the idea, that is the conviction, that he must and will conquer, the more he will strive to throw every weight into the scale in the first battle, hope and strive to win everything by it. Buonaparte hardly ever entered upon a War without thinking of conquering his enemy at once in the first battle,[44] and Frederick the Great, although in a more limited sphere, and with interests of less magnitude at stake, thought the same when, at the head of a small Army, he sought to disengage his rear from the Russians or the Federal Imperial Army.

The decision which is given by the great battle, depends, we have said, partly on the battle itself, that is on the number of troops engaged, and partly on the magnitude of the success.

44   This was Moltke's essential idea in his preparations for the War of 1870. See his secret memorandum issued to G.O.C.s on May 7. 1870, pointing to a battle on the Upper Saar as his primary purpose. – *Editor.*

How the General may increase its importance in respect to the first point is evident in itself and we shall merely observe that according to the importance of the great battle, the number of cases which are decided along with it increases, and that therefore Generals who, confident in themselves have been lovers of great decisions, have always managed to make use of the greater part of their troops in it without neglecting on that account essential points elsewhere.

As regards the consequences or speaking more correctly the effectiveness of a victory, that depends chiefly on four points:

1. On the tactical form adopted as the order of battle.
2. On the nature of the country.
3. On the relative proportions of the three arms.
4. On the relative strength of the two Armies.

A battle with parallel fronts and without any action against a flank will seldom yield as great success as one in which the defeated Army has been turned, or compelled to change front more or less. In a broken or hilly country the successes are likewise smaller, because the power of the blow is everywhere less.

If the cavalry of the vanquished is equal or superior to that of the victor, then the effects of the pursuit are diminished, and by that great part of the results of victory are lost.

Finally it is easy to understand that if superior numbers are on the side of the conqueror, and he uses his advantage in that respect to turn the flank of his adversary, or compel him to change front, greater results will follow than if the conqueror had been weaker in numbers than the vanquished. The battle of Leuthen may certainly be quoted as a practical refutation of this principle, but we beg permission for once to say what we otherwise do not like, *no rule without an exception.*

In all these ways, therefore, the Commander has the means of giving his battle a decisive character; certainly he thus exposes himself to an increased amount of danger, but his whole line of action is subject to that dynamic law of the moral world.

There is then nothing in War which can be put in comparison with the great battle in point of importance, *and the acme of strategic ability is displayed in the provision of means for this great event, in the skilful determination of place and time, and direction of troops, and its the good use made of success.*

But it does not follow from the importance of these things that they must be of a very complicated and recondite nature; all is here rather simple, the art of combination by no means great; but there is great need of quickness in judging of circumstances, need of energy, steady resolution, a youthful spirit of enterprise – heroic qualities, to which we shall often have to refer. There is, therefore, but little wanted here of that which can be taught by books and there is much that, if it can be taught at all, must come to the General through some other medium than printer's type.

The impulse towards a great battle, the voluntary, sure progress to it, must proceed from a feeling of innate power and a clear sense of the necessity; in other words, it must proceed from inborn courage and from perceptions sharpened by contact with the higher interests of life.

Great examples are the best teachers, but it is certainly a misfortune if a cloud of theoretical prejudices comes between, for even the sunbeam is refracted and tinted by the clouds. To destroy such prejudices, which many a time rise and spread themselves like a miasma, is an imperative duty of theory, for the misbegotten offspring of human reason can also be in turn destroyed by pure reason.

CHAPTER TWELVE
Strategic Means of Utilising Victory

THE MORE DIFFICULT part, viz., that of perfectly preparing the victory, is a silent service of which the merit belongs to Strategy and yet for which it is hardly sufficiently commended. It appears brilliant and full of renown by turning to good account a victory gained.

What may be the special object of a battle, how it is connected with the whole system of a War, whither the career of victory may lead according to the nature of circumstances, where its culminating-point lies – all these are things which we shall not enter upon until hereafter. But under any conceivable circumstances the fact holds good, that without a pursuit no victory can have a great effect, and that, however short the career of victory may be, it must always lead beyond the first steps in pursuit; and in order to avoid the frequent repetition of this, we shall now dwell for a moment on this necessary supplement of victory in general.

The pursuit of a beaten Army commences at the moment that Army, giving up the combat, leaves its position; all previous movements in one direction and another belong not to that but to the progress of the battle itself. Usually victory at the moment here described, even if it is certain, is still as yet small and weak in its proportions, and would not rank as an event of any great positive advantage if not completed by a pursuit on the first day. Then it is mostly, as we have before said, that the trophies which give substance to the victory begin to be gathered up. Of this pursuit we shall speak in the next place.

Usually both sides come into action with their physical powers considerably deteriorated, for the movements immediately preceding have generally the character of very urgent circumstances. The efforts which the forging out of a great combat costs, complete the exhaustion; from this it follows that the victorious party is very little less disorganised and out of his original formation than the vanquished, and therefore requires time to reform, to collect stragglers, and issue fresh ammunition to those who are without. All these things place the conqueror himself in the state of crisis of which we have already spoken. If now the defeated force is only a detached portion of the enemy's Army, or if it has otherwise to expect a considerable reinforcement, then the conqueror may easily run into the obvious danger of having to pay dear for his victory, and this consideration, in such a case, very soon puts an end to pursuit, or at least restricts it materially. Even when a strong accession of force by the enemy is not to be feared, the conqueror finds in the above circumstances a powerful check to the vivacity of his pursuit. There is no reason to fear that the victory will be snatched away, but adverse combats are still possible, and may diminish the advantages which up to the present have been gained. Moreover, at this moment the whole weight of all that is sensuous in an Army, its wants and weaknesses, are dependent on the will of the Commander. All the thousands under his command require rest and refreshment, and long to see a stop put to toil and danger for the present; only a few, forming an exception, can see and feel beyond the present moment, it is only amongst this little number that there is sufficient mental vigour to think, after what is absolutely necessary at the moment has been done, upon those results which at such a moment only appear to the rest as mere embellishments of victory – as a luxury of triumph. But all these thousands have a voice in the council of the General, for through the various steps of the military hierarchy these interests of the sensuous creature have their sure conductor into the heart of the Commander. He himself, through mental and bodily fatigue, is more or less weakened in his natural activity, and thus it happens then that, mostly from these causes, purely incidental to human nature, less is done than might have been done, and that generally what is done is to be ascribed entirely to the *thirst for glory*, the energy, indeed also the *hard-heartedness* of the General-in-Chief. It is only thus we can explain the hesitating manner in which many Generals follow up a victory which superior numbers have given them. The first pursuit of the enemy we limit in general to the extent of the first day, including the night following the victory. At the end of that period the necessity of rest ourselves prescribes a halt in any case.

This first pursuit has different natural degrees.

The first is, if cavalry alone are employed; in that case it amounts usually more to alarming and watching than to pressing the enemy in reality, because the smallest obstacle of ground is generally sufficient to check the pursuit. Useful as cavalry may be against single bodies of broken demoralised troops, still when opposed to the bulk of the beaten Army it becomes again only the auxiliary arm, because the troops in retreat can employ fresh reserves to cover the movement, and, therefore, at the next trifling obstacle of ground, by combining all arms they can make a stand with success. The only exception to this is in the case of an army in actual flight in a complete state of dissolution.

The second degree is, if the pursuit is made by a strong advance-guard composed of all arms, the greater part consisting naturally of cavalry. Such a pursuit generally drives the enemy as far as the nearest strong position for his rear-guard, or the next position affording space for his Army. Neither can usually be found at once, and, therefore, the pursuit can be carried further; generally, however, it does not extend beyond the distance of one or at most a couple of leagues, because otherwise the advance-guard would not feel itself sufficiently supported. The third and most vigorous degree is when the victorious Army itself continues to advance as far as its physical powers can endure. In this case the beaten Army will generally quit such ordinary positions as a country usually offers on the mere show of an attack, or of an intention to turn its flank; and the rear-guard will be still less likely to engage in an obstinate resistance.

In all three cases the night, if it sets in before the conclusion of the whole act, usually puts an end to it, and the few instances in which this has not taken place, and the pursuit has been continued throughout the night, must be regarded as pursuits in an exceptionally vigorous form.

If we reflect that in fighting by night everything must be, more or less, abandoned to chance, and that at the conclusion of a battle the regular cohesion and order of things in an army must inevitably be disturbed, we may easily conceive the reluctance of both Generals to carrying on their business under such disadvantageous conditions. If a complete dissolution of the vanquished Army, or a rare superiority of the victorious Army in military virtue does not ensure success, everything would in a manner be given up to fate, which can never be for the interest of any one, even of the most fool-hardy General. As a rule, therefore, night puts an end to pursuit, even when the battle has only been decided shortly before darkness sets in. This allows the conquered either time for rest and to rally immediately, or, if he retreats during the night it gives him a march in advance. After this break the conquered is decidedly in a better condition; much of that which had been thrown into confusion has been brought again into order, ammunition has been renewed, the whole has been put into a fresh formation. Whatever further encounter now takes place with the enemy is a new battle not a continuation of the old, and although it may be far from promising absolute success, still it is a fresh combat, and not merely a gathering up of the debris by the victor.

When, therefore, the conqueror can continue the pursuit itself throughout the night, if only with a strong advance-guard composed of all arms of the service, the effect of the victory is immensely increased, of this the battles of Leuthen and La Belle Alliance[45] are examples.

The whole action of this pursuit is mainly tactical, and we only dwell upon it here in order to make plain the difference which through it may be produced in the effect of a victory.

This first pursuit, as far as the nearest stopping-point, belongs as a right to every conqueror, and is hardly in any way connected with his further plans and combinations. These may considerably diminish the positive results of a victory gained with the main body of the Army, but they cannot make this first use of it impossible; at least cases of that kind, if conceivable at all, must be so uncommon that they should have no appreciable influence on theory. And here certainly we must say that the example afforded by modern Wars opens up quite a new field for energy. In preceding Wars, resting on a narrower basis, and altogether more circumscribed in their scope, there were many unnecessary conventional restrictions in various ways, but particularly in this point. *the conception, honour of victory* seemed to Generals so much by far the chief thing that they thought the less of the complete destruction of the enemy's military force, as in point of fact that destruction of force appeared to them only as one of the many means in War, not by any means as the principal, much less as the only means; so that they the more readily put the sword in its sheath the moment the enemy had lowered his. Nothing seemed more natural to them than to stop the combat as soon as the decision was obtained, and to regard all further carnage as unnecessary cruelty. Even if this false philosophy did not determine their resolutions entirely, still it was a point of view by which representations of the exhaustion of all powers, and physical impossibility of continuing the struggle, obtained readier evidence and greater weight. Certainly the sparing one's own instrument of victory is a vital question if we only possess this one, and foresee that soon the time may arrive when it will not be sufficient for all that remains to be done, for every continuation of the offensive must lead ultimately to complete exhaustion. But this calculation was still so far false, as the further loss of forces by a continuance of the pursuit could bear no

45 Waterloo.

proportion to that which the enemy must suffer. That view, therefore, again could only exist because the military forces were not considered the vital factor. And so we find that in former Wars real heroes only – such as Charles XII., Marlborough, Eugene, Frederick the Great – added a vigorous pursuit to their victories when they were decisive enough, and that other Generals usually contented themselves with the possession of the field of battle. In modern times the greater energy infused into the conduct of Wars through the greater importance of the circumstances from which they have proceeded has thrown down these conventional barriers; the pursuit has become an all-important business for the conqueror; trophies have on that account multiplied in extent, and if there are cases also in modern Warfare in which this has not been the case, still they belong to the list of exceptions, and are to be accounted for by peculiar circumstances.

At Gorschen[46] and Bautzen nothing but the superiority of the allied cavalry prevented a complete rout, at Gross Beeren and Dennewitz the ill-will of Bernadotte, the Crown Prince of Sweden; at Laon the enfeebled personal condition of Bluecher, who was then seventy years old and at the moment confined to a dark room owing to an injury to his eyes.

But Borodino is also an illustration to the point here, and we cannot resist saying a few more words about it, partly because we do not consider the circumstances are explained simply by attaching blame to Buonaparte, partly because it might appear as if this, and with it a great number of similar cases, belonged to that class which we have designated as so extremely rare, cases in which the general relations seize and fetter the General at the very beginning of the battle. French authors in particular, and great admirers of Buonaparte (Vaudancourt, Chambray, Se'gur), have blamed him decidedly because he did not drive the Russian Army completely off the field, and use his last reserves to scatter it, because then what was only a lost battle would have been a complete rout. We should be obliged to diverge too far to describe circumstantially the mutual situation of the two Armies; but this much is evident, that when Buonaparte passed the Niemen with his Army the same corps which afterwards fought at Borodino numbered 300,000 men, of whom now only 120,000 remained, he might therefore well be apprehensive that he would not have enough left to march upon Moscow, the point on which everything seemed to depend. The victory which

---

46   Gorschen or Lutzen, May 2, 1813; Gross Beeren and Dennewitz, August 22, 1813; Bautzen. May 22, 1913; Laon, March 10 1813.

he had just gained gave him nearly a certainty of taking that capital, for that the Russians would be in a condition to fight a second battle within eight days seemed in the highest degree improbable; and in Moscow he hoped to find peace. No doubt the complete dispersion of the Russian Army would have made this peace much more certain; but still the first consideration was to get to Moscow, that is, to get there with a force with which he should appear dictator over the capital, and through that over the Empire and the Government. The force which he brought with him to Moscow was no longer sufficient for that, as shown in the sequel, but it would have been still less so if, in scattering the Russian Army, he had scattered his own at the same time. Buonaparte was thoroughly alive to all this, and in our eyes he stands completely justified. But on that account this case is still not to be reckoned amongst those in which, through the general relations, the General is interdicted from following up his victory, for there never was in his case any question of mere pursuit. The victory was decided at four o'clock in the afternoon, but the Russians still occupied the greater part of the field of battle; they were not yet disposed to give up the ground, and if the attack had been renewed, they would still have offered a most determined resistance, which would have undoubtedly ended in their complete defeat, but would have cost the conqueror much further bloodshed. We must therefore reckon the Battle of Borodino as amongst battles, like Bautzen, left unfinished. At Bautzen the vanquished preferred to quit the field sooner; at Borodino the conqueror preferred to content himself with a half victory, not because the decision appeared doubtful, but because he was not rich enough to pay for the whole.

Returning now to our subject, the deduction from our reflections in relation to the first stage of pursuit is, that the energy thrown into it chiefly determines the value of the victory; that this pursuit is a second act of the victory, in many cases more important also than the first, and that strategy, whilst here approaching tactics to receive from it the harvest of success, exercises the first act of her authority by demanding this completion of the victory.

But further, the effects of victory are very seldom found to stop with this first pursuit; now first begins the real career to which victory lent velocity. This course is conditioned as we have already said, by other relations of which it is not yet time to speak. But we must here mention, what there is of a general character in the pursuit in order to avoid repetition when the subject occurs again.

In the further stages of pursuit, again, we can distinguish three degrees: the simple pursuit, a hard pursuit, and a parallel march to intercept.

The simple *following* or *pursuing* causes the enemy to continue his retreat, until he thinks he can risk another battle. It will therefore in its effect suffice to exhaust the advantages gained, and besides that, all that the enemy cannot carry with him, sick, wounded, and disabled from fatigue, quantities of baggage, and carriages of all kinds, will fall into our hands, but this mere following does not tend to heighten the disorder in the enemy's Army, an effect which is produced by the two following causes.

If, for instance, instead of contenting ourselves with taking up every day the camp the enemy has just vacated, occupying just as much of the country as he chooses to abandon, we make our arrangements so as every day to encroach further, and accordingly with our advance-guard organised for the purpose, attack his rear-guard every time it attempts to halt, then such a course will hasten his retreat, and consequently tend to increase his disorganisation. – This it will principally effect by the character of continuous flight, which his retreat will thus assume. Nothing has such a depressing influence on the soldier, as the sound of the enemy's cannon afresh at the moment when, after a forced march he seeks some rest; if this excitement is continued from day to day for some time, it may lead to a complete rout. There lies in it a constant admission of being obliged to obey the law of the enemy, and of being unfit for any resistance, and the consciousness of this cannot do otherwise than weaken the moral of an Army in a high degree. The effect of pressing the enemy in this way attains a maximum when it drives the enemy to make night marches. If the conqueror scares away the discomfited opponent at sunset from a camp which has just been taken up either for the main body of the Army, or for the rear-guard, the conquered must either make a night march, or alter his position in the night, retiring further away, which is much the same thing; the victorious party can on the other hand pass the night in quiet.

The arrangement of marches, and the choice of positions depend in this case also upon so many other things, especially on the supply of the Army, on strong natural obstacles in the country, on large towns, &c. &c., that it would be ridiculous pedantry to attempt to show by a geometrical analysis how the pursuer, being able to impose his laws on the retreating enemy, can compel him to march at night while he takes his rest. But nevertheless it is true and practicable that marches in pursuit may be so planned as to have this tendency, and that the efficacy of the pursuit is very much enchanced thereby. If this is seldom attended to in the execution, it is because such a procedure is more difficult for the pursuing Army, than a regular adherence to ordinary marches in the daytime. To start in good time in the morning, to encamp at mid-day, to occupy the rest of the day in providing for the ordinary wants of the Army, and to use the night for repose, is a much more convenient method than to regulate one's movements exactly according to those of the enemy, therefore to determine nothing till the last moment, to start on the march, sometimes in the morning, sometimes in the evening, to be always for several hours in the presence of the enemy, and exchanging cannon shots with him, and keeping up skirmishing fire, to plan manoeuvres to turn him, in short, to make the whole outlay of tactical means which such a course renders necessary. All that naturally bears with a heavy weight on the pursuing Army, and in War, where there are so many burdens to be borne, men are always inclined to strip off those which do not seem absolutely necessary. These observations are true, whether applied to a whole Army or as in the more usual case, to a strong advance-guard. For the reasons just mentioned, this second method of pursuit, this continued pressing of the enemy pursued is rather a rare occurrence; even Buonaparte in his Russian campaign, 1812, practised it but little, for the reasons here apparent, that the difficulties and hardships of this campaign, already threatened his Army with destruction before it could reach its object; on the other hand, the French in their other campaigns have distinguished themselves by their energy in this point also.

Lastly, the third and most effectual form of pursuit is, the parallel march to the immediate object of the retreat.

Every defeated Army will naturally have behind it, at a greater or less distance, some point, the attainment of which is the first purpose in view, whether it be that failing in this its further retreat might be compromised, as in the case of a defile, or that it is important for the point itself to reach it before the enemy, as in the case of a great city, magazines, &c., or, lastly, that the Army at this point will gain new powers of defence, such as a strong position, or junction with other corps.

Now if the conqueror directs his march on this point by a lateral road, it is evident how that may quicken the retreat of the beaten Army in a destructive manner, convert it into hurry, perhaps into flight.[47] The conquered has only three ways to counteract this: the first is to throw himself in front of the enemy, in order by an unexpected attack to gain that probability of success which is lost to him in general from his position; this plainly supposes an enterprising bold General, and an excellent Army, beaten but not utterly defeated; therefore, it can only be employed by a beaten Army in very few cases.

47 This point is exceptionally well treated by von Bernhardi in his "Cavalry in Future Wars." London: Murray, 1906.

The second way is hastening the retreat; but this is just what the conqueror wants, and it easily leads to immoderate efforts on the part of the troops, by which enormous losses are sustained, in stragglers, broken guns, and carriages of all kinds.

The third way is to make a detour, and get round the nearest point of interception, to march with more ease at a greater distance from the enemy, and thus to render the haste required less damaging. This last way is the worst of all, it generally turns out like a new debt contracted by an insolvent debtor, and leads to greater embarrassment. There are cases in which this course is advisable; others where there is nothing else left; also instances in which it has been successful; but upon the whole it is certainly true that its adoption is usually influenced less by a clear persuasion of its being the surest way of attaining the aim than by another inadmissible motive – this motive is the dread of encountering the enemy. Woe to the Commander who gives in to this! However much the moral of his Army may have deteriorated, and however well founded may be his apprehensions of being at a disadvantage in any conflict with the enemy, the evil will only be made worse by too anxiously avoiding every possible risk of collision. Buonaparte in 1813 would never have brought over the Rhine with him the 30,000 or 40,000 men who remained after the battle of Hanau,[48] if he had avoided that battle and tried to pass the Rhine at Mannheim or Coblenz. It is just by means of small combats carefully prepared and executed, and in which the defeated army being on the defensive, has always the assistance of the ground – it is just by these that the moral strength of the Army can first be resuscitated.

The beneficial effect of the smallest successes is incredible; but with most Generals the adoption of this plan implies great self-command. The other way, that of evading all encounter, appears at first so much easier, that there is a natural preference for its adoption. It is therefore usually just this system of evasion which best, promotes the view of the pursuer, and often ends with the complete downfall of the pursued; we must, however, recollect here that we are speaking of a whole Army, not of a single Division, which, having been cut off, is seeking to join the main Army by making a de'tour; in such a case circumstances are different, and success is not uncommon. But there is one condition requisite to the success of this race of two Corps for an object, which is that a Division of the pursuing army should follow by the same road

48 At Hanau (October 30, 1813), the Bavarians some 50,000 strong threw themselves across the line of Napoleon's retreat from Leipsic. By a masterly use of its artillery the French tore the Bavarians asunder and marched on over their bodies. – *Editor*.

which the pursued has taken, in order to pick up stragglers, and keep up the impression which the presence of the enemy never fails to make. Bluecher neglected this in his, in other respects unexceptionable, pursuit after La Belle Alliance.

Such marches tell upon the pursuer as well as the pursued, and they are not advisable if the enemy's Army rallies itself upon another considerable one; if it has a distinguished General at its head, and if its destruction is not already well prepared. But when this means can be adopted, it acts also like a great mechanical power. The losses of the beaten Army from sickness and fatigue are on such a disproportionate scale, the spirit of the Army is so weakened and lowered by the constant solicitude about impending ruin, that at last anything like a well organised stand is out of the question; every day thousands of prisoners fall into the enemy's hands without striking a blow. In such a season of complete good fortune, the conqueror need not hesitate about dividing his forces in order to draw into the vortex of destruction everything within reach of his Army, to cut off detachments, to take fortresses unprepared for defence, to occupy large towns, &c. &c. He may do anything until a new state of things arises, and the more he ventures in this way the longer will it be before that change will take place. There is no want of examples of brilliant results from grand decisive victories, and of great and vigorous pursuits in the wars of Buonaparte. We need only quote Jena 1806, Ratisbonne 1809, Leipsic 1813, and Belle- Alliance 1815.

CHAPTER THIRTEEN

Retreat After a Lost Battle

IN A LOST BATTLE the power of an Army is broken, the moral to a greater degree than the physical. A second battle unless fresh favourable circumstances come into play, would lead to a complete defeat, perhaps, to destruction. This is a military axiom. According to the usual course the retreat is continued up to that point where the equilibrium of forces is restored, either by reinforcements, or by the protection of strong fortresses, or by great defensive positions afforded by the country, or by a separation of the enemy's force. The magnitude of the losses sustained, the extent of the defeat, but still more the character of the enemy, will bring nearer or put off the instant of this equilibrium. How many instances may be found of a beaten Army rallied again at a short distance, without its circumstances having altered in any way since the battle. The cause of this may be traced to the moral weakness of the adversary, or to the preponderance gained in the battle not having been sufficient to make lasting impression.

To profit by this weakness or mistake of the enemy, not to yield one inch breadth more than the pressure of circumstances demands, but above all things, in order to keep up the moral forces to as advantageous a point as possible, a slow retreat, offering incessant resistance, and bold courageous counterstrokes, whenever the enemy seeks to gain any excessive advantages, are absolutely necessary. Retreats of great Generals and of Armies inured to War have always resembled the retreat of a wounded lion, such is, undoubtedly, also the best theory.

It is true that at the moment of quitting a dangerous position we have often seen trifling formalities observed which caused a waste of time, and were, therefore, attended with danger, whilst in such cases everything depends on getting out of the place speedily. Practised Generals reckon this maxim a very important one. But such cases must not be confounded with a general retreat after a lost battle. Whoever then thinks by a few rapid marches to gain a start, and more easily to recover a firm standing, commits a great error. The first movements should be as small as possible, and it is a maxim in general not to suffer ourselves to be dictated to by the enemy. This maxim cannot be followed without bloody fighting with the enemy at our heels, but the gain is worth the sacrifice; without it we get into an accelerated pace which soon turns into a headlong rush, and costs merely in stragglers more men than rear-guard combats, and besides that extinguishes the last remnants of the spirit of resistance.

A strong rear-guard composed of picked troops, commanded by the bravest General, and supported by the whole Army at critical moments, a careful utilisation of ground, strong ambuscades wherever the boldness of the enemy's advance-guard, and the ground, afford opportunity; in short, the preparation and the system of regular small battles, – these are the means of following this principle.

The difficulties of a retreat are naturally greater or less according as the battle has been fought under more or less favourable circumstances, and according as it has been more or less obstinately contested. The battle of Jena and La Belle-Alliance show how impossible anything like a regular retreat may become, if the last man is used up against a powerful enemy.

Now and again it has been suggested[49] to divide for the purpose of retreating, therefore to retreat in separate divisions or even eccentrically. Such a separation as is made merely for convenience, and along with which concentrated action continues possible and is kept in view, is not what we now refer to; any other kind is extremely dangerous, contrary to the nature of the thing, and therefore a great error. Every lost battle is a principle of weakness and disorganisation; and the first and immediate desideratum is to concentrate, and in concentration to recover order, courage, and confidence. The idea of harassing the enemy by separate corps on both flanks at the moment when he is following up his victory, is a perfect anomaly; a faint-hearted pedant might be overawed by his enemy in that manner, and for such a case it may answer; but where we are not sure of this failing in our opponent it is better let alone. If the strategic relations after a battle require that we should cover ourselves right and left by detachments, so much must be

49   Allusion is here made to the works of Lloyd Bullow and others.

done, as from circumstances is unavoidable, but this fractioning must always be regarded as an evil, and we are seldom in a state to commence it the day after the battle itself.

If Frederick the Great after the battle of Kollin,[50] and the raising of the siege of Prague retreated in three columns that was done not out of choice, but because the position of his forces, and the necessity of covering Saxony, left him no alternative, Buonaparte after the battle of Brienne,[51] sent Marmont back to the Aube, whilst he himself passed the Seine, and turned towards Troyes; but that this did not end in disaster, was solely owing to the circumstance that the Allies, instead of pursuing divided their forces in like manner, turning with the one part (Bluecher) towards the Marne, while with the other (Schwartzenberg), from fear of being too weak, they advanced with exaggerated caution.

50   June 19, 1757.
51   January 30, 1814.

CHAPTER FOURTEEN

Night Fighting

THE MANNER OF conducting a combat at night, and what concerns the details of its course, is a tactical subject; we only examine it here so far as in its totality it appears as a special strategic means.

Fundamentally every night attack is only a more vehement form of surprise. Now at the first look of the thing such an attack appears quite preeminently advantageous, for we suppose the enemy to be taken by surprise, the assailant naturally to be prepared for everything which can happen. What an inequality! Imagination paints to itself a picture of the most complete confusion on the one side, and on the other side the assailant only occupied in reaping the fruits of his advantage. Hence the constant creation of schemes for night attacks by those who have not to lead them, and have no responsibility, whilst these attacks seldom take place in reality.

These ideal schemes are all based on the hypothesis that the assailant knows the arrangements of the defender because they have been made and announced beforehand, and could not escape notice in his reconnaissances, and inquiries; that on the other hand, the measures of the assailant, being only taken at the moment of execution, cannot be known to the enemy. But the last of these is not always quite the case, and still less is the first. If we are not so near the enemy as to have him completely under our eye, as the Austrians had Frederick the Great before the battle of Hochkirch (1758), then all that we know of his position must always be imperfect, as it is obtained by reconnaissances, patrols, information from prisoners, and spies, sources on which no firm reliance can be placed because intelligence thus obtained is always more or less of an old date, and the position of the enemy may have been altered in the meantime. Moreover, with the tactics and mode of encampment of former times it was much easier than it is now to examine the position of the enemy. A line of tents is much easier to distinguish than a line of huts or a bivouac; and an encampment on a line of front, fully and regularly drawn out, also easier than one of Divisions formed in columns, the mode often used at present. We may have the ground on which a Division bivouacs in that manner completely under our eye, and yet not be able to arrive at any accurate idea.

But the position again is not all that we want to know the measures which the defender may take in the course of the combat are just as important, and do not by any means consist in mere random shots. These measures also make night attacks more difficult in modern Wars than formerly, because they have in these campaigns an advantage over those already taken. In our combats the position of the defender is more temporary than definitive, and on that account the defender is better able to surprise his adversary with unexpected blows, than he could formerly.[52]

Therefore what the assailant knows of the defensive previous to a night attack, is seldom or never sufficient to supply the want of direct observation.

But the defender has on his side another small advantage as well, which is that he is more at home than the assailant, on the ground which forms his position, and therefore, like the inhabitant of a room, will find his way about it in the dark with more ease than a stranger. He knows better where to find each part of his force, and therefore can more readily get at it than is the case with his adversary.

From this it follows, that the assailant in a combat at night feels the want of his eyes just as much as the defender, and that therefore, only particular reasons can make a night attack advisable.

Now these reasons arise mostly in connection with subordinate parts of an Army, rarely with the Army itself; it follows that a night attack also as a rule can only take place with secondary combats, and seldom with great battles.

We may attack a portion of the enemy's Army with a very superior force, consequently enveloping it with a view either to take the whole, or to inflict very severe loss on it by an unequal combat, provided that other circumstances are in our favour. But such a scheme can never succeed except by a great surprise, because no fractional part of the enemy's Army would engage in such an unequal combat, but would retire instead. But a surprise on an important scale except in rare instances in a very close country, can only be effected at night. If therefore we wish to gain such an advantage as this from the faulty disposition of a portion of the

---

52   All these difficulties obviously become increased as the power of the weapons in use tends to keep the combatants further apart. – *Editor*.

enemy's Army, then we must make use of the night, at all events, to finish the preliminary part even if the combat itself should not open till towards daybreak. This is therefore what takes place in all the little enterprises by night against outposts, and other small bodies, the main point being invariably through superior numbers, and getting round his position, to entangle him unexpectedly in such a disadvantageous combat, that he cannot disengage himself without great loss.

The larger the body attacked the more difficult the undertaking, because a strong force has greater resources within itself to maintain the fight long enough for help to arrive.

On that account the whole of the enemy's Army can never in ordinary cases be the object of such an attack for although it has no assistance to expect from any quarter outside itself, still, it contains within itself sufficient means of repelling attacks from several sides particularly in our day, when every one from the commencement is prepared for this very usual form of attack. Whether the enemy can attack us on several sides with success depends generally on conditions quite different from that of its being done unexpectedly; without entering here into the nature of these conditions, we confine ourselves to observing, that with turning an enemy, great results, as well as great dangers are connected; that therefore, if we set aside special circumstances, nothing justifies it but a great superiority, just such as we should use against a fractional part of the enemy's Army.

But the turning and surrounding a small fraction of the enemy, and particularly in the darkness of night, is also more practicable for this reason, that whatever we stake upon it, and however superior the force used may be, still probably it constitutes only a limited portion of our Army, and we can sooner stake that than the whole on the risk of a great venture. Besides, the greater part or perhaps the whole serves as a support and rallying-point for the portion risked, which again very much diminishes the danger of the enterprise.

Not only the risk, but the difficulty of execution as well confines night enterprises to small bodies. As surprise is the real essence of them so also stealthy approach is the chief condition of execution: but this is more easily done with small bodies than with large, and for the columns of a whole Army is seldom practicable. For this reason such enterprises are in general only directed against single outposts, and can only be feasible against greater bodies if they are without sufficient outposts, like Frederick the Great at Hochkirch.[53] This will happen seldomer in future to Armies themselves than to minor divisions.

53   October 14, 1758.

In recent times, when War has been carried on with so much more rapidity and vigour, it has in consequence often happened that Armies have encamped very close to each other, without having a very strong system of outposts, because those circumstances have generally occurred just at the crisis which precedes a great decision.

But then at such times the readiness for battle on both sides is also more perfect; on the other hand, in former Wars it was a frequent practice for armies to take up camps in sight of each other, when they had no other object but that of mutually holding each other in check, consequently for a longer period. How often Frederick the Great stood for weeks so near to the Austrians, that the two might have exchanged cannon shots with each other.

But these practices, certainly more favourable to night attacks, have been discontinued in later days; and armies being now no longer in regard to subsistence and requirements for encampment, such independent bodies complete in themselves, find it necessary to keep usually a day's march between themselves and the enemy. If we now keep in view especially the night attack of an army, it follows that sufficient motives for it can seldom occur, and that they fall under one or other of the following classes.

1. An unusual degree of carelessness or audacity which very rarely occurs, and when it does is compensated for by a great superiority in moral force.

2. A panic in the enemy's army, or generally such a degree of superiority in moral force on our side, that this is sufficient to supply the place of guidance in action.

3. Cutting through an enemy's army of superior force, which keeps us enveloped, because in this all depends on surprise, and the object of merely making a passage by force, allows a much greater concentration of forces.

4. Finally, in desperate cases, when our forces have such a disproportion to the enemy's, that we see no possibility of success, except through extraordinary daring.

But in all these cases there is still the condition that the enemy's army is under our eyes, and protected by no advance-guard.

As for the rest, most night combats are so conducted as to end with daylight, so that only the approach and the first attack are made under cover of darkness, because the assailant in that manner can better profit by the consequences of the state of confusion into which he throws his adversary; and combats of this description which do not commence until daybreak, in which the night therefore is only made use of to approach, are not to be counted as night combats.

BOOK FIVE
Military Forces

CHAPTER ONE

General Scheme

WE SHALL consider military forces:

1. As regards their numerical strength and organisation.
2. In their state independent of fighting.
3. In respect of their maintenance; and, lastly,
4. In their general relations to country and ground.

Thus we shall devote this book to the consideration of things appertaining to an army, which only come under the head of *necessary conditions of fighting*, but do not constitute the fight itself. They stand in more or less close connection with and react upon the fighting, and therefore, in considering the application of the combat they must often appear; but we must first consider each by itself, as a whole, in its essence and peculiarities.

CHAPTER TWO

Theatre of War, Army, Campaign

THE NATURE of the things does not allow of a completely satisfactory definition of these three factors, denoting respectively, space, mass, and time in war; but that we may not sometimes be quite misunderstood, we must try to make somewhat plainer the usual meaning of these terms, to which we shall in most cases adhere.

1. – *Theatre of War.*

This term denotes properly such a portion of the space over which war prevails as has its boundaries protected, and thus possesses a kind of independence. This protection may consist in fortresses, or important natural obstacles presented by the country, or even in its being separated by a considerable distance from the rest of the space embraced in the war. – Such a portion is not a mere piece of the whole, but a small whole complete in itself; and consequently it is more or less in such a condition that changes which take place at other points in the seat of war have only an indirect and no direct influence upon it. To give an adequate idea of this, we may suppose that on this portion an advance is made, whilst in another quarter a retreat is taking place, or that upon the one an army is acting defensively, whilst an offensive is being carried on upon the other. Such a clearly defined idea as this is not capable of universal application; it is here used merely to indicate the line of distinction.

2. – *Army.*

With the assistance of the conception of a Theatre of War, it is very easy to say what an Army is: it is, in point of fact, the mass of troops in the same Theatre of War. But this plainly does not include all that is meant by the term in its common usage. Blucher and Wellington commanded each a separate army in 1815, although the two were in the same Theatre of War. The chief command is, therefore, another distinguishing sign for the conception of an Army. At the same time this sign is very nearly allied to the preceding, for where things are well organised, there should only exist one supreme command in a Theatre of War, and the commander-in-chief in a particular Theatre of War should always have a proportionate degree of independence.

The mere absolute numerical strength of a body of troops is less decisive on the subject than might at first appear. For where several Armies are acting under one command, and upon one and the same Theatre of War, they are called Armies, not by reason of their strength, but from the relations antecedent to the war (1813, the Silesian Army, the Army of the North, etc), and although we should divide a great mass of troops intended to remain in the same Theatre into corps, we should never divide them into Armies, at least, such a division would be contrary to what seems to be the meaning which is universally attached to the term. On the other hand, it would certainly be pedantry to apply the term Army to each band of irregular troops acting independently in a remote province: still we must not leave unnoticed that it surprises no one when the Army of the Vendeans in the Revolutionary War is spoken of, and yet it was not much stronger.

The conceptions of Army and Theatre of War therefore, as a rule, go together, and mutually include each other.

3. – *Campaign.*

Although the sum of all military events which happen in all the Theatres of War in one year is often called a *Campaign*, still, however, it is more usual and more exact to understand by the term the events in *one single* Theatre of War. But it is worse still to connect the notion of a Campaign with the period of one year, for wars no longer divide themselves naturally into Campaigns of a year's duration by fixed and long periods in winter quarters. As, however, the events in a Theatre of War of themselves form certain great chapters – if, for instance, the direct effects of some more or less great catastrophe cease, and new combinations begin to develop themselves – therefore these natural subdivisions must be taken into consideration in order to allot to each year (Campaign) its complete share of events. No one would make the Campaign of 1812 terminate at Memel, where the armies were on the 1st January, and transfer the further retreat of the French until they recrossed the Elbe to the campaign of 1813, as that further retreat was plainly only a part of the whole retreat from Moscow.

That we cannot give these conceptions any greater degree of distinctness is of no consequence, because they cannot be used as philosophical definitions for the basis of any kind of propositions. They only serve to give a little more clearness and precision to the language we use.

CHAPTER THREE

Relation of Power

IN THE EIGHTH CHAPTER of the third book we have spoken of the value of superior numbers in battles, from which follows as a consequence the superiority of numbers in general in strategy. So far the importance of the relations of power is established: we shall now add a few more detailed considerations on the subject.

An unbiassed examination of modern military history leads to the conviction that the superiority in numbers becomes every day more decisive; the principle of assembling the greatest possible numbers for a decisive battle may therefore be regarded as more important than ever.

Courage and the spirit of an army have, in all ages, multiplied its physical powers, and will continue to do so equally in future; but we find also that at certain periods in history a superiority in the organisation and equipment of an army has given a great moral preponderance; we find that at other periods a great superiority in mobility had a like effect; at one time we see a new system of tactics brought to light; at another we see the art of war developing itself in an effort to make a skilful use of ground on great general principles, and by such means here and there we find one general gaining great advantages over another; but even this tendency has disappeared, and wars now go on in a simpler and more natural manner. – If, divesting ourselves of any preconceived notions, we look at the experiences of recent wars, we must admit that there are but little traces of any of the above influences, either throughout any whole campaign, or in engagements of a decisive character – that is, the great battle, respecting which term we refer to the second chapter of the preceding book.

Armies are in our days so much on a par in regard to arms, equipment, and drill, that there is no very notable difference between the best and the worst in these things. A difference may still be observed, resulting from the superior instruction of the scientific corps, but in general it only amounts to this, that one is the inventor and introducer of improved appliances, which the other immediately imitates. Even the subordinate generals, leaders of corps and divisions, in all that comes within the scope of their sphere, have in general everywhere the same ideas and methods, so that, except the talent of the commander-in-chief – a thing entirely dependent on chance, and not bearing a constant relation to the standard of education amongst the people and the army – there is nothing now but habituation to war which can give one army a decided superiority over another. The nearer we approach to a state of equality in all these things, the more decisive becomes the relation in point of numbers.

The character of modern battles is the result of this state of equality. Take for instance the battle of Borodino, where the first army in the world, the French, measured its strength with the Russian, which, in many parts of its organisation, and in the education of its special branches, might be considered the furthest behindhand. In the whole battle there is not one single trace of superior art or intelligence, it is a mere trial of strength between the respective armies throughout; and as they were nearly equal in that respect, the result could not be otherwise than a gradual turn of the scale in favour of that side where there was the greatest energy on the part of the commander, and the most experience in war on the part of the troops. We have taken this battle as an illustration, because in it there was an equality in the numbers on each side such as is rarely to be found.

We do not maintain that all battles exactly resemble this, but it shows the dominant tone of most of them.

In a battle in which the forces try their strength on each other so leisurely and methodically, an excess of force on one side must make the result in its favour much more certain. And it is a fact that we may search modern military history in vain for a battle in which an army has beaten another double its own strength, an occurrence by no means uncommon in former times. Buonaparte, the greatest general of modern times, in all his great victorious battles – with one exception, that of Dresden, 1813 – had managed to assemble an army superior in numbers, or at least very little inferior, to that of his opponent, and when it was impossible for him to do so, as at Leipsic, Brienne, Laon, and Belle-Alliance, he was beaten.

The absolute strength is in strategy generally a given quantity, which the commander cannot alter. But from this it by no means follows that it is impossible to carry on a war with a decidedly inferior force.

War is not always a voluntary act of state policy, and least of all is it so when the forces are very unequal: consequently, any relation of forces is imaginable in war, and it would be a strange theory of war which would wish to give up its office just where it is most wanted.

However desirable theory may consider a proportionate force, still it cannot say that no use can be made of the most disproportionate. No limits can be prescribed in this respect.

The weaker the force the more moderate must be the object it proposes to itself, and the weaker the force the shorter time it will last. In these two directions there is a field for weakness to give way, if we may use this expression. Of the changes which the measure of the force produces in the conduct of war, we can only speak by degrees, as these things present themselves; at present it is sufficient to have indicated the general point of view, but to complete that we shall add one more observation.

The more that an army involved in an unequal combat falls short of the number of its opponents, the greater must be the tension of its powers, the greater its energy when danger presses. If the reverse takes place, and instead of heroic desperation a spirit of despondency ensues, then certainly there is an end to every art of war.

If with this energy of powers is combined a wise moderation in the object proposed, then there is that play of brilliant actions and prudent forbearance which we admire in the wars of Frederick the Great.

But the less that this moderation and caution can effect, the more must the tension and energy of the forces become predominant. When the disproportion of forces is so great that no modification of our own object can ensure us safety from a catastrophe, or where the probable continuance of the danger is so great that the greatest economy of our powers can no longer suffice to bring us to our object, then the tension of our powers should be concentrated for one desperate blow; he who is pressed on all sides expecting little help from things which promise none, will place his last and only reliance in the moral ascendancy which despair gives to courage, and look upon the greatest daring as the greatest wisdom, – at the same time employ the assistance of subtle stratagem, and if he does not succeed, will find in an honourable downfall the right to rise hereafter.

CHAPTER FOUR

Relation of the Three Arms

WE SHALL ONLY SPEAK of the three principal arms: Infantry, Cavalry, and Artillery.

We must be excused for making the following analysis which belongs more to tactics, but is necessary to give distinctness to our ideas.

The combat is of two kinds, which are essentially different: the destructive principle of fire, and the hand to hand or personal combat. This latter, again, is either attack or defence. (As we here speak of elements, attack and defence are to be understood in a perfectly absolute sense.) Artillery, obviously, acts only with the destructive principle of fire. Cavalry only with personal combat. Infantry with both.

In close combat the essence of defence consists in standing firm, as if rooted to the ground; the essence of the attack is movement. Cavalry is entirely deficient in the first quality; on the other hand, it possesses the latter in an especial manner. It is therefore only suited for attack. Infantry has especially the property of standing firm, but is not altogether without mobility.

From this division of the elementary forces of war into different arms, we have as a result, the superiority and general utility of Infantry as compared with the other two arms, from its being the only arm which unites in itself all the three elementary forces. A further deduction to be drawn is, that the combination of the three arms leads to a more perfect use of the forces, by affording the means of strengthening at pleasure either the one or the other of the principles which are united in an unalterable manner in Infantry.

The destructive principle of fire is in the wars of the present time plainly beyond measure the most effective; nevertheless, the close combat, man to man, is just as plainly to be regarded as the real basis of combat. For that reason, therefore, an army of artillery only would be an absurdity in war, but an army of cavalry is conceivable, only it would possess very little intensity of force An army of infantry alone is not only conceivable but also much the strongest of the three. The three arms, therefore, stand in this order in reference to independent value – Infantry, Cavalry, Artillery.

But this order does not hold good if applied to the relative importance of each arm when they are all three acting in conjunction. As the destructive principle is much more effective than the principle of motion, therefore the complete want of cavalry would weaken an army less than the total want of artillery.

An army consisting of infantry and artillery alone, would certainly find itself in a disagreeable position if opposed to an army composed of all three arms; but if what it lacked in cavalry was compensated for by a proportionate increase of infantry, it would still, by a somewhat different mode of acting, be able to do very well with its tactical economy. Its outpost service would cause some embarrassment; it would never be able to pursue a beaten enemy with great vivacity, and it must make a retreat with greater hardships and efforts; but these inconveniences would still never be sufficient in themselves to drive it completely out of the field. – On the other hand, such an army opposed to one composed of infantry and cavalry only would be able to play a very good part, while it is hardly conceivable that the latter could keep the field at all against an army made up of all three arms.

Of course these reflections on the relative importance of each single arm result only from a consideration of the generality of events in war, where one case compensates another; and therefore it is not our intention to apply the truth thus ascertained to each individual case of a particular combat. A battalion on outpost service or on a retreat may, perhaps, choose to have with it a squadron in preference to a couple of guns. A body of cavalry with horse artillery, sent in rapid pursuit of, or to cut off, a flying enemy wants no infantry, etc., etc.

If we summarise the results of these considerations they amount to this.

1. That infantry is the most independent of the three arms.
2. Artillery is quite wanting in independence.
3. Infantry is the most important in the combination of the three arms.
4. Cavalry can the most easily be dispensed with.
5. A combination of the three arms gives the greatest strength.

Now, if the combination of the three gives the greatest strength, it is natural to inquire what is the best absolute proportion of each, but that is a question which it is almost impossible to answer.

If we could form a comparative estimate of the cost of organising in the first instance, and then provisioning and maintaining each of the three arms, and then again of the relative amount of service rendered by each in war, we should obtain a definite result which would give the best proportion in the abstract. But this is little more than a play of the imagination. The very first term in the comparison is difficult to determine, that is to say, one of the factors, the cost in money, is not difficult to find; but another, the value of men's lives, is a computation which no one would readily try to solve by figures.

Also the circumstance that each of the three arms chiefly depends on a different element of strength in the state – Infantry on the number of the male population, cavalry on the number of horses, artillery on available financial means – introduces into the calculation some heterogeneous conditions, the overruling influence of which may be plainly observed in the great outlines of the history of different people at various periods.

As, however, for other reasons we cannot altogether dispense with some standard of comparison, therefore, in place of the whole of the first term of the comparison we must take only that one of its factors which can be ascertained, namely, the cost in money. Now on this point it is sufficient for our purpose to assume that, in general, a squadron of 150 horsemen, a battalion of infantry 800 strong, a battery of artillery consisting of 8 six-pounders, cost nearly the same, both as respects the expense of formation and of maintenance.

With regard to the other member of the comparison, that is, how much service the one arm is capable of rendering as compared with the others, it is much less easy to find any distinct quantity. The thing might perhaps be possible if it depended merely on the destroying principle; but each arm is destined to its own particular use, therefore has its own particular sphere of action, which, again, is not so distinctly defined that it might not be greater or less through modifications only in the mode of conducting the war, without causing any decided disadvantage.

We are often told of what experience teaches on this subject, and it is supposed that military history affords the information necessary for a settlement of the question, but every one must look upon all that as nothing more than a way of talking, which, as it is not derived from anything of a primary and necessary nature, does not deserve attention in an analytical examination.

Now although a fixed ratio as representing the best proportion between the three arms is conceivable, but is an x which it is impossible to find, a mere imaginary quantity, still it is possible to appreciate the effects of having a great superiority or a great inferiority in one particular arm as compared with the same arm in the enemy's army.

Artillery increases the destructive principle of fire; it is the most redoubtable of arms, and its want, therefore, diminishes very considerably the intensive force of an army. On the other hand, it is the least moveable, consequently, makes an army more unwieldy; further, it always requires a force for its support, because it is incapable of close combat; if it is too numerous, so that the troops appointed for its protection are not able to resist the attacks of the enemy at every point, it is often lost, and from that follows a fresh disadvantage, because of the three arms it is the only one which in its principal parts, that is guns and carriages, the enemy can soon use against us.

Cavalry increases the principle of mobility in an army. If too few in number the brisk flame of the elements of war is thereby weakened, because everything must be done slower (on foot), everything must be organised with more care; the rich harvest of victory, instead of being cut with a scythe, can only be reaped with a sickle.

An excess of cavalry can certainly never be looked upon as a direct diminution of the combatant force, as an organic disproportion, but it may certainly be so indirectly, on account of the difficulty of feeding that arm, and also if we reflect that instead of a surplus of 10,000 horsemen not required we might have 50,000 infantry.

These peculiarities arising from the preponderance of one arm are the more important to the art of war in its limited sense, as that art teaches the use of whatever forces are forthcoming; and when forces are placed under the command of a general, the proportion of the three arms is also commonly already settled without his having had much voice in the matter.

If we would form an idea of the character of warfare modified by the preponderance of one or other of the three arms it is to be done in the following manner: –

An excess of artillery leads to a more defensive and passive character in our measures; our interest will be to seek security in strong positions, great natural obstacles of ground, even in mountain positions, in order that the natural impediments we find in the ground may undertake the defence and protection of our numerous artillery, and that the enemy's forces may come themselves and seek their own destruction. The whole war will be carried on in a serious formal minuet step.

On the other hand, a want of artillery will make us prefer the offensive, the active, the mobile principle; marching, fatigue, exertion, become our special weapons, thus the war will become more diversified, more lively, rougher; small change is substituted for great events.

With a very numerous cavalry we seek wide plains, and take to great movements. At a greater distance from the enemy we enjoy more rest and greater conveniences without conferring the same advantages on our adversary. We may venture on bolder measures to outflank him, and on more daring movements generally, as we have command over space. In as far as diversions and invasions are true auxiliary means of war we shall be able to make use of them with greater facility.

A decided want of cavalry diminishes the force of mobility in an army without increasing its destructive power as an excess of artillery does. Prudence and method become then the leading characteristics of the war. Always to remain near the enemy in order to keep him constantly in view – no rapid, still less hurried movements, everywhere a slow pushing on of well concentrated masses – a preference for the defensive and for broken country, and, when the offensive must be resorted to, the shortest road direct to the centre of force in the enemy's army – these are the natural tendencies or principles in such cases.

These different forms which warfare takes according as one or other of the three arms preponderates, seldom have an influence so complete and decided as alone, or chiefly to determine the direction of a whole undertaking. Whether we shall act strategically on the offensive or defensive, the choice of a theatre of war, the determination to fight a great battle, or adopt some other means of destruction, are points which must be determined by other and more essential considerations, at least, if this is not the case, it is much to be feared that we have mistaken minor details for the chief consideration. But although this is so, although the great questions must be decided before on other grounds, there still always remains a certain margin for the influence of the preponderating arm, for in the offensive we can always be prudent and methodical, in the defensive bold and enterprising, etc., etc., through all the different stages and gradations of the military life.

On the other hand, the nature of a war may have a notable influence on the proportions of the three arms.

First, a national war, kept up by militia and a general levy (Landsturm), must naturally bring into the field a very numerous infantry; for in such wars there is a greater want of the means of equipment than of men, and as the equipment consequently is confined to what is indisputably necessary, we may easily imagine, that for every battery of eight pieces, not only one, but two or three battalions might be raised.

Second, if a weak state opposed to a powerful one cannot take refuge in a general call of the male population to regular military service, or in a militia system resembling it, then the increase of its artillery is certainly the shortest way of bringing up its weak army nearer to an equality with that of the enemy, for it saves men, and intensifies the essential principle of military force, that is, the destructive principle. Any way, such a state will mostly be confined to a limited theatre, and therefore this arm will be better suited to it. Frederick the Great adopted this means in the later period of the Seven Years' War.

Third, cavalry is the arm for movement and great decisions; its increase beyond the ordinary proportions is therefore important if the war extends over a great space, if expeditions are to be made in various directions, and great and decisive blows are intended. Buonaparte is an example of this.

That the offensive and defensive do not properly in themselves exercise an influence on the proportion of cavalry will only appear plainly when we come to speak of these two methods of acting in war; in the meantime, we shall only remark that both assailant and defender as a rule traverse the same spaces in war, and may have also, at least in many cases, the same decisive intentions. We remind our readers of the campaign of 1812.

It is commonly believed that, in the middle ages, cavalry was much more numerous in proportion to infantry, and that the difference has been gradually on the decrease ever since. Yet this is a mistake, at least partly. The proportion of cavalry was, according to numbers, on the average perhaps, not much greater; of this we may convince ourselves by tracing, through the history of the middle ages, the detailed statements of the armed forces then employed. Let us only think of the masses of men on foot who composed the armies of the Crusaders, or the masses who followed the Emperors of Germany on their Roman expeditions. It was in reality the importance of the cavalry which was so much greater in those days; it was the stronger arm, composed of the flower of the people, so much so that, although always very much weaker actually in numbers, it was still always looked upon as the chief thing, infantry was little valued, hardly spoken of; hence has arisen the belief that its numbers were few. No doubt it happened oftener than it does now, that in incursions of small importance in France, Germany, and Italy, a small army was composed entirely of cavalry; as it was the chief arm, there is nothing inconsistent in that; but these cases decide nothing if we take a general view, as they are greatly outnumbered by cases of greater armies of the period constituted differently. It was only when the obligations to military service imposed by the feudal laws had ceased, and wars were carried on by soldiers enlisted, hired, and paid – when, therefore, wars depended on money and enlistment, that is, at the time of the Thirty

Years' War, and the wars of Louis XIV. – that this employment of great masses of almost useless infantry was checked, and perhaps in those days they might have fallen into the exclusive use of cavalry, if infantry had not just then risen in importance through the improvements in fire-arms, by which means it maintained its numerical superiority in proportion to cavalry; at this period, if infantry was weak, the proportion was as one to one, if numerous as three to one.

Since then cavalry has always decreased in importance according as improvements in the use of fire-arms have advanced. This is intelligible enough in itself, but the improvement we speak of does not relate solely to the weapon itself and the skill in handling it; we advert also to greater ability in using troops armed with this weapon. At the battle of Mollwitz the Prussian army had brought the fire of their infantry to such a state of perfection, that there has been no improvement since then in that sense. On the other hand, the use of infantry in broken ground and as skirmishers has been introduced more recently, and is to be looked upon as a very great advance in the art of destruction.

Our opinion is, therefore, that the relation of cavalry has not much changed as far as regards numbers, but as regards its importance, there has been a great alteration. This seems to be a contradiction, but is not so in reality. The infantry of the middle ages, although forming the greater proportion of an army, did not attain to that proportion by its value as compared to cavalry, but because all that could not be appointed to the very costly cavalry were handed over to the infantry; this infantry was, therefore, merely a last resource; and if the number of cavalry had depended merely on the value set on that arm, it could never have been too great. Thus we can understand how cavalry, in spite of its constantly decreasing importance, may still, perhaps, have importance enough to keep its numerical relation at that point which it has hitherto so constantly maintained.

It is a remarkable fact that, at least since the wars of the Austrian succession, the proportion of cavalry to infantry has changed very little, the variation being constantly between a fourth, a fifth or a sixth; this seems to indicate that those proportions meet the natural requirements of an army, and that these numbers give the solution which it is impossible to find in a direct manner. We doubt, however, if this is the case, and we find the principal instances of the employment of a numerous cavalry sufficiently accounted for by other causes.

Austria and Russia are states which have kept up a numerous cavalry, because they retain in their political condition the fragments of a Tartar organisation. Buonaparte for his purposes could never be strong enough in cavalry; when he had made use of the conscription as far as possible, he had no ways of strengthening his armies, but by increasing the auxiliary arms, as they cost him more in money than in men. Besides this, it stands to reason that in military enterprises of such enormous extent as his, cavalry must have a greater value than in ordinary cases.

Frederick the Great it is well known reckoned carefully every recruit that could be saved to his country; it was his great business to keep up the strength of his army, as far as possible at the expense of other countries. His reasons for this are easy to conceive, if we remember that his small dominions did not then include Prussia and the Westphalian provinces. Cavalry was kept complete by recruitment more easily than infantry, irrespective of fewer men being required; in addition to which, his system of war was completely founded on the mobility of his army, and thus it was, that while his infantry diminished in number, his cavalry was always increasing itself till the end of the Seven Years' War. Still at the end of that war it was hardly more than a fourth of the number of infantry that he had in the field.

At the period referred to there is no want of instances, also of armies entering the field unusually weak in cavalry, and yet carrying off the victory. The most remarkable is the battle of Gross-gorschen. If we only count the French divisions which took part in the battle, Buonaparte was 100,000 strong, of which 5,000 were cavalry, 90,000 infantry; the Allies had 70,000, of which 25,000 were cavalry and 40,000 infantry. Thus, in place of the 20,000 cavalry on the side of the Allies in excess of the total of the French cavalry, Buonaparte had only 50,000 additional infantry when he ought to have had 100,000. As he gained the battle with that superiority in infantry, we may ask whether it was at all likely that he would have lost it if the proportions had been 140,000 to 40,000.

Certainly the great advantage of our superiority in cavalry was shown immediately after the battle, for Buonaparte gained hardly any trophies by his victory. The gain of a battle is therefore not everything, – but is it not always the chief thing?

If we put together these considerations, we can hardly believe that the numerical proportion between cavalry and infantry which has existed for the last eighty years is the natural one, founded solely on their absolute value; we are much rather inclined to think, that after many fluctuations, the relative proportions of these arms will change further in the same direction as hitherto, and that the fixed number of cavalry at last will be considerably less.

With respect to artillery, the number of guns has naturally increased since its first invention, and according as it has been made lighter and otherwise improved; still since the time of Frederick the Great, it has also kept very much to the same proportion of two or three guns per 1,000 men, we mean at the commencement of a campaign; for during its course artillery does not melt away as fast as infantry, therefore at the end of a campaign the proportion is generally notably greater, perhaps three, four, or five guns per 1,000 men. Whether this is the natural proportion, or that the increase of artillery may be carried still further, without prejudice to the whole conduct of war, must be left for experience to decide.

The principal results we obtain from the whole of these considerations, are –

1. That infantry is the chief arm, to which the other two are subordinate.

2. That by the exercise of great skill and energy in command, the want of the two subordinate arms may in some measure be compensated for, provided that we are much stronger in infantry; and the better the infantry the easier this may be done.

3. That it is more difficult to dispense with artillery than with cavalry, because it is the chief principle of destruction, and its mode of fighting is more amalgamated with that of infantry.

4. That artillery being the strongest arm, as regards destructive action, and cavalry the weakest in that respect, the question must in general arise, how much artillery can we have without inconvenience, and what is the least proportion of cavalry we require?

CHAPTER FIVE

Order of Battle of an Army

THE ORDER OF BATTLE is that division and formation of the different arms into separate parts or sections of the whole Army, and that form of general position or disposition of those parts which is to be the norm throughout the whole campaign or war.

It consists, therefore, in a certain measure, of an arithmetical and a geometrical element, *the division* and the *form of disposition*. The first proceeds from the permanent peace organisation of the army; adopts as units certain parts, such as battalions, squadrons, and batteries, and with them forms units of a higher order up to the highest of all, the whole army, according to the requirements of predominating circumstances. In like manner, the form of disposition comes from the elementary tactics, in which the army is instructed and exercised in time of peace, which must be looked upon as a property in the troops that cannot be essentially modified at the moment war breaks out, the disposition connects these tactics with the conditions which the use of the troops in war and in large masses demands, and thus it settles in a general way the rule or norm in conformity with which the troops are to be drawn up for battle.

This has been invariably the case when great armies have taken the field, and there have been times when this form was considered as the most essential part of the battle.

In the seventeenth and eighteenth centuries, when the improvements in the firearms of infantry occasioned a great increase of that arm, and allowed of its being deployed in such long thin lines, the order of battle was thereby simplified, but, at the same time it became more difficult and more artificial in the carrying out, and as no other way of disposing of cavalry at the commencement of a battle was known but that of posting them on the wings, where they were out of the fire and had room to move, therefore in the order of battle the army always became a closed inseparable whole. If such an army was divided in the middle, it was like an earthworm cut in two: the wings had still life and the power of motion, but they had lost their natural functions. The army lay, therefore, in a manner under a spell of unity, and whenever any parts of it had to be placed in a separate position, a small organisation and disorganisation became necessary. The marches which the whole army had to make were a condition in which, to a certain extent, it found itself out of rule. If the enemy was at hand, the march had to be arranged in the most artificial manner, and in order that one line or one wing might be always at the prescribed distance from the other, the troops had to scramble over everything: marches had also constantly to be stolen from the enemy, and this perpetual theft only escaped severe punishment through one circumstance, which was, that the enemy lay under the same ban.

Hence, when, in the latter half of the eighteenth century, it was discovered that cavalry would serve just as well to protect a wing if it stood in rear of the army as if it were placed on the prolongation of the line, and that, besides this, it might be applied to other purposes than merely fighting a duel with the enemy's cavalry, a great step in advance was made, because now the army in its principal extension or front, which is always the breadth of its order of battle (position), consisted entirely of homogeneous members, so that it could be formed of any number of parts at pleasure, each part like another and like the whole. In this way it ceased to be one single piece and became an articulated whole, consequently pliable and manageable: the parts might be separated from the whole and then joined on again without difficulty, the order of battle always remained the same. – Thus arose the corps consisting of all arms, that is, thus such an organisation became possible, for the want of it had been felt long before.

That all this relates to the combat is very natural. The battle was formerly the whole war, and will always continue to be the principal part of it; but, the order of battle belongs generally more to tactics than strategy, and it is only introduced here to show how tactics in organising the whole into smaller wholes made preparations for strategy.

The greater armies become, the more they are distributed over wide spaces and the more diversified the action and reaction of the different parts amongst themselves, the wider becomes the field of strategy, and, therefore, then the order of battle, in the sense of our definition, must also come into a kind of reciprocal action with strategy, which manifests itself chiefly at the extreme points where tactics and strategy meet, that is, at those moments when the general distribution of the combatant forces passes into the special dispositions for the combat.

We now turn to those three points, the *division, combination of arms*, and *order of battle (disposition)* in a strategic point of view.

1. – *Division.*

In strategy we must never ask what is to be the strength of a division or a corps, but how many corps or division an army should have. There is nothing more unmanageable than an army divided into three parts, except it be one divided into only two, in which case the chief command must be almost neutralised.

To fix the strength of great and small corps, either on the grounds of elementary tactics or on higher grounds, leaves an incredibly wide field for arbitrary judgment, and heaven knows what strange modes of reasoning have sported in this wide field. On the other hand, the necessity of forming an independent whole (army) into a certain number of parts is a thing as obvious as it is positive, and this idea furnishes real strategic motives for determining the number of the greater divisions of an army, consequently their strength, whilst the strength of the smaller divisions, such as companies, battalions, etc., is left to be determined by tactics.

We can hardly imagine the smallest independent body in which there are not at least three parts to be distinguished, that one part may be thrown out in advance, and another part be left in rear: that four is still more convenient follows of itself, if we keep in view that the middle part, being the principal division, ought to be stronger than either of the others; in this way, we may proceed to make out eight, which appears to us to be the most suitable number for an army if we take one part for an advanced guard as a constant necessity, three for the main body, that is a right wing, centre and left wing, two divisions for reserve, and one to detach to the right, one to the left. Without pedantically ascribing a great importance to these numbers and figures, we certainly believe that they represent the most usual and frequently recurring strategic disposition, and on that account one that is convenient.

Certainly it seems that the supreme direction of an army (and the direction of every whole) must be greatly facilitated if there are only three or four subordinates to command, but the commander-in-chief must pay dearly for this convenience in a twofold manner. In the first place, an order loses in rapidity, force, and exactness if the gradation ladder down which it has to descend is long, and this must be the case if there are corps-commanders between the division leaders and the chief; secondly, the chief loses generally in his own proper power and efficiency the wider the spheres of action of his immediate subordinates become. A general commanding 100,000 men in eight divisions exercises a power which is greater in intensity than if the 100,000 men were divided into only three corps. There are many reasons for this, but the most important is that each commander looks upon himself as having a kind of proprietary right in his own corps, and always opposes the withdrawal from him of any portion of it for a longer or shorter time. A little experience of war will make this evident to any one.

But on the other hand the number of divisions must not be too great, otherwise disorder will ensue. It is difficult enough to manage eight divisions from one head quarter, and the number should never be allowed to exceed ten. But in a division in which the means of circulating orders are much less, the smaller normal number four, or at most five, may be regarded as the more suitable.

If these factors, five and ten, will not answer, that is, if the brigades are too strong, then *corps d'armée* must be introduced; but we must remember that by so doing, a new power is created, which at once very much lowers all other factors.

But now, what is too strong a brigade? The custom is to make them from 2,000 to 5,000 men strong, and there appear to be two reasons for making the latter number the limit; the first is that a brigade is supposed to be a subdivision which can be commanded by one man directly, that is, through the compass of his voice: the second is that any larger body of infantry should not be left without artillery, and through this first combination of arms a special division of itself is formed.

We do not wish to involve ourselves in these tactical subtilties, neither shall we enter upon the disputed point, where and in what proportions the combination of all three arms should take place, whether with divisions of 8,000 to 12,000 men, or with corps which are 20,000 to 30,000 men strong. The most decided opponent of these combinations will scarcely take exception at the mere assertion, that nothing but this combination of the three arms can make a division independent, and that therefore, for such as are intended to be frequently detached separately, it is at least very desirable.

An army of 200,000 men in ten divisions, the divisions composed of five brigades each, would give brigades 4,000 strong. We see here no disproportion. Certainly this army might also be divided into five corps, the corps into four divisions, and the division into four brigades, which makes the brigade 2,500 men strong; but the first distribution, looked at in the abstract, appears to us preferable, for besides that, in the other, there is one more gradation of rank, five parts are too few to make an army manageable; four divisions, in like manner, are too few for a corps, and 2,500 men is a weak brigade, of which, in this manner, there are eighty, whereas the first formation has only fifty, and is therefore simpler. All these advantages are given up merely for the sake of having only to send orders to half as many generals. Of course the distribution into corps is still more unsuitable for smaller armies.

This is the abstract view of the case. The particular case may present good reasons for deciding otherwise. Likewise, we must admit that, although eight or ten divisions may be directed when united in a level country, in widely extended mountain positions the thing might perhaps be impossible. A great river which divides an army into halves, makes a commander for each half indispensable; in short, there are a hundred local and particular objects of the most decisive character, before which all rules must give way.

But still, experience teaches us, that these abstract grounds come most frequently into use and are seldomer overruled by others than we should perhaps suppose.

We wish further to explain clearly the scope of the foregoing considerations by a simple outline, for which purpose we now place the different points of most importance next to each other.

As we mean by the term numbers, or parts of a whole, only those which are made by the primary, therefore the immediate division, we say.

1. If a whole has too few members it is unwieldy.

2. If the parts of a whole body are too large, the power of the superior will is thereby weakened.

3. With every additional step through which an order has to pass, it is weakened in two ways: in one way by the loss of force, which it suffers in its passage through an additional step; in another way by the longer time in its transmission.

The tendency of all this is to show that the number of co-ordinate divisions should be as great, and the gradational steps as few as possible; and the only limitation to this conclusion is, that in armies no more than from eight to ten, and in subordinate corps no more than from four or at most six, subdivisions can be conveniently directed.

2. – *Combination of Arms.*

For strategy the combination of the three arms in the order of battle is only important in regard to those parts of the army which, according to the usual order of things, are likely to be frequently employed in a detached position, where they may be obliged to engage in an independent combat. Now it is in the nature of things, that members of the first class, and for the most part only these, are destined for detached positions, because, as we shall see elsewhere, detached positions are most generally adopted upon the supposition and the necessity of a body independent in itself.

In a strict sense strategy would therefore only require a permanent combination of arms in army corps, or where these do not exist, in divisions, leaving it to circumstances to determine when a provisional combination of the three arms shall be made in subdivisions of an inferior order.

But it is easy to see that, when corps are of considerable size, such as 30,000 or 40,000 men, they can seldom find themselves in a situation to take up a completely connected position in mass. With corps of such strength, a combination of the arms in the divisions is therefore necessary. No one who has had any experience in war, will treat lightly the delay which occurs when pressing messages have to be sent to some other perhaps distant point before cavalry can be brought to the support of infantry – to say nothing of the confusion which takes place.

The details of the combination of the three arms, how far it should extend, how low down it should be carried, what proportions should be observed, the strength of the reserves of each to be set apart – these are all purely tactical considerations.

3. – *The Disposition.*

The determination as to the relations in space, according to which the parts of an army amongst themselves are to be drawn up in order of battle, is likewise completely a tactical subject, referring solely to the battle. No doubt there is also a strategic disposition of the parts; but it depends almost entirely on determinations and requirements of the moment, and what there is in it of the rational, does not come within the meaning of the term "order of battle." We shall therefore treat of it in the following chapter under the head of *Disposition of an Army.*

The order of battle of an army is therefore the organisation and disposition of it in mass ready prepared for battle. Its parts are united in such a manner that both the tactical and strategical requirements of the moment can be easily satisfied by the employment of single parts drawn from the general mass. When such momentary exigency has passed over, these parts resume their original place, and thus the order of battle becomes the first step to, and principal foundation of, that wholesome methodicism which, like the beat of a pendulum, regulates the work in war, and of which we have already spoken in the fourth chapter of the Second Book.

CHAPTER SIX

General Disposition of an Army

Between the moment of the first assembling of military forces, and that of the solution arrived at maturity when strategy has brought the army to the decisive point, and each particular part has had its position and rôle pointed out by tactics, there is in most cases a long interval; it is the same between one decisive catastrophe and another.

Formerly these intervals in a certain measure did not belong to war at all. Take for example the manner in which Luxemburg encamped and marched. We single out this general because he is celebrated for his camps and marches, and therefore may be considered a representative general of his period, and from the *Histoire de la Flandre militaire*, we know more about him than about other generals of the time.

The camp was regularly pitched with its rear close to a river, or morass, or a deep valley, which in the present day would be considered madness. The direction in which the enemy lay had so little to do with determining the front of the army, that cases are very common in which the rear was towards the enemy and the front towards their own country. This now unheard of mode of proceeding is perfectly unintelligible, unless we suppose that in the choice of camps the convenience of the troops was the chief, indeed almost the only consideration, and therefore look upon the state of being in camp as a state outside of the action of war, a kind of withdrawal behind the scenes, where one is quite at ease. The practice of always resting the rear upon some obstacle may be reckoned the only measure of security which was then taken, of course, in the sense of the mode of conducting war in that day, for such a measure was quite inconsistent with the possibility of being compelled to fight in that position. But there was little reason for apprehension on that score, because the battles generally depended on a kind of mutual understanding, like a duel, in which the parties repair to a convenient rendezvous. As armies, partly on account of their numerous cavalry, which in the decline of its splendour was still regarded, particularly by the French, as the principal arm, partly on account of the unwieldy organisation of their order of battle, could not fight in every description of country, an army in a close broken country was as it were under the protection of a neutral territory, and as it could itself make but little use of broken ground, therefore, it was deemed preferable to go to meet an enemy seeking battle. We know, indeed, that Luxemburg's battles at Fleurus, Stienkirk, and Neerwinden, were conceived in a different spirit; but this spirit had only just then under this great general freed itself from the old method, and it had not yet reacted on the method of encampment. Alterations in the art of war originate always in matters of a decisive nature, and then lead by degrees to modifications in other things. The expression *il va à la guerre*, used in reference to a partizan setting out to watch the enemy, shows how little the state of an army in camp was considered to be a state of real warfare.

It was not much otherwise with the marches, for the artillery then separated itself completely from the rest of the army, in order to take advantage of better and more secure roads, and the cavalry on the wings generally took the right alternately, that each might have in turn its share of the honour of marching on the right.

At present (that is, chiefly since the Silesian wars) the situation out of battle is so thoroughly influenced by its connection with battle that the two states are in intimate correlation, and the one can no longer be completely imagined without the other. Formerly in a campaign the battle was the real weapon, the situation at other times only the handle – the former the steel blade, the other the wooden haft glued to it, the whole therefore composed of heterogeneous parts, – now the battle is the edge, the situation out of the battle the back of the blade, the whole to be looked upon as metal completely welded together, in which it is impossible any longer to distinguish where the steel ends and the iron begins.

This state in war outside of the battle is now partly regulated by the organisation and regulations with which the army comes prepared from a state of peace, partly by the tactical and strategic arrangements of the moment. The three situations in which an army may be placed are in quarters, on a march, or in camp. All three belong as much to tactics as to strategy, and these two branches, bordering on each other here in many ways, often seem to, or actually do, incorporate themselves with each other, so that many dispositions may be looked upon at the same time as both tactical and strategic.

We shall treat of these three situations of an army outside of the combat in a general way, before any special objects come into connection with them; but we must, first of all, consider the general disposition of the forces, because that is a superior and more comprehensive measure, determining as respects camps, cantonments, and marches.

If we look at the disposition of the forces in a general way, that is, leaving out of sight any special object, we can only imagine it as a unit, that is, as a whole, intended to fight all together, for any deviation from this simplest form would imply a special object. Thus arises, therefore, the conception of an army, let it be small or large.

Further, when there is an absence of any special end, there only remains as the sole object the preservation of the army itself, which of course includes its security. That the army shall be able to exist without inconvenience, and that it shall be able to concentrate without difficulty for the purpose of fighting, are, therefore, the two requisite conditions. From these result, as desirable, the following points more immediately applying to subjects concerning the existence and security of the army.

1. Facility of subsistence.
2. Facility of providing shelter for the troops.
3. Security of the rear.
4. An open country in front.
5. The position itself in a broken country.
6. Strategic points d'appui.
7. A suitable distribution of the troops.

Our elucidation of these several points is as follows:

The first two lead us to seek out cultivated districts, and great towns and roads. They determine measures in general rather than in particular.

In the chapter on lines of communication will be found what we mean by security of the rear. The first and most important point in this respect is that the centre of the position should be at a right angle with the principal line of retreat adjoining the position.

Respecting the fourth point, an army certainly cannot look over an expanse of country in its front as it overlooks the space directly before it when in a tactical position for battle. But the strategic eyes are the advanced guard, scouts and patrols sent forward, spies, etc., etc., and the service will naturally be easier for these in an open than in an intersected country. The fifth point is merely the reverse of the fourth.

Strategical points d'appui differ from tactical in these two respects, that the army need not be in immediate contact with them, and that, on the other hand, they must be of greater extent. The cause of this is that, according to the nature of the thing, the relations to time and space in which strategy moves are generally on a greater scale than those of tactics. If, therefore, an army posts itself at a distance of a mile from the sea coast or the banks of a great river, it leans strategically on these obstacles, for the enemy cannot make use of such a space as this to effect a strategic turning movement. Within its narrow limits he cannot adventure on marches miles in length, occupying days and weeks. On the other hand, in strategy, a lake of several miles in circumference is hardly to be looked upon as an obstacle; in its proceedings, a few miles to the right or left are not of much consequence. Fortresses will become strategic points d'appui, according as they are large, and afford a wide sphere of action for offensive combinations.

The disposition of the army in separate masses may be done with a view either to special objects and requirements, or to those of a general nature; here we can only speak of the latter.

The first general necessity is to push forward the advanced guard and the other troops required to watch the enemy.

The second is that, with very large armies, the reserves are usually placed several miles in rear, and consequently occupy a separate position.

Lastly, the covering of both wings of an army usually requires a separate disposition of particular corps.

By this covering it is not at all meant that a portion of the army is to be detached to defend the space round its wings, in order to prevent the enemy from approaching these weak points, as they are called: who would then defend the wings of these flanking corps? This kind of idea, which is so common, is complete nonsense. The wings of an army are in themselves not weak points of an army for this reason, that the enemy also has wings, and cannot menace ours without placing his own in jeopardy. It is only if circumstances are unequal, if the enemy's army is larger than ours, if his lines of communication are more secure (see Lines of Communication), it is only then that the wings become weak parts; but of these special cases we are not now speaking, therefore, neither of a case in which a flanking corps is appointed in connection with other combinations to defend effectually the space on our wings, for that no longer belongs to the category of general dispositions.

But although the wings are not particularly weak parts still they are particularly important, because here, on account of flanking movements the defence is not so simple as in front, measures are more complicated and require more time and preparation. For this reason it is necessary in the majority of cases to protect the wings specially against unforeseen enterprises on the part of the enemy, and this is done by placing stronger masses on the wings than would be required for mere purposes of observation. To press heavily these masses, even if they oppose no very serious resistance, more time is required, and the stronger they are the more the enemy must develop his forces and his intentions, and by that means the object of the measure is attained; what is to be done further depends on the particular plans of the moment. We may therefore regard corps placed on the wings as lateral advanced guards, intended to retard the advance of the enemy through the space beyond our wings and give us time to make dispositions to counteract his movement.

If these corps are to fall back on the main body and the latter is not to make a backward movement at the same time, then it follows of itself that they must not be in the same line with the front of the main body, but thrown out somewhat forwards, because when a retreat is to be made, even without being preceded by a serious engagement, they should not retreat directly on the side of the position.

From these reasons of a subjective nature, as they relate to the inner organisation of an army, there arises a natural system of disposition, composed of four or five parts according as the reserve remains with the main body or not.

As the subsistence and shelter of the troops partly decide the choice of a position in general, so also they contribute to a disposition in separate divisions. The attention which they demand comes into consideration along with the other considerations above mentioned; and we seek to satisfy the one without prejudice to the other. In most cases, by the division of an army into five separate corps, the difficulties of subsistence and quartering will be overcome, and no great alteration will afterwards be required on their account.

We have still to cast a glance at the distances at which these separated corps may be allowed to be placed, if we are to retain in view the advantage of mutual support, and, therefore, of concentrating for battle. On this subject we remind our readers of what is said in the chapters on the duration and decision of the combat, according to which no absolute distance, but only the most general, as it were, average rules can be given, because absolute and relative strength of arms and country have a great influence.

The distance of the advanced guard is the easiest to fix, as in retreating it falls back on the main body of the army, and, therefore, may be at all events at a distance of a long day's march without incurring the risk of being obliged to fight an independent battle. But it should not be sent further in advance than the security of the army requires, because the further it has to fall back the more it suffers.

Respecting corps on the flanks, as we have already said, the combat of an ordinary division of 8000 to 10,000 men usually lasts for several hours, even for half a day before it is decided; on that account, therefore, there need be no hesitation in placing such a division at a distance of some leagues or one or two miles, and for the same reason, corps of three or four divisions may be detached a day's march or a distance of three or four miles.

From this natural and general disposition of the main body, in four or five divisions at particular distances, a certain method has arisen of dividing an army in a mechanical manner whenever there are no strong special reasons against this ordinary method.

But although we assume that each of these distinct parts of an army shall be competent to undertake an independent combat, and it may be obliged to engage in one, it does not therefore by any means follow that the real object of fractioning an army is that the parts should fight separately; the necessity for this distribution of the army is mostly only a condition of existence imposed by time. If the enemy approaches our position to try the fate of a general action, the strategic period is over, everything concentrates itself into the one moment of the battle, and therewith terminates and vanishes the object of the distribution of the army. As soon as the battle commences, considerations about quarters and subsistence are suspended; the observation of the enemy before our front and on our flanks has fulfilled the purpose of checking his advance by a partial resistance, and now all resolves itself into the one great unit – the great battle. The best criterion of skill in the disposition of an army lies in the proof that the distribution has been considered merely as a condition, as a necessary evil, but that united action in battle has been considered the object of the disposition.

CHAPTER SEVEN

Advanced Guard and Out-Posts

THESE TWO BODIES belong to that class of subjects into which both the tactical and strategic threads run simultaneously. On the one hand we must reckon them amongst those provisions which give form to the battle and ensure the execution of tactical plans; on the other hand, they frequently lead to independent combats, and on account of their position, more or less distant from the main body, they are to be regarded as links in the strategic chain, and it is this very feature which obliges us to supplement the preceding chapter by devoting a few moments to their consideration.

Every body of troops, when not completely in readiness for battle, requires an advanced guard to learn the approach of the enemy, and to gain further particulars respecting his force before he comes in sight, for the range of vision, as a rule, does not go much beyond the range of firearms. But what sort of man would he be who could not see farther than his arms can reach! The foreposts are the eyes of the army, as we have already said. The want of them, however, is not always equally great; it has its degrees. The strength of armies and the extent of ground they cover, time, place, contingencies, the method of making war, even chance, are all points which have an influence in the matter; and, therefore, we cannot wonder that military history, instead of furnishing any definite and simple outlines of the method of using advanced guards and outposts, only presents the subject in a kind of chaos of examples of the most diversified nature.

Sometimes we see the security of an army intrusted to a corps regularly appointed to the duty of advanced guard; at another time a long line of separate outposts; sometimes both these arrangements co-exist, sometimes neither one nor the other; at one time there is only one advanced guard in common for the whole of the advancing columns; at another time, each column has its own advanced guard. We shall endeavour to get a clear idea of what the subject really is, and then see whether we can arrive at some principles capable of application.

If the troops are on the march, a detachment of more or less strength forms its van or advanced guard, and in case of the movement of the army being reversed, this same detachment will form the rearguard. If the troops are in cantonments or camp, an extended line of weak posts, forms the vanguard, *the outposts*. It is essentially in the nature of things, that, when the army is halted, a greater extent of space can and must be watched than when the army is in motion, and therefore in the one case the conception of a chain of posts, in the other that of a concentrated corps arises of itself.

The actual strength of an advanced guard, as well as of outposts, ranges from a considerable corps, composed of an organisation of all three arms, to a regiment of hussars, and from a strongly entrenched defensive line, occupied by portions of troops from each arm of the service, to mere outlying pickets, and their supports detached from the camp. The services assigned to such vanguards range also from those of mere observation to an offer of opposition or resistance to the enemy, and this opposition may not only be to give the main body of the army the time which it requires to prepare for battle, but also to make the enemy develop his plans, and intentions, which consequently makes the observation far more important.

According as more or less time is required to be gained, according as the opposition to be offered is calculated upon and intended to meet the special measures of the enemy, so accordingly must the strength of the advanced guard and outposts be proportioned.

Frederick the Great, a general above all others ever ready for battle, and who almost directed his army in battle by word of command, never required strong outposts. We see him therefore constantly encamping close under the eyes of the enemy, without any great apparatus of outposts, relying for his security, at one place on a hussar regiment, at another on a light battalion, or perhaps on the pickets, and supports furnished from the camp. On the march, a few thousand horse, generally furnished by the cavalry on the flanks of the first line, formed his advanced guard, and at the end of the march rejoined the main body. He very seldom had any corps permanently employed as advanced guard.

When it is the intention of a small army, by using the whole weight of its mass with great vigour and activity, to make the enemy feel the effect of its superior discipline and the greater resolution of its commander, then almost every thing must be done *sous la barbe de l'ennemi*, in the same way as Frederick the Great did when opposed to Daun. A system of holding back from the enemy, and a very formal, and extensive system of outposts would neutralise all the advantages of the above kind of superiority. The circumstance that an error of another kind, and the carrying out Frederick's system too far, may lead to a battle of Hochkirch, is no argument against this method of acting; we should rather say, that as there was only one battle of Hochkirch in all the Silesian war, we ought to recognise in this system a proof of the King's consummate ability.

Napoleon, however, who commanded an army not deficient in discipline and firmness, and who did not want for resolution himself, never moved without a strong advanced guard. There are two reasons for this.

The first is to be found in the alteration in tactics. A whole army is no longer led into battle as one body by mere word of command, to settle the affair like a great duel by more or less skill and bravery; the combatants on each side now range their forces more to suit the peculiarities of the ground and circumstances, so that the order of battle, and consequently the battle itself, is a whole made up of many parts, from which there follows, that the simple determination to fight becomes a regularly formed plan, and the word of command a more or less long preparatory arrangement. For this time and data are required.

The second cause lies in the great size of modern armies. Frederick brought thirty or forty thousand men into battle; Napoleon from one to two hundred thousand.

We have selected these examples because every one will admit, that two such generals would never have adopted any systematic mode of proceeding without some good reason. Upon the whole, there has been a general improvement in the use of advanced guards and outposts in modern wars; not that every one acted as Frederick, even in the Silesian wars, for at that time the Austrians had a system of strong outposts, and frequently sent forward a corps as advanced guard, for which they had sufficient reason from the situation in which they were placed. Just in the same way we find differences enough in the mode of carrying on war in more modern times. Even the French Marshals Macdonald in Silesia, Oudinot and Ney in the Mark (Brandenburg), advanced with armies of sixty or seventy thousand men, without our reading of their having had any advanced guard. – We have hitherto been discussing advanced guards and outposts in relation to their numerical strength; but there is another difference which we must settle. It is that, when an army advances or retires on a certain breadth of ground, it may have a van and rear guard in common for all the columns which are marching side by side, or each column may have one for itself. In order to form a clear idea on this subject, we must look at it in this way.

The fundamental conception of an advanced guard, when a corps is so specially designated, is that its mission is the security of the main body or centre of the army. If this main body is marching upon several contiguous roads so close together that they can also easily serve for the advanced guard, and therefore be covered by it, then the flank columns naturally require no special covering.

But those corps which are moving at great distances, in reality as detached corps, must provide their own van-guards. The same applies also to any of those corps which belong to the central mass, and owing to the direction that the roads may happen to take, are too far from the centre column. Therefore there will be as many advanced guards, as there are columns virtually separated from each other; if each of these advanced guards is much weaker than one general one would be, then they fall more into the class of other tactical dispositions, and there is no advanced guard in the strategic tableau. But if the main body or centre has a much larger corps for its advanced guard, then that corps will appear as the advanced guard of the whole, and will be so in many respects.

But what can be the reason for giving the centre a van-guard so much stronger than the wings? The following three reasons.

1. Because the mass of troops composing the centre is usually much more considerable.

2. Because plainly the central point of a strip of country along which the front of an army is extended must always be the most important point, as all the combinations of the campaign relate mostly to it, and therefore the field of battle is also usually nearer to it than to the wings.

3. Because, although a corps thrown forward in front of the centre does not directly protect the wings as a real vanguard, it still contributes greatly to their security indirectly. For instance, the enemy cannot in ordinary cases pass by such a corps within a certain distance in order to effect any enterprise of importance against one of the wings, because he has to fear an attack in flank and rear. Even if this check which a corps thrown forward in the centre imposes on the enemy is not sufficient to constitute complete security for the wings, it is at all events sufficient to relieve the flanks from all apprehension in a great many cases.

The van-guard of the centre, if much stronger than that of a wing, that is to say, if it consists of a special corps as advanced guard, has then not merely the mission of a van-guard intended to protect the troops in its rear from sudden surprise; it also operates in more general strategic relations as an army corps thrown forward in advance.

The following are the purposes for which such a corps may be used, and therefore those which determine its duties in practice.

1. To insure a stouter resistance, and make the enemy advance with more caution; consequently to do the duties of a van-guard on a greater scale, whenever our arrangements are such as to require time before they can be carried into effect.

2. If the central mass of the army is very large, to be able to keep this unwieldy body at some distance from the enemy, while we still remain close to him with a more moveable body of troops.

3. That we may have a corps of observation close to the enemy, if there are any other reasons which require us to keep the principal mass of the army at a considerable distance.

The idea that weaker look-out posts, mere partisan corps, might answer just as well for this observation is set aside at once if we reflect how easily a weak corps might be dispersed, and how very limited also are its means of observation as compared with those of a considerable corps.

4. In the pursuit of the enemy. A single corps as advanced guard, with the greater part of the cavalry attached to it, can move quicker, arriving later at its bivouac, and moving earlier in the morning than the whole mass.

5. Lastly, on a retreat, as rearguard, to be used in defending the principal natural obstacles of ground. In this respect also the centre is exceedingly important. At first sight it certainly appears as if such a rearguard would be constantly in danger of having its flanks turned. But we must remember that, even if the enemy succeeds in overlapping the flanks to some extent, he has still to march the whole way from there to the centre before he can seriously threaten the central mass, which gives time to the rearguard of the centre to prolong its resistance, and remain in rear somewhat longer. On the other hand, the situation becomes at once critical if the centre falls back quicker than the wings; there is immediately an appearance as if the line had been broken through, and even the very idea or appearance of that is to be dreaded. At no time is there a greater necessity for concentration and holding together, and at no time is this more sensibly felt by every one than on a retreat. The intention always is, that the wings in case of extremity should close upon the centre; and if, on account of subsistence and roads, the retreat has to be made on a considerable width (of country), still the movement generally ends by a concentration on the

centre. If we add to these considerations also this one, that the enemy usually advances with his principal force in the centre and with the greatest energy against the centre, we must perceive that the rear guard of the centre is of special importance.

Accordingly, therefore, a special corps should always be thrown forward as an advanced guard in every case where one of the above relations occurs. These relations almost fall to the ground if the centre is not stronger than the wings, as, for example, Macdonald when he advanced against Blucher, in Silesia, in 1813, and the latter, when he made his movement towards the Elbe. Both of them had three corps, which usually moved in three columns by different roads, the heads of the columns in line. On this account no mention is made of their having had advanced guards.

But this disposition in three columns of equal strength is one which is by no means to be recommended, partly on that account, and also because the division of a whole army into three parts makes it very unmanageable, as stated in the fifth chapter of the third book.

When the whole is formed into a centre with two wings separate from it, which we have represented in the preceding chapter as the most natural formation as long as there is no particular object for any other, the corps forming the advanced guard, according to the simplest notion of the case, will have its place in front of the centre, and therefore before the line which forms the front of the wings; but as the first object of corps thrown out on the flanks is to perform the same office for the sides as the advanced guard for the front, it will very often happen that these corps will be in line with the advanced guard, or even still further thrown forward, according to circumstances.

With respect to the strength of an advanced guard we have little to say, as now very properly it is the general custom to detail for that duty one or more component parts of the army of the first class, reinforced by part of the cavalry: so that it consists of a corps, if the army is formed in corps; of a division, if the organisation is in divisions.

It is easy to perceive that in this respect also the great number of higher members or divisions is an advantage.

How far the advanced guard should be pushed to the front must entirely depend on circumstances; there are cases in which it may be more than a day's march in advance, and others in which it should be immediately before the front of the army. If we find that in most cases between one and three miles is the distance chosen, that shows certainly that circumstances have usually pointed out this distance as the best; but we cannot make of it a rule by which we are to be always guided.

In the foregoing observations we have lost sight altogether of *outposts*, and therefore we must now return to them again.

In saying, at the commencement, that the relations between outposts and stationary troops is similar to that between advanced guards and troops in motion, our object was to refer the conceptions back to their origin, and keep them distinct in future; but it is clear that if we confine ourselves strictly to the words we should get little more than a pedantic distinction.

If an army on the march halts at night to resume the march next morning, the advanced guard must naturally do the same, and always organise the outpost duty, required both for its own security and that of the main body, without on that account being changed from an advanced guard into a line of outposts. To satisfy the notion of that transformation, the advanced guard would have to be completely broken up into a chain of small posts, having either only a very small force, or none at all in a form approaching to a mass. In other words, the idea of a line of outposts must predominate over that of a concentrated corps.

The shorter the time of rest of the army, the less complete does the covering of the army require to be, for the enemy has hardly time to learn from day to day what is covered and what is not. The longer the halt is to be the more complete must be the observation and covering of all points of approach. As a rule, therefore, when the halt is long, the vanguard becomes always more and more extended into a line of posts. Whether the change becomes complete, or whether the idea of a concentrated corps shall continue uppermost, depends chiefly on two circumstances. The first is the proximity of the contending armies, the second is the nature of the country.

If the armies are very close in comparison to the width of their front, then it will often be impossible to post a vanguard between them, and the armies are obliged to place their dependence on a chain of outposts.

A concentrated corps, as it covers the approaches to the army less directly, generally requires more time and space to act efficiently; and therefore, if the army covers a great extent of front, as in cantonments, and a corps standing in mass is to cover all the avenues of approach, it is necessary that we should be at a considerable distance from the enemy; on this account winter quarters, for instance, are generally covered by a cordon of posts.

The second circumstance is the nature of the country; where, for example, any formidable obstacle of ground affords the means of forming a strong line of posts with but few troops, we should not neglect to take advantage of it.

Lastly, in winter quarters, the rigour of the season may also be a reason for breaking up the advanced guard into a line of posts, because it is easier to find shelter for it in that way.

The use of a reinforced line of outposts was brought to great perfection by the Anglo-Dutch army, during the campaign of 1794 and 1795, in the Netherlands, when the line of defence was formed by brigades composed of all arms, in single posts, and supported by a reserve. Scharnhorst, who was with that army, introduced this system into the Prussian army on the Passarge in 1807. Elsewhere in modern times, it has been little adopted, chiefly because the wars have been too rich in movement. But even when there has been occasion for its use it has been neglected, as for instance, by Murat, at Tarutino. A wider extension of his defensive line would have spared him the loss of thirty pieces of artillery in a combat of out-posts.

It cannot be disputed that in certain circumstances, great advantages may be derived from this system. We propose to return to the subject on another occasion.

CHAPTER EIGHT

Mode of Action of Advanced Corps

WE HAVE JUST SEEN how the security of the army is expected, from the effect which an advanced guard and flank corps produce on an advancing enemy. Such corps are always to be considered as very weak whenever we imagine them in conflict with the main body of the enemy, and therefore a peculiar mode of using them is required, that they may fulfil the purpose for which they are intended, without incurring the risk of the serious loss which is to be feared from this disproportion in strength.

The object of a corps of this description, is to observe the enemy, and to delay his progress.

For the first of these purposes a smaller body would never be sufficient, partly because it would be more easily driven back, partly because its means of observation – that is its eyes – could not reach as far.

But the observation must be carried to a high point; the enemy must be made to develop his whole strength before such a corps, and thereby reveal to a certain extent, not only his force, but also his plans.

For this its mere presence would be sufficient, and it would only be necessary to wait and see the measures by which the enemy seeks to drive it back, and then commence its retreat at once.

But further, it must also delay the advance of the enemy, and that implies actual resistance.

Now how can we conceive this waiting until the last moment, as well as this resistance, without such a corps being in constant danger of serious loss? Chiefly in this way, that the enemy himself is preceded by an advanced guard, and therefore does not advance at once with all the outflanking and overpowering weight of his whole force. Now, if this advance guard is also from the commencement superior to our advanced corps, as we may naturally suppose it is intended it should be, and if the enemy's main body is also nearer to his advanced guard than we are to ours, and if that main body, being already on the march, will soon be on the spot to support the attack of his advanced guard with all his strength, still this first act, in which our advanced corps has to contend with the enemy's advanced guard, that is with a force not much exceeding its own, ensures at once a certain gain of time, and thus allows of our watching the adversary's movements for some time without endangering our own retreat.

But even a certain amount of resistance which such a corps can offer in a suitable position is not attended with such disadvantage as we might anticipate in other cases through the disproportion in the strength of the forces engaged. The chief danger in a contest with a superior enemy consists always in the possibility of being turned and placed in a critical situation by the enemy enveloping our position; but in the case to which our attention is now directed, a risk of this description is very much less, owing to the advancing enemy never knowing exactly how near there may be support from the main body of his opponent's army itself, which may place his advanced column between two fires. The consequence is, that the enemy in advancing keeps the heads of his single columns as nearly as possible in line, and only begins very cautiously to attempt to turn one or other wing after he has sufficiently reconnoitred our position. While the enemy is thus feeling about and moving guardedly, the corps we have thrown forward has time to fall back before it is in any serious danger.

As for the length of the resistance which such a corps should offer against the attack in front, or against the commencement of any turning movement, that depends chiefly on the nature of the ground and the proximity of the enemy's supports. If this resistance is continued beyond its natural measure, either from want of judgment or from a sacrifice being necessary in order to give the main body the time it requires, the consequence must always be a very considerable loss.

It is only in rare instances, and more especially when some local obstacle is favourable, that the resistance actually made in such a combat can be of importance, and the duration of the little battle of such a corps would in itself be hardly sufficient to gain the time required; that time is really gained in a threefold manner, which lies in the nature of the thing, viz.:

1. By the more cautious, and consequently slower advance of the enemy.
2. By the duration of the actual resistance offered.
3. By the retreat itself.

This retreat must be made as slowly as is consistent with safety. If the country affords good positions they should be made use of, as that obliges the enemy to organise fresh attacks and plans for turning movements, and by that means more time is gained. Perhaps in a new position a real combat even may again be fought.

We see that the opposition to the enemy's progress by actual fighting and the retreat are completely combined with one another, and that the shortness of the duration of the fights must be made up for by their frequent repetition.

This is the kind of resistance which an advanced corps should offer. The degree of effect depends chiefly on the strength of the corps, and the configuration of the country; next on the length of the road which the corps has to march over, and the support which it receives.

A small body, even when the forces on both sides are equal can never make as long a stand as a considerable corps; for the larger the masses the more time they require to complete their action, of whatever kind it may be. In a mountainous country the mere marching is of itself slower, the resistance in the different positions longer, and attended with less danger, and at every step favourable positions may be found.

As the distance to which a corps is pushed forward increases so will the length of its retreat, and therefore also the absolute gain of time by its resistance; but as such a corps by its position has less power of resistance in itself, and is less easily reinforced, its retreat must be made more rapidly in proportion than if it stood nearer the main body, and had a shorter distance to traverse.

The support and means of rallying afforded to an advanced corps must naturally have an influence on the duration of the resistance, as all the time that prudence requires for the security of the retreat is so much taken from the resistance, and therefore diminishes its amount.

There is a marked difference in the time gained by the resistance of an advanced corps when the enemy makes his first appearance after midday; in such a case the length of the night is so much additional time gained, as the advance is seldom continued throughout the night. Thus it was that, in 1815, on the short distance from Charleroi to Ligny, not more than two miles,[54] the first Prussian corps under General Ziethen, about 30,000 strong, against Buonaparte at the head of 120,000 men, was enabled to gain twenty-four hours for the Prussian army then engaged in concentrating. The first attack was made on General Ziethen

54 Here, as well as elsewhere, by the word mile, the German mile is meant. – Tr.

about nine o'clock on the morning of 15th June, and the battle of Ligny did not commence until about two on the afternoon of 16th. General Ziethen suffered, it is true, very considerable loss, amounting to five or six thousand men killed, wounded or prisoners.

If we refer to experience the following are the results, which may serve as a basis in any calculations of this kind.

A division of ten or twelve thousand men, with a proportion of cavalry, a day's march of three or four miles in advance in an ordinary country, not particularly strong, will be able to detain the enemy (including time occupied in the retreat) about half as long again as he would otherwise require to march over the same ground, but if the division is only a mile in advance, then the enemy ought to be detained about twice or three times as long as he otherwise would be on the march.

Therefore supposing the distance to be a march of four miles, for which usually ten hours are required, then from the moment that the enemy appears in force in front of the advanced corps, we may reckon upon fifteen hours before he is in a condition to attack our main body. On the other hand, if the advanced guard is posted only a mile in advance, then the time which will elapse before our army can be attacked will be more than three or four hours, and may very easily come up to double that, for the enemy still requires just as much time to mature his first measures against our advanced guard, and the resistance offered by that guard in its original position will be greater than it would be in a position further forward.

The consequence is, that in the first of these supposed cases the enemy cannot easily make an attack on our main body on the same day that he presses back the advanced corps, and this exactly coincides with the results of experience. Even in the second case the enemy must succeed in driving our advanced guard from its ground in the first half of the day to have the requisite time for a general action.

As the night comes to our help in the first of these supposed cases, we see how much time may be gained by an advanced guard thrown further forward.

With reference to corps placed on the sides or flanks, the object of which we have before explained, the mode of action is in most cases more or less connected with circumstances which belong to the province of immediate application. The simplest way is to look upon them as advanced guards placed on the sides, which being at the same time thrown out somewhat in advance, retreat in an oblique direction upon the army.

As these corps are not immediately in the front of the army, and cannot be so easily supported as a regular advanced guard, they would, therefore, be exposed to greater danger if it was not that the enemy's offensive power in most cases is somewhat less at the outer extremities of his line, and in the worst cases such corps have sufficient room to give way without exposing the army so directly to danger as a flying advanced guard would in its rapid retreat.

The most usual and best means of supporting an advanced corps is by a considerable body of cavalry, for which reason, when necessary from the distance at which the corps is advanced, the reserve cavalry is posted between the main body and the advanced corps.

The conclusion to be drawn from the preceding reflections is, that an advanced corps effects more by its presence than by its efforts, less by the combats in which it engages than by the possibility of those in which it might engage: that it should never attempt to stop the enemy's movements, but only serve like a pendulum to moderate and regulate them, so that they may be made matter of calculation.

CHAPTER NINE
Camps

WE ARE NOW considering the three situations of an army outside of the combat only strategically, that is, so far as they are conditioned by place, time, and the number of the effective force. All those subjects which relate to the internal arrangement of the combat and the transition into the state of combat belong to tactics.

The disposition in camps, under which we mean every disposition of an army except in quarters, whether it be in tents, huts, or bivouac, is strategically completely identical with the combat which is contingent upon such disposition. Tactically, it is not so always, for we can, for many reasons, choose a site for encamping which is not precisely identical with the proposed field of battle. Having already said all that is necessary on the disposition of an army, that is, on the position of the different parts, we have only to make some observations on camps in connection with their history.

In former times, that is, before armies grew once more to considerable dimensions, before wars became of greater duration, and their partial acts brought into connection with a whole or general plan, and up to the time of the war of the French Revolution, armies always used tents. This was their normal state. With the commencement of the mild season of the year they left their quarters, and did not again take them up until winter set in. Winter quarters at that time must to a certain extent be looked upon as a state of no war, for in them the forces were neutralised, the whole clockwork stopped, quarters to refresh an army which preceded the real winter quarters, and other temporary cantonments, for a short time within contracted limits were transitional and exceptional conditions.

This is not the place to enquire how such a periodical voluntary neutralisation of power consisted with, or is now consistent with the object and being of war; we shall come to that subject hereafter. Enough that it was so.

Since the wars of the French Revolution, armies have completely done away with the tents on account of the encumbrance they cause.

Partly it is found better for an army of 100,000 men to have, in place of 6,000 tent horses, 5,000 additional cavalry, or a couple of hundred extra guns, partly it has been found that in great and rapid operations a load of tents is a hindrance, and of little use.

But this change is attended with two drawbacks, viz., an increase of casualties in the force, and greater wasting of the country.

However slight the protection afforded by a roof of common tent cloth, – it cannot be denied that on a long continuance it is great relief to the troops. For a single day the difference is small, because a tent is little protection against wind and cold, and does not completely exclude wet; but this small difference, if repeated two or three hundred times in a year, becomes important. A greater loss through sickness is just a natural result.

How the devastation of the country is increased through the want of tents for the troops requires no explanation.

One would suppose that on account of these two reactionary influences the doing away with tents must have diminished again the energy of war in another way, that troops must remain longer in quarters, and from want of the requisites for encampment must forego many positions which would have been possible had tents been forthcoming.

This would indeed have been the case had there not been, in the same epoch of time, an enormous revolution in war generally, which swallowed up in itself all these smaller subordinate influences.

The elementary fire of war has become so overpowering, its energy so extraordinary, that these regular periods of rest also have disappeared, and every power presses forward with persistent force towards the great decision, which will be treated of more fully in the ninth book. Under these circumstances, therefore, any question about effects on an army from the discontinuance of the use of tents in the field is quite thrown into the shade. Troops now occupy huts, or bivouac under the canopy of heaven, without regard to season of the year, weather, or locality, just according as the general plan and object of the campaign require.

Whether war will in the future continue to maintain, under all circumstances and at all times, this energy, is a question we shall consider hereafter; where this energy is wanting, the want of tents is calculated to exercise some influence on the conduct of war; but that this reaction will ever be strong enough to bring back the use of tents is very doubtful, because now that much wider limits have been opened for the elements of war it will never return within its old narrow bounds, except occasionally for a certain time and under certain circumstances, only to break out again with the all-powerful force of its nature. Permanent arrangements for an army must, therefore, be based only upon that nature.

CHAPTER TEN

Marches

MARCHES ARE A mere passage from one position to another under two primary conditions.

The first is the due care of the troops, so that no forces shall be squandered uselessly when they might be usefully employed; the second, is precision in the movements, so that they may fit exactly. If we marched 100,000 men in one single column, that is, upon *one* road without intervals of time, the rear of the column would never arrive at the proposed destination on the same day with the head of the column; we must either advance at an unusually slow pace, or the mass would, like a thread of water, disperse itself in drops; and this dispersion, together with the excessive exertion laid upon those in rear owing to the length of the column, would soon throw everything into confusion.

If from this extreme we take the opposite direction, we find that the smaller the mass of troops in one column the greater the ease and precision with which the march can be performed. The result of this is the need of a *division* quite irrespective of that division of an army in separate parts which belongs to its position; therefore, although the division into columns of march originates in the strategic disposition in general, it does not do so in every particular case. A great mass which is to be concentrated at any one point must necessarily be divided for the march. But even if a disposition of the army in separate parts causes a march in separate divisions, sometimes the conditions of the primitive disposition, sometimes those of the march, are paramount. For instance, if the disposition of the troops is one made merely for rest, one in which a battle is not expected, then the conditions of the march predominate, and these conditions are chiefly the choice of good, well-frequented roads. Keeping in view this difference, we choose a road in the one case on account of the quarters and camping ground, in the other we take the quarters and camps such as they are, on account of the road. When a battle is expected, and everything depends on our reaching a particular point with a mass of troops, then we should think nothing of getting to that point by even the worst by-roads, if necessary; if, on the other hand, we are still on the journey to the theatre of war, then the nearest great roads are selected for the columns, and we look out for the best quarters and camps that can be got near them.

Whether the march is of the one kind or the other, if there is a possibility of a combat, that is within the whole region of actual war, it is an invariable rule in the modern art of war to organise the columns so that the mass of troops composing each column is fit of itself to engage in an independent combat. This condition is satisfied by the combination of the three arms, by an organised subdivision of the whole, and by the appointment of a competent commander. Marches, therefore, have been the chief cause of the new order of battle, and they profit most by it.

When in the middle of the last century, especially in the theatre of war in which Frederick II. was engaged, generals began to look upon movement as a principle belonging to fighting, and to think of gaining the victory by the effect of unexpected movements, the want of an organised order of battle caused the most complicated and laborious evolutions on a march. In carrying out a movement near the enemy, an army ought to be always ready to fight; but at that time they were never ready to fight unless the whole army was collectively present, because nothing less than the army constituted a complete whole. In a march to a flank, the second line, in order to be always at the regulated distance, that is about a quarter of a mile from the first, had to march up hill and down dale, which demanded immense exertion, as well as a great stock of local knowledge; for where can one find two good roads running parallel at a distance of a quarter of a mile from each other? The cavalry on the wings had to encounter the same difficulties when the march was direct to the front. There was other difficulty with the artillery, which required a road for itself, protected by infantry; for the lines of infantry required to be continuous lines, and the artillery increased the length of their already long trailing columns still more, and threw all their regulated distances into disorder. It is only necessary to read the dispositions for marches in Tempelhof's History of the Seven Years' War, to be satisfied of all these incidents and of the restraints thus imposed on the action of war.

But since then the modern art of war has subdivided armies on a regular principle, so that each of the principal parts forms in itself a complete whole, of small proportions, but capable of acting in battle precisely like the great whole, except in one respect, which is, that the duration of its action must be shorter. The consequence of this change is, that even when it is intended that the whole force should take part in a battle, it is no longer necessary to have the columns so close to each other that they may unite before the commencement of the combat; it is sufficient now if the concentration takes place in the course of the action.

The smaller a body of troops the more easily it can be moved, and therefore the less it requires that subdivision which is not a result of the separate disposition, but of the unwieldiness of the mass. A small body, therefore, can march upon one road, and if it is to advance on several lines it easily finds roads near each other which are as good as it requires. The greater the mass the greater becomes the necessity for subdividing, the greater becomes the number of columns, and the want of made roads, or even great high roads, consequently also the distance of the columns from each other. Now the danger of this subdivision is – arithmetically expressed – in an inverse ratio to the necessity for it. The smaller the parts are, the more readily must they be able to render assistance to each other; the larger they are, the longer they can be left to depend on themselves. If we only call to mind what has been said in the preceding book on this subject, and also consider that in cultivated countries at a few miles distance from the main road there are always other tolerably good roads running in a parallel direction, it is easy to see that, in regulating a march, there are no great difficulties which make rapidity and precision in the advance incompatible with the proper concentration of force. – In a mountainous country parallel roads are both scarce, and the difficulties of communication between them great; but the defensive powers of a single column are very much greater.

In order to make this idea clearer let us look at it for a moment in a concrete form.

A division of 8, 000 men, with its artillery and other carriages, takes up, as we know by experience in ordinary cases, a space of one league; if, therefore, two divisions march one after the other on the same road, the second arrives one hour after the first; but now, as said in the sixth chapter of the fourth book, a division of this strength is quite capable of maintaining a combat for several hours, even against a superior force, and, therefore, supposing the worst, that is, supposing the first had to commence a fight instantaneously, still the second division would not arrive too late. Further, within a league right and left of the road on which we march, in the cultivated countries of central Europe there are, generally, lateral roads which can be used for a march, so that there is no necessity to go across country, as was so often done in the Seven Years' War.

Again, it is known by experience that the head of a column composed of four divisions and a reserve of cavalry, even on indifferent roads, generally gets over a march of three miles in eight hours; now, if we reckon for each division one league in depth, and the same for the reserve cavalry and artillery, then the whole march will last thirteen hours. This is no great length of time, and yet in this case forty thousand men would have marched over the same road. But with such a mass as this we can make use of lateral roads, which are to be found at a greater distance, and therefore easily shorten the march. If the mass of troops marching on the same road is still greater than above supposed, then it is a case in which the arrival of the whole on the same day is no longer indispensable, for such masses never give battle now the moment they meet, usually not until the next day.

We have introduced these concrete cases, not as exhausting considerations of this kind, but to make ourselves more intelligible, and by means of this glance at the results of experience to show that in the present mode of conducting war the organisation of marches no longer offers such great difficulties; that the most rapid marches, executed with the greatest precision, no longer require either that peculiar skill or that exact knowledge of the country which was needed for Frederick's rapid and exact marches in the Seven Years' War. Through the existing organisation of armies, they rather go on now almost of themselves, at least without any great preparatory plans. In times past, battles were conducted by mere word of command, but marches required a regular plan, now the order of battle requires the latter, and for a march the word of command almost suffices.

As is well known, all marches are either perpendicular [to the front] or parallel. The latter, also called flank marches, alter the geometrical position of the divisions; those parts which, in position, were in line, will follow one another, and *vice versa*. Now, although the line of march may be at any angle with the front, still the order of the march must decidedly be of one or other of these classes.

This geometrical alteration could only be completely carried out by tactics, and by it only through the file-march as it is called, which, with great masses, is impossible. Far less is it possible for strategy to do it. The parts which changed their geometrical relation in the old order of battle were only the centre and wings; in the new they are the divisions of the first rank – corps, divisions, or even brigades, according to the organisation of the army. Now, the consequences above deduced from the new order of battle have an influence here also, for as it is no longer so necessary, as formerly, that the whole army should be assembled before action commences, therefore the greater care is taken that those troops which march together form one whole (a unit). If two divisions were so placed that one formed the reserve to the other, and that they were to advance against the enemy upon two roads, no one would think of sending a portion of each division by each of the roads, but a road would at once be assigned to each division; they would therefore march side by side, and each general of division would be left to provide a reserve for himself in case of a combat. Unity of command is much more important than the original geometrical relation; if the divisions reach their new position without a combat, they can resume their previous relations. Much less if two divisions, standing together, are to make a *parallel* (flank) march upon two roads should we think of placing the second line or reserve of each division on the rear road; instead of that, we should allot to each of the divisions one of the roads, and therefore during the march consider one division as forming the reserve to the other. If an army in four divisions, of which three form the front line and the fourth the reserve, is to march against the enemy in that order, then it is natural to assign a road to each of the divisions in front, and cause the reserve to follow the centre. If there are not three roads at a suitable distance apart, then we need not hesitate at once to march upon two roads, as no serious inconvenience can arise from so doing.

It is the same in the opposite case, the flank march.

Another point is the march off of columns from the right flank or left. In parallel marches (marches to a flank) the thing is plain in itself. No one would march off from the right to make a movement to the left flank. In a march to the front or rear, the order of march should properly be chosen according to the direction of the lines of roads in respect to the future line of deployment. This may also be done frequently in tactics, as its spaces are smaller, and therefore a survey of the geometrical relations can be more easily taken. In strategy it is quite impossible, and therefore although we have seen here and there a certain analogy brought over into strategy from tactics, it was mere pedantry. Formerly the whole order of march was a purely tactical affair, because the army on a march remained always an indivisible whole, and looked to nothing but a combat of the whole; yet nevertheless Schwerin, for example, when he marched off from his position near Brandeis, on the 5th of May, could not tell whether his future field of battle would be on his right or left, and on this account he was obliged to make his famous countermarch.

If an army in the old order of battle advanced against the enemy in four columns, the cavalry in the first and second lines on each wing formed the two exterior columns, the two lines of infantry composing the wings formed the two central columns. Now these columns could march off all from the right or all from the left, or the right wing from the right, the left wing from the left, or the left from the right, and the right from the left. In the latter case it would have been called "double column from the centre." But all these forms, although they ought to have had a relation directly to the future deployment, were really all quite indifferent in that respect. When Frederick the Great entered on the battle of Leuthen, his army had been marched off by wings from the right in four columns, therefore the wonderful transition to a march off in order of battle, as described by all writers of history, was done with the greatest ease, because it happened that the king chose to attack the left wing of the Austrians; had he wanted to turn their right, he must have countermarched his army, as he did at Prague.

If these forms did not meet that object in those days, they would be mere trifling as regards it now. We know now just as little as formerly the situation of the future battle-field in reference to the road we take; and the little loss of time occasioned by marching off in inverted order is now infinitely less important than formerly. The new order of battle has further a beneficial influence in this respect, that it is now immaterial which division arrives first or which brigade is brought under fire first.

Under these circumstances the march off from the right or left is of no consequence now, otherwise than that when it is done alternately it tends to equalise the fatigue which the troops undergo. This, which is the only object, is certainly an important one for retaining both modes of marching off with large bodies.

The advance from the centre as a definite evolution naturally comes to an end on account of what has just been stated, and can only take place accidentally. An advance from the centre by one and the same column in strategy is, in point of fact, nonsense, for it supposes a double road.

The order of march belongs, moreover, more to the province of tactics than to that of strategy, for it is the division of a whole into parts, which, after the march, are once more to resume the state of a whole. As, however, in modern warfare the formal connection of the parts is not required to be constantly kept up during a march, but on the contrary, the parts during the march may become further separated, and therefore be left more to their own resources, therefore it is much easier now for independent combats to happen in which the parts have to sustain themselves, and which, therefore must be reckoned as complete combats in themselves, and on that account we have thought it necessary to say so much on the subject.

Further, an order of battle in three parts in juxtaposition being, as we have seen in the second[55] chapter of this book, the most natural where no special object predominates, from that results also that the order of march in three columns is the most natural.

It only remains to observe that the notion of a column in strategy does not found itself mainly on the line of march of one body of troops. The term is used in strategy to designate masses of troops marching on the same road on different days as well. For the division into columns is made chiefly to shorten and facilitate the march, as a small number marches quicker and more conveniently than large bodies. But this end may, be attained by marching troops on different days, as well as by marching them on different roads.

55   5th Chap.? – tr.

CHAPTER ELEVEN

Marches (Continued)

RESPECTING THE LENGTH of a march and the time it requires, it is natural for us to depend on the general results of experience.

For our modern armies it has long been settled that a march of three miles should be the usual day's work which, on long distances, may be set down as an average distance of two miles per day, allowing for the necessary rest days, to make such repairs of all kinds as may be required.

Such a march in a level country, and on tolerable roads will occupy a division of 8,000 men from eight to ten hours; in a hilly country from ten to twelve hours. If several divisions are united in one column, the march will occupy a couple of hours longer, without taking into account the intervals which must elapse between the departure of the first and succeeding divisions.

We see, therefore, that the day is pretty well occupied with such a march; that the fatigue endured by a soldier loaded with his pack for ten or twelve hours is not to be judged of by that of an ordinary journey of three miles on foot which a person, on tolerable roads, might easily get over in five hours.

The longest marches to be found in exceptional instances are of five, or at most six miles a day; for a continuance four.

A march of five miles requires a halt for several hours; and a division of 8,000 men will not do it, even on a good road, in less than sixteen hours. If the march is one of six miles, and that there are several divisions in the column, we may reckon upon at least twenty hours.

We here mean the march of a number of whole divisions at once, from one camp to another, for that is the usual form of marches made on a theatre of war. When several divisions are to march in one column, the first division to move is assembled and marched off earlier than the rest, and therefore arrives at its camping ground so much the sooner. At the same time this difference can still never amount to the whole time, which corresponds to the depth of a division on the line of march, and which is so well expressed in French, as the time it requires for its *découlement* (running down). The soldier is, therefore, saved very little fatigue in this way, and every march is very much lengthened in duration in proportion as the number of troops to be moved increases. To assemble and march off the different brigades of a division, in like manner at different times, is seldom practicable, and for that reason we have taken the division itself as the unit.

In long distances, when troops march from one cantonment into another, and go over the road in small bodies, and without points of assembly, the distance they go over daily may certainly be increased, and in point of fact it is so, from the necessary detours in getting to quarters.

But those marches, on which troops have to assemble daily in divisions, or perhaps in corps, and have an additional move to get into quarters, take up the most time, and are only advisable in rich countries, and where the masses of troops are not too large, as in such cases the greater facility of subsistence and the advantage of the shelter which the troops obtain compensate sufficiently for the fatigue of a longer march. The Prussian army undoubtedly pursued a wrong system in their retreat in 1806 in taking up quarters for the troops every night on account of subsistence. They could have procured subsistence in bivouacs, and the army would not have been obliged to spend fourteen days in getting over fifty miles of ground, which, after all, they only accomplished by extreme efforts.

If a bad road or a hilly country has to be marched over, all these calculations as to time and distance undergo such modifications that it is difficult to estimate, with any certainty, in any particular case, the time required for a march; much less, then, can any general theory be established. All that theory can do is to direct attention to the liability to error with which we are here beset. To avoid it the most careful calculation is necessary, and a large margin for unforeseen delays. The influence of weather and condition of the troops also come into consideration.

Since the doing away with tents and the introduction of the system of subsisting troops by compulsory demands for provisions on the spot, the baggage of an army has been very sensibly diminished, and as a natural and most important consequence we look first for an acceleration in the movements of an army, and, therefore, of course, an increase in the length of the day's march. This, however, is only realized under certain circumstances.

Marches within the theatre of war have been very little accelerated by this means, for it is well known that for many years whenever the object required marches of unusual length it has always been the practice to leave the baggage behind or send it on beforehand, and, generally, to keep it separate from the troops during the continuance of such movements, and it had in general no influence on the movement, because as soon as it was out of the way, and ceased to be a direct impediment, no further trouble was taken about it, whatever damage it might suffer in that way. Marches, therefore, took place in the Seven Years' War, which even now cannot be surpassed; as an instance we cite Lascy's march in 1760, when he had to support the diversion of the Russians on Berlin, on that occasion he got over the road from Schweidnitz to Berlin through Lusatia, a distance of forty-five miles, in ten days, averaging, therefore, 4½ miles a day, which, for a corps of 15,000, would be an extraordinary march even in these days.

On the other hand, through the new method of supplying troops the movements of armies have acquired a new *retarding* principle. If troops have partly to procure supplies for themselves, which often happens, then they require more time for the service of supply than would be necessary merely to receive rations from provision wagons. Besides this, on marches of considerable duration troops cannot be encamped in such large numbers at any one point; the divisions must be separated from one another, in order the more easily to manage for them. Lastly, it almost always happens that it is necessary to place part of the army, particularly the cavalry, in quarters. All this occasions on the whole a sensible delay. We find, therefore, that Buonaparte in pursuit of the Prussians in 1806, with a view to cut off their retreat, and Blucher in 1815, in pursuit of the French, with a like object, only accomplished thirty miles in ten days, a rate which Frederick the Great was able to attain in his marches from Saxony to Silesia and back, notwithstanding all the train that he had to carry with him.

At the same time the mobility and handiness, if we may use such an expression, of the parts of an army, both great and small, on the theatre of war have very perceptibly gained by the diminution of baggage. Partly, inasmuch as while the number of cavalry and guns is the same, there are fewer horses, and therefore, there is less forage required; partly, inasmuch as we are no longer so much tied to any one position, because we have not to be for ever looking after a long train of baggage dragging after us.

Marches such as that, which, after raising the siege of Olmutz, 1758, Frederick the Great made with 4,000 carriages, the escort of which employed half his army broken up into single battalions and companies, could not be effected now in presence of even the most timid adversary.

On long marches, as from the Tagus to the Niemen, that lightening of the army is more sensibly felt, for although the usual measure of the day's march remains the same on account of the carriages still remaining, yet, in cases of great urgency, we can exceed that usual measure at a less sacrifice.

Generally the diminution of baggage tends more to a saving of power than to the acceleration of movement.

CHAPTER TWELVE
Marches (Continued)

WE HAVE NOW to consider the destructive influence which marches have upon an army. It is so great that it may be regarded as an active principle of destruction, just as much as the combat.

One single moderate march does not wear down the instrument, but a succession of even moderate marches is certain to tell upon it, and a succession of severe ones will, of course, do so much sooner.

At the actual scene of war, want of food and shelter, bad broken-up roads, and the necessity of being in a perpetual state of readiness for battle, are causes of an excessive strain upon our means, by which men, cattle, carriages of every description as well as clothing are ruined.

It is commonly said that a long rest does not suit the physical health of an army; that at such a time there is more sickness than during moderate activity. No doubt sickness will and does occur if soldiers are packed too close in confined quarters; but the same thing would occur if these were quarters taken up on the march, and the want of air and exercise can never be the cause of such sicknesses, as it is so easy to give the soldier both by means of his exercises.

Only think for a moment, when the organism of a human being is in a disordered and fainting state, what a difference it must make to him whether he falls sick in a house or is seized in the middle of a high road, up to his knees in mud, under torrents of rain, and loaded with a knapsack on his back; even if he is in a camp he can soon be sent to the next village, and will not be entirely without medical assistance, whilst on a march he must be for hours without any assistance, and then be made to drag himself along for miles as a straggler. How many trifling illnesses by that means become serious, how many serious ones become mortal. Let us consider how an ordinary march in the dust, and under the burning rays of a summer sun may produce the most excessive heat, in which state, suffering from intolerable thirst, the soldier then rushes to the fresh spring of water, to bring back for himself sickness and death.

It is not our object by these reflections to recommend less activity in war; the instrument is there for use, and if the use wears away the instrument that is only in the natural order of things; we only wish to see every thing put in its right place, and to oppose that theoretical bombast according to which the most astonishing surprises the most rapid movements, the most incessant activity cost nothing, and are painted as rich mines which the indolence of the general leaves un-worked. It is very much the same with these mines as with those from which gold and silver are obtained; nothing is seen but the produce, and no one asks about the value of the work which has brought this produce to light.

On long marches outside a theatre of war, the conditions under which the march is made are no doubt usually easier, and the daily losses smaller, but on that account men with the slightest sickness are generally lost to the army for some time, as it is difficult for convales-cents to overtake an army constantly advancing.

Amongst the cavalry the number of lame horses and horses with sore backs rises in an increasing ratio, and amongst the carriages many break down or require repair. It never fails, therefore, that at the end of a march of 100 miles or more, an army arrives much weakened, par-ticularly as regards its cavalry and train.

If such marches are necessary on the theatre of war, that is under the eyes of the enemy, then that disadvantage is added to the other, and from the two combined the losses with large masses of troops, and under conditions otherwise unfavourable may amount to some-thing incredible.

Only a couple of examples in order to illustrate our ideas.

When Buonaparte crossed the Niemen on 24th June, 1812, the enor-mous centre of his army with which he subsequently marched against Moscow numbered 301,000 men. At Smolensk, on the 15th August, he detached 13,500, leaving, it is to be supposed, 287,500. The actual state of his army however at that date was only 182,000; he had therefore lost 105,000.[56] Bearing in mind that up to that time only two engagements to speak of had taken place, one between Davoust and Bragathion, the other between Murat and Tolstoy-Osterman, we may put down the losses of the French army in action at 10,000 men at most, and there-

56   All these figures are taken from Chambray. Vergl. Bd. vii. 2te Auflage,§ 80, ff.

fore the losses in sick and stragglers within fifty-two days on a march of about seventy miles direct to his front, amounted to 95,000, that is a third part of the whole army.

Three weeks later, at the time of the battle of Borodino, the loss amounted to 144,000 (including the casualties in the battle), and eight days after that again, at Moscow, the number was 198,000. The losses of this army in general were at the commencement of the campaign at the rate of 1/150 daily, subsequently they rose to 1/120, and in the last period they increased to 1/19 of the original strength.

The movement of Napoleon from the passage of the Niemen up to Moscow certainly may be called a persistent one; still, we must not forget that it lasted eighty-two days, in which time he only accomplished 120 miles, and that the French army upon two occasions made regular halts, once at Wilna for about fourteen days, and the other time at Witebsk for about eleven days, during which periods many stragglers had time to rejoin. This fourteen weeks' advance was not made at the worst season of the year, nor over the worst of roads, for it was summer, and the roads along which they marched were mostly sand. It was the immense mass of troops collected on one road, the want of sufficient subsistence, and an enemy who was on the retreat, but by no means in flight, which were the adverse conditions.

Of the retreat of the French army from Moscow to the Niemen, we shall say nothing, but this we may mention, that the Russian army following them left Kaluga 120,000 strong, and reached Wilna with 30,000. Every one knows how few men were lost in actual combats during that period.

One more example from Blucher's campaign of 1813 in Silesia and Saxony, a campaign very remarkable not for any long march but for the amount of marching to and fro. York's corps of Blucher's army began this campaign 16th August about 40,000 strong, and was reduced to 12,000 at the battle of Leipsic, 19th October. The principal combats which this corps fought at Goldberg, Lowenberg, on the Katsbach, at Wartenburg, and Mockern (Leipsic) cost it, on the authority of the best writers, 12,000 men. According to that their losses from other causes in eight weeks amounted to 16,000, or two-fifths of the whole.

We must, therefore, make up our minds to great wear and tear of our own forces, if we are to carry on a war rich in movements, we must arrange the rest of our plan accordingly, and above all things the reinforcements which are to follow.

CHAPTER THIRTEEN
Cantonments

IN THE MODERN system of war cantonments have become again indispensable, because neither tents nor a complete military train make an army independent of them. Huts and open-air camps (bivouacs as they are called), however far such arrangements may be carried, can still never become the usual way of locating troops without sickness gaining the upper hand, and prematurely exhausting their strength, sooner or later, according to the state of the weather or climate. The campaign in Russia in 1812 is one of the few in which, in a very severe climate, the troops, during the six months that it lasted hardly ever lay in cantonments. But what was the consequence of this extreme effort, which should be called an extravagance, if that term was not much more applicable to the political conception of the enterprise!

Two things interfere with the occupation of cantonments – the proximity of the enemy, and the rapidity of movement. For these reasons they are quitted as soon as the decision approaches, and cannot be again taken up until the decision is over.

In modern wars, that's, in all campaigns during the last twenty-five years which occur to us at this moment, the military element has acted with full energy. Nearly all that was possible has generally been done in them, as far as regards activity and the utmost effort of force; but all these campaigns have been of short duration, they have seldom exceeded half a year; in most of them a few months sufficed to bring matters to a crisis, that is, to a point where the vanquished enemy saw himself compelled to sue for an armistice or at once for peace, or to a point where, on the conqueror's part, the impetus of victory had exhausted itself. During this period of extreme effort there could be little question of cantonments, for even in the victorious march of the pursuer, if there was no longer any danger, the rapidity of movement made that kind of relief impossible.

But when from any cause the course of events is less impetuous, when a more even oscillation and balancing of forces takes place, then the housing of troops must again become a foremost subject for attention. This want has some influence even on the conduct of war itself, partly in this way, that we seek to gain more time and security by a stronger system of outposts, by a more considerable advanced guard thrown further forward; and partly in this way, that our measures are governed more by the richness and fertility of the country than by the tactical advantages which the ground affords in the geometrical relations of lines and points. A commercial town of twenty or thirty thousand inhabitants, a road thickly studded with large villages or flourishing towns give such facilities for the assembling in one position large bodies of troops, and this concentration gives such a freedom and such a latitude for movement as fully compensate for the advantages which the better situation of some point may otherwise present.

On the form to be followed in arranging cantonments we have only a few observations to make, as this subject belongs for the most part to tactics.

The housing of troops comes under two heads, inasmuch as it can either be the main point or only a secondary consideration. If the disposition of the troops in the course of a campaign is regulated by grounds purely tactical and strategical, and if, as is done more especially with cavalry, they are directed for their comfort to occupy the quarters available in the vicinity of the point of concentration of the army, then the quarters are subordinate considerations and substitutes for camps; they must, therefore, be chosen within such a radius that the troops can reach the point of assembly in good time. But if an army takes up quarters to rest and refresh, then the housing of the troops is the main point, and other measures, consequently also the selection of the particular point of assembly, will be influenced by that object.

The first question for examination here is as to the general form of the cantonments as a whole. The usual form is that of a very long oval, a mere widening as it were of the tactical order of battle. The point of assembly for the army is in front, the head-quarters in rear. Now these three arrangements are, in point of fact, adverse, indeed almost opposed, to the safe assembly of the army on the approach of the enemy.

The more the cantonments form a square, or rather a circle, the quicker the troops can concentrate at one point, that is the centre. The further the place of assembly is placed in rear, the longer the enemy will be in reaching it, and, therefore, the more time is left us to assemble. A point of assembly in rear of the cantonments can never be in danger. And, on the other hand, the farther the head-quarters are in advance, so much the sooner reports arrive, therefore so much the better is the commander informed of everything. At the same time, the first named arrangements are not devoid of points which deserve some attention.

By the extension of cantonments in width, we have in view the protection of the country which would otherwise be laid under contributions by the enemy. But this motive is neither thoroughly sound, nor is it very important. It is only sound as far as regards the country on the extremity of the wings, but does not apply at all to intermediate spaces existing between separate divisions of the army, if the quarters of those divisions are drawn closer round their point of assembly, for no enemy will then venture into those intervals of space. And it is not very important, because there are simpler means of shielding the districts in our vicinity from the enemy's requisitions than scattering the army itself.

The placing of the point of assembly in front is with a view to covering the quarters, for the following reasons: – In the first place, a body of troops, suddenly called to arms, always leaves behind it in cantonments a tail of stragglers – sick, baggage, provisions, etc., etc. – which may easily fall into the enemy's hands if the point of assembly is placed in rear. In the second place, we have to apprehend that if the enemy with some bodies of cavalry passes by the advanced guard, or if it is defeated in any way, he may fall upon scattered regiments or battalions. If he encounters a force drawn up in good order, although it is weak, and in the end must be overpowered, still he is brought to a stop, and in that way time is gained.

As respects the position of the head-quarters, it is generally supposed that it cannot be made too secure.

According to these different considerations, we may conclude that the best arrangement for districts of cantonments is where they take an oblong form, approaching the square or circle, have the point of assembly in the centre, and the head-quarters placed on the front line, well protected by considerable masses of troops.

What we have said as to covering of the wings in treating of the disposition of the army in general, applies here also; therefore corps detached from the main body, right and left, although intended to fight in conjunction with the rest, will have particular points of assembly of their own in the same line with the main body.

Now, if we reflect that the nature of a country, on the one hand, by favourable features in the ground determines the most natural point of assembly, and on the other hand, by the positions of towns and villages determines the most suitable situation for cantonments, then we must perceive how very rarely any geometrical form can be decisive in our present subject. But yet it was necessary to direct attention to it, because, like all general laws, it affects the generality of cases in a greater or less degree.

What now remains to be said as to an advantageous position for cantonments is that they should be taken up behind some natural obstacle of ground affording cover, whilst the sides next the enemy can be watched by small but numerous detached parties; or they may be taken up behind fortresses, which, when circumstances prevent any estimate being formed of the strength of their garrisons, impose upon the enemy a greater feeling of respect and and caution.

We reserve the subject of winter quarters, covered by defensive works for a separate article.

The quarters taken up by troops on a march differ from those called standing cantonments in this way, that, in order to save the troops from unnecessary marching, cantonments on a march are taken up as much as possible along the lines of march, and are not at any considerable distance on either side of these roads; if their extension in this sense does not exceed a short day's march, the arrangement is not one at all unfavourable to the quick concentration of the army.

In all cases in presence of the enemy, according to the technical phrase in use, that is in all cases where there is no considerable interval between the advance guards of the two armies respectively, the extent of the cantonments and the time required to assemble the army determine the strength and position of the advanced guard and outposts; but when these must be suited to the enemy and circumstances, then, on the contrary, the extent of the cantonments must depend on the time which we can count upon by the resistance of the advance guard.

In the third1 chapter of this book, we have stated how this resistance, in the case of an advanced corps, may be estimated. From the time of that resistance we must deduct the time required for transmission of reports and getting the men under arms, and the remainder only is the time available for assembling at the point of concentration.

We shall conclude here also by establishing our ideas in the form of a result, such as is usual under ordinary circumstances. If the distance at which the advanced guard is detached is the same as the radius of the cantonments, and the point of assembly is fixed in the centre of the cantonments, the time which is gained by checking the enemy's advance would be available for the transmission of intelligence and getting under arms, and would in most cases be sufficient, even although the communication is not made by means of signals, cannon-shots, etc., but simply by relays of orderlies, the only really sure method.

With an advanced guard pushed forward three miles in front, our cantonments might therefore cover a space of thirty square miles. In a moderately-peopled country there would be 10,000 houses in this space, which for an army of 50,000, after deducting the advanced guard, would be four men to a billet, therefore very comfortable quarters; and for an army of twice the strength nine men to a billet, therefore still not very close quarters. On the other hand, if the advanced guard is only one mile in front, we could only occupy a space of four square miles; for although the time gained does not diminish exactly in proportion as the distance of the advanced guard diminishes, and even with a distance of one mile we may still calculate on a gain of six hours, yet the necessity for caution increases when the enemy is so close. But in such a space an army of 50,000 men could only find partial accommodation, even in a very thickly populated country.

From all this we see what an important part is played here by great or at least considerable towns, which afford convenience for sheltering 10,000 or even 20,000 men almost at one point.

From this result it follows that, if we are not very close to the enemy, and have a suitable advanced guard we might remain in cantonments, even if the enemy is concentrated, as Frederick the Great did at Breslau in the beginning of the year 1762, and Buonaparte at Witebsk in 1812. But although by preserving a right distance and by suitable arrangements we have no reason to fear not being able to assemble in time, even opposite an enemy who is concentrated, yet we must not forget that an army engaged in assembling itself in all haste can do nothing else in that time; that it is therefore, for a time at least, not in a condition to avail itself in an instant of fortuitous opportunities, which deprives it of the greater part of its really efficient power. The consequence of this is, that an army should only break itself up completely in cantonments under some one or other of the three following cases:

1. If the enemy does the same.
2. If the condition of the troops makes it unavoidable.
3. If the more immediate object with the army is completely limited to the maintenance of a strong position, and therefore the only point of importance is concentrating the troops at that point in good time.

The campaign of 1815 gives a very remarkable example of the assembly of an army from cantonments. General Ziethen, with Blucher's advanced guard, 30,000 men, was posted at Charleroi, only two miles from Sombreff, the place appointed for the assembly of the army. The farthest cantonments of the army were about eight miles from Sombreff, that is, on the one side beyond Ciney, and on the other near Liége. Notwithstanding this, the troops cantoned about Ciney were assembled at Ligny several hours before the battle began, and those near Liége (Bulow's Corps) would have been also, had it not been for accident and faulty arrangements in the communication of orders and intelligence.

Unquestionably, proper care for the security of the Prussian army was not taken; but in explanation we must say that the arrangements were made at a time when the French army was still dispersed over widely extended cantonments, and that the real fault consisted in not altering them the moment the first news was received that the enemy's troops were in movement, and that Buonaparte had joined the army.

Still it remains noteworthy that the Prussian army was able in any way to concentrate at Sombreff before the attack of the enemy. Certainly, on the night of the 14th, that is, twelve hours before Ziethen was actually attacked, Blucher received information of the advance of the enemy, and began to assemble his army; but on the 15th at nine in the morning, Ziethen was already hotly engaged, and it was not until the same moment that General Thielman at Ciney first received orders to march to Namur. He had therefore then to assemble his divisions, and to march six and a half miles to Sombreff, which he did in 24 hours. General Bulow would also have been able to arrive about the same time, if the order had reached him as it should have done.

But Buonaparte did not resolve to make his attack on Ligny until two in the afternoon of the 16th. The apprehension of having Wellington on the one side of him, and Blucher on the other, in other words, the disproportion in the relative forces, contributed to this slowness; still we see how the most resolute commander may be detained by the cautious feeling of the way which is always unavoidable in cases which are to a certain degree complicated.

Some of the considerations here raised are plainly more tactical than strategic in their nature; but we have preferred rather to encroach a little than to run the risk of not being sufficiently explicit.

CHAPTER FOURTEEN
Subsistence

THIS SUBJECT has acquired much greater importance in modern warfare from two causes in particular. First, because the armies in general are now much greater than those of the middle ages, and even those of the old world; for, although formerly armies did appear here and there which equalled or even surpassed modern ones in size, still these were only rare and transient occurrences, whilst in modern military history, since the time of Louis XIV, armies have always been very strong in number. But the second cause is still more important, and belongs entirely to modern times. It is the very much closer inner connection which our wars have in themselves, the constant state of readiness for battle of the belligerents engaged in carrying them on. Almost all old wars consist of single unconnected enterprises, which are separated from each other by intervals during which the war in reality either completely rested, and only still existed in a political sense, or when the armies at least had removed so far from each other that each, without any care about the army opposite, only occupied itself with its own wants.

Modern wars, that is, the wars which have taken place since the Peace of Westphalia, have, through the efforts of respective governments, taken a more systematic connected form; the military object, in general, predominates everywhere, and demands also that arrangements for subsistence shall be on an adequate scale. Certainly there were long periods of inaction in the wars of the seventeenth and eighteenth centuries, almost amounting to a cessation of war; these are the regular periods passed in cantonments; still even those periods were subordinate to the military object; they were caused by the inclemency of the season, not by any necessity arising out of the subsistence of the troops, and as they regularly terminated with the return of summer, therefore we may say at all events uninterrupted action was the rule of war during the fine season of the year.

As the transition from one situation or method of action to another always takes place gradually so it was in the case before us. In the wars against Louis XIV. the allies used still to send their troops into winter cantonments in distant provinces in order to subsist them the more easily; in the Silesian war that was no longer done.

This systematic and connected form of carrying on war only became possible when states took regular troops into their service in place of the feudal armies. The obligation of the feudal law was then commuted into a fine or contribution: personal service either came to an end, enlistment being substituted, or it was only continued amongst the lowest classes, as the nobility regarded the furnishing a quota of men (as is still done in Russia and Hungary) as a kind of tribute, a tax in men. In every case, as we have elsewhere observed, armies became henceforward, an instrument of the cabinet, their principal basis being the treasury or the revenue of the government.

Just the same kind of thing which took place in the mode of raising and keeping up an establishment of troops could not but follow in the mode of subsisting them. The privileged classes having been released from the first of these services on payment of a contribution in money, the expense of the latter could not be again imposed on them quite so easily. The cabinet and the treasury had therefore to provide for the subsistence of the army, and could not allow it to be maintained in its own country at the expense of the people. Administrations were therefore obliged to look upon the subsistence of the army as an affair for which they were specially responsible. The subsistence thus became more difficult in two ways: first, because it was an affair belonging to government, and next, because the forces required to be permanently embodied to confront those kept up in other states.

Thus arose a separate military class in the population, with an independent organisation provided for its subsistence, and carried out to the utmost possible perfection.

Not only were stores of provisions collected, either by purchase or by deliveries in kind from the landed estates (Dominiallieferungen), consequently from distant points, and lodged in magazines, but they were also forwarded from these by means of special wagons, baked near the quarters of the troops in ovens temporarily established, and from thence again carried away at last by the troops, by means of another system of transport attached to the army itself. We take a glance at this system not merely from its being characteristic of the military arrangements of the period, but also because it is a system which can never be entirely done away; some parts of it must continually reappear.

Thus military organisation strove perpetually towards becoming more independent of people and country.

The consequence was that in this manner war became certainly a more systematic and more regular affair, and more subordinated to the military, that is the political object; but it was at the same time also much straitened and impeded in its movement, and infinitely weakened in energy. For now an army was tied to its magazines, limited to the working powers of its transport service, and it naturally followed that the tendency of everything was to economise the subsistence of the troops. The soldier fed on a wretched pittance of bread, moved about like a shadow, and no prospect of a change for the better comforted him under his privations.

Whoever treats this miserable way of feeding soldiers as a matter of no moment, and points to what Frederick the Great did with soldiers subsisted in this manner, only takes a partial view of the matter. The power of enduring privations is one of the finest virtues in a soldier, and without it no army is animated with the true military spirit; but such privation must be of a temporary kind, commanded by the force of circumstances, and not the consequence of a wretchedly bad system, or of a parsimonious abstract calculation of the smallest ration that a man can exist upon. When such is the case the powers of the men individually will always deteriorate physically and morally. What Frederick the Great managed to do with his soldiers cannot be taken as a standard for us, partly because he was opposed to those who pursued a similar system, partly because we do not know how much more he might have effected if he had been able to let his troops live as Buonaparte allowed his whenever circumstances permitted.

The feeding of horses by an artificial system of supply is, however, an experiment which has not been tried, because forage is much more difficult to provide on account of its bulk. A ration for a horse weighs about ten times as much as one for a man, and the number of horses with an army is more than one-tenth the number of men, at present it is one-fourth to one-third, and formerly it was one-third to one-half, therefore the weight of the forage required is three, four, or five times as much as that of the soldier's rations required for the same period of time; on this account the shortest and most direct means were taken to meet the wants of an army in this respect, that is by foraging expeditions. Now these expeditions occasioned great inconvenience in the conduct of war in other ways, first by making it a principal object to keep the war in the enemy's country; and next because they made it impossible to remain very long in one part of the country. However, at the time of the Silesian war, foraging expeditions were much less frequent, they were found to occasion a much greater drain upon the country, and much greater waste than if the requirements were satisfied by means of requisitions and imposts.

When the French Revolution suddenly brought again upon the war stage a national army, the means which governments could command were found insufficient, and the whole system of war, which had its origin in the limited extent of these means, and found again its security in this limitation, fell to pieces, and of course in the downfall of the whole was included that of the branch of which we are now speaking, the system of subsistence. Without troubling themselves about magazines, and still less about such an organisation as the artificial clockwork of which we have spoken, by which the different divisions of the transport service went round like a wheel, the leading spirits of the revolution sent their soldiers into the field, forced their generals to fight, subsisted, reinforced their armies, and kept alive the war by a system of exaction, and of helping themselves to all they required by robbery and plunder.

Between these two extremes the war under Buonaparte, and against him, preserved a sort of medium, that is to say, it just made use of such means as suited it best amongst all that were available; and so it will be also in future.

The modern method of subsisting troops, that is, seizing every thing which is to be found in the country without regard to *meum et tuum* may be carried out in four different ways: that is, subsisting on the inhabitant, contributions which the troops themselves look after, general contributions and magazines. All four are generally applied together, one generally prevailing more than the others: still it sometimes happens that only one is applied entirely by itself.

1. – *Living on the inhabitant, or on the community, which is the same thing.*

If we bear in mind that in a community consisting even as it does in great towns, of consumers only, there must always be provisions enough to last for several days, we may easily see that the most densely populated place can furnish food and quarters for a day for about as many troops as there are inhabitants, and for a less number of troops for several days without the necessity of any particular previous preparation. In towns of considerable size this gives a very satisfactory result, because it enables us to subsist a large force at one point. But in

smaller towns, or even in villages, the supply would be far from sufficient; for a population of 3,000 or 4,000 in a square mile which would
be large in such a space, would only suffice to feed 3,000 or 4,000 soldiers, and if the whole mass of troops is great they would have to be
spread over such an extent of country at this rate as would hardly be
consistent with other essential points. But in level countries, and even
in small towns, the quantity of those kinds of provisions which are
essential in war is generally much greater; the supply of bread which
a peasant has is generally adequate to the consumption of his family
for several, perhaps from eight to fourteen days; meat can be obtained
daily, vegetable productions are generally forthcoming in sufficient
quantity to last till the following crop. Therefore in quarters which
have never been occupied there is no difficulty in subsisting troops
three or four times the number of the inhabitants for several days,
which again is a very satisfactory result. According to this, where the
population is about 2,000 or 3,000 per square mile, and if no large
town is included, a column of 30,000 would require about four square
miles, which would be a length of side of two miles. Therefore for an
army of 90,000, which we may reckon at about 75,000 combatants, if
marching in three columns contiguous to each other, we should require to take up a front six miles in breadth in case three roads could
be found within that breadth.

If several columns follow one another into these cantonments, then
special measures must be adopted by the civil authorities, and in that
way there can be no great difficulty in obtaining all that is required for
a day or two more. Therefore if the above 90,000 are followed the day
after by a like number, even these last would suffer no want; this makes
up the large number of 150,000 combatants.

Forage for the horses occasions still less difficulty, as it neither requires grinding nor baking, and as there must be forage forthcoming in
sufficient quantity to last the horses in the country until next harvest,
therefore even where there is little stall-feeding, still there should be no
want, only the deliveries of forage should certainly be demanded from
the community at large, not from the inhabitants individually. Besides,
it is supposed that some attention is, of course, paid to the nature of the
country in making arrangements for a march, so as not to send cavalry
mostly into places of commerce and manufactures, and into districts
where there is no forage.

The conclusion to be drawn from this hasty glance is, therefore, that
in a moderately populated country, that is, a country of from 2,000 to
3,000 souls per square mile, an army of 150,000 combatants may be

subsisted by the inhabitants and community for one or two days within such a narrow space as will not interfere with its concentration for battle, that is, therefore, that such an army can be subsisted on a continuous march without magazines or other preparation.

On this result were based the enterprises of the French army in the revolutionary war, and under Buonaparte. They marched from the Adige to the Lower Danube, and from the Rhine to the Vistula, with little means of subsistence except upon the inhabitants, and without ever suffering want. As their undertakings depended on moral and physical superiority, as they were attended with certain results, and were never delayed by indecision or caution, therefore their progress in the career of victory was generally that of an uninterrupted march.

If circumstances are less favourable, if the population is not so great, or if it consists more of artisans than agriculturists, if the soil is bad, the country already several times overrun – then of course the results will fall short of what we have supposed. Still, we must remember that if the breadth of the front of a column is extended from two miles to three, we get a superficial extent of country more than double in size, that is, instead of four we command nine square miles, and that this is still an extent which in ordinary cases will always admit of concentration for action; we see therefore that even under unfavourable circumstances this method of subsistence will still be always compatible with a continuous march.

But if a halt of several days takes place, then great distress must ensue if preparations have not been made beforehand for such an event in other ways. Now these preparatory measures are of two kinds, and without them a considerable army even now cannot exist. The first is equipping the troops with a wagon train, by means of which bread or flour, as the most essential part of their subsistence, can be carried with them for a few, that is, for three or four days; if to this we add three or four days' rations which the soldier himself can carry, then we have provided what is most indispensable in the way of subsistence for eight days.

The second arrangement is that of a regular commissariat, which whenever there is a moment's halt gathers provisions from distant localities, so that at any moment we can pass over from the system of quartering on the inhabitants to a different system.

Subsisting in cantonments has the immense advantage that hardly any transport is required, and that it is done in the shortest time, but certainly it supposes as a prior condition that cantonments can be provided for all the troops.

2. – *Subsistence through exactions enforced by the troops themselves.*

If a single battalion occupies a camp, this camp may be placed in the vicinity of some villages, and these may receive notice to furnish subsistence; then the method of subsistence would not differ essentially from the preceding mode. But, as is most usual, if the mass of troops to be encamped at some one point is much larger, there is no alternative but to make a collection in common within the circle of districts marked out for the purpose, collecting sufficient for the supply of one of the parts of the army, a brigade or division, and afterwards to make a distribution from the common stock thus collected.

The first glance shows that by such a mode of proceeding the subsistence of a large army would be a matter of impossibility. The collection made from the stores in any given district in the country will be much less than if the troops had taken up their quarters in the same district, for when thirty or forty men take possession of a farmer's house they can if necessary collect the last mouthful, but one officer sent with a few men to collect provisions has neither time nor means to hunt out all the provisions that may be stored in a house, often also he has not the means of transport; he will therefore only be able to collect a small proportion of what is actually forthcoming. Besides, in camps the troops are crowded together in such a manner at one point, that the range of country from which provisions can be collected in a hurry is not of sufficient extent to furnish the whole of what is required. What could be done in the way of supplying 30,000 men, within a circle of a mile in diameter, or from an area of three or four square miles? Moreover it would seldom be possible to collect even what there is, for the most of the nearest adjacent villages would be occupied by small bodies of troops, who would not allow anything to be removed. Lastly, by such a measure there would be the greatest waste, because some men would get more than they required, whilst a great deal would be lost, and of no benefit to any one.

The result is, therefore, that the subsistence of troops by forced contributions in this manner can only be adopted with success when the bodies of troops are not too large, not exceeding a division of 8,000 or 10,000 men, and even then it is only to be resorted to as an unavoidable evil.

It cannot in general be avoided in the case of troops directly in front of the enemy, such as advanced guards and outposts, when the army is advancing, because these bodies must arrive at points where no preparations could have been made, and they are usually too far from the stores collected for the rest of the army; further, in the case of moveable

ENGAGE BOOKS | *On War: Book Five*

columns acting independently; and lastly, in all cases where by chance there is neither time nor means to procure subsistence in any other way.

The more troops are accustomed to live by regular requisitions, the more time and circumstances permit the adoption of that way of subsisting, then the more satisfactory will be the result. But time is generally wanting, for what the troops get for themselves directly is got much quicker.

3. – *By regular requisitions.*

This is unquestionably the simplest and most efficacious means of subsisting troops, and it has been the basis of all modern wars.

It differs from the preceding way chiefly by its having the co-operation of the local authorities. The supply in this case must not be carried off forcibly just from the spot where it is found, but be regularly delivered according to an equitable division of the burden. This division can only be made by the recognised official authorities of the country.

In this all depends on time. The more time there is, the more general can the division be made, the less will it press on individuals, and the more regular will be the result. Even purchases may be made with ready money to assist, in which way it will approach the mode which follows next in order (Magazines). In all assemblages of troops in their own country there is no difficulty in subsisting by regular requisitions; neither, as a rule, is there any in retrograde movements. On the other hand, in all movements into a country of which we are not in possession, there is very little time for such arrangements, seldom more than the one day which the advanced guard is in the habit of preceding the army. With the advanced guard the requisitions are sent to the local officials, specifying how many rations they are to have ready at such and such places. As these can only be furnished from the immediate neighbourhood, that is, within a circuit of a couple of miles round each point, the collections so made in haste will never be nearly sufficient for an army of considerable strength, and consequently, if the troops do not carry with them enough for several days, they will run short. It is therefore the duty of the commissariat to economise what is received, and only to issue to those troops who have nothing. With each succeeding day, however, the embarrassment diminishes; that is to say, if the distances from which provisions can be procured increase in proportion to the number of days, then the superficial area over which the contributions can be levied increases as the squares of the distances gained. If on the first day only four square miles have been drawn upon, on the next day we shall have sixteen, on the third, thirty-six; therefore on the second day twelve more than on the first, and on the third day twenty more than on the second.

Of course this is a mere rough estimate of what may take place, subject to many modifying circumstances which may intervene, of which the principal is, that one district may not be capable of contributing like another. But on the other hand, we must also remember that the radius within which we can levy may increase more than two miles a day in width, perhaps three or four, or in many places still more.

The due execution of these requisitions is enforced by detachments placed under the orders of the official functionaries, but still more by the fear of responsibility, punishment, and ill-treatment which, in such cases, like a general weight, presses on the whole population.

However, it is not our intention to enter into details – into the whole machinery of commissariat and army subsistence; we have only results in view.

The result to be derived from a common-sense view of all the circumstances in general, and the view which the experience of the wars since the French revolution tends to confirm is, – that even the largest army, if it carries with it provisions for a few days, may undoubtedly be subsisted by contributions which, commencing at the moment of entering a country, affect at first only the districts in the immediate vicinity of the army, but afterwards, in the course of time, are levied on a greater scale, over a range of country always increasing, and with an ever increasing weight of authority.

This resource has no limits except those of the exhaustion, impoverishment, and devastation of the country. When the stay of an invading army is of some duration, the administration of this system at last is handed over to those in the highest official capacity; and they naturally do all they can to equalise its pressure as much as possible, and to alleviate the weight of the tax by purchases; at the same time, even an invader, when his stay is prolonged in his enemy's country, is not usually so barbarous and reckless as to lay upon that country the entire burden of his support; thus the system of contributions of itself gradually approaches to that of magazines, at the same time without ever ceasing altogether, or sensibly losing any of that influence which it exercises on the operations of the war; for there is a wide difference between a case in which some of the resources which have been drawn from a country are replaced by supplies brought from more distant parts (the country, however, still remaining substantially the source on which the army depends for its supplies), and the case of an army which – as in the eighteenth century – provides for all its wants from its own resources, the country in which it is operating contributing, as a rule, nothing towards its support.

The great difference consists in two things, – namely, the employment of the transport of the country, and its ovens. In this way, that enormous burden of any army, that incubus which is always destroying its own work, a military transport train, is almost got rid of.

It is true that even now no army can do entirely without some subsistence wagons, but the number is immensely diminished, and little more is required than sufficient to carry the surplus of one day on till the next. Peculiar circumstances, as in Russia in 1812, may even again compel an army to carry an enormous train, and also field-ovens; but in the first place these are exceptional cases; for how seldom will it happen that 300,000 men make a hostile advance of 130 miles upon almost a single road, and that through countries such as Poland and Russia, and shortly before the season of harvest; and in the next place, any means of supply attached to an army in such cases, may be looked upon as only an assistance in case of need, the contributions of the country being always regarded as the groundwork of the whole system of supply.

Since the first campaigns of the French revolutionary war, the requisition system has formed constantly the mainstay of their armies, the armies opposed to them were also obliged to adopt the same system, and it is not at all likely that it will ever be abandoned. There is no other which can be substituted for it with the same results, both as regards its simplicity and freedom from restraint, and also as respects energy in the prosecution of the war. As an army is seldom distressed for provisions during the first three or four weeks of a campaign whatever direction it takes, and afterwards can be assisted by magazines, we may very well say that by this method war has acquired the most perfect freedom of action. Certainly difficulties may be greater in one direction than in another, and that may carry weight in preliminary deliberation; but we can never encounter an absolute impossibility, and the attention which is due to the subject of subsistence can never decide a question imperatively. To this there is only one exception, which is a retreat through an enemy's country. In such a case many of the inconveniences connected with subsistence meet together. The operation is one of a continuous nature, generally carried on without a halt worth speaking of; there is, therefore, no time to procure provisions; the circumstances under which the operation commences are generally unfavourable, it is therefore necessary to keep the troops in masses, and a dispersion in cantonments, or even any considerable extension in the width of the column cannot be allowed; the hostile feeling of the country precludes the chance of any collection of contributions by mere orders issued without the support of a force capable of executing the order; and, lastly, the moment is most auspicious for the inhabitants to give vent to their feelings by acts of hostility. On account of all this, an army so situated is generally obliged to confine itself strictly to its previously prepared lines of communication and retreat.

When Buonaparte had to retreat in 1812, it was impossible for him to do so by any other line but the one upon which he had advanced, on account of the subsistence of his army; and if he had attempted any other he would only have plunged into more speedy and certain destruction; all the censure therefore passed on him by even French writers as well as by others with regard to this point is sheer nonsense.

4. – *Subsistence from Magazines.*

If we are to make a generic distinction between this method of subsisting troops and the preceding, it must be by an organisation such as existed for about thirty years at the close of the seventeenth and during the eighteenth century. Can this organisation ever reappear?

Certainly we cannot conceive how it can be dispensed with if great armies are to be bound down for seven, ten, or twelve years long to one spot, as they have been formerly in the Netherlands, on the Rhine, in Upper Italy, Silesia, and Saxony; for what country can continue for such a length of time to endure the burden of two great armies, making it the entire source of their supplies, without being utterly ruined in the end, and therefore gradually becoming unable to meet the demands?

But here naturally arises the question: shall the war prescribe the system of subsistence, or shall the latter dictate the nature of the war? To this we answer: the system of subsistence will control the war, in the first place, as far as the other conditions on which it depends permit; but when the latter are encroached upon, the war will react on the subsistence system, and in such case determine the same.

A war carried on by means of the system of requisitions and local supplies furnished on the spot has such an advantage over one carried on in dependence on issues from magazines, that the latter does not look at all like the same instrument. No state will therefore venture to encounter the former with the latter; and if any war minister should be so narrow-minded and blind to circumstances as to ignore the real relation which the two systems bear to each other, by sending an army into the field to live upon the old system, the force of circumstances would carry the commander of that army along with it in its course, and the requisition system would burst forth of itself. If we consider besides, that the great expense attending such an organisation must necessarily reduce the extent of the armament in other respects, including of course the actual number of combatant soldiers, as no state has a superabundance of wealth, then there seems no probability of any such organisation being again resorted to unless it should be adopted by the belligerents by mutual agreement, an idea which is a mere play of the imagination.

Wars therefore may be expected henceforward always to commence with the requisition system; how much one or other government will do to supplement the same by an artificial organisation to spare their own country, etc., etc., remains to be seen; that it will not be overmuch we may be certain, for at such moments the tendency is to look to the most urgent wants, and an artificial system of subsisting troops does not come under that category.

But now, if a war is not so decisive in its results, if its operations are not so comprehensive as is consistent with its real nature, then the requisition system will begin to exhaust the country in which it is carried on to that degree that either peace must be made, or means must be found to lighten the burden on the country, and to become independent of it for the supplies of the army. The latter was the case of the French army under Buonaparte in Spain, but the first happens much more frequently. In most wars the exhaustion of the state increases to that degree that, instead of thinking of prosecuting the war at a still greater expense, the necessity for peace becomes so urgent as to be imperative. Thus from this point of view the modern method of carrying on war has a tendency to shorten the duration of wars.

At the same time we shall not positively deny the possibility of the old system of subsistence reappearing in future wars; it will perhaps be resorted to by belligerents hereafter, where the nature of their mutual relations urge them to it, and circumstances are favourable to its adoption; but we can never perceive in that system a natural organisation; it is much rather an abnormal growth permitted by circumstances, but which can never spring from war in its true sense. Still less can we consider that form or system as any improvement in war on the ground of its being more humane, for war itself is not a humane proceeding.

Whatever method of providing subsistence may be chosen, it is but natural that it should be more easily carried out in rich and well-peopled countries, than in the midst of a poor and scanty population. That the population should be taken into consideration, lies in the double relation which that element bears to the quantity of provisions to be found in a country: first because, where the consumption is large, the provision to meet that consumption is also large; and in the next place, because as a rule a large population produces also largely. From this we must certainly except districts peopled chiefly by manufacturers, particularly when, as is often the case, such districts lie in mountain valleys surrounded by unproductive land; but in the generality of cases it is always very much easier to feed troops in a well populated than in a thinly inhabited country. An army of 100,000 men cannot be supported on four hundred square miles inhabited by 400,000 people, as well as it would be on four hundred square miles with a population of 2,000,000 inhabitants, even supposing the soil equally good in the two cases. Besides, the roads and means of water-carriage are much better in rich countries and afford a greater choice, being more numerous, the means of transport are more abundant, the commercial relations easier and more certain. In a word, there is infinitely less difficulty in supporting an army in Flanders than in Poland.

The consequence is, that war with its manifold suckers fixes itself by preference along high roads, near populous towns, in the fertile valleys of large rivers, or along such sea-coasts as are well frequented.

This shows clearly how the subsistence of troops may have a general influence upon the direction and form of military undertakings, and upon the choice of a theatre of war and lines of communication.

The extent of this influence, what weight shall attach to the facility or difficulty of provisioning the troops, all that in the calculation depends very much on the way in which the war is to be conducted. If it is to be carried on in its real spirit, that is, with the unbridled force which belongs to its element, with a constant pressing forward to, or seeking for the combat and decisive solution, then the sustenance of the troops although an important, is but a subordinate, affair; but if there is to be a state of equilibrium during which the armies move about here and there in the same province for several years, then the subsistence must often become the principal thing, the intendant the commander-in-chief, and the conduct of the war an administration of wagons.

There are numberless campaigns of this kind in which nothing took place; the plans miscarried, the forces were used to no purpose, the only excuse being the plea of a want of subsistence; on the other hand Buonaparte used to say "*Qu'on ne me parle pas des vivres!*" ["Let no one speak to me about food!"]

Certainly that general in the Russian campaign proved that such recklessness may be carried too far, for not to say that perhaps his whole campaign was ruined through that cause alone, which at best would be only a supposition, still it is beyond doubt that to his want of regard to the subsistence of his troops he was indebted for the extraordinary melting away of his army on his advance, and for its utter ruin on the retreat.

But while fully recognising in Buonaparte the eager gambler who ventures on many a mad extreme, we may justly say that he and the revolutionary generals who preceded him dispelled a powerful prejudice in respect to the subsistence of troops, and showed that it should never be looked upon in any other light than as a *condition* of war, never as an object.

Besides, it is with privation in war just as with physical exertion and danger; the demands which the general can make on his army are without any defined bounds; an iron character demands more than a feeble sensitive man; also the endurance of an army differs in degree, according as habit, military spirit, confidence in and affection towards the commander, or enthusiasm for the cause of fatherland, sustain the will and energy of the soldier. But this we may look upon as an established principle, that privation and want, however far they may be carried, should never be otherwise regarded than as transition-states which should be succeeded by a state of abundance, indeed even by superfluity. Can there be any thing more touching than the thought of so many thousand soldiers, badly clothed, with packs on their backs weighing thirty or forty pounds, toiling over every kind of road, in every description of weather, for days and days continually on the march, health and life for ever in peril, and for all that unable to get a sufficiency of dry bread. Any one who knows how often this happens in war, is at a loss to know how it does not oftener lead to a refusal of the will and powers to submit any longer to such exactions, and how the mere bent constantly given to the imagination of human beings in one direction, is capable of first calling forth, and then supporting such incredible efforts.

Let any one then, who imposes great privations on his men because great objects demand such a trial of endurance, always bear in mind as a matter of prudence, if not prompted to it by his own feelings, that there is a recompence for such sacrifices which he is bound to pay at some other time.

We have now to consider the difference which takes place in respect to the question of subsistence in war, according as the action is offensive or defensive.

The defensive is in a position to make uninterrupted use of the subsistence which he has been able to lay in beforehand, as long as his defensive act continues. The defensive side therefore can hardly be in want of the necessaries of life, particularly if he is in his own country; but even in the enemy's this holds good. The offensive on the other hand is moving away from his resources, and as long as he is advancing, and even during the first weeks after he stops, must procure from day to day what he requires, and this can very rarely be done without want and inconvenience being felt.

This difficulty is felt in its fullest force at two particular periods, first in the advance, before the decision takes place; then the supplies of the defensive side are all at hand, whilst the assailant has been obliged to leave his behind; he is obliged to keep his masses concentrated, and therefore cannot spread his army over any considerable space; even his transport cannot keep close to him when he commences his movements preliminary to a battle. If his preparations have not been very well made, it may easily happen at this moment that his army may be in want of supplies for several days before the decisive battle, which certainly is not a means of bringing them into the fight in the highest state of efficiency.

The second time a state of want arises is at the end of a victorious career, if the lines of communication begin to be too long, especially if the war is carried on in a poor, sparsely-populated country, and perhaps also in the midst of a people whose feelings are hostile. What an enormous difference between a line of communication from Wilna to Moscow, on which every carriage must be forcibly seized, and a line from Cologne by Liége, Louvain, Brussels, Mons, and Valenciennes to Paris, where a mercantile contract or a bill of exchange would suffice to procure millions of rations.

Frequently has the difficulty we are now speaking of resulted in obscuring the splendour of the most brilliant victories, reduced the powers of the victorious army, rendered retreat necessary, and then by degrees ended in producing all the symptoms of a real defeat.

Forage, of which, as we have before said, there is usually at first the least deficiency, will run short soonest if a country begins to become exhausted, for it is the most difficult supply to procure from a distance, on account of its bulk, and the horse feels the effect of low feeding much sooner than the man. For this reason, an over-numerous cavalry and artillery may become a real burden, and an element of weakness to an army.

CHAPTER FIFTEEN
Base of Operations

IF AN ARMY sets out on any expedition, whether it be to attack the enemy and his theatre of war, or to take post on its own frontier, it continues in a state of necessary dependence on the sources from which it
draws its subsistence and reinforcements, and must maintain its communication with them, as they are the conditions of its existence and
preservation. This dependence increases in intensity and extent in proportion to the size of the army. But now it is neither always possible nor
requisite that the army should continue in direct communication with
the whole of its own country; it is sufficient if it does so with that portion immediately in its rear, and which is consequently covered by its
position. In this portion of the country then, as far as necessary, special
depôts of provisions are formed, and arrangements are made for regularly forwarding reinforcements and supplies. This strip of territory is
therefore the foundation of the army and of all its undertakings, and
the two must be regarded as forming in connection only one whole. If
the supplies for their greater security are lodged in fortified places, the
idea of a base becomes more distinct; but the idea does not originate
in any arrangement of that kind, and in a number of cases no such arrangement is made.

But a portion of the enemy's territory may also become a base for our
army, or, at least, form part of it; for when an army penetrates into an
enemy's land, a number of its wants are supplied from that part of the
country which is taken possession of; but it is then a necessary condition that we are completely masters of this portion of territory, that
is, certain of our orders being obeyed within its limits. This certainty,
however, seldom extends beyond the reach of our ability to keep the
inhabitants in awe by small garrisons, and detachments moving about

from place to place, and that is not very far in general. The consequence is, that in the enemy's country, the part of territory from which we can draw supplies is seldom of sufficient extent to furnish all the supplies we require, and we must therefore still depend on our own land for much, and this brings us back again to the importance of that part of our territory immediately in rear of our army as an indispensable portion of our base.

The wants of an army may be divided into two classes, first those which every cultivated country can furnish; and next those which can only be obtained from those localities where they are produced. The first are chiefly provisions, the second the means of keeping an army complete in every way. The first can therefore be obtained in the enemy's country; the second, as a rule, can only be furnished by our own country, for example men, arms, and almost all munitions of war. Although there are exceptions to this classification in certain cases, still they are few and trifling, and the distinction we have drawn is of standing importance, and proves again that the communication with our own country is indispensable.

Depôts of provisions and forage are generally formed in open towns, both in the enemy's and in our own country, because there are not as many fortresses as would be required for these bulky stores continually being consumed, and wanted sometimes here, sometimes there, and also because their loss is much easier to replace; on the other hand, stores to keep the army complete, such as arms, munition of war, and articles of equipment are never lodged in open places in the vicinity of the theatre of war if it can be avoided, but are rather brought from a distance, and in the enemy's country never stored anywhere but in fortresses. From this point, again, it may be inferred that the base is of more importance in relation to supplies intended to refit an army than in relation to provisions for food.

Now, the more means of each kind are collected together in great magazines before being brought into use, the more, therefore, all separate streams unite in great reservoirs, so much the more may these be regarded as taking the place of the whole country, and so much the more will the conception of a base fix itself upon these great depôts of supply; but this must never go so far that any such place becomes looked upon as constituting a base in itself alone.

If these sources of supply and refitment are abundant, that is, if the tracts of territory are wide and rich, if the stores are collected in great depôts to be more speedily brought into use, if these depôts are covered in a military sense in one way or another, if they are in close proximity to the army and accessible by good roads, if they extend along a considerable width in the rear of the army or surround it in part as well – then follows a greater vitality for the army, as well as a greater freedom in its movements. Attempts have been made to sum up all the advantages which an army derives from being so situated in one single conception, that is, the extent of the base of operations. By the relation which this base bears to the object of the undertakings, by the angle which its extremities make with this object (supposed as a point), it has been attempted to express the whole sum of the advantages and disadvantages which accrue to an army from the position and nature of its sources of supply and equipment; but it is plain this elegant piece of geometrical refinement is merely a play of fancy, as it is founded on a series of substitutions which must all be made at the expense of truth. As we have seen, the base of an army is a triple formation in connection with the situation in which an army is placed: the resources of the country adjacent to the position of the army, the depôts of stores which have been made at particular points, and the *province* from which these stores are derived or collected. These three things are separated in space, and cannot be collected into one whole, and least of all can we substitute for them a line which is to represent the width of the base, a line which is generally imagined in a manner perfectly arbitrary, either from one fortress to another or from one capital of a province to another, or along a political boundary of a country. Neither can we determine precisely the mutual relation of these three steps in the formation of a base, for in reality they blend themselves with each other always more or less. In one case the surrounding country affords largely the means of refitting an army with things which otherwise could only be obtained from a long distance; in another case we are obliged to get even food from a long distance. Sometimes the nearest fortresses are great arsenals, ports, or commercial cities, which contain all the military resources of a whole state, sometimes they are nothing but old, feeble ramparts, hardly sufficient for their own defence.

The consequence is that all deductions from the length of the base of operations and its angles, and the whole theory of war founded on these data, as far as its geometrical phase, have never met with any attention in real war, and in theory they have only caused wrong tendencies. But as the basis of this chain of reasoning is a truth, and only the conclusions drawn are false, this same view will easily and frequently thrust itself forward again.

We think, therefore, that we cannot go beyond acknowledging generally the influence of a base on military enterprises, that at the same time there are no means of framing out of this maxim any serviceable rules by a few abstract ideas; but that in each separate case the whole of the things which we have specified must be *kept in view together*.

When once arrangements are made within a certain radius to provide the means of subsisting an army and keeping it complete in every respect, and with a view to operations in a certain direction, then, even in our own country, this district only is to be regarded as the base of the army; and as any alteration of a base requires time and labour, therefore an army cannot change its base every day, even in its own country, and this again limits it always more or less in the direction of its operations. If, then, in operating against an enemy's country we take the whole line of our own frontier, where it forms a boundary between the two countries as our base, we may do so in a general sense, in so far that we might make those preparations which constitute a base anywhere on that frontier; but it will not be a base at any moment if preparations have not been already made everywhere. When the Russian army retreated before the French in 1812, at the beginning of the campaign the whole of Russia might have been considered as its base, the more so because the vast extent of the country offered the army abundance of space in any direction it might select. This is no illusory notion, as it was actually realised at a subsequent time, when other Russian armies from different quarters entered the field; but still at every period throughout the campaign the base of the Russian army was not so extensive; it was principally confined to the road on which the whole train of transport to and from their army was organised. This limitation prevented the Russian army, for instance, from making the further retreat which became necessary after the three days' fighting at Smolensk in any direction but that of Moscow, and so hindered their turning suddenly in the direction of Kaluga, as was proposed in order to draw the enemy away from Moscow. Such a change of direction could only have been possible by having been prepared for long beforehand.

We have said that the dependence on the base increases in intensity and extent with the size of the army, which is easy to understand. An army is like a tree. From the ground out of which it grows it draws its nourishment; if it is small it can easily be transplanted, but this becomes more difficult as it increases in size. A small body of troops has also its channels, from which it draws the sustenance of life, but it strikes root easily where it happens to be; not so a large army. When, therefore, we talk of the influence of the base on the operations of an army, the dimensions of the army must always serve as the scale by which to measure the magnitude of that influence.

Further it is consistent with the nature of things that for the immediate wants of the present hour the *subsistence* is the main point, but for the general efficiency of the army through a long period of time the *refitment* and *recruitment* are the more important, because the latter can only be done from particular sources while the former may be obtained in many ways; this again defines still more distinctly the influence of the base on the operations of the army.

However great that influence may be, we must never forget that it belongs to those things which can only show a decisive effect after some considerable time, and that therefore the question always remains what may happen in that time. The value of a base of operations will seldom determine the choice of an undertaking in the first instance. Mere difficulties which may present themselves in this respect must be put side by side and compared with other means actually at our command; obstacles of this nature often vanish before the force of decisive victories.

CHAPTER SIXTEEN

Lines of Communication

THE ROADS which lead from the position of an army to those points in its rear where its depôts of supply and means of recruiting and refitting its forces are principally united, and which it also in all ordinary cases chooses for its retreat, have a double signification; in the first place, they are its *lines of communication* for the constant nourishment of the combatant force, and next they are *roads of retreat.*

We have said in the preceding chapter, that, although according to the present system of subsistence, an army is chiefly fed from the district in which it is operating, it must still be looked upon as forming a whole with its base. The lines of communication belong to this whole; they form the connection between the army and its base, and are to be considered as so many great vital arteries. Supplies of every kind, convoys of munitions, detachments moving backwards and forwards, posts, orderlies, hospitals, depôts, reserves of stores, agents of administration, all these objects are constantly making use of these roads, and the total value of these services is of the utmost importance to the army.

These great channels of life must therefore neither be permanently severed, nor must they be of too great length, or beset with difficulties, because there is always a loss of strength on a long road, which tends to weaken the condition of an army.

By their second purpose, that is as lines of retreat, they constitute in a real sense the strategic rear of the army.

For both purposes the value of these roads depends on their *length*, their *number*, their *situation*, that is their general direction, and their direction specially as regards the army, their *nature* as roads, *difficulties* of *ground*, the *political relations and feeling of local population*, and lastly, on the *protection* they derive from fortresses or natural obstacles in the country.

But all the roads which lead from the point occupied by an army to its sources of existence and power, are not on that account necessarily lines of communication for that army. They may no doubt be used for that purpose, and may be considered as supplementary of the system of communication, but that system is confined to the lines regularly prepared for the purpose. Only those roads on which magazines, hospitals, stations, posts for despatches and letters are organised under commandants with police and garrisons, can be looked upon as real lines of communication. But here a very important difference between our own and the enemy's army makes its appearance, one which is often overlooked. An army, even in its own country, has its prepared lines of communication, but it is not completely limited to them, and can in case of need change its line, taking some other which presents itself, for it is every where at home, has officials in authority, and the friendly feeling of the people. Therefore, although other roads may not be as good as those at first selected there is nothing to prevent their being used, and the use of them is not to be regarded as *impossible* in case the army is turned and obliged to change its front. An army in an enemy's country on the contrary can as a rule only look upon those roads as lines of communication upon which it has advanced; and hence arises through small and almost invisible causes a great difference in operating. The army in the enemy's country takes under its protection the organisation which, as it advances, it necessarily introduces to form its lines of communication; and in general, inasmuch as terror, and the presence of an enemy's army in the country invests these measures in the eyes of the inhabitants with all the weight of unalterable necessity, the inhabitants may even be brought to regard them as an alleviation of the evils inseparable from war. Small garrisons left behind in different places support and maintain this system. But if these commissaries, commandants of stations, police, fieldposts, and the rest of the apparatus of administration, were sent to some distant road upon which the army had not been seen, the inhabitants then would look upon such measures as a burden which they would gladly get rid of, and if the most complete defeats and catastrophes had not previously spread terror throughout the land, the probability is that these functionaries would be treated as enemies, and driven away with very rough usage. Therefore in the first place it would be necessary to establish garrisons to subjugate the new line, and these garrisons would require to be of more than ordinary strength, and still there would always be a danger of the inhabitants rising and attempting to overpower them. In short, an army marching into an enemy's country is destitute of the mechanism through which obedience is rendered; it has to institute its officials into their places, which can only be done by a strong hand, and this cannot be effected thoroughly without sacrifices and difficulties, nor is it the work of a moment – From this it follows that a change of the system of communication is much less easy of accomplishment in an enemy's country than in our own, where it is at least possible; and it also follows that the army is more restricted in its movements, and must be much more sensitive about any demonstrations against its communications.

But the choice and organisation of lines of communication is from the very commencement subject also to a number of conditions by which it is restricted. Not only must they be in a general sense good high roads, but they will be the more serviceable the wider they are, the more populous and wealthy towns they pass through, the more strong places there are which afford them protection. Rivers, also, as means of water communication, and bridges as points of passage, have a decisive weight in the choice. It follows from this that the situation of a line of communication, and consequently the road by which an army proceeds to commence the offensive, is only a matter of free choice up to a certain point, its situation being dependent on certain geographical relations.

All the foregoing circumstances taken together determine the strength or weakness of the communication of an army with its base, and this result, compared with one similarly obtained with regard to the enemy's communications, decides which of the two opponents is in a position to operate against the other's lines of communication, or to cut off his retreat, that is, in technical language to *turn him.* Setting aside all considerations of moral or physical superiority, that party can only effectually accomplish this whose communications are the strongest of the two, for otherwise the enemy saves himself in the shortest mode, by a counterstroke.

Now this turning can, by reason of the double signification of these lines, have also two purposes. Either the communications may be interfered with and interrupted, that the enemy may melt away by degrees from want, and thus be compelled to retreat, or the object may be directly to cut off the retreat.

With regard to the first, we have to observe that a mere momentary interruption will seldom have any effect while armies are subsisted as they now are; a certain time is requisite to produce an effect in this way in order that the losses of the enemy by frequent repetition may compensate in number for the small amount he suffers in each case. One single enterprise against the enemy's flank, which might have been a decisive stroke in those days when thousands of bread-waggons traversed the lines of communication, carrying out the systematised method then in force for subsisting troops, would hardly produce any effect now, if ever so successful; one convoy at most might be seized, which would cause the enemy some partial damage, but never compel him to retreat.

The consequence is, that enterprises of this description on a flank, which have always been more in fashion in books than in real warfare, now appear less of a practical nature than ever, and we may safely say that there is no danger in this respect to any lines of communication but such as are very long, and otherwise unfavourably circumstanced, more especially by being exposed everywhere and at any moment to attacks from an *insurgent population.*

With respect to the cutting off an enemy's retreat, we must not be overconfident in this respect either of the consequences of threatening or closing the enemy's lines of retreat, as recent experience has shown that, when troops are good and their leader resolute, it is *more difficult* to make them prisoners, than it is for them to cut their way through the force opposed to them.

The means of shortening and protecting long lines of communication are very limited. The seizure of some fortresses adjacent to the position taken up by the army, and on the roads leading to the rear – or in the event of there being no fortresses in the country, the construction of temporary defences at suitable points – the kind treatment of the people of the country, strict discipline on the military roads, good police, and active measures to improve the roads, are the only means by which the evil may be diminished, but it is one which can never be entirely removed.

Furthermore, what we said when treating of the question of subsistence with respect to the roads which the army should chose by preference, applies also particularly to lines of communication. The best lines of communication are roads leading through the most flourishing towns and the most important provinces; they ought to be preferred, even if considerably longer, and in most cases they exercise an important influence on the definitive disposition of the army.

CHAPTER SEVENTEEN

On Country and Ground

QUITE IRRESPECTIVE of their influence as regards the means of subsistence of an army, country and ground bear another most intimate and never-failing relation to the business of war, which is their decisive influence on the battle, both upon what concerns its course, as well as upon the preparation for it, and the use to be made of it. We now proceed to consider country and ground in this phase, that is, in the full meaning of the French expression "*Terrain.*"

The way to make use of them is a subject which lies mostly within the province of tactics, but the effects resulting from them appear in strategy; a battle in the mountains is, in its consequences as well as in itself, quite a different thing from a battle on a level plain.

But until we have studied the distinction between offensive and defensive, and examined the nature of each separately and fully, we cannot enter upon the consideration of the principal features of the ground in their effects; we must therefore for the present confine ourselves to an investigation of its general properties. There are three properties through which the ground has an influence on action in war; that is, as presenting an obstacle to approach, as an obstacle to an extensive view, and as protection against the effect of fire-arms; all other effects may be traced back to these three.

Unquestionably this threefold influence of ground has a tendency to make warfare more diversified, more complicated, and more scientific, for they are plainly three more quantities which enter into military combinations.

A completely level plain, quite open at the same time, that is, a tract of country which cannot influence war at all, has no existence except in relation to small bodies of troops, and with respect to them only for the duration of some given moment of time. When larger bodies are concerned, and a longer duration of time, accidents of ground mix themselves up with the action of such bodies, and it is hardly possible in the case of a whole army to imagine any particular moment, such as a battle, when the ground would not make its influence felt.

This influence is therefore never in abeyance, but it is certainly stronger or weaker according to the nature of the country.

If we keep in view the great mass of topographical phenomena we find that countries deviate from the idea of perfectly open level plains principally in three ways: first by the form of the ground, that is, hills and valleys; then by woods, marshes, and lakes as natural features; and lastly, by such changes as have been introduced by the hand of man. Through each of these three circumstances there is an increase in the influence of ground on the operations of war. If we trace them up to a certain distance we have mountainous country, a country little cultivated and covered with woods and marshes, and the well cultivated. The tendency in each case is to render war more complicated and connected with art.

The degree of influence which cultivation exercises is greater or less according to the nature of the cultivation; the system pursued in Flanders, Holstein, and some other countries, where the land is intersected in every direction with ditches, dykes, hedges, and walls, interspersed with many single dwellings and small woods has the greatest effect on war.

The conduct of war is therefore of the easiest kind in a level moderately-cultivated country. This however only holds good in quite a general sense, leaving entirely out of consideration the use which the defensive can make of obstacles of ground.

Each of these three kinds of ground has an effect in its own way on movement, on the range of sight, and in the cover it affords.

In a thickly-wooded country the obstacle to sight preponderates; in a mountainous country, the difficulty of movement presents the greatest obstacle to an enemy; in countries very much cultivated both these obstacles exist in a medium degree.

As thick woods render great portions of ground in a certain manner impracticable for military movements, and as, besides the difficulty which they oppose to movement they also obstruct the view, thereby preventing the use of means to clear a passage, the result is that they simplify the measures to be adopted on one side in proportion as they increase the difficulties with which the other side has to contend. Although it is difficult practically to concentrate forces for action in a wooded country, still a partition of forces does not take place to the same extent as it usually does in a mountainous country, or in a country very much intersected with canals, rivers, &c.: in other words, the partition of forces in such a country is more unavoidable but not so great.

In mountains, the obstacles to movement preponderate and take effect in two ways, because in some parts the country is quite impassable, and where it is practicable we must move slower and with greater difficulty. On this account the rapidity of all movements is much diminished in mountains, and all operations are mixed up with a larger quantity of the element of time. But the ground in mountains has also the special property peculiar to itself, that one point commands another. We shall devote the following chapter to the discussion of the subject of commanding heights generally, and shall only here remark that it is this peculiarity which causes the great partition of forces in operations carried on amongst mountains, for particular points thus acquire importance from the influence they have upon other points in addition to any intrinsic value which they have in themselves.

As we have elsewhere observed, each of these three kinds of ground in proportion as its own special peculiarity has a tendency to an extreme, has in the same degree a tendency to lower the influence of the supreme command, increasing in like manner the independent action of subordinates down to the private soldier. The greater the partition of any force, the less an undivided control is possible, so much the more are subordinates left to themselves; that is self-evident. Certainly when the partition of a force is greater, then through the diversity of action and greater scope in the use of means the influence of intelligence must increase, and even the commander-in-chief may show his talents to advantage under such circumstances; but we must here repeat what has been said before, that in war the sum total of single results decides more than the form or method in which they are connected, and therefore, if we push our present considerations to an extreme case, and suppose a whole army extended in a line of skirmishers so that each private soldier fights his own little battle, more will depend on the sum of single victories gained than on the form in which they are connected; for the benefit of good combinations can only follow from positive results, not from negative. Therefore in such a case the courage, the dexterity, and the spirit of individuals will prove decisive. It is only when two opposing armies are on a par as regards military qualities, or that their peculiar properties hold the balance even, that the talent and judgment of the commander become again decisive. The consequence is that national armies and insurgent levies, etc., etc., in which, at least in the individual, the warlike spirit is highly excited, although they are not superior in skill and bravery, are still able to maintain a superiority by a great dispersion of their forces favoured by a difficult country, and that they can only maintain themselves for a continuance upon that kind of system, because troops of this description are generally destitute of all the qualities and virtues which are indispensable when tolerably large numbers are required to act as a united body.

Also in the nature of forces there are many gradations between one of these extremes and the other, for the very circumstance of being engaged in the defence of its own country gives to even a regular standing army something of the character of a national army, and makes it more suited for a war waged by an army broken up into detachments.

Now the more these qualifications and influences are wanting in an army, the greater they are on the side of its opponent, so much the more will it dread being split into fractions, the more it will avoid a broken country; but to avoid fighting in such a description of country is seldom a matter of choice; we cannot choose a theatre of war like a piece of merchandise from amongst several patterns, and thus we find generally that armies which from their nature fight with advantage in concentrated masses, exhaust all their ingenuity in trying to carry out their system as far as possible in direct opposition *to the nature of the country*. They must in consequence submit to other disadvantages, such as scanty and difficult subsistence for the troops, bad quarters, and in the combat numerous attacks from all sides; but the disadvantage of giving up their own special advantage would be greater.

These two tendencies in opposite directions, the one to concentration the other to dispersion of forces, prevail more or less according as the nature of the troops engaged incline them more to one side or the other, but however decided the tendency, the one side cannot always remain with his forces concentrated, neither can the other expect success by following his system of warfare in scattered bodies on all occasions. The French were obliged to resort to partitioning their forces in Spain, and the Spaniards, whilst defending their country by means of an insurgent population, were obliged to try the fate of great battles in the open field with part of their forces.

Next to the connection which country and ground have with the general, and especially with the political, composition of the forces engaged, the most important point is the relative proportion of the three arms.

In all countries which are difficult to traverse, whether the obstacles are mountains, forests, or a peculiar cultivation, a numerous cavalry is useless: that is plain in itself; it is just the same with artillery in wooded countries; there will probably be a want of room to use it with effect, of roads to transport it, and of forage for the horses. For this arm highly cultivated countries are less disadvantageous, and least of all a mountainous country. Both, no doubt, afford cover against its fire, and in that respect they are unfavourable to an arm which depends entirely on its fire: both also often furnish means for the enemy's infantry to place the heavy artillery in jeopardy, as infantry can pass anywhere; but still in neither is there in general any want of space for the use of a numerous artillery, and in mountainous countries it has this great advantage, that its effects are prolonged and increased in consequence of the movements of the enemy being slower.

But it is undeniable that infantry has a decided advantage over every other arm in difficult country, and that, therefore, in such a country its number may considerably exceed the usual proportion.

CHAPTER EIGHTEEN

Command of Ground

THE WORD "COMMAND" has a charm in the art of war peculiar to itself, and in fact to this element belongs a great part, perhaps half the influence which ground exercises on the use of troops. Here many of the sacred relics of military erudition have their root, as, for instance, commanding positions, key positions, strategic manœuvres, etc. We shall take as clear a view of the subject as we can without prolixity, and pass in review the true and the false, reality and exaggeration.

Every exertion of physical force if made upwards is more difficult than if it is made in the contrary direction (downwards); consequently it must be so in fighting; and there are three evident reasons why it is so. First, every height may be regarded as an obstacle to approach; secondly, although the range is not perceptibly greater in shooting down from a height, yet, all geometrical relations being taken into consideration, we have a better chance of hitting than in the opposite case; thirdly, an elevation gives a better command of view. How all these advantages unite themselves together in battle we are not concerned with here; we collect the sum total of the advantages which tactics derives from elevation of position and combine them in one whole which we regard as the first strategic advantage.

But the first and last of these advantages that have been enumerated must appear once more as advantages of strategy itself, for we march and reconnoitre in strategy as well as in tactics; if, therefore, an elevated position is an obstacle to the approach of those on lower ground, that is the second; and the better command of view which this elevated position affords is the third advantage which strategy may derive in this way.

Of these elements is composed the power of dominating, overlooking, commanding; from these sources springs the sense of superiority and security which is felt in standing on the brow of a hill and looking at the enemy below, and the feeling of weakness and apprehension which pervades the minds of those below. Perhaps the total impression made is at the same time stronger than it ought to be, because the advantage of the higher ground strikes the senses more than the circumstances which modify that advantage. Perhaps the impression made surpasses that which the truth warrants, in which case the effect of imagination must be regarded as a new element, which exaggerates the effect produced by an elevation of ground.

At the same time the advantage of greater facility of movement is not absolute, and not always in favour of the side occupying the higher position; it is only so when his opponent wishes to attack him; it is not if the combatants are separated by a great valley, and it is actually in favour of the army on the lower ground if both wish to fight in the plain (battle of Hohenfriedberg). Also the power of overlooking, or command of view, has likewise great limitations. A wooded country in the valley below, and often the very masses of the mountains themselves on which we stand, obstruct the vision. Countless are the cases in which we might seek in vain on the spot for those advantages of an elevated position which a map would lead us to expect; and we might often be led to think we had only involved ourselves in all kinds of disadvantages, the very opposite of the advantages we counted upon. But these limitations and conditions do not abrogate or destroy the superiority which the more elevated position confers, both on the defensive and offensive. We shall point out, in a few words, how this is the case with each.

Out of the three strategic advantages of the more elevated ground, *the greater tactical strength, the more difficult approach,* and *the better view,* the first two are of such a nature that they belong really to the defensive only; for it is only in holding firmly to a position that we can make use of them, whilst the other side (offensive) in moving cannot remove them and take them with him; but the third advantage can be made use of by the offensive just as well as by the defensive.

From this it follows that the more elevated ground is highly important to the defensive, and as it can only be maintained in a decisive way in mountainous countries, therefore it would seem to follow, as a consequence, that the defensive has an important advantage in mountain positions. How it is that, through other circumstances, this is not so in reality, we shall show in the chapter on the defence of mountains.

We must first of all make a distinction if the question relates merely to commanding ground at one single point, as, for example, a position for an army; in such case the strategic advantages rather merge in the tactical one of a battle fought under advantageous circumstances; but if now we imagine a considerable tract of country – suppose a whole province – as a regular slope, like the declivity at a general watershed, so that we can make several marches, and always hold the upper ground, then the strategic advantages become greater, because we can now use the advantages of the more elevated ground not only in the combination of our forces with each other for one particular combat, but also in the combination of several combats with one another. Thus it is with the defensive.

As regards the offensive, it enjoys to a certain extent the same advantages as the defensive from the more elevated ground; for this reason that the stragetic attack is not confined to one act like the tactical. The strategic advance is not the continuous movement of a piece of wheel-work; it is made in single marches with a longer or shorter interval between them, and at each halting point the assailant is just as much acting on the defensive as his adversary.

Through the advantage of a better view of the surrounding country, an elevated position confers, in a certain measure, on the offensive as well as the defensive, a power of action which we must not omit to notice; it is the facility of operating with separate masses. For each portion of a force separately derives the same advantages which the whole derives from this more elevated position; by this – a separate corps, let it be strong or weak in numbers, is stronger than it would otherwise be, and we can venture to take up a position with less danger than we could if it had not that particular property of being on an elevation. The advantages which are to be derived from such separate bodies of troops is a subject for another place.

If the possession of more elevated ground is combined with other geographical advantages which are in our favour, if the enemy finds himself cramped in his movements from other causes, as, for instance, by the proximity of a large river, such disadvantages of his position may prove quite decisive, and he may feel that he cannot too soon relieve himself from such a position. No army can maintain itself in the valley of a great river if it is not in possession of the heights on each side by which the valley is formed.

The possession of elevated ground may therefore become virtually command, and we can by no means deny that this idea represents a reality. But nevertheless the expressions "commanding ground," "sheltering position," "key of the country," in so far as they are founded on the nature of heights and descents, are hollow shells without any sound kernel. These imposing elements of theory have been chiefly resorted to in order to give a flavour to the seeming commonplace of military combinations; they have become the darling themes of learned soldiers, the magical wands of adepts in strategy, and neither the emptiness of these fanciful conceits, nor the frequent contradictions which have been given to them by the results of experience have sufficed to convince authors, and those who read their books, that with such phraseology they are drawing water in the leaky vessel of the Danaides. The conditions have been mistaken for the thing itself, the instrument for the hand. The occupation of such and such a position or space of ground, has been looked upon as an exercise of power like a thrust or a cut, the ground or position itself as a substantive quantity; whereas the one is like the lifting of the arm, the other is nothing but the lifeless instrument, a mere property which can only realise itself upon an object, a mere sign of plus or minus which wants the figures or quantities. This cut and thrust, this object, this quantity, is *a victorious battle;* it alone really counts; with it only can we reckon; and we must always have it in view, as well in giving a critical judgment in literature as in real action in the field.

Consequently, if nothing but the number and value of victorious combats decides in war, it is plain that the comparative value of the opposing armies and ability of their respective leaders again rank as the first points for consideration, and that the part which the influence of ground plays can only be one of an inferior grade.

BOOK SIX
Defence

CHAPTER ONE

Offence and Defence

1. – *Conception of Defence.*

WHAT IS DEFENCE in conception? The warding off a blow. What is then its characteristic sign? The state of expectancy (or of waiting for this blow). This is the sign by which we always recognise an act as of a defensive character, and by this sign alone can the defensive be distinguished from the offensive in war. But inasmuch as an absolute defence completely contradicts the idea of war, because there would then be war carried on by one side only, it follows that the defence in war can only be relative and the above distinguishing signs must therefore only be applied to the essential idea or general conception: it does not apply to all the separate acts which compose the war. A partial combat is defensive if we receive the onset, the charge of the enemy; a battle is so if we receive the attack, that is, wait for the appearance of the enemy before our position and within range of our fire; a campaign is defensive if we wait for the entry of the enemy into our theatre of war. In all these cases the sign of waiting for and warding off belongs to the general conception, without any contradiction arising with the conception of war, for it may be to our advantage to wait for the charge against our bayonets, or the attack on our position or our theatre of war. But as we must return the enemy's blows if we are really to carry on war on our side, therefore this offensive act in defensive war takes place more or less under the general title defensive – that is to say, the offensive of which we make use falls under the conception of position or theatre of war. We can, therefore, in a defensive campaign fight offensively, in a defensive battle we may use some divisions for offensive purposes, and lastly, while remaining in position awaiting the enemy's onslaught, we still make use of the offensive by sending at the same time balls into the enemy's ranks. The defensive form in war is therefore no mere shield but a shield formed of blows delivered with skill.

2. – *Advantages of the Defensive.*

What is the object of defence? *To preserve.* To preserve is easier than to acquire; from which follows at once that the means on both sides being supposed equal, the defensive is easier than the offensive. But in what consists the greater facility of preserving or keeping possession? In this, that all time which is not turned to any account falls into the scale in favour of the defence. He reaps where he has not sowed. Every suspension of offensive action, either from erroneous views, from fear or from indolence, is in favour of the side acting defensively. This advantage saved the State of Prussia from ruin more than once in the Seven Years' War. It is one which derives itself from the conception and object of the defensive, lies in the nature of all defence, and in ordinary life, particularly in legal business which bears so much resemblance to war, it is expressed by the Latin proverb, *Beati sunt possidentes.* Another advantage arising from the nature of war and belonging to it exclusively, is the aid afforded by locality or ground; this is one of which the defensive form has a preferential use.

Having established these general ideas we now turn more directly to the subject.

In tactics every combat, great or small, is *defensive* if we leave the initiative to the enemy, and wait for his appearance in our front. From that moment forward we can make use of all offensive means without losing the said two advantages of the defence, namely, that of waiting for, and that of ground. In strategy, at first, the campaign represents the battle, and the theatre of war the position; but afterwards the whole war takes the place of the campaign, and the whole country that of the theatre of war, and in both cases the defensive remains that which it was in tactics.

It has been already observed in a general way that the defensive is easier than the offensive; but as the defensive has a negative object, that of *preserving*, and the offensive a positive object that of *conquering*, and as the latter increases our own means of carrying on war, but the preserving does not, therefore in order to express ourselves distinctly, we must say, *that the defensive form of war is in itself stronger than the offensive.* This is the result we have been desirous of arriving at; for although it lies completely in the nature of the thing, and has been confirmed by experience a thousand times, still it is completely contrary to prevalent opinion – a proof how ideas may be confused by superficial writers.

If the defensive is the stronger form of conducting war, but has a negative object, it follows of itself that we must only make use of it so long as our weakness compels us to do so, and that we must give up that form as soon as we feel strong enough to aim at the positive object. Now as the state of our circumstances is usually improved in the event of our gaining a victory through the assistance of the defensive, it is therefore, also, the natural course in war to begin with the defensive, and to end with the offensive. It is therefore just as much in contradiction with the conception of war to suppose the defensive the ultimate object of the war as it was a contradiction to understand passivity to belong to all the parts of the defensive, as well as to the defensive as a whole. In other words: a war in which victories are merely used to ward off blows, and where there is no attempt to return the blow, would be just as absurd as a battle in which the most absolute defence (passivity) should everywhere prevail in all measures.

Against the justice of this general view many examples might be quoted in which the defensive continued defensive to the last, and the assumption of the offensive was never contemplated; but such an objection could only be urged if we lost sight of the fact that here the question is only about general ideas (abstract ideas), and that examples in opposition to the general conception we are discussing are all of them to be looked upon as cases in which the time for the possibility of offensive reaction had not yet arrived.

In the Seven Years' War, at least in the last three years of it, Frederick the Great did not think of an offensive; indeed we believe further, that generally speaking, he only acted on the offensive at any time in this war as the best means of defending himself; his whole situation compelled him to this course, and it is natural that a general should aim more immediately at that which is most in accordance with the situation in which he is placed for the time being. Nevertheless, we cannot look at this example of a defence upon a great scale without supposing that the idea of a possible counterstroke against Austria lay at the bottom of the whole of it, and saying to ourselves, the moment for that counterstroke had not arrived before the war came to a close. The conclusion of peace shows that this idea is not without foundation even in this instance; for what could have actuated the Austrians to make peace except the thought that they were not in a condition with their own forces alone to make head against the talent of the king; that to maintain an equilibrium their exertions must be greater than heretofore, and that the slightest relaxation of their efforts would probably lead to fresh losses of territory. And, in fact, who can doubt that if Russia, Sweden, and the army of the German Empire had ceased to act together against Frederick the Great he would have tried to conquer the Austrians again in Bohemia and Moravia?

Having thus defined the true meaning of the defensive, having defined its boundaries, we return again to the assertion that the defensive *is the stronger form of making war.*

Upon a closer examination, and comparison of the offensive and defensive, this will appear perfectly plain; but for the present we shall confine ourselves to noticing the contradiction in which we should be involved with ourselves, and with the results of experience by maintaining the contrary to be the fact. If the offensive form was the stronger there would be no further occasion ever to use the defensive, as it has merely a negative object, every one would be for attacking, and the defensive would be an absurdity. On the other hand, it is very natural that the higher object should be purchased by greater sacrifices. Whoever feels himself strong enough to make use of the weaker form has it in his power to aim at the greater object; whoever sets before himself the smaller object can only do so in order to have the benefit of the stronger form – If we look to experience, such a thing is unheard of as any one carrying on a war upon two different theatres – offensively on one with the weaker army, and defensively on the other with his strongest force But if the reverse of this has everywhere and at all times taken place that shows plainly that generals although their own inclination prompts them to the offensive, still hold the defensive to be the stronger form. We have still in the next chapters to explain some preliminary points.

CHAPTER TWO

The Relations of the Offensive and Defensive to each other in Tactics

FIRST OF ALL we must inquire into the circumstances which give the victory in a battle.

Of superiority of numbers, and bravery, discipline, or other qualities of an army, we say nothing here, because, as a rule, they depend on things which lie out of the province of the art of war in the sense in which we are now considering it; besides which they exercise the same effect in the offensive as the defensive; and, moreover also, the superiority in *numbers in general* cannot come under consideration here, as the number of troops is likewise a given quantity or condition, and does not depend on the will or pleasure of the general. Further, these things have no particular connection with attack and defence. But, irrespective of these things, there are other three which appear to us of decisive importance, these are: *surprise, advantage of ground*, and *the attack from several quarters*. The surprise produces an effect by opposing to the enemy a great many more troops than he expected at some particular point. The superiority in numbers in this case is very different to a general superiority of numbers; it is the most powerful agent in the art of war. – The way in which the advantage of ground contributes to the victory is intelligible enough of itself, and we have only one observation to make which is, that we do not confine our remarks to obstacles which obstruct the advance of an enemy, such as scarped grounds, high hills, marshy streams, hedges, inclosures, etc.; we also allude to the advantage which ground affords as cover, under which troops are concealed from view. Indeed we may say that even from ground which is quite unimportant a person acquainted with the locality may derive assistance. The attack from several quarters includes in itself all tactical turning movements great and small, and its effects are derived partly from the double execution obtained in this way from fire-arms, and partly from the enemy's dread of his retreat being cut off.

Now how do the offensive and defensive stand respectively in relation to these things?

Having in view the three principles of victory just described, the answer to this question is, that only a small portion of the first and last of these principles is in favour of the offensive, whilst the greater part of them, and the whole of the second principle, are at the command of the party acting defensively.

The offensive side can only have the advantage of one complete surprise of the whole mass with the whole, whilst the defensive is in a condition to surprise incessantly, throughout the whole course of the combat, by the force and form which he gives to his partial attacks.

The offensive has greater facilities than the defensive for surrounding and cutting off the whole, as the latter is in a manner in a fixed position while the former is in a state of movement having reference to that position. But the superior advantage for an enveloping movement, which the offensive possesses, as now stated, is again limited to a movement against the whole mass; for during the course of the combat, and with separate divisions of the force, it is easier for the defensive than for the offensive to make attacks from several quarters, *because, as we have already said, the former is in a better situation to surprise by the force and form of his attacks.*

That the defensive in an especial manner enjoys the assistance which ground affords is plain in itself; as to what concerns the advantage which the defensive has in surprising by the force and form of his attacks, that results from the offensive being obliged to approach by roads and paths where he may be easily observed, whilst the defensive conceals his position, and, until almost the decisive moment, remains invisible to his opponent. – Since the true method of defence has been adopted, reconnaissances have gone quite out of fashion, that is to say, they have become impossible. Certainly reconnaissances are still made at times, but they seldom bring home much with them. Immense as is the advantage of being able to examine well a position, and become perfectly acquainted with it before a battle, plain as it is that he (the defensive) who lies in wait near such a chosen position can much more easily effect a surprise than his adversary, yet still to this very hour the old notion is not exploded that a battle which is accepted is half lost. This comes from the old kind of defensive practised twenty years ago, and partly also in the Seven Years' War, when the only assistance expected from the ground was that it should be difficult of approach in front (by steep mountain slopes, etc., etc.), when the little depth of the positions and the difficulty of moving the flanks produced such weakness that the armies dodged one another from one hill to another, which increased the evil. If some kind of support were found on which to rest the wings, then all depended on preventing the army stretched along between these points, like a piece of work on an embroidery frame, from being broken through at any point. The ground occupied possessed a direct value at every point, and therefore a direct defence was required everywhere. Under such circumstances, the idea of making a movement or attempting a surprise during the battle could not be entertained; it was the exact reverse of what constitutes a good defence, and of that which the defence has actually become in modern warfare.

In reality, contempt for the defensive has always been the result of some particular method of defence having become worn out (outlived its period); and this was just the case with the method we have now mentioned, for in times antecedent to the period we refer to, that very method was superior to the offensive.

If we go through the progressive development of the modern art of war, we find that at the commencement – that is the Thirty Years' War and the war of the Spanish Succession – the deployment and drawing up of the army in array, was one of the great leading points connected with the battle. It was the most important part of the plan of the battle. This gave the defensive, as a rule, a great advantage, as he was already drawn up and deployed. As soon as the troops acquired greater capability of manœuvring, this advantage ceased, and the superiority passed over to the side of the offensive for a time. Then the defensive sought shelter behind rivers or deep valleys, or on high land. The defensive thus recovered the advantage, and continued to maintain it until the offensive acquired such increased mobility and expertness in manœuvring that he himself could venture into broken ground and attack in separate columns, and therefore became able *to turn* his adversary. This led to a gradual increase in the length of positions, in consequence of which, no doubt, it occurred to the offensive to concentrate at a few points, and break through the enemy's thin line. The offensive thus, for a third time, gained the ascendancy, and the defence was again obliged to alter its system. This it has done in recent wars by keeping its forces concentrated in large masses, the greater part not deployed, and, where possible, concealed, thus merely taking up a position in readiness to act according to the measures of the enemy as soon as they are sufficiently revealed.

This does not preclude a partially passive defence of the ground; its advantage is too great for it not to be used a hundred times in a campaign. But that kind of passive defence of the ground is usually no longer the principal affair: that is what we have to do with here.

If the offensive should discover some new and powerful element which it can bring to its assistance – an event not very probable, seeing the point of simplicity and natural order to which all is now brought – then the defence must again alter its method. But the defensive is always certain of the assistance of ground, which insures to it in general its natural superiority, as the special properties of country and ground exercise a greater influence than ever on actual warfare.

CHAPTER THREE

The Relations of the Offensive and Defensive to each other in Strategy

LET US ASK AGAIN, first of all, what are the circumstances which insure a successful result in strategy?

In strategy there is no victory, as we have before said. On the one hand, the strategic success is the successful preparation of the tactical victory; the greater this strategic success, the more probable becomes the victory in the battle. On the other hand, strategic success lies in the making use of the victory gained. The more events the strategic combinations can in the sequel include in the consequences of a battle gained, the more strategy can lay hands on amongst the wreck of all that has been shaken to the foundation by the battle, the more it sweeps up in great masses what of necessity has been gained with great labour by many single hands in the battle, the grander will be its success. – Those things which chiefly lead to this success, or at least facilitate it, consequently the leading principles of efficient action in strategy, are as follow: –

1. The advantage of ground.

2. The surprise, let it be either in the form of an actual attack by surprise or by the unexpected display of large forces at certain points.

3. The attack from several quarters (all three, as in tactics).

4. The assistance of the theatre of war by fortresses, and everything belonging to them.

5. The support of the people.

6. The utilisation of great moral forces.

Now, what are the relations of offensive and defensive with respect to these things?

The party on the defensive has the advantage of ground; the offensive side that of the attack by surprise in strategy, as in tactics But respecting the surprise, we must observe that it is infinitely more efficacious and important in strategy than in tactics. In the latter, a surprise seldom rises to the level of a great victory, while in strategy it often finishes the war at one stroke. But at the same time we must observe that the advantageous use of this means supposes some *great* and *uncommon*, as well as *decisive* error committed by the adversary, therefore it does not alter the balance much in favour of the offensive.

The surprise of the enemy, by placing superior forces in position at certain points, has again a great resemblance to the analogous case in tactics. Were the defensive compelled to distribute his forces upon several points of approach to his theatre of war, then the offensive would have plainly the advantage of being able to fall upon one point with all his weight. But here also, the new art of acting on the defensive by a different mode of proceeding has imperceptibly brought about new principles. If the defensive side does not apprehend that the enemy, by making use of an undefended road, will throw himself upon some important magazine or depôt, or on some unprepared fortification, or on the capital itself. – and if he is not reduced to the alternative of opposing the enemy on the road he has chosen, or of having his retreat cut off, then there are no peremptory grounds for dividing his forces; for if the offensive chooses a different road from that on which the defensive is to be found, then some days later the latter can march against his opponent with his whole force upon the road he has chosen; besides, he may at the same time, in most cases, rest satisfied that the offensive will do him the honour to seek him out. – If the offensive is obliged to advance with his forces divided, which is often unavoidable on account of subsistence, then plainly the defensive has the advantage on his side of being able to fall in force upon a fraction of the enemy.

Attacks in flank and rear, which in strategy mean on the sides and reverse of the theatre of war, are of a very different nature to attacks so called in tactics.

1st. There is no bringing the enemy under two fires, because we cannot fire from one end of a theatre of war to the other.

2nd. The apprehension of losing the line of retreat is very much less, for the spaces in strategy are so great that they cannot be barred as in tactics.

3rd. In strategy, on account of the extent of space embraced, the efficacy of interior, that is of shorter lines, is much greater, and this forms a great safeguard against attacks from several directions.

4th. A new principle makes its appearance in the sensibility, which is felt as to lines of communication, that is in the effect which is produced by merely interrupting them.

Now it confessedly lies in the nature of things, that on account of the greater spaces in strategy, the enveloping attack, or the attack from several sides, as a rule is only possible for the side which has the initiative, that is the offensive, and that the defensive is not in a condition, as he is in tactics, in the course of the action, to turn the tables on the enemy by surrounding him, because he has it not in his power either to draw up his forces with the necessary depth relatively, or to conceal them sufficiently: but then, of what use is the facility of enveloping to the offensive, if its advantages are not forthcoming? We could not therefore bring forward the enveloping attack in strategy as a principle of victory in general, if its influence on the lines of communication did not come into consideration. But this factor is seldom great at the first moment, when attack and defence first meet, and while they are still opposed to each other in their original position; it only becomes great as a campaign advances, when the offensive in the enemy's country is by degrees brought into the condition of defensive; then the lines of communication of this new party acting on the defensive, become weak, and the party originally on the defensive, in assuming the offensive can derive advantage from this weakness. But who does not see that this casual superiority of the attack is not to be carried to the credit of the offensive in general, for it is in reality created out of the superior relations of the defensive.

The fourth principle, the *Assistance of the Theatre of War*, is naturally an advantage on the side of the defensive. If the attacking army opens the campaign, it breaks away from its own theatre, and is thus weakened, that is, it leaves fortresses and depôts of all kinds behind it. The greater the sphere of operations which must be traversed, the more it will be weakened (by marches and garrisons); the army on the defensive continues to keep up its connection with everything, that is, it enjoys the support of its fortresses, is not weakened in any way, and is near to its sources of supply.

The support of the population as a fifth principle is not realised in every defence, for a defensive campaign may be carried on in the enemy's country, but still this principle is only derived from the idea of the defensive, and applies to it in the majority of cases. Besides by this is meant chiefly, although not exclusively, the effect of calling out the last Reserves, and even of a national armament, the result of which is that all friction is diminished, and that all resources are sooner forthcoming and flow in more abundantly.

The campaign of 1812, gives as it were in a magnifying glass a very clear illustration of the effect of the means specified under principles 3 and 4. 500,000 men passed the Niemen, 120,000 fought at Borodino, and much fewer arrived at Moscow.

We may say that the effect itself of this stupendous attempt was so disastrous that even if the Russians had not assumed any offensive at all, they would still have been secure from any fresh attempt at invasion for a considerable time. It is true that with the exception of Sweden there is no country in Europe which is situated like Russia, but the efficient principle is always the same, the only distinction being in the greater or less degree of its strength.

If we add to the fourth and fifth principles, the consideration that these forces of the defensive belong to the original defensive, that is the defensive carried on in our own soil, and that they are much weaker if the defence takes place in an enemy's country and is mixed up with an offensive undertaking, then from that there is a new disadvantage for the offensive, much the same as above, in respect to the third principle; for the offensive is just as little composed entirely of active elements, as the defensive of mere warding off blows; indeed every attack which does not lead directly to peace must inevitably end in the defensive.

Now, if all defensive elements which are brought into use in the attack are weakened by its nature, that is by belonging to the attack, then this must also be considered as a general disadvantage of the offensive.

This is far from being an idle piece of logical refinement, on the contrary we should rather say that in it lies the chief disadvantage of the offensive in general, and therefore from the very commencement of, as well as throughout every combination for a strategic attack, most particular attention ought to be directed to this point, that is to the defensive, which may follow, as we shall see more plainly when we come to the book on plans of campaigns.

The great moral forces which at times saturate the element of war, as it were with a leaven of their own, which therefore the commander in certain cases can use to assist the other means at his command, are to be supposed just as well on the side of the defensive as of the offensive; at least those which are more especially in favour of the attack, such as confusion and disorder in the enemy's ranks – do not generally appear until after the decisive stroke is given, and consequently seldom contribute beforehand to produce that result.

We think we have now sufficiently established our proposition, that the *defensive is a stronger form of war than the offensive;* but there still remains to be mentioned one small factor hitherto unnoticed. It is the high spirit, the feeling of superiority in an army which springs from a consciousness of belonging to the attacking party. The thing is in itself a fact, but the feeling soon merges into the more general and more powerful one which is imparted by victory or defeat, by the talent or incapacity of the general.

CHAPTER FOUR

Convergence of Attack and Divergence of Defence

THESE TWO CONCEPTIONS, these forms in the use of offensive and defensive, appear so frequently in theory and reality, that the imagination is involuntarily disposed to look upon them as intrinsic forms, necessary to attack and defence, which, however, is not really the case, as the smallest reflection will show. We take the earliest opportunity of examining them, that we may obtain once for all clear ideas respecting them, and that, in proceeding with our consideration of the relations of attack and defence, we may be able to set these conceptions aside altogether, and not have our attention for ever distracted by the appearance of advantage and the reverse which they cast upon things. We treat them here as pure abstractions, extract the conception of them like an essence, and reserve our remarks on the part which it has in actual things for a future time.

The defending party, both in tactics and in strategy, is supposed to be waiting in expectation, therefore standing, whilst the assailant is imagined to be in movement, and in movement expressly directed against that standing adversary. It follows from this, necessarily, that turning and enveloping is at the option of the assailant only, that is to say, as long as his movement and the immobility of the defensive continue. This freedom of choice of the mode of attack, whether it shall be convergent or not, according as it shall appear advantageous or otherwise, ought to be reckoned as an advantage to the offensive in general. But this choice is free only in tactics; it is not always allowed in strategy. In the first, the points on which the wings rest are hardly ever absolutely secure; but they are very frequently so in strategy, as when the front to be defended stretches in a straight line from one sea to another, or from one neutral territory to another. In such cases, the attack cannot be made in a convergent form, and the liberty of choice is limited. It is limited in a still more embarrassing manner if the assailant is obliged to operate by converging lines. Russia and France cannot attack Germany in any other way than by converging lines; therefore they cannot attack with their forces united. Now if we assume as granted that the concentric form in the action of forces in the majority of cases is the weaker form, then the advantage which the assailant possesses in the greater freedom of choice may probably be completely outweighed by the disadvantage, in other cases, of being compelled to make use of the weaker form.

We proceed to examine more closely the action of these forms, both in tactics and in strategy.

It has been considered one of the chief advantages of giving a concentric direction to forces, that is, operating from the circumference of a circle towards the centre, that the further the forces advance, the nearer they approach to each other; the fact is true, but the supposed advantage is not; for the tendency to union is going on equally on both sides; consequently, the equilibrium is not disturbed. It is the same in the dispersion of force by eccentric movements.

But another and a real advantage is, that forces operating on converging lines direct their action towards a *common point*, those operating on diverging lines do not. – Now what are the effects of the action in the two cases? Here we must separate tactics from strategy.

We shall not push the analysis too far, and therefore confine ourselves to the following points as the advantages of the action in tactics.

1. A cross fire, or, at least, an increased effect of fire, as soon as all is brought within a certain range.

2. Attack of one and the same point from several sides.

3. The cutting off the retreat.

The interception of a retreat may be also conceived strategically, but then it is plainly much more difficult, because great spaces are not easily blocked. The attack upon one and the same body from several quarters is generally more effectual and decisive, the smaller this body is, the nearer it approaches to the lowest limit – that of a single combatant. An army can easily give battle on several sides, a division less easily, a battalion only when formed in mass, a single man not at all. Now strategy, in its province, deals with large masses of men, extensive spaces, and considerable duration of time; with tactics, it is the reverse. From this follows that the attack from several sides in strategy cannot have the same results as in tactics.

The effect of fire does not come within the scope of strategy; but in its place there is something else. It is that tottering of the base which every army feels when there is a victorious enemy in its rear, whether near or far off.

It is, therefore, certain that the concentric action of forces has an advantage in this way, that the action or effect against *a* is at the same time one against *b*, without its force against *a* being diminished, and that the action against *b* is likewise action against *a*. The whole, therefore, is not *a* + *b*, but something more; and this advantage is produced both in tactics and strategy, although somewhat differently in each.

Now what is there in the eccentric or divergent action of forces to oppose to this advantage? Plainly the advantage of having the forces in greater proximity to each other, and the moving on *interior lines*. It is unnecessary to demonstrate how this can become such a multiplier of forces that the assailant cannot encounter the advantage it gives his opponent unless he has a great superiority of force. – When once the defensive has adopted the principle of movement (movement which certainly commences later than that of the assailant, but still time enough to break the chains of paralysing inaction), then this advantage of greater concentration and the interior lines tends much more decisively, and in most cases more effectually, towards victory than the concentric form of the attack. But victory must precede the realisation of this superiority; we must conquer before we can think of cutting off an enemy's retreat. In short, we see that there is here a relation similar to that which exists between attack and defence generally; the concentric form leads to brilliant results, the advantages of the eccentric are more secure: the former is the weaker form with the positive object; the latter, the stronger form with the negative object. In this way these two forms seem to us to be brought nearly to an even balance. Now if we add to this that the defence, not being always absolute, is also not always precluded from using its forces on converging lines, we have no longer a right to believe that this converging form is alone sufficient to ensure to the offensive a superiority over the defensive universally, and thus we set ourselves free from the influence which that opinion usually exercises over the judgment, whenever there is an opportunity.

What has been said up to the present, relates to both tactics and strategy; we have still a most important point to bring forward, which applies to strategy only. The advantage of interior lines increases with the distances to which these lines relate. In distances of a few thousand yards, or a half mile, the time which is gained, cannot of course be as much as in distances of several days' march, or indeed, of twenty or thirty miles; the first, that is, the small distances, concerns tactics, the greater ones belong to strategy. But, although we certainly require more time, to reach an object in strategy, than in tactics, and an army is not so quickly defeated as a battalion, still, these periods of time in strategy can only increase up to a certain point; that is, they can only last until a battle takes place, or, perhaps, over and above that, for the few days during which a battle may be avoided without serious loss. Further, there is a much greater difference in the real start in advance, which is gained in one case, as compared with the other. Owing to the insignificance of the distances in tactics, the movements of one army in a battle, take place almost in sight of the other; the army, therefore, on the exterior line, will generally very soon be made aware of what his adversary is doing. From the long distances, with which strategy has to deal, it very seldom happens, that the movement of one army, is not concealed from the other for at least a day, and there are numerous instances, in which especially if the movement is only partial, such as a considerable detachment, that it remains secret for weeks. – It is easy to see, what a great advantage this power of concealing movements must be to that party, who through the nature of his position has reason to desire it most.

We here close our considerations on the convergent and divergent use of forces, and the relation of those forms to attack and defence, proposing to return to the subject at another time.

CHAPTER FIVE

Character of Strategic Defensive

WE HAVE ALREADY explained what the defensive is generally, namely, nothing more than a stronger form of carrying on war (page 69), by means of which we endeavour to wrest a victory, in order, after having gained a superiority, to pass over to the offensive, that is to the positive object of war.

Even if the intention of a war is only the maintenance of the existing situation of things, the *status quo*, still a mere parrying of a blow is something quite contradictory to the conception of the term war, because the conduct of war is unquestionably no mere state of endurance. If the defender has obtained an important advantage, then the defensive form has done its part, and under the protection of this success he must give back the blow, otherwise he exposes himself to certain destruction; common sense points out that iron should be struck while it is hot, that we should use the advantage gained to guard against a second attack. How, when and where this reaction shall commence is subject certainly to a number of other conditions, which we can only explain hereafter. For the present we keep to this, that we must always consider this transition to an offensive return as a natural tendency of the defensive, therefore as an essential element of the same, and always conclude that there is something wrong in the management of a war when a victory gained through the defensive form is not turned to good account in any manner, but allowed to wither away.

A swift and vigorous assumption of the offensive – the flashing sword of vengeance – is the most brilliant point in the defensive; he who does not at once think of it at the right moment, or rather he who does not from the first include this transition in his idea of the defensive will never understand the superiority of the defensive as a form of war; he will be for ever thinking only of the means which will be consumed by the enemy and gained by ourselves through the offensive, which means however depend not on tying the knot, but on untying it. Further, it is a stupid confusion of ideas if, under the term offensive, we always understand sudden attack or surprise, and consequently under defensive imagine nothing but embarrassment and confusion.

It is true that a conqueror makes his determination to go to war sooner than the unconscious defender, and if he knows how to keep his measures properly secret, he may also perhaps take the defender unawares; but that is a thing quite foreign to war itself, for it should not be so. War actually takes place more for the defensive than for the conqueror, for invasion only calls forth resistance, and it is not until there is resistance that there is war. A conqueror is always a lover of peace (as Buonaparte always asserted of himself); he would like to make his entry into our state unopposed; in order to prevent this, we must choose war, and therefore also make preparations, that is in other words, it is just the weak, or that side which must defend itself, which should be always armed in order not to be taken by surprise; so it is willed by the art of war.

The appearance of one side sooner than the other in the theatre of war depends, besides, in most cases on things quite different from a view to offensive or defensive. But although a view to one or other of these forms is not the cause, it is often the result of this priority of appearance. Whoever is first ready will on that account go to work offensively, if the advantage of surprise is sufficiently great to make it expedient; and the party who is the last to be ready can only then in some measure compensate for the disadvantage which threatens him by the advantages of the defensive.

At the same time, it must be looked upon in general as an advantage for the offensive, that he can make that good use of being the first in the field which has been noticed in the third book; only this general advantage is not an absolute necessity in every case.

If, therefore, we imagine to ourselves a defensive, such as it should be, we must suppose it with every possible preparation of all means, with an army fit for, and inured to, war, with a general who does not wait for his adversary with anxiety from an embarrassing feeling of uncertainty, but from his own free choice, with cool presence of mind, with fortresses which do not dread a siege, and lastly, with a loyal people who fear the enemy as little as he fears them. With such attributes the defensive will act no such contemptible part in opposition to the offensive, and the latter will not appear such an easy and certain form of war, as it does in the gloomy imaginations of those who can only see in the offensive courage, strength of will, and energy; in the defensive, helplessness and apathy.

CHAPTER SIX
Extent of the Means of Defence

WE HAVE SHOWN in the second and third chapters of this book how the defence has a natural advantage in the employment of those things, which, – irrespective of the absolute strength and qualities of the combatant force, – influence the tactical as well as the strategic result, namely, the advantage of ground, sudden attack, attack from several directions (converging form of attack), the assistance of the theatre of war, support of the people, and the utilising great moral forces. We think it useful now to cast again a glance over the extent of the means which are at command of the defensive in particular, and which are to be regarded as the columns of the different orders of architecture in his edifice.

1. – *Landwehr (Militia).*

This force has been used in modern times to combat the enemy on foreign soil; and it is not to be denied that its organisation in many states, for instance in Prussia, is of such a kind, that it may almost be regarded as part of the standing army, therefore it does not belong to the defensive exclusively. At the same time, we must not overlook the fact, that the very great use made of it in 1813-1415 was the result of defensive war; that it is organised in very few places to the same degree as in Prussia, and that always when its organisation falls below the level of complete efficiency, it is better suited for the defensive than for the offensive. But besides that, there always lies in the idea of a militia the notion of a very extensive more or less voluntary co-operation of the whole mass of the people in support of the war, with all their physical powers, as well as with their feelings, and a ready sacrifice of all they possess. The more its organisation deviates from this, so much the more the force thus created will become a standing army under another name, and the more it will have the advantages of such a force; but it will also lose in proportion the advantages which belong properly to the militia, those of being a force, the limits of which are undefined, and capable of being easily increased by appealing to the feelings and patriotism of the people. In these things lies the essence of a militia; in its organisation, latitude must be allowed for this co-operation of the whole people; if we seek to obtain something extraordinary from a militia, we are only following a shadow.

But now the close relationship between this essence of a militia system, and the conception of the defensive, is not to be denied, neither can it be denied that such a militia will always belong more to the defensive form than to the offensive, and that it will manifest chiefly in the defensive, those effects through which it surpasses the attack.

2. – *Fortresses.*

The assistance afforded by fortresses to the offensive does not extend beyond what is given by those close upon the frontiers, and is only feeble in influence; the assistance which the defensive can derive from this reaches further into the heart of the country, and therefore more of them can be brought into use, and their utility itself differs in the degree of its intensity. A fortress which is made the object of a regular siege, and holds out, is naturally of more considerable weight in the scales of war, than one which by the strength of its works merely forbids the idea of its capture, and therefore neither occupies nor consumes any of the enemy's forces.

3. – *The People.*

Although the influence of a single inhabitant of the theatre of war on the course of the war in most cases is not more perceptible than the co-operation of a drop of water in a whole river, still even in cases where there is no such thing as a general rising of the people, the *total influence* of the inhabitants of a country in war is anything but imperceptible. Every thing goes on easier in our own country, provided it is not opposed by the general feeling of the population. All contributions great and small, are only yielded to the enemy under the compulsion of direct force; that operation must be undertaken by the troops, and cost the employment of many men as well as great exertions. The defensive receives all he wants, if not always voluntarily, as in cases of enthusiastic devotion, still through the long-used channels of submission to the state on the part of the citizens, which has become second nature, and which besides that, is enforced by the terrors of the law with which the army has nothing to do. But the spontaneous co-operation of the people proceeding from true attachment is in all cases most important, as it never fails in all those points where service can be rendered without any sacrifice. We shall only notice one point, which is of the highest importance in war, that is *intelligence*, not so much special, great and important information through persons employed, as that respecting the innumerable little matters in connection with which the daily service of an army is carried on in uncertainty, and with regard to which a good understanding with the inhabitants gives the defensive a general advantage.

If we ascend from this quite general and never failing beneficial influence, up to special cases in which the populace begins to take part in the war, and then further up to the highest degree, where as in Spain, the war, as regards its leading events is chiefly a war carried on by the people themselves, we may see that we have here virtually a new power rather than a manifestation of increased cooperation on the part of the people, and therefore that –

4. – *The National Armament,*

or general call to arms, may be considered as a particular means of defence.

5. – *Allies.*

Finally, we may further reckon *allies* as the last support of the defensive. Naturally we do not mean ordinary allies, which the assailant may likewise have; we speak of those *essentially interested in maintaining* the integrity of the country. If for instance we look at the various states composing Europe at the present time, we find (without speaking of a systematically regulated balance of power and interests, as that does not exist, and therefore is often with justice disputed, still, unquestionably) that the great and small states and interests of nations are interwoven with each other in a most diversified and changeable manner, each of these points of intersection forms a binding knot, for in it the direction of the one gives equilibrium to the direction of the other; by all these knots therefore, evidently a more or less compact connection of the whole will be formed, and this general connection must be partially overturned by every change. In this manner the whole relations of all states to each other serve rather to preserve the stability of the whole than to produce changes, that is to say, *this tendency* to stability exists in general.

This we conceive to be the true notion of a balance of power, and in this sense it will always of itself come into existence, wherever there are extensive connections between civilised states.

How far this tendency of the general interests to the maintenance of the existing state of things is efficient is another question; at all events we can conceive some changes in the relations of single states to each other, which promote this efficiency of the whole, and others which obstruct it. In the first case they are efforts to perfect the political balance, and as these have the same tendency as the universal interests, they will also be supported by the majority of these interests. But in the other case, they are of an abnormal nature, undue activity on the part of some single states, real maladies; still that these should make their appearance in a whole with so little cohesion as an assemblage of great and little states is not to be wondered at, for we see the same in that marvellously organised whole, the natural world.

If in answer we are reminded of instances in history where single states have effected important changes, solely for their own benefit, without any effort on the part of the whole to prevent the same, or cases where a single state has been able to raise itself so much above others as to become almost the arbiter of the whole, – then our answer is that these examples by no means prove that a tendency of the interests of the whole in favour of stability does not exist, they only show that its action was not powerful enough at the moment. The effort towards an object is a different thing from the motion towards it. At the same time it is anything but a nullity, of which we have the best exemplification in the dynamics of the heavens.

We say, the tendency of equilibrium is to the maintenance of the existing state, whereby we certainly assume that rest, that is equilibrium, existed in this state; for where that has been already disturbed, tension has already commenced, and there the equilibrium may certainly also tend to a change. But if we look to the nature of the thing, this change can only affect some few separate states, never the majority, and therefore it is certain that the preservation of the latter is supported and secured through the collective interests of the whole – certain also that each single state which has not against it a tension of the whole will have more interest in favour of its defence than opposition to it.

Whoever laughs at these reflections as utopian dreams, does so at the expense of philosophical truth. Although we may learn from it the relations which the essential elements of things bear to each other, it would be rash to attempt to deduce laws from the same by which each individual case should be governed without regard to any accidental disturbing influences. But when a person, in the words of a great writer, *"never rises above anecdote,"* builds all history on it, begins always with the most individual points, with the climaxes of events, and only goes down just so deep as he finds a motive for doing, and therefore never reaches to the lowest foundation of the predominant general relations, his opinion will never have any value beyond the one case, and to him, that which philosophy proves to be applicable to cases in general, will only appear a dream.

Without that general striving for rest and the maintenance of the existing condition of things, a number of civilised states could not long live quietly side by side; they must necessarily become fused into one. Therefore, as Europe has existed in its present state for more than a thousand years, we can only regard the fact as a result of that tendency of the collective interests; and if the protection afforded by the whole has not in every instance proved strong enough to preserve the independence of each individual state, such exceptions are to be regarded as irregularities in the life of the whole, which have not destroyed that life, but have themselves been mastered by it.

It would be superfluous to go over the mass of events in which changes which would have disturbed the balance too much have been prevented or reversed by the opposition more or less openly declared of other states. They will be seen by the most cursory glance at history. We only wish to say a few words about a case which is always on the lips of those who ridicule the idea of a political balance, and because it appears specially applicable here as a case in which an unoffending state, acting on the defensive, succumbed without receiving any foreign aid. We allude to Poland. That a state of eight millions of inhabitants should disappear, should be divided amongst three others without a sword being drawn by any of the rest of the European states, appears, at first sight, a fact which either proves conclusively the general inefficiency of the political balance, or at least shows that it is inefficient to a very great extent in some instances. That a state of such extent should disappear, a prey to others, and those already the most powerful (Russia and Austria), appears such a very extreme case that it will be said, if an event of this description could not rouse the collective interests of all free states, then the efficient action which this collective interest should display for the benefit of individual states is imaginary. But we still maintain that a single case, however striking, does not negative the general truth, and we assert next that the downfall of Poland is also not so unaccountable as may at first sight appear. Was Poland really to be regarded as a European state, as a homogeneous member of the community of nations in Europe? No! It was a Tartar state, which instead of being located, like the Tartars of the Crimea, on the Black Sea, on the confines of the territory inhabited by the European community, had its habitation in the midst of that community on the Vistula. We neither desire by this to speak disrespectfully of the Poles, nor to justify the partition of their country, but only to look at things as they really are. For a hundred years this country had ceased to play any independent part in European politics, and had been only an apple of discord for the others. It was impossible that for a continuance it could maintain itself amongst the others with its state and constitution unaltered: an essential alteration in its Tartar nature would have been the work of not less than half, perhaps a whole century, supposing the chief men of that nation had been in favour of it. But these men were far too thorough Tartars to wish any such change. Their turbulent political condition, and their unbounded levity went hand in hand, and so they tumbled into the abyss. Long before the partition of Poland the Russians had become quite at home there, the idea of its being an independent state, with boundaries of its own, had ceased, and nothing is more certain than that Poland, if it had not been partitioned, must have become a Russian province. If this had not been so, and if Poland had been a state capable of making a defence, the three powers would not so readily have proceeded to its partition, and those powers most interested in maintaining its integrity, like France, Sweden and Turkey, would have been able to co-operate in a very different manner towards its preservation. But if the maintenance of a state is entirely dependent on external support, then certainly too much is asked.

The partition of Poland had been talked of frequently for a hundred years, and for that time the country had been not like a private house, but like a public road, on which foreign armies were constantly jostling one another. Was it the business of other states to put a stop to this; were they constantly to keep the sword drawn to preserve the political inviolability of the Polish frontier? That would have been to demand a moral impossibility. Poland was at this time politically little better than an uninhabited steppe; and as it is impossible that defenceless steppes, lying in the midst of other countries should be guarded for ever from invasion, therefore it was impossible to preserve the integrity of this state, as it was called. For all these reasons there is as little to cause wonder in the noiseless downfall of Poland as in the silent conquest of the Crimean Tartars; the Turks had a greater interest in upholding the latter than any European state had in preserving the independence of Poland, but they saw that it would be a vain effort to try to protect a defenceless steppe. –

We return to our subject, and think we have proved that the defensive in general may count more on foreign aid than the offensive; he may reckon the more certainly on it in proportion as his existence is of importance to others, that is to say, the sounder and more vigorous his political and military condition.

Of course the subjects which have been here enumerated as means properly belonging to the defensive will not be at the command of each particular defensive. Sometimes one, sometimes another, may be wanting; but they all belong to the idea of the defensive as a whole.

CHAPTER SEVEN

Mutual Action and Reaction of Attack and Defence

WE SHALL NOW consider attack and defence separately, as far as they can be separated from each other. We commence with the defensive for the following reasons: – It is certainly very natural and necessary to base the rules for the defence upon those of the offensive, and *vicè versâ*; but one of the two must still have a third point of departure, if the whole chain of ideas is to have a beginning, that is, to be possible. The first question concerns this point.

If we reflect upon the commencement of war philosophically, the conception of war properly does not originate with the *offensive*, as that form has for its absolute object, not so much *fighting* as the *taking possession of something*. The idea of war arises first by the *defensive*, for that form has the battle for its direct object, as warding off and fighting plainly are one and the same. The warding off is directed entirely against the attack; therefore supposes it, necessarily; but the attack is not directed against the warding off; it is directed upon something else – the *taking possession*; consequently does not presuppose the warding off. It lies, therefore, in the nature of things, that the party who first brings the element of war into action, the party from whose point of view two opposite parties are first conceived, also establishes the first laws of war, and that party is the *defender*. We are not speaking of any individual case; we are only dealing with a general, an abstract case, which theory imagines in order to determine the course it is to take.

By this we now know where to look for this fixed point, outside and independent of the reciprocal effect of attack and defence, and that it is in the defensive.

If this is a logical consequence, the defensive must have motives of action, even when as yet he knows nothing of the intentions of the offensive; and these motives of action must determine the organisation of the means of fighting. On the other hand, as long as the offensive knows nothing of the plans of his adversary, there are no motives of action for him, no grounds for the application of his military means. He can do nothing more than take these means along with him, that is, take possession by means of his army. And thus it is also in point of fact; for to carry about the apparatus of war is not to use it; and the offensive who takes such things with him, on the quite general supposition that he may require to use them, and who, instead of taking possession of a country by official functionaries and proclamations, does so with an army, has not as yet committed, properly speaking, any act of warfare; but the defensive who both collects his apparatus of war, and disposes of it with a view to fighting, is the first to exercise an act which really accords with the conception of war.

The second question is now: what is theoretically the nature of the motives which must arise in the mind of the defensive first, before the attack itself is thought of? Plainly the advance made with a view to taking possession, which we have imagined extraneous to the war, but which is the foundation of the opening chapter. The defence is to oppose this advance; therefore in idea we must connect this advance with the land (country); and thus arise the first most general measures of the defensive. When these are once established, then upon them the application of the offensive is founded, and from a consideration of the means which the offensive then applies, new principles again of defence are derived. Now here is the reciprocal effect which theory can follow in its inquiry, as long as it finds the fresh results which are produced are worth examination.

This little analysis was necessary in order to give more clearness and stability to what follows, such as it is; it is not made for the field of battle, neither is it for the generals of the future; it is only for the army of theorists, who have made a great deal too light of the subject hitherto.

CHAPTER EIGHT
Methods of Resistance

THE CONCEPTION of the defence is warding off; in this warding off lies the state of expectance, and this state of expectance we have taken as the chief characteristic of the defence, and at the same time as its principal advantage.

But as the defensive in war cannot be a state of endurance, therefore this state of expectation is only a relative, not an absolute state; the subjects with which this waiting for is connected are, as regards space, either the country, or the theatre of war, or the position, and, as regards time, the war, the campaign, or the battle. That these subjects are no immutable units, but only the centres of certain limited regions, which run into one another and are blended together, we know; but in practical life we must often be contented only to group things together, not rigidly to separate them; and these conceptions have, in the real world itself, sufficient distinctness to be made use of as centres round which we may group other ideas.

A defence of the country, therefore, only waits for attack on the country; a defence of a theatre of war an attack on the theatre of war; and the defence of a position the attack of that position. Every positive, and consequently more or less offensive, kind of action which the defensive uses after the above period of waiting for, does not negative the idea of the continuance of the defensive; for the state of expectation, which is the chief sign of the same, and its chief advantage, has been realised.

The conception of war, campaign, and battle, in relation to time, are coupled respectively with the ideas of country, theatre of war, and position, and on that account they have the same relations to the present subject.

The defensive consists, therefore, of two heterogeneous parts, the state of expectancy and that of action. By having referred the first to a definite subject, and therefore given it precedence of action, we have made it possible to connect the two into one whole. But an act of the defensive, especially a considerable one, such as a campaign or a whole war, does not, as regards time, consist of two great halves, the first the state of mere expectation, the second entirely of a state of action; it is a state of alternation between the two, in which the state of expectation can be traced through the whole act of the defensive like a continuous thread.

We give to this state of expectation so much importance simply because it is demanded by the nature of the thing. In preceding theories of war it has certainly never been brought forward as an independent conception, but in reality it has always served as a guide, although often unobserved. It is such a fundamental part of the whole act of war, that the one without the other appears almost impossible; and we shall therefore often have occasion to recur to it hereafter by calling attention to its effects in the dynamic action of the powers called into play.

For the present we shall employ ourselves in explaining how the principle of the state of expectation runs through the act of defence, and what are the successive stages in the defence itself which have their origin in this state.

In order to establish our ideas on subjects of a more simple kind, we shall defer the defence of a country, a subject on which a very great diversity of political influences exercises a powerful effect, until we come to the Book on the Plan of War; and as on the other hand, the defensive act in a position or in a battle is matter of tactics, which only forms a starting point for strategic action as a *whole*, we shall take the defence of a *theatre, of war* as being the subject, in which we can best show the relations of the defensive.

We have said, that the state of expectation and of action – which last is always a counterstroke, therefore a reaction – are both essential parts of the defensive; for without the first, there would be no defensive, without the second no war. This view led us before to the idea of the defensive being nothing but the *stronger form of war, in order the more certainly to conquer the enemy;* this idea we must adhere to throughout, partly because it alone saves us in the end from absurdity, partly, because the more vividly it is impressed on the mind, so much the greater is the energy it imparts to the whole act of the defensive.

If therefore we should make a distinction between the reaction, constituting the second element of the defensive, and the other element which consists in reality in the repulse only of the enemy; – if we should look at expulsion from the country, from the theatre of war, in such a light as to see in it alone the *necessary thing* by itself, the ultimate object beyond the attainment of which our efforts should not be carried, and on the other hand, regard the possibility of a reaction carried still further, and *passing into the real strategic attack*, as a subject foreign to and of no consequence to the defence, – such a view would be *in opposition to* the nature of the idea above represented, and therefore we cannot look upon this distinction as really existing, and we must adhere to our assertion, that the idea of *revenge* must always be at the bottom of every defensive; for otherwise, however much damage might be occasioned to the enemy, by a successful issue of the first reaction, there would always be a deficiency in the necessary balance of the dynamic relations of the attack and defence.

We say, then, the defensive is the more powerful form of making war, in order to overcome the enemy more easily, and we leave to circumstances to determine whether this victory over the object against which the defence was commenced is sufficient or not.

But as the defensive is inseparable from the idea of the state of expectation, that object, *the defeat of the enemy*, only exists conditionally, that is, only if the offensive takes place; and otherwise (that is, if the offensive stroke does not follow) of course the defensive is contented with the maintenance of its possessions; this maintenance is therefore its object in the state of expectation, that is, its immediate object; and it is only as long as it contents itself with this more modest end, that it preserves the advantages of the stronger form of war.

If we suppose an army with its theatre of war intended for defence, the defence may be made as follows:

1. By attacking the enemy the moment he enters the theatre of war. (Mollwitz, Hohenfriedberg).

2. By taking up a position close on the frontier, and waiting till the enemy appears with the intention of attacking it, in order then to attack him (Czaslau, Soor, Rosbach). Plainly this second mode of proceeding, partakes more of endurance, we "wait for" longer; and although the *time* gained by it as compared with that gained in the first, may be very little, or none at all if the enemy's attack actually takes place, still, the battle which in the first case was certain, is in the second much less certain, perhaps the enemy may not be able to make up his mind to attack; the advantage of the "waiting for," is then at once greater.

3. By the army in such position not only awaiting the decision of the enemy to fight a battle, that is his appearance in front of the position, but also waiting to be actually assaulted (in order to keep to the same

general, Bunzelwitz). In such case, we fight a regular defensive battle, which however, as we have before said, may include offensive movements with one or more parts of the army. Here also, as before, the gain of time does not come into consideration, but the determination of the enemy is put to a new proof; many a one has advanced to the attack, and at the last moment, or after one attempt given it up, finding the position of the enemy too strong.

4. By the army transferring its defence to the heart of the country. The object of retreating into the interior is to cause a diminution in the enemy's strength, and to wait until its effects are such that his forward march is of itself discontinued, or at least until the resistance which we can offer him at the end of his career is such as he can no longer overcome.

This case is exhibited in the simplest and plainest manner, when the defensive can leave one or more of his fortresses behind him, which the offensive is obliged to besiege or blockade. It is clear in itself, how much his forces must be weakened in this way, and what a chance there is of an opportunity for the defensive to attack at some point with superior forces.

But even when there are no fortresses, a retreat into the interior of the country may procure by degrees for the defender that necessary equilibrium or that superiority which was wanting to him on the frontier; for every forward movement in the strategic attack lessens its force, partly absolutely, partly through the separation of forces which becomes necessary, of which we shall say more under the head of the "Attack." We anticipate this truth here as we consider it as a fact sufficiently exemplified in all wars.

Now in this fourth case the gain of time is to be looked upon as the principal point of all. If the assailant lays siege to our fortresses, we have time till their probable fall, (which may be some weeks or in some cases months); but if the weakening, that is the expenditure, of the force of the attack is caused by the advance, and the garrisoning or occupation of certain points, therefore merely through the length of the assailant's march, then the time gained in most cases becomes greater, and our action is not so much restricted in point of time.

Besides the altered relations between offensive and defensive in regard to power which is brought about at the end of this march, we must bring into account in favour of the defensive an *increased* amount of the *advantage* of the state of "waiting for." Although the assailant by this advance may not in reality be weakened to such a degree that he is unfit to attack our main body where he halts, still he will probably want resolution to do so, for that is an act requiring more resolution in the position in which he is now placed, than would have sufficed when operations had not extended beyond the frontier: partly, because the powers are weakened, and no longer in fresh vigour, while the danger is increased; partly, because with an irresolute commander the possession of that portion of the country which has been obtained is often sufficient to do away with all idea of a battle, because he either really believes or assumes as a pretext, that it is no longer necessary. By the offensive thus declining to attack, the defensive certainly does not acquire, as he would on the frontier, a sufficient result of a negative kind, but still there is a great gain of time.

It is plain that, in all the four methods indicated, the defensive has the benefit of the ground or country, and likewise that he can by that means bring into cooperation his fortresses and the people; moreover these efficient principles increase at each fresh stage of the defence, for they are a chief means of bringing about the weakening of the enemy's force in the fourth stage. Now as the advantages of the "state of expectation" increase in the same direction, therefore it follows of itself that these stages are to be regarded as a real intensifying of the defence, and that this form of war always gains in strength the more it differs from the offensive. We are not afraid on this account of any one accusing us of holding the opinion that the most passive defence would therefore be the best. The action of resistance is not weakened at each new stage, it is only *delayed, postponed.* But the assertion that a stouter resistance can be offered in a strong judiciously entrenched position, and also that when the enemy has exhausted his strength in fruitless efforts against such a position a more effective counterstroke may be levelled at him, is surely not unreasonable. Without the advantage of position Daun would not have gained the victory at Kollin, and as Frederick the Great only brought off 18,000 men from the field of battle, if Daun had pursued him with more energy the victory might have been one of the most brilliant in military history.

We therefore maintain, that at each new stage of the defensive the preponderance, or more correctly speaking, the counterpoise increases in favour of the defensive, and consequently there is also a gain in power for the counterstroke.

Now are these advantages of the increasing force of the defensive to be had for nothing? By no means, for the sacrifice with which they are purchased increases in the same proportion.

If we wait for the enemy within our own theatre of war, however near the border of our territory the decision takes place, still this theatre of war is entered by the enemy, which must entail a sacrifice on our part; whereas, had we made the attack, this disadvantage would have fallen on the enemy. If we do not proceed at once to meet the enemy and attack him, our loss will be the greater, and the extent of the country which the enemy will overrun, as well as the time which he requires to reach our position, will continually increase. If we wish to give battle on the defensive, and we therefore leave its determination and the choice of time for it to the enemy, then perhaps he may remain for some time in occupation of the territory which he has taken, and the time which through his deferred decision we are allowed to gain will in that manner be paid for by us. The sacrifices which must be made become still more burdensome if a retreat into the heart of the country takes place.

But all these sacrifices on the part of the defensive, at most only occasion him in general a loss of power which merely diminishes his military force *indirectly*, therefore, at a later period, and not directly, and often so indirectly that its effect is hardly felt at all. The defensive, therefore, strengthens himself for the present moment at the expense of the future, that is to say, he borrows, as every one must who is too poor for the circumstances in which he is placed.

Now, if we would examine the result of these different forms of resistance, we must look to the *object of the aggression*. This is, to obtain possession of our theatre of war, or, at least, of an important part of it, for under the conception of the whole, at least the greater part must be understood, as the possession of a strip of territory few miles in extent is, as a rule, of no real consequence in strategy. As long, therefore, as the aggressor is not in possession of this, that is, as long as from fear of our force he has either not yet advanced to the attack of the theatre of war, or has not sought to find us in our position, or has declined the combat we offer, the object of the defence is fulfilled, and the effects of the measures taken for the defensive have therefore been successful. At the same time this result is only a *negative one*, which certainly cannot directly give the force for a real counterstroke. But it may give it *indirectly*, that is to say, it is on the way to do so; for the time which elapses *the aggression loses*, and every loss of time is a disadvantage, and must weaken in some way the party who suffers the loss.

Therefore in the first three stages of the defensive, that is, if it takes place on the frontier, *the non-decision is already a result in favour of the defensive.*

But it is not so with the fourth.

If the enemy lays siege to our fortresses we must relieve them in time, to do this we must therefore bring about the decision by positive action.

This is likewise the case if the enemy follows us into the interior of the country without besieging any of our places. Certainly in this case we have more time; we can wait until the enemy's weakness is extreme, but still it is always an indispensable condition that we are at last to act. The enemy is now, perhaps, in possession of the whole territory which was the object of his aggression, but it is only lent to him; the tension continues, and the decision is yet pending. As long as the defensive is gaining strength and the aggressor daily becoming weaker, the postponement of the decision is in the interest of the former: but as soon as the culminating point of this progressive advantage has arrived, as it must do, were it only by the ultimate influence of the general loss to which the offensive has exposed himself, it is time for the defender to proceed to action, and bring on a solution, and the advantage of the "waiting for" may be considered as completely exhausted.

There can naturally be no point of time fixed generally at which this happens, for it is determined by a multitude of circumstances and relations; but it may be observed that the winter is usually a natural turning point. If we cannot prevent the enemy from wintering in the territory which he has seized, then, as a rule, it must be looked upon as given up. We have only, however, to call to mind Torres Vedras, to see that this is no general rule.

What is now the solution generally?

We have always supposed it in our observations in the form of a battle; but in reality, this is not necessary, for a number of combinations of battles with separate corps may be imagined, which may bring about a change of affairs, either because they have really ended with bloodshed, or because their probable result makes the retreat of the enemy necessary.

Upon the theatre of war itself there can be no other solution; that is a necessary consequence of our view of war; for, in fact, even if an enemy's army, merely from want of provisions, commences his retreat, still it takes place from the state of restraint in which our sword holds him; if our army was not in the way he would soon be able to provision his forces.

Therefore, even at the end of his aggressive course, when the enemy is suffering the heavy penalty of his attack, when detachments, hunger, and sickness have weakened and worn him out, it is still always the dread of our sword which causes him to turn about, and allow everything to go on again as usual. But nevertheless, there is a great difference between such a solution and one which takes place on the frontier.

In the latter case our arms only were opposed to his to keep him in check, or carry destruction into his ranks; but at the end of the aggressive career the enemy's forces, by their own exertions, are half destroyed, by which our arms acquire a totally different value, and therefore, although they are the final they are not the only means which have produced the solution. This destruction of the enemy's forces in the advance prepares the solution, and may do so to this extent, that the mere possibility of a reaction on our part may cause the retreat, consequently a reversal of the situation of affairs. In this case, therefore, we can practically ascribe the solution to nothing else than the efforts made in the advance. Now, in point of fact we shall find no case in which the sword of the defensive has not co-operated; but, for the practical view, it is important to distinguish which of the two principles is the predominating one.

In this sense we think we may say that there is a double solution in the defensive, consequently a double kind of reaction, according as the aggressor is ruined by the *sword of the defensive,* or *by his own efforts.*

That the first kind of solution predominates in the first three steps of the defence, the second in the fourth, is evident in itself; and the latter will, in most cases, only come to pass by the retreat being carried deep into the heart of the country, and nothing but the prospect of that result can be a sufficient motive for such a retreat, considering the great sacrifices which it must cost.

We have, therefore, ascertained that there are two different principles of defence; there are cases in military history where they each appear as separate and distinct as it is possible for an elementary conception to appear in practical life. When Frederick the Great attacked the Austrians at Hohenfriedberg, just as they were descending from the Silesian mountains, their force could not have been weakened in any sensible manner by detachments or fatigue; when, on the other hand, Wellington, in his entrenched camp at Torres Vedras, waited till hunger, and the severity of the weather, had reduced Massena's army to such extremities that they commenced to retreat of themselves, the sword of the defensive party had no share in the weakening of the enemy's army. In other cases, in which they are combined with each other in a variety of ways, still, one of them distinctly predominates. This was the case in the year 1812. In that celebrated campaign such a number of bloody encounters took place as might, under other circumstances, have sufficed for a most complete decision by the sword; nevertheless, there is hardly any campaign in which we can so plainly see how the aggressor may be ruined by his own efforts. Of the 300,000 men composing the French centre only about 90,000 reached Moscow; not more than 13,000 were detached; consequently there had been a loss of 197,000 men, and certainly not a third of that loss can be put to account of battles.

All campaigns which are remarkable for temporising, as it is called, like those of the famous Fabius Cunctator, have been calculated chiefly on the destruction of the enemy by his own efforts. This principle has been the leading one in many campaigns without that point being almost ever mentioned; and it is only when we disregard the specious reasoning of historians, and look at things clearly with our own eyes, that we are led to this real cause of many a solution.

By this we believe we have unravelled sufficiently those ideas which lie at the root of the defensive, and that in the two great kinds of defence we have shown plainly and made intelligible how the principle of the waiting for runs through the whole system and connects itself with positive action in such a manner that, sooner or later, action does take place, and that then the advantage of the attitude of waiting for appears to be exhausted.

We think, now, that in this way we have gone over and brought into view everything comprised in the province of the defensive. At the same time, there are subjects of sufficient importance in themselves to form separate chapters, that is, points for consideration in themselves, and these we must also study; for example, the nature and influence of fortified places, entrenched camps, defence of mountains and rivers, operations against the flank, etc., etc. We shall treat of them in subsequent chapters, but none of these things lie outside of the preceding sequence of ideas; they are only to be regarded as a closer application of it to locality and circumstances. That order of ideas has been deduced from the conception of the defensive, and from its relation to the offensive; we have connected these simple ideas with reality, and therefore shown the way by which we may return again from the reality to those simple ideas, and obtain firm ground, and not be forced in reasoning to take refuge on points of support which themselves vanish in the air.

But resistance by the sword may wear such an altered appearance, assume such a different character, through the multiplicity of ways of combining battles, especially in cases where these are not actually realised, but become effectual merely through their possibility, that we might incline to the opinion that there must be some other efficient active principle still to be discovered; between the sanguinary defeat in a simple battle, and the effects of strategic combinations which do not bring the thing nearly so far as actual combat, there seems such a difference, that it is necessary to suppose some fresh force, something in the same way as astronomers have decided on the existence of other planets from the great space between Mars and Jupiter.

If the assailant finds the defender in a strong position which he thinks he cannot take, or behind a large river which he thinks he cannot cross, or even if he fears that by advancing further he will not be able to subsist his army, in all these cases it is nothing but the sword of the defensive which produces the effect; for it is the fear of being conquered by this sword, either in a great battle or at some specially important points, which compels the aggressor to stop, only he will either not admit that at all, or does not admit it in a straightforward way.

Now even if it is granted that, where there has been a decision without bloodshed, the combat merely *offered*, but not accepted, has been the ultimate cause of the decision, it will still be thought that in such cases the really effectual principle is the *strategic combination of* these combats and not their tactical decision, and that this superiority of the strategic combination could only have been thought of because there are other defensive means which may be considered besides an actual appeal to the sword. We admit this, and it brings us just to the point we wished to arrive at, which is as follows: if the tactical result of a battle must be the *foundation* of all strategic combinations, then it is always possible and to be feared that the assailant may lay hold of this principle, and above all things direct his efforts to be superior in the hour of decision, in order to baffle the strategic combination; and that therefore this strategic combination can *never be regarded as something all-sufficient in itself;* that it only has a value when either on one ground or another we can look forward to the tactical solution without any misgivings. In order to make ourselves intelligible in a few words, we shall merely call to our readers' recollection how such a general as Buonaparte marched without hesitation through the whole web of his opponents' strategic plans, to seek for the battle itself, because he had no doubts as to its issue. Where, therefore, strategy had not directed its whole effort to ensure a preponderance over him in this battle, where it engaged in finer (feebler) plans, there it was rent asunder like a cobweb. But a general like Daun might be checked by such measures; it would therefore be folly to offer Buonaparte and his army what the Prussian army of the Seven Years' War dared to offer Daun and his contemporaries. Why? – Because Buonaparte knew right well that all depended on the tactical issue, and made certain of gaining it; whereas with Daun it was very different in both respects.

On this account we hold it therefore to be serviceable to show that every strategic combination rests only upon the tactical results, and that these are everywhere, in the bloody as well as in the bloodless solution, the real fundamental grounds of the ultimate decision. It is only if we

have no reason to fear that decision, whether on account of the character or the situation of the enemy, or on account of the moral and physical equality of the two armies, or on account of our own superiority – it
is only then that we can expect something from strategic combinations
in themselves without battles.

Now if a great many campaigns are to be found within the compass of military history in which the assailant gives up the offensive
without any blood being spilt in fight, in which, therefore, strategic
combinations show themselves effectual to that degree, this may lead
to the idea that these combinations have at least great inherent force
in themselves, and might in general decide the affair alone, where too
great a preponderance in the tactical results is not supposed on the
side of the aggressor. To this we answer that, if the question is about
things which have their origin in the theatre of war, and consequently
belong to the war itself, this idea is also equally false; and we add that
the cause of the failure of most attacks is to be found in the higher, the
political relations of war.

The general relations out of which a war springs, and which naturally
constitute its foundation, determine also its character; on this subject
we shall have more to say hereafter, in treating of the plan of a war.
But these general relations have converted most wars into half-and-
half things, into which real hostility has to force its way through such a
conflict of interests, that it is only a very weak element at the last. This
effect must naturally show itself chiefly and with most force on the side
of the offensive, *the side of positive action.* One cannot therefore wonder
if such a short-winded, consumptive attack is brought to a standstill by
the touch of a finger. Against a weak resolution so fettered by a thousand considerations, that it has hardly any existence, a mere show of
resistance is often enough.

It is not the number of unassailable positions in all directions, not
the formidable look of the dark mountain masses encamped round the
theatre of war, or the broad river which passes through it, not the ease
with which certain combinations of battles can effectually paralyse the
muscle which should strike the blow against us – none of these things
are the true causes of the numerous successes which the defensive gains
on bloodless fields; the cause lies in the weakness of the will with which
the assailant puts forward his hesitating feet.

These counteracting influences may and ought to be taken into consideration, but they should only be looked upon in their true light, and
their effects should not be ascribed to other things, namely the things
of which alone we are now treating. We must not omit to point out in

an emphatic manner how easily military history in this respect may become a perpetual liar and deceiver if criticism is not careful about taking a correct point of view.

Let us now consider, in what we may call their ordinary form, the many offensive campaigns which have miscarried without a bloody solution.

The assailant advances into the enemy's country, drives back his opponent a little way, but finds it too serious a matter to bring on a decisive battle. He therefore remains standing opposite to him; acts as if he had made a conquest, and had nothing else to do but to protect it; as if it was the enemy's business to seek the battle, as if he offered it to him daily, etc., etc. These are the *representations* with which the commander deludes his army, his government, the world, even himself. But the truth is, that he finds the enemy in a position too strong for him. We do not now speak of a case where an aggressor does not proceed with his attack because he can make no use of a victory, because at the end of his first bound he has not enough impulsive force left to begin another. Such a case supposes an attack which has been successful, a real conquest; but we have here in view the case where an assailant sticks fast half way to his intended conquest.

He is now waiting to take advantage of favourable circumstances, of which favourable circumstances there is in general no prospect, for the aggression now intended shows at once that there is no better prospect from the future than from the present; it is, therefore, a further illusion. If now, as is commonly the case, the undertaking is in connection with other simultaneous operations, then what they do not want to do themselves is transferred to other shoulders, and their own inactivity is ascribed to want of support and proper co-operation. Insurmountable obstacles are talked of, and motives in justification are discovered in the most confused and subtil considerations. Thus the forces of the assailant are wasted away in inactivity, or rather in a partial activity, destitute of any utility. The defensive gains time, the greatest gain to him; bad weather arrives, and the aggression ends by the return of the aggressor to winter quarters in his own theatre of war.

A tissue of false representations thus passes into history in place of the simple real ground of absence of any result, namely *fear of the enemy's sword*. When criticism takes up such a campaign, it wearies itself in the discussion of a number of motives and counter-motives, which give no satisfactory result, because they all dwindle into vapour, and we have not descended to the real foundation of the truth. The opposition through which the elementary energy of war, and therefore of the offensive in particular, becomes weakened, lies for the most part in the relations and views of states, and these are always concealed from the world, from the mass of the people belonging to the state, as well as from the army, and very often from the general-in-chief. No one will account for his faint-heartedness by the admission that he feared he could not attain the desired object with the force at his disposal, or that new enemies would be roused, or that he did not wish to make his allies too powerful, etc. Such things are hushed up; but as occurrences have to be placed before the world in a presentable form, therefore the commander is obliged, either on his own account or on that of his government to pass off a tissue of fictitious motives. This ever-recurring deception in military dialectics has ossified into systems in theory, which, of course, are equally devoid of truth. Theory can never be deduced from the essence of things except by following the simple thread of cause and effect, as we have tried to do.

If we look at military history with this feeling of suspicion, then a great parade of mere words about offensive and defensive collapses, and the simple idea of it, which we have given, comes forward of itself. We believe it therefore to be applicable to the whole domain of the defensive, and that we must adhere closely to it in order to obtain that clear view of the mass of events by which alone we can form correct judgments.

We have still to inquire into the question of the employment of these different forms of defence.

As they are merely gradations of the same which must be purchased by a higher sacrifice, corresponding to the increased intensity of the form, there would seem to be sufficient in that view to indicate always to the general which he should choose, provided there are no other circumstances which interfere. He would, in fact, choose that form which appeared sufficient to give his force the requisite degree of defensive power and no more, that there might be no unnecessary waste of his force. But we must not overlook the circumstance that the room given for choice amongst these different forms is generally very circumscribed, because other circumstances which must be attended to necessarily urge a preference for one or other of them. For a retreat into the interior of the country a considerable superficial space is required, or such a condition of things as existed in Portugal (1810), where one ally (England) gave support in rear, and another (Spain) with its wide territory, considerably diminished the impulsive force of the enemy. The position of the fortresses more on the frontier or more in the interior may likewise decide for or against such a plan; but still more the nature of the country and ground, the character, habits, and feelings of the inhabitants. The choice between an offensive or defensive battle may be decided by the plans of the enemy, by the peculiar qualities of both armies and their generals; lastly, the possession of an excellent position or line of defence, or the want of them may determine for one or the other; – in short, at the bare mention of these things, we can perceive that the choice of the form of defensive must in many cases be determined more by them than by the mere relative strength of the armies. As we shall hereafter enter more into detail on the more important subjects which have just been touched upon, the influence which they must have upon the choice will then develop itself more distinctly, and in the end the whole will be methodised in the Book on Plans of Wars and Campaigns.

But this influence will not, in general, be decisive unless the inequality in the strength of the opposing armies is trifling; in the opposite case (as in the generality of cases), the relation of the numerical strength will be decisive. There is ample proof, in military history, that it has done so heretofore, and that without the chain of reasoning by which it has been brought out here; therefore in a manner intuitively by *mere tact of judgment*, like most things that happen in war. It was the same general who at the head of the same army, and on the same theatre of war, fought the battle of Hohenfriedberg, and at another time took up the camp of Bunzelwitz. Therefore even Frederick the Great, a general above all inclined to the offensive as regards the battle, saw himself compelled at last, by a great disproportion of force, to resort to a real defensive position; and Buonaparte, who was once in the habit of falling on his enemy like a wild boar, have we not seen him, when the proportion of force turned against him, in August and September, 1813, turn himself hither and thither as if he had been pent up in a cage, instead of rushing forward recklessly upon some one of his adversaries? And in October of the same year, when the disproportion reached its climax, have we not seen him at Leipsic, seeking shelter in the angle formed by the Parth, the Elster, and Pleiss, as it were waiting for his enemy in the corner of a room, with his back against the wall?

We cannot omit to observe, that from this chapter, more than from any other in our book, it is plainly shown that our object is not to lay down new principles and methods of conducting war, but merely to investigate what has long existed in its innermost relations, and to reduce it to its simplest elements.

CHAPTER NINE
Defensive Battle

WE HAVE SAID, in the preceding chapter, that the defender, in his defensive, would make use of a battle, technically speaking, of a purely offensive character, if, at the moment the enemy invades his theatre of war, he marches against him and attacks him; but that he might also wait for the appearance of the enemy in his front, and then pass over to the attack; in which case also the battle tactically would be again an offensive battle, although in a modified form; and lastly, that he might wait till the enemy attacked his position, and then oppose him both by holding a particular spot, and by offensive action with portions of his force. In all this we may imagine several different gradations and shades, deviating always more from the principle of a positive counterstroke, and passing into that of the defence of a spot of ground. We cannot here enter on the subject of how far this should be carried, and which is the most advantageous proportion of the two elements of offensive and defensive, as regards the winning a decisive victory. But we maintain that when such a result is desired, the offensive part of the battle should never be completely omitted, and we are convinced that all the effects of a decisive victory may and must be produced by this offensive part, just as well as in a purely tactical offensive battle.

In the same manner as the field of battle is only a point in strategy, the duration of a battle is only, strategically, an instant of time, and the end and result, not the course of a battle, constitutes a strategic quantity.

Now, if it is true that a complete victory may result from the offensive elements which lie in every defensive battle, then there would be no fundamental difference between an offensive and a defensive battle, as far as regards strategic combinations; we are indeed convinced that this is so, but the thing wears a different appearance. In order to fix the subject more distinctly in the eye, to make our view clear and thereby remove the appearance now referred to, we shall sketch, hastily, the picture of a defensive battle, such as we imagine it.

The defensive waits the attack in a position; for this he has selected proper ground, and turned it to the best account, that is, he has made himself well acquainted with the locality, thrown up strong entrenchments at some of the most important points, opened and levelled communications, constructed batteries, fortified villages, and looked out places where he can draw up his masses under cover, etc., etc., etc. Whilst the forces on both sides are consuming each other at the different points where they come into contact, the advantage of a front more or less strong, the approach to which is made difficult by one or more parallel trenches or other obstacles, or also by the influence of some strong commanding points, enables him with a *small part of his force* to destroy *great numbers of the enemy* at every stage of the defence up to the heart of the position. The points of support which he has given his wings secure him from any sudden attack from several quarters; the covered ground which he has chosen for his masses makes the enemy cautious, indeed timid, and affords the defensive the means of diminishing by partial and successful attacks the general backward movement which goes on as the combat becomes gradually concentrated within narrower limits. The defender therefore casts a contented look at the battle as it burns in a moderate blaze before him; – but he does not reckon that his resistance in front can last for ever; – he does not think his flanks impregnable; – he does not expect that the whole course of the battle will be changed by the successful charge of a few battalions or squadrons. His position is *deep*, for each part in the scale of gradation of the order of battle, from the division down to the battalion, has its reserve for unforeseen events, and for a renewal of the fight; and at the same time an important mass, one fifth to a quarter of the whole, is kept quite in the rear out of the battle, so far back as to be quite out of fire, and if possible so far as to be beyond the circuitous line by which the enemy might attempt to turn either flank. With this corps he intends to cover his flanks from wider and greater turning movements, secure himself against unforeseen events, and in the latter stage of the battle, when the assailant's plan is fully developed, when the most of his troops have been brought into action, he will throw this mass on a part of the enemy's army, and open at that part of the field a smaller offensive battle on his own part, using all the elements of attack, such as charges, surprise, turning movements, and by means of this pressure against the centre of gravity of the battle, now only resting on a point, make the whole recoil.

This is the normal idea which we have formed of a defensive battle, based on the tactics of the present day. In this battle the general turning movement made by the assailant in order to assist his attack, and at the same time with a view to make the results of victory more complete, is replied to by a partial turning movement on the part of the defensive, that is, by the turning of that part of the assailant's force used by him in the attempt to turn. This partial movement may be supposed sufficient to destroy the effect of the enemy's attempt, but it cannot lead to a like general enveloping of the assailant's army; and there will always be a distinction in the features of a victory on this account, that the side fighting an offensive battle encircles the enemy's army, and acts towards the centre of the same, while the side fighting on the defensive acts more or less from the centre to the circumference, in the direction of the radii.

On the field of battle itself, and in the first stages of the pursuit, the enveloping form must always be considered the most effectual; we do not mean on account of its form generally, we only mean in the event of its being carried out to such an extreme as to limit very much the enemy's means of retreat during the battle. But it is just against this extreme point that the enemy's positive counter-effort is directed, and in many cases where this effort is not sufficient to obtain a victory, it will at least suffice to protect him from such an extreme as we allude to. But we must always admit that this danger, namely, of having the line of retreat seriously contracted, is particularly great in defensive battles, and if it cannot be guarded against, the results in the battle itself, and in the first stage of the retreat are thereby very much enhanced in favour of the enemy.

But as a rule this danger does not extend beyond the first stage of the retreat, that is, until night-fall; on the following day enveloping is at an end, and both parties are again on an equality in this respect.

Certainly the defender may have lost his principal line of retreat, and therefore be placed in a disadvantageous strategic situation for the future; but in most cases the turning movement itself will be at an end, because it was only planned to suit the field of battle, and therefore cannot apply much further. But what will take place, on the other hand, if the *defender* is victorious? A division of the defeated force. This may facilitate the retreat at the first moment, but *next day a concentration of all parts* is the one thing most needful. Now if the victory is a most decisive one, if the defender pursues with great energy, this concentration will often become impossible, and from this separation of the beaten force the worst consequences may follow, which may go on step by step to a complete rout. If Buonaparte had conquered at Leipsic, the allied army would have been completely cut in two, which would have considerably lowered their relative strategic position. At Dresden, although Buonaparte certainly did not fight a regular defensive battle, the attack had the geometrical form of which we have been speaking, that is, from the centre to the circumference; the embarrassment of the Allies in consequence of their separation, is well known, an embarrassment from which they were only relieved by the victory on the Katzbach, the tidings of which caused Buonaparte to return to Dresden with the Guard.

This battle on the Katzbach itself is a similar example. In it the defender, at the last moment passes over to the offensive, and consequently operates on diverging lines; the French corps were thus wedged asunder, and several days after, as the fruits of the victory, Puthod's division fell into the hands of the Allies.

The conclusion we draw from this is, that if the assailant, by the concentric form which is homogeneous to him, has the means of giving expansion to his victory, on the other hand the defender also, by the divergent form which is homogeneous to the defence, acquires a a means of giving greater results to his victory than would be the case by a merely parallel position and perpendicular attack, and we think that one means is at least as good as the other.

If in military history we rarely find such great victories resulting from the defensive battle as from the offensive, that proves nothing against our assertion that the one is as well suited to produce victory as the other; the real cause is in the very different relations of the defender. The army acting on the defensive is generally the weaker of the two, not only in the amount of his forces, but also in every other respect; he either is, or thinks he is, not in a condition to follow up his victory with great results, and contents himself with merely fending off the danger and saving the honour of his arms. That the defender by inferiority of force and other circumstances may be tied down to that degree we do not dispute, but there is no doubt that this, which is only the consequence of a contingent necessity, has often been assumed to be the consequence of that part which every defender has to play: and thus in an absurd manner it has become a prevalent view of the defensive that its battles should really be confined to warding off the attacks of the enemy, and not directed to the destruction of the enemy. We hold this to be a prejudicial error, a regular substitution of the form for the thing itself; and we maintain unreservedly that in the form of war which we call *defence*, the victory may not only be more probable, but may also attain the same magnitude and efficacy as in the attack, and that this may be the case not only in the *total result* of all the combats which constitute campaign, but also in any *particular* battle, if the necessary degree of force and energy is not wanting.

CHAPTER TEN

Fortresses

FORMERLY, and up to the time of great standing armies, fortresses, that is castles and fortified towns, were only built for the defence and protection of the inhabitants. The baron, if he saw himself pressed on all sides, took refuge in his castle to gain time and wait a more favourable moment; and towns sought by their walls to keep off the passing hurricane of war. This simplest and most natural object of fortresses did not continue to be the only one; the relation which such a place acquired with regard to the whole country and to troops acting here and there in the country soon gave these fortified points a wider importance, a signification which made itself felt beyond their walls, and contributed essentially to the conquest or occupation of the country, to the successful or unsuccessful issue of the whole contest, and in this manner they even became a means of making war more of a connected whole. Thus fortresses acquired that strategic significance which for a time was regarded as so important that it dictated the leading features of the plans of campaigns, which were more directed to the taking of one or more fortresses than the destruction of the enemy's army in the field. Men reverted to the cause of the importance of these places, that is to the connection between a fortified point, and the country, and the armies; and then thought that they could not be sufficiently particular or too philosophical in choosing the points to be fortified. In these abstract objects the original one was almost lost sight of, and at length they came to the idea of fortresses without either towns or inhabitants.

On the other hand, the times are past in which the mere enclosure of a place with walls, without any military preparations, could keep a place dry during an inundation of war sweeping over the whole country. Such a possibility rested partly on the division of nations formerly into small states, partly on the periodical character of the incursions then in vogue, which had fixed and very limited duration, almost in accordance with the seasons, as either the feudal forces hastened home, or the pay for the condottieri used regularly to run short. Since large standing armies, with powerful trains of artillery mow down the opposition of walls or ramparts as it were with a machine, neither town nor other small corporation has any longer an inclination to hazard all their means only to be taken a few weeks or months later, and then to be treated so much the worse. Still less can it be the interest of an army to break itself up into garrisons for a number of strong places, which may for a time retard the progress of the enemy, but must in the end submit. We must always keep enough forces, over and above those in garrison, to make us equal to the enemy in the open field, unless we can depend on the arrival of an ally, who will relieve our strong places and set our army free. Consequently the number of fortresses has necessarily much diminished, and this has again led to the abandonment of the idea of directly protecting the population and property in towns by fortifications, and promoted the other idea of regarding the fortresses as an *indirect* protection to the country, which they secure by their strategic importance as knots which hold together the strategic web.

Such has been the course of ideas, not only in books but also in actual experience, at the same time, as usually happens, it has been much more spun out in books.

Natural as was this tendency of things, still these ideas were carried out to an extreme, and mere crotchets and fancies displaced the sound core of a natural and urgent want. We shall look into these simple and important wants when we enumerate the objects and conditions of fortresses all together; we shall thereby advance from the simple to the more complicated, and in the succeeding chapter we shall see what is to be deduced therefrom as to the determination of the position and number of fortresses.

The efficacy of a fortress is plainly composed of two different elements, the passive and the active. By the first it shelters the place, and all that it contains; by the other it possesses a certain influence over the adjacent country, even beyond the range of its guns.

This active element consists in the attacks which the garrison may undertake upon every enemy who approaches within a certain distance. The larger the garrison, so much the stronger numerically will be the detachments that may be employed on such expeditions, and the stronger such detachments the wider as a rule will be the range of their operations; from which it follows that the sphere of the active influence of a great fortress is not only greater in intensity but also more extensive than that of a small one. But the active element itself is again, to a certain extent, of two kinds, consisting namely of enterprises of the garrison proper, and of enterprises which other bodies of troops, great and small, not belonging to the garrison but in co-operation with it, may be able to carry out. For instance, corps which independently would be too weak to face the enemy, may, through the shelter which, in case of necessity, the walls of a fortress afford them, be able to maintain themselves in the country, and to a certain extent to command it.

The enterprises which the garrison of a fortress can venture to undertake are always somewhat restricted. Even in the case of large places and strong garrisons, the bodies of troops which can be employed on such operations are mostly inconsiderable as compared with the forces in the field, and their average sphere of action seldom exceeds a couple of days' marches. If the fortress is small, the detachments it can send out are quite insignificant and the range of their activity will generally be confined to the nearest villages. But corps which do not belong to the garrison, and therefore are not under the necessity of returning to the place, are thereby much more at liberty in their movements, and by their means, if other circumstances are favourable, the external zone of action of a fortress may be immensely extended. Therefore if we speak of the active influence of fortresses in general terms, we must always keep this feature of the same principally in view.

But even the smallest active element of the weakest garrison, is still essential for the different objects which fortresses are destined to fulfil, for strictly speaking even the most passive of all the functions of a fortress (defence against attack) cannot be imagined exclusive of that active agency. At the same time it is evident that amongst the different purposes which a fortress may have to answer generally, or in this or that moment, the passive element will be most required at one time, the active at another. The role which a fortress is to fulfil may be perfectly simple, and the action of the place will in such case be to a certain extent direct; it may be partly complicated, and the action then becomes more or less indirect. We shall examine these subjects separately, commencing with the first; but at the outset we must state that a fortress may be intended to answer several of these purposes, perhaps all of them, either at once, or at least at different stages of the war.

We say, therefore, that fortresses are great and most important supports of the defensive.

1. *As secure depots of stores of all kinds.* The assailant during his aggression subsists his army from day to day; the defensive usually must have made preparations long beforehand, he need not therefore draw provisions exclusively from the district he occupies, and which he no

doubt desires to spare. Storehouses are therefore for him a great necessity. The provisions of all kinds which the aggressor possesses are in his rear as he advances, and are therefore exempt from the dangers of the theatre of war, while those of the defensive are exposed to them. If these provisions of all kinds are not in *fortified places*, then a most injurious effect on the operations in the field is the consequence, and the most extended and compulsory positions often become necessary in order to cover depots or sources of supply.

An army on the defensive without fortresses has a hundred vulnerable spots; it is a body without armour.

2. *As a protection to great and wealthy towns.* This purpose is closely allied to the first, for great and wealthy towns, especially commercial ones, are the natural storehouses of an army; as such their possession and loss affects the army directly. Besides this, it is also always worth while to preserve this portion of the national wealth, partly on account of the resources which they furnish directly, partly because, in negotiations for peace, an important place is in itself a valuable weight thrown into the scale.

This use of fortresses has been too little regarded in modern times, and yet it is one of the most natural, and one which has a most powerful effect, and is the least liable to mistakes. If there was a country in which not only all great and rich cities, but all populous places as well were fortified, and defended by the inhabitants and the people belonging to the adjacent districts, then by that means the expedition of military operation would be so much reduced, and the people attacked would press with so great a part of their whole weight in the scales, that the talent as well as the force of will of the enemy's general would sink to nothing.

We just mention this ideal application of fortification to a country to do justice to what we have just supposed to be the proper use of fortresses, and that the importance of the *direct* protection which they afford may not be overlooked for a moment; but in any other respect this idea will not again interrupt our considerations, for amongst the whole number of fortresses there must always be some which must be more strongly fortified than others, to serve as the real supports of the active army.

The purposes specified under 1 and 2 hardly call forth any other but the passive action of fortresses.

3. *As real barriers*, they close the roads, and in most cases the rivers, on which they are situated.

It is not as easy as is generally supposed to find a practicable lateral road which passes round a fortress, for this turning must be made, not only out of reach of the guns of this place, but also by a detour greater or less, to avoid sorties of the garrison.

If the country is in the least degree difficult, there are often delays connected with the slightest deviation of the road which may cause the loss of a whole day's march, and, if the road is much used, may become of great importance.

How they may have an influence on enterprises by closing the navigation of a river is clear in itself.

4. *As tactical points d'appui.* As the diameter of the zone covered by the fire of even a very inferior class of fortifications is usually some leagues, fortresses may be considered always as the best points d'appui for the flanks of a position. A lake of several miles long is certainly an excellent support for the wing of an army, and yet a fortress of moderate size is better. The flank does not require to rest close upon it, as the assailant, for the sake of his retreat, would not throw himself between our flank and that obstacle.

5. *As a station (or stage).* If fortresses are on the line of communication of the defensive, as is generally the case, they serve as halting places for all that passes up and down these lines. The chief danger to lines of communication is from irregular bands, whose action is always of the nature of a shock. If a valuable convoy, on the approach of such a comet, can reach a fortress by hastening the march or quickly turning, it is saved, and may wait there till the danger is past. Further, all troops marching to or from the army, after halting here for a a few days, are better able to hasten the remainder of the march, and a halting day is just the time of greatest danger. In this way a fortress situated half way on a line of communication of 30 miles shortens the line in a manner one half.

6. *As places of refuge for weak or defeated corps.* Under the guns of a moderate sized fortress every corps is safe from the enemy's blows, even if no entrenched camp is specially prepared for them. No doubt such a corps must give up its further retreat if it waits too long; but this is no great sacrifice in cases where a further retreat would only end in complete destruction.

In many cases a fortress can ensure a few days' halt without the retreat being altogether stopped. For the slightly wounded and fugitives who precede a beaten army, it is especially suited as a place of refuge, where they can wait to rejoin their corps.

If Magdeburg had lain on the direct line of the Prussian retreat in 1806, and if that line had not been already lost at Auerstadt, the army could easily have halted for three or four days near that great fortress, and rallied and reorganised itself. But even as it was it served as a rallying point for the remains of Hohenlohe's corps, which there first resumed the appearance of an army.

It is only by actual experience in war itself that the beneficial influence of fortresses close at hand in disastrous times can be rightly understood. They contain powder and arms, forage and bread, give covering to the sick, security to the sound, and recovery of sense to the panic-stricken. They are like an hostelry in the desert.

In the four last named purposes it is evident that the active agency of fortresses is called more into requisition.

7. *As a real shield against the enemy's aggression.* Fortresses which the defender leaves in his front break the stream of the enemy's attack like blocks of ice. The enemy must at least invest them, and requires for that, if the garrisons are brave and enterprising, perhaps double their strength. But, besides, these garrisons may and do mostly consist in part of troops, who, although competent to duty in a garrison, are not fit for the field – half trained militia, invalids, convalescents, armed citizens, landsturm, etc. The enemy, therefore, in such case is perhaps weakened four times more than we are.

This disproportionate weakening of the enemy's power is the first and most important but not the only advantage which a besieged fortress affords by its resistance. From the moment that the enemy crosses our line of fortresses, all his movements become much more constrained; he is limited in his lines of retreat, and must constantly attend to the direct covering of the sieges which he undertakes.

Here, therefore, fortresses co-operate with the defensive act in a most extensive and decisive manner, and of all the objects that they can have, this may be regarded as the most important.

If this use of fortresses – far from being seen regularly repeating itself – seldom comparatively occurs in military history, the cause is to be found in the character of most wars, this means being to a certain extent far too decisive and too thoroughly effectual for them, the explanation of which we leave till hereafter.

In this use of fortresses it is chiefly their offensive power that is called for, at least it is that by which their effectual action is chiefly produced. If a fortress was no more to an aggressor than a point which could not be occupied by him, it might be an obstacle to him, but not to such a degree as to compel him to lay siege to it But as he cannot leave six, eight, or ten thousand men to do as they like in his rear, he is obliged to invest the place with a sufficient force, and if he desires that this investment should not continue to employ so large a detachment, he must convert the investment into a siege, and take the place. From the moment the siege commences, it is then chiefly the passive efficacy of the fortress which comes into action.

All the destinations of fortresses which we have been hitherto considering are fulfilled in a simple and mainly in a direct manner. On the other hand, in the next two objects the method of action is more complicated.

8. *As a protection to extended cantonments*. That a moderate-sized fortress closes the approach to cantonments lying behind it for a width of three or four miles is a simple result of its existence; but how such a place comes to have the honour of covering a line of cantonments fifteen or twenty miles in length, which we find frequently spoken of in military history as a fact – that requires investigation as far as it has really taken place, and refutation so far as it may be mere illusion.

The following points offer themselves for consideration: –

(1.) That the place in itself blocks one of the main roads, and really covers a breadth of three or four miles of country.

(2.) That it may be regarded as an exceptionally strong advanced post, or that it affords a more complete observation of the country, to which may be added facilities in the way of secret information through the ordinary relations of civil life which exist between a great town and the adjacent districts It is natural that in a place of six, eight or ten thousand inhabitants, one should be able to learn more of what is going on in the neighbourhood than in a mere village, the quarters of an ordinary outpost.

(3.) That smaller corps are appuyed on it, derive from it protection and security, and from time to time can advance towards the enemy, it may be to bring in intelligence, or, in case he attempts to turn the fortress, to underdertake something against his rear; that therefore although a fortress, cannot quit its place, still it may have the efficacy of an advanced corps (Fifth Book, eighth Chapter).

(4.) That the defender, after assembling his corps, can take up his position at a point directly behind this fortress, which the assailant cannot reach without becoming exposed to danger from the fortress in his rear.

No doubt every attack on a line of cantonments as such is to be taken in the sense of a surprise, or rather, we are only speaking here of that kind of attack; now it is evident in itself that an attack by surprise accomplishes its effect in a much shorter space of time than a regular attack on a theatre of war. Therefore, although in the latter case, a fortress which is to be passed by must necessarily be invested and kept in check, this investment will not be so indispensable in the case of a mere sudden attack on cantonments, and therefore in the same proportion the fortress will be less an obstacle to the attack of the cantonments. That is true enough; also the cantonments lying at a distance of six to eight miles from the fortress cannot be directly protected by it; but the object of such a sudden attack does not consist alone in the attack of a few cantonments. Until we reach the book on attack we cannot describe circumstantially the real object of such a sudden attack and what may be expected from it; but this much we may say at present, that its principal results are obtained, not by the actual attack on some isolated quarters, but by the series of combats which the aggressor forces on single corps not in proper order, and more bent upon hurrying to certain points than upon fighting. But this attack and pursuit will always be in a direction more or less towards the centre of the enemy's cantonments, and, therefore, an important fortress lying *before* this centre will certainly prove a very great impediment to the attack.

If we reflect on these four points in the whole of their effects, we see that an important fortress in a direct and in an indirect way certainly gives some security to a much greater extent of cantonments than we should think at first sight. "Some security" we say, for all these indirect agencies do not render the advance of the enemy *impossible;* they only make it *more difficult,* and a *more serious consideration;* consequently less probable and less of a danger for the defensive. But that is also all that was required, and all that should be understood in this case under the term covering. The real direct security must be attained by means of outposts and the arrangement of the cantonments themselves.

There is, therefore, some truth in ascribing to a great fortress the capability of covering a wide extent of cantonments lying in rear of it; but it is also not to be denied that often in plans of real campaigns, but still oftener in historical works, we meet with vague and empty expressions, or illusory views in connection with this subject. For if that covering is only realised by the co-operation of several circumstances, if it then also only produces a diminution of the danger, we can easily see that, in particular cases, through special circumstances, above all, through the boldness of the enemy, this whole covering may prove an illusion, and therefore in actual war we must not content ourselves with assuming hastily at once the efficacy of such and such a fortress, but carefully examine and study each single case on its own merits.

9. *As covering a province not occupied.* If during war province is either not occupied at all, or only occupied by an insufficient force, and likewise exposed more or less to incursions from flying columns, then a fortress, if not too unimportant in size, may be looked upon as a covering, or, if we prefer, as a security for this province. As a security it may at all events be regarded, for an enemy cannot become master of the province until he has taken it, and that gives us time to hasten to its defence.

But the actual covering can certainly only be supposed very indirect, or as *not preperly belonging to it*. That is, the fortress by its active opposition can only in some measure check the incursions of hostile bands. If this opposition is limited to merely what the garrison can effect, then the result must be little indeed, for the garrisons of such places are generally weak and usually consist of infantry only, and that not of the best quality. The idea gains a little more reality if small columns keep themselves in communication with the place, making it their base and place of retreat in case of necessity.

10. *As the focus of a general arming of the nation.* Provisions, arms, and munitions can never be supplied in a regular manner in a People's War; on the other hand, it is just in the very nature of such a war to do the best we can; in that way a thousand small sources furnishing means of resistance are opened which otherwise might have remained unused; and it is easy to see that a strong commodious fortress, as a great magazine of these things, can well give to the whole defence more force and intensity, more cohesion, and greater results.

Besides, a fortress is a place of refuge for wounded, the seat of the civil functionaries, the treasury, the point of assembly for the greater enterprises, etc., etc.; lastly, a nucleus of resistance which during the siege places the enemy's force in a condition which facilitates and favours the attacks of national levies acting in conjunction.

11. *For the defence of rivers and mountains.* Nowhere can a fortress answer so many purposes, undertake to play so many parts, as when it is situated on a great river. It secures the passage at any time at that spot, and hinders that of the enemy for several miles each way, it commands the use of the river for commercial purposes, receives all ships within its walls, blocks bridges and roads, and helps the indirect defence of the river, that is, the defence by a position on the enemy's side. It is evident that, by its influence in so many ways, it very greatly facilitates the defence of the river, and may be regarded as an essential part of that defence.

Fortresses in mountains are important in a similar manner. They there form the knots of whole systems of roads, which have their commencement and termination at that spot; they thus command the whole country which is traversed by these roads, and they may be regarded as the true buttresses of the whole defensive system.

CHAPTER ELEVEN

Fortresses – (Continued)

WE HAVE DISCUSSED the object of fortresses: now for their situation. At first the subject seems very complicated, when we think of the diversity of objects, each of which may again be modified by the locality; but such a view has very little foundation if we keep to the essence of the thing, and guard against unnecessary subtilties.

It is evident that all these demands are at once satisfied, if, in those districts of country which are to be regarded as the theatre of war, all the largest and richest towns on the great high roads connecting the two countries with each other are fortified, more particularly those adjacent to harbours and bays of the sea, or situated on large rivers and in mountains. Great towns and great roads always go hand in hand, and both have also a natural connection with great rivers and the coasts of the sea, all these four conditions, therefore, agree very well with each other, and give rise to no incongruity; on the other hand, it is not the same with mountains, for large towns are seldom found there. If, therefore, the position and direction of a mountain chain makes it favourable to a defensive line, it is necessary to close its roads and passes by small forts, built for this purpose only, and at the least possible cost, the great outlay on works of fortification being reserved for the important places of arms in the level country.

We have not yet noticed the frontiers of the state, nor said anything of the geometrical form of the whole system of fortresses, nor of the other geographical points in connection with their situation, because we regard the objects above mentioned as the most essential, and are of opinion that in many cases they alone are sufficient, particularly in small states. But, at the same time, other considerations may be admitted, and may be imperative in countries of a greater superficial extent, which either have a great many important towns and roads, or, on the contrary, are almost without any, which are either very rich, and, possessing already many fortresses, still want new ones, or those which, on the other hand, are very poor, and under the necessity of making a few answer, in short, in cases where the number of fortresses does not correspond with the number of important towns and roads which present themselves, being either considerably greater or less.

We shall now cast a glance at the nature of such other considerations. The chief questions which remain relate to –

1. The choice of the principal roads, if the two countries are connected by more roads than we wish to fortify.

2. Whether the fortresses are to be placed on the frontier only, or spread over the country. Or,

3. Whether they shall be distributed uniformly, or in groups.

4. Circumstances relating to the geography of the country to which it is necessary to pay attention.

A number of other points with respect to the geometrical form of the line of fortifications, such as whether they should be placed in a single line or in several lines, that is, whether they do more service when placed one behind another, or side by side in line with each other; whether they should be chequer-wise, or in a straight line; or whether they should take the form of a fortification itself, with salients and re-entering angles – all these we look upon as empty subtilties, that is, considerations so insignificant, that, compared with the really important points, they are not worth notice; and we only mention them here because they are not merely treated of in many books, but also a great deal more is made of this rubbish than it is worth.

As regards the first question, in order to place it in a clearer light we shall merely instance the relation of the south of Germany to France, that is, to the upper Rhine. If, without reference to the number of separate states composing this district of country, we suppose it a whole which is to be fortified strategically, much doubt will arise, for a great number of very fine roads lead from the Rhine into the interior of Franconia, Bavaria and Austria. Certainly, towns are not wanting which surpass others in size and importance, as Nuremburg, Wurzburg, Ulm, Augsburg, and Munich; but if we are not disposed to fortify all, there is no alternative but to make a selection. If, further, in accordance with our view, the fortification of the greatest and wealthiest is held to be the principal thing, still it is not to be denied that, owing to the distance between Nuremburg and Munich, the first has a very different strategic signification from the second; and therefore it always remains to be considered whether it would not be better, in place of Nuremburg, to fortify some other place in the neighbourhood of Munich, even if the place is one of less importance in itself.

As concerns the decision in such cases, that is, answering the first question, we must refer to what has been said in the chapters on the general plan of defence, and on the choice of points of attack. Wherever the most natural point of attack is situated, there the defensive arrangements should be made by preference.

Therefore, amongst a number of great roads leading from the enemy's country into ours, we should first of all fortify that which leads most directly to the heart of our dominions, or that which, traversing fertile provinces, or running parallel to navigable rivers, facilitates the enemy's undertaking, and then we may rest secure. The assailant then encounters these works, or should he resolve to pass them by, he will naturally offer a favourable opportunity for operations against his flank.

Vienna is the heart of South Germany, and plainly Munich or Augsburg, in relation to France alone (Switzerland and Italy being therefore supposed neutral) would be more efficient as a principal fortress than Nuremburg or Wurzburg. But if, at the same time, we look at the roads leading from Italy into Germany by Switzerland and the Tyrol, this will become still more evident, because, in relation to these, Munich and Augsburg will always be places of importance, whereas Wurzburg and Nuremburg are much the same, in this respect, as if they did not exist.

We turn now to the second question – Whether the fortresses should be placed on the frontier, or distributed over the country? In the first place, we must observe, that, as regards small states, this question is superfluous, for what are called *strategic frontiers* coincide, in their case, nearly with the whole country. The larger the state is supposed to be in the consideration of this question, the plainer appears the necessity for its being answered.

The most natural answer is, – that fortresses belong to the frontiers, for they are to defend the state, and the state is defended as long as the frontiers are defended. This argument may be valid in the abstract, but the following considerations will show that it is subject to very many modifications.

Every defence which is calculated chiefly on foreign assistance lays great value on gaining time; it is not a vigorous counterstroke, but a slow proceeding, in which the chief gain consists more in delay than in any weakening of the enemy which is effected. But now it lies in the nature of the thing that, supposing all other circumstances alike, fortresses which are spread over the whole country, and include between them a very considerable area of territory, will take longer to capture than those squeezed together in a close line on the frontier. Further, in all cases in which the object is to overcome the enemy through the length of his communications, and the difficulty of his existence therefore in countries which can chiefly reckon on this kind of reaction, it would be a complete contradiction to have the defensive preparations of this kind only on the frontier. Lastly, let us also remember that, if circumstances will in any way allow of it, the fortification of the capital is a main point; that according to our principles the chief towns and places of commerce in the provinces demand it likewise; that rivers passing through the country, mountains, and other irregular features of ground, afford advantages for new lines of defence; that many towns, through their strong natural situation, invite fortification; moreover, that certain accessories of war, such as manufactories of arms, &c., are better placed in the interior of the country than on the frontier, and their value well entitles them to the protection of works of fortification; then we see that there is always more or less occasion for the construction of fortresses in the interior of a country; on this account we are of opinion, that although states which possess a great number of fortresses are right in placing the greater number on the frontier, still it would be a great mistake if the interior of the country was left entirely destitute of them. We think that this mistake has been made in a remarkable degree in France. – A great doubt may with reason arise if the border provinces of a country contain no considerable towns, such towns lying further back towards the interior, as is the case in South Germany in particular, where Swabia is almost destitute of great towns, whilst Bavaria contains a large number. We do not hold it to be necessary to remove these doubts once for all on general grounds, believing that in such cases, in order to arrive at a solution, reasons derived from the particular situation must come into consideration. Still we must call attention to the closing remarks in this chapter.

The third question – Whether fortresses should be disposed in groups, or more equally distributed? – will, if we reflect upon it, seldom arise; still we must not, for that reason, set it down as a useless subtilty, because certainly a group of two, three, or four fortresses, which are only a few days' march from a common centre, give that point and the army placed there such strength, that, if other conditions allowed of it, in some measure one would be very much tempted to form such a strategic bastion.

The last point concerns the other geographical properties of the points to be chosen. That fortresses on the sea, on streams and great rivers, and in mountains, are doubly effective, has been already stated to be one of the principal considerations; but there are a number of other points in connection with fortresses to which regard must be paid.

If a fortress cannot lie on the river itself, it is better not to place it near, but at a distance of ten or twelve miles from it; otherwise, the river intersects, and lowers the value of the sphere of action of the fortress in all those points above mentioned.[57]

This is not the same in mountains, because there the movement of large or small masses upon particular points is not restricted in the same degree as it is by a river. But fortresses on the enemy's side of a mountain are not well placed, because they are difficult to succour. If they are on our side, the difficulty of laying siege to them is very great, as the mountains cut across the enemy's line of communication. We give Olmutz, 1758, as an example.

It is easily seen that impassable forests and marshes have a similar effect to that of rivers.

The question has been often raised as to whether towns situated in a very difficult country are well or ill suited for fortresses. As they can be fortified and defended at a small expense, or be made much stronger, often impregnable, at an equal expenditure, and the services of a fortress are always more passive than active, it does not seem necessary to attach much importance to the objection that they can easily be blockaded.

If we now, in conclusion, cast a retrospective glance over our simple system of fortification for a country, we may assert that it rests on comprehensive data, lasting in their nature, and directly connected with the foundations of the state itself, not on transient views on war, fashionable for a day; not on imaginary strategic niceties, nor on requirements completely singular in character, an error which might be attended with irreparable consequences if allowed to influence the construction of fortresses intended to last five hundred, perhaps a thousand, years. Silberberg, in Silesia, built by Frederick the Great on one of the ridges of the Sudetics, has, from the complete alteration in circumstances which has since taken place, lost almost entirely its importance and object, whilst Breslau, if it had been made a strong place of arms, and continued to be so, would have always maintained its value against the French, as well as against the Russians, Poles, and Austrians.

Our reader will not overlook the fact that these considerations are not raised on the supposed case of a state providing itself with a set of new fortifications; they would be useless if such was their object, as such a case seldom, if ever, happens; but they may all arise at the designing of each single fortification.

---

57 Philippsburg was the pattern of a badly-placed fortress; it resembled a fool standing with his nose close to a wall.

CHAPTER TWELVE
Defensive Position

EVERY POSITION in which we accept battle, at the same time making use of the ground as a means of protection, is a *defensive position*, and it makes no difference in this respect whether we act more passively or more offensively in the action. This follows from the general view of the defensive which we have given.

Now we may also apply the term to every position in which an army whilst marching to encounter the enemy would certainly accept battle if the latter sought for it. In point of fact, most battles take place in this way, and in all the middle ages no other was ever thought of. That is, however, not the kind of position of which we are now speaking; by far the greater number of positions are of this kind, and the conception of a *position* in contradistinction to a *camp taken up on the march* would suffice for that. A position which is specially called a *defensive position* must therefore have some other distinguishing characteristics.

In the decisions which take place in an ordinary position, the idea of *time* evidently predominates; the armies march against each other in order to come to an engagement: the place is a subordinate point, all that is required from it is that it should not be unsuitable. But in a real defensive position the idea of *place* predominates; the decision is to be realised on this *spot*, or rather, chiefly *through* this spot. That is the only kind of position we have here in view.

Now the connection of place is a double one; that is, in the first instance, inasmuch as a force posted at this point exercises a certain influence upon the war in general; and next, inasmuch as the local features of the ground contribute to the strength of the army and afford protection: in a word, a strategic and a tactical connection.

Strictly speaking, the term *defensive position* has its origin only in connection with tactics, for its connection with strategy, namely, that an army posted at this point by its presence serves to defend the country, will also suit the case of an army acting offensively.

The strategic effect to be derived from a position cannot be shown completely until hereafter, when we discuss the defence of a theatre of war; we shall therefore only consider it here as far as can be done at present, and for that end we must examine more closely the nature of two ideas which have a similarity and are often mistaken for one another, that is, the *turning a position*, and *the passing by it*.

The turning a position relates to its front, and is done either by an attack upon the side of the position or on its rear, or by acting against its lines of retreat and communication.

The first of these, that is, an attack on flank or rear is tactical in its nature. In our days in which the mobility of troops is so great, and all plans of battles have more or less in view the turning or enveloping the enemy, every position must accordingly be adapted to meet such measures, and one to deserve the name of strong must, with a strong front, allow at least of good combinations for battle on the sides and rear as well, in case of their being menaced. In this way a position will not become untenable by the enemy turning it with a view to an attack on the flank or rear, as the battle which then takes place was provided for in the choice of the position, and should ensure the defender all the advantages which he could expect from this position generally.

If the position *is turned* by the enemy with a view to acting against the lines of retreat and communication, this is a *strategic* relation, and the question is how long the position can be maintained, and whether we cannot outbid the enemy by a scheme like his own, both these questions depend on the situation of the point (strategically), that is, chiefly on the relations of the lines of communication of both combatants. A good position should secure to the army on the defensive the advantage in this point. In any case the position will not be rendered of no effect in this way, as the enemy is neutralised by the position when he is occupied by it in the manner supposed.

But if the assailant, without troubling himself about the existence of the army awaiting his attack in a defensive position, advances with his main body by another line in pursuit of his object, then he *passes by the position;* and if he can do this with impunity, and really does it, he will immediately enforce the abandonment of the position, consequently put an end to its usefulness.

There is hardly any position in the world which, in the simple sense of the words, cannot be passed by, for cases such as the isthmus of Perekop are so rare that they are hardly worth attention. The impossibility of passing by must therefore be understood as merely applying to the disadvantages in which the assailant would become involved if he set about such an operation. We shall have a more fitting opportunity to state these disadvantages in the twenty-seventh chapter; whether small or great, in every case they are the equivalent of the tactical effect which the position is capable of producing but which has not been realised, and in common with it constitute the object of the position.

From the preceding observations, therefore, two strategic properties of the defensive position have resulted:

1. That it cannot be passed round.

2. That in the struggle for the lines of communication it gives the defender advantages.

Here we have to add two other strategic properties, namely –

3. That the relation of the lines of communication may also have a favourable influence on the form of combat; and

4. That the general influence of the country is advantageous.

For the relation of the lines of communication has an influence not only upon the possibility or impossibility of passing by a position or of cutting off the enemy's supplies, but also on the whole course of the battle. An oblique line of retreat facilitates a tactical turning movement on the part of the assailant, and paralyses our own tactical movements during the battle. But an oblique position in relation to the lines of communication is often not the fault of tactics but a consequence of a defective strategic point; it is, for example, not to be avoided when the road changes direction in the vicinity of the position (Borodino, 1812); the assailant is then in such a position that he can turn our line *without deviating from, his own perpendicular disposition.*

Further, the aggressor has much greater freedom for tactical movement if he commands several roads for his retreat whilst we are limited to one. In such cases the tactical skill of the defensive will be exerted in vain to overcome the disadvantageous influence resulting from the strategic relations.

Lastly as regards the fourth point, such a disadvantageous general influence may predominate in the other characteristics of ground, that the most careful choice, and the best use of tactical means, can do nothing to combat them. Under such circumstances the chief points are as follows:

1. The defensive must particularly seek for the advantage of being able to overlook his adversary, so that he may be able swiftly to throw himself upon him inside the limits of his position. It is only when the local difficulties of approach combine with these two conditions that the ground is really favourable to the defensive.

On the other hand, those points which are under the influence of commanding ground are disadvantageous to him; also most positions in mountains (of which we shall speak more particularly in the chapters on mountain warfare). Further, positions which rest one flank on mountains, for such a position certainly makes the *passing by* more difficult, but facilitates a *turning movement*. Of the same kind are all positions which have a mountain immediately in their front, and generally all those which bear relation to the description of ground above specified.

As an example of the opposite of these disadvantageous properties, we shall only instance the case of a position which has a mountain in rear; from this so many advantages result that it may be assumed in general to be one of the most favourable of all positions for the defensive.

2. A country may correspond more or less to the character and composition of an army. A very numerous cavalry is a proper reason for seeking an open country. Want of this arm, perhaps also of artillery, while we have at command a courageous infantry inured to war, and acquainted with the country, make it advisable to take advantage of a difficult, close country.

We do not here enter into particulars respecting the tactical relation which the local features of a defensive position bear to the force which is to occupy it. We only speak of the total result, as that only is a strategic quantity.

Undoubtedly a position in which an army is to await the full force of the hostile attack, should give the troops such an important advantage of ground as may be considered a multiplier of its force. Where nature does much, but not to the full as much as we want, the art of entrenchment comes to our help. In this way it happens not unfrequently that some parts become *unassailable*, and not unusually the whole is made so: plainly in this last case, the whole nature of the measure is changed. It is then no longer a battle under advantageous conditions which we seek, and in this battle the issue of the campaign, but an issue without a battle. Whilst we occupy with our force an unassailable position, we directly refuse the battle, and oblige our enemy to seek for a solution in some other way.

We must, therefore, completely separate these two cases, and shall speak of the latter in the following chapter, under the title of a *strong position*.

But the defensive position with which we have now to do is nothing more than a field of battle with the addition of advantages in our favour; and that it should become a field of battle, the advantages in our favour must not be *too great*. But now what degree of strength may such a position have? Plainly more in proportion as our enemy is more determined on the attack, and that depends on the nature of the individual case. Opposed to a Buonaparte, we may and should withdraw behind stronger ramparts than before a Daun or a Schwartzenburg.

If certain portions of a position are unattackable, say the front, then that is to be taken as a separate factor of its whole strength, for the forces not required at that point are available for employment else-where; but we must not omit to observe that whilst the enemy is kept completely off such impregnable points, the form of his attack assumes quite a different character, and we must ascertain, in the first instance, how this alteration will suit our situation.

For instance, to take up a position, as has often been done, so close behind a great river that it is to be looked upon as covering the front, is nothing else but to make the river a point of support for the right or left flank; for the enemy is naturally obliged to cross further to the right or left, and cannot attack without changing his front: the chief question, therefore, is what advantages or disadvantages does that bring to us?

According to our opinion, a defensive position will come the nearer to the true ideal of such a position the more its strength is hid from ob-servation, and the more it is favourable to our surprising the enemy by our combinations in the battle. Just as we advisably endeavour to con-ceal from the enemy the whole strength of our forces and our real in-tentions, so in the same way we should seek to conceal from the enemy the advantages which we expect to derive from the form of the ground. This of course can only be done to a certain degree, and requires, per-haps, a peculiar mode of proceeding, hitherto but little attempted.

The vicinity of a considerable fortress, in whatever direction it may be, confers on every position a great advantage over the enemy in the move-ment and use of the forces belonging to it. By suitable field-works, the want of natural strength at particular points may be remedied, and in that man-ner the great features of the battle may be settled beforehand at will; these are the means of strengthening by art; if with these we combine a good selection of those natural obstacles of ground which impede the effective action of the enemy's forces without making action absolutely impossible, if we turn to the best account the advantage we have over the enemy in knowing the ground, which he does not, so that we succeed in conceal-ing our movements better than he does his, and that we have a general superiority over him in unexpected movements in the course of the battle, then from these advantages united, there may result in our favour an over-powering and decisive influence in connection with the ground, under the power of which the enemy will succumb, without knowing the real cause of his defeat. This is what we understand under *defensive position*, and we consider it one of the greatest advantages of defensive war.

Leaving out of consideration particular circumstances, we may as-sume that an undulating, not too well, but still not too little, cultivated country affords the most positions of this kind.

CHAPTER THIRTEEN

Strong Positions and Entrenched Camps

WE HAVE SAID in the preceding chapter that a position so strong through nature, assisted by art, that it is unassailable, does not come under the meaning of an advantageous field of battle, but belongs to a peculiar class of things. We shall in this chapter take a review of what constitutes the nature of this peculiarity, and on account of the analogy between such positions and fortresses, call them *strong positions*.

Merely by entrenchments alone they can hardly be formed, except as entrenched camps resting on fortresses; but still less are they to be found ready formed entirely by natural obstacles. Art usually lends a hand to assist nature, and therefore they are frequently designated as *entrenched* camps or positions. At the same time, that term may really be applied to any position strengthened more or less by field works, which need have nothing in common with the nature of the position we are now considering.

The object of a strong position is to make the force there stationed in point of fact unattackable, and by that means, either really to cover a certain space directly, or only the troops which occupy that space in order then, through them, in another way to effect the covering of the country indirectly. The first was the signification of the *lines* of former times, for instance, those on the French frontier; the latter, is that of *entrenched camps* laid out near fortresses, and showing a front in every direction.

If, for instance, the front of a position is so strong by works and hindrances to approach that an attack is impossible, then the enemy is compelled to turn it, to make his attack on a side of it or in rear. Now to prevent this being easily done, *points d'appui* were sought for these lines, which should give them a certain degree of support on the side, such as the Rhine and the Vosges give the lines in Alsace. The longer the front of such a line the more easily it can be protected from being turned, because every movement to turn it is attended with danger to the side attempting the movement, the danger increasing in proportion as the required movement causes a greater deviation from the normal direction of the attacking force. Therefore, a considerable length of front, which can be made unassailable, and good flank-supports, ensure the possibility of protecting a large space of territory directly from hostile invasion: at least, that was the view in which works of this class originated; that was the object of the lines in Alsace, with their right flank on the Rhine and the left on the Vosges; and the lines in Flanders, fifteen miles long, resting their right on the Scheldt and the fortress of Tournay, their left on the sea.

But when we have not the advantages of such a long well-defended front, and good flank-supports, if the country is to be held generally by a force well entrenched, then that force (and its position) must be protected against being turned by such an arrangement that it can show a front in every direction. But then the idea of *a thoroughly covered tract of country* vanishes, for such a position is only strategically a point which covers the force occupying it, and thus secures to that force the power of keeping the field, that is to say, *maintaining itself in the country*. Such a camp cannot be *turned*, that is, cannot be attacked in flank or rear by reason of those parts being weaker than its front, for it can show front in all directions, and is equally strong everywhere. But such a camp can be *passed by*, and that much easier than a fortified line, because its extent amounts to nothing.

Entrenched camps connected with fortresses are in reality of this second kind, for the object of them is to protect the troops assembled in them; but their further strategic meaning, that is, the application of this protected force, is somewhat different from that of other fortified camps.

Having given this explanation of the origin of these three different defensive means, we shall now proceed to consider the value of each of them separately, under the heads of *strong lines, strong positions*, and *entrenched camps resting on fortresses*.

1. *Lines.* – They are the worst kind of cordon war: the obstacle which they present to the aggressor is of no value at all unless they are defended by a powerful fire; in themselves they are simply worthless. But now the extent to which an army can furnish an effective fire is generally very small in proportion to the extent of country to be defended;

the lines can, therefore, only be short, and consequently cover only a small extent of country, or the army will not be able really to defend the lines at all points. In consequence of this, the idea was started of not occupying all points in the line, but only watching them, and defending them by means of strong reserves, in the same way as a small river may be defended; but this procedure is in opposition to the nature of the means. If the natural obstacles of the ground are so great that such a method of defence could be applied, then the entrenchments were needless, and entail danger, for that method of defence is not local, and entrenchments are only suited to a strictly local defence; but if the entrenchments themselves are to be considered the chief impediments to approach, then we may easily conceive that an *undefended* line will not have much to say as an obstacle to approach. What is a twelve or fifteen feet ditch, and a rampart ten or twelve feet high, against the united efforts of many thousands, if these efforts are not hindered by the fire of an enemy? The consequence, therefore, is, that if such lines are short and tolerably well defended by troops, they can be *turned;* but if they are extensive, and not sufficiently occupied, they can be attacked in front, and taken without much difficulty.

Now as lines of this description tie the troops down to a local defence, and take away from them all mobility, they are a bad and senseless means to use against an enterprising enemy. If we find them long retained in modern wars in spite of these objections, the cause lies entirely in the low degree of energy impressed on the conduct of war, one consequence of which was, that seeming difficulties often effected quite as much as real ones. Besides, in most campaigns these lines used merely for a secondary defence against irregular incursions; if they have been found not wholly inefficacious for that purpose, we must only keep in view, at the same time, how much more usefully the troops required for their defence might have been employed at other points. In the latest wars such lines have been out of the question, neither do we find any trace of them; and it is doubtful if they will ever re-appear.

2. *Positions.* – he defence of a tract of country continues (as we shall show more plainly in the 27th chapter) as long as the force designated for it maintains itself there, and only ceases if that force removes and abandons it.

If a force is to maintain itself in any district of country which is attacked by very superior forces, the means of protecting this force against the power of the sword by a position which is unassailable is a first consideration.

Now such a position, as before said, must be able to show a front in all directions; and in conformity with the *usual* extent of tactical positions, if the force is not *very large* (and a large force would be contrary to the nature of the supposed case) it would take up a very small space, which, in the course of the combat, would be exposed to so many disadvantages that, even if strengthened in every possible way by entrenchments, we could hardly expect to make a successful defence. Such a camp, showing front in every direction, must therefore necessarily have an extent of sides proportionably great; but these sides must likewise be as good as unassailable; to give this requisite strength, notwithstanding the required extension, is not within the compass of the art of field fortification; it is therefore a fundamental condition that such a camp must derive part of its strength from natural impediments of ground which render many places impassable and others difficult to pass. In order, therefore, to be able to apply this defensive means, it is necessary to find such a spot, and when that is wanting, the object cannot be attained merely by field works. These considerations relate more immediately to tactical results in order that we may first establish the existence of this strategic means; we mention as examples for illustration, Pirna, Bunzelwitz, Colberg, Torres Vedras, and Drissa. Now, as respects the strategic properties and effects. The first condition is naturally that the force which occupies this camp shall have its subsistence secured for some time, that is, for as long as we think the camp will be required, and this is only possible when the position has behind it a port, like Colberg and Torres Vedras, or stands in connection with a fortress like Bunzelwitz and Pirna, or has large depôts within itself or in the immediate vicinity, like Drissa.

It is only in the first case that the provisioning can be ensured for any time we please; in the second and third cases, it can only be so for a more or less limited time, so that in this point there is always danger. From this appears how the difficulty of subsistence debars the use of many strong points which otherwise would be suitable for entrenched positions, and, therefore, makes those that are eligible *scarce*.

In order to ascertain the eligibility of a position of this description, its advantages and defects, we must ask ourselves what the aggressor can do against it.

a. The assailant can pass by this strong position, pursue his enterprise, and watch the position with a greater or less force.

We must here make a distinction between the cases of a position which is occupied by the main body, and one only occupied by an inferior force.

In the first case the passing by the position can only benefit the as-sailant, if, besides the principal force of the defendant, there is also some other attainable and *decisive object of attack*, as, for instance, the capture of a fortress or a capital city, etc. But even if there is such an object, he can only follow it if the strength of his base and the direction of his lines of communication are such that he has no cause to fear op-erations against his strategic flanks.

The conclusions to be drawn from this with respect to the admis-sibility and eligibility of a strong position for the main body of the de-fender's army are, that it is only an advisable position when either the possibility of operating against the strategic flank of the aggressor is so decisive that we may be sure beforehand of being able in that way to keep him at a point where his army can effect nothing, or in a case where there is no object attainable by the aggressor for which the de-fence need be uneasy. If there is such an object, and the strategic flank of the assailant cannot be seriously menaced, then such position should not be taken up, or if it is it should only be as a feint to see whether the assailant can be imposed upon respecting its value; this is always at-tended with the danger, in case of failure, of being too late to reach the point which is threatened.

If the strong position is only held by an inferior force, then the ag-gressor can never be at a loss for a further object of attack, because he has it in the main body itself of the enemy's army; in this case, there-fore, the value of the position is entirely limited to the means which it affords of operating against the enemy's strategic flank, and depends upon that condition.

b. If the assailant does not venture to pass by a position, he can invest it and reduce it by famine. But this supposes two conditions beforehand: first, that the position is not open in rear, and secondly, that the assailant is sufficiently strong to be able to make such an in-vestment. If these two conditions are united then the assailant's army certainly would be neutralised for a time by this strong position, but at the same time, the defensive pays the price of this advantage by a loss of his defensive force.

From this, therefore, we deduce that the occupation of such a strong position with the main body is a measure only to be taken, –

aa. When the rear is perfectly safe (Torres Vedras).

bb. When we foresee that the enemy's force is not strong enough for-mally to invest us in our camp. Should the enemy attempt the invest-ment with insufficient means, then we should be able to sally out of the camp and beat him in detail.

cc. When we can count upon relief like the Saxons at Pirna, 1756, and as took place in the main at Prague, because Prague could only be regarded as an entrenched camp in which Prince Charles would not have allowed himself to be shut up if he had not known that the Moravian army could liberate him.

One of these three conditions is therefore absolutely necessary to justify the choice of a strong position for the main body of an army; at the same time we must add that the two last are bordering on a great danger for the defensive.

But if it is a question of exposing an inferior corps to the risk of being sacrificed for the benefit of the whole, then these conditions disappear, and the only point to decide is whether by such a sacrifice a greater evil may be avoided. This will seldom happen; at the same time it is certainly not inconceivable. The entrenched camp at Pirna prevented Frederick the Great from attacking Bohemia, as he would have done, in the year 1756. The Austrians were at that time so little prepared, that the loss of that kingdom appears beyond doubt; and perhaps, a greater loss of men would have been connected with it than the 17,000 allied troops who capitulated in the Pirna camp.

c. If none of those possibilities specified under *a* and *b* are in favour of the aggressor; if, therefore, the conditions which we have there laid down for the defensive are fulfilled, then there remains certainly nothing to be done by the assailant but to fix himself before the position, like a setter before a covey of birds, to spread himself, perhaps, as much as possible by detachments over the country, and contenting himself with these small and indecisive advantages to leave the real decision as to the possession of territory to the future. In this case the position has fulfilled its object.

3. *Entrenched camps near fortresses.* – They belong, as already said, to the class of entrenched positions generally, in so far, as they have for their object to cover not a tract of territory, but an armed force against a hostile attack, and only differ in reality from the other in this, that with the fortress they make up an inseparable whole, by which they naturally acquire much greater strength.

But there follows further from the above the undermentioned special points.

a. That they may also have the particular object of rendering the siege of the fortress either impossible or extremely difficult. This object may be worth a great sacrifice of troops if the place is a port which cannot be blockaded, but in any other case we have to take care lest the place is one which may be reduced by hunger so soon that the sacrifice of any considerable number of troops is not justifiable.

b. Entrenched camps can be formed near fortresses for smaller bodies of troops than those in the open field. Four or five thousand men may be invincible under the walls of a fortress, when, on the contrary, in the strongest camp in the world, formed in the open field, they would be lost.

c. They may be used for the assembly and organisation of forces which have still too little solidity to be trusted in contact with the enemy, without the support afforded by the works of the place, as for example, recruits, militia, national levies, etc.

They might, therefore, be recommended as a very useful measure, in many ways, if they had not the immense disadvantage of injuring the fortress, more or less, when they cannot be occupied; and to provide the fortress always with a garrison, in some measure sufficient to occupy the camp also, would be much too onerous a condition.

We are, therefore, very much inclined to consider them only advisable for places on a sea coast, and as more injurious than useful in all other cases.

If, in conclusion, we should summarise our opinion in a general view, then strong and entrenched positions are –

1. The more requisite the smaller the country, the less the space afforded for a retreat.

2. The less dangerous the more surely we can reckon on succouring or relieving them by other forces, or by the inclemency of season, or by a rising of the nation, or by want, &c.

3. The more efficacious, the weaker the elementary force of the enemy's attack.

CHAPTER FOURTEEN
Flank Positions

WE HAVE ONLY allotted to this prominent conception, in the world of ordinary military theory, a special chapter in dictionary fashion, that it may the more easily be found; for we do not believe that anything independent in itself is denoted by the term.

Every position which is to be held, even if the enemy passes by it, is a flank position; for from the moment that he does so it can have no other efficacy but that which it exercises on the enemy's strategic flank. Therefore, necessarily, all *strong positions* are flank positions as well; for as they cannot be attacked, the enemy accordingly is driven to pass them by, therefore they can only have a value by their influence on his strategic flank. The direction of the proper front of a strong position is quite immaterial, whether it runs parallel with the enemy's strategic flank, as Colberg, or at right angles as Bunzelwitz and Drissa, for a strong position must front every way.

But it may also be desirable still to maintain a position which is *not* unassailable, even if the enemy passes by it, should its situation, for instance, give us such a preponderating advantage in the comparative relations of the lines of retreat and communication, that we can not only make an efficacious attack on the strategic flank of the advancing enemy, but also that the enemy alarmed for his own retreat is unable to seize ours entirely; for if that last is not the case, then because our position is not a strong, that is not an *unassailable one*, we should run the risk of being obliged to fight without having the command of any retreat.

The year 1806 affords an example which throws a light on this. The disposition of the Prussian army, on the right bank of the Saal, might in respect to Buonaparte's advance by Hof, have become in every sense a flank position, if the army had been drawn up with its front parallel to the Saal, and there, in that position, waited the progress of events.

If there had not been here such a disproportion of moral and physical powers, if there had only been a Daun at the head of the French army, then the Prussian position might have shown its efficacy by a most brilliant result. To pass it by was quite impossible; that was acknowledged by Buonaparte, by his resolution to attack it; in severing from it the line of retreat even Buonaparte himself did not *completely* succeed, and if the disproportion in physical and moral relations had not been quite so great, that would have been just as little practicable as the passing it by, for the Prussian army was in much less danger from its left wing being overpowered than the French army would have been by the defeat of their left wing. Even with the disproportion of physical and moral power as it existed, a resolute and sagacious exercise of the command would still have given great hopes of a victory. There was nothing to prevent the Duke of Brunswick from making arrangements on the 13th, so that on the morning of the 14th, at day-break, he might have opposed 80,000 men to the 60,000 with which Buonaparte passed the Saal, near Jena and Dornburg. Had even this superiority in numbers, and the steep valley of the Saal behind the French not been sufficient to procure a decisive victory, still it was a fortunate concurrence of circumstances, and if with such advantages no successful decision could be gained, no decision was to be expected in that district of country; and we should, therefore, have retreated further, in order to gain reinforcements and weaken the enemy.

The Prussian position on the Saal, therefore, although assailable, might have been regarded as a flank position in respect to the great road through Hof; but like every position which can be attacked, that property is not to be attributed to it absolutely, because it would only have become so if the enemy had not attempted to attack it.

Still less would it bespeak a clear idea if those positions which *cannot* be maintained after the enemy has passed by them, and from which, in consequence of that, the defensive seeks to attack the assailant's flank, were called *flank positions* merely because his attack is directed against a flank; for this flank attack has hardly anything to do with the position itself, or, at least, is not mainly produced by its properties, as is the case in the action against a strategic flank.

It appears from this that there is nothing new to establish with regard to the properties of a flank position. A few words only on the character of the measure may properly be introduced here; we set aside, however, completely strong positions in the true sense, as we have said enough about them already.

A flank position which is not assailable is an extremely efficacious instrument, but certainly just on that account a dangerous one. If the assailant is checked by it, then we have obtained a great effect by a small expenditure of force; it is the pressure of the finger on the long lever of a sharp bit. But if the effect is too insignificant, if the assailant is not stopped, then the defensive has more or less imperilled his retreat, and must seek to escape either in haste and by a detour – consequently under very unfavourable circumstances, or he is in danger of being compelled to fight without any line of retreat being open to him. Against a bold adversary, having the moral superiority, and seeking a decisive solution, this means is therefore extremely hazardous and entirely out of place, as shown by the example of 1806 above quoted. On the other hand, when used against a cautious opponent in a war of mere observation, it may be reckoned one of the best means which the defensive can adopt. The Duke Ferdinand's defence of the Weser by his position on the left bank, and the well-known positions of Schmotseifen and Landshut are examples of this; only the latter, it is true, by the catastrophe which befell Fouque's corps in 1760, also shows the danger of a false application.

CHAPTER FIFTEEN

Defence of Mountains

THE INFLUENCE of mountains on the conduct of war is very great; the subject, therefore, is very important for theory. As this influence introduces into action a retarding principle, it belongs chiefly to the defensive. We shall therefore discuss it here in a wider sense than that conveyed by the simple conception, defence of mountains. As we have discovered in our consideration of the subject results which run counter to general opinion in many points, we shall therefore be obliged to enter into rather an elaborate analysis of it.

We shall first examine the tactical nature of the subject, in order to gain the point where it connects itself with strategy.

The endless difficulty attending the march of large columns on mountain roads, the extraordinary strength which a small post obtains by a steep scarp covering its front, and by ravines right and left supporting its flanks, are unquestionably the principal causes why such efficacy and strength are universally attributed to the defence of mountains, so that nothing but the peculiarities in armament and tactics at certain periods has prevented large masses of combatants from engaging in it.

When a column, winding like a serpent, toils its way through narrow ravines up to the top of a mountain, and passes over it at a snail's pace, artillery and train-drivers, with oaths and shouts, flogging their over-driven cattle through the narrow rugged roads, each broken waggon has to be got out of the way with indescribable trouble, whilst all behind are detained, cursing and blaspheming, every one then thinks to himself, Now if the enemy should appear with only a few hundred men, he might disperse the whole. From this has originated the expression used by historical writers, when they describe a narrow pass as a place where "a handful of men might keep an army in check." At the same time, every one who has had any experience in war knows, or ought to know, that such a march through mountains has little or nothing in common with *the attack* of these same mountains, and that therefore to infer from the *difficulty* of marching through mountains that the difficulty of attacking them must be much greater is a false conclusion.

It is natural enough that an inexperienced person should thus argue, and it is almost as natural that the art of war itself for a certain time should have been entangled in the same error, for the fact which it related to was almost as new at that time to those accustomed to war as to the uninitiated. Before the Thirty Years' War, owing to the deep order of battle, the numerous cavalry, the rude fire-arms, and other peculiarities, it was quite unusual to make use of formidable obstacles of ground in war, and a formal defence of mountains, at least by regular troops, was almost impossible. It was not until a more extended order of battle was introduced, and that infantry and their arms became the chief part of an army, that the use which might be made of hills and valleys occurred to men's minds. But it was not until a hundred years afterwards, or about the middle of the eighteenth century, that the idea became fully developed.

The second circumstance, namely, the great defensive capability which might be given to a small post planted on a point difficult of access, was still more suited to lead to an exaggerated idea of the strength of mountain defences. The opinion arose that it was only necessary to multiply such a post by a certain number to make an army out of a battalion, a chain of mountains out of a mountain.

It is undeniable that a small post acquires an extraordinary strength by selecting a good position in a mountainous country. A small detachment, which would be driven off in the level country by a couple of squadrons, and think itself lucky to save itself from rout or capture by a hasty retreat, can in the mountains stand up before a whole army, and, as one might say, with a kind of tactical effrontery exact the military honour of a regular attack, of having its flank turned, etc., etc. How it obtains this defensive power, by obstacles to approach, *points d'appui* for its flanks, and new positions which it finds on its retreat, is a subject for tactics to explain; we accept it as an established fact.

It was very natural to believe that a number of such posts placed in a line would give a very strong, almost unassailable front, and all that remained to be done was to prevent the position from being turned by extending it right and left until either flank-supports were met with commensurate with the importance of the whole, or until the extent of the position itself gave security against turning movements. A mountainous country specially invites such a course by presenting such a succession of defensive positions, each one apparently better than another, that one does not know where to stop; and therefore it ended in all and every approach to the mountains within a certain distance being guarded, with a view to defence, and ten or fifteen single posts, thus spread over a space of about ten miles or more, were supposed to bid defiance to that odious turning movement. Now as the connection between these posts was considered sufficiently secure by the intervening spaces, being ground of an impassable nature (columns at that time not being able to quit the regular roads), it was thought a wall of brass was thus presented to the enemy. As an extra precaution, a few battalions, some horse artillery, and a dozen squadrons of cavalry, formed a reserve to provide against the event of the line being unexpectedly burst through at any point.

No one will deny that the prevalence of this idea is shown by history, and it is not certain that at this day we are completely emancipated from these errors.

The course of improvement in tactics since the Middle Ages, with the ever increasing strength of armies, likewise contributed to bring mountainous districts in this sense more within the scope of military action.

The chief characteristic of mountain defence is its complete passivity; in this light the tendency towards the defence of mountains was very natural before armies attained to their present capability of movement. But armies were constantly becoming greater, and on account of the effect of fire-arms began to extend more and more into long thin lines connected with a great deal of art, and on that account very difficult, often almost impossible, to move. To dispose, in order of battle, such an artistic machine, was often half a day's work, and half the battle; and almost all which is now attended to in the preliminary plan of the battle was included in this first disposition or drawing up. After this work was done it was therefore difficult to make any modifications to suit new circumstances which might spring up; from this it followed that the assailant, being the last to form his line of battle, naturally adapted it to the order of battle adopted by the enemy, without the latter being able in turn to modify his in accordance. The attack thus acquired a general superiority, and the defensive had no other means of reinstating the balance than that of seeking protection from the impediments of ground, and for this nothing was so favourable in general as mountainous ground. Thus it became an object to couple, as it were, the army with a formidable obstacle of ground, and the two united then made common cause. The battalion defended the mountain, and the mountain the battalion; so the passive defence through the aid of mountainous ground became highly efficacious, and there was no other evil in the thing itself except that it entailed a greater loss of freedom of movement, but of that quality they did not understand the particular use at that time.

When two antagonistic systems act upon each other, the exposed, that is, the weak point on the one side always draws upon itself the blows from the other side. If the defensive becomes fixed, and as it were, spell-bound in posts, which are in themselves strong, and can not be taken, the aggressor then becomes bold in turning movements, because he has no apprehension about his own flanks. This is what took place – The *turning*, as it was called, soon became the order of the day: to counteract this, positions were extended more and more; they were thus weakened in front, and the offensive suddenly turned upon that part: instead of trying to outflank by extending, the assailant now concentrated his masses for attack at some one point, and the line was broken. This is nearly what took place in regard to mountain defences according to the latest modern history.

The offensive had thus again gained a preponderance through the greater mobility of troops; and it was only through the same means that the defence could seek for help. But mountainous ground by its nature is opposed to mobility, and thus the whole theory of mountain defence experienced, if we may use the expression, a defeat like that which the armies engaged in it in the Revolutionary war so often suffered.

But that we may not reject the good with the bad, and allow ourselves to be carried along by the stream of commonplace to assertions which, in actual experience, would be refuted a thousand times by the force of circumstances, we must distinguish the effects of mountain defence according to the nature of the cases.

The principal question to be decided here, and that which throws the greatest light over the whole subject is, whether the resistance which is intended by the defence of mountains is to be *relative* or *absolute* – whether it is only intended to last for a time, or is meant to end in a decisive victory. For a resistance of the first kind mountainous ground is in a high degree suitable, and introduces into it a very powerful element of strength; for one of the latter kind, on the contrary, it is in general not at all suitable, or only so in some special cases.

In mountains every movement is slower and more difficult, costs also more time, and more men as well, if within the sphere of danger. But the loss of the assailant in time and men is the standard by which the defensive resistance is measured. As long as the movement is all on the side of the offensive so long the defensive has a marked advantage; but as soon as the defensive resorts to this principle of movement also, that advantage ceases. Now from the nature of the thing, that is to say, on tactical grounds, a relative resistance allows of a much greater degree of passivity than one which is intended to lead to a decisive result, and it allows this passivity to be carried to an extreme, that is, to the end of the combat, which in the other case can never happen. The impeding element of mountain ground, which as a medium of greater density weakens all positive activity, is, therefore, completely suited to the passive defence.

We have already said that a small post acquires an extraordinary strength by the nature of the ground; but although this tactical result in general requires no further proof, we must add to what we have said some explanation. We must be careful here to draw a distinction between what is relatively and what is absolutely small. If a body of troops, let its size be what it may, isolates a portion of itself in a position, this portion may possibly be exposed to the attack of the whole body of the enemy's troops, therefore of a superior force, in opposition to which it is itself small. There, as a rule, no absolute but only a relative defence can be the object. The smaller the post in relation to the whole body from which it is detached and in relation to the whole body of the enemy, the more this applies.

But a post also which is small in an absolute sense, that is, one which is not opposed by an enemy superior to itself, and which, therefore, may aspire to an absolute defence, a real victory, will be infinitely better off in mountains than a large army, and can derive more advantage from the ground as we shall show further on.

Our conclusion, therefore, is, that a small post in mountains possesses great strength. How this may be of decisive utility in all cases which depend entirely on a *relative* defence is plain of itself; but will it be of the same decisive utility for the *absolute* defence by a whole army? This is the question which we now propose to examine.

First of all we ask whether a front line composed of several posts has, as has hitherto been assumed, the same strength proportionally as each post singly. This is certainly not the case, and to suppose so would involve one of two errors.

In the first place, a country *without roads* is often confounded with one which is *quite impassable*. Where a column, or where artillery and cavalry cannot *march*, infantry may still, in general, be able to pass, and even artillery may often be brought there as well, for the movements made in a battle by excessive efforts of short duration are not to be judged of by the same scale as marches. The secure connection of the single posts with one another rests therefore on an illusion, and the flanks are in reality in danger.

Or next it is supposed, a line of small posts, which are very strong in front, are also equally strong on their flanks, because a ravine, a precipice, etc., etc., form excellent supports for a small post. But why are they so? – not because they make it impossible to turn the post, but because they cause the enemy an expenditure of time and of force, which gives scope for the effectual action of the post. The enemy who, in spite of the difficulty of the ground, wishes, and in fact is obliged, to turn such a post, because the front is unassailable requires, perhaps, half-a-day to execute his purpose, and cannot after all accomplish it without some loss of men. Now if such a post can be succoured, or if it is only designed to resist for a certain space of time, or lastly, if it is able to cope with the enemy, then the flank supports have done their part, and we may say the position had not only a strong front, but strong flanks as well. But it is not the same if it is a question of a line of posts, forming part of an extended mountain position. None of these three conditions are realised in that case. The enemy attacks one point with an overwhelming force, the support in rear is perhaps slight, and yet it is a question of absolute resistance. Under such circumstances the flank supports of such posts are worth nothing.

Upon a weak point like this the attack usually directs its blows. The assault with concentrated, and therefore very superior forces, upon a point in front, may certainly *be met by a resistance, which is very violent as regards that point, but which is unimportant as regards the whole.* After it is overcome, the line is pierced, and the object of the attack attained.

From this it follows that the *relative* resistance in mountain warfare is, in general, greater than in a level country, that it is comparatively greatest in small posts, and does not increase in the same measure as the masses increase.

Let us now turn to the real object of great battles generally – to the *positive victory* which may also be the object in the defence of mountains. If the whole mass, or the principal part of the force, is employed for that purpose, then *the defence of mountains* changes itself *eo ipso* into a *defensive battle in the mountains.* A battle, that is the application of all our powers to the destruction of the enemy is now the form, a victory the object of the combat. The defence of mountains which takes place in this combat, appears now a subordinate consideration, for it is no longer the object, it is only the means. Now in this view, how does the ground in mountains answer to the object?

The character of a defensive battle is a passive reaction in front, and an increased active reaction in rear; but for this the ground in mountains is a paralysing principle. There are two reasons for this: first, want of roads affording means of rapidly moving in all directions, from the rear towards the front, and even the sudden tactical attack is hampered by the unevenness of ground; secondly, a free view over the country, and the enemy's movements is not to be had. The ground in mountains, therefore, ensures in this case to the enemy the same advantages which it gave to us in the front, and deadens all the better half of the resistance. To this is to be added a third objection, namely the danger of being cut off. Much as a mountainous country is favourable to a retreat, made under a pressure exerted along the whole front, and great as may be the loss of time to an enemy who makes a turning movement in such a country, still these again are only advantages in the case of a *relative defence*, advantages which have no connection with the decisive battle, the resistance to the last extremity. The resistance will last certainly somewhat longer, that is until the enemy has reached a point with his flank-columns which menaces or completely bars our retreat. Once he has gained such a point then relief is a thing hardly possible. No act of the offensive which we can make from the rear can drive him out again from the *points which threaten us;* no desperate assault with our whole mass can clear the passage *which he blocks.* Whoever thinks he discovers in this a contradiction, and believes that the advantages which the assailant has in mountain warfare, must also accrue to the defensive in an attempt to cut his way through, forgets the difference of circumstances. The corps which opposes the passage is not engaged in an *absolute* defence, a few hours' resistance will probably be sufficient; it is, therefore, in the situation of a small post. Besides this, its opponent is no longer in full possession of all his fighting powers; he is thrown into disorder, wants ammunition, etc. Therefore, in any view, the chance of cutting through is small, and this is the danger that the defensive fears above all; this fear is at work even during the battle, and enervates every fibre of the struggling athlete. A nervous sensibility springs up on the flanks, and every small detachment which the aggressor makes a display of on any wooded eminence in our rear, is for him a new lever, helping on the victory.

These disadvantages will, for the most part, disappear, leaving all the advantages, if the defence of a mountain district consists in the concentrated disposition of the army on an extensive mountain plateau. There we may imagine a very strong front; flanks very difficult of approach, and yet the most perfect freedom of movement, both within and in rear of the position. Such a position would be one of the strongest that there can be, but it is little more than an illusion, for although most mountains are more easily traversed along their crests than on their declivities, yet most plateaux of mountains are either too small for such a purpose, or they have no proper right to be called plateaux, and are so termed more in a geological, than in a geometrical sense.

For smaller bodies of troops, the disadvantages of a defensive position in mountains diminish as we have already remarked. The cause of this is, that such bodies take up less space, and require fewer roads for retreat, etc., etc. A single hill is not a mountain system, and has not the same disadvantages. The smaller the force, the more easily it can establish itself on a single ridge or hill, and the less will be the necessity for it to get entangled in the intricacies of countless steep mountain gorges.

CHAPTER SIXTEEN

Defence of Mountains – (Continued)

WE NOW PROCEED to the strategic use of the tactical results developed in the preceding chapter.

We make a distinction between the following points: –

1. A mountainous district as a battle-field.

2. The influence which the possession of it exercises on other parts of the country.

3. Its effect as a strategic barrier.

4. The attention which it demands in respect to the supply of the troops.

The first and most important of these heads, we must again subdivide as follows: –

a. A general action.

b. Inferior combats.

1. *A mountain system as a battle-field.*

We have shown in the preceding chapter how unfavourable *mountain ground* is to the defensive in a *decisive battle*, and, on the other hand, how much it favours the assailant. This runs exactly counter to the generally received opinion; but then how many other things there are which general opinion confuses; how little does it draw distinctions between things which are of the most opposite nature! From the powerful resistance which small bodies of troops may offer in a mountainous country, common opinion becomes impressed with an idea that all mountain defence is extremely strong, and is astonished when any one denies that this great strength is communicated to the greatest act of all defence, the defensive battle. On the other hand, it is instantly ready, whenever a battle is lost by the defensive in mountain warfare, to point out the inconceivable error of a system of cordon war, without any regard to the fact that in the nature of things such a system is unavoidable in mountain warfare. We do not hesitate to put ourselves in direct opposition to such an opinion, and at the same time we must mention, that to our great satisfaction, we have found our views supported in the works of an author whose opinion ought to have great weight in this matter; we allude to the history of the campaigns of 1796 and 1797, by the Archduke Charles, himself a good historical writer, a good critic, and above all, a good general.

We can only characterise it as a lamentable position when the weaker defender, who has laboriously, by the greatest effort, assembled all his forces, in order to make the assailant feel the effect of his love of Fatherland, of his enthusiasm and his ability, in a decisive battle – when he on whom every eye is fixed in anxious expectation, having betaken himself to the obscurity of thickly veiled mountains, and hampered in every movement by the obstinate ground, stands exposed to the thousand possible forms of attack which his powerful adversary can use against him. Only towards one single side is there still left an open field for his intelligence, and that is in making all possible use of every obstacle of ground; but this leads close to the borders of the disastrous war of cordons, which, under all circumstances, is to be avoided. Very far therefore from seeing a refuge for the defensive, in a mountainous country, when a decisive battle is sought, we should rather advise a general in such a case to avoid such a field by every possible means.

It is true, however, that this is sometimes impossible; but the battle will then necessarily have a very different character from one in a level country: the disposition of the troops will be much more extended – in most cases twice or three times the length; the resistance more passive, the counter blow much less effective. These are influences of mountain ground which are inevitable; still, in such a battle the defensive is not to be converted into a mere defence of mountains; the predominating character must be a concentrated order of battle in the mountains, in which everything unites into *one* battle, and passes as much as possible under the eye of *one* commander, and in which there are sufficient reserves to make the decision something more than a mere warding off, a mere holding up of the shield. This condition is indispensable, but difficult to realise; and the drifting into the pure defence of mountains comes so naturally, that we cannot be surprised at its often happening; the danger in this is so great that theory cannot too urgently raise a warning voice.

Thus much as to a decisive battle with the main body of the army. –

For combats of minor significance and importance, a mountainous country, on the other hand, may be very favourable, because the main point in them is not absolute defence, and because no decisive results are coupled with them. We may make this plainer by enumerating the objects of this reaction.

a. Merely to gain time. This motive occurs a hundred times: always in the case of a defensive line formed with the view of observation; besides that, in all cases in which a reinforcement is expected.

b. The repulse of a mere demonstration or minor enterprise of the enemy. If a province is guarded by mountains which are defended by troops, then this defence, however weak, will always suffice to prevent partisan attacks and expeditions intended to plunder the country. Without the mountains, such a weak chain of posts would be useless.

c. To make demonstrations on our own part. It will be some time yet before general opinion with respect to mountains will be brought to the right point; until then an enemy may at any time be met with who is afraid of them, and shrinks back from them in his undertakings. In such a case, therefore, the principal body may also be used for the defence of a mountain system. In wars carried on with little energy or movement, this state of things will often happen; but it must always be a condition then that we neither design to accept a general action in this mountain position, nor can be compelled to do so.

d. In general, a mountainous country is suited for all positions in which we do not intend to accept any great battle, for each of the separate parts of the army is stronger there, and it is only the whole that is weaker; besides, in such a position, it is not so easy to be suddenly attacked and forced into a decisive battle.

e. Lastly, a mountainous country is the true region for the efforts of a people in arms. But while national risings should always be supported by small bodies of regular troops, on the other hand, the proximity of a great army seems to have an unfavourable effect upon movements of this kind; this motive, therefore, as a rule, will never give occasion for transferring the whole army to the mountains.

Thus much for mountains in connection with the positions which may be taken up there for battle.

2. *The influence of mountains on other parts of the country.*

Because, as we have seen, it is so easy in mountainous ground to secure a considerable tract of territory by small posts, so weak in numbers that in a district easily traversed they could not maintain themselves, and would be continually exposed to danger; because every step forward in mountains which have been occupied by the enemy must be made much more slowly than in a level country, and therefore cannot be made at the same rate with him – therefore the question, Who is in possession? – is also much more important in reference to mountains than to any other tract of country of equal extent. In an open country, the possession may change from day to day. The mere advance of strong detachments compels the enemy to give up the country we want to occupy. But it is not so in mountains; there a very stout resistance is possible by much inferior forces, and for that reason, if we require a portion of country which includes mountains, enterprises of a special nature, formed for the purpose, and often necessitating a considerable expenditure of time as well as of men, are always required in order to obtain possession. If, therefore, the mountains of a country are not the theatre of the principal operations of a war, we cannot, as we should were it the case of a district of level country, look upon the possession of the mountains as dependent on and a necessary consequence of our success at other parts.

A mountainous district has therefore much more independence, and the possession of it is much firmer and less liable to change. If we add to this that a ridge of mountains from its crests affords a good view over the adjacent open country, whilst it remains itself veiled in obscurity, we may therefore conceive that when we are close to mountains, without being in actual possession of them, they are to be regarded as a constant source of disadvantage – a sort of laboratory of hostile forces; and this will be the case in a still greater degree if the mountains are not only occupied by the enemy, but also form part of his territory. The smallest bodies of adventurous partisans always find shelter there if pursued, and can then sally forth again with impunity at other points; the largest bodies, under their cover, can approach unperceived, and our forces must, therefore, always keep at a sufficient distance if they would avoid getting within reach of their dominating influence – if they would not be exposed to disadvantageous combats and sudden attacks which they cannot return.

In this manner every mountain system, as far as a certain distance, exercises a very great influence over the lower and more level country adjacent to it. Whether this influence shall take effect momentarily, for instance in a battle (as at Maltsch on the Rhine, 1796) or only after some time upon the lines of communication, depends on the local relations; – whether or not it shall be overcome through some decisive event happening in the valley or level country, depends on the relations of the armed forces to each other respectively.

Buonaparte, in 1805 and 1809, advanced upon Vienna without troubling himself much about the Tyrol; but Moreau had to leave Swabia in 1796, chiefly because he was not master of the more elevated parts of the country, and too many troops were required to watch them. In campaigns, in which there is an evenly balanced series of alternate successes on each side, we shall not expose ourselves to the constant disadvantage of the mountains remaining in possession of the enemy: we need, therefore, only endeavour to seize and retain possession of that portion of them which is required on account of the direction of the principal lines of our attack; this generally leads to the mountains being the arena of the separate minor combats which take place between forces on each side. But we must be careful of overrating the importance of this circumstance, and being led to consider a mountain-chain as the key to the whole in all cases, and its possession as the main point. When a victory is the object sought; then it is the principal, object; and if the victory is gained, other things can be regulated according to the paramount requirement of the situation.

3. *Mountains considered in their aspect of a strategic barrier.*

We must divide this subject under two heads.

The first is again that of a decisive battle. We can, for instance, consider the mountain chain as a river, that is, as a barrier with certain points of passage, which may afford us an opportunity of gaining a victory, because the enemy will be compelled by it to divide his forces in advancing, and is tied down to certain roads, which will enable us with our forces concentrated behind the mountains to fall upon fractions of his force. As the assailant on his march through the mountains, irrespective of all other considerations, cannot march in a single column because he would thus expose himself to the danger of getting engaged in a decisive battle with only one line of retreat, therefore, the defensive method recommends itself certainly on substantial grounds. But as the conception of mountains and their outlets is very undefined, the question of adopting this plan depends entirely on the nature of the country itself, and it can only be pointed out as possible whilst it must also be considered as attended with two disadvantages, the first is, that if the enemy receives a severe blow, he soon finds shelter in the mountains; the second is, that he is in possession of the higher ground, which, although not decisive, must still always be regarded as a disadvantage for the pursuer.

We know of no battle given under such circumstances unless the battle with Alvinzi in 1796 can be so classed. But that the case *may* occur is plain from Buonaparte's passage of the Alps in the year 1800, when Melas might and should have fallen on him with his whole force before he had united his columns.

The second influence which mountains may have as a barrier is that which they have upon the lines of communication if they cross those lines. Without taking into account what may be done by erecting forts at the points of passage and by arming the people, the bad roads in mountains at certain seasons of the year may of themselves alone prove at once destructive to an army; they have frequently compelled a retreat after having first sucked all the marrow and blood out of the army. If, in addition, troops of active partisans hover round, or there is a national rising to add to the difficulties, then the enemy's army is obliged to make large detachments, and at last driven to form strong posts in the mountains and thus gets engaged in one of the most disadvantageous situations that can be in an offensive war.

4. *Mountains in their relation to the provisioning an army.*

This is a very simple subject, easy to understand. The opportunity to make the best use of them in this respect is when the assailant is either obliged to remain in the mountains, or at least to leave them close in his rear.

These considerations on the defence of mountains, which, in the main, embrace all mountain warfare, and, by their reflection, throw also the necessary light on offensive war, must not be deemed incorrect or impracticable because we can neither make plains out of mountains, nor hills out of plains, and the choice of a theatre of war is determined by so many other things that it appears as if there was little margin left for considerations of this kind. In affairs of magnitude it will be found that this margin is not so small. If it is a question of the disposition and effective employment of the principal force, and that, even in the moment of a decisive battle, by a few marches more to the front or rear an army can be brought out of mountain ground into the level country, then a resolute concentration of the chief masses in the plain will neutralise the adjoining mountains.

We shall now once more collect the light which has been thrown on the subject, and bring it to a focus in one distinct picture.

We maintain and believe we have shown, that mountains, both tactically and strategically, are in general unfavourable to the defensive, meaning thereby, that kind of defensive which is *decisive*, on the result of which the question of the possession or loss of the country depends. They limit the view and prevent movements in every direction; they force a state of passivity, and make it necessary to stop every avenue or passage, which always leads more or less to a war of cordons. We should therefore, if possible, avoid mountains with the principal mass of our force, and leave them on one side, or keep them before or behind us.

At the same time, we think that, for minor operations and objects, there is an element of increased strength to be found in mountain ground; and after what has been said, we shall not be accused of inconsistency in maintaining that such a country is the real place of refuge for the weak, that is, for those who dare not any longer seek an absolute decision. On the other hand again, the advantages derived from a mountainous country by troops acting an inferior rôle cannot be participated in by large masses of troops.

Still all these considerations will hardly counteract the impressions made on the senses. The imagination not only of the inexperienced but also of all those accustomed to bad methods of war will still feel in the concrete case such an overpowering dread of the difficulties which the inflexible and retarding nature of mountainous ground opposes to all the movements of an assailant, that they will hardly be able to look upon our opinion as anything but a most singular paradox. Then again, with those who take a general view, the history of the last century (with its peculiar form of war) will take the place of the impressions of the senses, and therefore there will be but few who will not still adhere to the belief that Austria, for example, should be better able to defend her states on the Italian side than on the side of the Rhine. On the other hand, the French who carried on war for twenty years under a leader both energetic and indifferent to minor considerations, and have constantly before their eyes the successful results thus obtained, will, for some time to come, distinguish themselves in this as well as in other cases by the tact of a practised judgment.

Does it follow from this that a state would be better protected by an open country than by mountains, that Spain would be stronger without the Pyrenees; Lombardy more difficult of access without the Alps, and a level country such as North Germany more difficult to conquer than a mountainous country? To these false deductions we shall devote our concluding remarks.

We do not assert that Spain would be stronger *without* the Pyrenees than *with* them, but we say that a Spanish army, feeling itself strong enough to engage in a decisive battle, would do better by concentrating itself in a position behind the Ebro, than by fractioning itself amongst the fifteen passes of the Pyrenees. But the influence of the Pyrenees on war is very far from being set aside on that account. We say the same respecting an Italian army. If it divided itself in the High Alps it would be vanquished by each resolute commander it encountered, without even the alternative of victory or defeat; whilst in the plains of Turin it would have the same chance as every other army. But still no one can on that account suppose that it is desirable for an aggressor to have to march over masses of mountains such as the Alps, and to leave them behind. Besides, a determination to accept a great battle in the plains, by no means excludes a preliminary defence of the mountains by subordinate forces, an arrangement very advisable in respect to such masses as the Alps and Pyrenees. Lastly, it is far from our intention to argue that the conquest of a mountainous country is easier than that of a level[58] one, unless a single victory sufficed to prostrate the enemy completely. After this victory ensues a state of defence for the conqueror, during which the mountainous ground must be as disadvantageous to the assailant as it was to the defensive, and even more so. If the war continues, if foreign assistance arrives, if the people take up arms, this reaction will gain strength from a mountainous country.

It is here as in dioptrics, the image represented becomes more luminous when moved in a certain direction, not, however, as far as one pleases, but only until the focus is reached, beyond that the effect is reversed.

If the defensive is weaker in the mountains, that would seem to be a reason for the assailant to prefer a line of operations in the mountains. But this will seldom occur, because the difficulties of supporting an army, and those arising from the roads, the uncertainty as to whether the enemy will accept battle in the mountains, and even whether he will take up a position there with his principal force, tend to neutralise that possible advantage.

58 As it is conceived that the words *"ebenen"* and *"gebirgigen"* in this passage in the original have by some means become transposed, their equivalents – *level* and *mountainous* – are here placed in the order in which it is presumed the author intended the words to stand. – Tr.

CHAPTER SEVENTEEN

Defence of Mountains (Continued)

IN THE FIFTEENTH chapter we spoke of the nature of combats in mountains, and in the sixteenth of the use to be made of them by strategy, and in so doing we often came upon the idea of *mountain defence*, without stopping to consider the form and details of such a measure. We shall now examine it more closely.

As mountain systems frequently extend like streaks or belts over the surface of the earth, and form the division between streams flowing in different directions, consequently the separation between whole water systems, and as this general form repeats itself in the parts composing that whole, inasmuch as these parts diverge from the main chain in branches or ridges, and then form the separation between lesser water systems; hence the idea of a system of mountain defence has naturally founded itself in the first instance, and afterwards developed itself, upon the conception of the general form of mountains, that of an obstacle, like a great barrier, having greater length than breadth. Although geologists are not yet agreed as to the origin of mountains and the laws of their formation, still in every case the course of the waters indicates in the shortest and surest manner the general form of the system, whether the action of the water has contributed to give that general form (according to the aqueous theory), or that the course of the water is a consequence of the form of the system itself. It was, therefore, very natural again, in devising a system of mountain defence, to take the course of the waters as a guide, as those courses form a natural series of levels, from which we can obtain both the general height and the general profile of the mountain, while the valleys formed by the streams present also the best means of access to the heights, because so much of the effect of the erosive and alluvial action of the water is permanent, that the inequalities of the slopes of the mountain are smoothed down by it to one regular slope. Hence, therefore, the idea of mountain defence would assume that, when a mountain ran about parallel with the front to be defended, it was to be regarded as a great obstacle to approach, as a kind of rampart, the gates of which were formed by the valleys. The real defence was then to be made on the crest of this rampart, (that is, on the edge of the plateau which crowned the mountain) and cut the valleys transversely. If the line of the principal mountain-chain formed somewhat of a right angle with the front of defence, then one of the principal branches would be selected to be used instead; thus the line chosen would be parallel to one of the principal valleys, and run up to the principal ridge, which might be regarded as the extremity.

We have noticed this scheme for mountain defence founded on the geological structure of the earth, because it really presented itself in theory for some time, and in the so-called "theory of ground" the laws of the process of aqueous action have been mixed up with the conduct of war.

But all this is so full of false hypotheses and incorrect substitutions, that when these are abstracted, nothing in reality remains to serve as the basis of any kind of a system.

The principal ridges of real mountains are far too impracticable and inhospitable to place large masses of troops upon them; it is often the same with the adjacent ridges, they are often too short and irregular. Plateaux do not exist on all mountain ridges, and where they are to be found they are mostly narrow, and therefore unfit to accommodate many troops; indeed, there are few mountains which, closely examined, will be found surmounted by an uninterrupted ridge, or which have their sides at such an angle that they form in some measure practicable slopes, or, at least, a succession of terraces. The principal ridge winds, bends, and splits itself; immense branches launch into the adjacent country in curved lines, and lift themselves often just at their termination to a greater height than the main ridge itself; promontories then join on, and form deep valleys which do not correspond with the general system. Thus it is that, when several lines of mountains cross each other, or at those points from which they branch out, the conception of a small band or belt is completely at an end, and gives place to mountain and water lines radiating from a centre in the form of a star.

From this it follows, and it will strike those who have examined mountain-masses in this manner the more forcibly, that the idea of a systematic disposition is out of the question, and that to adhere to such an idea as a fundamental principle for our measures would be wholly impracticable. There is still one important point to notice belonging to the province of practical application.

If we look closely at mountain warfare in its tactical aspects, it is evident that these are of two principal kinds, the first of which is the defence of steep slopes, the second is that of narrow valleys. Now this last, which is often, indeed almost generally, highly favourable to the action of the defence, is not very compatible with the disposition on the principal ridge, for the occupation of the valley *itself* is often required and that at its outer extremity nearest to the open country, not at its commencement, because there its sides are steeper. Besides, this defence of valleys offers a means of defending mountainous districts, even when the ridge itself affords no position which can be occupied; the rôle which it performs is, therefore, generally greater in proportion as the masses of the mountains are higher and more inaccessible.

The result of all these considerations is, that we must entirely give up the idea of a defensible line more or less regular, and coincident with one of the geological lines, and must look upon a mountain range as merely a surface intersected and broken with inequalities and obstacles strewed over it in the most diversified manner, the features of which we must try to make the best use of which circumstances permit; that therefore, although a knowledge of the geological features of the ground is indispensable to a clear conception of the form of mountain masses, it is of little value in the organisation of defensive measures.

Neither in the war of the Austrian Succession, nor in the Seven Years' War, nor in those of the French Revolution, do we find military dispositions which comprehended a whole mountain system, and in which the defence was systematised in accordance with the leading features of that system. Nowhere do we find armies on the principal ridges always in position on the slopes. Sometimes at a greater, sometimes at a lower elevation; sometimes in one direction, sometimes in another; parallel, at right angles, and obliquely; with and against the watercourse; in lofty mountains, such as the Alps, frequently extended along the valleys; amongst mountains of a inferior class, like the Sudetics (and this is the strangest anomaly), at the middle of the declivity, as it sloped towards the defender, therefore with the principal ridge in front, like the position in which Frederick the Great, in 1762, covered the siege of Schwednitz, with the "hohe Eule" before the front of his camp.

The celebrated positions, Schmotseifen and Landshut, in the Seven Years' War, are for the most part in the bottoms of valleys. It is the same with the position of Feldkirch, in the Vorarlsberg. In the campaigns of 1799 and 1800, the chief posts, both of the French and Austrians, were always quite in the valleys, not merely across them so as to close them, but also parallel with them, whilst the ridges were either not occupied at all, or merely by a few single posts.

The crests of the higher Alps in particular are so difficult of access, and afford so little space for the accommodation of troops, that it would be impossible to place any considerable bodies of men there. Now if we must positively have armies in mountains to keep possession of them, there is nothing to be done but to place them in the valleys. At first sight this appears erroneous, because, in accordance with the prevalent theoretical ideas, it will be said, the heights command the valleys. But that is really not the case. Mountain ridges are only accessible by a few paths and rude tracks, with a few exceptions only passable for infantry, whilst the carriage roads are in the valleys. The enemy can only appear there at certain points with infantry; but in these mountain masses the distances are too great for any effective fire of small arms, and therefore a position in the valleys is less dangerous than it appears. At the same time, the valley defence is exposed to another great danger, that of being cut off. The enemy can, it is true, only descend into the valley with infantry, at certain points, slowly and with great exertion; he cannot, therefore, take us by surprise; but none of the positions we have in the valley defend the outlets of such paths into the valley. The enemy can, therefore, bring down large masses gradually, then spread out, and burst through the thin and from that moment weak line, which, perhaps, has nothing more for its protection than the rocky bed of a shallow mountain-stream. But now retreat, which must always be made piecemeal in a valley, until the outlet from the mountains is reached, is impossible for many parts of the line of troops; and that was the reason that the Austrians in Switzerland almost always lost a third, or a half of their troops taken prisoners. –

Now a few words on the usual way of dividing troops in such a method of defence.

Each of the subordinate positions is in relation with a position taken up by the principal body of troops, more or less in the centre of the whole line, on the principal road of approach. From this central position, other corps are detached right and left to occupy the most important points of approach, and thus the whole is disposed in a line, as it were, of three, four, five, six posts, &c. How far this fractioning and extension of the line shall be carried, must depend on the requirements of each individual case. An extent of a couple of marches, that is, six to eight miles is of moderate length, and we have seen it carried as far as twenty or thirty miles.

Between each of these separate posts, which are one or two leagues from each other, there will probably be some approaches of inferior importance, to which afterwards attention must be directed. Some very good posts for a couple of battalions each are selected, which form a good connection between the chief posts, and they are occupied. It is easy to see that the distribution of the force may be carried still further, and go down to posts occupied only by single companies and squadrons; and this has often happened. There are, therefore, in this no general limits to the extent of fractioning. On the other hand, the strength of each post must depend on the strength of the whole; and therefore we can say nothing as to the possible or natural degree which should be observed with regard to the strength of the principal posts. We shall only append, as a guide, some maxims which are drawn from experience and the nature of the case.

1. The more lofty and inaccessible the mountains are, so much the further this separation of divisions of the force not only may be, *but also must be*, carried; for the less any portion of a country can be kept secure by combinations dependent on the movement of troops, so much the more must the security be obtained by direct covering. The defence of the Alps requires a much greater division of force, and therefore approaches nearer to the cordon system, than the defence of the Vosges or the Giant mountains.

2. Hitherto, wherever defence of mountains has taken place, such a division of the force employed has been made that the chief posts have generally consisted of only one line of infantry, and in a second line, some squadrons of cavalry; at all events, only the chief post established in the centre has perhaps had some battalions in a second line.

3. A strategic reserve, to reinforce any point attacked, has very seldom been kept in rear, because the extension of front made the line feel too weak already in all parts. On this account the support which a post attacked has received, has generally been furnished from other posts in the line not themselves attacked.

4. Even when the division of the forces has been relatively moderate, and the strength of each single post considerable, the principal resistance has been always confined to a local defence; and if once the enemy succeeded in wresting a post, it has been impossible to recover it by any supports afterwards arriving.

How much, according to this, may be expected from mountain defence, in what cases this means may be used, how far we can and may go in the extension and fractioning of the forces – these are all questions which theory must leave to the tact of the general. It is enough if it tells him what these means really are, and what rôle they can perform in the active operations of the army.

A general who allows himself to be beaten in an extended mountain position deserves to be brought before a court martial.

CHAPTER EIGHTEEN

Defence of Streams and Rivers

Streams and large rivers, in so far as we speak of their defence, belong, like mountains, to the category of strategic barriers. But they differ from mountains in two respects. The one concerns their relative, the other their absolute defence.

Like mountains, they strengthen the relative defence; but one of their peculiarities is, that they are like implements of hard and brittle metal, they either stand every blow without bending, or their defence breaks and then ends altogether. If the river is very large, and the other conditions are favourable, then the passage may be absolutely impossible. But if the defence of any river is forced at one point, then there cannot be, as in mountain warfare, a persistent defence afterwards; the affair is finished with that one act, unless that the river itself runs between mountains.

The other peculiarity of rivers in relation to war is, that in many cases they admit of very good, and in general of better combinations than mountains for a decisive battle.

Both again have this property in common, that they are dangerous and seductive objects which have often led to false measures, and placed generals in awkward situations. We shall notice these results in examining more closely the defence of rivers.

Although history is rather bare in examples of rivers defended with success, and therefore the opinion is justified that rivers and streams are no such formidable barriers as was once supposed, when an absolute defensive system seized all means of strengthening itself which the country offered, still the influence which they exercise to the advantage of the battle, as well as of the defence of a country, cannot be denied.

In order to look over the subject in a connected form, we shall specify the different points of view from which we propose to examine it.

First and foremost, the strategic results which streams and rivers produce through their defence, must be distinguished from the influence which they have on the defence of a country, even when not themselves specially defended.

Further, the defence itself may take three different forms: –

1. An absolute defence with the main body.

2. A mere demonstration of resistance.

3. A relative resistance by subordinate bodies of troops, such as outposts, covering lines, flanking corps, etc.

Lastly, we must distinguish three different degrees or kinds of defence, in each of its forms, namely –

1. A direct defence by opposing the passage.

2. A rather indirect one, by which the river and its valley are only used as a means towards a better combination for the battle.

3. A completely direct one, by holding an unassailable position on the enemy's side of the river.

We shall subdivide our observations, in conformity with these three degrees, and after we have made ourselves acquainted with each of them in its relation to the first, which is the most important of the forms, we shall then proceed to do the same in respect to their relations to the other two. Therefore, first, the direct defence, that is, such a defence as is to prevent the passage of the enemy's army itself.

This can only come into the question in relation to large rivers, that is, great bodies of water.

The combinations of space, time, and force, which require to be looked into as elements of this theory of defence, make the subject somewhat complicated, so that it is not easy to gain a sure point from which to commence. The following is the result at which every one will arrive on full consideration.

The time required to build a bridge determines the distance from each other at which the corps charged with the defence of the river should be posted. If we divide the whole length of the line of defence by this distance, we get the number of corps required for the defence; if with that number we divide the mass of troops disposable, we shall get the strength of each corps. If we now compare the strength of each single corps with the number of troops which the enemy, by using all the means in his power, can pass over during the construction of his bridge, we shall be able to judge how far we can expect a successful resistance. For we can only assume the forcing of the passage to be impossible when the defender is able to attack the troops passed over with a *considerable numerical superiority*, say *the double*, before the bridge is completed. An illustration will make this plain.

If the enemy requires twenty-four hours for the construction of a bridge, and if he can by other means only pass over 20,000 men in those twenty-four hours, whilst the defender within twelve hours can appear at any point whatever with 20,000 men, in such case the passage cannot be forced; for the defender will arrive when the enemy engaged in crossing has only passed over the half of 20,000. Now as in twelve hours, the time for conveying intelligence included, we can march four miles, therefore every eight miles 20,000 men would be required, which would make 60,000 for the defence of a length of twenty-four miles of river. These would be sufficient for the appearance of 20,000 men at any point, even if the enemy attempted the passage at two points at the same time; if at only one point twice 20,000 could be brought to oppose him at that single point.

Here, then, there are three circumstances exercising a decisive influence: (1) the breadth of the river; (2) the means of passage, for the two determine both the time required to construct the bridge, and the number of troops that can cross during the time the bridge is being built; (3) the strength of the defender's army. The strength of the enemy's force itself does not as yet come into consideration. According to this theory we may say that there is a point at which the possibility of crossing completely stops, and that no numerical superiority on the part of the enemy would enable him to force a passage.

This is the simple theory of the direct defence of a river, that is, of a defence intended to prevent the enemy from finishing his bridge and from making the passage itself; in this there is as yet no notice taken of the effect of demonstrations which the enemy may use. We shall now bring into consideration particulars in detail, and measures requisite for such a defence.

Setting aside, in the first place, geographical peculiarities, we have only to say that the corps as proposed by the present theory, must be posted close to the river, and each corps in itself concentrated. It must be close to the river, because every position further back lengthens unnecessarily and uselessly the distance to be gone over to any point menaced; for as the waters of the river give security against any important movement on the part of the enemy, a reserve in rear is not required, as it is for an ordinary line of defence, where there is no river in front. Besides, the roads running parallel to and near a river up and down, are generally better than transverse roads from the interior leading to any particular points on the river. Lastly, the river is unquestionably better watched by corps thus placed than by a mere chain of posts, more particularly as the commanders are all close at hand. – Each of these corps must be concentrated in itself, because otherwise all the calculation as to time would require alteration. He who knows the loss of time in effecting a concentration, will easily comprehend that just in this concentrated position lies the great efficacy of the defence. No doubt, at first sight, it is very tempting to make the crossing, even in boats, impossible for the enemy by a line of posts; but with a few exceptions of points, specially favourable for crossing, such a measure would be extremely prejudicial. To say nothing of the objection that the enemy can generally drive off such a post by bringing a superior force to bear on it from the opposite side, it is, as a rule, a waste of strength, that is to say, the most that can be obtained by any such post, is to compel the enemy to choose another point of passage. If, therefore, we are not so strong that we can treat and defend the river like a ditch of a fortress, a case for which no new precept is required, such a method of directly defending the bank of a river leads necessarily away from the proposed object. Besides these general principles for positions, we have to consider – first, the examination of the special peculiarities of the river; second, the removal of all means of passage; third, the influence of any fortresses situated on the river.

A river, considered as a line of defence, must have at the extremities of the line, right and left, *points d'appui*, such as, for instance, the sea, or a neutral territory; or there must be other causes which make it impracticable for the enemy to turn the line of defence by crossing beyond its extremities. Now, as neither such flank supports nor such impediments are to be found, unless at considerable distances, we see at once that the defence of a river must embrace a considerable portion of its length, and that, therefore, the possibility of a defence by placing a large body of troops behind a relatively short length of the river vanishes from the class of possible facts (to which we must always confine ourselves). We say *a relatively short length of the river,* by which we mean a length which does not very much exceed that which the same number of troops would usually occupy on an ordinary position in line without a river. Such cases, we say, do not occur, and every direct defence of a river always becomes a kind of cordon system, at least as far as regards the extension of the troops, and therefore is not at all adapted to oppose a turning movement on the part of the enemy in the same manner which is natural to an army in a concentrated position. Where, therefore, such turning movement is possible, the direct defence of the river, however promising its results in other respects, is a measure in the highest degree dangerous.

Now, as regards the portion of the river between its extreme points, of course we may suppose that all points within that portion are not equally well suited for crossing. This subject admits of being somewhat more precisely determined in the abstract, but not positively fixed, for the very smallest local peculiarity often decides more than all which looks great and important in books. Besides, it is wholly unnecessary to lay down any rules on this subject, for the appearance of the river, and the information to be obtained from those residing near it, will always amply suffice, without referring back to books.

As matters of detail, we may observe that roads leading down upon a river, its affluents, the great towns through which it passes, and lastly above all, its islands, generally favour a passage the most; that on the other hand, the elevation of one bank over another, and the bend in the course of the river at the point of passage, which usually act such a prominent rôle in books, are seldom of any consequence. The reason of this is, that the presumed influence of these two things rests on the limited idea of an absolute defence of the river bank – a case which seldom or never happens in connection with great rivers.

Now, whatever may be the nature of the circumstances which make it easier to cross a river at particular points, they must have an influence on the position of the troops, and modify the general geometrical law; but it is not advisable to deviate too far from that law, relying on the difficulties of the passage at many points. The enemy would choose exactly those spots which are the least favourable by nature for crossing, if he knew that these are the points where there is the least likelihood of meeting us.

In any case the strongest possible occupation of islands is a measure to be recommended, because a serious attack on an island indicates in the surest way the intended point of passage.

As the corps stationed close to a river must be able to move either up or down along its banks according as circumstances require, therefore if there is no road parallel to the river, one of the most essential preparatory measures for the defence of the river is to put the nearest small roads running in a parallel direction into suitable order, and to construct such short roads of connection as may be necessary.

The second point on which we have to speak, is the removal of the means of crossing. – On the river itself the thing is no easy matter, at least requires considerable time; but on the affluents which fall into the river, particularly those on the enemy's side, the difficulties are almost insurmountable, as these branch rivers are generally already in the hands of the enemy. For that reason it is important to close the mouths of such rivers by fortifications.

As the equipment for crossing rivers which an enemy brings with him, that is his pontoons, are rarely sufficient for the passage of great rivers, much depends on the means to be found on the river itself, its affluents, and in the great towns adjacent, and lastly, on the timber for building boats and rafts in forests near the river. There are cases in which all these circumstances are so unfavourable, that the crossing of a river is by that means almost an impossibility.

Lastly, the fortresses, which lie on both sides, or on the enemy's side of the river, serve both to prevent any crossing at any points near them, up or down the river, and as a means of closing the mouths of affluents, as well as to receive immediately all craft or boats which may be seized.

So much as to the direct defence of a river, on the supposition that it is one containing a great volume of water. If a deep valley with precipitous sides or marshy banks, are added to the barrier of the river itself, then the difficulty of passing and the strength of the defence are certainly increased; but the volume of water is not made up for by such obstacles, for they constitute no absolute severance of the country, which is an *indispensable* condition of direct defence.

If we are asked what rôle such a direct river defence can play in the strategic plan of the campaign, we must admit that it can never lead to a decisive victory, partly because the object is not to let the enemy pass over to our side at all, or to crush the first mass of any size which passes; partly because the river prevents our being able to convert the advantages gained into a decisive victory by sallying forth in force.

On the other hand, the defence of a river in this way may produce a great gain of time, which is generally all important for the defensive. The collecting the means of crossing, takes up often much time; if several attempts fail a good deal more time is gained. If the enemy, on account of the river, gives his forces an entirely different direction, then still further advantages may be gained by that means. Lastly, whenever the enemy is not in downright earnest about advancing, a river will occasion a stoppage in his movements and thereby afford a durable protection to the country.

A direct defence of a river, therefore, when the masses of troops engaged are considerable, the river large, and other circumstances favourable, may be regarded as a very good defensive means, and may yield results to which commanders in modern times (influenced only by the thought of unfortunate attempts to defend rivers, which failed from insufficient means), have paid too little attention. For if, in accordance with the supposition just made (which may easily be realized in connection with such rivers as the Rhine or the Danube), an efficient defence of 24 miles of river is possible by 60,000 men in face of a very considerably superior force, we may well say that such a result deserves consideration.

We say, in opposition to a *considerably superior force*, and must again recur to that point. According to the theory we have propounded, all depends on the means of crossing, and nothing on the numerical strength of the force seeking to cross, always supposing it is not less than the force which defends the river. This appears very extraordinary, and yet it is true. But we must take care not to forget that most defences of rivers, or, more properly speaking, the whole, have no absolute *points d'appui*, therefore, may be turned, and this turning movement will be very much easier if the enemy has very superior numbers.

If now we reflect that such a direct defence of a river, even if overcome by the enemy, is by no means to be compared to a lost battle, and can still less lead to a complete defeat, since only a part of our force has been engaged, and the enemy, detained by the tedious crossing over of his troops on a single bridge, cannot immediately follow up his victory, we shall be the less disposed to despise this means of defence.

In all the practical affairs of human life it is important to hit the right point; and so also, in the defence of a river, it makes a great difference whether we rightly appreciate our situation in all its relations; an apparently insignificant circumstance may essentially alter the case, and make a measure which is wise and effective in one instance, a disastrous mistake in another. This difficulty of forming a right judgment and of avoiding the notion that "a river is a river" is perhaps greater here than anywhere else, therefore we must especially guard against false applications and interpretations; but having done so, we have also no hesitation in plainly declaring that we do not think it worth while to listen to the cry of those who, under the influence of some vague feeling, and without any fixed idea, expect everything from attack and movement, and think they see the most true picture of war in a hussar at full gallop brandishing his sword over his head.

Such ideas and feelings are not always all that is required (we shall only instance here the once famous dictator Wedel, at Zullichau, in 1759); but the worst of all is that they are seldom durable, and they forsake the general at the last moment if great complex cases branching out into a thousand relations bear heavily upon him.

We therefore believe that a direct defence of a river with large bodies of troops, under favourable conditions, can lead to successful results if we content ourselves with a moderate negative: but this does not hold good in the case of smaller masses. Although 60,000 men on a certain length of river could prevent an army of 100,000 or more from passing, a corps of 10,000 on the same length would not be able to oppose the passage of a corps of 10,000 men, indeed, probably, not of one half that strength if such a body chose to run the risk of placing itself on the same side of the river with an enemy so much superior in numbers. The case is clear, as the means of passing do not alter.

We have as yet said little about feints or demonstrations of crossing, as they do not essentially come into consideration in the direct defence of a river, for partly such defence is not a question of concentration of the army at one point, but each corps has the defence of a portion of the river distinctly allotted to it; partly such simulated intentions of crossing are also very difficult under the circumstances we have supposed. If, for instance, the means of crossing in themselves are already limited, that is, not in such abundance as the assailant must desire to ensure the success of his undertaking, he will then hardly be able or willing to apply a large share to a mere demonstration: at all events the mass of troops to be passed over at the true point of crossing must be so much the less, and the defender gains again in time what through uncertainty he may have lost.

This direct defence, as a rule, seems only suitable to large rivers, and on the last half of their course.

The second form of defence is suitable for smaller rivers with deep valleys, often also for very unimportant ones. It consists in a position taken up further back from the river at such a distance that the enemy's army may either be caught in detail after the passage (if it passes at several points at the same time) or if the passage is made by the whole at one point, then near the river, hemmed in upon one bridge and road. An army with the rear pressed close against a river or a deep valley, and confined to one line of retreat, is in a most disadvantageous position for battle; in the making proper use of this circumstance, consists precisely the most efficacious defence of rivers of moderate size, and running in deep valleys.

The disposition of an army in large corps close to a river which we consider the best in a direct defence, supposes that the enemy cannot pass the river unexpectedly and in great force, because otherwise, by making such a disposition, there would be great danger of being beaten in detail. If, therefore, the circumstances which favour the defence are not sufficiently advantageous, if the enemy has already in hand ample means of crossing, if the river has many islands or fords, if it is not broad enough, if we are too weak, etc., etc., then the idea of that method may be dismissed: the troops for the more secure connection with each other must be drawn back a little from the river, and all that then remains to do is to ensure the most rapid concentration possible upon that point where the enemy attempts to cross, so as to be able to attack him before he has gained so much ground that he has the command of several passages. In the present case the river or its valley must be watched and partially defended by a chain of outposts whilst the army is disposed in several corps at suitable points and at a certain distance (usually a few leagues) from the river.

The most difficult point lies here in the passage through the narrow way formed by the river and its valley. It is not now only the volume of water in the river with which we are concerned, but the whole of the defile, and, as a rule, a deep rocky valley is a greater impediment to pass than a river of considerable breadth. The difficulty of the march of a large body of troops through a long defile is in reality much greater than appears at first consideration. The time required is very considerable; and the danger that the enemy during the march may make himself master of the surrounding heights must cause disquietude. If the troops in front advance too far, they encounter the enemy too soon, and are in danger of being overpowered; if they remain near the point of passage then they fight in the worst situation. The passage across such an obstacle of ground with a view to measure strength with the enemy on the opposite side is, therefore, a bold undertaking, or it implies very superior numbers and great confidence in the commander.

Such a defensive line cannot certainly be extended to such a length as in the direct defence of a great river, for it is intended to fight with the whole force united, and the passages, however difficult, cannot be compared in that respect with those over a large river; it is, therefore, much easier for the enemy to make a turning movement against us. But at the same time, such a movement carries him out of his natural direction (for we suppose, as is plain in itself, that the valley crosses that direction at about right angles), and the disadvantageous effect of a confined line of retreat only disappears gradually, not at once, so that the defender will still always have some advantage over the advancing foe, although the latter is not caught exactly at the crisis of the passage, but by the detour he makes is enabled to get a little more room to move.

As we are not speaking of rivers in connection only with the mass of their waters, but have rather more in view the deep cleft or channel formed by their valleys, we must explain that under the term we do not mean any regular mountain gorge, because then all that has been said about mountains would be applicable. But, as every one knows, there are many level districts where the channels of even the smallest streams have deep and precipitous sides; and, besides these, such as have marshy banks, or whose banks are otherwise difficult of approach, belong to the same class.

Under these conditions, therefore, an army on the defensive, posted behind a large river or deep valley with steep sides, is in a very excellent position, and this sort of river defence is a strategic measure of the best kind.

Its defect (the point on which the defender is very apt to err) is the over-extension of the defending force. It is so natural in such a case to be drawn on from one point of passage to another, and to miss the right point where we ought to stop; but then, if we do not succeed in fighting with the whole army united, we miss the intended effect; a defeat in battle, the necessity of retreat, confusion in many ways and losses reduce the army nearly to ruin, even although the resistance has not been pushed to an extremity.

In saying that the defensive, under the above conditions, should not extend his forces widely, that he should be in any case able to assemble all his forces on the evening of the day on which the enemy passes, enough is said, and it may stand in place of all combinations of time, power, and space, things which, in this case, must depend on many local points.

The battle to which these circumstances lead must have a special character – that of the greatest impetuosity on the side of the defender. The feigned passages by which the enemy will keep him for some time in uncertainty – will, in general prevent his discovering the real point of crossing a moment too soon. The peculiar advantages of the situation of the defender consist in the disadvantageous situation of the enemy's corps just immediately in his front; if other corps, having passed at other points, menace his flank, he cannot, as in a defensive battle, counteract such movements by vigorous blows from his rear, for that would be to sacrifice the above-mentioned advantage of his situation; he must, therefore, decide the affair in his front before such other corps can arrive and become dangerous, that is, he must attack what he has before him as swiftly and vigorously as possible, and decide all by its defeat.

But the object of *this* form of river defence can never be the repulse of a very greatly superior force, as is conceivable in the direct defence of a large river; for as a rule we have really to deal with the bulk of the enemy's force, and although we do so under favourable circumstances, still it is easy to see the relation between the forces must soon be felt.

This is the nature of the defence of rivers of a moderate size and deep valleys when the principal masses of the armies are concerned, for in respect to them the considerable resistance which can be offered on the ridges or scarps of the valley stands no comparison with the disadvantages of a scattered position, and to them a decisive victory is a matter of necessity. But if nothing more is wanted but the reinforcement of a secondary line of defence which is intended to hold out for a short time, and which can calculate on support, then certainly a direct defence of the scarps of the valley, or even of the river bank, may be made; and although the same advantages are not to be expected here as in mountain positions, still the resistance will always last longer than in an ordinary country. Only one circumstance makes this measure very dangerous, if not impossible: it is when the river has many windings and sharp turnings, which is just what is often the case when a river runs in a deep valley, Only look at the course of the Mosel. In a case of its defence, the corps in advance on the salients of the bends would almost inevitably be lost in the event of a retreat.

That a great river allows the same defensive means, the same form of defence, which we have pointed out as best suited for rivers of a moderate size, in connection with the mass of an army, and also under much more favourable circumstances, is plain of itself. It will come into use more especially when the point with the defender is to gain a decisive victory (Aspern).

The case of an army drawn up with its front close on a river, or stream, or deep valley, in order by that means to command a tactical obstacle to the approach to its position, or to strengthen its front, is quite a different one, the detailed examination of which belongs to tactics. Of the effect of this we shall only say this much, that it is founded on a delusion. – If the cleft in the ground is very considerable, the front of the position becomes absolutely unassailable. Now, as there is no more difficulty in passing round such a position than any other, it is just the same as if the defender had himself gone out of the way of the assailant, yet that could hardly be the object of the position. A position of this kind can, therefore, only be advisable when, as a consequence of its position, it threatens the communications of the assailant, so that every deviation by him from the direct road is fraught with consequences altogether too serious to be risked.

In this second form of defence, feigned passages are much more dangerous, for the assailant can make them more easily, while, on the other hand, the proposition for the defender is, to assemble his whole army at the right point. But the defender is certainly not quite so much limited for time here, because the advantage of his situation lasts until the assailant has massed his whole force, and made himself master of several crossings; moreover, also, the simulated attack has not the same degree of effect here as in the defence of a cordon, where all must be held, and where, therefore, in the application of the reserve, it is not merely a question, as in our proposition, where the enemy has his principal force, but the much more difficult one, Which is the point he will first seek to force?

With respect to both forms of defence of large and small rivers, we must observe generally, that if they are undertaken in the haste and confusion of a retreat, without preparation, without the removal of all means of passage, and without an exact knowledge of the country, they cannot certainly fulfil what has been here supposed; in most such cases, nothing of the kind is to be calculated upon; and therefore it will be always a great error for an army to divide itself over extended positions.

As everything usually miscarries in war, if it is not done upon clear convictions and with the whole will and energy, so a *river defence* will generally end badly when it is only resorted to because we have not the heart to meet the enemy in the open field, and hope that the broad river or the deep valley will stop him. When that is the case, there is so little confidence in the actual situation that both the general and his army are usually filled with anxious forebodings, which are almost sure to be realized quick enough. A battle in the open field does not suppose a perfectly equal state of circumstances beforehand, like a duel; and the defender who does not know how to gain for himself any advantages, either through the special nature of the defence, through rapid marches, or by knowledge of the country and freedom of movement, is one whom nothing can save, and least of all will a river or its valley be able to help him.

The third form of defence – by a strong position taken up on the enemy's side of the river – founds its efficacy on the danger in which it places the enemy of having his communications cut by the river, and being thus limited to some bridges. It follows, as a matter of course, that we are only speaking of great rivers with a great volume of water, as these alone can lead to such results, whilst a river which is merely in a deep ravine usually affords such a number of passages that all danger of the above disappears.

But the position of the defensive must be very strong, almost unassailable; otherwise he would just meet the enemy half way, and give up his advantages. But if it is of such strength that the enemy resolves not to attack it, he will, under certain circumstances, be confined thereby to the same bank with the defender. If the assailant crosses, he exposes his communications; but certainly, at the same time, he threatens ours. Here, as in all cases in which one army passes by another, the great point is, whose communications, by their number, situation, and other circumstances, are the best secured, and which has also, in other respects, most to lose, therefore can be outbid by his opponent; lastly, which possesses still in his army the most power of victory upon which he can depend in an extreme case. The influence of the river merely amounts to this, that it augments the danger of such a movement for both parties, as both are dependent on bridges. Now, in so far as we can assume that, according to the usual course of things, the passage of the defender, as well as of his depôts of all kinds, are better secured by fortresses than those of the offensive, in so far is such a defence conceivable, and one which might be substituted for the direct defence when circumstances are not favourable to that form. Certainly then the river is not defended by the army, nor the army by the river, but by the connection between the two the country is defended, which is the main point.

At the same time it must be granted that this mode of defence, without a decisive blow, and resembling the state of tension of two electric currents, of which the atmospheres only are as yet in contact, cannot stop any very powerful impulsive force. It might be applicable against even a great superiority of force on the side of the enemy, if their army is commanded by a cautious general, wanting in decision, and never disposed to push forward with energy; it might also answer when a kind of oscillation towards equality between the contending forces has previously arisen, and nothing but small advantages are looked for on either side. But if we have to deal with superior forces, led by a bold general, we are upon a dangerous course, very close to an abyss.

This form of defence looks so bold, and at the same time so scientific, that it might be called the elegant; but as elegance easily merges into folly, and as it is not so easily excused in war as in society, therefore we have had as yet few instances of this elegant art. From this third mode a special means of assistance for the first two forms is developed, that is, by the permanent occupation of a bridge and a *tête du pont* to keep up a constant threat of crossing.

Besides the object of an absolute defence with the main body, each of the three modes of defence may also have that of *a feigned defence.*

This show of a resistance, which it is not intended really to offer, is an act which is combined with many other measures, and fundamentally with every position which is anything more than a camp of route; but the feigned defence of a great river becomes a complete stratagem in this way, that it is necessary to adopt actually more or less a number of measures of detail, and that its action is usually on a greater scale and of longer duration than that of any other; for the act of passing a great river in sight of an army is always an important step for the assailant, one over which he often ponders long, or which he postpones to a more favourable moment.

For such a feigned defence it is therefore requisite that the main army should divide and post itself along the river, (much in the same manner as for a real defence); but as the intention of a mere demonstration shows that circumstances are not favourable enough for a real defence, therefore, from that measure as it always occasions a more or less extended and scattered disposition, the danger of serious loss may very easily arise if the corps should get engaged in a real resistance, even if not carried to an extremity; it would then be in the true sense a half measure. In a demonstration of defence, therefore, arrangement must be made for a sure concentration of the army at a point considerably (perhaps several days' march) in rear, and the defence should not be carried beyond what is consistent with this arrangement.

In order to make our views plainer, and to show the importance of such a defensive demonstration, let us refer to the end of the campaign of 1813. Buonaparte repassed the Rhine with forty or fifty thousand men. To attempt to defend this river with such a force at all points where the Allies, according to the direction of their forces, might easily pass, that is, between Manheim and Nimeguen, would have been to attempt an impossibility. The only idea which Buonaparte could therefore entertain was to offer his first real resistance somewhere on the French Meuse, where he could make his appearance with his army in some measure reinforced. Had he at once withdrawn his forces to that point, the Allies would have followed close at his heels; had he placed his army in cantonments for rest behind the Rhine, the same thing must have taken place almost as soon, for at the least show of desponding caution on his part, the Allies would have sent over swarms of Cossacks and other light troops in pursuit, and, if that measure produced good results, other corps would have followed. The French corps had therefore nothing for it but to take steps to defend the Rhine in earnest. As Buonaparte could foresee that this defence must end in nothing whenever, the Allies seriously undertook to cross the river, it may therefore be regarded in the light of a mere demonstration, in which the French corps incurred hardly any danger, as their point of concentration lay on the Upper Moselle. Only Macdonald, who, as is known, was at Nimeguen with twenty thousand men, committed a mistake in deferring his retreat till fairly compelled to retire, for this delay prevented his joining Buonaparte before the battle of Brienne, as the retreat was not forced on him until after the arrival of Winzurgerode's corps in January. This defensive demonstration on the Rhine, therefore, produced the result of checking the Allies in their advance, and induced them to postpone the crossing of the river until their reinforcements arrived, which did not take place for six weeks. These six weeks were of infinite value to Buonaparte. Without this defensive demonstration on the Rhine, Paris would have become the next immediate object after the victory of Leipsic, and it would have been impossible for the French to have given battle on that side of their capital.

In a river defence of the second class, therefore, in that of rivers of a smaller size, such demonstrations may also be used, but they will generally be less effectual, because mere attempts to cross are in such a case easier, and therefore the spell is sooner broken.

In the third kind of river defence, a demonstration would in all probability be still less effectual, and produce no more result than that of the occupation of any other temporary position.

Lastly, the two first forms of defence are very well suited to give a chain of outposts, or any other defensive line (cordon) established for a secondary object, or to a corps of observation, much greater and more reliable strength than it would have without the river. In all these cases the question is limited to a relative resistance, and that must naturally be considerably strengthened by such a great natural obstacle. At the same time, we must not think only of the relative quantity of time gained by the resistance in fight in a case of this sort, but also of the many anxieties which such undertakings usually excite in the mind of the enemy, and which in ninety-nine cases out of a hundred lead to his giving up his plans if not urged or pressed by necessity.

CHAPTER NINETEEN
Defence of Streams and Rivers (Continued.)

WE HAVE STILL to add something respecting the influence of streams and rivers on the defence of a country, even when they are not themselves defended.

Every important river, with its main valley and its adjacent valleys, forms a very considerable obstacle in a country, and in that way it is, therefore, advantageous to defence in general; but its peculiar influence admits of being more particularly specified in its principal effects.

First we must distinguish whether it flows parallel to the frontier, that is, the general strategic front, or at an oblique or a right angle to it. In the case of the parallel direction we must observe the difference between having our own army or that of the enemy behind it, and in both cases again the distance between it and the army.

An army on the defensive, having behind it a large river within easy reach (but not less than a day's march), and on that river an adequate number of secure crossings, is unquestionably in a much stronger situation than it would be without the river; for if it loses a little in freedom of movement by the requisite care for the security of the crossings, still it gains much more by the security of its strategic rear, that means chiefly of its lines of communication. In all this we allude to a defence in *our own country;* for in the enemy's country, although his army might be before us, we should still have always more or less to apprehend his appearance behind us on the other side of the river, and then the river, involving as it does narrow defiles in roads, would be more disadvantageous than otherwise in its effect on our situation. The further the river is behind the army, the less useful it will be, and at certain distances its influence disappears altogether.

If an advancing army has to leave a river in its rear, the river cannot be otherwise than prejudicial to its movements, for it restricts the communications of the army to a few single passages. When Prince Henry marched against the Russians on the right bank of the Oder near Breslau, he had plainly a *point d'appui* in the Oder flowing behind him at a day's march; on the other hand, when the Russians under Cznernitschef passed the Oder subsequently, they were in a very embarrassing situation, just through the risk of losing their line of retreat, which was limited to one bridge.

If a river crosses the theatre of war more or less at a right angle with the strategic front, then the advantage is again on the side of the defensive; for, in the first place, there are generally a number of good positions leaning on the river, and covered in front by the transverse valleys connected with the principal valley (like the Elbe for the Prussians in the Seven Years' War); secondly, the assailant must leave one side of the river or the other unoccupied, or he must divide his forces; and such division cannot fail to be in favour again of the defensive, because he will be in possession of more well secured passages than the assailant. We need only cast a glance over the whole Seven Years' War, to be convinced that the Oder and Elbe were very useful to Frederick the Great in the defence of his theatre of war (namely Silesia, Saxony and the Mark), and consequently a great impediment to the conquest of these provinces by the Austrians and Russians, although there was no real defence of those rivers in the whole Seven Years' War, and their course is mostly, as connected with the enemy, at an oblique or a right angle rather than parallel with the front.

It is only the convenience of a river as a means of transport, when its course is more or less in a perpendicular direction, which can, in general, be advantageous to the assailant; in that respect it may be so for this reason, that as he has the longer line of communication, and, therefore, the greater difficulty in the transport of all he requires, water carriage may relieve him of a great deal of trouble and prove very useful. The defender, on his side, certainly has it in his power to close the navigation within his own frontier by fortresses; still even by that means the advantages which the river affords the assailant will not be lost so far as regards its course up to that frontier. But if we reflect upon the fact that many rivers are often not navigable, even where they are of no unimportant breadth as respects other military relations, that others are not navigable at all seasons, that the ascent against the stream is tedious, that the winding of a river often doubles its length, that the chief communications between countries now are high roads, and that now more than ever the wants of an army are supplied from the country adjacent to the scene of its operations, and not by carriage from distant parts, – we can well see that the use of a river does not generally play such a prominent part in the subsistence of troops as is usually represented in books, and that its influence on the march of events is therefore very remote and uncertain.

CHAPTER TWENTY

A. Defence of Swamps

VERY LARGE WIDE swamps, such as the Bourtang Moor in North Germany, are so uncommon that it is not worth while to lose time over them; but we must not forget that certain lowlands and marshy banks of small rivers are more common, and form very considerable obstacles of ground which may be, and often have been, used for defensive purposes.

Measures for their defence are certainly very like those for the defence of rivers, at the same time there are some peculiarties to be specially noticed. The first and principal one is, that a marsh which except on the causeway is impracticable for infantry is much more difficult to cross than any river; for, in the first place, a causeway is not so soon built as a bridge; secondly, there are no means at hand by which the troops to cover the construction of the dyke or causeway can be sent across. No one would begin to build a bridge without using some of the boats to send over an advanced guard in the first instance; but in the case of a morass no similar assistance can be employed; the easiest way to make a crossing for infantry over a morass is by means of planks, but when the morass is of some width, this is a much more tedious process than the crossing of the first boats on a river. If now, besides, there is in the middle of the morass a river which cannot be passed without a bridge, the crossing of the first detachment of troops becomes a still more difficult affair, for although single passengers may get across on boards, the heavy material required for bridge building cannot be so transported. This difficulty on many occasions may be insurmountable.

A second peculiarity of a swamp is, that the means used to cross cannot be completely removed like those, used for passing a river; bridges may be broken, or so completely destroyed that they can never be used again; the most that can be done with dykes is to cut them, which is not doing much. If there is a river in the middle, the bridge can of course be taken away, but the whole passage will not by that means be destroyed in the same degree as that of a large river by the destruction of a bridge. The natural consequence is that dykes which exist must always be occupied in force and strenuously defended if we desire to derive any general advantage from the morass.

On the one hand, therefore, we are compelled to adopt a local defence, and on the other, such a defence is favoured by the difficulty of passing at other parts. From these two peculiarities the result is, that the defence of a swamp must be more local and passive than that of a river.

It follows from this that we must be stronger in a relative degree than in the direct defence of a river, consequently that the line of defence must not be of great length, especially in cultivated countries, where the number of passages, even under the most favourable circumstances for defence, is still very great.

In this respect, therefore, swamps are inferior to great rivers, and this is a point of great importance, for all local defence is illusory and dangerous to an extreme. But if we reflect that such swamps and low grounds generally have a breadth with which that of the largest rivers in Europe bears no comparison, and that consequently a post stationed for the defence of a passage is never in danger of being overpowered by the fire from the other side, that the effects of its own fire over a long narrow dyke is greatly increased, and that the time required to pass such a defile, perhaps a quarter or half a mile long, is much longer than would suffice to pass an ordinary bridge: if we consider all this, we must admit that such low lands and morasses, if means of crossing are not too numerous, belong to the strongest lines of defence which can be formed.

An indirect defence, such as we made ourselves acquainted with in the case of streams and rivers, in which obstacles of ground are made use of to bring on a great battle under advantageous circumstances, is generally quite as applicable to morasses.

The third method of a river-defence by means of a position on the enemy's side would be too hazardous on account of the toilsome nature of the crossing.

It is extremely dangerous to venture on the defence of such morasses, soft meadows, bogs, etc., as are not quite impassable beyond the dykes. One single line of crossing discovered by the enemy is sufficient to pierce the whole line of defence which, in case of a serious resistance, is always attended with great loss to the defender.

B. Inundations

Now we have still to consider inundations. As defensive means and also as phenomena in the natural world they have unquestionably the nearest resemblance to morasses.

They are not common certainly; perhaps Holland is the only country in Europe where they constitute a phenomenon which makes them worth notice in connection with our object; but just that country, on account of the remarkable campaigns of 1672 and 1787, as well as on account of its important relation in itself to both France and Germany, obliges us to devote some consideration to this matter.

The character of these Dutch inundations differs from ordinary swampy and impassable wet low lands in the following respects: –

1. The soil itself is dry and consists either of dry meadows or of cultivated fields.

2. For purposes of irrigation or of drainage, a number of small ditches of greater or loss depth and breadth intersect the country in such a way that they may be seen running in lines in parallel directions.

3. Larger canals, inclosed by dykes and intended for irrigation, drainage, and transit of vessels, run through the country in all possible directions and are of such a size that they can only be passed on bridges.

4. The level of the ground throughout the whole district subject to inundation, lies perceptibly under the level of the sea, therefore, of course, under that of the canals.

5. The consequence of this is, that by means of cutting the dams, closing and opening the sluices, the whole country can be laid under water, so that there are no dry roads except on the tops of the dykes, all others being either entirely under water or, at least, so soaked that they become no longer fit for use. Now, if even the inundation is only three or four feet deep, so that, perhaps, for short distances it might be waded through, still even that is made impossible on account of the smaller ditches mentioned under No. 2, which are not visible. It is only where these ditches have a corresponding direction, so that we can move between two of them without crossing either, that the inundation does not constitute in effect an absolute bar to all communication. It is easy to conceive that this exception to the general obstruction can only be for short distances, and, therefore, can only be used for tactical purposes of an entirely special character.

From all this we deduce –

1. That the assailant's means of moving are limited to a more or less small number of practicable lines, which run along very narrow dykes, and usually have a wet ditch on the right and left, consequently form very long defiles.

2. That every defensive preparation upon such a dam may be easily strengthened to such a degree as to become impregnable.

3. But that, because the defensive is so hemmed in, he must confine himself to the most passive resistance as respects each isolated point, and consequently must look for his safety entirely from passive resistance.

4. That in such a country it is not a system of a single defensive line, closing the country like a simple barrier, but that as in every direction the same obstacle to movement exists, and the same security for flanks may be found, new posts may incessantly be formed, and in this manner any portion of the first defensive line, if lost, may be replaced by a new piece. We may say that the number of combinations here, like those on a chessboard, are infinite.

5. But while this general condition of a country is only conceivable along with the supposition of a high degree of cultivation and a dense population, it follows of itself that the number of passages, and therefore the number of posts required or their defence, must be very great in comparison to other strategetic dispositions; from which again we have, as a consequence, that such a defensive line must not be long.

The principal line of defence in Holland is from Naarden on the Zuyder Zee (the greater part of the way behind the Vecht), to Gorcum on the Waal, that is properly to the Biesbosch, its extent being about eight miles. For the defence of this line a force of 25,000 to 30,000 was employed in 1672, and again in 1787. If we could reckon with certainty upon an invincible resistance, the results would certainly be very great, at least for the provinces of Holland lying behind that line.

In 1672 the line actually withstood very superior forces led by great generals, first Condé, and afterwards Luxembourg, who had under their command 40,000 to 50,000 men, and yet would not assault, preferring to wait for the winter, which did not prove severe enough. On the other hand, the resistance which was made on this first line in 1787 amounted to nothing, and even that which was made by a second line much shorter, between the Zuyder Zee and the lake of Haarlem, although somewhat more effective, was overcome by the Duke of Brunswick in one day, through a very skilful tactical disposition well adapted to the locality, and this although the Prussian force actually engaged in the attack was little, if at all, superior in numbers to the troops guarding the lines.

The different result in the two cases is to be attributed to the difference in the supreme command. In the year 1672 the Dutch were surprised by Louis XIV., while everything was on a peace establishment, in which, as is well known, there breathed very little military spirit as far as concerned land forces. For that reason the greater number of the fortresses were deficient in all articles of material and equipment, garrisoned only by weak bodies of hired troops, and defended by governors who were either native-born incapables, or treacherous foreigners. Thus all the Brandenburg fortresses on the Rhine, garrisoned by Dutch, as well as all their own places situated to the east of the line of defence above described, except Groningen, very soon fell into the hands of the French, and for the most part without any real defence. And in the conquest of this great number of places consisted the chief exertions of the French army, 150,000 strong, at that time.

But when, after the murder of the brothers De Witt, in August 1672, the Prince of Orange came to the head of affairs, bringing unity to the measures for national defence, there was still time to close the defensive line above-mentioned, and all the measures then adopted harmonised so well with each other that neither Condé nor Luxembourg, who commanded the French armies left in Holland after the departure of the two armies under Turenne and Louis in person, would venture to attempt anything against the separate posts.

In the year 1787 all was different. It was not the Republic of seven united provinces, but only the province of Holland which had to resist the invasion. The conquest of all the fortresses, which had been the principal object in 1672, was therefore not the question; the defence was confined at once to the line we have described. But the assailant this time, instead of 150,000 men, had only 25,000, and was no mighty sovereign of a great country adjoining Holland, but the subordinate general of a distant prince, himself by no means independent in many respects. The people in Holland, like those everywhere else at that time, were divided into two parties, but the republican spirit in Holland was decidedly predominant, and had at the same time attained even to a kind of enthusiastic excitement. Under these circumstances the resistance in the year 1787 ought to have ensured at least as great results as that of 1672. But there was one important difference, which is, that in the year 1787 unity of command was entirely wanting. What in 1672 had been left to the wise, skilful, and energetic guidance of the Prince of Orange, was entrusted to a so called Defence Commission in 1787, which although it included in its number men of energy, was not in a position to infuse into its work the requisite unity of measures, and to inspire others with that confidence which was wanted to prevent the whole instrument from proving imperfect and inefficient in use.

We have dwelt for a moment on this example, in order to give more distinctness to the conception of this defensive measure, and at the same time to show the difference in the effects produced, according as more or less unity and sequence prevail in the direction of the whole.

Although the organisation and method of defence of such a defensive line are tactical subjects, still, in connection with the latter, which is the nearest allied to strategy, we cannot omit to make an observation to which the campaign of 1787 gives occasion.

We think, namely, that however passive the defence must naturally be at each point in a line of this kind, still an offensive action from some one point of the line is not impossible, and may not be unproductive of good results if the enemy, as was the case in 1787, is not decidedly very superior. For although such an attack must be executed by means of dykes, and on that account cannot certainly have the advantage of much freedom of movement or of any great impulsive force, nevertheless, it is impossible for the offensive side to occupy all the dykes and roads which he does not require for his own purposes, and therefore the defensive with his better knowledge of the country, and being in possession of the strong points, should be able by some of the unoccupied dykes to effect a real flank attack against the columns of the assailant, or to cut them off from their sources of supply. If now, on the other hand, we reflect for a moment on the constrained position in which the assailant is placed, how much more dependent he is on his communications than in almost any other conceivable case, we may well imagine that every sally on the part of the defensive side which has the remotest possibility of success must at once as a demonstration be most effective. We doubt very much if the prudent and cautious duke of Brunswick would have ventured to approach Amsterdam if the Dutch had only made such a demonstration, from Utrecht for instance.

CHAPTER TWENTY ONE
Defence of Forests

ABOVE ALL THINGS we must distinguish thick tangled and impassable forests from extensive woods under a certain degree of culture, which are partly quite clear, partly intersected by numerous roads.

Whenever the object is to form a defensive line, the latter should be left in rear or avoided as much as possible. The defensive requires more than the assailant to see clearly round him, partly because, as a rule, he is the weaker, partly because the natural advantages of his position cause him to develop his plans later than the assailant. If he should place a woody district before him he would be fighting like a blind man against one with his eyesight. If he should place himself in the middle of the wood then both would be blind, but that equality of condition is just what would not answer the natural requirements of the defender.

Such a wooded country can therefore not be brought into any favourable connection with the defensive except it is kept in rear of the defender's army, so as to conceal from the enemy all that takes place behind that army, and at the same time to be available as an assistance to cover and facilitate the retreat.

At present we only speak of forests in level country, for where the decided mountain character enters into combination, its influence becomes predominant over tactical and strategic measures, and we have already treated of those subjects elsewhere.

But impassable forests, that is, such as can only be traversed on certain roads, afford advantages in an indirect defence similar to those which the defence derives from mountains for bringing on a battle under favourable circumstances; the army can await the enemy behind the wood in a more or less concentrated position with a view to falling on him the moment he debouches from the road defiles. Such a forest resembles mountain in its effects more than a river: for it affords, it is true, only one very long and difficult defile, but it is in respect to the retreat rather advantageous than otherwise.

But a direct defence of forests, let them be ever so impracticable, is a very hazardous piece of work for even the thinnest chain of outposts; for abattis are only imaginary barriers, and no wood is so completely impassable that it cannot be penetrated in a hundred places by small detachments, and these, in their relation to a chain of defensive posts, may be likened to the first drops of water which ooze through a roof and are soon followed by a general rush of water.

Much more important is the influence of great forests of every kind in connection with the arming of a nation; they are undoubtedly the true element for such levies; if, therefore, the strategic plan of defence can be so arranged that the enemy's communications pass through great forests, then, by that means, another mighty lever is brought into use in support of the work of defence.

CHAPTER TWENTY TWO

The Cordon

THE TERM CORDON is used to denote every defensive plan which is intended directly to cover a whole district of country by a line of posts in connection with each other. We say *directly*, for several corps of a great army posted in line with each other might protect a large district of country from invasion without forming a cordon; but then this protection would not be direct, but through the effect of combinations and movements.

It is evident at a glance that such a long defensive line as that must be, which is to cover an extensive district of country directly, can only have a very small degree of defensive stamina. Even when very large bodies of troops occupy the lines this would be the case if they were attacked by corresponding masses. The object of a cordon can therefore only be to resist a weak blow, whether that the weakness proceeds from a feeble will or the smallness of the force employed.

With this view the wall of China was built: a protection against the inroads of Tartars. This is the intention of all lines and frontier defences of the European States bordering on Asia and Turkey. Applied in this way the cordon system is neither absurd nor does it appear unsuitable to its purpose. Certainly it is not sufficient to stop all inroads, but it will make them more difficult and therefore of less frequent occurrence, and this is a point of considerable importance where relations subsist with people like those of Asia, whose passions and habits have a perpetual tendency to war.

Next to this class of cordons come the lines, which, in the wars of modern times have been formed between European States, such as the French lines on the Rhine and in the Netherlands. These were originally formed only with a view to protect a country against inroads made for the purpose of levying contributions or living at the expense of the enemy. They are, therefore, only intended to check minor operations, and consequently it is also meant that they should be defended by small bodies of troops. But, of course, in the event of the enemy's principal force taking its direction against these lines, the defender must also use his principal force in their defence, an event by no means conducive to the best defensive arrangements. On account of this disadvantage and because the protection against incursions in temporary war is quite a minor object, by which through the very existence of these lines an excessive expenditure of troops may easily be caused, their formation is looked upon in our day as a pernicious measure. The more power and energy thrown into the prosecution of the war the more useless and dangerous this means becomes.

Lastly, all very extended lines of outposts covering the quarters of an army and intended to offer a certain amount of resistance come under the head of cordons.

This defensive measure is chiefly designed as an impediment to raids, and other such minor expeditions directed against single cantonments, and for this purpose it may be quite sufficient if favoured by the country. Against an advance of the main body of the enemy the opposition offered can be only relative, that is, intended to gain time: but as this gain of time will be but inconsiderable in most cases, this object may be regarded as a very minor consideration in the establishment of these lines. The assembling and advance of the enemy's army itself can never take place so unobservedly that the defender gets his first information of it through his outposts; when such is the case he is much to be pitied.

Consequently, in this case also, the cordon is only intended to resist the attack of a weak force, and the object, therefore, in this and in the other two cases is not at variance with the means.

But that an army formed for the defence of a country should spread itself out in a long line of defensive posts opposite to the enemy, that it should disperse itself in a cordon form, seems to be so absurd that we must seek to discover the circumstances and motives which lead to and accompany such a proceeding.

Every position in a mountainous country, even if taken up with the view of a battle with the whole force united, is and must necessarily be more extended than a position in a level country. It *may be* because the aid of the ground augments very much the force of the resistance; it *must be* because a wider basis of retreat is required, as we have shown in the chapter on mountain defences. But if there is no near prospect of a battle, if it is probable that the enemy will remain in his position opposite to us for some time without undertaking anything unless tempted by some very favourable opportunity which may present itself (the usual state of things in most wars formerly), then it is also natural not to limit ourselves merely to the occupation of so much country as is absolutely necessary, but to hold as much right or left as is consistent with the security of the army, by which we obtain many advantages, as we shall presently show. In open countries with plenty of communications, this object may be effected to a greater extent than in mountains, through the principle of *movement*, and for that reason the extension and dispersion of the troops is less necessary in an open country; it would also be much more dangerous there on account of the inferior capability of resistance of each part.

But in mountains where all occupation of ground is more dependent on local defence, where relief cannot so soon be afforded to a point menaced, and where, when once the enemy has got possession of a point, it is more difficult to dislodge him by a force slightly superior – in mountains, under these circumstances, we shall always come to a form of position which, if not strictly speaking a cordon, still approaches very near to it, being a line of defensive posts. From such a disposition, consisting of several detached posts, to the cordon system, there is still certainly a considerable step, but it is one which generals, nevertheless, often take without being aware of it, being drawn on from one step to another. First, the covering and the possession of the country is the object of the dispersion; afterwards it is the security of the army itself. Every commander of a post calculates the advantage which may be derived from this or that point connected with the approach to his position on the right or the left, and thus the whole progresses insensibly from one degree of subdivision to another.

A cordon war, therefore, carried on by the principal force of an army, is not to be considered a form of war designedly chosen with a view to stopping every blow which the enemy's forces might attempt, but a situation which the army is drawn into in the pursuit of a very different object, namely, the holding and covering the country against an enemy who has no decisive undertaking in view. Such a situation must always be looked upon as a mistake; and the motives through which generals have been lured by degrees into allowing one small post after another, are contemptible in connection with the object of a large army; this point of view shows, at all events, the possibility of such a mistake. That it is really an error, namely, a mistaken appreciation of our own position, and that of the enemy is sometimes not observed, and it is spoken of as an erroneous *system*. But this same system, when it is pursued with advantage, or, at all events, without causing damage, is quietly approved. Every one praises the *faultless* campaigns of Prince Henry in the Seven Years' War, because they have been pronounced so by the king, although these campaigns exhibit the most decided and most incomprehensible examples of chains of posts so extended that they may just with as much propriety be called cordons as any that ever were. We may completely justify these positions by saying, the prince knew his opponent; he knew that he had no enterprises of a decisive character to apprehend from that quarter, and as the object of his position besides was to occupy always as much territory as possible, he therefore carried out that object as far as circumstances in any way permitted. If the prince had once been unfortunate with one of these cobwebs, and had met with a severe loss, we should not say that he had pursued a faulty system of warfare, but that he had been mistaken about a measure and had applied it to a case to which it was not suited.

While we thus seek to explain how the cordon system, as it is called, may be resorted to by the principal force in a theatre in war, and how it may even be a judicious and useful measure, and, therefore, far from being an absurdity, we must, at the same time, acknowledge that there appear to have been instances where generals or their staff have overlooked the real meaning or object of a cordon system, and assumed its relative value to be a general one; conceiving it to be really suited to afford protection against every kind of attack, instances, therefore, where there was no mistaken application of the measure but a complete misunderstanding of its nature; we shall further allow that this very absurdity amongst others seems to have taken place in the defence of the Vosges by the Austrian and Prussian armies in 1793 and 1794.

CHAPTER TWENTY THREE

Key of the Country

THERE IS NO theoretical idea in the art of war which has played such a part in criticism as that we are now entering upon. It is the "great war steed" in all accounts of battles and campaigns; the most frequent point of view in all arguments, and one of those fragments of scientific form with which critics make a show of learning. And yet the conception embodied in it has never yet been established, nor has it ever been clearly explained.

We shall try to ascertain its real meaning, and then see how far it can be made available for practical use.

We treat of it here because the defence of mountains, river defences, as well as the conceptions of strong and entrenched camps with which it closely connects itself, required to have precedence.

The indefinite confused conception which is concealed behind this ancient military metaphor has sometimes signified the most exposed part of a country at other times the strongest.

If there is any spot without the *possession of which no one dare venture to penetrate into an enemy's country* that may, with propriety, be called the key of that country. But this simple, though certainly at the same time also, barren notion has not satisfied theorists, and they have amplified it, and under the term key of a country imagined *points* which *decide upon the possession of the whole country.*

When the Russians wanted to advance into the Crimean peninsula, they were obliged to make themselves masters of the isthmus of Perekop and its lines, not so much to gain an entrance generally – for Lascy turned it twice (1737 and 1738) – but to be able to establish themselves with tolerable security in the Crimea. That is very simple, but we gain very little in this through the conception of a key-point. But if it might be said, Whoever has possession of the district of Langres commands all France as far as Paris – that is to say, it only rests with himself to take possession – that is plainly a very different thing, something of much higher importance. According to the first kind of conception the possession of the country cannot be thought of without the possession of the point which we have called key; that is a thing which is intelligible to the most ordinary capacity: but according to the second kind of conception, the possession of the point which we have called key, cannot be imagined without the possession of the country following as a necessary consequence; that is plainly, something marvellous, common sense is no longer sufficient to grasp this, the magic of the occult sciences must be called into requisition. This cabala came into existence in works published fifty years ago, and reached its zenith at the end of the last century; and notwithstanding the irresistible force, certainty and distinctness with which Buonaparte's method of conducting war carried conviction generally, this cabala has, nevertheless, still managed, we say, to spin out the thread of its tenacious existence through the medium of books.

(Setting aside for a moment *our* conception of the key-point) it is self-evident that in every country there are points of *commanding* importance, where several roads meet, where our means of subsistence may be conveniently collected, which have the advantage of being centrally situated with reference to other important points, the possession of which in short meets many requirements and affords many advantages. Now, if generals wishing to express the importance of such a point by one word have called it the *key of the land*, it would be pedantic affectation to take offence at their using that term; on the contrary we should rather say the term is very expressive and pleasing. But if we try to convert this mere flower of speech into the germ of a system branching out like a tree into many ramifications, common sense rises in opposition, and demands that the expression should be restricted to its true value.

In order to develop a system out of the expression, it was necessary to resort to something more distinct and absolute than the practical, but certainly very indefinite, meaning attaching to the term in the narrations of generals when speaking of their military enterprises. And from amongst all its various relations, that of high ground was chosen.

Where a road traverses a mountain ridge, we thank heaven when we get to the top and have only to descend. This feeling so natural to a single traveller is still more so in the case of an army All difficulties seem to be overcome, and so they are indeed in most instances; we find that the descent is easy, and we are conscious of a kind of feeling of superiority over any one who would stop us; we have an extensive view over the country, and command it with a look beforehand. Thus the highest point on a road over a mountain is always considered to possess a decisive importance, and it does in fact in the majority of cases, but by no means in all. Such points are very often described in the despatches of generals by the name of key-points; but certainly again in a somewhat different and generally in a more restricted sense. This idea has been the starting point of a false theory (of which, perhaps, Lloyd may be regarded as the founder); and on this account, elevated points from which several roads descend into the adjacent country, came to be regarded as the keypoints of the country – as points which *command* the country. It was natural that this view should amalgamate itself with one very nearly connected with it, that of a *systematic defence of mountains*, and that the matter should thus be driven still further into the regions of the illusory; added to which many tactical elements connected with the defence of mountains came into play, and thus the idea of the highest *point in the road* was soon abandoned, and the highest point generally of the whole mountain system, that is the point of the *watershed*, was substituted for it as the key of the country.

Now just at that time, that is the latter half of the preceding century, more definite ideas on the forms given to the surface of the earth through aqueous action became current; thus natural science lent a hand to the theory of war by this geological system, and then every barrier of practical truth was broken through, and reasoning floated in the illusory system of a geological analogy. In consequence of this, about the end of the eighteenth century we heard, or rather we *read*, of nothing but the sources of the Rhine and Danube. It is true that this nuisance prevailed mostly in books, for only a small portion of book wisdom ever reaches the real world, and the more foolish a theory the less it will attain to practice; but this of which we are now speaking has not been unproductive of injury to Germany by its practical effects, therefore we are not fighting with a windmill, in proof of which we shall quote two examples; first, the important but very scientific campaigns of the Prussian army, 1793 and 1794 in the Vosges, the theoretical key to which will be found in the works of Gravert and Massenbach; secondly, the campaign of 1814, when, on the principle of the same theory, an army of 200,000 men was led by the nose through Switzerland on to the plateau of Langres as it is called.

But a high point in a country from which all its waters flow, is generally nothing more than a high point; and all that in exaggeration and false application of ideas, true in themselves, was written at the end of the eighteenth and commencement of the nineteenth centuries, about its influence on military events, is completely imaginary. If the

Rhine and Danube and all the six rivers of Germany had their common source on the top of *one* mountain, that mountain would not on that account have any claim to any greater military value than being suited for the position of a trigonometrical point. For a signal tower it would be less useful, still less so for a vidette, and for a whole army worth just nothing at all.

To seek for a *key-position* therefore in the so called *key country*, that is where the different branches of the mountains diverge from a common point, and at the highest source of its waters, is merely an idea in books, which is overthrown by nature itself, because nature does not make the ridges and valleys so easy to descend as is assumed by the hitherto so called theory of ground, but distributes peaks and gorges, in the most irregular manner, and not unfrequently the lowest water level is surrounded by the loftiest masses of mountain. If any one questions military history on the subject, he will soon convince himself that the leading geological points of a country exercise very little regular influence on the use of the country for the purposes of war, and that little is so over-balanced by other local circumstances, and other requirements, that a line of positions may often run quite close to one of the points we are discussing without having been in any way attracted there by that point.

We have only dwelt so long upon this false idea because a whole – and very pretentious – system has built itself upon it. We now leave it, and turn back to our own views.

We say, then, that if the expression, *key-position*, is to represent an independent conception in strategy, it must only be that of a locality the possession of which is indispensable before daring to enter the enemy's country. But if we choose to designate by that term every convenient point of entrance to a country, or every advantageous central point in the country, then the term loses its real meaning (that is, its value), and denotes something which may be found anywhere more or less. It then becomes a mere pleasing figure of speech.

But positions such as the term conveys to our mind are very rarely indeed to be found. In general, the best key to the country lies in the enemy's army; and when the idea of country predominates over that of the armed force, some very specially advantageous circumstances must prevail. These, according to our opinion, may be recognised by their tending to two principal results: first, that the force occupying the position, through the help of the ground, obtains extraordinary capability of tactical resistance; second, that the enemy's lines of communication can be sooner effectively threatened from this position than he can threaten ours.

CHAPTER TWENTY FOUR

Operating Against a Flank

WE NEED HARDLY observe that we speak of the strategic flank, that is, a side of the theatre of war, and that the attack from one side in battle, or the tactical movement against a flank, must not be confounded with it; and even in cases in which the strategic operation against a flank, in its last stage, ends in the tactical operation, they can quite easily be kept separate, because the one never follows necessarily out of the other.

These flanking movements, and the flanking positions connected with them, belong also to the mere useless pageantry of theory, which is seldom met with in actual war. Not that the means itself is either ineffectual or illusory, but because both sides generally seek to guard themselves against its effects; and cases in which this is impossible are rare. Now in these uncommon cases this means has often also proved highly efficacious, and for this reason, as well as on account of the constant watching against it which is required in war, it is important that it should be clearly explained in theory. Although the strategic operation against a flank can naturally be imagined, not only on the part of the defensive, but also on that of the offensive, still it has much more affinity with the first, and therefore finds its place under the head of defensive means.

Before we enter into the subject, we must establish the simple principle, which must never be lost sight of afterwards in the consideration of the subject, that troops which are to act against the rear or flank of the enemy cannot be employed against his front, and that, therefore, whether it be in tactics or strategy, it is a completely false kind of notion to consider that *coming on the rear* of the enemy is at once an advantage in itself. In itself, it is as yet nothing; but it will become something in connection with other things, and something either advantageous or the reverse, according to the nature of these things, the examination of which now claims our attention.

First, in the action against the strategic flank, we must make a distinction between two objects of that measure – between the action merely against the *communications*, and that against the *line of retreat*, with which, at the same time, an effect upon the communications may also be combined.

When Daun, in 1758, sent a detachment to seize the convoys on their way to the siege of Olmutz, he had plainly no intention of impeding the king's retreat into Silesia; he rather wished to bring about that retreat, and would willingly have opened the line to him.

In the campaign of 1812, the object of all the expeditionary corps that were detached from the Russian army in the months of September and October, was only to intercept the communications, not to stop the retreat; but the latter was quite plainly the design of the Moldavian army which, under Tschitschagof, marched against the Beresina, as well as of the attack which General Wittgenstein was commissioned to make on the French corps stationed on the Dwina.

These examples are merely to make the exposition clearer.

The action against the lines of communication is directed against the enemy's convoys, against small detachments following in rear of the army, against couriers and travellers, small depôts, etc.; in fact, against all the means which the enemy requires to keep his army in a vigorous and healthy condition; its object is, therefore, to weaken the condition of the enemy in this respect, and by this means to cause him to retreat.

The action against the enemy's line of retreat is to cut his army off from that line. It cannot effect this object unless the enemy really determines to retreat; but it may certainly cause him to do so by threatening his line of retreat, and, therefore, it may have the same effect as the action against the line of communication, by working as a demonstration. But as already said, none of these effects are to be expected from the mere turning which has been effected, from the mere geometrical form given to the disposition of the troops, they only result from the conditions suitable to the same.

In order to learn more distinctly these conditions, we shall separate completely the two actions against the flank, and first consider that which is directed against the communications.

Here we must first establish two principal conditions, one or other of which must always be forthcoming.

The first is, that the forces used for this action against the flank of the enemy must be so insignificant in numbers that their absence is not observed in front.

The second, that the enemy's army has run its career, and therefore can neither make use of a fresh victory over our army, nor can he pursue us if we evade a combat by moving out of the way.

This last case, which is by no means so uncommon as might be supposed, we shall lay aside for the moment, and occupy ourselves with the accessory conditions of the first.

The first of these is, that the communications have a certain length, and cannot be protected by a few good posts; the second point is, that the situation of the line is such as exposes it to our action.

This weakness of the line may arise in two ways – either by its direction, if it is not perpendicular to the strategic front of the enemy's army, or because his lines of communication pass through our territory; if both these circumstances exist, the line is so much the more exposed. These two relations require a closer examination.

One would think that when it is a question of covering a line of communication forty or fifty miles long, it is of little consequence whether the position occupied by an army standing at one extremity of this line forms an oblique angle or a right angle in reference to it, as the breadth of the position is little more than a mere point in comparison to the line; and yet it is not so unimportant as it may seem. When an army is posted at a right angle with its communications, it is difficult, even with a considerable superiority, to interrupt the communications by any detachments or partisans sent out for the purpose. If we think only of the difficulty of covering absolutely a certain space, we should not believe this, but rather suppose, on the contrary, that it must be very difficult for an army to protect its rear (that is, the country behind it) against all expeditions which an enemy superior in numbers may undertake. Certainly, if we could look at everything in war as it is on a sheet of paper! Then the party covering the line, in his uncertainty as to the point where light troops or partisans may appear, would be in a certain measure blind, and only the partisans would see. But if we think of the uncertainty and insufficiency of intelligence gained in war, and know that both parties are incessantly groping in the dark, then we easily perceive that a detached corps sent round the enemy's flank to gain his rear is in the position of a man engaged in a fray with numbers in a dark room. In the end he must fall; and so must it also be with bands who get round an army occupying a perpendicular position, and who therefore place themselves near to the enemy, but widely separated from their own people. Not only is there danger of losing numbers in this way; there is also a risk of the whole instrument itself being blunted immediately; for the very first misfortune which happens to one such party will make all the others timid, and instead of bold attacks and insolent dodging, the only play will be constant running away.

Through this difficulty, therefore, an army occupying a perpendicular position covers the nearest points on its line of communication for a distance of two or three marches, according to the strength of the army; but those nearest points are just those which are most in danger, as they are the nearest to the enemy.

On the other hand, in the case of a decidedly oblique position, no such part of the line of communication is covered; the smallest pressure, the most insignificant attempt on the part of the enemy, leads at once to a vulnerable point.

But now, what is it which determines the front of a position, if it is not just the direction perpendicular to the line of communication? The front of the enemy; but then, again, this may be equally as well supposed as dependent on our front. Here there is a reciprocal effect, for the origin of which we must search.

If we suppose the lines of communication of the assailant, *a b*, so situated with respect to those of the enemy, *c d*, that the two lines form a considerable angle with each other, it is evident that if the defensive wishes to take up a position at *e*, where the two lines intersect, the assailant from *b*, by the mere geometrical relation, could compel him to form front opposite to him, and thus to lay bare his communications. The case would be reversed if the defensive took up his position on this side of the point of junction, about *d;* then the assailant must make front towards him, if so be that his line of operations, which closely depends on geographical conditions, cannot be arbitrarily changed, and moved, for instance, to the direction *a d*. From this it would seem to follow that the defender has an advantage in this system of reciprocal action, because he only requires to take a position on this side of the intersection of the two lines. But very far from attaching any importance to this geometrical element, we only brought it into consideration to make ourselves the better understood; and we are rather of opinion that local and generally individual relations have much more to do with determining the position of the defender; that, therefore, it is quite impossible to lay down in general which of two belligerents will be obliged soonest to expose his communications.

If the lines of communication of both sides lie in one and the same direction, then whichever of the two parties takes up an oblique position will certainly compel his adversary to do the same. But then there is nothing gained geometrically by this, and both parties attain the same advantages and disadvantages.

In the continuation of our considerations we shall, therefore, confine ourselves to the case of the line of communication of one side only being exposed.

Now as regards the second disadvantageous relation of a line of communication, that is to say, when it runs through an enemy's country, it is clear in itself how much the line is compromised by that circumstance, if the inhabitants of the country have taken up arms; and consequently the case must be looked at as if a body of the enemy was posted all along the line; this body, it is true, is in itself weak without solidity or intensive force; but we must also take into consideration what the close contact and influence of such a hostile force may nevertheless effect through the number of points which offer themselves one after another on long lines of communication. That requires no further explanation. But even if the enemy's subjects have *not* taken up arms, and even if there is no militia in the country, or other military organisation, indeed if the people are even very unwarlike in spirit, still the mere relation of the people as subjects to a hostile government is a disadvantage for the lines of communication of the other side which is always felt. The assistance which expeditionary forces and partisans derive merely through a better understanding with the people, through a knowledge of the country and its inhabitants, through good information, through the support of official functionaries, is, for them, of decided value; and this support every such body will enjoy without any special effort on its own part. Added to this, within a certain distance there will not be wanting fortresses, rivers, mountains, or other places of refuge, which of ordinary right belong to the enemy, if they have not been formally taken possession of and occupied by our troops.

Now in such a case as is here supposed, especially if attended with other favourable circumstances, it is possible to act against the communications of an army, although their direction is perpendicular to the position of that army; for the detachments employed for the purpose do not then require to fall back always on their own army, because being in their own country they are safe enough if they only make their escape.

We have, therefore, now ascertained that –

1. A considerable length,
2. An oblique direction,
3. An enemy's province,

are the principal circumstances under which the lines of communication of an army may be interrupted by a relatively small proportion of armed forces on the side of the enemy; in order to make this interruption effectual, a fourth condition is still requisite, which is a certain duration of time. Respecting this point, we beg attention to what has been said in the fifteenth chapter of the fifth book.

But these four conditions are only the chief points which relate to the subject; a number of local and special circumstances attach themselves to these, and often attain to an influence more decisive and important than that of the principal ones themselves. Selecting only the most essential, we mention the state of the roads, the nature of the country through which they pass, the means of cover which are afforded by rivers, mountains, and morasses, the seasons and weather, the importance of particular convoys, such as siege trains, the number of light troops, etc., etc.

On all these circumstances, therefore, will depend the effect with which a general can act on his opponent's communications; and by comparing the result of the whole of these circumstances on the one side with the result of the whole on the other, we obtain a just estimate of the relative advantages of both systems of communication, on which will depend which of the two generals can play the highest game.

What here seems so prolix in the explanation is often decided in the concrete case at first sight; but still, the tact of a practised judgment is required for that, and person must have thought over every one of the cases now developed in order to see in its true light the absurdity of those critical writers who think they have settled something by the mere words "turning" and "acting on a flank," without giving their reasons.

We now come to the *second chief condition*, under which the strategic action against the enemy's flank may take place.

If the enemy is hindered from advancing by any other cause but the resistance which our army opposes, let that cause be what it may, then our army has no reason to be apprehensive about weakening itself by sending out detachments to harass the enemy; for if the enemy should attempt to chastise us by an attack, we have only to yield some ground and decline the combat. This is what was done by the chief Russian army at Moscow in 1812. But it is not at all necessary that everything should be again on the same great scale as in that campaign for such a case to happen again. In the first Silesian war, Frederick the Great was each time in this situation, on the frontiers of Bohemia and Moravia, and in the complex affairs relating to generals and their armies, many causes of different kinds, particularly political ones, may be imagined, which make further advance an impossibility.

As in the case now supposed more forces may be spared to act against the enemy's flank, the other conditions need not be quite so favourable: even the nature of our communications in relation to those of the enemy need not give us the advantage in that respect, as an enemy who is not in a condition to make any particular use of our further retreat is not likely to use his right to retaliate, but will rather be anxious about the direct covering of his own line of retreat.

Such a situation is therefore very well suited to obtain for us, by means less brilliant and complete but less dangerous than a victory, those results which it would be too great a risk to seek to obtain by a battle.

As in such a case we feel little anxiety about exposing our own line of communications, by taking up a position on one or other flank, and as the enemy by that means may always be comspelled to form front obliquely to his line of communications, therefore *this one* of the conditions above named will seldom fail to occur. The more the rest of the conditions, as well as other circumstances, co-operate, so much the more certain are we of success from the means now in question; but the fewer favourable circumstances exist, the more will all depend on superior skill in combination, and promptitude and precision in the execution.

Here is the proper field for strategic manœuvres, such as are to be found so frequently in the Seven Years' War, in Silesia and Saxony, and in the campaigns of 1760 and 1762. If, in many wars in which only a moderate amount of elementary force is displayed, such strategic manœuvring very often appears, this is not because the commander on each occasion found himself at the end of his career, but because want of resolution and courage, and of an enterprising spirit, and dread of responsibility, have often supplied the place of real impediments; for a case in point, we have only to call to mind Field Marshal Daun.

As a summary of the results of our considerations, we may say, that the action against a flank is most effectual –

1. In the defensive;
2. Towards the end of a campaign;
3. Above all, in a retreat into the heart of the country; and
4. In connection with a general arming of the people.

On the mode of executing this action against the communications, we have only a few words to say.

The enterprises must be conducted by skilful detachment leaders, who, at the head of small bodies, by bold marches and attacks, fall upon the enemy's weak garrisons, convoys, and small detachments on the march here and there, encourage the national levies (landsturm), and sometimes join with them in particular undertakings. These parties must be more numerous than strong individually, and so organised that it may be possible to unite several of them for any greater undertaking without any obstacle from the vanity or caprice of any of the single leaders.

We have now to speak of the action against the enemy's line of retreat.

Here we must keep in view, above all things, the principle with which we commenced, that forces destined to operate in rear cannot be used in front; that, therefore, the action against the rear or flanks is not an increase of force in itself; it is only to be regarded as a more powerful application (or employment) of the same; increasing the degree of success in prospect, but also increasing the degree of risk.

Every opposition offered with the sword which is not of a direct and simple nature, has a tendency to raise the result at the cost of its certainty. An operation against the enemy's flank, whether with one compact force, or with separate bodies converging from several quarters, belongs to this category.

But now, if cutting off the enemy's retreat is not to be a mere demonstration, but is seriously intended, the real solution is a decisive battle, or, at least, the conjunction of all the conditions for the same; and just in this solution we find again the two elements above-mentioned – the greater result and the greater danger. Therefore, if a general is to stand justified in adopting this method of action, his reasons must be favourable conditions.

In this method of resistance we must distinguish the two forms already mentioned. The first is, if a general with his whole force intends to attack the enemy in rear, either from a position taken up on the flank for that purpose, or by a formal turning movement; the second is, if he divides his forces, and, by an enveloping position with one part, threatens the enemy's rear, with the other part his front.

The result is intensified in both cases alike, that is – either there is a real interception of the retreat, and consequently the enemy's army taken prisoners, or the greater part scattered, or there may be a long and hasty retreat of the enemy's force to escape the danger.

But the intensified risk is different in the two cases.

If we turn the enemy with our whole force, the danger lies in the laying open our own rear; and hence the question again depends on the relation of the mutual lines of retreat, just as in the action against the lines of communication, it depended on the relation of those lines.

Now certainly the defender, if he is in his own country, is less restricted than the assailant, both as to his lines of retreat and communication, and in so far is therefore in a better position to turn his adversary strategically; but this general relation is not of a sufficiently decisive character to be used as the foundation of a practical method; therefore, nothing but the whole of the relations in each individual case can decide.

Only so much we may add, that favourable conditions are naturally more common in wide spheres of action than in small; more common, also, on the side of independent states than on that of weak ones, dependent on foreign aid, and whose armies must, therefore, constantly have their attention bent on the point of junction with the auxiliary army; lastly, they become most favorable for the defender towards the close of the campaign, when the impulsive force of the assailant is somewhat spent; very much, again, in the same manner as in the case of the lines of communication.

Such a flank position as the Russians took up with such advantage on the road from Moscow to Kaluga, when Buonaparte's aggressive force was spent, would have brought them into a scrape at the commencement of the campaign at the camp of Drissa, if they had not been wise enough to change their plan in good time.

The other method of turning the enemy, and cutting off his retreat by dividing our force, entails the risk attending a division of our own force, whilst the enemy, having the advantage of interior lines, retains his forces united, and therefore has the power of acting with superior numbers against one of our divisions. This is a disadvantage which nothing can remove, and in exposing ourselves to it, we can only be justified by one of three principal reasons: –

1. The original division of the force which makes such a method of action necessary, unless we incur a great loss of time.

2. A great moral and physical superiority, which justifies the adoption of a decisive method.

3. The want of impulsive force in the enemy as soon as he has arrived at the culminating point of his career.

When Frederick the Great invaded Bohemia, 1757, on converging lines, he had not in view to combine an attack in front with one on the strategic rear, at all events, this was by no means his principal object, as we shall more fully explain elsewhere, but in any case it is evident that there never could have been any question of a concentration of forces in Silesia or Saxony before the invasion, as he would thereby have sacrificed all the advantages of a surprise.

When the allies formed their plan for the second part of the campaign of 1813, looking to their great superiority in numbers, they might very well at that time entertain the idea of attacking Buonaparte's right on the Elbe with their main force, and of thus shifting the theatre of war from the Oder to the Elbe. Their ill-success at Dresden is to be ascribed not to this general plan but to their faulty dispositions both strategic and tactical. They could have concentrated 220,000 men at Dresden against Buonaparte's 130,000, a proportion of numbers eminently favourable (at Leipsic, at least, the proportion was as 285 : 157). It is true that Buonaparte had distributed his forces too evenly for the particular system of a defence upon one line (in Silesia 70,000 against 90,000, in the Mark – Brandenburg – 70,000 against 110,000), but at all events it would have been difficult for him, without completely abandoning Silesia, to assemble on the Elbe a force which could have contended with the principal army of the allies in a decisive battle. The allies could also have easily called up the army of Wrede to the Maine, and employed it to try to cut Buonaparte off from the road to Mayence.

Lastly, in 1812, the Russians might have directed their army of Moldavia upon Volhynia and Lithuania in order to move it forward afterwards against the rear of the principal French army, because it was quite certain that Moscow must be the extreme point of the French line of operations. For any part of Russia beyond Moscow there was nothing to fear in that campaign, therefore the Russian main army had no cause to consider itself too weak.

This same scheme formed part of the disposition of the forces laid down in the first defensive plan proposed by General Phul, according to which the army of Barclay was to occupy the camp at Drissa, whilst that under Bragathion was to press forward against the rear of the main French army. But what a difference of circumstances in the two cases! In the first of them the French were three times as strong as the Russians; in the second, the Russians were decidedly superior. In the first, Buonaparte's great army had in it an impulsive force which carried it to Moscow 80 miles beyond Drissa: in the second, it is unfit to make a day's march beyond Moscow; in the first, the line of retreat on the Niemen did not exceed 30 miles: in the second it was 112. The same action against the enemy's retreat therefore, which was so successful in the second case, would, in the first, have been the wildest folly.

As the action against the enemy's line of retreat, if it is more than a demonstration, becomes a formal attack from the rear, there remains therefore still a good deal to be said on the subject, but it will come in more appropriately in the book upon the attack; we shall therefore break off here and content ourselves with having given the conditions under which this kind of reaction may take place.

Very commonly the design of causing the enemy to retreat by menacing his line of retreat, is understood to imply rather a mere demonstration than the actual execution of the threat. If it was necessary that every efficacious demonstration should be founded on the actual practicability of real action, which seems a matter of course at first sight, then it would accord with the same in all respects. But this is not the case: on the contrary, in the chapter on demonstrations we shall see that they are connected with conditions somewhat different, at all events in some respects, we therefore refer our readers to that chapter.

CHAPTER TWENTY FIVE

Retreat into the Interior
of the Country

WE HAVE CONSIDERED the voluntary retreat into the heart of the country as a particular indirect form of defence through which it is expected the enemy will be destroyed, not so much by the sword as by exhaustion from his own efforts. In this case, therefore, a great battle is either not supposed, or it is assumed to take place when the enemy's forces are considerably reduced.

Every assailant in advancing diminishes his military strength by the advance; we shall consider this more in detail in the seventh book; here we must assume that result which we may the more readily do as it is clearly shown by military history in every campaign in which there has been a considerable advance.

This loss in the advance is increased if the enemy has not been beaten, but withdraws of his own accord with his forces intact, and offering a steady continuous resistance, sells every step of ground at a bloody price, so that the advance is a continuous combat for ground and not a mere pursuit.

On the other hand, the losses which a party on the defensive suffers on a retreat, are much greater if his retreat has been preceded by a defeat in battle than if his retreat is voluntary. For if he is able to offer the pursuer the daily resistance which we expect on a voluntary retreat, his losses would be *at least* the same in that way, over and above which those sustained in the battle have still to be added. But how contrary to the nature of the thing such a supposition as this would be! The best army in the world if obliged to retire far into the country after the loss of a battle, will suffer losses on the retreat, *beyond measure out of proportion;* and if the enemy is considerably superior, as we suppose him, in the case of which we are now speaking, if he pursues with great energy as has almost always been done in modern wars, then there is the highest probability that a regular flight takes place by which the army is usually completely ruined.

A *regularly measured* daily resistance, that is, one which each time only lasts as long as the balance of success in the combat can be kept wavering, and in which we secure ourselves from defeat by giving up the ground which has been contested at the right moment, will cost the assailant at least as many men as the defender in these combats, for the loss which the latter by retiring now and again must unavoidably suffer in prisoners, will be balanced by the losses of the other under fire, as the assailant must always fight against the advantages of the ground. It is true that the retreating side loses entirely all those men who are badly wounded, but the assailant likewise loses all his in the same case for the present, as they usually remain several months in the hospitals.

The result will be that the two armies will wear each other away in nearly equal proportions in these perpetual collisions.

It is quite different in the pursuit of a beaten army. Here the troops lost in battle, the general disorganisation, the broken courage, the anxiety about the retreat, make such a resistance on the part of the retreating army very difficult, in many cases impossible; and the pursuer who, in the former case, advances extremely cautiously, even hesitatingly, like a blind man, always groping about, presses forward in the latter case with the firm tread of the conqueror, with the overweening spirit which good fortune imparts, with the confidence of a demigod, and the more daringly he urges the pursuit so much the more he hastens on things in the direction which they have already taken, because here is the true field for the moral forces which intensify and multiply themselves without being restricted to the rigid numbers and measures of the physical world.

It is therefore very plain how different will be the relations of two armies according as it is by the first or the second of the above ways, that they arrive at that point which may be regarded as the end of the assailant's course.

This is merely the result of the mutual destruction; to this must now be added the reductions which the advancing party suffers otherwise in addition, and respecting which, as already said, we refer to the seventh book; further, on the other hand, we have to take into account reinforcements which the retreating party receives in the great majority of cases, by forces subsequently joining him either in the form of help from abroad or through persistent efforts at home.

Lastly, there is, in the means of subsistence, such a disproportion between the retreating side and the advancing, that the first not uncommonly lives in superfluity when the other is reduced to want.

The army in retreat has the means of collecting provisions everywhere, and he marches towards them, whilst the pursuer must have everything brought after him, which, as long as he is in motion, even with the shortest lines of communication, is difficult, and on that account begets scarcity from the very first.

All that the country yields will be taken for the benefit of the retreating army first, and will be mostly consumed. Nothing remains but wasted villages and towns, fields from which the crops have been gathered, or which are trampled down, empty wells, and muddy brooks.

The pursuing army, therefore, from the very first day, has frequently to contend with the most pressing wants. On taking the enemy's supplies he cannot reckon; it is only through accident, or some unpardonable blunder on the part of the enemy, that here and there some little falls into his hands.

Thus there can be no doubt that in countries of vast dimensions, and when there is no extraordinary disproportion between the belligerent powers, a relation may be produced in this way between the military forces, which holds out to the defensive an immeasurably greater chance of a final result in his favour than he would have had if there had been a great battle on the frontier. Not only does the probability of gaining a victory become greater through this alteration in the proportions of the contending armies, but the prospects of great results from the victory are increased as well, through the change of position. What a difference between a battle lost close to the frontier of our country and one in the middle of the enemy's country! Indeed, the situation of the assailant is often such at the end of his first start, that even a battle *gained* may force him to retreat, because he has neither enough impulsive power left to complete and make use of a victory, nor is he in a condition to replace the forces he has lost.

There is, therefore, an immense difference between a decisive blow at the commencement and at the end of the attack.

To the great advantage of this mode of defence are opposed two drawbacks. The first is the loss which the country suffers through the presence of the enemy in his advance, the other is the moral impression.

To protect the country from loss can certainly never be looked upon as the object of the whole defence. That object is an advantageous peace. To obtain that as surely as possible is the endeavour, and for it no momentary sacrifice must he considered too great. At the same time, the above loss, although it may not be decisive, must still be laid in the balance, for it always affects our interests.

This loss does not affect our army directly; it only acts upon it in a more or less roundabout way, whilst the retreat itself directly reinforces our army. It is, therefore, difficult to draw a comparison between the advantage and disadvantage in this case; they are things of a different kind, the action of which is not directed towards any common point. We must, therefore, content ourselves with saying that the loss is greater when we have to sacrifice fruitful provinces well populated, and large commercial towns; but it arrives at a maximum when at the same time we lose war-means either ready for use or in course of preparation.

The second counterpoise is the moral impression. There are cases in which the commander must be above regarding such a thing, in which he must quietly follow out his plans, and run the risk of the objections which short-sighted despondency may offer; but nevertheless, this impression is no phantom which should be despised. It is not like a force which acts upon one point: but like a force which, with the speed of lightning, penetrates every fibre, and paralyses all the powers which should be in full activity, both in a nation and in its army. There are indeed cases in which the cause of the retreat into the interior of the country is quickly understood by both nation and army, and trust, as well as hope, are elevated by the step; but such cases are rare. More usually, the people and the army cannot distinguish whether it is a voluntary movement or a precipitate retreat, and still less whether the plan is one wisely adopted, with a view to ensure ulterior advantages, or the result of fear of the enemy's sword. The people have a mingled feeling of sympathy and dissatisfaction at seeing the fate of the provinces sacrificed; the army easily loses confidence in its leaders, or even in itself, and the constant combats of the rear-guard during the retreat, tend always to give new strength to its fears. *These are consequences* of the retreat about which we must never deceive ourselves. And it certainly is – considered in itself – more natural, simpler, nobler, and more in accordance with the moral existence of a nation, to enter the lists at once, that the enemy may out cross the frontiers of its people without being opposed by its genius, and being called to a bloody account.

These are the advantages and disadvantages of this kind of defence; now a few words on its conditions and the circumstances which are in its favour.

A country of great extent, or at all events, a long line of retreat, is the first and fundamental condition; for an advance of a few marches will naturally not weaken the enemy seriously. Buonaparte's centre, in the year 1812, at Witepsk, was 250,000 strong, at Smolensk, 182,000, at Borodino it had only diminished to 130,000, that is to say, had fallen to about an equality with the Russian centre. Borodino is ninety miles from the frontier; but it was not until they came near Moscow that the Russians reached that decided superiority in numbers, which of itself reversed the situation of the combatants so assuredly, that the French victory at Malo Jaroslewetz could not essentially alter it again.

No other European state has the dimensions of Russia, and in very few can a line of retreat 100 miles long be imagined. But neither will a power such as that of the French in 1812, easily appear under different circumstances, still less such a superiority in numbers as existed at the commencement of the campaign, when the French army had more than double the numbers of its adversary, besides its undoubted moral superiority. Therefore, what was here only effected at the end of 100 miles, may perhaps, in other cases, be attained at the end of 50 or 30 miles.

The circumstances which favour this mode of defence are –

1. A country only little cultivated.
2. A loyal and warlike people.
3. An inclement season.

All these things increase the difficulty of maintaining an army, render great convoys necessary, many detachments, harassing duties, cause the spread of sickness, and make operations against the flanks easier for the defender.

Lastly, we have yet to speak of the absolute mass alone of the armed force, as influencing the result.

It lies in the nature of the thing itself that, irrespective of the mutual relation of the forces opposed to each other, a small force is sooner exhausted than a larger, and, therefore, that its career cannot be so long, nor its theatre of war so wide. There is, therefore, to a certain extent, a constant relation between the absolute size of an army and the space which that army can occupy. It is out of the question to try to express this relation by any figures, and besides, it will always be modified by other circumstances; it is sufficient for our purpose to say that these things necessarily have this relation from their very nature. We may be able to march upon Moscow with 500,000 but not with 50,000, even if the relation of the invader's army to that of the defender in point of numbers were much more favourable in the latter case.

Now if we assume that there is this relation of absolute power to space in two different cases, then it is certain that the effect of our retreat into the interior in weakening the enemy will increase with the masses.

1. Subsistence and lodging of the troops become more difficult – for, supposing the space which an army covers to increase in proportion to the size of the army, still the subsistence for the army will never be obtainable from this space alone, and everything which has to be brought after an army is subject to greater loss also; the whole space occupied is never used for covering for the troops, only a small part of it is required, and this does not increase in the same proportion as the masses.

2. The advance is in the same manner more tedious in proportion as the masses increase, consequently, the time is longer before the career of aggression is run out, and the sum total of the daily losses is greater.

Three thousand men driving two thousand before them in an ordinary country, will not allow them to march at the rate of 1, 2, or at most 3 miles a day, and from time to time to make a few days' halt. To come up with them, to attack them, and force them to make a further retreat is the work of a few hours; but if we multiply these masses by 100, the case is altered. Operations for which a few hours sufficed in the first case, require now a whole day, perhaps two. The contending forces cannot remain together near one point; thereby, therefore, the diversity of movements and combinations increases, and, consequently, also the time required. But this places the assailant at a disadvantage, because his difficulty with subsistence being greater, he is obliged to extend his force more than the pursued, and, therefore, is always in danger of being overpowered by the latter at some particular point, as the Russians tried to do at Witepsk.

3. The greater the masses are, the more severe are the exertions demanded from each individual for the daily duties required strategically and tactically. A hundred thousand men who have to march to and from the point of assembly every day, halted at one time, and then set in movement again, now called to arms, then cooking or receiving their rations – a hundred thousand who must not go into their bivouac until the necessary reports are delivered in from all quarters – these men, as a rule, require for all these exertions connected with the actual march, twice as much time as 50,000 would require, but there are only twenty-four hours in the day for both. How much the time and fatigue of the march itself differs according to the size of the body of troops to be moved, has been shown in the ninth chapter of the preceding book. Now, the retreating army, it is true, partakes of these fatigues as well as the advancing, but they are much greater for the latter: –

1, because the mass of his troops is greater on account of the superiority which we supposed,

2, because the defender, by being always the party to yield ground, purchases by this sacrifice the right of the initiative, and, therefore, the right always to give the law to the other. He forms his plan beforehand, which, in most cases, he can carry out unaltered, but the aggressor, on the other hand, can only make his plans conformably to those of his adversary, which he must in the first instance find out.

We must, however, remind our readers that we are speaking of the pursuit of an enemy who has not suffered a defeat, who has not even lost a battle. It is necessary to mention this, in order that we may not be supposed to contradict what was said in the twelfth chapter of our fourth book.

But this privilege of giving the law to the enemy makes a difference in saving of time, expenditure of force, as well as in respect of other minor advantages which, in the long run, becomes very important.

3, because the retreating force on the one hand does all he can to make his own retreat easy, repairs roads, and bridges, chooses the most convenient places for encampment, etc., and, on the other hand again, does all he can to throw impediments in the way of the pursuer, as he destroys bridges, by the mere act of marching makes bad roads worse, deprives the enemy of good places for encampment by occupying them himself, etc.

Lastly, we must add still, as a specially favourable circumstance, the war made by the people. This does not require further examination here, as we shall allot a chapter to the subject itself.

Hitherto, we have been engaged upon the advantages which such a retreat ensures, the sacrifices which it requires, and the conditions which must exist; we shall now say something of the mode of executing it.

The first question which we have to propose to ourselves is with reference to the direction of the retreat.

It should be made into the *interior* of the country, therefore, if possible, towards a point where the enemy will be surrounded on all sides by our provinces; there he will be exposed to their influence, and we shall not be in danger *of being separated from the principal mass of our territory*, which might happen if we chose a line too near the frontier, as would have happened to the Russians in 1812 if they had retreated to the south instead of the east.

This is the condition which lies in the object of the measure itself. Which point in the country is the best, how far the choice of that point will accord with the design of covering the capital or any other important point directly, or drawing the enemy away from the direction of such important places depends on circumstances.

If the Russians had well considered their retreat in 1812 beforehand, and, therefore, made it completely in conformity with a regular plan, they might easily, from Smolensk, have taken the road to Kaluga, which they only took on leaving Moscow; it is very possible that under these circumstances Moscow would have been entirely saved.

That is to say, the French were about 130,000 strong at Borodino, and there is no ground for assuming that they would have been any stronger if this battle had been fought by the Russians half way to Kaluga instead; now, how many of these men could they have spared to detach to Moscow? Plainly, very few; but it is not with a few troops that an expedition can be sent a distance of fifty miles (the distance from Smolensk to Moscow) against such a place as Moscow.

Supposing Buonaparte when at Smolensk, where he was 160,000 strong, had thought he could venture to detach against Moscow before engaging in a great battle, and had used 40,000 men for that purpose, leaving 120,000 opposite the principal Russian army, in that case, these 120,000 men would not have been more than 90,000 in the battle, that is 40,000 less than the number which fought at Borodino; the Russians, therefore, would have had a superiority in numbers of 30,000 men. Taking the course of the battle of Borodino as a standard, we may very well assume that with such a superiority they would have been victorious. At all events, the relative situation of the parties would have been more favourable for the Russians than it was at Borodino. But the retreat of the Russians was not the result of a well-matured plan; they retreated as far as they did because each time that they were on the point of giving battle they did not consider themselves strong enough yet for a great action; all their supplies and reinforcements were on the road from Moscow to Smolensk, and it could not enter the head of anyone at Smolensk to leave that road. But, besides, a victory between Smolensk and Kaluga would never have excused, in the eyes of the Russians, the offence of having left Moscow uncovered, and exposed it to the possibility of being captured.

Buonaparte, in 1813, would have secured Paris with more certainty from an attack if he had taken up a position at some distance in a lateral direction, somewhere behind the canal of Burgundy, leaving only with the large force of National Guard in Paris a few thousand regular troops. The allies would never have had the courage to march a corps of 50,000 or 60,000 against Paris whilst Buonaparte was in the field at Auxerre with 100,000 men. If the case is supposed reversed, and the allies in Buonaparte's place, then no one, indeed, would have advised them to leave the road open to their own capital with *Buonaparte* for their opponent. With such a preponderance he would not have hesitated a moment about marching on the capital. So different is the effect under the same circumstances but under different moral relations.

As we shall have hereafter to return to this subject when treating of the plan of a war, we shall only at present add that, when such a lateral position is taken, the capital or place which it is the object to protect, must, in every case, be capable of making some resistance that it may not be occupied and laid under contribution by every flying column or irregular band.

But we have still to consider another peculiarity in the direction of such a line of retreat, that is, a sudden *change of direction*. After the Russians had kept the same direction as far as Moscow they left that direction which would have taken them to Wladimir, and after first taking the road to Riazan for some distance, they then transferred their army to the Kaluga road. If they had been obliged to continue their retreat they could easily have done so in this new direction which would have led them to Kiew, therefore much nearer again to the enemy's frontier. That the French, even if they had still preserved a large numerical superiority over the Russians, could not have maintained their line of communication by Moscow under such circumstances is clear in itself; they must have given up not only Moscow but, in all probability, Smolensk also, therefore have again abandoned the conquests obtained with so much toil, and contented themselves with a theatre of war on this side the Beresina.

Now, certainly, the Russian army would thus have got into the same difficulty to which it would have exposed itself by taking the direction of Kiew at first, namely, that of being separated from the mass of its own territory; but this disadvantage would now have become almost insignificant, for how different would have been the condition of the French army if it had marched straight upon Kiew without making the detour by Moscow.

It is evident that such a sudden *change of direction* of a line of retreat, which is very practicable in a spacious country, ensures remarkable advantages.

1. It makes it impossible for the enemy (the advancing force) to maintain his old line of communication: but the organisation of a new one is always a difficult matter, in addition to which the change is made gradually, therefore, probably, he has to try more than one new line.

2. If both parties in this manner approach the frontier again; the position of the aggressor no longer covers his conquests, and he must in all probability give them up.

Russia with its enormous dimensions, is a country in which two armies might in this manner regularly play at prisoners' base (Zeck jagen).

But such a change of the line of retreat is also possible in smaller countries, when other circumstances are favourable, which can only be judged of in each individual case, according to its different relations.

When the direction in which the enemy is to be drawn into the country is once fixed upon, then it follows of itself that our principal army should take that direction, for otherwise the enemy would not advance in that direction, and if he even did we should not then be able to impose upon him all the conditions above supposed. The question then only remains whether we shall take this direction with our forces undivided, or whether considerable portions should spread out laterally and therefore give the retreat a divergent (eccentric) form.

To this we answer that this latter form in itself is to be rejected.

1. Because it divides our forces, whilst their concentration on one point is just one of the chief difficulties for the enemy.

2. Because the enemy gets the advantage of operating on interior lines, can remain more concentrated than we are, consequently can appear in so much the greater force at any one point. Now certainly this superiority is less to be dreaded when we are following a system of constantly giving way; but the very condition of this constantly yielding, is always to continue formidable to the enemy and not to allow him to beat us in detail, which might easily happen. A further object of such a retreat, is to bring our principal force by degrees to a superiority of numbers, and with this superiority to give a decisive blow, but that by a partition of forces would become an uncertainty.

3. Because as a general rule the concentric (convergent) action against the enemy is not adapted to the weaker forces.

4. Because many disadvantages of the weak points of the aggression disappear when the defender's army is divided into separate parts.

The weakest features in a long advance on the part of the aggressor are for instance; – the length of the lines of communication, and the exposure of the strategic flanks. By the divergent form of retreat, the aggressor is compelled to cause a portion of his force to show a front to the flank, and this portion properly destined only to neutralise our force immediately in his front, now effects to a certain extent something else in addition, by covering a portion of the lines of communication.

For the mere strategic effect of the retreat, the divergent form is therefore not favourable; but if it is to prepare an action hereafter against the enemy's line of retreat, then we must refer to what has been said about that in the last chapter.

There is *only one* object which can give occasion to a divergent retreat, that is when we can by that means protect provinces which otherwise the enemy would occupy.

What sections of territory the advancing foe will occupy right and left of his course, can with tolerable accuracy be discerned by the point of assembly of, and directions given to, his forces, by the situation of his own provinces, fortresses, etc., in respect to our own. To place troops in those districts of territory which he will in all probability leave unoccupied, would be dangerous waste of our forces. But now whether *by any disposition of our forces we shall be able to hinder him* from occupying those districts which in all probability he will desire to occupy, is more difficult to decide, and it is therefore a point, the solution of which depends much on tact of judgment.

When the Russians retreated in 1812, they left 30,000 men under Tormassow in Volhynia, to oppose the Austrian force which was expected to invade that province. The size of the province, the numerous obstacles of ground which the country presents, the near proportion between the forces likely to come into conflict justified the Russians in their expectations, that they would be able to keep the upper hand in that quarter, or at least to maintain themselves near to their frontier. By this, very important advantages might have resulted in the sequel, which we shall not stop here to discuss; besides this, it was almost impossible for these troops to have joined the main army in time if they had wished. For these reasons, the determination to leave these troops in Volhynia to carry on there a distinct war of their own, was right. Now on the other hand, if according to the proposed plan of campaign submitted by General Phul, only the army of Barclay (80,000 men), was to retire to Drissa, and Bragathion's army (40,000 men) was to remain on the right flank of the French, with a view to subsequently falling on their rear, it is evident at once that this corps could not possibly maintain itself in South Lithuania so near to the rear of the main body of the French army, and would soon have been destroyed by their overwhelming masses.

That the defender's interest in itself is to give up as few provinces as possible to the assailant is intelligible enough, but this is always a secondary consideration; that the attack is also made more difficult the smaller or rather narrower the theatre of war is to which we can confine the enemy, is likewise clear in itself; but all this is subordinate to the condition that in so doing we have the probability of a result in our favour, and that the main body of the force on the defensive will not be too much weakened; for upon that force we must chiefly depend for the final solution, because the difficulties and distress suffered by the main body of the enemy, first call forth his determination to retreat, and increase in the greatest degree the loss of physical and moral power therewith connected.

The retreat into the interior of the country should therefore as a rule be made directly before the enemy, and as slowly as possible, with an army which has not suffered defeat and is undivided; and by its incessant resistance it should force the enemy to a constant state of readiness for battle, and to a ruinous expenditure of forces in tactical and strategical measures of precaution.

When both sides have in this manner reached the end of the aggressor's first start, the defender should then dispose his army in a position, if such can be found, forming an oblique angle with the route of his opponent, and operate against the enemy's rear with all the means at his command.

The campaign of 1812 in Russia shows all these measures on a great scale, and their effects, as it were, in a magnifying glass. Although it was not a voluntary retreat, we may easily consider it from that point of view. If the Russians with the experience they now have of the results to be thus produced, had to undertake the defence of their country over again, exactly under the same circumstances, they would do voluntarily and systematically what in great part was done without a definite plan in 1812; but it would be a great mistake to suppose that there neither is nor can be any instance elsewhere of the same mode of action where the dimensions of the Russian empire are wanting.

Whenever a strategic attack, without coming to the issue of a battle, is wrecked merely on the difficulties encountered, and the aggressor is compelled to make a more or less disastrous retreat, there the chief conditions and principal effects of this mode of defence will be found to have taken place, whatever may be the modifying circumstances otherwise with which it is accompanied. Frederick the Great's campaign of 1742 in Moravia, of 1744 in Bohemia, the French campaign of 1743 in Austria and Bohemia, the Duke of Brunswick's campaign of 1792 in France, Massena's winter campaign of 1810 – 11 in Portugal, are all cases in which this is exemplified, although in smaller proportions and relations; there are besides innumerable fragmentary operations of this kind, the results of which, although not wholly, are still partly to be ascribed to the principle which we here uphold; these we do not bring forward, because it would necessitate a development of circumstances which would lead us into too wide a field.

In Russia, and in the other cases cited, the crisis or turn of affairs took place without any successful battle, having given the decision at the culminating point; but even when such an effect is not to be expected, it is always a matter of immense importance in this mode of defence to bring about such a relation of forces as makes victory possible, and through that victory, as through a first blow, to cause a movement which usually goes on increasing in its disastrous effects according to the laws applicable to falling bodies.

CHAPTER TWENTY SIX
Arming the Nation

A PEOPLE'S WAR in civilised Europe is a phenomenon of the nineteenth century. It has its advocates and its opponents: the latter either considering it in a political sense as a revolutionary means, a state of anarchy declared lawful, which is as dangerous as a foreign enemy to social order at home; or on military grounds, conceiving that the result is not commensurate with the expenditure of the nation's strength. The first point does not concern us here, for we look upon a people's war merely as a means of fighting, therefore, in its connection with the enemy; but with regard to the latter point, we must observe that a people's war in general is to be regarded as a consequence of the outburst which the military element in our day has made through its old formal limits; as an expansion and strengthening of the whole fermentation-process which we call war. The requisition system, the immense increase in the size of armies by means of that system, and the general liability to military service, the utilizing militia, are all things which lie in the same direction, if we make the limited military system of former days our starting point; and the *levée en masse*, or arming of the people, now lies also in the same direction. If the first named of these new aids to war are the natural and necessary consequences of barriers thrown down; and if they have so enormously increased the power of those who first used them, that the enemy has been carried along in the current, and obliged to adopt them likewise, this will be the case also with people-wars. In the generality of cases, the people who make judicious use of this means, will gain a proportionate superiority over those who despise its use. If this be so, then the only question is whether this modern intensification of the military element is, upon the whole, salutary for the interests of humanity or otherwise, – a question which it would be about as easy to answer as the question of war itself –

we leave both to philosophers. But the opinion may be advanced, that the resources swallowed up in people's wars might be more profitably employed, if used in providing other military means; no very deep investigation, however, is necessary to be convinced that these resources are for the most part not disposable, and cannot be utilized in an arbitrary manner at pleasure. One essential part that is the moral element, is not called into existence until this kind of employment for it arises.

We therefore do not ask again: how much does the resistance which the whole nation in arms is capable of making, cost that nation? but we ask: what is the effect which such a resistance can produce? What are its conditions, and how is it to be used?

It follows from the very nature of the thing that defensive means thus widely dispersed, are not suited to great blows requiring concentrated action in time and space. Its operation, like the process of evaporation in physical nature, is according to the surface. The greater that surface and the greater the contact with the enemy's army, consequently the more that army spreads itself out, so much the greater will be the effects of arming the nation. Like a slow gradual heat, it destroys the foundations of the enemy's army. As it requires time to produce its effects, therefore whilst the hostile elements are working on each other, there is a state of tension which either gradually wears out if the people's war is extinguished at some points, and burns slowly away at others, or leads to a crisis, if the flames of this general conflagration envelop the enemy's army, and compel it to evacuate the country to save itself from utter destruction. In order that this result should be produced by a national war alone, we must suppose either a surface-extent of the dominions invaded, exceeding that of any country in Europe, except Russia, or suppose a disproportion between the strength of the invading army and the extent of the country, such as never occurs in reality. Therefore, to avoid following a phantom, we must imagine a people-war always in combination, with a war carried on by a regular army, and both carried on according to a plan embracing the operations of the whole.

The conditions under which alone the people's war can become effective are the following –

1. That the war is carried on in the heart of the country.
2. That it cannot be decided by a single catastrophe.
3. That the theatre of war embraces a considerable extent of country.
4. That the national character is favourable to the measure.
5. That the country is of a broken and difficult nature, either from being mountainous, or by reason of woods and marshes, or from the peculiar mode of cultivation in use.

Whether the population is dense or otherwise, is of little consequence, as there is less likelihood of a want of men than of anything else. Whether the inhabitants are rich or poor is also a point by no means decisive, at least it should not be; but it must be admitted that a poor population accustomed to hard work and privations usually shows itself more vigorous and better suited for war.

One peculiarity of country which greatly favors the action of war carried on by the people, is the scattered sites of the dwellings of the country people, such as is to be found in many parts of Germany. The country is thus more intersected an dcovered; the roads are worse, although more numerous; the lodgement of troops is attended with endless difficulties, but especially that peculiarity repeats itself on a small scale, which a people-war possesses on a great scale, namely that the principle of resistance exists everywhere, but is nowhere tangible. If the inhabitants are collected in villages, the most troublesome have troops quartered on them, or they are plundered as a punishment, and their houses burnt, etc, a system which could not be very easily carried out with a peasant community of Westphalia.

National levies and armed peasantry cannot and should not be employed against the main body of the enemy's army, or even against any considerable corps of the same, they must not attempt to crack the nut, they must only gnaw on the surface and the borders. They should rise in the provinces situated at one of the sides of the theatre of war, and in which the assailant does not appear in force, in order to withdraw these provinces entirely from his influence. Where no enemy is to be found, there is no want of courage to oppose him, and at the example thus given, the mass of the neighboring population gradually takes fire. Thus the fire spreads as it does in heather, and reaching at last that part of the surface of the soil on which the aggressor is based, it seizes his lines of communication and preys upon the vital thread by which his existence is supported. For although we entertain no exaggerated ideas of the omnipotence of a people's war, such as that it is an inexhaustible, unconquerable element, over which the mere force of an army has as little control as the human will has over the wind or the rain; in short, although our opinion is not founded on flowery ephemeral literature, still we must admit that armed peasants are not to be driven before us in the same way as a body of soldiers who keep together like a herd of cattle, and usually follow their noses. Armed peasants, on the contrary, when broken, disperse in all directions, for which no formal plan is required; through this circumstance, the march of every small body of troops in a mountainous, thickly wooded, or even broken country, becomes a service of a very dangerous character, for at any moment a combat may arise on the march; if in point of fact no armed bodies have even been seen for some time, yet the same peasants already driven off by the head of a column, may at any hour make their appearance in its rear. If it is an object to destroy roads or to block up a defile; the means which outposts or detachments from an army can apply to that purpose, bear about the same relation to those furnished by a body of insurgent peasants, as the action of an automaton does to that of a human being. The enemy has no other means to oppose to the action of national levies except that of detaching numerous parties to furnish escorts for convoys to occupy military stations, defiles, bridges, etc. In proportion as the first efforts of the national levies are small, so the detachments sent out will be weak in numbers, from the repugnance to a great dispersion of forces; it is on these weak bodies that the fire of the national war usually first properly kindles itself, they are overpowered by numbers at some points, courage rises, the love of fighting gains strength, and the intensity of this struggle increases until the crisis approaches which is to decide the issue.

According to our idea of a people's war, it should, like a kind of nebulous vapoury essence, never condense into a solid body; otherwise the enemy sends an adequate force against this core, crushes it, and makes a great many prisoners; their courage sinks; every one thinks the main question is decided, any further effort useless, and the arms fall from the hands of the people. Still, however, on the other hand, it is necessary that this mist should collect at some points into denser masses, and form threatening clouds from which now and again a formidable flash of lightning may burst forth. These points are chiefly on the flanks of the enemy's theatre of war, as already observed. There the armament of the people should be organised into greater and more systematic bodies, supported by a small force of regular troops, so as to give it the appearance of a regular force and fit it to venture upon enterprises on a larger scale. From these points, the irregular character in the organisation of these bodies should diminish in proportion as they are to be employed more in the direction of the rear of the enemy, where he is exposed to their hardest blows. These better organised masses, are for the purpose of falling upon the larger garrisons which the enemy leaves behind him. Besides, they serve to create a feeling of uneasiness and dread, and increase the moral impression of the whole, without them the total action would be wanting in force, and the situation of the enemy upon the whole would not be made sufficiently uncomfortable.

The easiest way for a general to produce this more effective form of a national armament, is to support the movement by small detachments sent from the army. Without the support of a few regular troops as an encouragement, the inhabitants generally want an impulse, and the confidence to take up arms. The stronger these detachments are, the greater will be their power of attraction, the greater will be the avalanche which is to fall down. But this has its limits; partly, first, because it would be detrimental to the army to cut it up into detachments, for this secondary object to dissolve it, as it were, into a body of irregulars, and form with it in all directions a weak defensive line, by which we may be sure both the regular army and national levies alike would become completely ruined; partly, secondly, because experience seems to tell us that when there are too many regular troops in a district, the people-war loses in vigour and efficacy; the causes of this are in the first place, that too many of the enemy's troops are thus drawn into the district, and, in the second place, that the inhabitants then rely on their own regular troops, and, thirdly, because the presence of such large bodies of troops makes too great demands on the powers of the people in other ways, that is, in providing quarters, transport, contributions, etc., etc.

Another means of preventing any serious reaction on the part of the enemy against this popular movement constitutes, at the same time, a leading principle in the method of using such levies; this is, that as a rule, with this great strategic means of defence, a tactical defence should seldom or ever take place. The character of a *combat with national levies* is the same as that of all combats of masses of troops of an inferior quality, great impetuosity and fiery ardour at the commencement, but little coolness or tenacity if the combat is prolonged. Further, the defeat and dispersion of a body of national levies is of no material consequence, as they lay their account with that, but a body of this description must not be broken up by losses in killed, wounded, and prisoners; a defeat of that kind would soon cool their ardour. But both these peculiarities are entirely opposed to the nature of a tactical defensive. In the defensive combat a persistent slow systematic action is required, and great risks must be run; a mere attempt, from which we can desist as soon as we please, can never lead to results in the defensive. If, therefore, the national levies are entrusted with the defence of any particular portion of territory, care must be taken that the measure does not lead to a regular great defensive combat; for if the circumstances were ever so favourable to them, they would be sure to be defeated. They may, and should, therefore, defend the approaches to mountains, dykes, over marshes, river-passages, as long as possible; but when once they are broken, they should rather disperse, and continue their defence by sudden attacks, than concentrate and allow themselves to be shut up in some narrow last refuge in a regular defensive position. – However brave a nation may be, however warlike its habits, however intense its hatred of the enemy, however favourable the nature of the country, it is an undeniable fact that a people's war cannot be kept up in an atmosphere too full of danger. If, therefore, its combustible material is to be fanned by any means into a considerable flame it must be at remote points where there is more air, and where it cannot be extinguished by one great blow.

After these reflections, which are more of the nature of subjective impressions than an objective analysis, because the subject is one as yet of rare occurrence generally, and has been but imperfectly treated of by those who have had actual experience for any length of time, we have only to add that the strategic plan of defence can include in itself the cooperation of a general arming of the people in two different ways, that is, either as a last resource after a lost battle, or as a natural assistance before a decisive battle has been fought. The latter case supposes a retreat into the interior of the country, and that indirect kind of reaction of which we have treated in the eighth and twenty-fourth chapters of this book. We have, therefore, here only to say a few words on the mission of the national levies after a battle has been lost.

No State should believe its fate, that is, its entire existence, to be dependent upon one battle, let it be even the most decisive. If it is beaten, the calling forth fresh power, and the natural weakening which every offensive undergoes with time, may bring about a turn of fortune, or assistance may come from abroad. No such urgent haste to die is needed yet; and as by instinct the drowning man catches at a straw, so in the natural course of the moral world a people should try the last means of deliverance when it sees itself hurried along to the brink of an abyss.

However small and weak a State may be in comparison to its enemy, if it foregoes a last supreme effort, we must say there is no longer any soul left in it. This does not exclude the possibility of saving itself from complete destruction by the purchase of peace at a sacrifice; but neither does such an aim on its part do away with the utility of fresh measures for defence; they will neither make peace more difficult nor more onerous, but easier and better. They are still more necessary if there is an expectation of assistance from those who are interested in maintaining our political existence. Any government, therefore, which, after the loss of a great battle, only thinks how it may speedily place the nation in the lap of peace, and unmanned by the feeling of great hopes disappointed, no longer feels in itself the courage or the desire to stimulate to the utmost every element of force, completely stultifies itself in such case through weakness, and shows itself unworthy of victory, and, perhaps, just on that account, was incapable of gaining one.

However decisive, therefore, the overthrow may be which is experienced by a State, still by a retreat of the army into the interior, the efficacy of its fortresses and an arming of the people may be brought into use. In connection with this it is advantageous if the flank of the principal theatre of war is fenced in by mountains, or otherwise very difficult tracts of country, which stand forth as bastions, the strategic enfilade of which is to check the enemy's progress.

If the victorious enemy is engaged in siege works, if he has left strong garrisons behind him everywhere to secure his communications, or detached corps to make himself elbow-room, and to keep the adjacent provinces in subjection, if he is already weakened by his various losses in active means and material of war, then the moment is arrived when the defensive army should again enter the lists, and by a well-directed blow make the assailant stagger in his disadvantageous position.

CHAPTER TWENTY SEVEN
Defence of a Theatre of War

HAVING TREATED of the *most important defensive means,* we might perhaps be contented to leave the manner in which these means attach themselves to the plan of defence as a whole to be discussed in the last Book, which will be devoted to the *Plan of a War;* for from this every secondary scheme, either of attack or defence, emanates and is determined in its leading features; and moreover in many cases the plan of the war itself is nothing more than the plan of the attack or defence of the principal theatre of war. But we have not been able to commence with war as a whole, although in war more than in any other phase of human activity, the parts are shaped by the whole, imbued with and essentially altered by its character; instead of that, we have been obliged to make ourselves thoroughly acquainted, in the first instance, with each single subject as a separate part. Without this progress from the simple to the complex, a number of undefined ideas would have overpowered us, and the manifold phases of reciprocal action in particular would have constantly confused our conceptions. We shall therefore still continue to advance towards the whole by one step at a time; that is, we shall consider the defence of a theatre in itself, and look for the thread by which the subjects already treated of connect themselves with it.

The defensive, according to our conception, is nothing *but the stronger form of combat.* The preservation of our own forces and the destruction of those of the enemy – in a word, the *victory* – is the aim of this contest, but at the same time not its ultimate object.

That object is the preservation of our own political state and the subjugation of that of the enemy; or again, in one word, the *desired peace,* because it is only by it that this conflict adjusts itself, and ends in a common result.

But what is the enemy's state in connection with war? Above all things its military force is important, then its territory; but certainly there are also still many other things which, through particular circumstances, may obtain a predominant importance; to these belong, before all, foreign and domestic political relations, which sometimes decide more than all the rest. But although the military force and the territory of the enemy alone are still not the state itself, nor are they the only connections which the state may have with the war, still these two things are always preponderating, mostly immeasurably surpassing all other connections in importance. Military force is to protect the territory of the state, or to conquer that of an enemy; the territory on the other hand, constantly nourishes and renovates the military force. The two, therefore, depend on each other, mutually support each other, are equal in importance one to the other. But still there is a difference in their mutual relations. If the military force is destroyed, that is completely defeated, rendered incapable of further resistance, then the loss of the territory follows of itself; but on the other hand, the destruction of the military force by no means follows from the conquest of the country, because that force may of its own accord evacuate the territory, in order afterwards to reconquer it the more easily. Indeed, not only does the *complete* destruction of its army decide the fate of a country, but even every *considerable weakening* of its military force leads regularly to a loss of territory; on the other hand, every considerable loss of territory does not cause a proportionate diminution of military power; in the long run it will do so, but not always within the space of time in which a war is brought to a close.

From this it follows that the preservation of our own military power, and the diminution or destruction of that of the enemy, take precedence in importance over the occupation of territory, and, therefore, is the *first object* which a general should strive for. The possession of territory only presses for consideration *as an object* if that means (diminution or destruction of the enemy's military force) has not effected it.

If the whole of the enemy's military power was united in *one army*, and if the whole war consisted of *one battle*, then the possession of the country would depend on the issue of that battle; destruction of the enemy's military forces, conquest of his country and security of our own, would follow from that result, and, in a certain measure, be identical with it. Now the question is, what can induce the defensive to deviate from this simplest form of the act of warfare, and distribute his power in space? The answer is, the insufficiency of the victory which he might gain with all his forces united. Every victory has its sphere of influence. If this extends over the whole of the enemy's state, consequently over the whole of his military force and his territory, that is, if all the parts are carried along in the same movement, which we have impressed upon the core of his power, then such a victory is all that we require, and a division of our forces would not be justified by sufficient grounds. But if there are portions of the enemy's military force, and of country belonging to either party, over which our victory would have no effect, then we must give particular attention to those parts; and as we cannot unite territory like a military force in one point, therefore we must divide our forces for the purpose of attacking or defending those portions.

It is only in small, compactly shaped states that it is possible to have such a unity of military force, and that probably all depends upon a victory over *that force*. Such a unity is practically impossible when larger tracts of country, having for a great extent boundaries conterminious with our own, are concerned, or in the case of an alliance of several surrounding states against us. In such cases, divisions of force must necessarily take place, giving occasion to different theatres of war.

The effect of a victory will naturally depend on its *greatness*, and that on the mass of the *conquered troops*. Therefore *the blow* which, if successful, will produce the greatest effect, must be made against *that part* of the country where the greatest number of the enemy's forces are collected together; and the greater the mass of our own forces which we use for this blow, so much the surer shall we be of this success. This natural sequence of ideas leads us to an illustration by which we shall see this truth more clearly; it is the nature and effect of the centre of gravity in mechanics.

As the centre of gravity is always situated where the greatest mass of matter is collected, and as a shock against the centre of gravity of a body always produces the greatest effect, and further, as the most effective blow is struck with the centre of gravity of the power used, so it is also in war. The armed forces of every belligerent, whether of a single state or of an alliance of states, have a certain unity, and in that way, connection; but where connection is there come in analogies of the centre of gravity. There are, therefore, in these armed forces certain centres of gravity, the movement and direction of which decide upon other points, and these centres of gravity are situated where the greatest bodies of troops are assembled. But just as, in the world of inert matter, the action against the centre of gravity has its measure and limits in the connection of the parts, so it is in war, and here as well as there the force exerted may easily be greater than the resistance requires, and then there is a blow in the air, a waste of force.

What a difference there is between the solidity of an army under *one* standard, led into battle under the personal command of *one* general, and that of an *allied army* extended over 50 or 100 miles, or it may be even based upon quite different sides (of the theatre of war). There we see coherence in the strongest degree, unity most complete; here unity in a very remote degree often only existing in the political view held in common, and in that also in a miserable and insufficient degree, the cohesion of parts mostly very weak, often quite an illusion.

Therefore, if on the one hand, the violence with which we wish to strike the blow prescribes the greatest concentration of force, so in like manner, on the other hand, we have to fear every undue excess as a real evil, because it entails a waste of power, and that in turn a *deficiency* of power at other points.

To distinguish these *"centra gravitatis"* in the enemy's military power, to discern their spheres of action is, therefore, a supreme act of strategic judgment. We must constantly ask ourselves, what effect the advance or retreat of part of the forces on either side will produce on the rest.

We do not by this lay claim in any way to the discovery of a new method, we have only sought to explain the foundation of the method of all generals, in every age, in a manner which may place its connection with the nature of things in a clearer light.

How this conception of the centre of gravity of the enemy's force affects the whole plan of the war, we shall consider in the last book, for that is the proper place for the subject, and we have only borrowed it from there to avoid leaving any break in the sequence of ideas. By the introduction of this view we have seen the motives which occasion a partition of forces in general. These consist fundamentally of two interests which are in opposition to each other; the one, *the possession of territory* strives to divide the forces; the other, *the effort of force against the centre of gravity of the enemy's military power*, combines them again up to a certain point.

Thus it is that theatres of war or particular army regions originate. These are those boundaries of the area of the country and of the forces thereon distributed, within which every decision given by the principal force of such a region extends itself *directly* over the whole, and carries on the whole with it in its own direction. We say *directly*, because a decision on one theatre of war must naturally have also an influence more or less over those adjoining it.

Although it lies quite in the nature of the thing, we must again remind our readers expressly that here as well as everywhere else our definitions are only directed at the centres of certain speculative regions, the limits of which we neither desire to, nor can we, define by sharp lines.

We think, therefore, a theatre of war, whether large or small, with its military force, whatever may be the size of that, represents a unity which maybe reduced to one centre of gravity. At this centre of gravity the decision must take place, and to be conqueror here means to defend the theatre of war in the widest sense.

CHAPTER TWENTY EIGHT

Defence of a Theatre of War – (Continued)

DEFENCE, however, consists of two different elements, these are the *decision* and the *state of expectation*. The combination of these two elements forms the subject of this chapter.

First we must observe that the state of expectation is not, in point of fact, the complete defence; it is only that province of the same in which it proceeds to its aim. As long as a military force has not abandoned the portion of territory placed under its guardianship, the tension of forces on both sides created by the attack continues, and this lasts until there is a decision. The decision itself can only be regarded as having actually taken place when either the assailant or defender has left the theatre of war.

As long as an armed force maintains itself within its theatre, the defence of the same continues, and in this sense the defence of the theatre of war is identical with the defence *in the same*. Whether the enemy in the meantime has obtained possession of much or little of that section of country is not essential, for it is only lent to him until the decision.

But this kind of idea by which we wish to settle the proper relation of the state of expectation to the whole is only correct when a decision is really to take place, and is regarded by both parties as inevitable. For it is only by that decision that the centres of gravity of the respective forces, and the theatre of war determined through them are *effectually* hit. Whenever the idea of a decisive solution disappears, then the centres of gravity are neutralised, indeed, in a certain sense, the whole of the armed forces become so also, and now the possession of territory, which forms the second principal branch of the whole theatre of war, comes forward as the direct object. In other words, the less a decisive blow is sought for by both sides in a war, and the more it is merely a mutual observation of one another, so much the more important becomes the possession of territory, so much the more the defensive seeks to cover all directly, and the assailant seeks to extend his forces in his advance.

Now we cannot conceal from ourselves the fact that the majority of wars and campaigns approach much more to a state of observation than to a struggle for life or death, that is, a contest in which one at least of the combatants uses every effort to bring about a complete decision. This last character is only to be found in the wars of the nineteenth century to such a degree that a theory founded on this point of view can be made use of in relation to them. But as all future wars will hardly have this character, and it is rather to be expected that they will again show a tendency to the observation character, therefore any theory to be practically useful must pay attention to that. Hence we shall commence with the case in which the desire of a decision permeates and guides the whole, therefore with *real,* or if we may use the expression, *absolute war;* then in another chapter we shall examine those modifications which arise through the approach, in a greater or less degree, to the state of a war of observation.

In the first case (whether the decision is sought by the aggressor or the defender) the defence of the theatre of war must consist in the defender establishing himself there in such a manner, that in a decision he will have an advantage on his side at any moment. This decision may be either a battle, or a series of great combats, but it may also consist in the resultant of mere relations, which arise from the situation of the opposing forces, that is, *possible combats.*

If the battle were not also the most powerful, the most usual and most effectual means of a decision in war, as we think we have already shown on several occasions, still the mere fact of its being in a general way one of the means of reaching this solution, would be sufficient to enjoin *the greatest concentration of our forces* which circumstances will in any way permit. A great battle upon the theatre of war is the blow of the centre of force against the centre of force; the more forces can be collected in the one or the other, the surer and greater will be the effect. Therefore every separation of forces which is not called for by an object (which either cannot itself be attained by the successful issue of a battle, or which itself is necessary to the successful issue of the battle) is *blameable.*

But the greatest concentration of forces is not the only fundamental condition; it is also requisite that they should have such a position and place that the battle may be fought under favourable circumstances.

The different steps in the defence which we have become acquainted with in the chapter on the methods of defence, are completely homogeneous with these fundamental conditions; there will therefore be no difficulty in connecting them with the same, according to the special requirements of each case. But there is one point which seems at first sight to involve a contradiction in itself, and which, as one of the most important in the defence, requires explanation so much the more. It is the hitting upon the exact centre of gravity of the enemy's force.

If the defender ascertains in time the roads by which the enemy will advance, and upon which in particular the great mass of his force will be found for a certainty, he may march against him on that road. This will be the most usual case, for although the defence precedes the attack in measures of a general nature, in the establishment of strong places, great arsenals, and depôts, and in the peace establishment of his army, and thus gives a line of direction to the assailant in his preparations, still, when the campaign really opens, the defender, in relation to the aggressor, has the peculiar advantage in general of playing the last hand.

To attack a foreign country with a large army, very considerable preparations are required. Provisions, stores, and articles of equipment of all kinds must be collected, which is a work of time. While these preparations are going on, the defender has time to prepare accordingly, in regard to which we must not forget that the defensive requires less time, generally speaking, because in every state things are prepared rather for the defensive than the offensive.

But although this may hold good in the majority of cases, there is always a possibility that, in particular cases, the defensive may remain in uncertainty as to the principal line by which the enemy intends to advance; and this case is more likely to occur when the defence is dependent on measures which of themselves take a good deal of time, as for example, the preparation of a strong position. Further, supposing the defender places himself on the line by which the aggressor is advancing, then, unless the defender is prepared to take the initiative by attacking the aggressor, the latter may avoid the position which the defender has taken up, by only altering a little his line of advance, for in the cultivated parts of Europe we can never be so situated that there are not roads to the right or left by which any position may be avoided. Plainly, in such a case the defender could not wait for his enemy in a position, or at least could not wait there in the expectation of giving battle.

But before entering on the means available to the defensive in this case, we must inquire more particularly into the nature of such a case, and the probability of its occurrence.

Naturally there are in every State, and also in every theatre of war (of which alone we are at present speaking), objects and points upon which an attack is likely to be more efficacious than anywhere else. Upon this we think it will be better to speak when we come to the attack. Here we shall confine ourselves to observing that, if the most advantageous object and point of attack is the motive for the assailant in the direction of his blow, this motive reacts on the defensive, and must be his guide in cases in which he knows nothing of the intentions of his adversary. If the assailant does not take this direction which is favourable to him, he foregoes part of his natural advantages. It is evident that, if the defender has taken up a position in that direction, the evading his position, or passing round, is not to be done for nothing; it costs a sacrifice. From this it follows that there is not on the side of the defender such a risk of *missing the direction of his enemy;* neither on the other hand, is it so easy for the assailant *to pass round his adversary* as appears at first sight, because there exists beforehand a very distinct, and in most cases preponderating, motive in favour of one or the other direction, and that consequently the defender, although his preparations are fixed to one spot, will not fail in most cases to come in contact with the mass of the enemy's forces. In other words, *if the defender has put himself in the right position, he may be almost sure that the assailant will come to meet him.*

But by this we shall not and cannot deny the possibility of the defender sometimes not meeting with the assailant after all these arrangements, and therefore the question arises, what he should then do, and how much of the real advantages of his position still remain available to him.

If we ask ourselves what means still remain generally to the defender when the assailant passes by his position, they are the following: –

1. To divide his forces instantly, so as to be certain to find the assailant with one portion, and then to support that portion with the other.

2. To take up a position with his force united, and in case the assailant passes by him, to push on rapidly in front of him by a lateral movement. In most cases there will not be time to make such a movement directly to a flank, it will therefore be necessary to take up the new position somewhat further back.

3. With his whole force to attack the enemy in flank.

4. To operate against his communications.

5. By a counter attack on *his* theatre of war, to do exactly what the enemy has done in passing by us.

We introduce this last measure, because it is possible to imagine a case in which it may be efficacious; but as it is in contradiction to the object of the defence, that is, the grounds on which that form has been chosen, therefore it can only be regarded as an abnormity, which can only take place because the enemy has made some great mistake, or because there are other special features in a particular case.

Operating against the enemy's communications implies that our own are superior, which is also one of the fundamental requisites of a good defensive position. But although on that ground this action may promise the defender a certain amount of advantage, still, in the defence of a theatre of war, it is seldom an operation suited to *lead to a decision,* which we have supposed to be the object of the campaign.

The dimensions of a single theatre of war are seldom so large that the line of communications is exposed to much danger by their length, and even if they were in danger, still the time which the assailant requires for the execution of his blow is usually too short for his progress to be arrested by the slow effects of the action against his communications.

Therefore this means (that is the action against the communications) will prove quite inefficacious in most cases against an enemy determined upon a decision, and also in case the defender seeks such a solution.

The object of the three other means which remain for the defender, is a direct decision – a meeting of centre of force with centre of force; they correspond better, therefore, with the thing required. But we shall at once say that we decidedly prefer the third to the other two, and without quite rejecting the latter, we hold the former to be in the majority of cases the true means of defence.

In a position where our forces are divided, there is always a danger of getting involved in a war of posts, from which, if our adversary is resolute, can follow, under the best of circumstances, only *a relative defence on a large scale,* never a decision such as we desire; and even if by superior tact we should be able to avoid this mistake, still, by the preliminary resistance being with divided forces, the first shock is sensibly weakened, and we can never be sure that the advanced corps first engaged will not suffer disproportionate losses. To this is to be added that the resistance of this corps which usually ends in its falling back on the main body, appears to the troops in the light of a lost combat, or miscarriage of plans, and the moral force suffers accordingly.

The second means, that of placing our whole force in front of the enemy, in whichever direction he may bend his march, involves a risk of our arriving too late, and thus between two measures, falling short of both. Besides this, a defensive battle requires coolness and consideration, a knowledge, indeed intimate knowledge of the country, which cannot be expected in a hasty oblique movement to a flank. Lastly, positions suitable for a good defensive battle-field are too rarely to be met with to reckon upon them at every point of every road.

On the other hand, the third means, namely to attack the enemy in flank, therefore to give battle with a change of front, is attended with great advantages.

Firstly, there is always in this case, as we know, an exposure of the lines of communication, here the lines of retreat, and in this respect the defender has one advantage in his general relations as defender, and next and chiefly, the advantage which we have claimed for the strategic properties of his position at present.

Secondly, – and this is the principal thing, – every assailant who attempts to pass by his opponent is placed between two opposite tendencies. His first desire is to advance to attain the object of his attack; but the possibility of being attacked in flank at any moment, creates a necessity for being prepared, at any moment, to deliver a blow in that direction, and that too a blow with the mass of his forces. These two tendencies are contradictory, and beget such a complication in the internal relations (of his army), such a difficulty in the choice of measures, if they are to suit every event, that there can hardly be a more disagreeable position strategically. If the assailant knew with certainty the moment when he would be attacked, he might prepare to receive the enemy with skill and ability; but in his uncertainty on this point, and pressed by the necessity of advancing, it is almost certain that when the moment for battle arrives, it finds him in the midst of hurried and half-finished preparations, and therefore by no means in an advantageous relation to his enemy.

If then there are favourable moments for the defender to deliver an offensive battle, it is surely at such a moment as this, above all others, that we may look for success. If we consider, further, that the knowledge of the country and choice of ground are on the side of the defender, that he can prepare his movements, and can time them, no one can doubt that he possesses in such a situation a decided superiority, strategically, over his adversary.

We think, therefore, that a defender occupying a well chosen position, with his forces united, may quietly wait for the enemy passing by his army; should the enemy not attack him in his position, and that an operation against the enemy's communications does not suit the circumstances, there still remains for him an excellent means of bringing about a decision by resorting to a flank attack.

If cases of this kind are hardly to be found in military history, the reason is, partly, that the defender has seldom had the courage to remain firm in such a position, but has either divided his forces, or rashly thrown himself in front of his enemy by a cross or diagonal march, or that no assailant dares to venture past the defender under such circumstances, and in that way his movement usually comes to a stand still.

The defender is in this case compelled to resort to an offensive battle: the further advantages of *the state of expectation of a strong position, of good entrenchments*, etc., etc., he must give up; in most cases the situation in which he finds the advancing enemy will not quite make up for these advantages, for it is just to evade their influence that the assailant has placed himself in his present situation; still it always offers him *a certain compensation*, and theory is therefore not just obliged to see a quantity disappear at once from the calculation, to see the pro and contra mutually cancel each other, as so often happens when critical writers of history introduce a little bit of theory.

It must not, in fact, be supposed that we are now dealing with logical subtilties; the subject is rather one which the more it is practically considered, the more it appears as an idea embracing the whole essence of defensive war, everywhere dominating and regulating it.

It is only by the determination on the part of the defender to assail his opponent with all his force, the moment he passes by him, that he avoids two pitfalls, close to which he is led by the defensive form; that is a division of his force, and a hasty flank march to intercept the assailant in front. In both he accepts the law of the assailant; in both he seeks to aid himself through measures of a very critical nature, and with a most dangerous degree of haste; and wherever a resolute adversary, thirsting for victory and a decision, has encountered such a system of defence, he has knocked it on the head. But when the defender has assembled his forces at the right point to fight a general action, if he is determined with this force, come what will, to attack his enemy in flank, he has done right, and is in the *right* course, and he is supported by all the advantages which the defence can give in his situation; his actions will then bear the *stamp of good preparation, coolness, security, unity and simplicity*.

We cannot here avoid mentioning a remarkable event in history, which has a close analogy with the ideas now developed; we do so to anticipate its being used in a wrong application.

When the Prussian army was, in October, 1806, waiting in Thuringia for the French under Buonaparte, the former was posted between the two great roads on which the latter might be expected to advance, that is, the road to Berlin by Erfurth, and that by Hof and Leipsic. The first intention of breaking into Franconia straight through the Thuringian Forest, and afterwards, when that plan was abandoned, the uncertainty as to which of the roads the French would choose for their advance, caused this intermediate position. *As such*, it must therefore have led to the adoption of the measure we have been discussing, a hasty interception of the enemy in front by a lateral movement.

This was in fact the idea in case the enemy marched by Erfurth, for the roads in that direction were good; on the other hand, the idea of a movement of this description on the road by Hof could not be entertained, partly because the army was two or three marches away from that road, partly because the deep valley of the Saale interposed; neither did this plan ever enter into the views of the Duke of Brunswick, so that there was no kind of preparation made for carrying it into effect, but it was always contemplated by Prince Hohenlohe, that is, by Colonel Massenbach, who exerted all his influence to draw the Duke into this plan. Still less could the idea be entertained of leaving the position which had been taken on the left bank of the Saale to try an offensive battle against Buonaparte on his advance, that is, to such an attack in flank as we have been considering; for if the Saale was an obstacle to intercepting the enemy in the last moment (*à fortiori*) it would be a still greater obstacle to assuming the offensive at a moment when the enemy would be in possession of the opposite side of the river, at least partially. The Duke, therefore, determined to wait behind the Saale to see what would happen, that is to say, if we can call anything a determination which emanated from this many-headed Headquarters' Staff, and in this time of confusion and utter indecision.

Whatever may have been the true condition of affairs during this state of expectation, the consequent situation of the army was this: –

1. That the enemy might be attacked if he crossed the Saale to attack the Prussian army.

2. That if he did not march against that army, operations might be commenced against his communications.

3. If it should be found practicable and advisable, he might be intercepted near Leipsic by a rapid flank march.

In the first case, the Prussian army possessed a great strategic and tactical advantage in the deep valley of the Saale. In the second, the strategic advantage was just as great, for the enemy had only a very narrow base between our position and the neutral territory of Bohemia, whilst ours was extremely broad; even in the third case, our army, covered by the Saale, was still by no means in a disadvantageous situation.

All these three measures, in spite of the confusion and want of any clear perception at head-quarters, *were really discussed;* but certainly we cannot wonder that, although a right idea may have been entertained, it should have entirely failed in the *execution* by the complete want of resolution and the confusion generally prevailing.

In the two first cases, the position on the left bank of the Saale is to be regarded as a real flank position, and it had undoubtedly as such very great qualities; but in truth, against a very superior enemy, *against a Buonaparte,* a flank position with an army that is not very sure about what it is doing, *is a very bold measure.*

After long hesitation, the Duke on the 13th adopted the last of the plans proposed, but it was too late, Buonaparte had already commenced to pass the Saale, and the battles of Jena and Auerstadt were inevitable. The Duke, through his indecision, had set himself between two stools; he quitted his first position too late *to push his army in before the enemy,* and too soon for a battle suited to the object. Nevertheless, the natural strength of this position proved itself so far that the Duke was able to destroy the right wing of the enemy's army at Auerstadt, whilst Prince Hohenlohe, by a bloody retreat, was still able to back out of the scrape; but at Auerstadt they did not venture to realise the victory, which was *quite certain;* and at Jena they thought they might reckon upon one which was *quite impossible.*

In any case, Buonaparte felt the strategic importance of the position on the Saale so much, that he did not venture to pass it by, but determined on a passage of the Saale in sight of the enemy.

By what we have now said we think we have sufficiently specified the relations between the defence and the attack when a decisive course of action is intended, and we believe we have shown also the threads to which, according to their situation and connection, the different subjects of the plan of defence attach themselves. To go through the different arrangements more in detail does not come within our views, for that would lead us into a boundless field of particular cases. When a general has laid down for his direction a distinct point, he will see how far it agrees with geographical, statistical, and political circumstances, the material and personal relations of his own army and that of the enemy, and how the one or the other may require that his plans should be modified in carrying them into effect.

But in order more distinctly to connect and look closer at the gradations in the defence specified in the chapter on the different kinds of defence, we shall here lay before our readers what seems to us most important, in relation to the same generally.

1. Reasons for marching against the enemy with a view to an offensive battle, may be as follows: –

(*a*) If we know that the enemy is advancing with his forces very much divided, and therefore we have reason to expect a victory, although we are, upon the whole, much weaker.

But such an advance on the part of the assailant is in itself very improbable, and consequently, unless we know of it upon certain information, the plan is not good; for to reckon upon it, and rest all our hopes on it through a *mere supposition*, and without sufficient motive, leads generally to a very dangerous situation. We do not, then, find things as we expected; we are obliged to give up the offensive battle, we are not prepared to fight on the defensive, we are obliged to commence with a retreat against our will, and leave almost everything to chance.

This is very much what occurred in the defence, conducted by the army under Dohna against the Russians, in the campaign of 1759, and which, under General Wedel, ended in the unfortunate battle of Zullichau.

This measure shortens matters so much that plan-makers are only too ready to propose it, without taking much trouble to inquire how far the hypothesis on which it rests is well founded.

(*b*) If we are generally in sufficient strength for battle, and –

(*c*) If a blundering, irresolute adversary specially invites an attack.

In this case the effect of surprise may be worth more than any assistance furnished by the ground through a good position. It is the real essence of good generalship thus to bring into play the power of the moral forces; – but theory can never say loud enough nor often enough there must be an *objective foundation* for these suppositions; without *such foundation* to be always talking of surprises and the superiority of novel or unusual modes of attack, and thereon to found plans, considerations, criticisms, is acting without any grounds, and is altogether objectionable.

(*d*) When the nature of our army makes it specially suited for the offensive.

It was certainly not a visionary or false idea when Frederick the Great conceived that in his mobile, courageous army, full of confidence in him, obedient by habit, trained to precision, animated and elevated by pride, and with its perfection in the oblique attack, he possessed an instrument which, in his firm and daring hand, was much more suited to attack than defence; all these qualities were wanting in his opponents, and in this respect, therefore, he had the most decided superiority; to make use of this was worth more to him, in most cases, than to take to his assistance entrenchments and obstacles of ground. – But such a superiority will always be rare; a well-trained army, thoroughly practised in great movements, has only part of the above advantages. If Frederick the Great maintained that the Prussian army was particularly adapted for attack – and this has been incessantly repeated since his time – still we should not attach too much weight to any such saying; in most cases in war we feel more exhilarated, more courageous when acting offensively than defensively: but this is a feeling which all troops have in common, and there is hardly an army respecting which its generals and leaders have not made the same assertion (as Frederick). We must, therefore, not too readily rely on an appearance of superiority, and through that neglect real advantages.

A very natural and weighty reason for resorting to an offensive battle may be the composition of the army as regards the three arms, for instance, a numerous cavalry and little artillery.

We continue the enumeration of reasons.

(e.) When we can nowhere find a good position.

(f.) When we must hasten with the decision.

(g.) Lastly, the combined influence of several or all of these reasons.

2. The waiting for the enemy in a locality where it is intended to attack him (Minden, 1759) naturally proceeds from –

a, there being no such disproportion of force to our disadvantage as to make it necessary to seek a strong position and strengthen it by entrenchments.

b, a locality having been found particularly adapted to the purpose. The properties which determine this belong to tactics; we shall only observe that these properties chiefly consist in an easy approach for the defender from his side, and in all kinds of obstacles on the side next to the enemy.

3. A position will be taken with the express intention of there waiting the attack of the enemy –

a. If the disproportion of forces compels us to seek cover from natural obstacles or behind field-works.

b. When the country affords an excellent position for our purpose.

The two modes of defence, 2 and 3, will come more into consideration according as we do not seek the decision itself, but content ourselves with a negative result, and have reason to think that our opponent is wavering and irresolute, and that he will in the end fail to carry out his plans.

4. An entrenched unassailable camp only fulfils the object –

a. If it is situated at an extremely important strategic point.

The character of such a position consists in this, that we cannot be driven out of it; the enemy is therefore obliged to try some other means, that is, to pursue his object without touching this camp, or to blockade it and reduce it by starvation: if it is impossible for him to do this, then the strategic qualities of the position must be very great.

b. If we have reason to expect aid from abroad.

Such was the case with the Saxon army in its position at Pirna. Notwithstanding all that has been said against the measure on account of the ill-success which attended it in this instance, it is perfectly certain that 17,000 Saxons could never have been able to neutralise 40,000 Prussians in any other way. If the Austrians were unable to make better use of the superiority obtained at Lowositz, that only shows the badness of their whole method of war, as well as of their whole military organisation; and there cannot be a doubt that if the Saxons instead of taking post in the camp at Pirna had retired into Bohemia, Frederick the Great would have driven both Austrians and Saxons beyond Prague, and taken that place in the same campaign. Whoever does not admit the value of this advantage, and limits his consideration to the capture of the whole Saxon army, shows himself incapable of making a calculation of all the circumstances in a case of this kind, and without calculation no certain deduction can be obtained.

But as the cases *a* and *b* very rarely occur, therefore, the entrenched camp is a measure which requires to be well considered, and which is very seldom suitable in practice. The hope of *inspiring* the enemy *with respect* by such a camp, and thus reducing him to a state of complete inactivity, is attended with too much danger, namely, with the danger of being obliged to fight without the possibility of retreat. If Frederick the Great gained his object in this way at Bunzelwitz, we must admire the correct judgment he formed of his adversary, but we must certainly also lay more stress than usual on the resources which he would have found at the last moment to clear a road for the remnants of his army, and also on the *irresponsibility* of a king.

5. If there is one or if there are several fortresses near the frontier, then the great question arises, whether the defender should seek an action before or behind them. The latter recommends itself –

a, by the superiority of the enemy in numbers, which forces us to break his power before coming to a final struggle.

b, by these fortresses being near, so that the sacrifice of territory is not greater than we are compelled to make.

c, by the fitness *of the fortresses for defence.*

One principal use of fortresses is unquestionably, or should be, to break the enemy's force in his advance and to weaken considerably that portion which we intend to bring to an engagement. If we so seldom see this use made of fortresses, that proceeds from the cases in which a decisive battle is sought for by one of the opposing parties being very rare. But that is the only kind of case which we treat of here. We therefore look upon it as a principle equally simple and important in all cases in which the defender has one or more fortresses near him, that he should keep them before him, and give the decisive battle behind them. We admit that a battle lost within the line of our fortresses will compel us to retreat further into the interior of the country than one lost on the other side, tactical results in both cases being the same, although the causes of the difference have their origin rather in the imagination than in real things; neither do we forget that a battle may be given beyond the fortresses in a well chosen position, whilst inside them the battle in most cases must be an offensive one, particularly if the enemy is laying siege to a fortress which is in danger of being lost; but what signify these nice shades of distinction, as compared to the advantage that, in the decisive battle, we meet the enemy weakened by a fourth or a third of his force, perhaps one half if there are many fortresses?

We think, therefore, that in all cases of *an inevitable decision*, whether sought for by the offensive or the defensive, and that the latter is not tolerably sure of a victory, or if the nature of the country does not offer some most decisive reason to give battle in a position further forward – in all these cases we say when a fortress is situated near at hand and capable of defence, the defender should by all means withdraw at once behind it, and let the decision take place on this side, consequently with its co-operation. If he takes up his position so close to the fortress that the assailant can neither form the siege of nor blockade the place without first driving him off, he places the assailant under the necessity of attacking him, the defender, in his position. To us, therefore, of all defensive measures in a critical situation, none appears so simple and efficacious as the choice of a good position near to and behind a strong fortress.

At the same time, the question would wear a different aspect if the fortress was situated far back; for then it would be necessary to abandon a considerable part of our theatre of war, a sacrifice which, as we know, should not be made unless in a case of great urgency. In such a case the measure would bear more resemblance to a retreat into the interior of the country.

Another condition is, the fitness of the place for defence. It is well known that there are fortified places, especially large ones, which are not fit to be brought into contact with an enemy's army, because they could not resist the sudden assault of a powerful force. In this case, our position must at all events be so close behind that we could support the garrison.

Lastly, the retreat into the interior of the country is only a natural resource under the following circumstances: –

a, when owing to the physical and moral relation in which we stand as respects the enemy, the idea of a successful resistance on the frontier or near it cannot be entertained.

b, when it is a principal object to gain time.

c, when there are peculiarities in the country which are favourable to the measure, a subject on which we have already treated in the twenty-fifth chapter.

We thus close the chapter on the defence of a theatre of war if a decisive solution is sought for by one or other party, and is therefore inevitable. But it must be particularly borne in mind, that events in war do not exhibit themselves in such a pure abstract form, and that therefore, if our maxims and arguments should be used in reasoning on actual war, our thirtieth chapter should also be kept in view, and we must suppose the general, in the majority of cases, as placed between two tendencies, urged *more* towards one or the other, according to circumstances.

CHAPTER TWENTY NINE

Defence of a Theatre of War – (Continued)

Successive Resistance.

WE HAVE PROVED, in the twelfth and thirteenth chapters, that in strategy a successive resistance is inconsistent with the nature of the thing, and that all forces available should be used simultaneously.

As regards forces which are moveable, this requires no further demonstration; but when we look at the seat of war itself, with its fortresses, the natural divisions of the ground, and even the extent of its surface as being also elements of war, then, these being immovable, we can only either bring them gradually into use, or we must at once place ourselves so far back, that all agencies of this kind which are to be brought into activity are in our front. Then everything which can contribute to weaken the enemy in the territory which he has occupied, comes at once into activity, for the assailant must at least blockade the defender's fortresses, he must keep the country in subjection by garrisons and other posts, he has long marches to make, and everything he requires must be brought from a distance, etc. All these agencies commence to work, whether the assailant makes *his advance before or after* a decision, but in the former case their influence is somewhat greater. From this, therefore, it follows, that if the defender chooses to transfer his decision to a point further back, he has thus the means of bringing at once into play all these immovable elements of military force.

On the other hand, it is clear that this *transfer of the solution* (on the part of the defender) does not alter the extent of the influence of a victory which the assailant gains. In treating of the attack, we shall examine more closely the extent of the influence of a victory; here we shall only observe that it reaches to the exhaustion of the superiority, that is, the resultant of the physical and moral relations. Now this superiority exhausts itself in the first place by the duties required from the forces on the theatre of war, and secondly by losses in combats; the diminution of force arising from these two causes cannot be essentially altered, whether the combats take place at the commencement or at the end, near the frontier, or further towards the interior of the country (vom oder hinten). We think, for example, that a victory gained by Buonaparte over the Russians at Wilna, 1812, would have carried him just as far as that of Borodino – assuming that it was equally great – and that a victory at Moscow would not have carried him any further; Moscow was, in either case, the limit of this sphere of victory. Indeed, it cannot be doubted for a moment that a decisive battle on the frontier (for other reasons) would have produced much greater results through victory, and then, perhaps, the sphere of its influence would have been wider. Therefore, in this view, also, the transfer of the decision to a point further back is not necessary for the defence.

In the chapter on the various means of resistance, that method of delaying the decision, which may be regarded as an extreme form, was brought before us under the name of *retreat into the interior*, and as a particular method of defence, in which the object is rather that the assailant should wear himself out, than that he should be destroyed by the sword on the field of battle. But it is only when such an intention predominates that the delaying of the decisive battle can be regarded as *a peculiar method of resistance;* for otherwise it is evident that an infinite number of gradations may be conceived in this method, and that these may be combined with all other means of defence. We therefore look upon the greater or less co-operation of the theatre of war, not as a special form of defence, but as nothing more than a discretionary introduction into the defence of the immovable means of resistance, just according as circumstances and the nature of the situation may appear to require.

But now, if the defender does not think he requires any assistance from these immovable forces for his purposed decision, or if the further sacrifice connected with the use of them is too great, then they are kept in reserve for the future, and form a sort of succession of reinforcements, which perhaps ensure the possibility of keeping the moveable forces in such a condition that they will be able to follow up the first favourable decision with a second, or perhaps in the same manner even with a third, that is to say, in this manner a *successive* application of his forces becomes possible.

If the defender loses a battle on the frontier, which does not amount to a complete defeat, we may very well imagine that, by placing himself behind the nearest fortress, he will then be in a condition to accept battle again; indeed, if he is only dealing with an opponent who has not much resolution, then, perhaps, some considerable obstacle of ground will be quite sufficient as a means of stopping the enemy.

There is, therefore, in strategy, in the use of the theatre of war as well as in everything else, *an economy of force;* the less one can make suffice the better: but there must be sufficient, and here, as well as in commerce, there is something to be thought of besides mere niggardliness.

But in order to prevent a great misconception, we must draw attention to this, that the subject of our present consideration is not how much resistance an army can offer, or the enterprises which it can undertake after a lost battle, but only the result which we can promise ourselves *beforehand* from this second act in our defence; consequently, how high we can estimate it in our plan. Here there is only one point almost which the defender has to look to, which is the character and the situation of his opponent. An adversary weak in character, with little self-confidence, without noble ambition, placed under great restrictions, will content himself, in case he is successful, with a moderate advantage, and timidly hold back at every fresh offer of a decision which the defender ventures to make. In this case the defender may count upon the beneficial use of all the means of resistance of his theatre of war in succession, in constantly fresh, although in themselves small, combats, in which the prospect always brightens of an ultimate decision in his favour.

But who does not feel that we are now on the road to campaigns devoid of decision, which are much more the field of a successive application of force. Of these we shall speak in the following chapter.

CHAPTER THIRTY

Defence of a Theatre of War (Continued)

When no Decision is Sought for.

WHETHER and how far a war is possible in which neither party acts on the offensive, therefore in which neither combatant has a *positive aim*, we shall consider in the last book; here it is not necessary for us to occupy ourselves with the contradiction which this presents, because on a single theatre of war we can easily suppose reasons for such a defensive on both sides, consequent on the relations of each of these parts to a whole.

But in addition to the examples which history furnishes of particular campaigns that have taken place without the focus of a necessary solution, history also tells us of many others in which there was no want of an assailant, consequently no want of a *positive will* on one side, but in which that will was so weak that instead of striving to attain the object at any price, and forcing the *necessary* decision, it contented itself with such advantages as arose in a manner spontaneously out of circumstances. Or the assailant pursued *no* self-selected end *at all*, but made his object depend on circumstances, in the meanwhile gathering such fruits as presented themselves from time to time.

Although such an offensive which deviates very much from the strict logical necessity of a direct march towards the object, and which, almost like a lounger sauntering through the campaign, looking out right and left for the cheap fruits of opportunity, differs very little from the defensive itself, which allows the general to pick up what he can in this way, still we shall give the closer philosophical consideration of this kind of warfare a place in the book on the attack. Here we shall confine ourselves to the conclusion that in such a campaign the settlement of the whole question is not looked for by either assailant or defender through a decisive battle, that, therefore, the great battle is no longer the key-stone of the arch, towards which all the lines of the strategic superstructure are directed. Campaigns of this kind (as the history of all times and all countries shows us) are not only numerous, but form such an overwhelming majority, that the remainder only appear as exceptions. Even if this proportion should alter in the future, still it is certain that there will always be many such campaigns; and, therefore, in studying the theory of the defence of a theatre of war, they must be brought into consideration. We shall endeavour to describe the peculiarities by which they are characterised. Real war will generally be in a medium between the two different tendencies, sometimes approaching nearer to one, sometimes to the other, and we can, therefore, only see the practical effect of these peculiarities in the modification which is produced, in the *absolute form* of war by their counteraction. We have already said in the third chapter of this book, that the *state of expectation* is one of the greatest advantages which the defensive has over the offensive; as a general rule, it seldom happens in life, and least of all in war, that *all* that circumstances would lead us to expect does actually take place. The imperfection of human insight, the fear of evil results, accidents which derange the development of designs in their execution, are causes through which many of the transactions enjoined by circumstances are never realised in the execution. In war where insufficiency of knowledge, the danger of a catastrophe, the number of accidents are incomparably greater than in any other branch of human activity, the number of shortcomings, if we may so call them, must necessarily also be much greater. This is then the rich field where the defensive gathers fruits which grow for it spontaneously. If we add to this result of experience the substantial importance of the possession of the surface of the ground in war, then that maxim which has become a proverb, *beati sunt possidentes*, holds good here as well as in peace. It is *this maxim* which here takes the place of the decision, that focus of all action in every war directed to *mutual destruction*. It is fruitful beyond measure, not in actions which it calls forth, but in motives for not acting, and for all that action which is done in the interest of inaction. When no decision is to be sought for or expected, there is no reason for giving up anything, for that could only be done to gain thereby some advantage in the decision. The consequence is that the defender keeps all, or at least as much as he can (that is as much as he can cover), and the assailant takes possession of so much as he can without involving himself in a decision, (that is, he will extend himself laterally as much as possible). We have only to deal with the first in this place.

Wherever the defender is not present with his military forces, the assailant can take possession, and then the advantage of the state of expectation is on *his side;* hence the endeavour to cover the country everywhere directly, and to take the chance of the assailant attacking the troops posted for this purpose.

Before we go further into the special properties of the defence, we must extract from the book on the attack those objects which the assailant usually aims at when the decision (by battle) is not sought. They are as follows: –

1. The seizure of a considerable strip of territory, as far as that can be done without a decisive engagement.

2. The capture of an important magazine under the same condition.

3. The capture of a fortress not covered. No doubt a siege is more or less a great operation, often requiring great labour; but it is an undertaking which does not contain the elements of a catastrophe. If it comes to the worst, the siege can be raised without thereby suffering a great positive loss.

4. Lastly, a successful combat of some importance, but in which there is not much risked, and consequently not much to be gained; a combat which takes place not as the cardinal knot of a whole strategic bond, but on its own account for the sake of trophies or honour of the troops. For such an object, of course, a combat is not fought *at any price;* we either wait for the chance of a favourable opportunity, or seek to bring one about by skill.

These four objects of attack give rise to the following efforts on the part of the defence: –

1. To cover the fortresses by keeping them behind us.

2. To cover the country by extending the troops over it.

3. Where the extension is not sufficient, to throw the army rapidly in front of the enemy by a flank march.

4. To guard against disadvantageous combats.

It is clear that the object of the first three measures is to force on the enemy the initiative, and to derive the utmost advantage from the state of expectation, and this object is so deeply rooted in the nature of the thing that it would be great folly to despise it *prima facie.* It must necessarily occupy a higher place the less a decision is expected, and it is the ruling principle in all such campaigns, even although, apparently, a considerable degree of activity may be manifested in small actions of an indecisive character.

Hannibal as well as Fabius, and both Frederick the Great and Daun, have done homage to this principle whenever they did not either seek for or expect a decision. The fourth effort serves as a corrective to the three others, it is their *conditio sine quâ non.*

We shall now proceed to examine these subjects a little more closely.

At first sight it appears somewhat preposterous to protect a fortress from the enemy's attack by placing an army in *front of it;* such a measure looks like a kind of pleonasm, as fortifications are built to resist a hostile attack of themselves. Yet it is a measure which we see resorted to thousands and thousands of times. But thus it is in the conduct of war; the most common things often seem the most incomprehensible. Who would presume to pronounce these thousands of instances to be so many blunders on the ground of this seeming inconsistency? The constant repetition of the measure shows that it must proceed from some deep-seated motive. This reason is, however, no other than that pointed out above, emanating from moral sluggishness and inactivity.

If the defender places himself in front of his fortress, the enemy cannot attack it unless he first beats the army in front of it; but a battle is a decision; if that is *not* the enemy's object then there will be no battle, and the defender will remain in possession of his fortress without striking a blow; consequently, whenever we do not believe the enemy intends to fight a battle, we should venture on the chance of his not making up his mind to do so, especially as in most cases we still retain the power of withdrawing behind the fortress in a moment, if, contrary to our expectation, the enemy should march to attack us; the position before the fortress is in this way free from danger, and the probability of maintaining the *status quo* without any sacrifice, is not even attended with the *slightest* risk.

If the defender places himself behind the fortress, he offers the assailant an object which is exactly suited to the circumstances in which the latter is placed. If the fortress is not of great strength, and he is not quite unprepared, he will commence the siege: in order that this may not end in the fall of the place, the defender must march to its relief. The positive action, the initiative, is now laid on him, and the adversary who by his siege is to be regarded as advancing towards his object, is in the situation of occupier.

Experience teaches that the matter always takes this turn, and it does so naturally. A catastrophe, as we have before said, is not necessarily bound up with a siege. Even a general, devoid of either the spirit of enterprise or energy, who would never make up his mind to a battle, will proceed to undertake a siege with perhaps nothing but field artillery, when he can approach a fortress without risk. At the worst he can abandon his undertaking without any positive loss. There always remains to be considered the danger to which most fortresses are more or less exposed, that of being taken by assault, or in some other irregular manner, and this circumstance should certainly not be overlooked by the defender in his calculation of probabilities.

In weighing and considering the different chances, it seems natural that the defender should look upon the probability of not having to fight at all as more for his advantage than the probability of fighting even *under favourable* circumstances. And thus it appears to us that the practice of placing an army in the field before its fortress, is both natural and fully explained. Frederick the Great, for instance, at Glogau, against the Russians, at Schwednitz, Neiss, and Dresden, against the Austrians, almost always adopted it. This measure, however, brought misfortune on the Duke of Bevern at Breslau; *behind* Breslau he could not have been attacked; the superiority of the Austrians in the king's absence would soon cease, as he was approaching; and therefore, by a position *behind* Breslau, a battle might have been avoided until Frederick's arrival. No doubt the Duke would have preferred that course if it had not been that it would have exposed that important place to a bombardment, at which the king, who was anything but tolerant on such occasions, would have been highly displeased. *The attempt made* by the Duke to protect Breslau by an entrenched position taken up for the purpose, cannot after all be disapproved, for it was very possible that Prince Charles of Lorraine, contented with the capture of Schwednitz, and threatened by the march of the king, would, by that position, have been prevented from advancing farther. The best thing he could have done would have been to refuse the battle at the last by withdrawing through Breslau at the moment that the Austrians advanced to the attack; in this way he would have got all the advantages of the state of expectation without paying for them by a great danger.

If we have here traced the position *before* a fortress to reasons of a superior and absolute order, and defended its adoption on those grounds, we have still to observe that there is a motive of a secondary class which, though a more obvious one, is not sufficient of itself alone, not being absolute; we refer to the use which is made by armies of the nearest fortress as a depôt of provisions and munitions of war. This is so convenient, and presents so many advantages, that a general will not easily make up his mind to draw his supplies of all kinds from more distant places, or to lodge them in open towns. But if a fortress is the great magazine of an army, then the position before it is frequently a matter of absolute necessity, and in most cases is very natural. But it is easy to see that this obvious motive, which is easily over-valued by those who are not in the habit of looking far before them, is neither sufficient to explain all cases, nor are the circumstances connected with it of sufficient importance to entitle it to give a final decision.

The capture of one or more fortresses without risking a battle, is such a very natural object of all attacks which do not aim at a decision on the field of battle, that the defender makes it his principal business to thwart this design. Thus it is that on theatres of war, containing a number of fortresses, we find these places made the pivots of almost all the movements; we find the assailant seeking to approach one of them unexpectedly, and employing various feints to aid his purpose, and the defender immediately seeking to stop him by well-prepared movements. Such is the general character of almost all the campaigns of Louis XIV. in the Netherlands up to the time of Marshal Saxe.

So much for the covering of fortresses.

The covering of a country by an extended disposition of forces, is only conceivable in combination with very considerable obstacles of ground. The great and small posts which must be formed for the purpose, can only get a certain capability of resistance through strength of position; and as natural obstacles are seldom found sufficient, therefore field fortification is made use of as an assistance. But now it is to be observed that, the power of resistance which is thus obtained at any one point, is always only *relative* (see the chapter on the signification of the combat), and never to be regarded as *absolute*. It may certainly happen that one such post may remain proof against all attacks made upon it, and that therefore in a single instance there may be an absolute result; but from the great number of posts, any single one, in comparison to the whole, appears weak, and exposed to the possible attack of an overwhelming force, and consequently it would be unreasonable to place one's dependence for safety on the resistance of any one single post. In such an extended position, we can therefore only count on a resistance of relative length, and not upon a victory, properly speaking. This value of single posts, at the same time, is also sufficient for the object, and for a general calculation. In campaigns in which no great decision, no irresistible march, towards the complete subjugation of the whole force is to be feared, there is little risk in a combat of posts, even if it ends in the loss of a post. There is seldom any further result in connection with it than the loss of the post and a few trophies; the influence of victory penetrates no further into the situation of affairs, it does not tear down any part of the foundation to be followed by a mass of building in ruin. In the worst case, if, for instance, the whole defensive system is disorganised by the loss of a single post, the defender has always time to concentrate his corps, and with his whole force to *offer battle*, which the assailant, according to our supposition, does not desire. Therefore also it usually happens that with this concentration of force the act closes, and the further advance of the assailant is stopped. A strip of land, a few men and guns, are the losses of the defender, and with these results the assailant is satisfied.

To such a risk we say the defender may very well expose himself, if he has, on the other hand, the possibility, or rather the probability, in his favour, that the assailant from excessive caution will halt before his posts without attacking them. Only in regard to this we must not lose sight of the fact, that we are now supposing an assailant who will not venture upon any great stroke, a moderate sized, but strong post will very well serve to stop such an adversary, for although he can undoubtedly make himself master of it, still the question arises as to the price it will cost, and whether that price is not too high for any use that he can make of the victory.

In this way we may see how the powerful relative resistance which the defender can obtain from an extended disposition, consisting of a number of posts in juxtaposition with each other, may constitute a satisfactory result in the calculation of his whole campaign. In order to direct at once to the right point the glance which the reader, with his mind's eye, will here cast upon military history, we must observe that these extended positions appear most frequently in the latter half of a campaign, because by that time the defender has become thoroughly acquainted with his adversary, with his projects, and his situation; and the little quantity of the spirit of enterprise with which the assailant started, is usually exhausted.

In this defensive, in an extended position by which the *country*, the *supplies, the fortresses* are to be covered, all great natural obstacles, such as streams, rivers, mountains, woods, morasses, must naturally play a great part, and acquire a predominant importance. Upon their use we refer to what has been already said on these subjects.

It is through this predominant importance of the topographical element that the knowledge and activity which are looked upon as the speciality of the general staff of an army are more particularly called into requisition. Now, as the staff of the army is usually that branch which writes and publishes most, it follows that these parts of campaigns are recorded more fully in history; and then again from that there follows a not unnatural tendency to systematise them, and to frame out of the historical solution of one case a general solution for all succeeding cases. But this endeavour is futile, and therefore erroneous.

Besides, in this more passive kind of war, in this form of it which is tied to localities, each case is different to another, and must be differently treated. The ablest memoirs of a critical character respecting these subjects are therefore only suited to make one acquainted with facts, but never to serve as dictates.

Natural, and at the same time meritorious, as is this industry which, according to the general view, we have attributed to the staff in particular, still we must raise a warning voice against usurpations which often spring from it to the prejudice of the whole. The authority acquired by those who are at the head of, and best acquainted with, this branch of military service, gives them often a sort of general dominion over people's minds, beginning with the general himself, and from this then springs a routine of ideas which causes an undue bias of the mind. At last the general sees nothing but mountains and passes, and that which should be a measure of free choice guided by circumstances becomes mannerism, becomes second nature.

Thus in the year 1793 and 1794, Colonel Grawert of the Prussian army, who was the animating spirit of the staff at that time, and well known as a regular man for mountains and passes, persuaded two generals of the most opposite personal characteristics, the Duke of Brunswick and General Mollendorf, into exactly the same method of carrying on war.

That a defensive line parallel to the course of a formidable natural obstacle may lead to a cordon war is quite plain. It must, in most cases, necessarily lead to that if really the whole extent of the theatre of war could be directly covered in that manner. But most theatres of war have such an extent, that the normal tactical disposition of the troops destined for its defence would be by no means commensurate with that object; at the same time as the assailant, by his own dispositions and other circumstances, is confined to certain principal directions and great roads, and any great deviations from these directions, even if he is only opposed to a very inactive defender, would be attended with great embarrassment and disadvantage, therefore generally all that the defender has to do is to cover the country for a certain number of miles or marches right and left of these principal lines of direction of his adversary. But again to effect this covering, we may be contented with defensive posts on the principal roads and means of approach, and merely watch the country between by small posts of observation. The consequence of this is certainly that the assailant may then pass a column between two of these posts, and thus make the attack, which he has in view, upon one post from several quarters at once. Now, these posts are in some measure arranged to meet this, partly by their having supports for their flanks, partly by the formation of flank defences (called crochets), partly by their being able to receive assistance from a reserve posted in rear, or by troops detached from adjoining posts. In this manner the number of posts is reduced still more, and the result is that an army engaged in a defence of this kind, usually divides itself into four or five principal posts.

For important points of approach, beyond a certain distance, and yet in some measure threatened, special central points are established which, in a certain measure, form small theatres of war within the principal one. In this manner the Austrians, during the Seven Years' War, generally placed the main body of their army, in four or five posts in the mountains of Lower Silesia; whilst a small almost independent corps organised for itself a similar system of defence in Upper Silesia.

Now, the further such a defensive system diverges from direct covering, the more it must call to its assistance – mobility (active defence), and even offensive means. Certain corps are considered reserves; besides which, one post hastens to send to the help of another all the troops it can spare. This assistance may be rendered either by hastening up directly from the rear to reinforce and re-establish the passive defence, or by attacking the enemy in flank, or even by menacing his line of retreat. If the assailant threatens the flank of a post not with direct attack, but only by a position through which he can act upon the communications of this post, then either the corps which has been advanced for this purpose must be attacked in earnest, or the way of reprisal must be resorted to by acting in turn on the enemy's communications.

We see, therefore, that however passive this defence is in the leading ideas on which it is based, still it must comprise many active means, and in its organisation may be forearmed in many ways against complicated events. Usually those defences pass for the best which make the most use of active or even offensive means; but this depends in great part on the nature of the country, the characteristics of the troops, and even on the talent of the general; partly we are also very prone in general to expect too much from movement, and other auxiliary measures of an active nature, and to place too little reliance on the local defence of a formidable natural obstacle. We think we have thus sufficiently explained what we understand by an extended line of defence, and we now turn to the third auxiliary means, the placing ourselves in front of the enemy by a rapid march to a flank.

This means is necessarily one of those provided for that defence of a country which we are now considering. In the first place the defender, even with the most extended position, often cannot guard all the approaches to his country which are menaced; next, in many cases, he must be ready to repair with the bulk of his forces to any posts upon which the bulk of the enemy's force is about to be thrown, as otherwise those posts would be too easily overpowered; lastly, a general who has an aversion to confining his army to a passive resistance in an extended position, must seek to attain his object, the protection of the country, by rapid, well-planned, and well-conducted movements. The greater the spaces which he leaves exposed, the greater the talent required in planning the movements, in order to arrive anywhere at the right moment of time.

The natural consequence of striving to do this is, that in such a case, positions which afford sufficient advantages to make an enemy give up all idea of an attack as soon as our army, or only a portion of it, reaches them, are sought for and prepared in all directions. As these positions are again and again occupied, and all depends on reaching the same in right time, they are in a certain measure the vowels of all this method of carrying on war, which on that account has been termed a *war of posts*.

Just as an extended position, and the relative resistance in a war *without great decisions*, do not present the dangers which are inherent in its original nature, so in the same manner the intercepting the enemy in front by a march to a flank is not so hazardous as it would be in the immediate expectation of a great decision. To attempt at the last moment in greatest haste (by a lateral movement) to thrust in an army in front of an adversary of determined character, who is both able and willing to deal heavy blows, and has no scruples about an expenditure of forces, would be half way to a most decisive disaster; for against an unhesitating blow delivered with the enemy's whole strength, such running and stumbling into a position would not do. But against an opponent who, instead of taking up his work with his whole hand, uses only the tips of his fingers, who does not know how to make use of a great result, or rather of the opening for one, who only seeks a trifling advantage but at small expense, against such an opponent this kind of resistance certainly may be applied with effect.

A natural consequence is, that this means also in general occurs oftener in the last half of a campaign than at its commencement.

Here, also, the general staff has an opportunity of displaying its topographical knowledge in framing a system of combined measures, connected with the choice and preparation of the positions and the roads leading to them.

When the whole object of one party is to gain in the end a certain point, and the whole object of his adversary, on the other hand, is to prevent his doing so, then both parties are often obliged to make their movements under the eyes of each other; for this reason, these movements must be made with a degree of precaution and precision not otherwise required. Formerly, before the mass of an army was formed of independent divisions, and even on the march was always regarded as an indivisible whole, this precaution and precision was attended with much more formality, and with the copious use of tactical skill. On these occasions, certainly, single brigades were often obliged to leave the general line of battle to secure particular points, and act an independent part until the army arrived: but these were, and continued, *anomalous proceedings;* and the aim in the order of march generally was to move the army from one point to another as a whole, preserving its normal formation, and avoiding such exceptional proceedings as the above as far as possible. Now that the parts of the main body of an army are subdivided again into independent bodies, and those bodies can venture to enter into an engagement with the mass of the enemy's army, provided the rest of the force of which it is a member is sufficiently near to carry it on and finish it, – now such a flank march is attended with less difficulty even under the eye of the enemy. What formerly could only be effected through the actual mechanism of the order of march, can now be done by starting single divisions at an earlier hour, by hastening the march of others, and by the greater freedom in the employment of the whole.

By the means of defence just considered, the assailant can be prevented from taking any fortress, from occupying any important extent of country, or capturing magazines; and he will be prevented, if in every direction combats are offered to him in which he can see little probability of success, or too great danger of a reaction in case of failure, or in general, an expenditure of force too great for his object and existing relations.

If now the defender succeeds in this triumph of his art and skill, and the assailant, wherever he turns his eyes, sees prudent preparations through which he is cut off from any prospect of attaining his modest wishes: then the offensive principle often seeks to escape from the difficulty in the satisfaction of the mere honour of its arms. The gain of some combat of respectable importance, gives the arms of the victor a semblance of superiority, appeases the vanity of the general, of the court, of the army, and the people, and thus satisfies, to a certain extent, the expectations which are naturally always raised when the offensive is assumed.

An advantageous combat of some importance merely for the sake of the victory and some trophies, becomes, therefore, the last hope of the assailant. No one must suppose that we here involve ourselves in a contradiction, for we contend that we still continue within our *own supposition*, that the good measures of the defender have deprived the assailant of all expectation of attaining any one of those other objects by means of a *successful combat!* To warrant that expectation, two conditions are required, that is, *a favourable termination to the combat*, and next, *that the result shall lead really to the attainment of one of those objects.*

The first may very well take place without the second, and therefore the defenders' corps and posts singly are much more frequently in danger of getting involved in disadvantageous combats if the assailant merely aims at the *honour of the battle field*, than if he connects with that a view to further advantages as well.

If we place ourselves in Daun's situation, and with his way of thinking, then his venturing on the surprise of Hochkirch does not appear inconsistent with his character, as long as we suppose him aiming at nothing more than the trophies of the day. But a victory rich in results, which would have compelled the king to abandon Dresden and Neisse, appears an entirely different problem, one with which he would not have been inclined to meddle.

Let it not be imagined that these are trifling or idle distinctions; we have, on the contrary, now before us one of the deepest-rooted, leading principles of war. The signification of a combat is its very soul in strategy, and we cannot too often repeat, that in strategy the leading events always proceed from the ultimate views of the two parties, as it were, from a conclusion of the whole train of ideas. This is why there may be such a difference strategically between one battle and another, that they can hardly be looked upon as the same means.

Now, although the fruitless victory of the assailant can hardly be considered any serious injury to the defence, still as the defender will not willingly concede even *this* advantage, particularly as we never know what accident may also be connected with it, therefore the defender requires to keep an incessant watch upon the situation of all his corps and posts. No doubt here all greatly depends on the leaders of those corps making suitable dispositions; but any one of them may be led into an unavoidable catastrophe by injudicious orders imposed on him by the general-in-chief. Who is not reminded here of Fouque's corps at Landshut and of Fink's at Maxen?

In both cases Frederick the Great reckoned too much on customary ideas. It was impossible that he could suppose 10,000 men capable of successfully resisting 30,000 in the position of Landshut, or that Fink could resist a superior force pouring in and overwhelming him on all sides; but he thought the strength of the position of Landshut would be accepted, like a bill of exchange, as heretofore, and that Daun would see in the demonstration against his flank sufficient reason to exchange his uncomfortable position in Saxony for the more comfortable one in Bohemia. He misjudged Laudon in one case and Daun in the other, and therein lies the error in these measures.

But irrespective of such errors, into which even generals may fall who are not so proud, daring, and obstinate as Frederick the Great in some of his proceedings may certainly be termed, there is always, in respect to the subject we are now considering, a great difficulty in this way, that the general-in-chief cannot always expect all he desires from the sagacity, good-will, courage and firmness of character of his corps-commanders. He cannot, therefore, leave everything to their good judgment; he must prescribe rules on many points by which their course of action, being restricted, may easily become inconsistent with the circumstances of the moment. This is, however, an unavoidable inconvenience. Without an imperious commanding will, the influence of which penetrates through the whole army, war cannot be well conducted; and whoever would follow the practice of always expecting the best from his subordinates, would from that very reason be quite unfit for a good Commander of an army.

Therefore the situation of every corps and post must be for ever kept clearly in view, to prevent any of them being unexpectedly drawn into a catastrophe.

The aim of all these efforts is to preserve the *status quo*. The more fortunate and successful these efforts are, the longer will the war last at the same point; but the longer war continues at one point, the greater become the cares for subsistence.

In place of collections and contributions from the country, a system of subsistence from magazines commences at once, or in a very short time; in place of country waggons being collected upon each occasion, the formation, more or less, of a regular transport takes place, composed either of carriages of the country, or of those belonging to the army; in short, there arises an approach to that regular system of feeding troops from magazines, of which we have already treated in the fourteenth chapter (On Subsistence).

At the same time, it is not this which exercises a great influence on this mode of conducting war, for as this mode, by its object and character, is in fact already tied down to a limited space, therefore the question of subsistence may very well have a part in determining its action – and will do so in most cases – without altering the general character of the war. On the other hand, the action of the belligerents mutually against the lines of communications gains a much greater importance for two reasons. Firstly, because in such campaigns, there being no measures of a great and comprehensive kind, generals must apply their energies to those of an inferior order; and secondly, because here there is time enough to wait for the effect of this means. The security of his line of communications is therefore specially important to the defender, for although it is true that its interruption cannot be an object of the hostile operations which take place, yet it might compel him to retreat, and thus to leave other objects open to attack.

All the measures having for their object the protection of the area of the theatre of war itself, must naturally also have the effect of covering the lines of communication; their security is therefore in part provided for in that way, and we have only to observe that it is a principal condition in fixing upon a position.

A *special* means of security consists in the bodies of troops, both small and large, escorting convoys. First, the most extended positions are not sufficient to secure the lines of communication, and next, such an escort is particularly necessary when the general wishes to avoid a very extended position. Therefore, we find, in Tempelhof's History of the Seven Years' War, instances without end in which Frederick the Great caused his bread and flour waggons to be escorted by single regiments of infantry or cavalry, sometimes also by whole brigades. On the Austrian side we nowhere find mention of the same thing, which certainly may be partly accounted for in this way, that they had no such circumstantial historian on their side, but in part it is also to be ascribed just to this, that they always took up much more extended positions.

Having now touched upon the four efforts which form the foundation of a defensive *that does not aim at a decision*, and which are at the same time, altogether free upon the whole from all offensive elements, we must now say something of the offensive means with which they may become more or less mixed up, in a certain measure flavoured. These offensive means are chiefly: –

1. Operating against the enemy's communications, under which we likewise include enterprises against his places of supply.

2. Diversions and incursions within the enemy's territory.

3. Attacks on the enemy's corps and posts, and even upon his main body, under favourable circumstances, or the threat only of such intention.

The first of these means is incessantly in action in all campaigns of this kind, but in a certain measure quite quietly without actually making its appearance. Every suitable position for the defender derives a great part of its efficacy from the disquietude which it causes the assailant in connection with his communications; and as the question of subsistence in such warfare becomes, as we have already observed, one of vital importance, affecting the assailant equally, therefore, through this apprehension of offensive action, possibly resulting from the enemy's position, a great part of the strategic web is determined, as we shall again find in treating of the attack.

Not only this general influence, proceeding from the choice of positions, which, like pressure in mechanics, produces an effect *invisibly*, but also an actual offensive movement with part of the army against the enemy's lines of communication, comes within the compass of such a defensive. But that it may be done with effect, *the situation of the lines of communication, the nature of the country, and the peculiar qualities of the troops* must be specially propitious to the undertaking.

Incursions into the enemy's country which have as their object reprisals or levying contributions, cannot properly be regarded as defensive means, they are rather true offensive means; but they are usually combined with the object of a real diversion, which may be regarded as a real defensive measure, as it is intended to weaken the enemy's force opposed to us. But as the above means may be used just as well by the assailant, and in itself is a real attack, we therefore think more suitable to leave its further examination for the next book. Accordingly we shall only count it in here, in order to render a full account of the arsenal of small offensive arms belonging to the defender of a theatre of war, and for the present merely add that in extent and importance it may attain to such a point, as to give the whole war the *appearance*, and along with that the honour, of the offensive. Of this nature are Frederick the Great's enterprises in Poland, Bohemia and Franconia, before the campaign of 1759. His campaign itself is plainly a pure defence; these incursions into the enemy's territory, however, gave it the appearance of an aggression, which perhaps had a special value on account of the moral effect.

An attack on one of the enemy's corps or on his main body must always be kept in view as a necessary complement of the whole defence whenever the aggressor takes the matter too easily, and on that account shows himself very defenceless at particular points. Under this silent condition the whole action takes place. But here also the defender, in the same way as in operating against the communications of the enemy, may go a step further in the province of the offensive, and just as well as his adversary may make it his business to lie in wait *for a favourable stroke*. In order to ensure a result in this field, he must either be very decidedly superior in force to his opponent – which certainly is inconsistent with the defensive in general, but still may happen – or he must have a method and the talent of keeping his forces more concentrated, and make up by activity and mobility for the danger which he incurs in other respects.

The first was Daun's case in the Seven Years' War; the latter, the case of Frederick the Great. Still we hardly ever see Daun's offensive make its appearance except when Frederick the Great invited it by excessive boldness and a display of contempt for him (Hochkirch, Maxen, Landshut). On the other hand, we see Frederick the Great almost constantly on the move in order to beat one or other of Daun's corps with his main body. He certainly seldom succeeded, at least, the results were never great, because Daun, in addition to his great superiority in numbers, had also a rare degree of prudence and caution; but we must not suppose that, therefore, the king's attempts were altogether fruitless. In these attempts lay rather a very effectual resistance; for the care and fatigue, which his adversary had to undergo in order to avoid fighting at a disadvantage, neutralised those forces which would otherwise have aided in advancing the offensive action. Let us only call to mind the campaign of 1760, in Silesia, where Daun and the Russians, out of sheer apprehension of being attacked and beaten by the king, first here and then there, never could succeed in making one step in advance.

We believe we have now gone through all the subjects which form the predominant ideas, the principal aims, and therefore the main stay, of the whole action in the defence of a theatre of war when no idea of decision is entertained. Our chief, and, indeed, sole object in bringing them all close together, was to let the organism of the whole strategic action be seen in one view; the particular measures by means of which those subjects come to life, marches, positions, etc., etc., we have already considered in detail.

By now casting a glance once more at the whole of our subject, the idea must strike us forcibly, that with such a weak offensive principle, with so little desire for a decision on either side, with so little positive motive, with so many counteracting influences of a subjective nature, which stop us and hold us back, the essential difference between attack and defence must always tend more to disappear. At the opening of a campaign, certainly one party will enter the other's theatre of war, and in that manner, to a certain extent, such party puts on the form of offensive. But it may very well take place, and happens frequently that he must soon enough apply all his powers to defend his own country on the enemy's territory. Then both stand, in reality, opposite one another in a state of mutual observation. Both intent on losing nothing, perhaps both alike intent also on obtaining a positive advantage. Indeed it may happen, as with Frederick the Great, that the real defender aims higher in that way than his adversary.

Now the more the assailant gives up the position of an enemy making progress, the less the defender is menaced by him, and confined to a strictly defensive attitude by the pressing claims of a regard for mere safety, so much the more a similarity in the relations of the parties is produced in which then the activity of both will be directed towards gaining an advantage over his opponent, and protecting himself against any disadvantage, therefore to a true strategic *manœuvring;* and indeed this is the character into which all campaigns resolve themselves more or less, when the situation of the combatants or political views do not allow of any great decision.

In the following book we have allotted a chapter specially to the subject of strategic manœuvres; but as this equipoised play of forces has frequently been invested in theory with an importance to which it is not entitled, we find ourselves under the necessity of examining the subject more closely while we are treating of the defence, as it is in that form of warfare more particularly that this false importance is ascribed to strategic manœuvres.

We call it an *equipoised play of forces,* for when there is no movement of the whole body there is a state of equilibrium; where no great object impels, there is no movement of the whole; therefore, in such a case, the two parties, however unequal they may be, are still to be regarded as in a state of equilibrium. From this state of equilibrium of the whole now come forth the particular motives to actions of a minor class and secondary objects. They can here develop themselves, because they are no longer kept down by the pressure of a great decision and great danger. Therefore, what can be lost or won upon the whole is changed into small counters, and the action of the war, as a whole, is broken up into smaller transactions. With these smaller operations for smaller gains, a contest of skill now takes place between the two generals; but as it is impossible in war to shut out chance, and consequently good luck, therefore this contest will never be otherwise than a *game.* In the meantime, here arise two other questions, that is, whether in this manœuvring, chance will not have a smaller, and superior intelligence a greater, share in the decision, than where all concentrates itself into one single great act. The last of these questions we must answer in the affirmative. The more complete the organisation of the whole, the oftener time and space come into consideration – the former by single moments, the latter at particular points – so much the greater, plainly, will be the field for calculation, therefore the greater the sway exercised by superior intelligence. What the superior understanding gains is abstracted in part from chance, but not necessarily altogether, and therefore we are not obliged to answer the first question affirmatively. Moreover, we must not forget that a superior understanding is not the only mental quality of a general; courage, energy, resolution, presence of mind, etc., are qualities which rise again to a higher value when all depends on one single great decision; they will, therefore, have somewhat less weight when there is an equipoised play of forces, and the predominating ascendancy of sagacious calculation increases not only at the expense of chance, but also at the expense of these qualities. On the other hand, these brilliant qualities, at the moment of a great decision, may rob chance of a great part of its power, and therefore, to a certain extent, secure that which calculating intelligence in such cases would be obliged to leave to chance. We see by this that here a conflict takes place between several forces, and that we cannot positively assert that there is a greater field left open to chance in the case of a great decision, than in the total result when that equipoised play of forces takes place. If we, therefore, see more particularly in this play of forces a contest of mutual skill, that must only be taken to refer to skill in sagacious calculation, and not to the sum total of military genius.

Now it is just from this aspect of strategic manœuvring that the whole has obtained that false importance of which we have spoken above. In the first place, in this skilfulness the whole genius of a general has been supposed to consist; but this is a great mistake, for it is, as already said, not to be denied that in moments of great decisions other moral qualities of a general may have power to control the force of events. If this power proceeds more from the impulse of noble feelings and those sparks of genius which start up almost unconsciously, and therefore does not proceed from long chains of thought, still it is not the less a free citizen of the art of war, for that art is neither a mere act of the understanding, nor are the activities of the intellectual faculties its principal ones. Further, it has been supposed that every active campaign without results must be owing to that sort of skill on the part of one, or even of both generals, while in reality it has always had its general and principal foundation just in the general relations which have turned war into such a game.

As most wars between civilised states have had for their object rather the observation of the enemy than his destruction, therefore it was only natural that the greater number of the campaigns should bear the character of strategic manœuvring. Those amongst them which did not bring into notice any renowned generals, attracted no attention; but where there was a great commander on whom all eyes were fixed, or two opposed to each other, like Turenne and Montecuculi, there the seal of perfection has been stamped upon this whole art of manœuvring through the names of these generals. A further consequence has then been that this game has been looked upon as the summit of the art, as the manifestation of its highest perfection, and consequently also as the source at which the art of war must chiefly be studied.

This view prevailed almost universally in the theoretical world before the wars of the French Revolution. But when these wars at one stroke opened to view a quite different world of phenomena in war, at first somewhat rough and wild, but which afterwards, under Buonaparte systematised into a method on a grand scale, produced results which created astonishment amongst old and young, then people set themselves free from the old models, and believed that all the changes they saw resulted from modern discoveries, magnificent ideas, etc.; but also at the same time, certainly from the changes in the state of society. It was now thought that what was old would never more be required, and would never even reappear. But as in such revolutions in opinions two parties are always formed, so it was also in this instance, and the old views found their champions, who looked upon the new phenomena as rude blows of brute force, as a general decadence of the art; and held the opinion that, in the evenly-balanced, nugatory, fruitless war game, the perfection of the art is realised. There lies at the bottom of this last view such a want of logic and philosophy, that it can only be termed a hopeless, distressing confusion of ideas. But at the same time the opposite opinion, that nothing like the past will ever reappear, is very irrational. Of the novel appearances manifested in the domain of the art of war, very few indeed are to be ascribed to new discoveries, or to a change in the direction of ideas; they are chiefly attributable to the alterations in the social state and its relations. But as these took place just at the crisis of a state of fermentation, they must not be taken as a norm; and we cannot, therefore, doubt that a great part of the former manifestations of war, will again make their appearance. This is not the place to enter further into these matters; it is enough for us that by directing attention to the relation which this even-balanced play of forces occupies in the whole conduct of a war, and to its signification and connection with other objects, we have shown that it is always produced by constraint laid on both parties engaged in the contest, and by a military element greatly attenuated. In this game one general may show himself more skilful than his opponent; and therefore, if the strength of his army is equal, he may also gain many advantages over him; or if his force is inferior, he may, by his superior talent, keep the contest evenly balanced; but it is completely contradictory to the nature of the thing to look here for the highest honour and glory of a general; such a campaign is always rather a certain sign that neither of the generals has any great military talent, or that he who has talent is prevented by the force of circumstances from venturing on a great decision; but when this is the case, there is no scope afforded for the display of the highest military genius.

We have hitherto been engaged with the general character of strategic manœuvring; we must now proceed to a special influence which it has on the conduct of war, namely this, that it frequently leads the combatants away from the principal roads and places into unfrequented, or at least unimportant localities. When trifling interests, which exist for a moment and then disappear, are paramount, the great features of a country have less influence on the conduct of the war. We therefore often find that bodies of troops move to points where we should never look for them, judging only by the great and simple requirements of the war; and that consequently, also, the changefulness and diversity in the details of the contest as it progresses, are much greater here than in wars directed to a great decision. Let us only look how in the last five campaigns of the Seven Years' War, in spite of the relations in general remaining unchanged in themselves, each of these campaigns took a different form, and, closely examined, no single measure ever appears twice; and yet in these campaigns the offensive principle manifests itself on the side of the allied army much more decidedly than in most other earlier wars.

In this chapter on the defence of a theatre of war, if no great decision is proposed, we have only shown the tendencies of the action, together with its combination, and the relations and character of the same; the particular measures of which it is composed have been described in detail in a former part of our work. Now the question arises whether for these different tendencies of action no thoroughly general comprehensive principles, rules, or methods can be given. To this we reply that, as far as history is concerned, we have decidedly not been led to any deductions of that kind through constantly recurring forms; and at the same time, for a subject so diversified and changeful in its general nature, we could hardly admit any theoretical rule, except one founded on experience. A war directed to great decisions is not only much simpler, but also much more in accordance with nature; is more free from inconsistencies, more objective, more restricted by a law of inherent necessity; hence the mind can prescribe forms and laws for it; but for a war without a decision for its object, this appears to us to be much more difficult. Even the two fundamental principles of the earliest theories of strategy published in our times, the *Breadth of the Base*, in Bulow, and the *Position on Interior Lines*, in Jomini, if applied to the defence of a theatre of war, have in no instance shown themselves absolute and effective. But being mere forms, this is just where they should show themselves most efficacious, because forms are always more efficacious, always acquire a preponderance over other factors of the product, the more the action extends over time and space. Notwithstanding this, we find that they are nothing more than particular parts of the subject, and certainly anything but decisive advantages. It is very clear that the peculiar nature of the means and the relations must always from the first have a great influence adverse to all general principles. What Daun did by the extent and provident choice of positions, the king did by keeping his army always concentrated, always hugging the enemy close, and by being always ready to act extemporally with his whole army. The method of each general proceeded not only from the nature of the army he commanded, but also from the circumstances in which he was placed. To extemporise movements is always much easier for a king than for any commander who acts under responsibility. We shall here once more point out particularly that the critic has no right to look upon the different manners and methods which may make their appearance as different degrees on the road to perfection, the one inferior to the other; they are entitled to be treated as on an equality, and it must rest with the judgment to estimate their relative fitness for use in each particular case.

To enumerate these different manners which may spring from the particular nature of an army, of a country, or of circumstances, is not our object here; the influence of these things generally we have already noticed.

We acknowledge, therefore, that in this chapter we are unable to give any maxims, rules, or methods, because history does not furnish the means; and on the contrary, at almost every moment, we there meet with peculiarities such as are often quite inexplicable, and often also surprise us by their singularity. But it is not on that account unprofitable to study history in connection with this subject also. Where neither system nor any dogmatic apparatus can be found, there may still be truth, and this truth will then, in most cases, only be discovered by a practised judgment and the tact of long experience. Therefore, even if history does not here furnish any formula, we may be certain that here as well as everywhere else, it will give us *exercise for the judgment*.

We shall only set up one comprehensive general principle, or rather we shall reproduce, and present to view more vividly, in the form of a separate principle, the natural presupposition of all that has now been said.

All the means which have been here set forth have only a *relative* value; they are all placed under the legal ban of a certain disability on both sides; above this region a higher law prevails, and there is a totally different world of phenomena. The general must never forget this; he must never move in imaginary security within the narrower sphere, as if he were in an *absolute* medium; never look upon the means which he employs here as the *necessary* or as the *only means, and still adhere to them, even when he himself already trembles at their insufficiency.*

From the point of view at which we have here placed ourselves, such an error may appear to be almost impossible; but it is not impossible in the real world, because there things do not appear in such sharp contrast.

We must just again remind our readers that, for the sake of giving clearness, distinctness, and force to our ideas, we have always taken as the subject of our consideration only the complete antithesis, that is the two extremes of the question, but that the concrete case in war generally lies between these two extremes, and is only influenced by either of these extremes according to the degree in which it approaches nearer towards it.

Therefore, quite commonly, everything depends on the general making up his own mind before all things as to whether his adversary has the inclination and the means of outbidding him by the use of greater and more decisive measures. As soon as he has reason to apprehend this, he must give up small measures intended to ward off small disadvantages; and the course which remains for him then is to put himself in a better situation, by a voluntary sacrifice, in order to make himself equal to a greater solution. In other words, the first requisite is that the general should take the right scale in laying out his work.

In order to give these ideas still more distinctness through the help of real experience, we shall briefly notice a string of cases in which, according to our opinion, a false criterion was made use of, that is, in which one of the generals in the calculation of his operations very much underestimated the decisive action intended by his adversary. We begin with the opening of the campaign of 1757, in which the Austrians showed by the disposition of their forces that they had not counted upon so thorough an offensive as that adopted by Frederick the Great; even the delay of Piccolomini's corps on the Silesian frontier while Duke Charles of Lorraine was in danger of having to surrender with his whole army, is a similar case of complete misconception of the situation.

In 1758, the French were in the first place completely taken in as to the effects of the convention of Kloster Seeven (a fact, certainly, with which we have nothing to do here), and two months afterwards they were completely mistaken in their judgment of what their opponent might undertake, which, very shortly after, cost them the country between the Weser and the Rhine. That Frederick the Great, in 1759, at Maxen, and in 1760, at Landshut, completely misjudged his enemies in not supposing them capable of such decisive measures has been already mentioned.

But in all history we can hardly find a greater error in the criterion than that in 1792. It was then imagined possible to turn the tide in a national war by a moderate sized auxiliary army, which brought down on those who attempted it the enormous weight of the whole French people, at that time completely unhinged by political fanaticism. We only call this error a great one because it has proved so since, and not because it would have been easy to avoid it. As far as regards the conduct of the war itself, it cannot be denied that the foundation of all the disastrous years which followed was laid in the campaign of 1794. On the side of the allies in that campaign, even the powerful nature of the enemy's system of attack was quite misunderstood, by opposing to it a pitiful system of extended positions and strategic manœuvres; and further in the want of unanimity between Prussia and Austria politically, and the foolish abandonment of Belgium and the Netherlands, we may also see how little presentiment the cabinets of that day had of the force of the torrent which had just broken loose. In the year 1796, the partial acts of resistance offered at Montenotte, Lodi, etc., etc., show sufficiently how little the Austrians understood the main point when confronted by a Buonaparte.

In the year 1800 it was not by the direct effect of the surprise, but by the false view which Melas took of the possible consequences of this surprise, that his catastrophe was brought about.

Ulm, in the year 1805, was the last knot of a loose network of scientific but extremely feeble strategic combinations, good enough to stop a Daun or a Lascy but not a Buonaparte, the Revolution's Emperor.

The indecision and embarrassment of the Prussians in 1806, proceeded from antiquated, pitiful, impracticable views and measures being mixed up with some lucid ideas and a true feeling of the immense importance of the moment. If there had been a distinct consciousness and a complete appreciation of the position of the country, how could they have left 30,000 men in Prussia, and then entertained the idea of forming a special theatre of war in Westphalia, and of gaining any results from a trivial offensive such as that for which Ruchel's and the Weimar corps were intended? and how could they have talked of danger to magazines and loss of this or that strip of territory in the last moments left for deliberation?

Even in 1812, in that grandest of all campaigns, there was no want at first of unsound purposes proceeding from the use of an erroneous standard Scale. In the head quarters at Wilna there was a party of men of high mark who insisted on a battle on the frontier, in order that no hostile foot should tread on Russian ground with impunity. That this battle on the frontier *might* be lost, nay, that it *would* be lost, these men certainly admitted; for although they did not know that there would be 300,000 French to meet 80,000 Russians, still they knew that the enemy was considerably superior in numbers. The chief error was in the value which they ascribed to this battle; they thought it would be a lost battle, like many other lost battles, whereas it may with certainty be asserted that this great battle on the frontier would have produced a succession of events completely different to those which actually took place. Even the camp at Drissa was a measure at the root of which there lay a completely erroneous standard with regard to the enemy. If the Russian army had been obliged to remain there they would have been completely isolated and cut off from every quarter, and then the French army would not have been at a loss for means to compel the Russians to lay down their arms. The designer of that camp never thought of power and will on such a scale as that.

But even Buonaparte sometimes used a false standard. After the armistice of 1813 he thought to hold in check the subordinate armies of the allies under Blucher and the Crown Prince of Sweden by corps which were certainly not able to offer any effectual resistance, but which might impose sufficiently on the cautious to prevent their risking anything, as had so often been done in preceding wars. He did not reflect sufficiently on the reaction proceeding from the deep-rooted resentment with which both Blucher and Bulow were animated, and from the imminent danger in which they were placed.

In general, he under-estimated the enterprising spirit of old Blucher. At Leipsic Blucher alone wrested from him the victory; at Laon Blucher might have entirely ruined him, and if he did not do so the cause lay in circumstances completely out of the calculation of Buonaparte; lastly, at Belle-Alliance, the penalty of this mistake reached him like a thunderbolt.

BOOK SEVEN

The Attack

CHAPTER ONE

The Attack in Relation to the Defence

IF TWO IDEAS form an exact logical antithesis, that is to say if the one is the complement of the other, then, in fact, each one is implied in the other; and when the limited power of our mind is insufficient to apprehend both at once, and, by the mere antithesis, to recognise in the one perfect conception the totality of the other also, still, at all events, the one always throws on the other a strong, and in many parts a sufficient light Thus we think the first chapter on the defence throws a sufficient light on all the points of the attack which it touches upon. But it is not so throughout in respect of every point; the train of thought could nowhere be carried to a finality; it is, therefore, natural that where the opposition of ideas does not lie so immediately at the root of the conception as in the first chapters, all that can be said about the attack does not follow directly from what has been said on the defence. An alteration of our point of view brings us nearer to the subject, and it is natural for us to observe, at this closer point of view, that which escaped observation at our former standpoint. What is thus perceived will, therefore, be the complement of our former train of thought; and it will not unfrequently happen that what is said on the attack will throw a new light on the defence. In treating of the attack we shall, of course, very frequently have the same subjects before us with which our attention has been occupied in the defence. But we have no intention, nor would it be consistent with the nature of the thing, to adopt the usual plan of works on engineering, and in treating of the attack, to circumvent or upset all that we have found of positive value in the defence, by showing that against every means of defence, there is an infallible method of attack. The defence has its strong points and weak ones; if the first are even not unsurmountable, still they can only be overcome at a disproportionate price, and that must remain true from whatever point of view we look at it, or we get involved in a contradiction. Further, it is not our intention thoroughly to review the reciprocal action of the means; each means of defence suggests a means of attack; but this is often so evident, that there is no occasion to transfer oneself from our standpoint in treating of the defence to a fresh one for the attack, in order to perceive it; the one issues from the other of itself. Our object is, in each subject, to set forth the peculiar relations of the attack, so far as they do not directly come out of the defence, and this mode of treatment must necessarily lead us to many chapters to which there are no corresponding ones in the defence.

CHAPTER TWO

Nature of the Strategical Attack

WE HAVE SEEN that the defensive in war generally – therefore, also, the strategic defensive – is no absolute state of expectancy and warding off, therefore no completely passive state, but that it is a relative state, and consequently impregnated more or less with offensive principles. In the same way the offensive is no homogeneous whole, but incessantly mixed up with the defensive. But there is this difference between the two, that a defensive, without an offensive return blow, cannot be conceived; that this return blow is a necessary constituent part of the defensive, whilst in the attack, the blow or act is in itself one complete idea. The defence in itself is not necessarily a part of the attack; but time and space, to which it is inseparably bound, import into it the defensive as a necessary evil. For in the *first* place, the attack cannot be continued uninterruptedly up to its conclusion, it must have stages of rest, and in these stages, when its action is neutralised, the state of defence steps in of itself; in the *second* place, the space which a military force, in its advance, leaves behind it, and which is essential to its existence, cannot always be covered by the attack itself, but must be specially protected.

The act of attack in war, but particularly in that branch which is called strategy, is therefore a perpetual alternating and combining of attack and defence; but the latter is not to be regarded as an effectual preparation for attack, as a means by which its force is heightened, that is to say, not as an active principle, but purely as a necessary evil; as the retarding weight arising from the specific gravity of the mass; it is its original sin, its seed of mortality. We say: a *retarding* weight, because if the defence does not contribute to strengthen the attack, it must tend to diminish its effect by the very loss of time which it represents. But now, may not this defensive element, which is contained in every attack, have over it a *positively disadvantageous* influence? If we suppose the *attack is the weaker, the defence the stronger form of war*, it seems to follow that the latter can not act in a positive sense prejudicially on the former; for as long as we have sufficient force for the *weaker* form, we should have more than enough for the *stronger*. In general – that is, as regards the chief part – this is true: in its detail we shall analyse it more precisely in the chapter on the *culminating point* of *victory*; but we must not forget that that superiority of the *strategic defence* is partly founded in this, that the attack itself cannot take place without a mixture of defence, and of a defensive of a very weak kind; what the assailant has to carry about with him of this kind are its worst elements; with respect to these, that which holds good of the whole, in a general sense, cannot be maintained; and therefore it is conceivable that the defensive may act upon the attack positively as a weakening principle. It is just in these moments of weak defensive in the attack, that the positive action of the offensive principle in the *defensive* should be introduced. During the twelve hours rest which usually succeeds a day's work, what a difference there is between the situation of the defender in his chosen, well-known, and prepared position, and that of the assailant occupying a bivouac, into which – like a blind man – he has groped his way, or during a longer period of rest, required to obtain provisions and to await reinforcements, etc., when the defender is close to his fortresses and supplies, whilst the situation of the assailant, on the other hand, is like that of a bird on a tree. Every attack must lead to a defence; what is to be the result of that defence, depends on circumstances; these circumstances may be very favourable if the enemy's forces are destroyed; but they may be very unfavourable if such is not the case. Although this defensive does not belong to the attack itself, its nature and effects must re-act on the attack, and must take part in determining its value.

The deduction from this view is, that in every attack the defensive, which is necessarily an inherent feature in the same, must come into consideration, in order to see clearly the disadvantages to which it is subject, and to be prepared for them.

On the other hand, in another respect, the attack is always in itself one and the same. But the defensive has its gradations according as the principle of expectancy approaches to an end. This begets forms which differ essentially from each other, as has been developed in the chapter on the forms of defence.

As the principle of the attack is *strictly* active, and the defensive, which connects itself with it, is only a dead weight; there is, therefore, not the same kind of difference in it. No doubt, in the energy employed in the attack, in the rapidity and force of the blow, there may be a great difference, but only a difference in *degree*, not in *form*. – It is quite possible to conceive even that the assailant may choose a defensive form, the better to attain his object; for instance, that he may choose a strong position, that he may be attacked there; but such instances are so rare that we do not think it necessary to dwell upon them in our grouping of ideas and facts, which are always founded on the practical. We may, therefore, say that there are no such gradations in the attack as those which present themselves in the defence.

Lastly, as a rule, the extent of the means of attack consists of the armed force only; of course, we must add to these the fortresses, for if in the vicinity of the theatre of war, they have a decided influence on the attack. But this influence gradually diminishes as the attack advances; and it is conceivable that, in the attack, its own fortresses never can play such an important part as in the defence, in which they often become objects of primary importance. The assistance of the people may be supposed in co-operation with the attack, in those cases in which the inhabitants of the country are better disposed towards the invader of the country than they are to their own army; finally, the assailant may also have allies, but then they are only the result of special or accidental relations, not an assistance proceeding from the nature of the aggressive. Although, therefore, in speaking of the defence we have reckoned fortresses, popular insurrections, and allies as available means of resistance; we cannot do the same in the attack; there they belong to the nature of the thing; here they only appear rarely, and for the most part accidentally.

CHAPTER THREE

Of the Objects of Strategical Attack

THE OVERTHROW of the enemy is the aim in war; destruction of the hostile military forces, the means both in attack and defence. By the destruction of the enemy's military force, the defensive is led on to the offensive, the offensive is led by it to the conquest of territory. Territory is, therefore, the object of the attack; but that need not be a whole country, it may be confined to a part, a province, a strip of country, a fortress. All these things may have a substantial value from their political importance, in treating for peace, whether they are retained or exchanged.

The object of the strategic attack is, therefore, conceivable in an infinite number of gradations, from the conquest of the whole country down to that of some insignificant place. As soon as this object is attained, and the attack ceases, the defensive commences. We may, therefore, represent to ourselves the strategic attack as a distinctly limited unit. But it is not so if we consider the matter practically, that is in accordance with actual phenomena. Practically the moments of the attack, that is, its views and measures, often glide just as imperceptibly into the defence as the plans of the defence into the offensive. It is seldom, or at all events not always, that a general lays down positively for himself what he will conquer, he leaves that dependent on the course of events. His attack often leads him further than he had intended; after rest more or less, he often gets renewed strength, without our being obliged to make out of this two quite different acts; at another time he is brought to a standstill sooner than he expected, without, however, giving up his intentions, and changing to a real defensive. We see, therefore, that if the successful defence may change imperceptibly into the offensive; so on the other hand an attack may, in like manner, change into a defence. These gradations must be kept in view, in order to avoid making a wrong application of what we have to say of the attack in general.

CHAPTER FOUR

Decreasing Force of the Attack

THIS IS ONE of the principal points in strategy: on its right valuation in the concrete, depends our being able to judge correctly what we are able to do.

The decrease of absolute power arises –

1. Through the object of the attack, the occupation of the enemy's country; this generally commences first after the first decision, but the attack does not cease upon the first decision.

2. Through the necessity imposed on the attacking army to guard the country in its rear, in order to preserve its line of communication and means of subsistence.

3. Through losses in action and through sickness.

4. Distance of the various depôts of supplies and reinforcements.

5. Sieges and blockades of fortresses.

6. Relaxation of efforts.

7. Secession of allies.

But frequently, in opposition to these weakening causes, there may be many others which contribute to strengthen the attack. It is clear, at all events, that a net result can only be obtained by comparing these different quantities; thus, for example, the weakening of the attack may be partly or completely compensated, or even surpassed by the weakening of the defensive. This last is a case which rarely happens; we cannot always bring into the comparison any more forces than those in the immediate front or at decisive points, not the whole of the forces in the field. – Different examples: The French in Austria and Prussia, in Russia; the allies in France, the French in Spain.

CHAPTER FIVE

Culminating Point of the Attack

THE SUCCESS of the attack is the result of a present superiority of force, it being understood that the moral as well as physical forces are included. In the preceding chapter we have shown that the power of the attack gradually exhausts itself; possibly at the same time the superiority may increase, but in most cases it diminishes. The assailant buys up prospective advantages which are to be turned to account hereafter in negotiations for peace; but, in the meantime, he has to pay down on the spot for them a certain amount of his military force. If a preponderance on the side of the attack, although thus daily diminishing, is still maintained until peace is concluded, the object is attained. – There are strategic attacks which have led to an immediate peace – but such instances are rare; the majority, on the contrary, lead only to a point at which the forces remaining are just sufficient to maintain a defensive, and to wait for peace. – Beyond that point the scale turns, there is a reaction; the violence of such a reaction is commonly much greater than the force of the blow. This we call the culminating point of the attack. – As the object of the attack is the possession of the enemy's territory, it follows that the advance must continue till the superiority is exhausted; this cause, therefore, impels us towards the ultimate object, and may easily lead us beyond it. – If we reflect upon the number of the elements of which an equation of the forces in action is composed, we may conceive how difficult it is in many cases to determine which of two opponents has the superiority on his side. Often all hangs on the silken thread of imagination.

Everything then depends on discovering the culminating point by the fine tact of judgment. Here we come upon a seeming contradiction. The defence is stronger than the attack; therefore we should think that the latter can never lead us too far, for as long as the weaker form remains strong enough for what is required, the stronger form ought to be still more so.[59]

59   Here follows in the MS. this note: – "Development of this subject after Book 3, in the essay on the Culminating Point of Victory."
Under this title, in an envelope endorsed "*Various dissertations as materials*," an essay has been found which appears to be a revision of the chapter here only sketched, it will be found at the end of the seventh book. Editress' (Mrs. Clausewitz's) Note.

CHAPTER SIX

Destruction of the Enemy's Armies

THE DESTRUCTION of the enemy's armed forces is the means to the end –
What is meant by this – The price it costs – Different points of view which
are possible in respect to the subject.

1, only to destroy as many as the object of the attack requires.

2, or as many on the whole as is possible.

3, the sparing of our own forces as the principal point of view.

4, this may again be carried so far, that the assailant does nothing
towards the destruction of the enemy's force *except when a favourable
opportunity offers*, which may also be the case with regard to the object
of the attack, as already mentioned in the third chapter.

The only means of destroying the enemy's armed force is by combat,
but this may be done in two ways: 1, directly, 2, indirectly, through a
combination of combats. – If, therefore, the battle is the chief means,
still it is not the only means. The capture of a fortress or of a portion
of territory, is in itself really a destruction of the enemy's force, and it
may also lead to a still greater destruction, and therefore, also, be an
indirect means.

The occupation of an undefended strip of territory, therefore, in addition to the value which it has as a direct fulfilment of the end, may also
reckon as a destruction of the enemy's force as well. The manœuvring, so
as to draw an enemy out of a district of country which he has occupied, is
somewhat similar, and must, therefore, only be looked at from the same
point of view, and not as a success of arms, properly speaking – These
means are generally estimated at more than they are worth – they have
seldom the value of a battle; besides which it is always to be feared that
the disadvantageous position to which they lead, will be overlooked; they
are seductive through the low price which they cost.

We must always consider means of this description as small investments, from which only small profits are to be expected; as means suited only to very limited State relations and weak motives. Then they are certainly better than battles without a purpose – than victories, the results of which cannot be realised to the full.

CHAPTER SEVEN
The Offensive Battle

WHAT WE HAVE SAID about the defensive battle throws a strong light upon the offensive also.

We there had in view that class of battle in which the defensive appears most decidedly pronounced, in order that we might convey a more vivid impression of its nature; – but only the fewer number are of that kind; most battles are *demirencontres* in which the defensive character disappears to a great extent. It is otherwise with the offensive battle: it preserves its character under all circumstances, and can keep up that character the more boldly, as the defender is out of his proper *esse*. For this reason, in the battle which is not purely defensive and in the real *rencontres*, there always remains also something of the difference of the character of the battle on the one side and on the other. The chief distinctive characteristic of the offensive battle is the manœuvre to turn or surround, therefore, the initiative as well.

A combat in lines, formed to envelope, has evidently in itself great advantages; it is, however, a subject of tactics. The attack must not give up these advantages because the defence has a means of counteracting them; for the attack itself cannot make use of that means, inasmuch as it is one that is too closely dependent upon other things connected with the defence. To be able in turn to operate with success against the flanks of an enemy, whose aim is to turn our line, it is necessary to have a well chosen and well prepared position. But what is much more important is, that all the advantages which the defensive possesses, cannot be made use of; most defences are poor makeshifts; the greater number of defenders find themselves in a very harassing and critical position, in which, expecting the worst, they meet the attack half way. The consequence of this is, that battles formed with enveloping lines, or even with an oblique front, which should properly result from an advantageous relation of the lines of communication, are commonly the result of a moral and physical preponderance (Marengo, Austerlitz, Jena). Besides, in the first battle fought, the base of the assailant, if not superior to that of the defender, is still mostly very wide in extent, on account of the proximity of the frontier; he can, therefore, afford to venture a little. – The flank-attack, that is, the battle with oblique front, is moreover generally more efficacious than the enveloping form. It is an erroneous idea that an enveloping strategic advance from the very commencement must be connected with it, as at Prague. (That strategic measure has seldom anything in common with it, and is very hazardous; of which we shall speak further in the attack of a theatre of war.)

As it is an object with the commander in the defensive battle to delay the decision as long as possible, and gain time, because a defensive battle undecided at sunset is commonly one gained: therefore the commander, in the offensive battle, requires to hasten the decision; but, on the other hand, there is a great risk in too much haste, because it leads to a waste of forces. One peculiarity in the offensive battle is the uncertainty, in most cases, as to the position of the enemy; it is a complete groping about amongst things that are unknown (Austerlitz, Wagram, Hohenlinden, Jena, Katzbach). The more this is the case, so much the more concentration of forces becomes paramount, and turning a flank to be preferred to surrounding. That the principal fruits of victory are first gathered in the pursuit, we have already learnt in the twelfth chapter of the 4th Book. According to the nature of the thing, the pursuit is more an integral part of the whole action in the offensive than in the defensive battle.

CHAPTER EIGHT

Passage of Rivers

1. A LARGE RIVER which crosses the direction of the attack is always very inconvenient for the assailant: for when he has crossed it he is generally limited to one point of passage, and, therefore, unless he remains close to the river he becomes very much hampered in his movements. Whether he meditates bringing on a decisive battle after crossing, or may expect the enemy to attack him, he exposes himself to great danger; therefore, without a decided superiority, both in moral and physical force, a general will not place himself in such a position.

2. From this mere disadvantage of placing a river behind an army, a river is much oftener capable of defence than it would otherwise be. If we suppose that this defence is not considered the only means of safety, but is so planned that even if it fails, still a stand can be made near the river, then the assailant in his calculations must add to the resistance which he may experience in the defence of the river, all the advantages mentioned in No. 1, as being on the side of the defender of a river, and the effect of the two together is, that we usually see generals show great respect to a river before they attack it if it is defended.

3. But in the preceding book we have seen, that under certain conditions, the real defence of a river promises right good results; and if we refer to experience, we must allow that such results follow in reality much more frequently than theory promises, because in theory we only calculate with real circumstances as we find them take place, while in the execution, things commonly appear to the assailant much more difficult than they really are, and they become therefore a greater clog on his action.

Suppose, for instance, an attack which is not intended to end in a great solution, and which is not conducted with thorough energy, we may be sure that in carrying it out a number of little obstacles and accidents, which no theory could calculate upon, will start up to the disadvantage of the assailant, because he is the acting party, and must, therefore, come first into collision with such impediments. Let us just think for a moment how often some of the insignificant rivers of Lombardy have been successfully defended! – If, on the other hand, cases may also be found in military history, in which the defence of rivers has failed to realise what was expected of them, that lies in the extravagant results sometimes looked for from this means; results not founded in any kind of way on its tactical nature, but merely on its well-known efficacy, to which people have thought there were no bounds.

4. It is only when the defender commits the mistake of placing his entire dependence on the defence of a river, so that in case it is forced he becomes involved in great difficulty, in a kind of catastrophe, it is only then that the defence of a river can be looked upon as a form of defence favourable to the attack, for it is certainly easier to force the passage of a river than to gain an ordinary battle.

5. It follows of itself from what has just been said that the defence of a river may become of great value if no great solution is desired, but where that is to be expected, either from the superior numbers or energy of the enemy, then this means, if wrongly used, may turn to the positive advantage of the assailant.

6. There are very few river-lines of defence which cannot be turned either on the whole length or at some particular point. Therefore the assailant, superior in numbers and bent upon serious blows, has the means of making a demonstration at one point and passing at another, and then by superior numbers, and advancing, regardless of all opposition, he can repair any disadvantageous relations in which he may have been placed by the issue of the first encounters: for his general superiority will enable him to do so. It very rarely happens that the passage of a river is actually tactically forced by overpowering the enemy's principal post by the effect of superior fire and greater valour on the part of the troops, and the expression, *forcing a passage* is only to be taken in a strategic sense, in so far that the assailant by his passage at an undefended or only slightly defended point within the line of defence, braves all the dangers which, in the defender's view, should result to him through the crossing. – But the worst which an assailant can do, is to attempt a real passage at several points, unless they lie close to each other and admit of all the troops joining in the combat; for as the defender must necessarily have his forces separated, therefore, if the assailant fractions his in like manner, he throws away his natural advantage. In that way Bellegarde lost

the battle on the Mincio, 1814, where by chance both armies passed at different points at the same time, and the Austrians were more divided than the French.

7. If the defender remains on this side of the river, it necessarily follows that there are two ways to gain a strategic advantage over him: either to pass at some point, regardless of his position, and so to outbid him in the same means, or to give battle. In the first case, the relations of the base and lines of communications should chiefly decide, but it often happens that special circumstances exercise more influence than general relations; he who can choose the best positions, who knows best how to make his dispositions, who is better obeyed, whose army marches fastest, etc., may contend with advantage against general circumstances. As regards the second means, it presupposes on the part of the assailant the means, suitable relations, and the determination to fight; but when these conditions may be presupposed, the defender will not readily venture upon this mode of defending a river.

8. As a final result, we must therefore give as our opinion that, although the passage of a river in itself rarely presents great difficulties, yet in all cases not immediately connected with a great decision, so many apprehensions of the consequences and of future complications are bound up with it, that at all events the progress of the assailant may easily be so far arrested that he either leaves the defender on this side the river, or he passes, and then remains close to the river. For it rarely happens that two armies remain any length of time confronting one another on different sides of a river.

But also in cases of a great solution, a river is an important object; it always weakens and deranges the offensive; and the most fortunate thing, in this case is, if the defender is induced through that to look upon the river as a tactical barrier, and to make the particular defence of that barrier the principal act of his resistance, so that the assailant at once obtains the advantage of being able to strike a decisive blow in a very easy manner. – Certainly, in the first instance, this blow will never amount to a complete defeat of the enemy, but it will consist of several advantageous combats, and these bring about a state of general relations very adverse to the enemy, as happened to the Austrians on the Lower Rhine, 1796.

CHAPTER NINE
Attack of Defensive Positions

IN THE BOOK on the defence, it has been sufficiently explained how far defensive positions can compel the assailant either to attack them, or to give up his advance. Only those which can effect this are subservient to our object, and suited to wear out or neutralise the forces of the aggressor, either wholly or in part, and in so far the attack can do nothing against such positions, that is to say, there are no means at its disposal by which to counter-balance this advantage. But defensive positions are not all really of this kind. If the assailant sees he can pursue his object without attacking such a position, it would be an error to make the attack; if he cannot follow out his object, then it is a question whether he cannot manœuvre the enemy out of his position by threatening his flank. It is only if such means are ineffectual, that a commander determines on the attack of a good position, and then an attack directed against one side, always in general presents the less difficulty; but the choice of the side must depend on the position and direction of the mutual lines of retreat, consequently, on the threatening the enemy's retreat, and covering our own. Between these two objects a competition may arise, in which case the first is entitled to the preference, as it is of an offensive nature; therefore homogeneous with the attack, whilst the other is of a defensive character. But it is certain, and may be regarded as a truth of the first importance, that *to attack an enemy thoroughly inured to war, in a good position, is a critical thing.* No doubt instances are not wanting of such battles, and of successful ones too, as Torgau, Wagram (we do not say Dresden, because we cannot call the enemy there quite aguerried); but upon the whole, the danger is small, and it vanishes altogether, opposed to the infinite number of cases in which we have seen the most resolute commanders make their bow before such positions. (Torres Vedras.)

We must not, however, confuse the subject now before us with ordinary battles. Most battles are real "*rencontres,*" in which one party certainly occupies a position, but one which has not been prepared.

CHAPTER TEN
Attack of an Entrenched Camp

IT WAS FOR A TIME the fashion to speak with contempt of entrenchments and their utility. The cordon lines of the French frontier, which had been often burst through; the entrenched camp at Breslau in which the Duke of Bevern was defeated, the battle of Torgau, and several other cases, led to this opinion of their value; and the victories of Frederick the Great, gained by the principle of movement and the use of the offensive, threw a fresh light on all kind of defensive action, all fighting in a fixed position, particularly in intrenchments, and brought them still more into contempt. Certainly, when a few thousand men are to defend several miles of country, and when entrenchments are nothing more than ditches reversed, they are worth nothing, and they constitute a dangerous snare through the confidence which is placed in them. But is it not inconsistent, or rather nonsensical, to extend this view even to the *idea of field fortification*, in a mere swaggering spirit (as Templehof does)? What would be the object of entrenchments generally, if not to strengthen the defence? No, not only reason but experience, in hundreds and thousands of instances, show that a well-traced, sufficiently manned, and well defended entrenchment is, *as a rule, to be looked upon as an impregnable point*, and is also so regarded by the attack. Starting from this point of the efficiency of a single entrenchment, we argue that there can be no doubt as to the attack of an entrenched camp being a most difficult undertaking, and one in which generally it will be impossible for the assailant to succeed.

It is consistent with the nature of an entrenched camp that it should be weakly garrisoned; but with good, natural obstacles of ground and strong field works, it is possible to bid defiance to superior numbers. Frederick the Great considered the attack of the camp of Pirna as impracticable, although he had at his command double the force of the garrison; and although it has been since asserted, here and there, that it was quite possible to have taken it; the only proof in favour of this assertion is founded on the bad condition of the Saxon troops; an argument which does not at all detract in any way from the value of entrenchments. But it is a question, whether those who have since contended not only for the feasibility but also for the facility of the attack, would have made up their minds to execute it at the time.

We, therefore, think that the attack of an entrenched camp belongs to the category of quite exceptional means on the part of the offensive. It is only if the entrenchments have been thrown up in haste are not completed, still less strengthed by obstacles to prevent their being approached, or when, as is often the case taken altogether, the whole camp is only an outline of what it was intended to be, a half-finished ruin, that then an attack on it may be advisable, and at the same time become the road to gain an easy conquest over the enemy.

CHAPTER ELEVEN
Attack of a Mountain

FROM THE FIFTH and following chapters of the sixth book, may be deduced sufficiently the strategic relations of a mountain generally, both as regards the defence and the attack. We have also there endeavoured to explain the part which a mountain plays as a line of defence, properly so called, and from that naturally follows how it is to be looked upon in this signification from the side of the assailant. There remains, therefore, little for us to say here on this important subject. Our chief result was there that the defence must choose as his point of view a secondary combat, or the entirely different one of a great general action; that in the first case the attack of a mountain can only be regarded as a necessary evil, because all the circumstances are unfavourable to it; but in the second case the advantages are on the side of the attack.

An attack, therefore, armed with the means and the resolution for a battle, will give the enemy a meeting in the mountains, and certainly find his account in so doing.

But we must here once more repeat that it will be difficult to obtain respect for this conclusion, because it runs counter to appearances, and is also, at first sight, contrary to the experience of war. It has been observed, in most cases hitherto, that an army pressing forward to the attack (whether seeking a great general action or not), has considered it an unusual piece of good fortune if the enemy has not occupied the intervening mountains, and has itself then hastened to be beforehand in the occupation of them. No one will find this forestalling of the enemy in any way inconsistent with the interests of the assailant; in our view this is also quite admissible, only we must point out clearly a fine distinction here between circumstances.

An army advancing against the enemy, with the design of bringing him to a general action, if it has to pass over an unoccupied range of mountain, has naturally to apprehend that the enemy may, at the last moment, block up those very passes which it proposes to use on its march: in such a case, the assailant will by no means have the same advantages as if the enemy occupied merely an ordinary mountain position. The latter is, for instance, not then in a position extended beyond measure, nor is he in uncertainty as to the road which the assailant will take; the assailant has not been able to choose his road with reference to the enemy's position, and therefore this battle in the mountains is not then united with all those advantages on his side of which we have spoken in the sixth book; under such circumstances, the defender might be found in an impregnable position – According to this, the defender might even have means at his command of making advantageous use of the mountains for a great battle. – This is, at any rate, possible; but if we reflect on the difficulties which the defender would have to encounter in establishing himself in a strong position in the mountains just at the last moment, particularly if he has left it entirely unoccupied before, we may put down this means of defence as one upon which no dependence can be placed, and therefore as one, the *probability* of which the assailant has little reason to dread. But even if it is a very improbable case, yet still it is natural to fear it; for in war, many a thing is very natural, and yet in a certain measure superfluous.

But another measure which the assailant has to apprehend here is, a preliminary defence of the mountains by an advanced guard or chain of outposts. This means, also, will seldom accord with the interests of the defender; but the assailant has not the means of discerning how far it may be beneficial to the defender or otherwise, and therefore he has only to provide against the worst.

Further, our view by no means excludes the possibility of a position being quite unassailable from the mountainous character of the ground: there are such positions which are not, on that account, in the mountains (Pirna, Schmotseifen, Meissen, Feldkirch), and it is just because they are not in the mountains, that they are so well suited for defence. We may also very well conceive that positions may be found in mountains themselves where the defender might avoid the ordinary disadvantages of mountain-positions, as, for instance, on lofty *plateaux;* but they are not common, and we can only take into our view the generality of cases.

It is just in military history that we see how little mountain-positions are suited to decisive defensive battles, for great generals have always preferred a position in the plains, when it was their object to fight a battle of the first order; and throughout the whole range of military history, there are no examples of decisive battles in the mountains, except in the Revolutionary Wars, and even there it was plainly a false application and analogy which led to the use of mountain-positions, where of necessity a decisive battle had to be fought (1793 and 1794 in the Vosges, and 1795, 1796, and 1797 in Italy). Melas has been generally blamed for not having occupied the Alpine passes in 1800; but such criticisms are nothing more than "early notions" – we might say – childlike judgments founded on appearances. Buonaparte, in Mela's place, would just as little have thought of occupying the passes.

The dispositions for the attack of mountain-positions are mostly of a tactical nature; but we think it necessary to insert here the following remarks as to the general outline, consequently as to those parts which come into immediate contact with, and are coincident with, strategy.

1. As we cannot move wide of the roads in mountains as we can in other districts, and form two or three columns out of one, when the exigency of the moment requires that the mass of the troops should be divided; but, on the contrary, we are generally confined to long defiles; the advance in mountains must generally be made on several roads, or rather upon a somewhat broader front.

2. Against a mountain line of defence of wide extent, the attack must naturally be made with concentrated forces; to surround the whole cannot be thought of there, and if an important result is to be gained from victory, it must be obtained rather by bursting through the enemy's line, and separating the wings, than by surrounding the force, and so cutting it off. A rapid, continuous advance upon the enemy's principal line of retreat is there the natural endeavour of the assailant.

3. But if the enemy to be attacked occupies a position somewhat concentrated, turning movements are an essential part of the scheme of attack, as the front attacks fall upon the mass of the defender's forces; but the turning movements again must be made more with a view to cutting off the enemy's retreat, than as a tactical rolling up of the flank or attack on the rear; for mountain positions are capable of a prolonged resistance even in rear if forces are not wanting, and the quickest result is invariably to be expected only from the enemy's apprehension of losing his line of retreat; this sort of uneasiness arises sooner, and acts more powerfully in mountains, because, when it comes to the worst, it is not so easy to make room sword in hand. A mere demonstration is no sufficient means here; it might certainly manœuvre the enemy out of his position, but would not ensure any special result; the aim must therefore be to cut him off, in reality, from his line of retreat.

CHAPTER TWELVE

Attack of Cordon Lines

If a supreme decision should lie in their defence and their attack, they place the assailant in an advantageous situation, for their wide extent is still more in opposition to all the requirements of a decisive battle than the direct defence of a river or a mountain range. Eugene's lines of Denain, 1712, are an illustration to the point here, for their loss was quite equal to a complete defeat, but Villars would hardly have gained such a victory against Eugene in a concentrated position. If the offensive side does not possess the means required for a decisive battle, then even lines are treated with respect, that is, if they are occupied by the main body of an army; for instance, those of Stollhofen, held by Louis of Baden in the year 1703, were respected even by Villars. But if they are only held by a secondary force, then it is merely a question of the strength of the corps which we can spare for their attack. The resistance in such cases is seldom great, but at the same time the result of the victory is seldom worth much.

The circumvallation lines of a besieger have a peculiar character, of which we shall speak in the chapter on the attack of a theatre of war.

All positions of the cordon kind, as, for instance, entrenched lines of outposts, etc., etc., have always this property, that they can be easily broken through; but when they are not forced with a view of going further and bringing on a decision, there is so little to be gained in general by the attack, that it hardly repays the trouble expended.

CHAPTER THIRTEEN

Manœuvring

1. WE HAVE ALREADY touched upon this subject in the thirtieth chapter of the sixth book. It is one which concerns the defence and the attack in common; nevertheless it has always in it something more of the nature of the offensive than the defensive. We shall therefore now examine it more thoroughly.

2. Manœuvring is not only the opposite of executing the offensive by force, by means of great battles; it stands also opposed to every such execution of the offensive as proceeds directly from offensive means, let it be either an operation against the enemy's communications, or line of retreat, a diversion, etc., etc.

3. If we adhere to the ordinary use of the word, there is in the conception of manœuvring an effect which is first *produced*, to a certain extent, from nothing, that is, from a state of rest or *equilibrium* through the mistakes into which the enemy is enticed. It is like the first moves in a game of chess. It is, therefore, a game of evenly-balanced powers, to obtain results from favourable opportunity, and then to use these as an advantage over the enemy.

4. But those interests which, partly as the final object, partly as the principal supports (pivot) of action, must be considered in this matter, are chiefly: –

(*a.*) The subsistence from which it is our object to cut off the enemy, or to impede his obtaining.

(*b.*) The junction with other corps.

(*c*) The threatening other communications with the interior of the country, or with other armies or corps.

(*d.*) Threatening the retreat.

(*e.*) Attack of isolated points with superior forces

These five interests may establish themselves in the smallest features of detail belonging to any particular situation; and any such object then becomes, on that account, a point round which everything for a time revolves. A bridge, a road, or an entrenchment, often thus plays the principal part. It is easy to show in each case that it is only the relation which any such object has to one of the above interests which gives it importance.

(*f*) The result of a successful manœuvre, then, is for the offensive, or rather for the active party (which may certainly be just as well the defensive), a piece of land, a magazine, etc.

(*g.*) In a strategic manœuvre two converse propositions appear, which look like different manœuvres, and have sometimes served for the derivation of false maxims and rules, and have four branches, which are, however, in reality, all necessary constituents of the same thing, and are to be regarded as such. The first antithesis is the surrounding the enemy, and the operating on interior lines; the second is the concentration of forces, and their extension over several posts.

(*h*) As regards the first antithesis, we certainly cannot say that one of its members deserves a general preference over the other; for partly it is natural that action of one kind calls forth the other as its natural counterpoise, its true remedy; partly the enveloping form is homogeneous to the attack, but the use of interior lines to the defence; and therefore, in most cases, the first is more suitable to the offensive side, the latter to the defensive. That form will gain the upper hand which is used with the greatest skill.

(*i.*) The branches of the other antithesis can just as little be classed the one above the other. The stronger force has the choice of extending itself over several posts; by that means he will obtain for himself a convenient strategic situation, and liberty of action in many respects, and spare the physical powers of his troops. The weaker, on the other hand, must keep himself more concentrated, and seek by rapidity of movement to counteract the disadvantage of his inferior numbers. This greater mobility supposes greater readiness in marching. The weaker must therefore put a greater strain on his physical and moral forces, – a final result which we must naturally come upon everywhere if we would always be consistent, and which, therefore, we regard, to a certain extent, as the logical test of the reasoning. The campaigns of Frederick the Great against Daun, in the years 1759 and 1760, and against Laudon, 1761, and Montecuculis against Turenne in 1673, 1675, have always been reckoned the most scientific combinations of this kind, and from them we have chiefly derived our view.

(*k*.) Just as the four parts of the two antitheses above supposed must not be abused by being made the foundation of false maxims and rules, so we must also give a caution against attaching to other general relations, such as base, ground, etc., an importance and a decisive influence which they do not in reality possess. The smaller the interests at stake, so much the more important the details of time and place become, so much the more that which is general and great falls into the background, having, in a certain measure no place in small calculations. Is there to be found, viewed generally, a more absurd situation than that of Turenne in 1675, when he stood with his back close to the Rhine, his army along a line of three miles in extent, and with his bridge of retreat at the extremity of his right wing? But his measures answered their object, and it is not without reason that they are acknowledged to show a high degree of skill and intelligence. We can only understand this result and this skill when we look more closely into details, and judge of them according to the value which they must have had in this particular case.

We are convinced that there are no rules of any kind for strategic manœuvring; that no method, no general principle can determine the mode of action; but that superior energy, precision, order, obedience, intrepidity in the most special and trifling circumstances may find means to obtain for themselves signal advantages, and that, therefore, chiefly on those qualities will depend the victory in this sort of contest.

CHAPTER FOURTEEN

Attack of Morasses, Inundations, Woods

MORASSES, that is, impassable swamps, which are only traversed by a few embankments, present peculiar difficulties to the tactical attack, as we have stated in treating of the defence. Their breadth hardly ever admits of the enemy being driven from the opposite bank by artillery, and of the construction of a roadway across. The strategic consequence is that endeavours are made to avoid attacking them by passing round them. Where the state of culture, as in many low countries, is so great that the means of passing are innumerable, the resistance of the defender is still strong enough relatively, but it is proportionably weakened for an absolute decision, and, therefore, wholly unsuitable for it. On the other hand, if the low land (as in Holland) is aided by inundations, the resistance may become absolute, and defy every attack. This was shown in Holland in the year 1672, when, after the conquest and occupation of all the fortresses outside the margin of the inundation, 50,000 French troops became available, who, – first under Condé and then under Luxemburg, – were unable to force the line of inundation, although it was only defended by about 20,000 men. The campaign of the Prussians, in 1787, under the Duke of Brunswick, against the Dutch, ended, it is true, in a quite contrary way, as these lines were then carried by a force very little superior to the defenders, and with trifling loss; but the reason of that is to be found in the dissensions amongst the defenders from political animosities, and a want of unity in the command, and yet nothing is more certain than that the success of the campaign, that is, the advance through the last line of inundation up to the walls of Amsterdam depended on a point of such extreme nicety that it is impossible to draw any general deduction from this case. The point alluded to was the leaving unguarded the Sea of Haarlem. By means of this, the Duke turned the inundation line, and got in rear of the post of Amselvoen. If the Dutch had had a couple of armed vessels on this lake the duke would never have got to Amsterdam, for he was *"au bout de son latin."* What influence that might have had on the conclusion of peace does not concern us here, but it is certain that any further question of carrying the last line of inundation would have been put an end to completely.

The winter is, no doubt, the natural enemy of this means of defence, as the French have shown in 1794 and 1795, but it must be a *severe* winter.

Woods, which are scarcely passable, we have also included amongst the means which afford the defence powerful assistance. If they are of no great depth then the assailant may force his way through by several roads running near one another, and thus reach better ground, for no one point can have any great tactical strength, as we can never suppose a wood as absolutely impassable as a river or a morass. – But when, as in Russia and Poland, a very large tract of country is nearly everywhere covered with wood, and the assailant has not the power of getting beyond it, then, certainly, his situation becomes very embarrassing. We have only to think of the difficulties he must contend with to subsist his army, and how little he can do in the depths of the forest to make his ubiquitous adversary feel his superiority in numbers. Certainly this is one of the worst situations in which the offensive can be placed.

CHAPTER FIFTEEN

Attack of a Theatre of War
with the View to a Decision

MOST OF THE SUBJECTS have been already touched upon in the sixth book, and by their mere reflection, throw sufficient light on the attack.

Moreover, the conception of an enclosed theatre of war, has a nearer relation to the defence than to the attack. Many of the leading points, *the object of attack, the sphere of action of victory*, etc., have been already treated of in that book, and that which is most decisive and essential on the nature of the attack, cannot be made to appear until we get to the plan of war: still there remains a good deal to say here, and we shall again commence with the campaign, *in which a great decision is positively intended*.

1. The first aim of the attack is a victory. To all the advantages which the defender finds in the nature of his situation, the assailant can only oppose superior numbers; and, perhaps, in addition, the slight advantage which the feeling of being the offensive and advancing side gives an army. The importance of this feeling, however, is generally overrated; for it does not last long, and will not hold out against real difficulties. Of course, we assume that the defender is as faultless and judicious in all he does as the aggressor. Our object in this observation is to set aside those vague ideas of sudden attack and surprise, which, in the attack, are generally assumed to be fertile sources of victory, and which yet, in reality, never occur except under special circumstances. The nature of the real strategic surprise, we have already spoken of elsewhere. – If, then, the attack is inferior in physical power, it must have the ascendancy in moral power, in order to make up for the disadvantages which are inherent in the offensive form; if the superiority in that way is also wanting, then there are no good grounds for the attack, and it will not succeed.

2. As prudence is the real genius of the defender, so boldness and self-confidence must animate the assailant. We do not mean that the opposite qualities in each case may be altogether wanting, but that the qualities named have the greatest affinity to the attack and defence respectively. These qualities are only in reality necessary because action in war is no mere mathematical calculation; it is activity which is carried on if not in the dark, at all events in a feeble twilight, in which we must trust ourselves to the leader who is best suited to carry out the aim we have in view. – The weaker the defender shows himself morally, the bolder the assailant should become.

3. For victory, it is necessary that there should be a battle between the enemy's principal force and our own. This is less doubtful as regards the attack than in regard to the defence, for the assailant goes in search of the defender in his position. But we have maintained (in treating of the defensive) that the offensive should not seek the defender out if he has placed himself in a *false* position, because he may be sure that the defender will seek *him* out, and then he will have the advantage of fighting where the defender has not prepared the ground. Here all depends on the road and direction which have the greatest importance; this is a point which was not examined in the defence, being reserved for the present chapter. We shall, therefore, say what is necessary about it here.

4. We have already pointed out those objects to which the attack should be more immediately directed, and which, therefore, are the ends to be obtained by victory; now, if these are within the theatre of war which is attacked, and within the probable sphere of victory, then the road to them is the natural direction of the blow to be struck. But we must not forget that the object of the attack does not generally obtain its signification until victory has been gained, and therefore the mind must always embrace the idea of victory with it; the principal consideration for the assailant is, therefore, not so much merely to reach the object as to reach it a conqueror; therefore the direction of his blow should be not so much on the object itself as on the way which the enemy's army must take to reach it. This way is the immediate object of the attack. To fall in with the enemy before he has reached this object, to cut him off from it, and in that position to beat him – to do this is to gain an intensified victory. – If, for example, the enemy's capital is the object of the attack, and the defender has not placed himself between it and the assailant, the latter would be wrong in marching direct upon the capital, he would do much better by taking his direction upon the line connecting the defender's army with the capital, and seeking there the victory which shall place the capital in his hands.

If there is no great object within the assailant's sphere of victory, then the enemy's line of communication with the nearest great object to him is the point of paramount importance. The question, then, for every assailant to ask himself is, If I am successful in the battle, what is the first use I shall make of the victory? The object to be gained, as indicated by the answer to this question, shows the natural direction for his blow. If the defender has placed himself in that direction, he has done right, and there is nothing to do but to go and look for him there. If his position is too strong, then the assailant must seek to turn it, that is, make a virtue of necessity. But if the defender has not placed himself on this right spot, then the assailant chooses that direction, and as soon as he comes in line with the defender, if the latter has not in the mean time made a lateral movement, and placed himself across his path, he should turn himself in the direction of the defender's line of communication in order to seek an action there; if the defender remains quite stationary, then the assailant must wheel round towards him and attack him in rear.

Of all the roads amongst which the assailant has a choice, the great roads which serve the commerce of the country are always the best and the most natural to choose. To avoid any very great bends, more direct roads, even if smaller, must be chosen, for a line of retreat which deviates much from a direct line is always perilous.

5. The assailant, when he sets out with a view to a great decision, has seldom any reason for dividing his forces, and if, notwithstanding this, he does so, it generally proceeds from a want of clear views. He should therefore only advance with his columns on such a width of front as will admit of their all coming into action together. If the enemy himself has divided his forces, so much the better for the assailant, and to preserve this further advantage small demonstrations should be made against the enemy's corps which have separated from the main body; these are the strategic *fausses attaques;* a detachment of forces *for this purpose* would then be justifiable.

Such separation into several columns as is indispensably necessary must be made use of for the disposition of the tactical attack in the enveloping form, for that form is natural to the attack, and must not be disregarded without good reason. But it must be only of a tactical nature, for a strategic envelopment when a great blow takes place, is a complete waste of power. It can only be excused when the assailant is so strong that there can be no doubt at all about the result.

6. But the attack requires also prudence, for the assailant has also a rear, and has communications which must be protected. This service of protection must be performed as far as possible by the manner in which

the army advances, that is, *eo ipso* by the army itself. If a force must be specially detailed for this duty, and therefore a partition of forces is required, this cannot but naturally weaken the force of the blow itself. – As a large army is always in the habit of advancing with a front of a day's march at least in breadth, therefore, if the lines of retreat and communication do not deviate much from the perpendicular, the covering of those lines is in most cases attained by the front of the army.

Dangers of this description, to which the assailant is exposed, must be measured chiefly by the situation and character of the adversary. When everything lies under the pressure of an imminent great decision, there is little room for the defender to engage in undertakings of this description; the assailant has, therefore, in ordinary circumstances not much to fear. But if the advance is over, if the assailant himself is gradually passing into the defensive, then the covering of the rear becomes every moment more necessary, becomes more a thing of the first importance. For the rear of the assailant being naturally weaker than that of the defender, therefore the latter, long before he passes over to the real offensive, and even at the same time that he is yielding ground, may have commenced to operate against the communications of the assailant.

CHAPTER SIXTEEN

Attack of a Theatre of War without the View to a Great Decision

1. ALTHOUGH THERE is neither the will nor the power sufficient for a great decision, there may still exist a decided view in a strategic attack, but it is directed against some secondary object. If the attack succeeds, then, with the attainment of this object the whole falls again into a state of rest and equilibrium. If difficulties to a certain extent present themselves, the general progress of the attack comes to a standstill before the object is gained. Then in its place commences a mere occasional offensive or strategic manœuvring. This is the character of most campaigns.

2. The objects which may be the aim of an offensive of this description are: –

(a.) A strip of territory; gain in means of subsistence, perhaps contributions, sparing our own territory, equivalents in negotiations for peace – such are the advantages to be derived from this procedure. Sometimes an idea of the credit of the army is attached to it, as was perpetually the case in the wars of the French Marshals in the time of Louis XIV. It makes a very important difference whether a portion of territory can be kept or not. In general, the first is the case only when the territory is on the edge of our own theatre of war, and forms a natural complement of it. Only such portions come into consideration as an equivalent in negotiating a peace, others are usually only taken possession of for the duration of a campaign, and to be evacuated when winter begins.

(b.) One of the enemy's principal magazines. If it is not one of considerable importance, it can hardly be looked upon as the object of an offensive determining a whole campaign. It certainly in itself is a loss to the defender, and a gain to the assailant; the great advantage, however, from it for the latter, is that the loss may compel the defender to retire

a little and give up a strip of territory which he would otherwise have kept. The capture of a magazine is therefore in reality more a means, and is only spoken of here as an object, because, until captured, it becomes, for the time being, the immediate definite aim of action.

(c.) The capture of a fortress. – We have made the siege of fortresses the subject of a separate chapter, to which we refer our readers. For the reasons there explained, it is easy to conceive how it is that fortresses always constitute the best and most desirable objects in those offensive wars and campaigns in which views cannot be directed to the complete overthrow of the enemy or the conquest of an important part of his territory. We may also easily understand how it is that in the wars in the Low Countries, where fortresses are so abundant, everything has always turned on the possession of one or other of these fortresses, so much so, that the successive conquests of whole provinces *never once appear as leading features;* while, on the other hand, each of these strong places used to be regarded as a separate thing, which had an intrinsic value in itself, and more attention was paid to the convenience and facility with which it could be attacked than to the value of the place itself.

At the same time, the attack of a place of some importance is always a great undertaking, because it causes a very large expenditure; and, in wars in which the whole is not staked at once on the game, this is a matter which ought to be very much considered. Therefore, such a siege takes its place here as one of the most important objects of a strategic attack. The more unimportant a place is, or the less earnestness there is about the siege, the smaller the preparations for it, the more it is done as a thing *en passant,* so much the smaller also will be the strategic object, and the more it will be a service fit for small forces and limited views; and the whole thing then often sinks into a kind of sham fight, in order to close the campaign with honour, because as assailant it is incumbent to do something.

(d) A successful combat, encounter, or even battle, for the sake of trophies, or merely for the honour of the arms, sometimes even for the mere ambition of the commanders. That this does happen no one can doubt, unless he knows nothing at all of military history. In the campaigns of the French during the reign of Louis XIV., the most of the offensive battles were of this kind. But what is of more importance for us is to observe that these things are not without objective value, they are not the mere pastime of vanity; they have a very distinct influence on peace, and therefore lead as it were direct to the object. The military fame, the moral superiority of the army and of the general, are things, the influence of which, although unseen, never ceases to bear upon the whole action in war.

The aim of such a combat of course presupposes; (*a*) that there is an adequate prospect of victory, (*B*) that there is not a very heavy stake dependent on the issue. – Such a battle fought in straitened relations, and with a limited object, must naturally not be confounded with a victory which is not turned to profitable account merely from moral weakness.

3. With the exception of the last of these objects (d) they may all be attained without a combat of importance, and generally they are so obtained by the offensive. Now, the means which the assailant has at command without resorting to a decisive battle, are derived from the interests which the defensive has to protect in his theatre of war; they consist, therefore, in threatening his lines of communications, either through objects connected with subsistence, as magazines, fertile provinces, water communications, etc., or important points (bridges, defiles, and such like,) or also by placing other corps in the occupation of strong positions situated inconveniently near to him and from which he cannot again drive us out; the seizure of important towns, fertile districts, disturbed parts of the country, which may be excited to rebellion, the threatening of weak allies, etc., etc. Should the attack effectually interrupt the communications, and in such a manner that the defender cannot re-establish them but at a great sacrifice, it compels the defender to take up another position more to the rear or to a flank to cover the objects, at the same time giving up objects of secondary importance. Thus a strip of territory is left open; a magazine or a fortress uncovered: the one exposed to be overrun, the other to be invested. Out of this, combats greater or less may arise, but in such case they are not sought for and treated as an object of the war but as a necessary evil, and can never exceed a certain degree of greatness and importance.

4. The operation of the defensive on the communications of the offensive, is a kind of reaction which in wars waged for the great solution, can only take place when the lines of operation are very long; on the other hand, this kind of reaction lies more in accordance with the nature of things in wars which are not aimed at the great solution. The enemy's lines of communication are seldom very long in such a case; but then, neither is it here so much a question of inflicting great losses of this description on the enemy, a mere impeding and cutting short his means of subsistence often produces an effect, and what the lines want in length is made up for in some degree by the length of time which can be expended in this kind of contest with the enemy: for this reason, the covering his strategic flanks becomes an important object for the assailant. If, therefore, a contest (or rivalry) of this description takes place between the assailant and defender, then the assailant must seek

to compensate by numbers for his natural disadvantages. If he retains sufficient power and resolution still to venture a decisive stroke against one of the enemy's corps, or against the enemy's main body itself, the danger which he thus holds over the head of his opponent is his best means of covering himself.

5. In conclusion, we must notice another great advantage which the assailant certainly has over the defender in wars of this kind, which is that of being better able to judge of the intentions and force of his adversary than the latter can in turn of his. It is much more difficult to discover in what degree an assailant is enterprising and bold than when the defender has something of consequence in his mind. Practically viewed, there usually lies already in the choice of the defensive form of war a sort of guarantee that nothing positive is intended; besides this, the preparations for a great reaction differ much more from the ordinary preparations for defence than the preparations for a great attack differ from those directed against minor objects. Finally, the defender is obliged to take his measures soonest of the two, which gives the assailant the advantage of playing the last hand.

CHAPTER SEVENTEEN
Attack of Fortresses

THE ATTACK of fortresses cannot of course come before us here in its aspect as a branch of the science of fortification or military works; we have only to consider the subject, first, in its relation to the strategic object with which it is connected; secondly, as regards the choice among several fortresses; and thirdly, as regards the manner in which a siege should be covered.

That the loss of a fortress weakens the defence, especially in case it forms an essential part of that defence; that many conveniences accrue to the assailant by gaining possession of one, inasmuch as he can use it for magazines and depôts, and by means of it can cover districts of country cantonments, etc.; that if his offensive at last should have to be changed into the defensive, it forms the very best support for that defensive – all these relations which fortresses bear to theatres of war, in the course of a war, make themselves sufficiently evident by what has been said about fortresses in the book on the Defence, the reflection from which throws all the light required on these relations with the attack.

In relation to the taking of strong places, there is also a great difference between campaigns which tend to a great decision and others. In the first, a conquest of this description is always to be regarded as an evil which is unavoidable. As long as there is yet a decision to be made, we undertake no sieges but such as are positively unavoidable. When the decision has been already given – the crisis, the utmost tension of forces, some time passed – and when, therefore, a state of rest has commenced, then the capture of strong places serves as a consolidation of the conquests made, and then they can generally be carried out, if not without effort and expenditure of force, at least without danger. In the crisis itself the siege of a fortress heightens the intensity of the crisis to the prejudice of the offensive; it is evident that nothing so much weakens the force of the offensive, and therefore there is nothing so certain to rob it of its preponderance for a season. But there are cases in which the capture of this or that fortress is quite unavoidable, if the offensive is to be continued, and in such case a siege is to be considered as an intensified progress of the attack; the crisis will be so much greater the less there has been decided previously. All that remains now for consideration on this subject belongs to the book on the plan of the war.

In campaigns with a limited object, a fortress is generally not the means but the end itself; it is regarded as a small independent conquest, and as such has the following advantages over every other: –

1. That a fortress is a small, distinctly-defined conquest, which does not require a further expenditure of force, and therefore gives no cause to fear a reaction.

2. That in negotiating for peace, its value as an equivalent may be turned to account.

3. That a siege is a real progress of the attack, or at least seems so, without constantly diminishing the force like every other advance of the offensive.

4. That the siege is an enterprise without a catastrophe.

The result of these things is that the capture of one or more of the enemy's strong places, is very frequently the object of those strategic attacks which cannot aim at any higher object.

The grounds which decide the choice of the fortress which should be attacked, in case that may be doubtful, generally are –

(*a*) That it is one which can be easily kept, therefore stands high in value as an equivalent in case of negotiations for peace.

(*b*) That the means of taking it are at hand. Small means are only sufficient to take small places; but it is better to take a small one than to fail before a large one.

(*c*) Its strength in engineering respects, which obviously is not always in proportion to its importance in other respects. Nothing is more absurd than to waste forces before a very strong place of little importance, if a place of less strength may be made the object of attack.

(*d*) The strength of the armament and of the garrison as well. If a fortress is weakly armed and insufficiently garrisoned, its capture must naturally be easier; but here we must observe that the strength of the garrison and armament, are to be reckoned amongst those things which make up the total *importance* of the place, because garrison and armaments are directly parts of the enemy's military strength, which cannot be said in the same measure of works of fortification. The conquest of a fortress with a strong garrison can, therefore, much more readily repay the sacrifice it costs than one with very strong works.

(*e*) The facility of moving the siege train. Most sieges fail for want of means, and the means are generally wanting from the difficulty attending their transport. Eugene's siege of Landreci, 1712, and Frederick the Great's siege of Olmutz, 1758, are very remarkable instances in point.

(*f*) Lastly, there remains the facility of covering the siege as a point now to be considered.

There are two essentially different ways by which a siege may be covered: by entrenching the besieging force, that is, by a line of circumvallation, and by what is called lines of observation. The first of these methods has gone quite out of fashion, although evidently one important point speaks in its favour, namely, that by this method the force of the assailant does not suffer by division exactly that weakening which is so generally found a great disadvantage at sieges. But we grant there is still a weakening in another way, to a very considerable degree, because –

1. The position round the fortress, as a rule, is of too great extent for the strength of the army.

2. The garrison, the strength of which, added to that of the relieving army, would only make up the force originally opposed to us, *under these circumstances* is to be looked upon as an enemy's corps in the middle of our camp, which, protected by its walls, is *invulnerable*, or at least not to be overpowered, by which its power is immensely increased.

3. The defence of a line of circumvallation admits of nothing but the most absolute defensive, because the circular order, facing outwards, is the weakest and most disadvantageous of all possible orders of battle, and is particularly unfavourable to any advantageous counter-attacks. There is no alternative, in fact, but to defend ourselves to the last extremity within the entrenchments. That these circumstances may cause a greater diminution of the army than one-third which, perhaps, would be occasioned by forming an army of observation, is easy to conceive. If, added to that, we now think of the general preference which has existed since the time of Frederick the Great for the offensive, as it is called, (but which, in reality, is not always so) for movements and manœuvres, and the aversion to entrenchments, we shall not wonder at lines of circumvallation having gone quite out of fashion. But this weakening of the tactical resistance is by no means its only disadvantage; and we have only reckoned up the prejudices which

forced themselves into the judgment on the lines of circumvallation next in order after that disadvantage, because they are nearly akin to each other. A line of circumvallation only in reality covers that portion of the theatre of war which it actually encloses; all the rest is more or less given up to the enemy if special detachments are not made use of to cover it, in which way the very partition of force which it was intended to obviate takes place. Thus the besieging army will be always in anxiety and embarrassment on account of the convoys which it requires, and the covering the same by lines of circumvallation, is not to be thought of if the army and the siege supplies required are considerable, and the enemy is in the field in strong force, unless under such conditions as are found in the Netherlands, where there is a whole system of fortresses lying close to each other, and intermediate lines connecting them, which cover the rest of the theatre of war, and considerably shorten the lines by which transport can be affected. In the time of Louis the Fourteenth the conception of a theatre of war had not yet bound itself up with the position of an army. In the Thirty Years' War particularly, the armies moved here and there sporadically before this or that fortress, in the neighbourhood of which there was no enemy's corps at all, and besieged it as long as the siege equipment they had brought with them lasted, and until an enemy's army approached to relieve the place. Then lines of circumvallation had their foundation in the nature of circumstances.

In future it is not likely they will be often used again, unless where the enemy in the field is very weak, or the conception of the theatre of war vanishes before that of the siege. Then it will be natural to keep all the forces united in the siege, as a siege by that means unquestionably gains in energy in a high degree.

The lines of circumvallation in the reign of Louis XIV., at Cambray and Valenciennes, were of little use, as the former were stormed by Turenne, opposed to Condé, the latter by Condé opposed to Turenne; but we must not overlook the endless number of other cases in which they were respected, even when there existed in the place the most urgent need for relief; and when the commander on the defensive side was a man of great enterprise, as in 1708, when Villars did not venture to attack the allies in their lines at Lille. Frederick the Great at Olmutz, 1758, and at Dresden, 1760, although he had no regular lines of circumvallation, had a system which in all essentials was identical; he used the same army to carry on the siege, and also as a covering army. The distance of the Austrian army induced him to adopt this plan at Olmutz, but the loss of his convoy at Domstadtel made him repent it; at

Dresden in 1760 the motives which led him to this mode of proceeding, were his contempt for the German States' imperial army, and his desire to take Dresden as soon as possible.

Lastly, it is a disadvantage in lines of circumvallation, that in case of a reverse it is more difficult to save the siege train. If a defeat is sustained at a distance of one or more days' march from the place besieged, the siege may be raised before the enemy can arrive, and the heavy trains may, in the mean time, gain also a day's march.

In taking up a position for an army of observation, an important question to be considered is the distance at which it should be placed from the besieged place. This question will, in most cases, be decided by the nature of the country, or by the position of other armies or corps with which the besiegers have to remain in communication. In other respects, it is easy to see that, with a greater distance, the siege is better covered, but that by a smaller distance, not exceeding a few miles, the two armies are better able to afford each other mutual support.

CHAPTER EIGHTEEN

Attack of Convoys

THE ATTACK and defence of a convoy form a subject of tactics: we should, therefore, have nothing to say upon the subject here if it was not necessary, first, to demonstrate generally, to a certain extent, the possibility of the thing, which can only be done from strategic motives and relations. We should have had to speak of it in this respect before when treating of the defence, had it not been that the little which can be said about it can easily be framed to suit for both attack and defence, while at the same time the first plays the higher part in connection with it.

A moderate convoy of three or four hundred wagons, let the load be what it may, takes up half a mile, a large convoy is several miles in length. Now, how is it possible to expect that the few troops usually allotted to a convoy will suffice for its defence? If to this difficulty we add the unwieldy nature of this mass, which can only advance at the slowest pace, and which, besides, is always liable to be thrown into disorder, and lastly, that every part of a convoy must be equally protected, because the moment that one part is attacked by the enemy, the whole is brought to a stop, and thrown into a state of confusion, we may well ask, – how can the covering and defence of such a train be possible at all? Or, in other words, why are not all convoys taken when they are attacked, and why are not all attacked which require an escort, or, which is the same thing, all that come within reach of the enemy? It is plain that all tactical expedients, such as Templehof's most impracticable scheme of constantly halting and assembling the convoy at short distances, and then moving off afresh: and the much better plan of Scharnhorst, of breaking up the convoy into several columns, are only slight correctives of a radical evil.

The explanation consists in this, that by far the greater number of convoys derive more security from the strategic situation in general, than any other parts exposed to the attacks of the enemy, which bestows on their limited means of defence a very much increased efficacy. Convoys generally move more or less in rear of their own army, or, at least, at a great distance from that of the enemy. The consequence is, that only weak detachments can be sent to attack them, and these are obliged to cover themselves by strong reserves. Added to this the unwieldiness itself of the carriages used, makes it very difficult to carry them off; the assailant must therefore, in general, content himself with cutting the traces, taking away the horses, and blowing up powder-wagons, by which the whole is certainly detained and thrown into disorder, but not completely lost; by all this we may perceive, that the security of such trains lies more in these general relations than in the defensive power of its escort. If now to all this we add the defence of the escort, which, although it cannot by marching resolutely against the enemy directly cover the convoy, is still able to derange the plan of the enemy's attack; then, at last, the attack of a convoy, instead of appearing easy and sure of success, will appear rather difficult, and very uncertain in its result.

But there remains still a chief point, which is the danger of the enemy's army, or one of its corps, retaliating on the assailants of its convoy, and punishing it ultimately for the undertaking by defeating it. The apprehension of this, puts a stop to many undertakings, without the real cause ever appearing; so that the safety of the convoy is attributed to the escort, and people wonder how a miserable arrangement, such as an escort, should meet with such respect. In order to feel the truth of this observation, we have only to think of the famous retreat which Frederick the Great made through Bohemia after the siege of Olmutz, 1758, when the half of his army was broken into a column of companies to cover a convoy of 4,000 carriages. What prevented Daun from falling on this monstrosity? The fear that Frederick would throw himself upon him with the other half of his army, and entangle him in a battle which Daun did not desire; what prevented Laudon, who was constantly at the side of that convoy, from falling upon it at Zischbowitz sooner and more boldly than he did? The fear that he would get a rap over the knuckles. Ten miles from his main army, and completely separated from it by the Prussian army, he thought himself in danger of a serious defeat if the king, who had no reason at that time to be concerned about Daun, should fall upon him with the bulk of his forces.

It is only if the strategic situation of an army involves it in the unnatural necessity of connecting itself with its convoys by the flank or by its front that then these convoys are really in great danger, and become an advantageous object of attack for the enemy, if his position allows him to detach troops for that purpose. The same campaign of 1758 affords an instance of the most complete success of an undertaking of this description, in the capture of the convoy at Domstadtel. The road to Neiss lay on the left flank of the Prussian position, and the king's forces were so neutralised by the siege and by the corps watching Daun, that the partizans had no reason to be uneasy about themselves, and were able to make their attack completely at their ease.

When Eugene besieged Landrecy in 1712, he drew his supplies for the siege from Bouchain by Denain; therefore, in reality, from the front of the strategic position. It is well known what means he was obliged to use to overcome the difficulty of protecting his convoys on that occasion, and in what embarrassments he involved himself, ending in a complete change of circumstances.

The conclusion we draw, therefore, is that however easy an attack on a convoy may appear in its tactical aspect, still it has not much in its favour on strategic grounds, and only promises important results in the exceptional instances of lines of communication very much exposed.

CHAPTER NINETEEN
Attack on the Enemy's Army in its Cantonments

WE HAVE NOT treated of this subject in the defence, because a line of cantonments is not to be regarded as a defensive means, but as a mere existence of the army in a state which implies little readiness for battle. In respect to this readiness for battle, we therefore did not go beyond what we required to say in connection with this condition of an army in the 13th chapter of the 5th book.

But here, in considering the attack, we have to think of an enemy's army in cantonments in all respects as a special object; for, in the first place, such an attack is of a very peculiar kind in itself; and, in the next place, it may be considered as a strategic means of particular efficacy. Here we have before us, therefore, not the question of an onslaught on a single cantonment or a small corps dispersed amongst a few villages, as the arrangements for that are entirely of a tactical nature, but of the attack of a large army, distributed in cantonments more or less extensive; an attack in which the object is not the mere surprise of a single cantonment, but to prevent the assembly of the army.

The attack on an enemy's army in cantonments is therefore the surprise of an army not assembled. If this surprise succeeds fully, then the enemy's army is prevented from reaching its appointed place of assembly, and, therefore, compelled to choose another more to the rear; as this change of the point of assembly to the rear in a state of such emergency can seldom be effected in less than a day's march, but generally will require several days, the loss of ground which this occasions is by no means an insignificant loss; and this is the first advantage gained by the assailant.

But now, this surprise which is in connection with the general relations, may certainly at the same time, in its commencement, be an onslaught on some of the enemy's single cantonments, not certainly upon all, or upon a great many, because that would suppose a scattering of the attacking army to an extent which could never be advisable. Therefore, only the most advanced quarters, only those which lie in the direction of the attacking columns, can be surprised, and even this will seldom happen to many of them, as large forces cannot easily approach unobserved. However, this element of the attack is by no means to be disregarded; and we reckon the advantages which may be thus obtained, as the second advantage of the surprise.

A third advantage consists in the minor combats forced upon the enemy in which his losses will be considerable. A great body of troops does not assemble itself at once by single battalions at the spot appointed for the general concentration of the army, but usually forms itself by brigades, divisions, or corps, in the first place, and these masses cannot then hasten at full speed to the rendezvous; in case of meeting with an enemy's column in their course, they are obliged to engage in a combat; now, they may certainly come off victorious in the same, particularly if the enemy's attacking column is not of sufficient strength, but in conquering, they lose time, and, in most cases, as may be easily conceived, a corps, under such circumstances, and in the general tendency to gain a point which lies to the rear, will not make any beneficial use of its victory. On the other hand, they may be beaten, and that is the most probable issue in itself, because they have not time to organise a good resistance. We may, therefore, very well suppose that in an attack well planned and executed, the assailant through these partial combats will gather up a considerable number of trophies, which become a principal point in the general result.

Lastly, the fourth advantage, and the keystone of the whole, is a certain momentary disorganisation and discouragement on the side of the enemy, which, when the force is at last assembled, seldom allows of its being immediately brought into action, and generally obliges the party attacked to abandon still more ground to his assailant, and to make a change generally in his plan of operations.

Such are the proper results of a successful surprise of the enemy in cantonments, that is, of one in which the enemy is prevented from assembling his army without loss at the point fixed in his plan. But by the nature of the case, success has many degrees; and, therefore, the results may be very great in one case, and hardly worth mentioning in another. But even when, through the complete success of the enterprise, these results are considerable, they will seldom bear comparison with the gain of a great battle, partly because, in the first place, the trophies are seldom as great, and in the next, the moral impression never strikes so deep.

This general result must always be kept in view, that we may not promise ourselves more from an enterprise of this kind than it can give. Many hold it to be the *non plus ultra* of offensive activity; but it is not so by any means, as we may see from this analysis, as well as from military history.

One of the most brilliant surprises in history, is that made by the Duke of Lorraine in 1643, on the cantonments of the French, under General Ranzan, at Duttlingen. The corps was 16,000 men, and they lost the General commanding, and 7,000 men; it was a complete defeat. The want of outposts was the cause of the disaster.

The surprise of Turenne at Mergentheim (Mariendal, as the French call it,) in 1644, is in like manner to be regarded as equal to a defeat in its effects, for he lost 3,000 men out of 8,000, which was principally owing to his having been led into making an untimely stand after he got his men assembled. Such results we cannot, therefore, often reckon upon; it was rather the result of an ill-judged action than of the surprise, properly speaking, for Turenne might easily have avoided the action, and have rallied his troops upon those in more distant quarters.

A third noted surprise is that which Turenne made on the Allies under the great Elector, the Imperial General Bournonville and the Duke of Lorraine, in Alsace, in the year 1674. The trophies were very small, the loss of the Allies did not exceed 2,000 or 3,000 men, which could not decide the fate of a force of 50,000; but the Allies considered that they could not venture to make any further resistance in Alsace, and retired across the Rhine again. This strategic result was all that Turenne wanted, but we must not look for the causes of it entirely in the surprise. Turenne surprised the plans of his opponents more than the troops themselves; the want of unanimity amongst the allied generals and the proximity of the Rhine did the rest. This event altogether deserves a closer examination, as it is generally viewed in a wrong light.

In 1741, Neipperg surprised Frederick the Great in his quarters; the whole of the result was that the king was obliged to fight the battle of Mollwitz before he had collected all his forces, and with a change of front.

In 1745, Frederick the Great surprised the Duke of Lorraine in his cantonments in Lusatia; the chief success was through the real surprise of one of the most important quarters, that of Hennersdorf, by which the Austrians suffered a loss of 2,000 men; the general result was that the Duke of Lorraine retreated to Bohemia by Upper Lusatia, but that did not at all prevent his returning into Saxony by the left bank of the Elbe, so that without the battle of Kesselsdorf, there would have been no important result.

1758. The Duke Ferdinand surprised the French quarters; the immediate result was that the French lost some thousands of men, and were obliged to take up a position behind the Aller. The moral effect may have been of more importance, and may have had some influence on the subsequent evacuation of Westphalia.

If from these different examples we seek for a conclusion as to the efficacy of this kind of attack, then only the two first can be put in comparison with a battle gained. But the corps were only small, and the want of outposts in the system of war in those days was a circumstance greatly in favour of these enterprises. Although the four other cases must be reckoned completely successful enterprises, it is plain that not one of them is to be compared with a battle gained as respects its result. The general result could not have taken place in any of them except with an adversary weak in will and character, and therefore it did not take place at all in the case of 1741.

In 1806 the Prussian army contemplated surprising the French in this manner in Franconia. The case promised well for a satisfactory result. Buonaparte was not present, the French corps were in widely extended cantonments; under these circumstances, the Prussian army, acting with great resolution and activity, might very well reckon on driving the French back across the Rhine, with more or less loss. But this was also all; if they reckoned upon more, for instance, on following up their advantages beyond the Rhine, or on gaining such a moral ascendancy, that the French would not again venture to appear on the right bank of the river in the same campaign, such an expectation had no sufficient grounds whatever.

In the beginning of August, 1812, the Russians from Smolensk meditated falling upon the cantonments of the French when Napoleon halted his army in the neighbourhood of Witepsk. But they wanted courage to carry out the enterprise; and it was fortunate for them they did; for as the French commander with his centre was not only more than twice the strength of their centre, but also in himself the most resolute commander that ever lived, as further, the loss of a few miles of ground would have decided nothing, and there was no natural obstacle in any feature of the country near enough up to which they might pursue their success, and by that means, in some measure make it certain, and lastly, as the war of the year 1812 was not in any way a campaign of that kind, which draws itself in a languid way to a conclusion, but the serious plan of an assailant who had made up his mind to conquer his opponent completely, – therefore the trifling results to be expected from a surprise of the enemy in his quarters, appear nothing else than utterly disproportionate to the solution of the problem, they could not justify a hope of making good by their means the great inequality of forces and other relations. But this scheme serves to show how a confused idea of the effect of this means may lead to an entirely false application of the same.

What has been hitherto said, places the subject in the light of *a strategic means*. But it lies in its nature that its execution also is not purely tactical, but in part belongs again to strategy so far, particularly that such an attack is generally made on a front of considerable width, and the army which carries it out can, and generally will, come to blows before it is concentrated, so that the whole is an agglomeration of partial combats. We must now add a few words on the most natural organisation of such an attack.

The first condition is: –

(1.) To attack the front of the enemy's quarters in a certain width of front, for that is the only means by which we can really surprise several cantonments, cut off others, and create generally that disorganisation in the enemy's army which is intended. – The number of, and the intervals between, the columns must depend on circumstances.

(2.) The direction of the different columns must converge upon a point where it is intended they should unite; for the enemy ends more or less with a concentration of his force, and therefore we must do the same. This point of concentration should, if possible, be the enemy's point of assembly, or lie on his line of retreat, it will naturally be best where that line crosses an important obstacle in the country.

(3.) The separate columns when they come in contact with the enemy's forces must attack them with great determination, with dash and boldness, as they have general relations in their favour, and daring is always there in its right place. From this it follows that the commanders of the separate columns must be allowed freedom of action and full power in this respect.

(4.) The tactical plan of attack against those of the enemy's corps that are the first to place themselves in position, must always be directed to turn a flank, for the greatest result is always to be expected by separating the corps, and cutting them off.

(5.) Each of the columns must be composed of portions of the three arms, and must not be stinted in cavalry, it may even sometimes be well to divide amongst them the whole of the reserve cavalry; for it would be a great mistake to suppose that this body of cavalry could play any great part in a mass in an enterprise of this sort. The first village, the smallest bridge, the most insignificant thicket would bring it to a halt.

(6.) Although it lies in the nature of a surprise that the assailant should not send his advanced guard very far in front, that principle only applies to the first approach to the enemy's quarters. When the fight has commenced in the enemy's quarters, and therefore all that was to be expected from actual surprise has been gained, then the columns of the advanced guard of all arms should push on as far as possible, for they may greatly increase the confusion on the side of the enemy by more rapid movement. It is only by this means that it becomes possible to carry off here and there the mass of baggage, artillery, non-effectives, and camp-followers, which have to be dragged after a cantonment suddenly broken up, and these advanced guards must also be the chief instruments in turning and cutting off the enemy.

(7.) Finally, the retreat in case of ill-success must be thought of, and a rallying point be fixed upon beforehand.

CHAPTER TWENTY

Diversion

ACCORDING to the ordinary use of language, under the term diversion is understood such an incursion into the enemy's country as draws off a portion of his force from the principal point. It is only when this is the chief end in view, and not the gain of the object which is selected as the point of attack, that it is an enterprise of a special character, otherwise it is only an ordinary attack.

Naturally the diversion must at the same time always have an object of attack, for it is only the value of this object that will induce the enemy to send troops for its protection; besides, in case the undertaking does not succeed as a diversion, this object is a compensation for the forces expended in the attempt.

These objects of attack may be fortresses, or important magazines, or rich and large towns, especially capital cities, contributions of all kinds; lastly, assistance may be afforded in this way to discontented subjects of the enemy.

It is easy to conceive that diversions may be useful, but they certainly are not so always; on the contrary, they are just as often injurious. The chief condition is that they should withdraw from the principal theatre of the war more of the enemy's troops than we employ on the diversion; for if they only succeed in drawing off just the same number, then their efficacy as diversions, properly called, ceases, and the undertaking becomes a mere subordinate attack. Even where, on account of circumstances, we have in view to attain a very great end with a very small force, as, for instance, to make an easy capture of an important fortress, and another attack is made adjoining to the principal attack, to assist the latter, that is no longer a diversion. When two states are at war, and a third falls upon one of them, such an event is very commonly called a diversion – but such an attack differs in nothing from an ordinary attack except in its direction; there is, therefore, no occasion to give it a particular name, for in theory it should be a rule only to denote by particular names such things as are in their nature distinct.

But if small forces are to attract large ones, there must obviously be some special cause, and, therefore, for the object of a diversion it is not sufficient merely to detach some troops to a point not hitherto occupied.

If the assailant with a small corps of 1000 men overruns one of his enemy's provinces, not belonging to the theatre of war, and levies contribution, etc., it is easy to see beforehand that the enemy cannot put a stop to this by detaching 1000 men, but that if he means to protect the province from invaders, he must at all events send a considerably larger force. But it may be asked cannot a defender, instead of protecting his own province, restore the balance by sending a similar detachment to plunder a province in our country? Therefore, if an advantage is to be obtained by an aggressor in this way, it must first be ascertained that there is more to be got or to be threatened in the defender's provinces than in his own. If this is the case, then no doubt a weak diversion will occupy a force on the enemy's side greater than that composing the enterprise. On the other hand, this advantage naturally diminishes as the masses increase, for 50,000 men can defend a province of moderate extent not only against equal but even against somewhat superior numbers. The advantage of large diversions is, therefore, very doubtful, and the greater they become the more decisive must be the other circumstances which favour a diversion if any good is to come out of such an enterprise upon the whole.

Now these favourable circumstances may be: –

a. Forces which the assailant holds available for a diversion without weakening the great mass of his force.

b. Points belonging to the defender which are of vital importance to him and can be threatened by a diversion.

c. Discontented subjects of the same.

d. A rich province which can supply a considerable quantity of munitions of war.

If only these diversions are undertaken, which, when tested by these different considerations, promise results, it will be found that an opportunity of making a diversion does not offer frequently.

But now comes another important point. Every diversion brings war into a district into which the war would not otherwise have penetrated: for that reason it will always be the means, more or less, of calling forth military forces which would otherwise have continued in abeyance, this will be done in a way which will be very sensibly felt if the enemy has any organised militia, and means of arming the nation at large. It is quite in the natural order of things, and amply shown by experience, that if a district is suddenly threatened by an enemy's force, and nothing has been prepared beforehand for its defence, all the most efficient official functionaries immediately lay hold of and set in motion every extraordinary means that can be imagined, in order to ward off the impending danger. Thus, new powers of resistance spring up, such as are next to a people's war, and may easily excite one.

This is a point which should be kept well in view in every diversion, in order that we may not dig our own graves.

The expeditions to North Holland in 1799, and to Walcheren in 1809, regarded as diversions, are only to be justified in so far that there was no other way of employing the English troops; but there is no doubt that the sum total of the means of resistance of the French was thereby increased, and every landing in France, would have just the same effect. To threaten the French coast certainly offers great advantages, because by that means an important body of troops becomes neutralised in watching the coast, but a landing with a large force can never be justifiable unless we can count on the assistance of a province in opposition to the Government.

The less a great decision is looked forward to in war the more will diversions be allowable, but so much the smaller will also certainly be the gain to be derived from them. They are only a means of bringing the stagnant masses into motion.

Execution.

1. A diversion may include in itself a real attack, then the execution has no special character in itself except boldness and expedition.

2. It may also have as an object to appear more than it really is, being, in fact, a demonstration as well. The special means to be employed in such a case can only suggest themselves to a subtil mind well versed in men and in the existing state of circumstances. It follows from the nature of the thing that there must be a great fractioning of forces on such occasions.

3. If the forces employed are not quite inconsiderable, and the retreat is restricted to certain points, then a reserve on which the whole may rally is an essential condition.

CHAPTER TWENTY ONE

Invasion

ALMOST ALL THAT we have to say on this subject consists in an explanation of the term. We find the expression very frequently used by modern authors and also that they pretend to denote by it something particular. *Guerre d'invasion* occurs perpetually in French authors. They use it as a term for every attack which enters deep into the enemy's country, and perhaps sometimes mean to apply it as the antithesis to methodical attack, that is, one which only nibbles at the frontier. But this is a very unphilosophical confusion of language. Whether an attack is to be confined to the frontier or to be carried into the heart of the country, whether it shall make the seizure of the enemy's strong places the chief object, or seek out the core of the enemy's power, and pursue it unremittingly, is the result of circumstances, and not dependent on a system. In some cases, to push forward may be more methodical, and at the same time more prudent than to tarry on the frontier, but in most cases it is nothing else than just the fortunate result of a vigorous *attack*, and consequently does not differ from it in any respect.

CHAPTER TWENTY TWO

On the Culminating Point of Victory.[60]

THE CONQUEROR in a war is not always in a condition to subdue his adversary completely. Often, in fact, almost universally, there is a culminating point of victory. Experience shows this sufficiently; but as the subject is one especially important for the theory of war, and the pivot of almost all plans of campaigns, while, at the same time, on its surface some apparent contradictions glitter, as in ever-changing colours, we therefore wish to examine it more closely, and look for its essential causes.

Victory, as a rule, springs from a preponderance of the sum of all the physical and moral powers combined; undoubtedly it increases this preponderance, or it would not be sought for and purchased at a great sacrifice. Victory *itself* does this unquestionably; also its consequences have the same effect, but not to the utmost point generally only up to a certain point. This point may be very near at hand, and is sometimes so near that the whole of the results of a victorious battle are confined to an increase of the moral superiority. How this comes about we have now to examine.

In the progress of action in war, the combatant force is incessantly meeting with elements which strengthen it, and others which weaken it. Hence it is a question of superiority on one side or the other. As every diminution of power on one side is to be regarded as an increase on the opposite, it follows, of course, that this double current, this ebb and flow, takes place whether troops are advancing or retiring.

It is therefore necessary to find out the principal cause of this alteration in the one case to determine the other along with it.

60   See Chapters IV. and V.

In advancing, the most important causes of the *increase of strength* which the assailant gains, are:

1. The loss which the enemy's army suffers, because it is usually greater than that of the assailant.

2. The loss which the enemy suffers in inert military means, such as magazines, depôts, bridges, etc., and which the assailant does not share with him.

3. That from the moment the assailant enters the enemy's territory, there is a loss of provinces to the defence, consequently of the sources of new military forces.

4. That the advancing army gains a portion of those resources, in other words, gains the advantage of living at the expense of the enemy.

5. The loss of internal organisation and of the regular action of everything on the side of the enemy.

6. That the allies of the enemy secede from him, and others join the conqueror.

7. Lastly, the discouragement of the enemy who lets the arms, in some measure, drop out of his hands.

The causes of *decrease of strength* in an army advancing, are:

1. That it is compelled to lay siege to the enemy's fortresses, to blockade them or observe them; or that the enemy, who did the same before the victory, in his retreat draws in these corps on his main body.

2. That from the moment the assailant enters the enemy's territory, the nature of the theatre of war is changed; it becomes hostile; we must occupy it, for we cannot call any portion our own beyond what is in actual occupation, and yet it everywhere presents difficulties to the whole machine, which must necessarily tend to weaken its effects.

3. That we are removing further away from our resources, whilst the enemy is drawing nearer to his; this causes a delay in the replacement of expended power.

4. That the danger which threatens the state, rouses other powers to its protection.

5. Lastly, the greater efforts of the adversary, in consequence of the increased danger, on the other hand, a relaxation of effort on the side of the victorious state.

All these advantages and disadvantages can exist together, meet each other in a certain measure, and pursue their way in opposite directions, except that the last meet as real opposites, cannot pass, therefore mutually exclude each other. This alone shows how infinitely different may be the effect of a victory according as it stuns the vanquished or stimulates him to greater exertions.

We shall now try to characterise, in a few words, each of these points singly.

1. The loss of the enemy when defeated, may be at the greatest in the first moment of defeat, and then daily diminish in amount until it arrives at a point where the balance is restored as regards our force; but it may go on increasing every day in an ascending ratio. The difference of situation and relations determines this. We can only say that, in general, with a good army the first will be the case, with an indifferent army the second; next to the spirit of the army, the spirit of the Government is here the most important thing. It is of great consequence in war to distinguish between the two cases in practice, in order not to stop just at the point where we ought to begin in good earnest, and *vice versâ*.

2. The loss which the enemy sustains in that part of the apparatus of war which is inert, may ebb and flow just in the same manner, and this will depend on the accidental position and nature of the depôts from which supplies are drawn. This subject, however, in the present day, cannot be compared with the others in point of importance.

3. The third advantage must necessarily increase as the army advances; indeed, it may be said that it does not come into consideration until an army has penetrated far into the enemy's country; that is to say, until a third or a fourth of the country has been left in rear. In addition, the intrinsic value which a province has in connection with the war comes also into consideration.

In the same way the fourth advantage should increase with the advance.

But with respect to these two last, it is also to be observed that their influence on the combatant powers actually engaged in the struggle, is seldom felt so immediately; they only work slowly and by a circuitous course; therefore we should not bend the bow too much on their account, that is to say, not place ourselves in any dangerous position.

The fifth advantage, again, only comes into consideration if we have made a considerable advance, and if by the form of the enemy's country some provinces can be detached from the principal mass, as these, like limbs compressed by ligatures, usually soon die off.

As to six and seven, it is at least probable that they increase with the advance; furthermore, we shall return to them hereafter. Let us now pass on to the causes of weakness.

1. The besieging, blockade, and investment of fortresses, generally increase as the army advances. This weakening influence alone acts so powerfully on the *condition of the combatant force*, that it may soon outweigh all the advantages gained. No doubt, in modern times, a system has been introduced of blockading places with a small number of

troops, or of watching them with a still smaller number; and also the enemy must keep garrisons in them. Nevertheless, they remain a great element of security. The garrisons consist very often in half of people, who have taken no part in the war previously. Before those places which are situated near the line of communication, it is necessary for the assailant to leave a force at least double the strength of the garrison; and if it is desirable to lay formal siege to, or to starve out, one single considerable place, a small army is required for the purpose.

2. The second cause, the taking up a theatre of war in the enemy's country, increases necessarily with the advance, and if it does not further weaken the condition of the combatant force at the moment, it does so at all events in the long run.

We can only regard as our theatre of war, so much of the enemy's country as we actually possess; that is to say, where we either have small corps in the field, or where we have left here and there strong garrisons in large towns, or stations along the roads, etc.; now, however small the garrisons may be which are detached, still they weaken the combatant force considerably. But this is the smallest evil.

Every army has strategic flanks, that is, the country which borders both sides of its lines of communications; the weakness of these parts is not sensibly felt as long as the enemy is similarly situated with respect to his. But that can only be the case as long as we are in our own country; as soon as we get into the enemy's country, the weakness of these parts is felt very much, because the smallest enterprise promises some result when directed against a long line only feebly, or not all, covered; and these attacks may be made from any quarter in an enemy's country.

The further we advance, the longer these flanks become, and the danger arising from them is enhanced in an increased ratio, for not only are they difficult to cover, but the spirit of enterprise is also first roused in the enemy, chiefly by long insecure lines of communication, and the consequences which their loss may entail in case of a retreat are matter of grave consideration.

All this contributes to place a fresh load on an advancing army at every step of its progress; so that if it has not commenced with a more than ordinary superiority, it will feel itself always more and more cramped in its plans, gradually weakened in its impulsive force, and at last in a state of uncertainty and anxiety as to its situation.

3. The third cause, the distance from the source from which the incessantly diminishing combatant force is to be just as incessantly filled up, increases with the advance. A conquering army is like the light of a

lamp in this respect; the more the oil which feeds it sinks in the reservoir and recedes from the focus of light, the smaller the light becomes, until at length it is quite extinguished.

The richness of the conquered provinces may certainly diminish this evil very much, but can never entirely remove it, because there are always a number of things which can only be supplied to the army from its own country, men in particular; because the subsidies furnished by the enemy's country are, in most cases, neither so promptly nor so surely forthcoming as in our own country; because the means of meeting any unexpected requirement cannot be so quickly procured; because misunderstandings and mistakes of all kinds cannot so soon be discovered and remedied.

If a prince does not lead his army in person, as became the custom in the last wars, if he is not anywhere near it, then another and very great inconvenience arises in the loss of time occasioned by communications backwards and forwards; for the fullest powers conferred on a commander of an army, are never sufficient to meet every case in the wide expanse of his activity.

4. The change in political alliances. If these changes, produced by a victory, should be such as are disadvantageous to the conqueror, they will probably be so in a direct relation to his progress, just as is the case if they are of an advantageous nature. This all depends on the existing political alliances, interests, customs, and tendencies, on princes, ministers, etc. In general, we can only say that when a great state which has smaller allies is conquered, these usually secede very soon from their alliance, so that the victor, in this respect, with every blow becomes stronger; but if the conquered state is small, protectors much sooner present themselves when his very existence is threatened, and others, who have helped to place him in his present embarrassment, will turn round to prevent his complete downfall.

5. The increased resistance on the part of the enemy which is called forth. Sometimes the enemy drops his weapon out of his hands from terror and stupefaction; sometimes an enthusiastic paroxysm seizes him, every one runs to arms, and the resistance is much stronger after the first defeat than it was before. The character of the people and of the Government, the nature of the country and its political alliances, are here the data from which the probable effect must be conjectured.

What countless differences these two last points alone make in the plans which may and should be made in war in one case and another? Whilst one, through an excess of caution, and what is called methodical proceedings, fritters away his good fortune, another, from a want of rational reflection, tumbles into destruction.

In addition, we must here call to mind the supineness, which not unfrequently comes over the victorious side, when danger is removed; whilst, on the contrary, renewed efforts are then required in order to follow up the success. If we cast a general glance over these different and antagonistic principles, the deduction, doubtless is, that the profitable use of the onward march in a war of aggression, in the generality of cases, diminishes the preponderance with which the assailant set out, or which has been gained by victory.

Here the question must naturally strike us; if this be so, what is it which impels the conqueror to follow up the career of victory to continue the offensive? And can this really be called making further use of the victory? Would it not be better to stop where as yet there is hardly any diminution of the preponderance gained?

To this we must naturally answer: the preponderance of combatant forces is only the means, not the end. The end or object is to subdue the enemy, or at least to take from him part of his territory, in order thus to put ourselves in a condition to realize the value of the advantages we have gained when we conclude a peace. Even if our aim is to conquer the enemy completely, we must be content that, perhaps, every step we advance, reduces our preponderance, but it does not necessarily follow from this that it will be *nil* before the fall of the enemy: the fall of the enemy may take place before that, and if it is to be obtained by the last minimum of preponderance, it would be an error not to expend it for that purpose.

The preponderance which we have or acquire in war is, therefore, the means, not the end, and it must be staked to gain the latter. But it is necessary to know how far it will reach, in order not to go beyond that point, and instead of fresh advantages, to reap disaster.

It is not necessary to introduce special examples from experience in order to prove that this is the way in which the strategic preponderance exhausts itself in the strategic attack; it is rather the multitude of instances which has forced us to investigate the causes of it. It is only since the appearance of Buonaparte that we have known campaigns between civilized nations, in which the preponderance has led, without interruption, to the fall of the enemy; before his time, every campaign ended with the victorious army seeking to win a point where it could simply maintain itself in a state of equilibrium. At this point, the movement of victory stopped, even if a retreat did not become necessary. Now, this culminating point of victory will also appear in the future, in all wars in which the overthrow of the enemy is not the military object of the war; and the generality of wars will still be of this kind. The natural aim of all single plans of campaigns is the point at which the offensive changes into the defensive.

But now, to overstep this point, is more than simply a *useless* expenditure of power, yielding no further result, it is a *destructive* step which causes reaction; and this re-action is, according to all general experience, productive of most disproportionate effects. This last fact is so common, and appears so natural and easy to understand that we need not enter circumstantially into the causes. Want of organisation in the conquered land, and the very opposite effect which a serious loss instead of the looked-for fresh victory makes on the feelings, are the chief causes in every case. The moral forces, courage on the one side rising often to *audacity*, and extreme depression on the other, now begin generally their active play. The losses on the retreat are increased thereby, and the hitherto successful party now generally thanks providence if he can escape with only the surrender of all his gains, without losing some of his own territory.

We must now clear up an apparent contradiction.

It may be generally supposed that as long as progress in the attack continues, there must still be a preponderance; and, that as the defensive, which will commence at the end of the victorious career, is a stronger form of war than the offensive, therefore, there is so much the less danger of becoming unexpectedly the weaker party. But yet there is, and keeping history in view, we must admit that the greatest danger of a reverse is often just at the moment when the offensive ceases and passes into the defensive. We shall try to find the cause of this.

The superiority which we have attributed to the defensive form of war consists:

1. In the use of ground.
2. In the possession of a prepared theatre of war.
3. In the support of the people.
4. In the advantage of the state of expectancy.

It must be evident that these principles cannot always be forthcoming and active in a like degree; that, consequently, one defence is not always like another; and therefore, also, that the defence will not always have this same superiority over the offensive. This must be particularly the case in a defensive, which commences after the exhaustion of an offensive, and has its theatre of war usually situated at the apex of an offensive triangle thrust far forward into the country. Of the four principles above named, this defensive only enjoys the first the use of the ground undiminished, the second generally vanishes altogether, the third becomes negative, and the fourth is very much reduced. A few more words, only by way of explanation, respecting the last.

If the imagined equilibrium, under the influence of which whole campaigns have often passed without any results, because the side which should assume the initiative is wanting in the necessary resolution, and just therein lies, as we conceive, the advantage of the state of expectancy if this equilibrium is disturbed by an offensive act, the enemy's interests damaged, and his will stirred up to action, then the probability of his remaining in a state of indolent irresolution is much diminished. A defence, which is organised on conquered territory, has a much more irritating character than one upon our own soil; the offensive principle is engrafted on it in a certain measure, and its nature is thereby weakened. The quiet which Daun allowed Frederick II. in Silesia and Saxony, he would never have granted him in Bohemia.

Thus it is clear that the defensive, which is interwoven or mixed up with an offensive undertaking, is weakened in all its chief principles; and, therefore, will no longer have the preponderance which belongs to it originally.

As no defensive campaign is composed of purely defensive elements, so likewise no offensive campaign is made up entirely of offensive elements; because, besides the short intervals in every campaign, in which both armies are on the defensive, every attack which does not lead to a peace, must necessarily end in a defensive.

In this manner it is the defensive itself which contributes to the weakening of the offensive. This is so far from being an idle subtlety, that on the contrary, we consider it a chief disadvantage of the attack that we are afterwards reduced through it to a very disadvantageous defensive.

And this explains how the difference which originally exists between the strength of the offensive and defensive forms in war is gradually reduced. We shall now show how it may completely disappear, and the advantage for a short time may change into the reverse.

If we may be allowed to make use of an idea from nature, we shall be able sooner to explain ourselves. It is the time which every force in the material world requires to show its effect. A power, which if applied slowly by degrees, would be sufficient to check a body in motion, will be overcome by it if time fails. This law of the material world is a striking illustration of many of the phenomena in our inner life. If we are once roused to a certain train of thought, it is not every motive sufficient in itself which can change or stop that current of thought. Time, tranquillity and durable impressions on our senses are required. So it is also in war. When once the mind has taken a decided direction towards an object, or turned back towards a harbour of refuge, it may easily happen that the motives which in the one base naturally serve to restrain, and those which in the other as naturally excite to enterprise, are not felt at once in their full force; and as the progress of action in the mean time continues, one is carried along by the stream of movement beyond the line of equilibrium, beyond the culminating point, without being aware of it. Indeed, it may even happen that, in spite of the exhaustion of force, the assailant, supported by the moral forces which specially lie in the offensive, like a horse drawing a load uphill, finds it less difficult to advance than to stop. By this, we believe, we have now shown, without contradiction in itself, how the assailant may pass that point, where, if he had stopped at the right moment, he might still, through the defensive, have had a result, that is equilibrium. Rightly to determine this point is, therefore, important in framing a plan of a campaign, as well for the offensive, that he may not undertake what is beyond his powers (to a certain extent contract debts), as for the defensive, that he may perceive and profit by this error if committed by the assailant.

If now we look back at all the points which the commander should bear in mind in making his determination, and remember that he can only estimate the tendency and value of the most important of them through the consideration of many other near and distant relations, that he must to a certain extent *guess* at them guess whether the enemy's army, after the first blow, will show a stronger core and increasing solidity, or like a Bologna phial, will turn into dust as soon as the surface is injured; guess the extent of weakness and prostration which the drying up of certain sources, the interruption of certain communications will produce on the military state of the enemy; guess whether the enemy, from the burning pain of the blow which has been dealt him, will collapse powerless, or whether, like a wounded bull, he will rise to a state of fury; lastly, guess whether other powers will be dismayed or roused, what political alliances are likely to be dissolved, and what are likely to be formed. When we say that he must hit all this, and much more, with the tact of his judgment, as the rifleman hits a mark, it must be admitted that such an act of the human mind is no trifle. A thousand wrong roads running here and there, present themselves to the judgment; and whatever the number, the confusion and complexity of objects leaves undone, is completed by the sense of danger and responsibility.

Thus it happens that the majority of generals prefer to fall short of the mark rather than to approach too close; and thus it happens that a fine courage and great spirit of enterprise often go beyond the point, and therefore also fail to hit the mark. Only he that does great things with small means has made a successful hit.

BOOK EIGHT

Plan of War

CHAPTER ONE

Introduction

IN THE CHAPTER on the essence and object of war, we sketched, in a certain measure, its general conception, and pointed out its relations to surrounding circumstances, in order to commence with a sound fundamental idea. We there cast a glance at the manifold difficulties which the mind encounters in the consideration of this subject, whilst we postponed the closer examination of them, and stopped at the conclusion, that the overthrow of the enemy, consequently the destruction of his combatant force, is the chief object of the whole of the action of war. This put us in a position to show in the following chapter, that the means which the act of war employs is the combat alone. In this manner, we think, we have obtained at the outset a correct point of view.

Having now gone through singly all the principal relations and forms which appear in military action, but are extraneous to, or outside of, the combat, in order that we might fix more distinctly their value, partly through the nature of the thing, partly from the lessons of experience which military history affords, purify them from, and root out, those vague ambiguous ideas which are generally mixed up with them, and also to put prominently forward the real object of the act of war, the destruction of the enemy's combatant force as the primary object universally belonging to it; we now return to War as a whole, as we propose to speak of the Plan of War, and of campaigns; and that obliges us to revert to the ideas in our first book.

In these chapters, which are to deal with the whole question, is contained strategy, properly speaking, in its most comprehensive and important features. We enter this innermost part of its domain, where all other threads meet, not without a degree of diffidence, which, indeed, is amply justified.

If, on the one hand, we see how extremely simple the operations of war appear; if we hear and read how the greatest generals speak of it, just in the plainest and briefest manner, how the government and management of this ponderous machine, with its hundred thousand limbs, is made no more of in their lips than if they were only speaking of their own persons, so that the whole tremendous act of war is individualised into a kind of duel; if we find the motives also of their action brought into connection sometimes with a few simple ideas, sometimes with some excitement of feeling; if we see the easy, sure, we might almost say light manner, in which they treat the subject and now see, on the other hand, the immense number of circumstances which present themselves for the consideration of the mind; the long, often indefinite, distances to which the threads of the subject run out, and the number of combinations which lie before us; if we reflect that it is the duty of theory to embrace all this systematically, that is with clearness and fullness, and always to refer the action to the necessity of a sufficient cause, then comes upon us an overpowering dread of being dragged down to a pedantic dogmatism, to crawl about in the lower regions of heavy abstruse conceptions, where we shall never meet any great captain, with his natural *coup d'oeil.* If the result of an attempt at theory is to be of this kind, it would have been as well, or rather, it would have been better, not to have made the attempt; it could only bring down on theory the contempt of genius, and the attempt itself would soon be forgotten. And on the other hand, this facile *coup d'oeil* of the general, this simple art of forming notions, this personification of the whole action of war, is so entirely and completely the soul of the right method of conducting war, that in no other but this broad way is it possible to conceive that freedom of the mind which is indispensable if it is to dominate events, not to be overpowered by them.

With some fear we proceed again; we can only do so by pursuing the way which we have prescribed for ourselves from the first. Theory ought to throw a clear light on the mass of objects, that the mind may the easier find its bearings; theory ought to pull up the weeds which error has sown broadcast; it should show the relations of things to each other, separate the important from the trifling. Where ideas resolve themselves spontaneously into such a core of Truth as is called Principle, when they of themselves keep such a line as forms a rule, Theory should indicate the same.

Whatever the mind seizes, the rays of light which are awakened in it by this exploration amongst the fundamental notions of things, *that is the assistance which Theory affords the mind.* Theory can give no formu-

las with which to solve problems; it cannot confine the mind's course
to the narrow line of necessity by Principles set up on both sides. It lets
the mind take a look at the mass of objects and their relations, and then
allows it to go free to the higher regions of action, there to act according to the measure of its natural forces, with the energy of the whole
of those forces combined, and to grasp the *True* and the *Right*, as one
single clear idea, which shooting forth from under the united pressure
of all these forces, would seem to be rather a product of feeling than of
reflection.

CHAPTER TWO

Absolute and Real War

THE PLAN of the War comprehends the whole Military Act; through it that Act becomes a whole, which must have one final determinate object, in which all particular objects must become absorbed. No war is commenced, or, at least, no war should be commenced, if people acted wisely, without saying to themselves, What is to be attained by and in the same; the first is the final object; the other is the intermediate aim. By this chief consideration the whole course of the war is prescribed, the extent of the means and the measure of energy are determined; its influence manifests itself down to the smallest organ of action.

We said, in the first chapter, that the overthrow of the enemy is the natural end of the act of War; and that if we would keep within the strictly philosophical limits of the idea, there can be no other in reality.

As this idea must apply to both the belligerent parties, it must follow, that there can be no suspension in the Military Act, and peace cannot take place until one or other of the parties concerned is overthrown.

In the chapter on the suspension of the Belligerent Act, we have shown how the simple principle of hostility applied to its embodiment, man, and all circumstances out of which it makes a war, is subject to checks and modifications from causes which are inherent in the apparatus of war.

But this modification is not nearly sufficient to carry us from the original conception of War to the concrete form in which it almost everywhere appears. Most wars appear only as an angry feeling on both sides, under the influence of which, each side takes up arms to protect himself, and to put his adversary in fear, and – when opportunity offers, to strike a blow. They are, therefore, not like mutually destructive elements brought into collision, but like tensions of two elements still apart which discharge themselves in small partial shocks.

But what is now the non-conducting medium which hinders the complete discharge? Why is the philosophical conception not satisfied? That medium consists in the number of interests, forces, and circumstances of various kinds, in the existence of the State, which are affected by the war, and through the infinite ramifications of which the logical consequence cannot be carried out as it would on the simple threads of a few conclusions; in this labyrinth it sticks fast, and man, who in great things as well as in small, usually acts more on the impulse of ideas and feelings, than according to strictly logical conclusions, is hardly conscious of his confusion, unsteadiness of purpose, and inconsistency.

But if the intelligence by which the war is decreed, could even go over all these things relating to the war, without for a moment losing sight of its aim, still all the other intelligences in the State which are concerned may not be able to do the same; thus an opposition arises, and with that comes the necessity for a force capable of overcoming the inertia of the whole mass – a force which is seldom forthcoming to the full.

This inconsistency takes place on one or other of the two sides, or it may be on both sides, and becomes the cause of the war being something quite different to what it should be, according to the conception of it – a half and half production, a thing without a perfect inner cohesion.

This is how we find it almost everywhere, and we might doubt whether our notion of its absolute character or nature was founded in reality, if we had not seen real warfare make its appearence in this absolute completeness just in our own times. After a short introduction performed by the French Revolution, the impetuous Buonaparte quickly brought it to this point Under him it was carried on without slackening for a moment until the enemy was prostrated, and the counter stroke followed almost with as little remission. Is it not natural and necessary that this phenomenon should lead us back to the original conception of war with all its rigorous deductions?

Shall we now rest satisfied with this idea, and judge of all wars according to it, however much they may differ from it, – deduce from it all the requirements of theory?

We must decide upon this point, for we can say nothing trustworthy on the Plan of War until we have made up our minds whether war should only be of this kind, or whether it may be of another kind.

If we give an affirmative to the first, then our Theory will be, in all respects, nearer to the necessary, it will be a clearer and more settled thing. But what should we say then of all wars since those of Alexander up to the time of Buonaparte, if we except some campaigns of the Romans? We should have to reject them in a lump, and yet we cannot, perhaps, do so without being ashamed of our presumption. But an additional evil is, that we must say to ourselves, that in the next ten years there may perhaps be a war of that same kind again, in spite of our Theory; and that this Theory, with a rigorous logic, is still quite powerless against the force of circumstances. We must, therefore, decide to construe war as it is to be, and not from pure conception, but by allowing room for everything of a foreign nature which mixes up with it and fastens itself upon it – all the natural inertia and friction of its parts, the whole of the inconsistency, the vagueness and hesitation (or timidity) of the human mind: we shall have to grasp the idea that war, and the form which we give it, proceeds from ideas, feelings, and circumstances, which dominate for the moment; indeed, if we would be perfectly candid we must admit that this has even been the case where it has taken its absolute character, that is, under Buonaparte.

If we must do so, if we must grant that war originates and takes its form not from a final adjustment of the innumerable relations with which it is connected, but from some amongst them which happen to predominate; then it follows, as a matter of course, that it rests upon a play of possibilities, probabilities, good fortune and bad, in which rigorous logical deduction often gets lost, and in which it is in general a useless, inconvenient instrument for the head; then it also follows that war may be a thing which is sometimes war in a greater, sometimes in a lesser degree.

All this, theory must admit, but it is its duty to give the foremost place to the absolute form of war, and to use that form as a general point of direction, that whoever wishes to learn something from theory, may accustom himself never to lose sight of it, to regard it as the natural measure of all his hopes and fears, in order to approach it *where he can, or where he must.*

That a leading idea, which lies at the root of our thoughts and actions, gives them a certain tone and character, even when the immediately determining grounds come from totally different regions, is just as certain as that the painter can give this or that tone to his picture by the colours with which he lays on his ground.

Theory is indebted to the last wars for being able to do this effectually now. Without these warning examples of the destructive force of the element set free, she might have talked herself hoarse to no purpose; no one would have believed possible what all have now lived to see realised.

Would Prussia have ventured to penetrate into France in the year 1798 with 70,000 men, if she had foreseen that the reaction in case of failure would be so strong as to overthrow the old balance of power in Europe?

Would Prussia, in 1806, have made war with 100,000 against France, if she had supposed that the first pistol shot would be a spark in the heart of the mine, which would blow it into the air?

CHAPTER THREE

A. **Interdependence of the Parts in War**

ACCORDING AS WE have in view the absolute form of war, or one of the real forms deviating more or less from it, so likewise different notions of its result will arise.

In the absolute form, where everything is the effect of its natural and necessary cause, one thing follows another in rapid succession; there is, if we may use the expression, no neutral space; there is on account of the manifold reactionary effects which war contains in itself,[61] on account of the connection in which, strictly speaking, the whole series of combats,[62] follow one after another, on account of the culminating point which every victory has, beyond which losses and defeats commence[63] on account of all these natural relations of war there is, I say, only *one result*, to wit, the *final result*. Until it takes place nothing is decided, nothing won, nothing lost. Here we may say indeed: the end crowns the work. In this view, therefore, war is an indivisible whole, the parts of which (the subordinate results) have no value except in their relation to this whole. The conquest of Moscow, and of half Russia in 1812, was of no value to Buonaparte unless it obtained for him the peace which he desired. But it was only a part of his Plan of campaign; to complete that Plan, one part was still wanted, the destruction of the Russian army; if we suppose this, added to the other success, then the peace was as certain as it is possible for things of this kind to be. This second part Buonaparte missed at the right time, and he could never afterwards attain it, and so the whole of the first part was not only useless, but fatal to him.

To this view of the relative connection of results in war, which may be regarded as extreme, stands opposed another extreme, according to

61 Book I., Chapter I.
62 Book I., Chapter I.
63 Book VII., Chapters IV. and V. (Culminating Point of Victory).

which war is composed of single independent results, in which, as in any number of games played, the preceding has no influence on the next following; everything here, therefore, depends only on the sum total of the results, and we can lay up each single one like a counter at play.

Just as the first kind of view derives its truth from the nature of things, so we find that of the second in history. There are cases without number in which a small moderate advantage might have been gained without any very onerous condition being attached to it. The more the element of war is modified the more common these cases become; but as little as the first of the views now imagined was ever completely realised in any war, just as little is there any war in which the last suits in all respects, and the first can be dispensed with.

If we keep to the first of these supposed views, we must perceive the necessity of every war being looked upon as a whole from the very commencement, and that at the very first step forwards, the commander should have in his eye the object to which every line must converge.

If we admit the second view, then subordinate advantages may be pursued on their own account, and the rest left to subsequent events.

As neither of these forms of conception is entirely without result, therefore theory cannot dispense with either. But it makes this difference in the use of them, that it requires the first to be laid as a fundamental idea at the root of everything, and that the latter shall only be used as a modification which is justified by circumstances.

If Frederick the Great in the years 1742, 1744, 1757, and 1758, thrust out from Silesia and Saxony a fresh offensive point into the Austrian Empire, which he knew very well could not lead to a new and durable conquest like that of Silesia and Saxony, it was done not with a view to the overthrow of the Austrian Empire, but from a lesser motive, namely, to gain time and strength; and it was optional with him to pursue that subordinate object without being afraid that he should thereby risk his whole existence.[64] But if Prussia in 1806, and Austria in 1805, 1809, proposed to

---

64 Had Frederick the Great gained the Battle of Kollen, and taken prisoners the chief Austrian army with their two field marshals in Prague, it would have been such a tremendous blow that he might then have entertained the idea of marching to Vienna to make the Austrian Court tremble, and gain a peace directly. This, in these times, unparalleled result, which would have been quite like what we have seen in our day, only still more wonderful and brilliant from the contest being between a little David and a great Goliath, might very probably have taken place after the gain of this one battle; but that does not contradict the assertion above maintained, for it only refers to what the king originally looked forward to from his offensive. The surrounding and taking prisoners the enemy's army was an event which was beyond all calculation, and which the king never thought of, at least not until the Austrians laid themselves open to it by the unskilful position in which they placed themselves at Prague.

themselves a still more moderate object, that of driving the French over the Rhine, they would not have acted in a reasonable manner if they had not first scanned in their minds the whole series of events which either, in the case of success, or of the reverse, would probably follow the first step, and lead up to peace. This was quite indispensable, as well to enable them to determine with themselves how far victory might be followed up without danger, and how and where they would be in a condition to arrest the course of victory on the enemy's side.

An attentive consideration of history shows wherein the difference of the two cases consists. At the time of the Silesian War in the eighteenth century, war was still a mere Cabinet affair, in which the people only took part as a blind instrument; at the beginning of the nineteenth century the people on each side weighed in the scale. The commanders opposed to Frederick the Great were men who acted on commission, and just on that account men in whom caution was a predominant characteristic; the opponent of the Austrians and Prussians may be described in a few words as the very god of war himself.

Must not these different circumstances give rise to quite different considerations? Should they not in the year 1805, 1806, and 1809 have pointed to the extremity of disaster as a very close possibility, nay, even a very great probability, and should they not at the same time have led to widely different plans and measures from any merely aimed at the conquest of a couple of fortresses or a paltry province?

They did not do so in a degree commensurate with their importance, although both Austria and Prussia, judging by their armaments, felt that storms were brewing in the political atmosphere. They could not do so because those relations at that time were not yet so plainly developed as they have been since from history. It is just those very campaigns of 1805, 1806, 1809, and following ones, which have made it easier for us to form a conception of modern absolute war in its destroying energy.

Theory demands, therefore, that at the commencement of every war its character and main outline shall be defined according to what the political conditions and relations lead us to anticipate as probable. The more, that according to this probability its character approaches the form of absolute war, the more its outline embraces the mass of the belligerent states and draws them into the vortex, so much the more complete will be the relation of events to one another and the whole, but so much the more necessary it will also be not to take the first step without thinking what may be the last.

B. Of the Magnitude of the Object of the War, and the Efforts to be Made.

THE COMPULSION which we must use towards our enemy will be regulated by the proportions of our own and his political demands. In so far as these are mutually known they will give the measure of the mutual efforts; but they are not always quite so evident, and this may be a first ground of a difference in the means adopted by each.

The situation and relations of the states are not like each other; this may become a second cause.

The strength of will, the character and capabilities of the governments are as little like; this is a third cause.

These three elements cause an uncertainty in the calculation of the amount of resistance to be expected, consequently an uncertainty as to the amount of means to be applied and the object to be chosen.

As in war the want of sufficient exertion may result not only in failure but in positive harm, therefore, the two sides respectively seek to outstrip each other, which produces a reciprocal action.

This might lead to the utmost extremity of exertion, if it was possible to define such a point. But then regard for the amount of the political demands would be lost, the means would lose all relation to the end, and in most cases this aim at an extreme effort would be wrecked by the opposing weight of forces within itself.

In this manner, he who undertakes war is brought back again into a middle course, in which he acts to a certain extent upon the principle of only applying so much force and aiming at such an object in war as are just sufficient for the attainment of its political object. To make this principle practicable he must renounce every absolute necessity of a result, and throw out of the calculation remote contingencies.

Here, therefore, the action of the mind leaves the province of science, strictly speaking, of logic and mathematics, and becomes, in the widest sense of the term, an *art*, that is, skill in discriminating, by the tact of judgment among an infinite multitude of objects and relations, that which is the most important and decisive. This tact of judgment consists unquestionably more or less in some intuitive comparison of things and relations by which the remote and unimportant are more quickly set aside, and the more immediate and important are sooner discovered than they could be by strictly logical deduction.

In order to ascertain the real scale of the means which we must put forth for war, we must think over the political object both on our own side and on the enemy's side; we must consider the power and position of the enemy's state as well as of our own, the character of his government and of his people, and the capacities of both, and all that again on our own side, and the political connections of other states, and the effect which the war will produce on those States. That the determination of these diverse circumstances and their diverse connections with each other is an immense problem, that it is the true flash of genius which discovers here in a moment what is right, and that it would be quite out of the question to become master of the complexity merely by a methodical study, this it is easy to conceive.

In this sense Buonaparte was quite right when he said that it would be a problem in algebra before which a Newton might stand aghast.

If the diversity and magnitude of the circumstances and the uncertainty as to the right measure augment in a high degree the difficulty of obtaining a right result, we must not overlook the fact that although the incomparable *importance* of the matter does not increase the complexity and difficulty of the problem, still it very much increases the merit of its solution. In men of an ordinary stamp freedom and activity of mind are depressed not increased by the sense of danger and responsibility: but where these things give wings to strengthen the judgment, there undoubtedly must be unusual greatness of soul.

First of all, therefore, we must admit that the judgment on an approaching war, on the end to which it should be directed, and on the means which are required, can only be formed after a full consideration of the whole of the circumstances in connection with it: with which therefore must also be combined the most individual traits of the moment; next, that this decision, like all in military life, cannot be purely objective but must be determined by the mental and moral qualities of princes, statesmen, and generals, whether they are united in the person of one man or not.

The subject becomes general and more fit to be treated of in the abstract if we look at the general relations in which States have been placed by circumstances at different times. We must allow ourselves here a passing glance at history.

Half-civilised Tartars, the Republics of ancient times, the feudal lords and commercial cities of the Middle Ages, kings of the eighteenth century, and, lastly, princes and people of the nineteenth century, all carry on war in their own way, carry it on differently, with different means, and for a different object.

The Tartars seek new abodes. They march out as a nation with their wives and children, they are, therefore, greater than any other army in point of numbers, and their object is to make the enemy submit or expel him altogether. By these means they would soon overthrow everything before them if a high degree of civilisation could be made compatible with such a condition.

The old Republics with the exception of Rome were of small extent; still smaller their armies, for they excluded the great mass of the populace: they were too numerous and lay too close together not to find an obstacle to great enterprises in the natural equilibrium in which small separate parts always place themselves according to the general law of nature: therefore their wars were confined to devastating the open country and taking some towns in order to ensure to themselves in these a certain degree of influence for the future.

Rome alone forms an exception, but not until the later period of its history. For a long time, by means of small bands, it carried on the usual warfare with its neighbours for booty and alliances. It became great more through the alliances which it formed, and through which neighbouring peoples by degrees became amalgamated with it into one whole, than through actual conquests. It was only after having spread itself in this manner all over Southern Italy, that it began to advance as a really conquering power. Carthage fell, Spain and Gaul were conquered, Greece subdued, and its dominion extended to Egypt and Asia. At this period its military power was immense, without its efforts being in the same proportion. These forces were kept up by its riches; it no longer resembled the ancient republics, nor itself as it had been; it stands alone.

Just as peculiar in their way are the wars of Alexander. With a small army, but distinguished for its intrinsic perfection, he overthrew the decayed fabric of the Asiatic States; without rest, and regardless of risks, he traverses the breadth of Asia, and penetrates into India. No republics could do this. Only a king, in a certain measure his own condottiere, could get through so much so quickly.

The great and small monarchies of the middle ages carried on their wars with feudal armies. Everything was then restricted to a short period of time; whatever could not be done in that time was held to be impracticable. The feudal force itself was raised through an organisation of vassaldom; the bond which held it together was partly legal obligation, partly a voluntary contract; the whole formed a real confederation. The armament and tactics were based on the right of might, on single combat, and therefore little suited to large bodies. In fact, at no period has the union of States been so weak, and the individual citizen so independent. All this influenced the character of the wars at that period in the most distinct manner. They were comparatively rapidly carried out, there was little time spent idly in camps, but the object was generally only punishing, not subduing, the enemy. They carried off his cattle, burnt his towns, and then returned home again.

The great commercial towns and small republics brought forward the condottieri. That was an expensive, and therefore, as far as visible strength, a very limited military force; as for its intensive strength, it was of still less value in that respect; so far from their showing anything like extreme energy or impetuosity in the field, their combats were generally only sham fights. In a word, hatred and enmity no longer roused a state to personal activity, but had become articles of trade; war lost great part of its danger, altered completely its nature, and nothing we can say of the character it then assumed, would be applicable to it in its reality.

The feudal system condensed itself by degrees into a decided territorial supremacy; the ties binding the State together became closer; obligations which concerned the person were made subject of composition; by degrees gold became the substitute in most cases, and the feudal armies were turned into mercenaries. The condottieri formed the connecting link in the change, and were therefore, for a time, the instrument of the more powerful States; but this had not lasted long, when the soldier, hired for a limited term, was turned into a *standing mercenary*, and the military force of States now became an army, having its base in the public treasury.

It is only natural that the slow advance to this stage caused a diversified interweaving of all three kinds of military force. Under Henry IV. we find the feudal contingents, condottieri, and standing army all employed together. The condottieri carried on their existence up to the period of the Thirty Years' War, indeed there are slight traces of them even in the eighteenth century.

The other relations of the States of Europe at these different periods were quite as peculiar as their military forces. Upon the whole, this part of the world had split up into a mass of petty States, partly republics in a state of internal dissension, partly small monarchies in which the power of the government was very limited and insecure. A State in either of these cases could not be considered as a real unity; it was rather an agglomeration of loosely connected forces. Neither, therefore, could such a State be considered an intelligent being, acting in accordance with simple logical rules.

It is from this point of view we must look at the foreign politics and wars of the Middle Ages. Let us only think of the continual expeditions of the Emperors of Germany into Italy for five centuries, without any substantial conquest of that country resulting from them, or even having been so much as in view. It is easy to look upon this as a fault repeated over and over again as a false view which had its root in the nature of the times, but it is more in accordance with reason to regard it as the consequence of a hundred important causes which we can partially realise in idea, but the vital energy of which it is impossible for us to understand so vividly as those who were brought into actual conflict with them. As long as the great States which have risen out of this chaos required time to consolidate and organise themselves, their whole power and energy is chiefly directed to that point; their foreign wars are few, and those that took place bear the stamp of a State-unity not yet well cemented.

The wars between France and England are the first that appear, and yet at that time France is not to be considered as really a monarchy, but as an agglomeration of dukedoms and countships; England, although bearing more the semblance of a unity, still fought with the feudal organisation, and was hampered by serious domestic troubles.

Under Louis XI., France made its greatest step towards internal unity; under Charles VIII. it appears in Italy as a power bent on conquest; and under Louis XIV. it had brought its political state and its standing army to the highest perfection.

Spain attains to unity under Ferdinand the Catholic; through accidental marriage connections, under Charles V., suddenly arose the great Spanish monarchy, composed of Spain, Burgundy, Germany, and Italy united. What this colossus wanted in unity and internal political cohesion, it made up for by gold, and its standing army came for the first time into collision with the standing army of France. After Charles's abdication, the great Spanish colossus split into two parts, Spain and Austria. The latter, strengthened by the acquisition of Bohemia and Hungary, now appears on the scene as a great power, towing the German Confederation like a small vessel behind her.

The end of the seventeenth century, the time of Louis XIV., is to be regarded as the point in history at which the standing military power, such as it existed in the eighteenth century, reached its zenith. That military force was based on enlistment and money. States had organised themselves into complete unities; and the governments, by commuting the personal obligations of their subjects into a money payment, had concentrated their whole power in their treasuries. Through the rapid strides in social improvements, and a more enlightened system of government, this power had become very great in comparison to what it had been. France appeared in the field with a standing army of a couple of hundred thousand men, and the other powers in proportion.

The other relations of States had likewise altered. Europe was divided into a dozen kingdoms and two republics; it was now conceivable that two of these powers might fight with each other without ten times as many others being mixed up in the quarrel, as would certainly have been the case formerly. The possible combinations in political relations were still manifold, but they could be discerned and determined from time to time according to probability.

Internal relations had almost everywhere settle down into a pure monarchical form; the rights and influence of privileged bodies or estates had gradually died away, and the cabinet had become a complete unity, acting for the State in all its external relations. The time had therefore come that a suitable instrument and a despotic will could give war a form in accordance with the theoretical conception.

And at this epoch appeared three new Alexanders Gustavus Adolphus, Charles XII., and Frederick the Great, whose aim was by small but highly-disciplined armies, to raise little States to the rank of great monarchies, and to throw down everything that opposed them. If they had had only to deal with Asiatic States, they would have more closely resembled Alexander in the parts they acted. In any case, we may look upon them as the precursors of Buonaparte as respects that which may be risked in war.

But what war gained on the one side in force and consistency was lost again on the other side.

Armies were supported out of the treasury, which the sovereign regarded partly as his private purse, or at least as a resource belonging to the government, and not to the people. Relations with other states, except with respect to a few commercial subjects, mostly concerned only the interests of the treasury or of the government, not those of the people; at least ideas tended everywhere in that way. The cabinets, therefore, looked upon themselves as the owners and administrators of large estates, which they were continually seeking to increase without the tenants on these estates being particularly interested in this improvement. The people, therefore, who in the Tartar invasions were everything in war, who, in the old republics, and in the Middle Ages, (if we restrict the idea to those possessing the rights of citizens,) were of great consequence, were in the eighteenth century, absolutely nothing directly, having only still an indirect influence on the war through their virtues and faults.

In this manner, in proportion as the government separated itself from the people, and regarded itself as the state, war became more exclusively a business of the government, which it carried on by means of the money in its coffers and the idle vagabonds it could pick up in its own and neighbouring countries. The consequence of this was, that the means which the government could command had tolerably well defined limits, which could be mutually estimated, both as to their extent and duration; this robbed war of its most dangerous feature: namely the effort towards the extreme, and the hidden series of possibilities connected therewith.

The financial means, the contents of the treasury, the state of credit of the enemy, were approximately known as well as the size of his army. Any large increase of these at the outbreak of a war was impossible. Inasmuch as the limits of the enemy's power could thus be judged of, a State felt tolerably secure from complete subjugation, and as the State was conscious at the same time of the limits of its own means, it saw itself restricted to a moderate aim. Protected from an extreme, there was no necessity to venture on an extreme. Necessity no longer giving an impulse in that direction, that impulse could only now be given by courage and ambition. But these found a powerful counterpoise in the political relations. Even kings in command were obliged to use the instrument of war with caution. If the army was dispersed, no new one could be got, and except the army there was nothing. This imposed as a necessity great prudence in all undertakings. It was only when a decided advantage seemed to present itself that they made use of the costly instrument; to bring about such an opportunity was a general's art; but until it was brought about they floated to a certain degree in an absolute vacuum, there was no ground of action, and all forces, that is all designs, seemed to rest. The original motive of the aggressor faded away in prudence and circumspection.

Thus war, in reality, became a regular game, in which Time and Chance shuffled the cards; but in its signification it was only diplomacy somewhat intensified, a more vigorous way of negotiating, in which battles and sieges were substituted for diplomatic notes. To obtain some moderate advantage in order to make use of it in negotiations for peace, was the aim even of the most ambitious.

This restricted, shrivelled-up form of war proceeded, as we have said, from the narrow basis on which it was supported. But that excellent generals and kings, like Gustavus Adolphus, Charles XII., and Frederick the Great, at the head of armies just as excellent, could not gain more prominence in the general mass of phenomena that even these men were obliged to be contented to remain at the ordinary level of moderate results, is to be attributed to the balance of power in Europe. Now that States had become greater, and their centres further apart from each other, what had formerly been done through direct perfectly natural interests, proximity, contact, family connections, personal friendship, to prevent any one single State among the number from becoming suddenly great was effected by a higher cultivation of the art of diplomacy. Political interests, attractions and repulsions developed into a very refined system, so that a cannon shot could not be fired in Europe without all the cabinets having some interest in the occurrence.

A new Alexander must therefore try the use of a good pen as well as his good sword; and yet he never went very far with his conquests.

But although Louis XIV. had in view to overthrow the balance of power in Europe, and at the end of the seventeenth century had already got to such a point as to trouble himself little about the general feeling of animosity, he carried on war just as it had heretofore been conducted; for while his army was certainly that of the greatest and richest monarch in Europe, in its nature it was just like others.

Plundering and devastating the enemy's country, which play such an important part with Tartars, with ancient nations, and even in the Middle Ages, were no longer in accordance with the spirit of the age. They were justly looked upon as unnecessary barbarity, which might easily be retaliated, and which did more injury to the enemy's subjects than the enemy's government, therefore, produced no effect beyond throwing the nation back many stages in all that relates to peaceful arts and civilisation. War, therefore, confined itself more and more both as regards means and end, to the army itself. The army with its fortresses, and some prepared positions, constituted a State in a State, within which the element of war slowly consumed itself. All Europe rejoiced at its taking this direction, and held it to be the necessary consequence of the spirit of progress. Although there lay in this an error, inasmuch as the progress of the human mind can never lead to what is absurd, can never make five out of twice two, as we have already said, and must again repeat, still upon the whole this change had a beneficial effect for the people; only it is not to be denied that it had a tendency to make war still more an affair of the State, and to separate it still more from the interests of the people. The plan of a war on the part of the state assuming the offensive in those times consisted generally in the conquest of one or other of the enemy's provinces; the plan of the defender was to prevent this; the particular plan of campaign was to take one or other of the enemy's fortresses, or to prevent one of our own from being taken; it was only when a battle became unavoidable for this purpose that it was sought for and fought. Whoever fought a battle without this unavoidable necessity, from mere innate desire of gaining a victory, was reckoned a general with too much daring. Generally the campaign passed over with one siege, or if it was a very active one, with two sieges, and winter quarters, which were regarded as a necessity, and during which, the faulty arrangements of the one could never be taken advantage of by the other, and in which the mutual relations of the two parties almost entirely ceased, formed a distinct limit to the activity which was considered to belong to one campaign.

If the forces opposed were too much on an equality, or if the aggressor was decidedly the weaker of the two, then neither battle nor siege took place, and the whole of the operations of the campaign pivoted on the maintenance of certain positions and magazines, and the regular exhaustion of particular districts of country.

As long as war was universally conducted in this manner, and the natural limits of its force were so close and obvious, so far from anything absurd being perceived in it, all was considered to be in the most regular order; and criticism, which in the eighteenth century began to turn its attention to the field of art in war, addressed itself to details without troubling itself much about the beginning and the end. Thus there was eminence and perfection of every kind, and even Field Marshal Daun, to whom it was chiefly owing that Frederick the Great completely attained his object, and that Maria Theresa completely failed in hers, notwithstanding that could still pass for a great General. Only now and again a more penetrating judgment made its appearance, that is, sound common sense acknowledged that with superior numbers something positive should be attained or war is badly conducted, whatever art may be displayed.

Thus matters stood when the French Revolution broke out; Austria and Prussia tried their diplomatic art of war; this very soon proved insufficient. Whilst, according to the usual way of seeing things, all hopes were placed on a very limited military force in 1793, such a force as no one had any conception of, made its appearance. War had suddenly become again an affair of the people, and that of a people numbering thirty millions, every one of whom regarded himself as a citizen of the State. Without entering here into the details of circumstances with which this great phenomenon was attended, we shall confine ourselves to the results which interest us at present. By this participation of the people in the war instead of a cabinet and an army, a whole nation with its natural weight came into the scale. Henceforward, the means available the efforts which might be called forth had no longer any definite limits; the energy with which the war itself might be conducted had no longer any counterpoise, and consequently the danger for the adversary had risen to the extreme.

If the whole war of the revolution passed over without all this making itself felt in its full force and becoming quite evident; if the generals of the revolution did not persistently press on to the final extreme, and did not overthrow the monarchies in Europe; if the German armies now and again had the opportunity of resisting with success, and checking for a time the torrent of victory, the cause lay in reality in that technical incompleteness with which the French had to contend, which showed itself first amongst the common soldiers, then in the generals, lastly, at the time of the Directory, in the Government itself.

After all this was perfected by the hand of Buonaparte, this military power, based on the strength of the whole nation, marched over Europe, smashing everything in pieces so surely and certainly, that where it only encountered the old fashioned armies the result was not doubtful for a moment. A re-action, however, awoke in due time. In Spain, the war became of itself an affair of the people. In Austria, in the year 1809, the Government commenced extraordinary efforts, by means of Reserves and Landwehr, which were nearer to the true object, and far surpassed in degree what this State had hitherto conceived possible, In Russia, in 1812, the example of Spain and Austria was taken as a pattern, the enormous dimensions of that empire on the one hand allowed the preparations, although too long deferred, still to produce effect; and, on the other hand, intensified the effect produced. The result was brilliant. In Germany, Prussia rose up the first, made the war a national cause, and without either money or credit, and with a population reduced one half, took the field with an army twice as strong as that of 1806. The rest of Germany followed the example of Prussia sooner or later, and Austria, although less energetic than in 1809, still also came forward with more than its usual strength. Thus it was that Germany and Russia in the years 1813 and 1814, including all who took an active part in, or were absorbed in these two campaigns, appeared against France with about a million of men.

Under these circumstances, the energy thrown into the conduct of the war was quite different; and, although not quite on a level with that of the French, although at some points timidity was still to be observed, the course of the campaigns, upon the whole, may be said to have been in the new, not in the old, style. In eight months the theatre of war was removed from the Oder to the Seine. Proud Paris had to bow its head for the first time; and the redoubtable Buonaparte lay fettered on the ground.

Therefore, since the time of Buonaparte, war, through being first on one side, then again on the other, an affair of the whole nation, has assumed quite a new nature, or rather it has approached much nearer to its real nature, to its absolute perfection. The means then called forth had no visible limit, the limit losing itself in the energy and enthusiasm of the Government and its subjects. By the extent of the means, and the wide field of possible results, as well as by the powerful excitement of feeling which prevailed, energy in the conduct of war was immensely increased; the object of its action was the downfall of the foe; and not until the enemy lay powerless on the ground was it supposed to be possible to stop or to come to any understanding with respect to the mutual objects of the contest.

Thus, therefore, the element of war, freed from all conventional restrictions, broke loose, with all its natural force. The cause was the participation of the people in this great *affair of State*, and this participation arose partly from the effects of the French Revolution on the internal affairs of countries, partly from the threatening attitude of the French towards all nations.

Now, whether this will be the case always in future, whether all wars hereafter in Europe will be carried on with the whole power of the States, and, consequently, will only take place on account of great interests closely affecting the people, or whether a separation of the interests of the Government from those of the people will gradually again arise, would be a difficult point to settle; and, least of all, shall we take upon us to settle it. But every one will agree with us, that bounds, which to a certain extent existed only in an unconsciousness of what is possible, when once thrown down, are not easily built up again; and that, at least, whenever great interests are in dispute, mutual hostility will discharge itself in the same manner as it has done in our times.

We here bring our historical survey to a close, for it was not our design to give at a gallop some of the principles on which war has been carried on in each age, but only to show how each period has had its own peculiar forms of war, its own restrictive conditions, and its own prejudices. Each period would, therefore, also keep its own theory of war, even if every where, in early times, as well as in later, the task had been undertaken of working out a theory on philosophical principles. The events in each age must, therefore, be judged of in connection with the peculiarities of the time, and only he who, less through an anxious study of minute details than through an accurate glance at the whole, can transfer himself into each particular age, is fit to understand and appreciate its generals.

But this conduct of war, conditioned by the peculiar relations of States, and of the military force employed, must still always contain in itself something more general, or rather something quite general, with which, above everything, theory is concerned.

The latest period of past time, in which war reached its absolute strength, contains most of what is of general application and necessary. But it is just as improbable that wars henceforth will all have this grand character as that the wide barriers which have been opened to them will ever be completely closed again. Therefore, by a theory which only dwells upon this absolute war, all cases in which external influences alter the nature of war would be excluded or condemned as false. This cannot be the object of theory, which ought to be the science of war, not under ideal but under real circumstances. Theory, therefore, whilst casting a searching, discriminating and classifying glance at objects, should always have in view the manifold diversity of causes from which war may proceed, and should, therefore, so trace out its great features as to leave room for what is required by the exigencies of time and the moment.

Accordingly, we must add that the object which every one who undertakes war proposes to himself, and the means which he calls forth, are determined entirely according to the particular details of his position; and on that very account they will also bear in themselves the character of the time and of the *general* relations; lastly, *that they are always subject to the general conclusions to be deduced from the nature of war.*

CHAPTER FOUR

Ends in War More Precisely Defined Overthrow of the Enemy

THE AIM OF WAR in conception must always be the overthrow of the enemy; this is the fundamental idea from which we set out.

Now, what is this overthrow? It does not always imply as necessary the complete conquest of the enemy's country. If the Germans had reached Paris, in 1792, there – in all human probability – the war with the Revolutionary party would have been brought to an end at once for a season; it was not at all necessary at that time to beat their armies beforehand, for those armies were not yet to be looked upon as potent powers in themselves singly. On the other hand, in 1814, the allies would not have gained everything by taking Paris if Buonaparte had still remained at the head of a considerable army; but as his army had nearly melted away, therefore, also in the year 1814 and 1815 the taking of Paris decided all. If Buonaparte in the year 1812, either before or after taking Moscow, had been able to give the Russian army of 120,000 on the Kaluga road, a complete defeat, such as he gave the Austrians in 1805, and the Prussian army, 1806, then the possession of that capital would most probably have brought about a peace, although an enormous tract of country still remained to be conquered. In the year 1805 it was the battle of Austerlitz that was decisive; and, therefore, the previous possession of Vienna and two-thirds of the Austrian States, was not of sufficient weight to gain for Buonaparte a peace; but, on the other hand also, after that battle of Austerlitz, the integrity of Hungary, still intact, was not of sufficient weight to prevent the conclusion of peace. In the Russian campaign, the complete defeat of the Russian army was the last blow required: the Emperor Alexander had no other army at hand, and, therefore, peace was the certain consequence of victory. If the Russian army had been on the Danube along with the Austrian, and had shared in its defeat, then probably the conquest of Vienna would not have been necessary, and peace would have been concluded in Linz.

In other cases, the complete conquest of a country has not been sufficient, as in the year 1807, in Prussia, when the blow levelled against the Russian auxiliary army, in the doubtful battle of Eylau, was not decisive enough, and the undoubted victory of Friedland was required as a finishing blow, like the victory of Austerlitz in the preceding year.

We see that here, also, the result cannot be determined from general grounds; the individual causes, which no one knows who is not on the spot, and many of a moral nature which are never heard of, even the smallest traits and accidents, which only appear in history as anecdotes, are often decisive. All that theory can here say is as follows: – That the great point is to keep the overruling relations of both parties in view. Out of them a certain centre of gravity, a centre of power and movement, will form itself, on which everything depends; and against this centre of gravity of the enemy, the concentrated blow of all the forces must be directed.

The little always depends on the great, the unimportant on the important, and the accidental on the essential. This must guide our view.

Alexander had his centre of gravity in his army, so had Gustavus Adolphus, Charles XII., and Frederick the Great, and the career of any one of them would soon have been brought to a close by the destruction of his army: in States torn by internal dissensions, this centre generally lies in the capital; in small states dependent on greater ones, it lies generally in the army of these allies; in a confederacy, it lies in the unity of interests; in a national insurrection, in the person of the chief leader, and in public opinion; against these points the blow must be directed. If the enemy by this loses his balance, no time must be allowed for him to recover it; the blow must be persistently repeated in the same direction, or, in other words, the conqueror must always direct his blows upon the mass, but not against a fraction of the enemy. It is not by conquering one of the enemy's provinces, with little trouble and superior numbers, and preferring the more secure possession of this unimportant conquest to great results, but by seeking out constantly the heart of the hostile power, and staking everything in order to gain all, that we can effectually strike the enemy to the ground.

But whatever may be the central point of the enemy's power against which we are to direct our operations, still the conquest and destruction of his army is the surest commencement, and in all cases, the most essential.

Hence we think that, according to the majority of ascertained facts, the following circumstances chiefly bring about the overthrow of the enemy.

1. Dispersion of his army if it forms, in some degree, a potential force.

2. Capture of the enemy's capital city, if it is both the centre of the power of the State and the seat of political assemblies and actions.

3. An effectual blow against the principal ally, if he is more powerful than the enemy himself.

We have always hitherto supposed the enemy in war as a unity, which is allowable for considerations of a very general nature. But having said that the subjugation of the enemy lies in the overcoming his resistance, concentrated in the centre of gravity, we must lay aside this supposition and introduce the case, in which we have to deal with more than one opponent.

If two or more States combine against a third, that combination constitutes, in a political aspect, only *one* war, at the same time this political union has also its degrees.

The question is whether each State in the coalition possesses an independent interest in, and an independent force with which to prosecute, the war; or whether there is one amongst them on whose interests and forces those of the others lean for support. The more that the last is the case, the easier it is to look upon the different enemies as one alone, and the more readily we can simplify our principal enterprise to one great blow; and as long as this is in any way possible, it is the most thorough and complete means of success.

We may, therefore, establish it as a principle, that if we can conquer all our enemies by conquering one of them, the defeat of that one must be the aim of the war, because in that one we hit the common centre of gravity of the whole war.

There are very few cases in which this kind of conception is not admissible, and where this reduction of several centres of gravity to one cannot be made. But if this cannot be done, then indeed there is no alternative but to look upon the war as two or more separate wars, each of which has its own aim. As this case supposes the substantive independence of several enemies, consequently a great superiority of the whole, therefore in this case the overthrow of the enemy cannot, in general, come into question.

We now turn more particularly to the question, When is such an object possible and advisable?

In the first place, our forces must be sufficient, –

1. To gain a decisive victory over those of the enemy.

2. To make the expenditure of force which may be necessary to follow up the victory to a point at which it will no longer be possible for the enemy to regain his balance.

Next, we must feel sure that in our political situation, such a result will not excite against us new enemies, who may compel us on the spot to set free our first enemy.

France, in the year 1806, was able completely to conquer Prussia, although in doing so it brought down upon itself the whole military power of

Russia, because it was in a condition to cope with the Russians in Prussia.

France might have done the same in Spain in 1808 as far as regards England, but not as regards Austria. It was compelled to weaken itself materially in Spain in 1809, and must have quite given up the contest in that country if it had not had otherwise great superiority both physically and morally, over Austria.

These three cases should therefore be carefully studied, that we may not lose in the last the cause which we have gained in the former ones, and be condemned in costs.

In estimating the strength of forces, and that which may be effected by them, the idea very often suggests itself to look upon time by a dynamic analogy as a factor of forces, and to assume accordingly that half efforts, or half the number of forces would accomplish in two years what could only be effected in one year by the whole force united. This view which lies at the bottom of military schemes, sometimes clearly, sometimes less plainly, is completely wrong.

An operation in war, like everything else upon earth, requires its time; as a matter of course we cannot walk from Wilna to Moscow in eight days; but there is no trace to be found in war of any reciprocal action between time and force, such as takes place in dynamics.

Time is necessary to both belligerents, and the only question is: which of the two, judging by his position, has most reason to expect *special advantages* from time? Now (exclusive of peculiarities in the situation on one side or the other) the *vanquished* has plainly the most reason, at the same time certainly not by dynamic, but by psychological laws. Envy, jealousy, anxiety for self, as well as now and again magnanimity, are the natural intercessors for the unfortunate; they raise up for him on the one hand friends, and on the other hand weaken and dissolve the coalition amongst his enemies. Therefore, by delay something advantageous is more likely to happen for the conquered than for the conqueror. Further, we must recollect that to make right use of a first victory, as we have already shown, a great expenditure of force is necessary; this is not a mere outlay once for all, but has to be kept up like housekeeping, on a great scale; the forces which have been sufficient to give us possession of a province, are not always sufficient to meet this additional outlay; by degrees the strain upon our resources becomes greater, until at last it becomes insupportable; time, therefore, of itself may bring about a change.

Could the contributions which Buonaparte levied from the Russians and Poles, in money and in other ways, in 1812, have procured the hundreds of thousands of men that he must have sent to Moscow in order to retain his position there?

But if the conquered provinces are sufficiently important, if there are in them points which are essential to the well-being of those parts which are not conquered, so that the evil, like a cancer, is perpetually of itself gnawing further into the system, then it is possible that the conqueror, although nothing further is done, may gain more than he loses. Now in this state of circumstances, if no help comes from without, then time may complete the work thus commenced; what still remains unconquered will, perhaps, fall of itself. Therefore, thus time may also become a factor of his forces, but this can only take place if a return blow from the conquered is no longer possible, a change of fortune in his favour no longer conceivable, when therefore this factor of his forces is no longer of any value to the conqueror; for he has accomplished the chief object, the danger of the culminating point is past, in short, the enemy is already subdued.

Our object in the above reasoning has been to show clearly that no conquest can be finished too soon, that spreading it over a *greater space of time* than is absolutely necessary for its completion, instead of *facilitating* it, makes it more *difficult*. If this assertion is true, it is further true also that if we are strong enough to effect a certain conquest, we must also be strong enough to do it in one march without intermediate stations. Of course we do not mean by this without short halts, in order to concentrate the forces, and make other indispensable arrangements.

By this view, which makes the character of a speedy and persistent effort towards a decision essential to offensive war, we think we have completely set aside all grounds for *that* theory which in place of the irresistible continued following up of victory, would substitute a slow methodical system as being more sure and prudent. But even for those who have readily followed us so far, our assertion has, perhaps after all, so much the appearance of a paradox, is at first sight so much opposed and offensive to an opinion which, like an old prejudice, has taken deep root, and has been repeated a thousand times in books, that we considered it advisable to examine more closely the foundation of those plausible arguments which may be advanced.

It is certainly easier to reach an object near us than one at a distance, but when the nearest one does not suit our purpose it does not follow that dividing the work, that a resting point, will enable us to get over the second half of the road easier. A small jump is easier than a large one, but no one on that account, wishing to cross a wide ditch, would jump half of it first.

If we look closely into the foundation of the conception of the so-called methodical offensive war, we shall find it generally consists of the following things: –

1. Conquest of those fortresses belonging to the enemy which we meet with.

2. Laying in the necessary supplies.

3. Fortifying important points, as, *magazines, bridges, positions*, etc.

4. Resting the troops in quarters during winter, or when they require to be recruited in health and refreshed.

5. Waiting for the reinforcements of the ensuing year.

If for the attainment of all these objects we make a formal division in the course of the offensive action, a resting point in the movement, it is supposed that we gain a new base and renewed force, as if our own State was following up in the rear of the army, and that the latter laid in renewed vigour for every fresh campaign.

All these praiseworthy motives may make the offensive war more convenient, but they do not make its results surer, and are generally only make-believes to cover certain counteracting forces, such as the feelings of the commander or irresolution in the cabinet. We shall try to roll them up from the left flank.

1. The waiting for reinforcements suits the enemy just as well, and is, we may say, more to his advantage. Besides, it lies in the nature of the thing that a State can place in line nearly as many combatant forces in one year as in two; for all the actual increase of combatant force in the second year is but trifling in relation to the whole.

2. The enemy rests himself at the same time that we do.

3. The fortification of towns and positions is not the work of the army, and therefore no ground for any delay.

4. According to the present system of subsisting armies, magazines are more necessary when the army is in cantonments, than when it is advancing. As long as we advance with success, we continually fall into possession of some of the enemy's provision depots, which assist us when the country itself is poor.

5. The taking of the enemy's fortresses cannot be regarded as a suspension of the attack: it is an intensified progress, and therefore the seeming suspension which is caused thereby is not properly a case such as we allude to, it is neither a suspension nor a modifying of the use of force. But whether a regular siege, a blockade, or a mere observation of one or other is most to the purpose, is a question which can only be decided according to particular circumstances. We can only say this in general, that in answering this question another must be clearly decided, which is, whether the risk will not be too great if, while only blockading, we at the same time make a further advance. Where this is not the case, and when there is ample room to extend our forces, it

is better to postpone the formal siege till the termination of the whole offensive movement. We must therefore take care not to be led into the error of neglecting the essential, through the idea of immediately making secure that which is conquered.

No doubt it seems as if, by thus advancing, we at once hazard the loss of what has been already gained. Our opinion, however, is that no division of action, no resting point, no intermediate stations are in accordance with the nature of offensive war, and that when the same are unavoidable, they are to be regarded as an evil which makes the result not more certain, but, on the contrary, more uncertain; and further, that, strictly speaking, if from weakness or any cause we have been obliged to stop, a second spring at the object we have in view is, as a rule, impossible; but if such a second spring is possible, then the stoppage at the intermediate station was unnecessary, and that when an object at the very commencement is beyond our strength, it will always remain so.

We say, this appears to be the general truth, by which we only wish to set aside the idea that time of itself can do something for the advantage of the assailant. But as the political relations may change from year to year, therefore, on that account alone, many cases may happen which are exceptions to this general truth.

It may appear perhaps as if we had left our general point of view, and had nothing in our eye except offensive war; but it is not so by any means. Certainly, he who can set before himself the complete overthrow of the enemy as his object, will not easily be reduced to take refuge in the defensive, the immediate object of which is only to keep possession; but as we stand by the declaration throughout, that a defensive without any positive principle is a contradiction in strategy as well as in tactics, and therefore always come back to the fact that every defensive, according to its strength, will seek to change to the attack as soon as it has exhausted the advantages of the defensive, so therefore, however great or small the defence may be, we still also include in it contingently the overthrow of the enemy as an object which this attack may have, and which is to be considered as the proper object of the defensive, and we say that there may be cases in which the assailant, notwithstanding he has in view such a great object, may still prefer at first to make use of the defensive form. That this idea is founded in reality is easily shown by the campaign of 1812. The Emperor Alexander in engaging in the war did not perhaps think of ruining his enemy completely, as was done in the sequel; but is there anything which makes such an idea impossible? And yet, if so, would it not still remain very natural that the Russians began the war on the defensive?

CHAPTER FIVE

Ends in War More Precisely Defined – (Continued) Limited Object

IN THE PRECEDING chapter we have said that, under the expression "overthrow of the enemy," we understand the real absolute aim of the "act of war;" now we shall see what remains to be done when the conditions under which this object might be attained do not exist.

These conditions presuppose a great physical or moral superiority, or a great spirit of enterprise, an innate propensity to extreme hazards. Now where all this is not forthcoming, the aim in the act of war can only be of two kinds; either the conquest of some small or moderate portion of the enemy's country, or the defence of our own until better times; this last is the usual case in defensive war.

Whether the one or the other of these aims is of the right kind, can always be settled by calling to mind the expression used in reference to the last. *The waiting till more favourable times* implies that we have reason to expect such times hereafter, and this waiting for, that is, defensive war, is always based on this prospect; on the other hand, offensive war, that is, the taking advantage of the present moment, is always commanded when the future holds out a better prospect, not to ourselves, but to our adversary.

The third case, which is probably the most common, is when neither party has anything definite to look for from the future, when therefore it furnishes no motive for decision. In this case, the offensive war is plainly imperative upon him who is politically the aggressor, that is, who has the positive motive; for he has taken up arms with that object, and every moment of time which is lost without any good reason, is so much lost time *for him.*

We have here decided for offensive or defensive war on grounds which have nothing to do with the relative forces of the combatants respectively, and yet it may appear that it would be nearer right to make the choice of the offensive or defensive chiefly dependent on the mutual relations of combatants in point of military strength; our opinion is, that in doing so we should just leave the right road. The logical correctness of our simple argument no one will dispute; we shall now see whether in the concrete case it leads to the contrary.

Let us suppose a small State which is involved in a contest with a very superior power, and foresees that with each year its position will become worse: should it not, if war is inevitable, make use of the time when its situation is furthest from the worst? Then it must attack, not because the attack *in itself* ensures any advantages – it will rather increase the disparity of forces – but because this State is under the necessity of either bringing the matter completely to an issue before the worst time arrives, or of gaining, at least, in the mean time, some advantages which it may hereafter turn to account. This theory cannot appear absurd. But if this small State is quite certain that the enemy will advance against it, then, certainly, it can and may make use of the defensive against its enemy to procure a first advantage; there is then at any rate no danger of losing time.

If, again, we suppose a small State engaged in war with a greater, and that the future has no influence on their decisions, still, if the small State is politically the assailant, we demand of it also that it should go forward to its object.

If it has had the audacity to propose to itself a positive end in the face of superior numbers, then it must also act, that is, attack the foe, if the latter does not save it the trouble. Waiting would be an absurdity; unless at the moment of execution it has altered its political resolution, a case which very frequently occurs, and contributes in no small degree to give wars an indefinite character.

These considerations on the limited object apply to its connection both with offensive war and defensive war; we shall consider both in separate chapters. But we shall first turn our attention to another phase.

Hitherto we have deduced the modifications in the object of war solely from intrinsic reasons. The nature of the political view (or design) we have only taken into consideration in so far as it is or is not directed at something positive. Everything else in the political design is in reality something extraneous to war; but in the second chapter of the first book (End and Means in War) we have already admitted that the nature of the political object, the extent of our own or the enemy's demand, and our whole political relation practically have a most decisive influence on the conduct of the war, and we shall therefore devote the following chapter to that subject specially.

CHAPTER SIX

A. Influence of the Political Object on the Military Object

WE NEVER FIND that a State joining in the cause of another State, takes it up with the same earnestness as its own. An auxiliary army of moderate strength is sent; if it is not successful, then the ally looks upon the affair as in a manner ended, and tries to get out of it on the cheapest terms possible.

In European politics it has been usual for States to pledge themselves to mutual assistance by an alliance offensive and defensive, not so far that the one takes part in the interests and quarrels of the other, but only so far as to promise one another beforehand the assistance of a fixed, generally very moderate, contingent of troops, without regard to the object of the war, or the scale on which it is about to be carried on by the principals. In a treaty of alliance of this kind, the ally does not look upon himself as engaged with the enemy in a war properly speaking, which should necessarily begin with a declaration of war, and end with a treaty of peace. Still, this idea also is nowhere fixed with any distinctness, and usage varies one way and another.

The thing would have a kind of consistency, and it would be less embarrassing to the theory of war if this promised contingent of ten, twenty, or thirty thousand men was handed over entirely to the state engaged in war, so that it could be used as required; it might then be regarded as a subsidised force. But the usual practice is widely different. Generally the auxiliary force has its own commander, who depends only on his own government, and to whom they prescribe an object such as best suits the shilly-shally measures they have in view.

But even if two States go to war with a third, they do not always both look in like measure upon this common enemy as one that they must destroy or be destroyed by themselves, the business is often settled like a commercial transaction; each, according to the amount of the risk he incurs or the advantage to be expected, takes shares in the concern to the extent of 30,000 or 40,000 men, and acts as if he could not lose more than the amount of his investment.

Not only is this the point of view taken when a State comes to the assistance of another in a cause in which it has in a manner, little concern, but even when both allies have a common and very considerable interest at stake, nothing can be done except under diplomatic reservation, and the contracting parties usually only agree to furnish a small stipulated contingent, in order to employ the rest of the forces according to the special ends to which policy may happen to lead them.

This way of regarding wars entered into by reason of alliances was quite general, and was only obliged to give place to the natural way in quite modern times, when the extremity of danger drove men's minds into the natural direction (as in the wars *against* Buonaparte), and when the most boundless power compelled them to it (as *under* Buonaparte). It was an abnormal thing, an anomaly, for war and peace are ideas which in their foundation can have no gradations; nevertheless it was no mere diplomatic offspring which the reason could look down upon, but deeply rooted in the natural limitedness and weakness of human nature.

Lastly, even in wars carried on without allies, the political cause of a war has a great influence on the method in which it is conducted.

If we only require from the enemy a small sacrifice, then we content ourselves with aiming at a small equivalent by the war, and we expect to attain that by moderate efforts. The enemy reasons in very much the same way. Now, if one or the other finds that he has erred in his reckoning that in place of being slightly superior to the enemy, as he supposed, he is, if anything, rather weaker, still, at that moment, money and all other means, as well as sufficient moral impulse for greater exertions are very often deficient: in such a case he just does what is called "the best he can;" hopes better things in the future, although he has not the slightest foundation for such hope, and the war, in the mean time drags itself feebly along, like a body worn out with sickness.

Thus it comes to pass that the reciprocal action, the rivalry, the violence and impetuosity of war lose themselves in the stagnation of weak motives, and that both parties move with a certain kind of security in very circumscribed spheres.

If this influence of the political object is once permitted, as it then must be, there is no longer any limit, and we must be pleased to come down to such warfare as consists in a *mere threatening of the enemy* and in *negotiating*.

That the theory of war, if it is to be and to continue a philosophical study, finds itself here in a difficulty is clear. All that is essentially inherent in the conception of war seems to fly from it, and it is in danger of being left without any point of support. But the natural outlet soon shows itself. According as a modifying principle gains influence over the act of war, or rather, the weaker the motives to action become, the more the action will glide into a passive resistance, the less eventful it will become, and the less it will require guiding principles. All military art then changes itself into mere prudence, the principal object of which will be to prevent the trembling balance from suddenly turning to our disadvantage, and the half war from changing into a complete one.

B. War is an Instrument of Policy

HAVING MADE the requisite examination on both sides of that state of antagonism in which the nature of war stands with relation to other interests of men individually and of the bond of society, in order not to neglect any of the opposing elements, an antagonism which is founded in our own nature, and which, therefore, no philosophy can unravel, we shall now look for that unity into which, in practical life, these antagonistic elements combine themselves by partly neutralising each other. We should have brought forward this unity at the very commencement, if it had not been necessary to bring out this contradiction very plainly, and also to look at the different elements separately. Now, this unity is *the conception that war is only a part of political intercourse, therefore by no means an independent thing in itself.*

We know, certainly, that war is only called forth through the political intercourse of Governments and nations; but in general it is supposed that such intercourse is broken off by war, and that a totally different state of things ensues, subject to no laws but its own.

We maintain, on the contrary: that war is nothing but a continuation of political intercourse, with a mixture of other means. We say, mixed with other means, in order thereby to maintain at the same time that this political intercourse does not cease by the war itself, is not changed into something quite different, but that, in its essence, it continues to exist, whatever may be the form of the means which it uses, and that the chief lines on which the events of the war progress, and to which they are attached, are only the general features of policy which run all through the war until peace takes place. And how can we conceive it to be otherwise? Does the cessation of diplomatic notes stop the political relations between different nations and Governments? Is not war merely another kind of writing and language for political thoughts? It has certainly a grammar of its own, but its logic is not peculiar to itself.

Accordingly, war can never be separated from political intercourse, and if, in the consideration of the matter, this is done in any way, all the threads of the different relations are, to a certain extent, broken, and we have before us a senseless thing without an object.

This kind of idea would be indispensable even if war was perfect war, the perfectly unbridled element of hostility, for all the circumstances on which it rests, and which determine its leading features, viz., our own power, the enemy's power, allies on both sides, the characteristics of the people and their Governments respectively, etc., as enumerated in the first chapter of the first book, are they not of a political nature, and are they not so intimately connected with the whole political intercourse that it is impossible to separate them? But this view is doubly indispensable if we reflect that real war is no such consistent effort tending to an extreme, as it should be according to the abstract idea, but a half and half thing, a contradiction in itself; that, as such, it cannot follow its own laws, but must be looked upon as a part of another whole, and this whole is policy.

Policy in making use of war avoids all those rigorous conclusions which proceed from its nature; it troubles itself little about final possibilities, confining its attention to immediate probabilities. If much uncertainty in the whole action ensues therefrom, if it thereby becomes a sort of game, the policy of each cabinet places its confidence in the belief that in this game it will surpass its neighbour in skill and sharpsightedness.

Thus policy makes out of the all-overpowering element of war a mere instrument, changes the tremendous battle-sword, which should be lifted with both hands and the whole power of the body to strike once for all, into a light handy weapon, which is even sometimes nothing more than a rapier to exchange thrusts and feints and parries.

Thus the contradictions in which man, naturally timid, becomes involved by war, may be solved, if we choose to accept this as a solution.

If war belongs to policy, it will naturally take its character from thence. If policy is grand and powerful, so will also be the war, and this may be carried to the point at which war attains to *its absolute form*.

In this way of viewing the subject, therefore, we need not shut out of sight the absolute form of war, we rather keep it continually in view in the back ground.

Only through this kind of view, war recovers unity; only by it can we see all wars as things of *one* kind; and it is only through it that the judgment can obtain the true and perfect basis and point of view from which great plans may be traced out and determined upon.

It is true the political element does not sink deep into the details of war, Vedettes are not planted, patrols do not make their rounds from political considerations, but small as is its influence in this respect, it is great in the formation of a plan for a whole war, or a campaign, and often even for a battle.

For this reason we were in no hurry to establish this view at the commencement. While engaged with particulars, it would have given us little help; and, on the other hand, would have distracted our attention to a certain extent; in the plan of a war or campaign it is indispensable.

There is, upon the whole, nothing more important in life than to find out the right point of view from which things should be looked at and judged of, and then to keep to that point; for we can only apprehend the mass of events in their unity from *one* standpoint; and it is only the keeping to one point of view that guards us from inconsistency.

If, therefore, in drawing up a plan of a war it is not allowable to have a two-fold or three-fold point of view, from which things may be looked at, now with the eye of a soldier, then with that of an administrator, and then again with that of a politician, etc., then the next question is, whether *policy* is necessarily paramount, and everything else subordinate to it.

That policy unites in itself, and reconciles all the interests of internal administrations, even those of humanity, and whatever else are rational subjects of consideration, is presupposed, for it is nothing in itself, except a mere representative and exponent of all these interests towards other States. That policy may take a false direction, and may promote unfairly the ambitious ends, the private interests, the vanity of rulers, does not concern us here; for, under no circumstances can the art of war be regarded as its preceptor, and we can only look at policy here as the representative of the interests generally of the whole community.

The only question, therefore, is, whether in framing plans for a war the political point of view should give way to the purely military (if such a point is conceivable), that is to say, should disappear altogether, or subordinate itself to it, or whether the political is to remain the ruling point of view, and the military to be considered subordinate to it.

That the political point of view should end completely when war begins, is only conceivable in contests which are wars of life and death, from pure hatred: as wars are in reality, they are as we before said, only the expressions or manifestations of policy itself. The subordination of the political point of view to the military would be contrary to common sense, for policy has declared the war; it is the intelligent faculty, war only the instrument, and not the reverse. The subordination of the military point of view to the political is, therefore, the only thing which is possible.

If we reflect on the nature of real war, and call to mind what has been said in the third chapter of this book, *that every war should be viewed above all things according to the probability of its character, and its leading features as they are to be deduced from the political forces and proportions*, and that often indeed we may safely affirm, in our days, *almost* always war is to be regarded as an organic whole, from which the single branches are not to be separated, in which therefore every individual activity flows into the whole, and also has its origin in the idea of this whole, then it becomes certain and palpable to us that the superior stand-point for the conduct of the war, from which its leading lines must proceed, can be no other than that of policy.

From this point of view the plans come, as it were, out of a cast; the apprehension of them and the judgment upon them become easier and more natural, our convictions respecting them gain in force, motives are more satisfying, and history more intelligible.

At all events, from this point of view, there is no longer in the nature of things a necessary conflict between the political and military interests, and where it appears it is therefore to be regarded as imperfect knowledge only. That policy makes demands on the war which it cannot respond to, would be contrary to the supposition that it knows the instrument which it is going to use, therefore, contrary to a natural and indispensable supposition. But if it judges correctly of the march of military events, it is entirely its affair, and can be its only to determine what are the events and what the direction of events most favourable to the ultimate and great end of the war.

In one word, the art of war in its highest point of view is policy, but, no doubt, a policy which fights battles, instead of writing notes.

According to this view, to leave a great military enterprise, or the plan for one, to *a purely military judgment and decision*, is a distinction which cannot be allowed, and is even prejudicial; indeed, it is an irrational proceeding to consult professional soldiers on the plan of a war, that they may give a *purely military opinion* upon what the cabinet should do; but still more absurd is the demand of Theorists that a statement of the available means of war should be laid before the general, that he may draw out a purely military plan for the war or for a campaign, in accordance with those means. Experience in general also teaches us that notwithstanding the multifarious branches and scientific character of military art in the present day, still the leading outlines of a war are always determined by the cabinet, that is, if we would use technical language, by a political not a military functionary.

This is perfectly natural. None of the principal plans which are required for a war can be made without an insight into the political relations; and, in reality, when people speak, as they often do, of the prejudicial influence of policy on the conduct of a war, they say in reality something very different to what they intend. It is not this influence but the policy itself which should be found fault with. If policy is right, that is, if it succeeds in hitting the object, then it can only act on the war in its sense, with advantage also; and if this influence of policy causes a divergence from the object, the cause is only to be looked for in a mistaken policy.

It is only when policy promises itself a wrong effect from certain military means and measures, an effect opposed to their nature, that it can exercise a prejudicial effect on war by the course it prescribes. Just as a person in a language with which he is not conversant sometimes says what he does not intend, so policy, when intending right, may often order things which do not tally with its own views.

This has happened times without end, and it shows that a certain knowledge of the nature of war is essential to the management of political commerce.

But before going further, we must guard ourselves against a false interpretation of which this is very susceptible. We are far from holding the opinion that a war minister, smothered in official papers, a scientific engineer, or even a soldier who has been well tried in the field, would, any of them, necessarily make the best minister of State where the sovereign does not act for himself; or in other words, we do not mean to say that this acquaintance with the nature of war is the principal qualification for a war minister; elevation, superiority of mind, strength of character, these are the principal qualifications which he must possess; a knowledge of war may be supplied in one way or the other. France was never worse advised in its military and political affairs than by the two Brothers Belleisle and the Duke of Choiseul, although all three were good soldiers.

If war is to harmonise entirely with the political views and policy, to accommodate itself to the means available for war, there is only one alternative to be recommended when the statesman and soldier are not combined in one person, which is, to make the chief commander a member of the cabinet, that he may take part in its councils and decisions on important occasions. But then again, this is only possible when the cabinet, that is the government itself, is near the theatre of war, so that things can be settled without a serious waste of time.

This is what the Emperor of Austria did in 1809, and the allied sovereigns in 1813, 1814, 1815, and the arrangement proved completely satisfactory.

The influence of any military man except the General-in Chief in the cabinet, is extremely dangerous; it very seldom leads to able vigorous action. The example of France in 1793, 1794, 1795, when Carnot, while residing in Paris, managed the conduct of the war, is to be avoided, as a system of terror is not at the command of any but a revolutionary government.

We shall now conclude with some reflections derived from history.

In the last decennary of the past century, when that remarkable change in the art of war in Europe took place by which the best armies found that a part of their method of war had become utterly unserviceable, and events were brought about of a magnitude far beyond what any one had any previous conception of, it certainly appeared that a false calculation of everything was to be laid to the charge of the art of war. It was plain that while confined by habit within a narrow circle of conceptions, she had been surprised by the force of a new state of relations, lying, no doubt, outside that circle, but still not outside the nature of things.

Those observers who took the most comprehensive view, ascribed the circumstance to the general influence which policy had exercised for centuries on the art of war, and undoubtedly to its very great disadvantage, and by which it had sunk into a half-measure, often into mere sham fighting. They were right as to fact, but they were wrong in attributing it to something accidental, or which might have been avoided.

Others thought that everything was to be explained by the momentary influence of the particular policy of Austria, Prussia, England, etc., with regard to their own interests respectively.

But is it true that the real surprise by which men's minds were seized, was confined to the conduct of war, and did not rather relate to policy itself? That is, as we should say: did the ill success proceed from the influence of policy on the war, or from a wrong policy itself?

The prodigious effects of the French revolution abroad were evidently brought about much less through new methods and views introduced by the French in the conduct of war than through the changes which it wrought in state-craft and civil administration, in the character of governments, in the condition of the people, etc. That other governments took a mistaken view of all these things; that they endeavoured, with their ordinary means, to hold their own against forces of a novel kind, and overwhelming in strength; all that was a blunder in policy.

Would it have been possible to perceive and mend this error by a scheme for the war from a purely military point of view? Impossible. For if there had been, even in reality, a philosophical strategist, who merely from the nature of the hostile elements, had foreseen all the consequences, and prophesied remote possibilities, still it would have been purely impossible to have turned such wisdom to account.

If policy had risen to a just appreciation of the forces which had sprung up in France, and of the new relations in the political state of Europe, it might have foreseen the consequences, which must follow in respect to the great features of war, and it was only in this way that it could arrive at a correct view of the extent of the means required as well as of the best use to make of those means.

We may therefore say, that the twenty years' victories of the revolution are chiefly to be ascribed to the erroneous policy of the governments by which it was opposed.

It is true these errors first displayed themselves in the war, and the events of the war completely disappointed the expectations which policy entertained. But this did not take place because policy neglected to consult its military advisers. That art of war in which the politician of the day could believe, namely, that derived from the reality of war at that time, that which belonged to the policy of the day, that familiar instrument which policy had hitherto used *that* art of war, I say, was naturally involved in the error of policy, and therefore could not teach it anything better. It is true that war itself underwent important alterations both in its nature and forms, which brought it nearer to its absolute form; but these changes were not brought about because the French Government had, to a certain extent, delivered itself from the leading-strings of policy; they arose from an altered policy, produced by the French Revolution, not only in France, but over the rest of Europe as well. This policy had called forth other means and other powers, by which it became possible to conduct war with a degree of energy which could not have been thought of otherwise.

Therefore, the actual changes in the art of war are a consequence of alterations in policy; and, so far from being an argument for the possible separation of the two, they are, on the contrary, very strong evidence of the intimacy of their connexion.

Therefore, once more: war is an instrument of policy; it must necessarily bear its character, it must measure with its scale: the conduct of war, in its great features, is therefore policy itself, which takes up the sword in place of the pen, but does not on that account cease to think according to its own laws.

CHAPTER SEVEN

Limited Object – Offensive War

Even if the complete overthrow of the enemy cannot be the object, there may still be one which is directly positive, and this positive object can be nothing else than the conquest of a part of the enemy's country.

The use of such a conquest is this, that we weaken the enemy's resources generally, therefore, of course, his military power, while we increase our own; that we therefore carry on the war, to a certain extent, at his expense; further in this way, that in negotiations for peace, the possession of the enemy's provinces may be regarded as net gain, because we can either keep them or exchange them for other advantages.

This view of a conquest of the enemy's provinces is very natural, and would be open to no objection if it were not that the defensive attitude, which must succeed the offensive, may often cause uneasiness.

In the chapter on the culminating point of victory we have sufficiently explained the manner in which such an offensive weakens the combatant force, and that it may be succeeded by a situation causing anxiety as to the future.

This weakening of our combatant force by the conquest of part of the enemy's territory has its degrees, and these depend chiefly on the geographical position of this portion of territory. The more it is an annex of our own country, being contiguous to or embraced by it, the more it is in the direction of our principal force, by so much the less will it weaken our combatant force. In the Seven Years' War, Saxony was a natural complement of the Prussian theatre of war, and Frederick the Great's army, instead of being weakened, was strengthened by the possession of that province, because it lies nearer to Silesia than to the Mark, and at the same time covers the latter.

Even in 1740 and 1741, after Frederick the Great had once conquered Silesia, it did not weaken his army in the field, because, owing to its form and situation as well as the contour of its frontier line, it only presented a narrow point to the Austrians, as long as they were not masters of Saxony, and besides that, this small point of contact also lay in the direction of the chief operations of the contending forces.

If, on the other hand, the conquered territory is a strip running up between hostile provinces, has an eccentric position and unfavourable configuration of ground, then the weakening increases so visibly that a victorious battle becomes not only much easier for the enemy, but it may even become unnecessary as well.

The Austrians have always been obliged to evacuate Provence without a battle when they have made attempts on it from Italy. In the year 1744 the French were very well pleased even to get out of Bohemia without having lost a battle. In 1758 Frederick the Great could not hold his position in Bohemia and Moravia with the same force with which he had obtained such brilliant successes in Silesia and Saxony in 1757. Examples of armies not being able to keep possession of conquered territory solely because their combatant force was so much weakened thereby, are so common that it does not appear necessary to quote any more of them.

Therefore, the question whether we should aim at such an object depends on whether we can expect to hold possession of the conquest or whether a temporary occupation (invasion, diversion) would repay the expenditure of force required: especially, whether we have not to apprehend such a vigorous counterstroke as will completely destroy the balance of forces. In the chapter on the culmination point we have treated of the consideration due to this question in each particular case.

There is just one point which we have still to add.

An offensive of this kind will not always compensate us for what we lose upon other points. Whilst we are engaged in making a partial conquest, the enemy may be doing the same at other points, and if our enterprise does not greatly preponderate in importance then it will not compel the enemy to give up his. It is, therefore, a question for serious consideration whether we may not lose more than we gain in a case of this description.

Even if we suppose two provinces (one on each side) to be of equal value, we shall always lose more by the one which the enemy takes from us than we can gain by the one we take, because a number of our forces become to a certain extent like *faux frais*, non-effective. But as the same takes place on the enemy's side also, one would suppose that in reality there is no ground to attach more importance to the maintenance of what is our own than to the conquest. But yet there is. The maintenance of our own territory is always a matter which more deeply concerns us, and the suffering inflicted on our own state can not be outweighed, nor, to a certain extent, neutralised by what we gain in return, unless the latter promises a high percentage, that is, is much greater.

The consequence of all this is that a strategic attack directed against only a moderate object involves a greater necessity for steps to defend other points which it does not directly cover than one which is directed against the centre of the enemy's force; consequently, in such an attack the concentration of forces in time and space cannot be carried out to the same extent. In order that it may take place, at least as regards time, it becomes necessary for the advance to be made offensively from every point possible, and at the same moment exactly: and therefore this attack loses the other advantage of being able to make shift with a much smaller force by acting on the defensive at particular points. In this way the effect of aiming at a minor object is to bring all things more to a level: the whole act of the war cannot now be concentrated into one principal affair which can be governed according to leading points of view; it is more dispersed; the friction becomes greater everywhere, and there is everywhere more room for chance.

This is the natural tendency of the thing. The commanders weighed down by it, finds himself more and more neutralised. The more he is conscious of his own powers, the greater his resources subjectively, and his power objectively, so much the more he will seek to liberate himself from this tendency in order to give to some one point a preponderating importance, even if that should only be possible by running greater risks.

CHAPTER EIGHT

Limited Object – Defence

THE ULTIMATE AIM of defensive war can never be an absolute negation, as we have before observed. Even for the weakest there must be
some point in which the enemy may be made to feel, and which may
be threatened.

Certainly we may say that this object is the exhaustion of the adversary, for as he has a positive object, every one of his blows which
fails, if it has no other result than the loss of the force applied, still
may be considered a retrograde step *in reality*, whilst the loss which
the defensive suffers is not in vain, because his object was keeping
possession, and that he has effected. This would be tantamount to
saying that the defensive has his positive object in merely keeping
possession. Such reasoning might be good if it was certain that the assailant after a certain number of fruitless attempts must be worn out,
and desist from further efforts. But just this necessary consequence is
wanting. If we look at the exhaustion of forces, the defender is under
a disadvantage. The assailant becomes weaker, but only in the sense
that it may reach a turning point; if we set aside that supposition, the
weakening goes on certainly more rapidly on the defensive side than
on that of the assailant: for in the first place, he is the weaker, and,
therefore, if the losses on both sides are equal, he loses more actually
than the other; in the next place, he is deprived generally of a portion
of territory and of his resources. We have, therefore, here no ground
on which to build the expectation that the offensive will cease, and
nothing remains but the idea that if the assailant repeats his blows,
while the defensive does nothing but wait to ward them off, then the
defender has no counterpoise as a set off to the risk he runs of one of
these attacks succeeding sooner or later.

Although in reality the exhaustion, or rather the weakening of the stronger, has brought about a peace in many instances that is to be attributed to the indecision which is so general in war, but cannot be imagined philosophically as the general and ultimate object of any defensive war whatever, there is, therefore, no alternative but that the defence should find its object in the idea of the '*waiting for*,' which is besides its real character. This idea in itself includes that of an alteration of circumstances, of an improvement of the situation, which, therefore, when it cannot be brought about by internal means, that is, by defensive pure in itself, can only be expected through assistance coming from without. Now, this improvement from without can proceed from nothing else than a change in political relations; either new alliances spring up in favour of the defender, or old ones directed against him fall to pieces.

Here, then, is the object for the defender, in case his weakness does not permit him to think of any important counterstroke. But this is not the nature of every defensive war, according to the conception which we have given of its form. According to that conception it is the stronger form of war, and on account of that strength it can also be applied when a counterstroke more or less important is designed.

These two cases must be kept distinct from the very first, as they have an influence on the defence.

In the first case, the defender's object is to keep possession of his own country intact as long as possible, because in that way he gains most time; and gaining time is the only way to attain his object. The positive object which he can in most cases attain, and which will give him an opportunity of carrying out his object in the negotiations for peace, he cannot yet include in his plan for the war. In this state of strategic passiveness, the advantages which the defender can gain at certain points consist in merely repelling partial attacks; the preponderance gained at those points he tries to make of service to him at others, for he is generally hard pressed at all points. If he has not the opportunity of doing this, then there often only accrues to him the small advantage that the enemy will leave him at rest for a time.

If the defender is not altogether too weak, small offensive operations directed less towards permanent possession than a temporary advantage to cover losses, which may be sustained afterwards, invasions, diversions, or enterprises against a single fortress, may have a place in this defensive system without altering its object or essence.

But in the second case, in which a positive object is already grafted upon the defensive, the greater the counterstroke that is warranted by circumstances the more the defensive imports into itself of positive character. In other words, the more the defence has been adopted voluntarily, in order to make the first blow surer, the bolder may be the snares which the defender lays for his opponent. The boldest, and if it succeeds, the most effectual, is the retreat into the interior of the country; and this means is then at the same time that which differs most widely from the other system.

Let us only think of the difference between the position in which Frederick the Great was placed in the Seven Years' War, and that of Russia in 1812.

When the war began, Frederick, through his advanced state of preparation for war, had a kind of superiority, this gave him the advantage of being able to make himself master of Saxony, which was besides such a natural complement of his theatre of war, that the possession of it did not diminish, but increased, his combatant force.

At the opening of the campaign of 1757, the King endeavoured to proceed with his strategic attack, which seemed not impossible as long as the Russians and French had not yet reached the theatre of war in Silesia, the Mark and Saxony. But the attack miscarried, and Frederick was thrown back on the defensive for the rest of the campaign, was obliged to evacuate Bohemia and to rescue his own theatre from the enemy, in which he only succeeded by turning himself with one and the same army, first upon the French, and then upon the Austrians. This advantage he owed entirely to the defensive.

In the year 1758 when his enemies had drawn round him in a closer circle, and his forces were dwindling down to a very disproportionate relation, he determined on an offensive on a small scale in Moravia: his plan was to take Olmutz before his enemies were prepared; not in the expectation of keeping possession of, or of making it a base for further advance, but to use it as a sort of advanced work, a *counter-approach* against the Austrians, who would be obliged to devote the rest of the present campaign, and perhaps even a second, to recover possession of it. This attack also miscarried. Frederick then gave up all idea of a real offensive, as he saw that it only increased the disproportion of his army. A compact position in the heart of his own country in Saxony and Silesia, the use of short lines, that he might be able rapidly to increase his forces at any point which might be menaced, a battle when unavoidable, small incursions when opportunity offered, and along with this a patient state of waiting-for (expectation), a saving of his means for better times became now his general plan. By degrees the execution of it became more and more passive. As he saw that even a victory cost him too much, therefore he tried to manage at still less expense; everything depended on gaining time, and on keeping what he had got; he therefore became more tenacious of yielding any ground, and did not hesitate to adopt a perfect cordon system. The positions of Prince Henry in Saxony, as well as those of the King in the Silesian mountains, may be so termed. In his letters to the Marquis d'Argens, he manifests the impatience with which he looks forward to winter quarters, and the satisfaction he felt at being able to take them up again without having suffered any serious loss.

Whoever blames Frederick for this, and looks upon it as a sign that his spirit had sunk, would, we think, pass judgment without much reflection.

If the entrenched camp at Bunzelwitz, the positions taken up by Prince Henry in Saxony, and by the King in the Silesian mountains, do not appear to us now as measures on which a General should place his dependence in a last extremity because a Buonaparte would soon have thrust his sword through such tactical cobwebs, we must not forget that times have changed, that war has become a totally different thing, is quickened with new energies, and that therefore positions might have been excellent at that time, although they are not so now, and that in addition to all, the character of the enemy deserves attention. Against the army of the German States, against Daun and Butturlin, it might have been the height of wisdom to employ means which Frederick would have despised if used against himself.

The result justified this view: in the state of patient expectation, Frederick attained his object, and got round difficulties in a collision with which his forces would have been dashed to pieces.

The relation in point of numbers between the Russian and French armies opposed to each other at the opening of the campaign in 1812 was still more unfavourable to the former than that between Frederick and his enemies in the Seven Years' War. But the Russians looked forward to being joined by large reinforcements in the course of the campaign. All Europe was in secret hostility to Buonaparte, his power had been screwed up to the highest point, a devouring war occupied him in Spain, and the vast extent of Russia allowed of pushing the exhaustion of the enemy's military means to the utmost extremity by a retreat over a hundred miles of country. Under circumstances on this grand scale, a tremendous counterstroke was not only to be expected if the French enterprise failed (and how could it succeed if the Russian Emperor would not make peace, or his subjects did not rise in insurrection?) but this counterstroke might also end in the complete destruction of the enemy. The most profound sagacity could, therefore, not have devised a better plan of campaign than that which the Russians followed on the spur of the moment.

That this was not the opinion at the time, and that such a view would then have been looked upon as preposterous, is no reason for our now denying it to be the right one. If we are to learn from history, we must look upon things which have actually happened as also possible in the future, and that the series of great events which succeeded the march upon Moscow is not a succession of mere accidents every one will grant who can claim to give an opinion on such subjects. If it had been possible for the Russians, with great efforts, to defend their frontier, it is certainly probable that in such case also the French power would have sunk, and that they would have at last suffered a reverse of fortune; but the reaction then would certainly not have been so violent and decisive. By sufferings and sacrifices (which certainly in any other country would have been greater, and in most would have been impossible) Russia purchased this enormous success.

Thus a great positive success can never be obtained except through positive measures, planned not with a view to a mere state of "waiting-for," but with a view to a *decision*, in short, even on the defensive, there is no great gain to be won except by a great stake.

CHAPTER NINE

Plan of War when the Destruction of the Enemy is the Object

HAVING CHARACTERISED in detail the different aims to which war may be directed, we shall go through the organisation of war as a whole for each of the three separate gradations corresponding to these aims.

In conformity with all that has been said on the subject up to the present, two fundamental principles reign throughout the whole plan of the war, and serve as a guide for everything else.

The first is: to reduce the weight of the enemy's power into as few centres of gravity as possible, into one if it can be done; again, to confine the attack against these centres of force to as few principal undertakings as possible, to one if possible; lastly, to keep all secondary undertakings as subordinate as possible. In a word, the first principle is, *to act concentrated as much as possible.*

The second principle runs thus *to act as swiftly as possible;* therefore, to allow of no delay or detour without sufficient reason.

The reducing the enemy's power to one central point depends

1. On the nature of its political connection. If it consists of armies of one Power, there is generally no difficulty; if of allied armies, of which one is acting simply as an ally without any interest of its own, then the difficulty is not much greater; if of a coalition for a common object, then it depends on the cordiality of the alliance; we have already treated of this subject.

2. On the situation of the theatre of war upon which the different hostile armies make their appearance.

If the enemy's forces are collected in one army upon one theatre of war, they constitute in reality a unity, and we need not inquire further; if they are upon one theatre of war, but in separate armies, which belong to different Powers, there is no longer absolute unity; there is, however, a sufficient interdependence of parts for a decisive blow upon *one part* to throw down the other in the concussion. If the armies are posted in theatres of war adjoining each other, and not separated by any great natural obstacles, then there is in such case also a decided influence of the one upon the other; but if the theatres of war are wide apart, if there is neutral territory, great mountains, etc., intervening between them, then the influence is very doubtful and improbable as well; if they are on quite opposite sides of the State against which the war is made, so that operations directed against them must diverge on eccentric lines, then almost every trace of connection is at an end.

If Prussia was attacked by France and Russia at the same time, it would be as respects the conduct of the war much the same as if there were two separate wars; at the same time the unity would appear in the negotiations.

Saxony and Austria, on the contrary, as military powers in the Seven Years' War, were to be regarded as one; what the one suffered the other felt also, partly because the theatres of war lay in the same direction for Frederick the Great, partly because Saxony had no political independence.

Numerous as were the enemies of Buonaparte in Germany in 1813, still they all stood very much in one direction in respect to him, and the theatres of war for their armies were in close connection, and reciprocally influenced each other very powerfully. If by a concentration of all his forces he had been able to overpower the main army, such a defeat would have had a decisive effect on all the parts. If he had beaten the Bohemain grand army, and marched upon Vienna by Prague, Blucher, however willing, could not have remained in Saxony, because he would have been called upon to co-operate in Bohemia, and the Crown Prince of Sweden as well would have been unwilling to remain in the Mark.

On the other hand, Austria, if carrying on war against the French on the Rhine and Italy at the same time, will always find it difficult to give a decision upon one of those theatres by means of a successful stroke on the other. Partly because Switzerland, with its mountains, forms too strong a barrier between the two theatres, and partly because the direction of the roads on each side is divergent. France, again, can much sooner decide in the one by a successful result in the other, because the direction of its forces in both converges upon Vienna, the centre of the power of the whole Austrian empire; we may add further, that a decisive blow in Italy will have more effect on the Rhine theatre than a success on the Rhine would have in Italy, because the blow from Italy strikes nearer to the centre, and that from the Rhine more upon the flank, of the Austrian dominions.

It proceeds from what we have said that the conception of separated or connected hostile power extends through all degrees of relationship, and that therefore, in each case, the first thing is to discover the influence which events in one theatre may have upon the other, according to which we may then afterwards settle how far the different forces of the enemy may be reduced into one centre of force.

There is only one exception to the principle of directing all our strength against the centre of gravity of the enemy's power, that is, if ancillary expeditions promise *extraordinary advantages*, and still, in this case, it is a condition assumed, that we have such a decisive superiority as enables us to undertake such enterprises without incurring too great risk at the point which forms our great object.

When General Bulow marched into Holland in 1814, it was to be foreseen that the thirty thousand men composing his corps would not only neutralise the same number of Frenchmen, but would, besides, give the English and the Dutch an opportunity of entering the field with forces which otherwise would never have been brought into activity.

Thus, therefore, the first consideration in the combination of a plan for a war, is to determine the centres of gravity of the enemy's power, and, if possible, to reduce them to one. The second is to unite the forces which are to be employed against the centre of force into one great action.

Here now the following grounds for dividing our forces may present themselves:

1. The original position of the military forces, therefore also the situation of the States engaged in the offensive.

If the concentration of the forces would occasion detours and loss of time, and the danger of advancing by separate lines is not too great, then the same may be justifiable on those grounds; for to effect an unnecessary concentration of forces, with great loss of time, by which the freshness and rapidity of the first blow is diminished, would be contrary to the second leading principle we have laid down. In all cases in which there is a hope of surprising the enemy in some measure, this deserves particular attention.

But the case becomes still more important if the attack is undertaken by allied States which are not situated on a line directed towards the State attacked not one behind the other but situated side by side. If Prussia and Austria undertook a war against France, it would be a very erroneous measure, a squandering of time and force if the armies of the two powers were obliged to set out from the same point, as the natural line for an army operating from Prussia against the heart of France is from the Lower Rhine, and that of the Austrians is from the Upper Rhine. Concentration, therefore, in this case, could only be effected by a sacrifice; consequently in any particular instance, the question to be decided would be, Is the necessity for concentration so great that this sacrifice must be made?

2. The attack by separate lines may offer greater results.

As we are now speaking of advancing by separate lines against *one* centre of force, we are, therefore, supposing an advance by *converging lines*. A separate advance on parallel or eccentric lines belongs to the rubric of *accessory undertakings*, of which we have already spoken.

Now, every convergent attack in strategy, as well as in tactics, holds out the prospect of *great* results; for if it succeeds, the consequence is not simply a defeat, but more or less the cutting off of the enemy. The concentric attack is, therefore, always that which may lead to the greatest results; but on account of the separation of the parts of the force, and the enlargement of the theatre of war, it involves also the most risk; it is the same here as with attack and defence, the weaker form holds out the greater results in prospect.

The question, therefore, is, whether the assailant feels strong enough to try for this great result.

When Frederick the Great advanced upon Bohemia, in the year 1757, he set out from Saxony and Silesia with his forces divided. The two principal reasons for his doing so were, first, that his forces were so cantoned in the winter that a concentration of them at one point would have divested the attack of all the advantages of a surprise; and next, that by this concentric advance, each of the two Austrian theatres of war was threatened in the flanks and the rear. The danger to which Frederick the Great exposed himself on that occasion was that one of his two armies might have been completely defeated by superior forces; should the Austrians *not see this*, then they would have to give battle with their centre only, or run the risk of being thrown off their line of communication, either on one side or the other, and meeting with a catastrophe; this was the great result which the king hoped for by this advance. The Austrians preferred the battle in the centre, but Prague, where they took up their position, was in a situation too much under the influence of the convergent attack, which, as they remained perfectly passive in their position, had time to develop its efficacy to the utmost. The consequence of this was that when they lost the battle, it was a complete catastrophe; as is manifest from the fact that two-thirds of the army with the commander-in-chief were obliged to shut themselves up in Prague.

This brilliant success at the opening of the campaign was attained by the bold stroke with a concentric attack. If Frederick considered the precision of his own movements, the energy of his generals, the moral superiority of his troops, on the one side, and the sluggishness of the Austrians on the other, as sufficient to ensure the success of his plan, who can blame him? But as we cannot leave these moral advantages out of consideration, neither can we ascribe the success solely to the mere geometrical form of the attack. Let us only think of the not less brilliant campaign of Buonaparte's, in the year 1796, when the Austrians were so severely punished for their concentric march into Italy. The means which the French general had at command on that occasion, the Austrian general had also at his disposal in 1757 (with the exception of the moral), indeed, he had rather more, for he was not, like Buonaparte, weaker than his adversary. Therefore, when it is to be apprehended that the advance on separate converging lines may afford the enemy the means of counteracting the inequality of numerical forces by using interior lines, such a form of attack is not advisable; and if on account of the situation of the belligerents, it must be resorted to, it can only be regarded as a necessary evil.

If, from this point of view, we cast our eyes on the plan which was adopted for the invasion of France in 1814, it is impossible to give it approval. The Russian, Austrian, and Prussian armies were concentrated at a point near Frankfort on the Maine, on the most natural and most direct line to the centre of the force of the French monarchy. These armies were then separated, that one might penetrate into France from Mayence, the other from Switzerland. As the enemy's force was so reduced that a defence of the frontier was out of the question, the whole advantage to be expected from this concentric advance, if it succeeded, was that while Lorraine and Alsace were conquered by one army, Franche-Comte would be taken by the other. Was this trifling advantage worth the trouble of marching into Switzerland? We know very well that there were other (but just as insufficient) grounds which caused this march; but we confine ourselves here to the point which we are considering.

On the other side, Buonaparte was a man who thoroughly understood the defensive to oppose to a concentric attack, as he had already shown in his masterly campaign of 1796; and although the Allies were very considerably superior in numbers, yet the preponderance due to his superiority as a general was on all occasions acknowledged. He joined his army too late near Chalons, and looked down rather too much, generally, on his opponents, still he was very near hitting the two armies separately; and what was the state he found them in at Brienne? Blucher had only 27,000 of his 65,000 men with him, and the great army, out of 200,000, had only 100,000 present. It was impossible to make a better game for the adversary. And from the moment that active work began, no greater want was felt than that of re-union.

After all these reflections, we think that although the concentric attack is in itself a means of obtaining greater results, still it should generally only proceed from a previous separation of the parts composing the whole force, and that there are few cases in which we should do right in giving up the shortest and most direct line of operation for the sake of adopting that form.

3. The breadth of a theatre of war can be a motive for attacking on separate lines.

If an army on the offensive in its advance from any point, penetrates with success to some distance into the interior of the enemy's country, then, certainly, the space which it commands is not restricted exactly to the line of road by which it marches, it will command a margin on each side; still that will depend very much, if we may use the figure, on the solidity and cohesion of the opposing State. If the State only hangs loosely together, if its people are an effeminate race unaccustomed to war, then, without our taking much trouble, a considerable extent of country will open behind our victorious army; but if we have to deal with a brave and loyal population, the space behind our army will form a triangle, more or less acute.

In order to obviate this evil, the attacking force requires to regulate its advance on a certain width of front. If the enemy's force is concentrated at a particular point, this breadth of front can only be preserved so long as we are not in contact with the enemy, and must be contracted as we approach his position: that is easy to understand.

But if the enemy himself has taken up a position with a certain extent of front, then there is nothing absurd in a corresponding extension on our part. We speak here of one theatre of war, or of several, if they are quite close to each other. Obviously this is, therefore, the case when, according to our view, the chief operation is, at the same time, to be decisive on subordinate points

But now can we *always* run the chance of this? And may we expose ourselves to the danger which must arise if the influence of the chief operation is not sufficient to decide at the minor points? Does not the want of a certain breadth for a theatre of war deserve special consideration?

Here as well as everywhere else it is impossible to exhaust the number of combinations which *may take* place; but we maintain that, with few exceptions, the decision on the capital point will carry with it the decision on all minor points. Therefore, the action should be regulated in conformity with this principle, in all cases in which the contrary is not evident.

When Buonaparte invaded Russia, he had good reason to believe that by conquering the main body of the Russian army he would compel their forces on the Upper Dwina to succumb. He left at first only the corps of Oudinot to oppose them, but Wittgenstein assumed the offensive, and Buonaparte was then obliged to send also the sixth corps to that quarter.

On the other hand, at the beginning of the campaign, he directed a part of his forces against Bagration; but that general was carried along by the influence of the backward movement in the centre, and Buonaparte was enabled then to recall that part of his forces. If Wittgenstein had not had to cover the second capital, he would also have followed the retreat of the great army under Barclay.

In the years 1805 and 1809, Buonaparte's victories at Ulm and Ratisbon decided matters in Italy and also in the Tyrol, although the first was rather a distant theatre, and an independent one in itself. In the year 1806, his victories at Jena and Auerstadt were decisive in respect to everything that might have been attempted against him in Westphalia and Hesse, or on the Frankfort road.

Amongst the number of circumstances which may have an influence on the resistance at secondary points, there are two which are the most prominent.

The first is: that in a country of vast extent, and also relatively of great power, like Russia, we can put off the decisive blow at the chief point for some time, and are not obliged to do all in a hurry.

The second is: when a minor point (like Silesia in the year 1806), through a great number of fortresses, possesses an extraordinary degree of independent strength. And yet Buonaparte treated that point with great contempt, inasmuch as, when he had to leave such a point completely in his rear on the march to Warsaw, he only detached 20,000 men under his brother Jerome to that quarter.

If it happens that the blow at the capital point, in all probability, will not shake such a secondary point, or has not done so, and if the enemy has still forces at that point, then to these, as a necessary evil, an adequate force must be opposed, because no one can absolutely lay open his line of communication from the very commencement.

But prudence may go a step further; it may require that the advance upon the chief point shall keep pace with that on the secondary points, and consequently the principal undertaking must be delayed whenever the secondary points will not succumb.

This principle does not directly contradict ours as to uniting all action as far as possible in one great undertaking, but the spirit from which it springs is diametrically opposed to the spirit in which ours is conceived. By following such a principle there would be such a measured pace in the movements, such a paralysation of the impulsive force, such room for the freak of chance, and such a loss of time, as would be practically perfectly inconsistent with an offensive directed to the complete overthrow of the enemy.

The difficulty becomes still greater if the forces stationed at these minor points can retire on divergent lines. What would then become of the unity of our attack?

We must, therefore, declare ourselves completely opposed in principle to the dependence of the chief attack on minor attacks, and we maintain that an attack directed to the destruction of the enemy which has not the boldness to shoot, like the point of an arrow, direct at the heart of the enemy's power, can never hit the mark.

4. Lastly, there is still a fourth ground for a separate advance in the facility which it may afford for subsistence.

It is certainly much pleasanter to march with a small army through an opulent country, than with a large army through a poor one; but by suitable measures, and with an army accustomed to privations, the latter is not impossible, and, therefore, the first should never have such an influence on our plans as to lead us into a great danger.

We have now done justice to the grounds for a separation of forces which divides the chief operation into several, and if the separation takes place on any of these grounds, with a distinct conception of the object, and after due consideration of the advantages and disadvantages, we shall not venture to find fault.

But if, as usually happens, a plan is drawn out by a learned general staff, merely according to routine; if different theatres of war, like the squares on a chess board, must each have its piece first placed on it before the moves begin, if these moves approach the aim in complicated lines and relations by dint of an imaginary profundity in the art of combination, if the armies are to separate to-day in order to apply all their skill in reuniting at the greatest risk in fourteen days then we have a perfect horror of this abandonment of the direct simple common-sense road to rush intentionally into absolute confusion. This folly happens more easily the less the general-in-chief directs the war, and conducts it in the sense which we have pointed out in the first chapter as an act of his individuality invested with extraordinary powers; the more, therefore, the whole plan is manufactured by an inexperienced staff, and from the ideas of a dozen smatterers.

We have still now to consider the third part of our first principle; that is, to keep the subordinate parts as much as possible in subordination.

Whilst we endeavour to refer the whole of the operations of a war to one single aim, and try to attain this as far as possible by *one great effort*, we deprive the other points of contact of the States at war with each other of a part of their independence; they become subordinate actions. If we could concentrate everything absolutely into one action, then those points of contact would be completely neutralised; but this is seldom possible, and, therefore, what we have to do is to keep them so far within bounds, that they shall not cause the abstraction of too many forces from the main action.

Next, we maintain that the plan of the war itself should have this tendency, even if it is not possible to reduce the whole of the enemy's resistance to one point; consequently, in case we are placed in the position already mentioned, of carrying on two almost quite separate wars at the same time, the one must always be looked upon as the *principal affair* to which our forces and activity are to be chiefly devoted.

In this view, it is advisable only to proceed *offensively* against that one principal point, and to preserve the defensive upon all the others. The attack there being only justifiable when invited by very exceptional circumstances.

Further we are to carry on this defensive, which takes place at minor points, with as few troops as possible, and to seek to avail ourselves of every advantage which the defensive form can give.

This view applies with still more force to all theatres of war on which armies come forward belonging to different powers really, but still such as will be struck when the general centre of force is struck.

But against *the enemy* at whom the great blow is aimed, there must be, according to this, no defensive on minor theatres of war. The chief attack itself, and the secondary attacks, which for other reasons are combined with it, make up this blow, and make every defensive, on points not directly covered by it, superfluous. All depends on this principal attack; by it every loss will be compensated. If the forces are sufficient to make it reasonable to seek for that great decision, then the *possibility of failure* can be no ground for guarding oneself against injury at other points in any event; for just by *such a course* this failure will become more probable, and it therefore constitutes here a contradiction in our action.

This same predominance of the principal action over the minor, must be the principle observed in each of the separate branches of the attack. But as there are generally ulterior motives which determine what forces shall advance from one theatre of war, and what from another against the common centre of the enemy's power, we only mean here that there must be an *effort to make the chief action over-ruling*, for everything will become simpler and less subject to the influence of chance events the nearer this state of preponderance can be attained.

The second principle concerns the rapid use of the forces.

Every unnecessary expenditure of time, every unnecessary detour, is a waste of power, and therefore contrary to the principles of strategy.

It is most important to bear always in mind that almost the only advantage which the offensive possesses, is the effect of surprise at the opening of the scene. Suddenness and irresistible impetuosity are its strongest pinions; and when the object is the complete overthrow of the enemy, it can rarely dispense with them.

By this, therefore, theory demands the shortest way to the object, and completely excludes from consideration endless discussions about right and left here and there.

If we call to mind what was said in the chapter on the subject of the strategic attack respecting the pit of the stomach in a state, and further, what appears in the fourth chapter of this book, on the influence of time, we believe no further argument is required to prove that the influence which we claim for that principle really belongs to it.

Buonaparte never acted otherwise. The shortest high road from army to army, from one capital to another, was always the way he loved best.

And in what will now consist the principal action to which we have referred everything, and for which we have demanded a swift and straightforward execution?

In the fourth chapter we have explained as far as it is possible in a general way what the total overthrow of the enemy means, and it is unnecessary to repeat it. Whatever that may depend on at last in particular cases, still the first step is always the same in all cases, namely: *The destruction of the enemy's combatant force*, that is, *a great victory over the same and its dispersion*. The sooner, which means the nearer our own frontiers, this victory is sought for, *the easier* it is; the later, that is, the further in the heart of the enemy's country it is gained, the more *decisive* it is. Here, as well as everywhere, the facility of success and its magnitude balance each other.

If we are not so superior to the enemy that the victory is beyond doubt, then we should, when possible, seek him out, that is his principal force. We say *when possible*, for if this endeavour to find him led to great detours, false directions, and a loss of time, it might very likely turn out a mistake. If the enemy's principal force is not on our road, and our interests otherwise prevent our going in quest of him, we may be sure we shall meet with him hereafter, for he will not fail to place himself in our way. We shall then, as we have just said, fight under less advantageous circumstances an evil to which we must submit. However, if we gain the battle, it will be so much the more decisive.

From this it follows that, in the case now assumed, it would be an error to pass by the enemy's principal force designedly, if it places itself in our way, at least if we expect thereby to facilitate a victory.

On the other hand, it follows from what precedes, that if we have a decided superiority over the enemy's principal force, we may designedly pass it by in order at a future time to deliver a more decisive battle.

We have been speaking of a complete victory, therefore of a thorough defeat of the enemy, and not of a mere battle gained. But such a victory requires an enveloping attack, or a battle with an oblique front, for these two forms always give the result a decisive character. It is therefore an essential part of a plan of a war to make arrangements for this movement, both as regards the mass of forces required and the direction to be given them, of which more will be said in the chapter on the plan of campaign.

It is certainly not impossible, that even Battles fought with parallel fronts may lead to complete defeats, and cases in point are not wanting in military history; but such an event is uncommon, and will be still more so the more armies become on a par as regards discipline and handiness in the field. We no longer take twenty-one battalions in a village, as they did at Blenheim.

Once the great victory is gained, the next question is not about rest, not about taking breath, not about considering, not about reorganising, etc., etc., but only of pursuit of fresh blows wherever necessary, of the capture of the enemy's capital, of the attack of the armies of his allies, or of whatever else appears to be a rallying point for the enemy.

If the tide of victory carries us near the enemy's fortresses, the laying siege to them or not will depend on our means. If we have a great superiority of force, it would be a loss of time not to take them as soon as possible; but if we are not certain of the further events before us, we must keep the fortresses in check with as few troops as possible, which precludes any regular formal sieges. The moment that the siege of a fortress compels us to suspend our strategic advance, that advance, *as a rule*, has reached its culminating point. We demand, therefore, that the main body should press forward rapidly in pursuit without any rest; we have already condemned the idea of allowing the advance towards the principal point being made dependent on success at secondary points; the consequence of this is, that in all ordinary cases, our chief army only keeps behind it a narrow strip of territory which it can call its own, and which therefore constitutes its theatre of war. How this weakens the momentum at the head, and the dangers for the offensive arising therefrom, we have shown already. Will not this difficulty, will not this intrinsic counterpoise come to a point which impedes further advance? Certainly that may occur; but just as we have already insisted that it would be a mistake to try to avoid this contracted theatre of war at the commencement, and for the sake of that object to rob the advance of its elasticity, so we also now maintain, that as long as the commander has not yet overthrown his opponent, as long as he considers himself strong enough to effect that object, so long must he also pursue it. He does so perhaps at an increased risk, but also with the prospect of a greater success. If he reaches a point which he cannot venture to go beyond, where, in order to protect his rear, he must extend himself right and left well, then, this is most probably his culminating point. The power of flight is spent, and if the enemy is not subdued, most probably he will not be now.

All that the assailant now does to intensify his attack by conquest of fortresses, defiles, provinces, is no doubt still a slow advance, but it is only of a relative kind, it is no longer absolute. The enemy is no longer in flight, he is perhaps preparing a renewed resistance, and it is therefore already possible that, although the assailant still advances intensively, the position of the defence is every day improving. In short, we come back to this, that, as a rule, there is no second spring after a halt has once been necessary.

Theory, therefore, only requires that, as long as there is an intention of destroying the enemy, there must be no cessation in the advance of the attack; if the commander gives up this object because it is attended with too great a risk, he does right to stop and extend his force. Theory only objects to this when he does it with a view to more readily defeating the enemy.

We are not so foolish as to maintain that no instance can be found of States having been *gradually* reduced to the utmost extremity. In the first place, the principle we now maintain is no absolute truth, to which an exception is impossible, but one founded only on the ordinary and probable result; next, we must make a distinction between cases in which the downfall of a State has been effected by a slow gradual process, and those in which the event was the result of a first campaign. We are here only treating of the latter case, for it is only in such that there is that tension of forces which either overcomes the centre of gravity of the weight, or is in danger of being overcome by it. If in the first year we gain a moderate advantage, to which in the following we add another, and thus gradually advance towards our object, there is nowhere very imminent danger, but it is distributed over many points. Each pause between one result and another gives the enemy fresh chances: the effects of the first results have very little influence on those which follow, often none, often a negative only, because the enemy recovers himself, or is perhaps excited to increased resistance, or obtains foreign aid; whereas, when all is done in one march, the success of yesterday brings on with itself that of to-day, one brand lights itself from another. If there are cases in which States have been overcome by successive blows in which, consequently, *Time*, generally the patron of the defensive, has proved adverse how infinitely more numerous are the instances in which the designs of the aggressor have by that means utterly failed. Let us only think of the result of the Seven Years' War, in which the Austrians sought to attain their object so comfortably, cautiously, and prudently, that they completely missed it.

In this view, therefore, we cannot at all join in the opinion that the care which belongs to the preparation of a theatre of war, and the impulse which urges us onwards, are on a level in importance, and that the former must, to a certain extent, be a counterpoise to the latter; but we look upon any evil which springs out of the forward movement, as an unavoidable evil which only deserves attention when there is no longer hope for us a-head by the forward movement.

Buonaparte's case in 1812, very far from shaking our opinion, has rather confirmed us in it.

His campaign did not miscarry because he advanced too swiftly, or too far, as is commonly believed, but because the only means of success failed. The Russian Empire is no country which can be regularly conquered, that is to say, which can be held in possession, at least not by the forces of the present States of Europe, nor by the 500,000 men with which Buonaparte invaded the country. Such a country can only be subdued by its own weakness, and by the effects of internal dissension. In order to strike these vulnerable points in its political existence, the country must be agitated to its very centre. It was only by reaching Moscow with the force of his blow that Buonaparte could hope to shake the courage of the Government, the loyalty and steadfastness of the people. In Moscow he expected to find peace, and this was the only rational object which he could set before himself in undertaking such a war.

He therefore led his main body against that of the Russians, which fell back before him, trudged past the camp at Drissa, and did not stop until it reached Smolensk. He carried Bagration along in his movement, beat the principal Russia army, and took Moscow.

He acted on this occasion as he had always done: it was only in that way that he made himself the arbiter of Europe, and only in that way was it possible for him to do so.

He, therefore, who admires Buonaparte in all his earlier campaigns as the greatest of generals, ought not to censure him in this instance.

It is quite allowable to judge an event according to the result, as that is the best criticism upon it (see fifth chapter, 2nd book), but this judgment derived merely from the result, must not then be passed off as evidence of superior understanding. To seek out the causes of the failure of a campaign, is not going the length of making a criticism upon it; it is only if we show that these causes should neither have been overlooked nor disregarded that we make a criticism and place ourselves above the General.

Now we maintain that any one who pronounces the campaign of 1812 an absurdity merely on account of the tremendous reaction in it, and who, if it had been successful, would look upon it as a most splendid combination, shows an utter incapacity of judgment.

If Buonaparte had remained in Lithuania, as most of his critics think he should, in order first to get possession of the fortresses, of which, moreover, except Riga, situated quite at one side, there is hardly one, because Bobruisk is a small insignificant place of arms, he would have involved himself for the winter in a miserable defensive system: then the same people would have been the first to exclaim, This is not the old Buonaparte! How is it, he has not got even as far as a first great battle? he who used to put the final seal to his conquests on the last ramparts of the enemy's states, by victories such as Austerlitz and Friedland. Has his heart failed him that he has not taken the enemy's capital, the defenceless Moscow, ready to open its gates, and thus left a nucleus round which new elements of resistance may gather themselves? He had the singular luck to take this far-off and enormous colossus by surprise, as easily as one would surprise a neighbouring town, or as Frederick the Great entered the little state of Silesia, lying at his door, and he makes no use of his good fortune, halts in the middle of his victorious career, as if some evil spirit laid at his heels! This is the way in which he would have been judged of after the result, for this is the fashion of critics' judgments in general.

In opposition to this, we say, the campaign of 1812 did not succeed because the government remained firm, the people loyal and steadfast, because it therefore could not succeed. Buonaparte may have made a mistake in undertaking such an expedition; at all events, the result has shown that he deceived himself in his calculations, but we maintain that, supposing it necessary to seek the attainment of this object, it could not have been done in any other way upon the whole.

Instead of burthening himself with an interminable costly defensive war in the east, such as he had on his hands in the west, Buonaparte attempted the only means to gain his object: by one bold stroke to extort a peace from his astonished adversary. The destruction of his army was the danger to which he exposed himself in the venture; it was the stake in the game, the price of great expectations. If this destruction of his army was more complete than it need have been through his own fault, this fault was not in his having penetrated too far into the heart of the country, for that was his object, and unavoidable; but in the late period at which the campaign opened, the sacrifice of life occasioned by his tactics, the want of due care for the supply of his army, and for his line of retreat, and lastly, in his having too long delayed his march from Moscow.

That the Russians were able to reach the Beresina before him, intending regularly to cut off his retreat, is no strong argument against us. For in the first place, the failure of that attempt just shows how difficult it is really to cut off an army, as the army which was intercepted in this case under the most unfavourable circumstances that can be conceived, still managed at last to cut its way through; and although this act upon the whole contributed certainly to increase its catastrophe, still it was not essentially the cause of it. Secondly, it was only the very peculiar nature of the country which afforded the means to carry things as far as the Russians did; for if it had not been for the marshes of the Beresina, with its wooded impassable borders lying across the great road, the cutting off would have been still less possible. Thirdly, there is generally no means of guarding against such an eventuality except by making the forward movement with the front of the army of such a width as we have already disapproved; for if we proceed on the plan of pushing on in advance with the centre and covering the wings by armies detached right and left, then if either of these detached armies meets with a check, we must fall back with the centre, and then very little can be gained by the attack.

Moreover, it cannot be said that Buonaparte neglected his wings. A superior force remained fronting Wittgenstein, a proportionate siege-corps stood before Riga which at the same time was not needed there, and in the south Schwarzenberg had 50,000 men with which he was superior to Tormasoff and almost equal to Tschitschagow:

in addition, there were 30,000 men under Victor, covering the rear of the centre. Even in the month of November, therefore, at the decisive moment when the Russian armies had been reinforced, and the French were very much reduced, the superiority of the Russians in rear of the Moscow army was not so very extraordinary. Wittgenstein, Tschitschagow, and Sacken, made up together a force of 100,000. Schwartzenberg, Regmer, Victor, Oudinot, and St. Cyr, had still 80,000 effective. The most cautious general in advancing would hardly devote a greater proportion of his force to the protection of his flanks.

If out of the 600,000 men who crossed the Niemen in 1812, Buonaparte had brought back 250,000 instead of the 50,000 who repassed it under Schwartzenberg, Regmer, and Macdonald, which was possible, by avoiding the mistakes with which he has been reproached, the campaign would still have been an unfortunate one, but theory would have had nothing to object to it, for the loss of half an army in such a case is not at all unusual, and only appears so to us in this instance on account of the enormous scale of the whole enterprize.

So much for the principal operation, its necessary tendency, and the unavoidable risks. As regards the subordinate operations, there must be, above all things, a common aim for all; but this aim must be so situated as not to paralyse the action of any of the individual parts. If we invade France from the upper and middle Rhine and Holland, with the intention of uniting at Paris, neither of the armies employed to risk anything on the advance, but to keep itself intact until the concentration is effected, that is what we call a ruinous plan. There must be necessarily a constant comparison of the state of this threefold movement causing delay, indecision, and timidity in the forward movement of each of the armies. It is better to assign to each part its mission, and only to place the point of union wherever these several activities become unity of themselves.

Therefore, when a military force advances to the attack on separate theatres of war, to each army should be assigned an object against which the force of its shock is to be directed. Here *the point* is that *these shocks* should be given from all sides simultaneously, but not that proportional advantages should result from all of them.

If the task assigned to one army is found too difficult because the enemy has made a disposition of his force different to that which was expected, if it sustains a defeat, this neither should, nor must have, any influence on the action of the others, or we should turn the probability of the general success against ourselves at the very outset. It is only the unsuccessful issue of the majority of enterprises or of the principal one, which can and must have an influence upon the others: for then it comes under the head of a plan which has miscarried.

This same rule applies to those armies and portions of them which have originally acted on the defensive, and, owing to the successes gained, have assumed the offensive, unless we prefer to attach such spare forces to the principal offensive, a point which will chiefly depend on the geographical situation of the theatre of war.

But under these circumstances, what becomes of the geometrical form and unity of the whole attack, what of the flanks and rear of corps when those corps next to them are beaten.

That is precisely what we wish chiefly to combat. This glueing down of a great offensive plan of attack on a geometrical square, is losing one's way in the regions of fallacy.

In the fifteenth chapter of the Third Book we have shown that the geometrical element has less influence in strategy than in tactics; and we shall only here repeat the deduction there obtained, that in the attack especially, the actual results at the various points throughout deserve more attention than the geometrical figure, which may gradually be formed through the diversity of results.

But in any case, it is quite certain, that looking to the vast spaces with which strategy has to deal, the views and resolutions which the geometrical situation of the parts may create, should be left to the general-in-chief; that, therefore, no subordinate general has a right to ask what his neighbour is doing or leaving undone, but each is to be directed peremptorily to follow out his object. If any serious incongruity really arises from this, a remedy can always be applied in time by the supreme authority. Thus, then, may be obviated the chief evil of this separate mode of action, which is, that in the place of realities, a cloud of apprehensions and suppositions mix themselves up in the progress of an operation, that every accident affects not only the part it comes immediately in contact with, but also the whole, by the communication of impressions, and that a wide field of action is opened for the personal failings and personal animosities of subordinate commanders.

We think that these views will only appear paradoxical to those who have not studied military history long enough or with sufficient attention, who do not distinguish the important from the unimportant, nor make proper allowance for the influence of human weaknesses in general.

If even in tactics there is a difficulty, which all experienced soldiers admit there is, in succeeding in an attack in separate columns where it depends on the perfect connection of the several columns, how much more difficult, or rather how impossible, must this be in strategy, where the separation is so much wider. Therefore, if a constant connection of all parts was a necessary condition of success, a strategic plan of attack of that nature must be at once given up. But on the one hand, it is not left to our option to discard it completely, because circumstances, which we cannot control, may determine in favour of it; on the other hand, even in tactics, this constant close conjunction of all parts at every moment of the execution, is not at all necessary, and it is still less so in strategy. Therefore in strategy we should pay the less attention to this point, and insist the more upon a distinct piece of work being assigned to each part.

We have still to add one important observation: it relates to the proper allotment of parts.

In the year 1793 and 1794 the principal Austrian army was in the Netherlands, that of the Prussians, on the upper Rhine. The Austrians marched from Vienna to Condé and Valenciennes, crossing the line of march of the Prussians from Berlin to Landau. The Austrians had certainly to defend their Belgian provinces in that quarter, and any conquests made in French Flanders would have been acquisitions conveniently situated for them, but that interest was not strong enough. After the death of Prince Kaunitz, the Minister Thugut carried a measure for giving up the Netherlands entirely, for the better concentration of the Austrian forces. In fact, Austria is about twice as far from Flanders as from Alsace; and at a time when military resources were very limited, and everything had to be paid for in ready money, that was no trifling consideration. Still, the Minister Thugut had plainly something else in view; his object was, through the urgency of the danger to compel Holland, England, and Prussia, the powers interested in the defence of the Netherlands and Lower Rhine, to make greater efforts. He certainly deceived himself in his calculations, because nothing could be done with the Prussian cabinet at that time, but this occurrence always shows the influence of political interests on the course of a war.

Prussia had neither anything to conquer nor to defend in Alsace. In the year 1792 it had undertaken the march through Lorraine into Champagne in a sort of chivalrous spirit. But as that enterprise ended in nothing, through the unfavourable course of circumstances, it continued the war with a feeling of very little interest. If the Prussian troops had been in the Netherlands, they would have been in direct communication with Holland, which they might look upon almost as their own country, having conquered it in the year 1787; they would then have covered the Lower Rhine, and consequently that part of the Prussian monarchy which lay next to the theatre of war. Prussia on account of subsidies would also have had a closer alliance with England, which, under these circumstances, would not so easily have degenerated into the crooked policy of which the Prussian cabinet was guilty at that time.

A much better result, therefore, might have been expected if the Austrians had appeared with their principal force on the Upper Rhine, the Prussians with their whole force in the Netherlands, and the Austrians had left there only a corps of proportionate strength.

If, instead of the enterprising Blücher, General Barclay had been placed at the head of the Silesian army in 1814, and Blucher and Schwartzenberg had been kept with the grand army, the campaign would perhaps have turned out a complete failure.

If the enterprising Laudon, instead of having his theatre of war at the strongest point of the Prussian dominions, namely, in Silesia, had been in the position of the German States' army, perhaps the whole Seven Years' War would have had quite a different turn. In order to examine this subject more narrowly, we must look at the cases according to their chief distinctions.

The first is, if we carry on war in conjunction with other powers, who not only take part as our allies, but also have an independent interest as well.

The second is, if the army of the ally has come to our assistance.

The third is, when it is only a question with regard to the personal characteristics of the General.

In the two first cases, the point may be raised, whether it is better to mix up the troops of the different powers completely, so that each separate army is composed of corps of different powers, as was done in the wars 1813 and 1814, or to keep them separate as much as possible, so that the army of each power may continue distinct and act independently.

Plainly, the first is the most salutary plan; but it supposes a degree of friendly feeling and community of interests which is seldom found. When there is this close good fellowship between the troops, it is much more difficult for the cabinets to separate their interests; and as regards the prejudicial influence of the egotistical views of commanders, it can only show itself under these circumstances amongst the subordinate Generals, therefore, only in the province of tactics, and even there not so freely or with such impunity as when there is a complete separation. In the latter case, it affects the strategy, and therefore, makes decided marks. But, as already observed, for the first case there must be a rare spirit of conciliation on the part of the Governments. In the year 1813, the exigencies of the time impelled all Governments in that direction; and yet we cannot sufficiently praise this in the Emperor of Russia, that although he entered the field with the strongest army, and the change of fortune was chiefly brought about by him, yet he set aside all pride about appearing at the head of a separate and an independent Russian army, and placed his troops under the Prussian and Austrian Commanders.

If such a fusion of armies cannot be effected, a complete separation of them is certainly better than a half-and-half state of things; the worst of all is when two independent Commanders of armies of different powers find themselves on the same theatre of war, as frequently happened in the Seven Years' War with the armies of Russia, Austria, and the German States. When there is a complete separation of forces, the burdens which must be borne are also better divided, and each suffers only from what is his own, consequently is more impelled to activity by the force of circumstances; but if they find themselves in close connection, or quite on the same theatre of war, this is not the case, and besides that the ill will of one paralyses also the powers of the other as well.

In the first of the three supposed cases, there will be no difficulty in the complete separation, as the natural interest of each State generally indicates to it a separate mode of employing its force; this may not be so in the second case, and then, as a rule, there is nothing to be done but to place oneself completely under the auxiliary army, if its strength is in any way proportionate to that measure, as the Austrians did in the latter part of the campaign of 1815, and the Prussians in the campaign of 1807.

With regard to the personal qualifications of the General, everything in this passes into what is particular and individual; but we must not omit to make one general remark, which is, that we should not, as is generally done, place at the head of subordinate armies the most prudent and cautious Commanders, but the *most enterprising;* for we repeat that in strategic operations conducted separately, there is nothing more important than that every part should develop its powers to the full, in that way faults committed at one part may be compensated for by successes at others. This complete activity at all points, however, is only to be expected when the Commanders are spirited, enterprising men, who are urged forwards by natural impulsiveness by their own hearts, because a mere objective, coolly reasoned out, conviction of the necessity of action seldom suffices.

Lastly, we have to remark that, if circumstances in other respects permit, the troops and their commanders, as regards their destination, should be employed in accordance with their qualities and the nature of the country that is regular armies; good troops; numerous cavalry; old, prudent, intelligent generals in an open country; Militia; national levies; young enterprising commanders in wooded country, mountains and defiles; auxiliary armies in rich provinces where they can make themselves comfortable.

What we have now said upon a plan of a war in general, and in this chapter upon those in particular which are directed to the destruction of the enemy, is intended to give special prominence to the object of the same, and next to indicate principles which may serve as guides in the preparation of ways and means. Our desire has been in this way to give a clear perception of what is to be, and should be, done in such a war. We have tried to emphasise the necessary and general, and to leave a margin for the play of the particular and accidental; but to exclude all that is *arbitrary, unfounded, trifling, fantastical; or sophistical.* If we have succeeded in this object, we look upon our problem as solved.

Now, if any one wonders at finding nothing here about turning rivers, about commanding mountains from their highest points, about avoiding strong positions, and finding the keys of a country, he has not understood us, neither does he as yet understand war in its general relations according to our views.

In preceding books we have characterised these subjects in general, and we there arrived at the conclusion, they are much more insignificant in their nature than we should think from their high repute. Therefore, so much the less can or ought they to play a great part, that is, so far as to influence the whole plan of a war, when it is a war which has for its object the destruction of the enemy.

At the end of the book we shall devote a chapter specially to the consideration of the chief command; the present chapter we shall close with an example.

If Austria, Prussia, the German Con-federation, the Netherlands and England, determine on a war with France, but Russia remains neutral a case which has frequently happened during the last one hundred and fifty years they are able to carry on an offensive war, having for its object the overthrow of the enemy. For powerful and great as France is, it is still possible for it to see more than half its territory overrun by the enemy, its capital occupied, and itself reduced in its means to a state of complete inefficiency, without there being any power, except Russia, which can give it effectual support. Spain is too distant and too disadvantageously situated; the Italian States are at present too brittle and powerless.

The countries we have named have, exclusive of their possessions out of Europe, above 75,000,000 inhabitants,[65] whilst France has only 30,000,000; and the army which they could call out for a war against France really meant in earnest, would be as follows, without exaggeration:

Austria	250,000
Prussia	200,000
The rest of Germany	150,000
Netherlands	75,000
England	50,000
Total	725,000

Should this force be placed on a warfooting it would, in all probability, very much exceed that which France could oppose; for under Buonaparte the country never had an army of the like strength. Now, if we take into account the deductions required as garrisons for fortresses and depôts, to watch the coasts, etc., there can be no doubt the allies would have a great superiority in the principal theatre of war, and upon that the object or plan of overthrowing the enemy is chiefly founded.

The centre of gravity of the French power lies in its military force and in Paris. To defeat the former in one or more battles, to take Paris and drive the wreck of the French across the Loire, must be the object of the allies. The pit of the stomach of the French monarchy is between Paris and Brussels, on that side the frontier is only thirty miles from the capital. Part of the allies; the English, Netherlanders, Prussian, and North German States have their natural point of assembly in that direction, as these States lie partly in the immediate vicinity, partly in a direct line behind it. Austria and South Germany can only carry on their war conveniently from the upper Rhine. Their natural direction is upon Troyes and Paris, or it may be Orleans. Both shocks, therefore, that from the Netherlands and the other from the upper Rhine, are quite direct and natural, short and powerful; and both fall upon the centre of gravity of the enemy's power. Between these two points, therefore, the whole invading army should be divided.

But there are two considerations which interfere with the simplicity of this plan.

65　This chapter was probably written in 1828, since which time the numerical relations have considerably changed. A. d. H.

The Austrians would not lay bare their Italian dominions, they would wish to retain the mastery over events there, in any case, and therefore would not incur the risk of making an attack on the heart of France, by which they would leave Italy only indirectly covered. Looking to the political state of the country, this collateral consideration is not to be treated with contempt; but it would be a decided mistake if the old and oft-tried plan of an attack from Italy, directed against the South of France, was bound up with it, and if on that account the force in Italy was increased to a size not required for mere security against contingencies in the first campaign. Only the number needed for that security should remain in Italy, only that number should be withdrawn from the great undertaking, if we would not be unfaithful to that first maxim, *Unity of plan, concentration of force.* To think of conquering France by the Rhone, would be like trying to lift a musket by the point of its bayonet; but also as an auxiliary enterprise, an attack on the South of France is to be condemned, for it only raises new forces against us. Whenever an attack is made on distant provinces, interests and activities are roused, which would otherwise have lain dormant. It would only be in case that the forces left for the security of Italy were in excess of the number required, and, therefore, to avoid leaving them unemployed, that there would be any justification for an attack on the South of France from that quarter.

We therefore repeat that the force left in Italy must be kept down as low as circumstances will permit; and it will be quite large enough if it will suffice to prevent the Austrians from losing the whole country in one campaign. Let us suppose that number to be 50,000 men for the purpose of our illustration.

Another consideration deserving attention, is the relation of France in respect to its sea-coast. As England has the upper hand at sea, it follows that France must, on that account, be very susceptible with regard to the whole of her Atlantic coast; and, consequently, must protect it with garrisons of greater or less strength. Now, however weak this coast-defence may be, still the French frontiers are tripled by it; and large drafts, on that account, cannot fail to be withdrawn from the French army on the theatre of war. Twenty or thirty thousand troops disposable to effect a landing, with which the English threaten France, would probably absorb twice or three times the number of French troops; and, further, we must think not only of troops, but also of money, artillery, etc., etc., required for ships and coast batteries. Let us suppose that the English devote 25,000 to this object.

Our plan of war would then consist simply in this:

1. That in the Netherlands:

200,000 Prussians,

75,000 Netherlanders,

25,000 English,

50,000 North German Confederation,

Total. 350,000 be assembled, of whom about 50,000 should be set aside to garrison frontier fortresses, and the remaining 300,000 should advance against Paris, and engage the French Army in a decisive battle.

2. That 200,000 Austrians and 100,000 South German troops should assemble on the Upper Rhine to advance at the same time as the army of the Netherlands, their direction being towards the Upper Seine, and from thence towards the Loire, with a view, likewise, to a great battle. These two attacks would, perhaps, unite in one on the Loire.

By this the chief point is determined. What we have to add is chiefly intended to root out false conceptions, and is as follows:

1. To seek for the great battle, as prescribed, and deliver it with such a relation, in point of numerical strength and under such circumstances, as promise a decisive victory, is the course for the chief commanders to follow; to this object everything must be sacrificed; and as few men as possible should be employed in sieges, blockades, garrisons, etc. If, like Schwartzenberg in 1814, as soon as they enter the enemy's provinces they spread out in eccentric rays all is lost. That this did not take place in 1814 the Allies may thank the powerless state of France alone. The attack should be like a wedge well driven home, not like a soap bubble, which distends itself till it bursts.

2. Switzerland must be left to its own forces. If it remains neutral it forms a good point *d'appui* on the Upper Rhine; if it is attacked by France, let her stand up for herself, which in more than one respect she is very well able to do. Nothing is more absurd than to attribute to Switzerland a predominant geographical influence upon events in war because it is the highest land in Europe. Such an influence only exists under certain very restricted conditions, which are not to be found here. When the French are attacked in the heart of their country they can undertake no offensive from Switzerland, either against Italy or Swabia, and, least of all, can the elevated situation of the country come into consideration as a decisive circumstance. The advantage of a country which is dominating in a strategic sense, is, in the first place, chiefly important in the defensive, and any importance which it has in the offensive may manifest itself in a single encounter. Whoever does not know this has not thought over the thing and arrived at a clear perception of it, and in case that at any future council of potentates

and generals, some learned officer of the general staff should be found, who, with an anxious brow, displays such wisdom, we now declare it beforehand to be mere folly, and wish that in the same council some true Blade, some child of sound common-sense may be present who will stop his mouth.

3. The space between two attacks we think of very little consequence. When 600,000 assemble thirty or forty miles from Paris to march against the heart of France, would any one think of covering the middle Rhine as well as Berlin, Dresden, Vienna, and Munich? There would be no sense in such a thing. Are we to cover the communications? That would not be unimportant; but then we might soon be led into giving this covering the importance of an attack, and then, instead of advancing on two lines, as the situation of the States positively requires, we should be led to advance upon three, which is not required. These three would then, perhaps, become five, or perhaps seven, and in that way the old rigmarole would once more become the order of the day.

Our two attacks have each their object; the forces employed on them are probably very superior to the enemy in numbers. If each pursues his march with vigour, they cannot fail to react advantageously upon each other. If one of the two attacks is unfortunate because the enemy has not divided his force equally, we may fairly expect that the result of the other will of itself repair this disaster, and this is the true interdependence between the two. An interdependence extending to (so as to be affected by) the events of each day is impossible on account of the distance; neither is it necessary, and therefore the immediate, or, rather the direct connection, is of no such great value.

Besides, the enemy attacked in the very centre of his dominions will have no forces worth speaking of to employ in interrupting this connection; all that is to be apprehended is that this interruption may be attempted by a co-operation of the inhabitants with the partisans, so that this object does not actually cost the enemy any troops. To prevent that, it is sufficient to send a corps of 10,000 or 15,000 men, particularly strong in cavalry, in the direction from Trèves to Rheims. It will be able to drive every partisan before it, and keep in line with the grand army. This corps should neither invest nor watch fortresses, but march between them, depend on no fixed basis, but give way before superior forces in any direction, no great misfortune could happen to it, and if such did happen, it would again be no serious misfortune for the whole. Under these circumstances, such a corps might probably serve as an intermediate link between the two attacks.

4. The two subordinate undertakings, that is, the Austrian army in Italy, and the English army for landing on the coast, might follow their object as appeared best. If they do not remain idle, their mission is fulfilled as regards the chief point, and on no account should either of the two great attacks be made dependent in any way on these minor ones.

We are quite convinced that in this way France may be overthrown and chastised whenever it thinks fit to put on that insolent air with which it has oppressed Europe for a hundred and fifty years. It is only on the other side of Paris, on the Loire, that those conditions can be obtained from it which are necessary for the peace of Europe. In this way alone the natural relation between 30 millions of men and 75 millions will quickly make itself known, but not if the country from Dunkirk to Genoa is to be surrounded in the way it has been for 150 years by a girdle of armies, whilst fifty different small objects are aimed at, not one of which is powerful enough to overcome the inertia, friction, and extraneous influences which spring up and reproduce themselves everywhere, but more especially in allied armies.

How little the provisional organisation of the German federal armies is adapted to such a disposition, will strike the reader. By that organisation the federative part of Germany forms the nucleus of the German power, and Prussia and Austria thus weakened, lose their natural influence. But a federative state is a very brittle nucleus in war there is in it no unity, no energy, no rational choice of a commander, no authority, no responsibility.

Austria and Prussia are the two natural centres of force of the German empire; they form the pivot (or fulcrum), the forte of the sword; they are monarchical states, used to war; they have well-defined interests, independence of power; they are predominant over the others. The organisation should follow these natural lineaments, and not a false notion about unity, which is an impossibility in such a case; and he who neglects the possible in quest of the impossible is a fool.

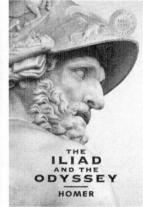
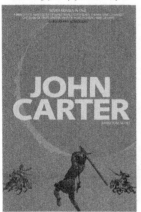

FOR OTHER GREAT TITLES VISIT
WWW.ENGAGEBOOKS.CA
1000 Copy Limited Editions

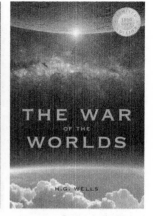
 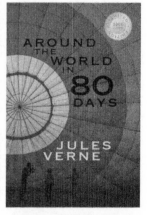
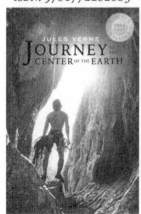 

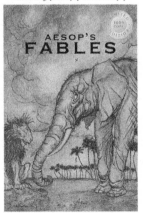

CPSIA information can be obtained at www.ICGtesting.com
Printed in the USA
BVOW08*1748271215

431107BV00002B/60/P